*The Microflora of Lakes
and Its Geochemical Activity*

THE MICROFLORA OF LAKES
and Its Geochemical Activity

By S. I. KUZNETSOV

Edited by Carl H. Oppenheimer

UNIVERSITY OF TEXAS PRESS, AUSTIN AND LONDON

Originally published in 1970 by "Nauka" Publishing House,
Leningrad Branch, Leningrad, USSR

**This volume was printed from camera-ready copy prepared by
Keter Publishing House Jerusalem Ltd.**

Translated for the National Science Foundation, Washington,
D.C., by the Israel Program for Scientific Translations,
Jerusalem, Israel

International Standard Book Number 0-292-75010-2
Library of Congress Catalog Card Number 73-21215
Printed in the United States of America

CONTENTS

FOREWORD

In this book S. I. Kuznetsov, the well-known Soviet microbiologist, provides a wealth of information on the microbial limnology of fresh-water lakes throughout the world and, especially, in the Soviet Union. This is a monumental work summarizing the geochemical activities as related to the geographic, geological, and physical relationships of fresh-water lakes.

The translator has produced an excellent translation, and I have attempted to keep the idioms of the original as much as possible and yet conform to proper English. Thus, some of the sentences may seem to have somewhat of a European flavor as a result of my effort to retain the author's identity. It was impossible to identify all the lakes that were mentioned in the text, and I ask the indulgence of the reader if certain errors in the identity of fresh-water lakes crept in due to translation and the passage of time. Names change quite quickly and I have not attempted to alter the translation of the names as they appear in the text.

The editing of a major work on microbial limnology has been stimulating and rewarding in its context. It is hoped that the text will be of value to the limnologist, biologist, and microbiologist in opening a new area of information. The text could serve as the nucleus for a course in microbial limnology or ecology on how the various activities of microorganisms influence most of the biological cycles that occur in fresh-water lakes. Also, there are many references to Soviet fresh-water lakes that will prove valuable for comparison with other environments of the world.

Carl H. Oppenheimer

*The Microflora of Lakes
and Its Geochemical Activity*

PREFACE

The geochemical processes that take place in water bodies do not stem entirely from the activity of bacteria, but are also determined by the biological activity of higher plants and animals. These processes are described in the book "Rol' mikroorganizmov v krugovorote veshchestv v ozerakh" [The role of microorganisms in the chemical cycle of lakes], published in 1952. The intervening years have witnessed major advances in research on the geochemical activities of bacteria, notably the sulfur and iron cycles in lakes and reservoirs. We decided accordingly to reexamine some aspects of the biology of microorganisms in water. All the information on chemical transformations in lakes has been revised in view of recent developments. The chapter on the cycle of calcium has been rewritten. A section is included on the use of radioactive isotopes for determining the rate of certain processes associated with the transformations of sulfur, carbon, and nitrogen in water bodies, as well as the rate of the exchange of phosphorus between the water and bottom sediments.

We have included a general outline of the ecology, the physical and chemical properties of water bodies, and a discussion of the whole complex of hydrobionts because of the great influence these factors exert on the microbial population. Fundamentals of limnology are briefly presented for the benefit of microbiologists.

The role of microorganisms in the chemical cycle cannot be understood without a thorough knowledge of their physiology. Regrettably, the physiology of autotrophic organisms appears to have been neglected in most of the recent textbooks. In fact, the physiology of microorganisms as a whole has not been given the attention it deserves in the Soviet scientific literature. In view of this, we found it necessary to devote one part of this book to a special study of this aspect. This section is largely compilatory and is based on American works (Carpenter, 1963; Oginsky and Umbreit, 1959; Stanier, Doudoroff, and Adelberg, 1958; Lis, 1958; Schlegel, 1969) and a number of Soviet publications.

Thus, the book consists of two separate but interrelated parts dealing respectively with the physiology and geochemical activity of aquatic microorganisms.

Procedures for sampling and analyzing microflora will not be included. These topics have been recently discussed (with V. I. Romanenko, 1963a) in a laboratory manual on the microbiological study of inland waters.

1

Elements of Limnology as Environmental
Factors in the Development of Microorganisms in Lakes

Lake waters vary widely in physical and chemical properties. In fact, it is impossible to find two water bodies with identical hydrological and biological features. The main properties that characterize a water body as an environment for organisms are the transparency of the water, the thermal regime, the salt composition (notably the presence of biogenic elements), and the gas regime. If the water body is to be considered as a whole, it is necessary to deal not only with the water mass but also with the silt sediments, which may contain up to 50% or more of organic matter in lake-type bodies of fresh water. Clearly, a comprehensive physico-chemical analysis is a crucial preliminary to an understanding of the biology of microorganisms inhabiting a particular water body.

Below we give an elementary outline of limnology, necessary for an adequate understanding of the environment of microbial life in lakes. Further information on limnology can be found in the works by D. A. Lastochkin (1925), S.G. Lepneva (1950), Welch (1948, 1952), B.B. Bogoslovskii (1960), Hutchinson (1957), V. I. Zhadin and S. V. Gerd (1961), Ruttner (1962), and many others.

Hydrological Elements of Lake-Type Water Bodies

Origin of a Water Body

The physical, chemical, and biological properties of a lake are determined by its morphometry, which in turn depends on the nature of the processes that act to form the lacustrine bed. Hutchinson (1957) gives specific examples of the formation of lake basins, which he classes in a number of categories. We shall outline the main types of lakes according to their origin, with particular reference to water bodies in the USSR.

Lakes formed by tectonic activity. Such lakes owe their existence to movements of the earth's crust that are not associated with volcanism. This category includes (a) relict lakes, such as the Caspian Sea and the Sea of Aral, which are remnants of the ancient Sarmatian Sea that have been cut off from the Black Sea by a rise of land; (b) lakes formed by faults, displacements, and folding of the earth's crust, such as Baikal, Teletskoe, and several lakes in central Africa — these lakes, notably Lake Baikal (Figure 1) and Lake Tanganyika, are characterized by great depths; and (c) lakes created by the Fennoscandia transgression with a subsequent glacial effect, for example, Ladoga and Onega.

Lakes associated with volcanic activity, situated in craters or calderas. Two such crater lakes — Kipyashchee and Goryachee ["Boiling Lake" and "Hot Lake"] — are on Kunashir Island on the summit of the extinct volcano Golovnina. The crater of this volcano gradually widened and filled up with eruptive material. Later its caldera filled with water, which formed the two lakes. The latter are surrounded by active fumaroles, some of which issue from the bottom of Lake Kipyashchee.

The Big Soda Lake in the state of Nevada, USA (Figure 2), has a similar history. During the Pleistocene its site was occupied by the large Lake Lahontan. Most of the water of this lake retreated in the course of time, leaving the recent Big Soda Lake in the deep basin of the ancient volcano.

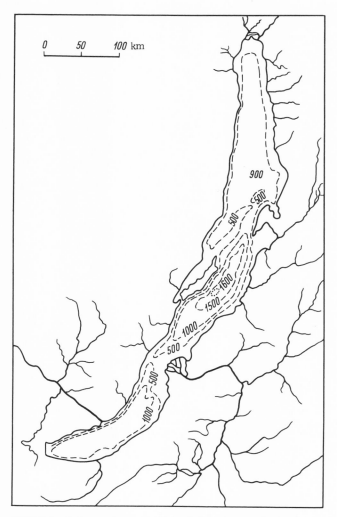

FIGURE 1. Bathymetric map of Lake Baikal, a water body of tectonic origin (after Rossolimo).

3

Numerous crater lakes situated in somewhat modified depressions within volcanic cones exist in Japan (for example, Lake Katanuma, Figure 3), northern Malawi, and New Zealand. Some of these lakes are temporary, since they lie in the craters of active volcanoes and their existence is confined to the intervals between eruptions.

Lakes formed by mountain landslides. An example is Lake Sarezskoe created in 1911 by a huge landslide that dammed up the Murgab River in a ravine near the village of Usoi. I. A. Preobrazhenskii (1920) believes that the landslide was the result of an earthquake. About six billion tons of slate in contact with marble created a slide. In 1946 the lake reached a length of 61 km and a maximal depth of 505 m, with a volume of 16.8 cubic kilometers.

Glacial lakes. No other lake-forming factor can be compared in magnitude to the effect of glaciers during their retreat in the Pleistocene. Because of climatic changes, many of the lakes formed at that time no longer exist. However, all the major types of glacial lakes can be illustrated with recent examples.

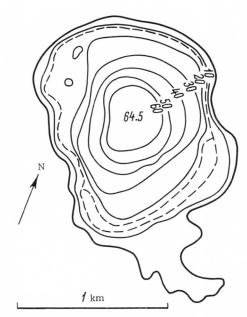

FIGURE 2. Bathymetric map of Big Soda Lake (Nevada, USA), situated in the crater of an ancient volcano on the site of the ancient Lake Lahontan.

1. In the permafrost zone of arctic regions, warming of the climate can convert blocks of melting ice into lakes. Such is the history of Lake Taimyr (Figure 4), situated in the tundra of the central part of Taimyr Peninsula (Greze, 1947). Lakes Vanyuty and Vatushkiny in the Bol'shezemel'-skaya tundra have flat, shallow basins. V. V. Kudryashov (1921) places in this category Lake Svyatoe (in Kosino), formed from ice masses during the retreat of the glacier at the time of the Würmian glaciation.

4

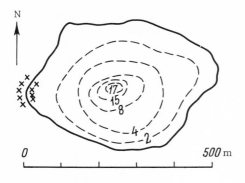

FIGURE 3. Bathymetric map of the crater lake Katanuma, Japan.

The crosses indicate fumarole sites.

If the ice masses are covered with moraine deposits at the time of the retreat of the glacier, their thawing causes a collapse of the overlying material. The result is a funnel-shaped lake basin. This process of lake formation is known as a thermokarst. The thoroughly studied Lake Glubokoe in Moscow Region (Figure 5) is said to be of this type (Shcherbakov, 1967).

2. The thawing ice forms powerful water currents in the wake of the retreating glacier. Such conditions are observed even today in alpine areas covered with permanent snow. It appears that a similar phenomenon took place during glacial time even in flatlands: currents of thaw water dug out basins in the surface deposits, carrying along sand and clay, which settled there as fluvioglacial sediments. The latter often dammed up the basins. Such is the origin of numerous glacial lakes in flatland regions. According to V.V.Kudryashov (1924), Lake Beloe (in Kosino) lies in a basin dug out by waters of a retreating glacier and dammed up by Sandr sands (Figure 6).

Most alpine lakes are believed to be of glacial origin. The same is true of the great lakes of subarctic Canada — Athabasca, Great Slave Lake, Great Bear Lake— the great lakes of Patagonia, the great lakes of the St. Lawrence Peninsula (Hough, 1962; Dussart, 1963), the lakes of Schleswig-Holstein (Ohle, 1934), the state of Wisconsin, USA (Frey, 1963).

3. A major factor in the formation of lakes is the combination of glacial activity with subsequent rise and sinking of land. Examples of this category are the lakes and fjords of Norway and Sweden.

4. The basins of many Karelian lakes were created by deep tectonic fissures and faults in the primary crustal rock. The formation of the basins was completed by the movement of the glacier, whose masses of sand and stone changed the profile of the fissure.

Many Karelian lakes have an elongate form because of the direction of the tectonic fissures and the movement of the glacier (Figure 7).

Sink lakes. Underground waters can dissolve a variety of sedimentary rocks, such as limestones, gypsum, or rock salt, leaving underground cavities or caves. The cave roof may sag under the weight of the overlying rocks, creating a funnel-shaped basin, which, according to the hydrogeologic circumstances, becomes filled with surface or underground waters. Such is the origin of the sink lakes. These are usually small in diameter but comparatively deep.

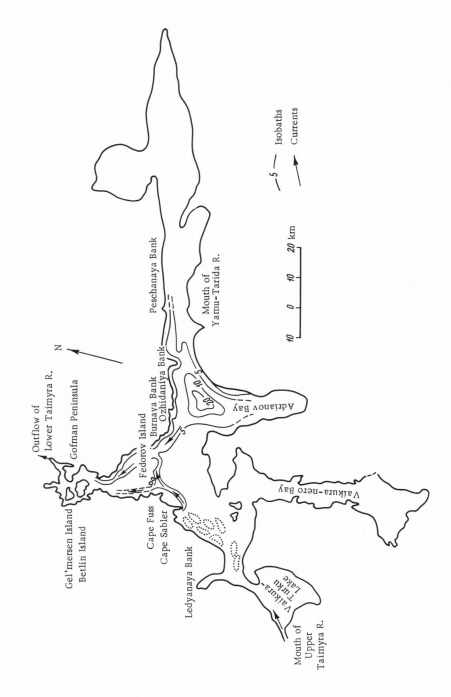

FIGURE 4. Scheme of Lake Taimyr, formed by a mass of thawed ice (after Greze, 1947).

Outflow of
Lower Taimyra R.

N

Gofman Peninsula

Gel'mersen Island

Betlin Island

Fedorov Island

Burnaya Bank

Ozhidaniya Bank

Cape Fuss

Cape Sabler

Ledyanaya Bank

Peschanaya Bank

Mouth of
Yamu–Tarida R.

Adrianov Bay

Valkuta-nero Bay

Valkuta-
Turku
Lake

Mouth of
Upper
Taimyra R.

Isobaths
Currents

10   0   10   20 km

6

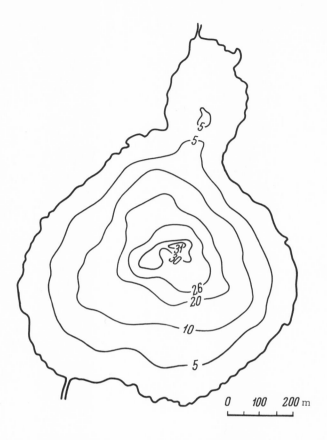

FIGURE 5. Scheme of Lake Glubokoe (Moscow Region), which
is of glacial origin and was formed by the collapse of moraine
sediments covering the ice of the retreating glacier (after
Shcherbakov, 1967).

Sink lakes (like Deep Lake) are widespread in calcareous rocks in
Florida, USA, in the Balkans, in Switzerland (Lünersee, depth 102 m), etc.;
in the USSR, such lakes are known in Gor'kii Region (Grichuk, 1937), the
Mari Autonomous SSR (Russkii, 1916), and elsewhere.

Less frequent are lakes formed by the solution of gypsum. Such is the
origin of Lake Belovod' (Figure 8), which lies in Vladimir Region and has
an area of 2 hectares and a depth of 25 m. The water of this lake is rich
in sulfates. Another lake of the same category is Girotte (Delbecque, 1898)
in the French Alps, with an area of 57 hectares and a depth of 99 m. This
is a meromictic lake with a high concentration of hydrogen sulfide in the
deep layers of water.

Among the lakes created by the solution of sodium chloride, those situated in
salt domes are of particular interest. Such are the lakes El'ton and Baskunchak,
and Lake Razval which lies in Sol-Iletsk and has a maximal depth of 17 m. Even
in summer water temperatures here are negative (Dzens-Litovskii, 1953).

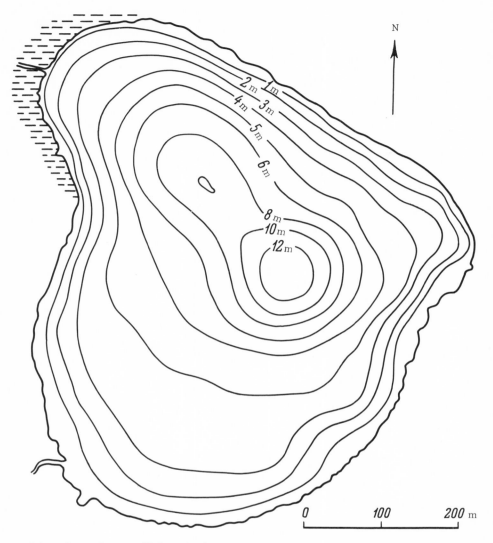

FIGURE 6. Bathymetric map of Lake Beloe (Kosino, Moscow Region), a lake of glacial origin formed by the damming effect of outwash sands in a basin dug out by the waters of the retreating glacier.

Finally, suffusion lakes are formed in small, dishlike basins left after the solution of salts in soil grounds deposited on former marine beds. Delbecque (1898) places in this group a number of lakes situated near Biarritz (western France) and formed by the solution of sodium chloride deposits in Tertiary salt-bearing sediments. Such brackish lakes are common in the Baraba forest-steppe and steppe zones.

River or oxbow lakes. Rivers flowing in flatland areas usually have meandering middle reaches. Lowering of the erosion base straightens the river bed, leaving the meanders as separate lakes that are usually narrow, comparatively shallow, and similar morphometrically to different sectors of the river.

8

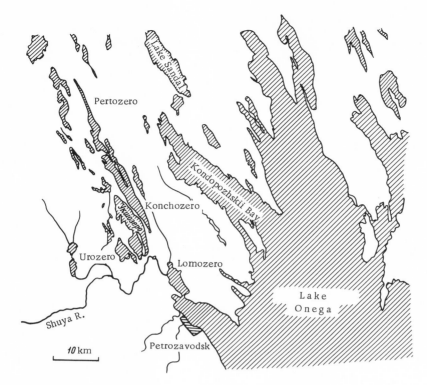

FIGURE 7. Map of the distribution of the lakes in the basin of Shuya River in Karelia. These lakes were formed by the appearance of tectonic fissures in the crystalline shield and a subsequent glacial effect (from the Great Soviet Encyclopedia).

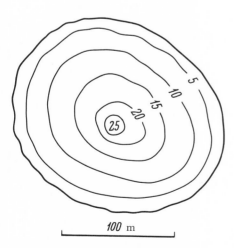

FIGURE 8. Bathymetric map of Lake Belovod', a sink lake formed by the solution of gypsiferous rocks in the Oka-Tsna bank.

FIGURE 9. Map of Kara Bogaz Gol Bay in the Caspian Sea.

Other lakes of river origin are those situated in river deltas. Large deltas are usually formed by rivers reaching the sea in an area of land elevations. Such are the deltas of the Lena, Volga, Amu-Dar'ya, etc. In the delta area, the river bed usually splits into numerous arms, which are of a temporary nature. The accumulation of river alluvia often isolates an arm from the river, converting it into a lake. During high water, such lakes may be reconnected with the river; in low water they again become isolated. Several thoroughly studied lakes of this category are situated in the Damchik Nature Reserve in the Volga Delta (Gorbunov, 1953).

Lakes situated in the marginal zone of seas or large lakes. Such lakes are usually created by bars and damlike formations in a rough coastline. Currents flowing along the coastline carry sand and suspended materials, which settle out forming a bank. The result is a smoother coastline. Eventually the bank traverses the bay, forming a coastal lake or lagoon.

Lakes of this type exist along the Atlantic coast, in France, southeastern Australia, on the south coast of Africa, along the Gulf of Mexico, North America, etc. In the USSR, such lakes are situated along the coast of the Caspian Sea, on Kerch Peninsula, and elsewhere, including, as it appears, Lake Mogil'noe on Kil'din Island.

The lakes of this type may retain their link with the sea if supplied with a sufficient amount of water to prevent the formation of a continuous bar, as is the case with many limans on the Black Sea coast, or if their water level is lower than that of the sea, as in Kara Bogaz Gol or Sivash, where evaporation is much greater than in the Caspian Sea and Sea of Azov and a powerful current of sea water is available to the lakes (Figures 9, 10).

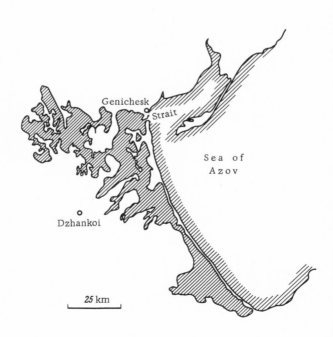

FIGURE 10. Scheme of Lake Sivash (Crimean Region).

Man-made lakes or artificial reservoirs. The art of river damming for the creation of artificial lakes or reservoirs was known even to the ancient Egyptians as long ago as 1000 B. C. Huge artificial reservoirs were built in Syria and Mesopotamia. Today, many artificial reservoirs are being constructed all over the world for irrigation, transport, production of electric energy, and other uses.

In most cases the dam is built across a river, resulting in a flooded river valley. The type of artificial reservoir obtained depends on the landscape, the climate, and the river itself. For example, artificial reservoirs situated in the upper reaches of mountain rivers carrying masses of terrigenic particles become completely silted-up within a few years. Such is the case with the artificial reservoirs on the Murgab River. In the flatlands, the trophic properties of the artificial reservoir depend largely on the nature of the flooded soils (Figure 11).

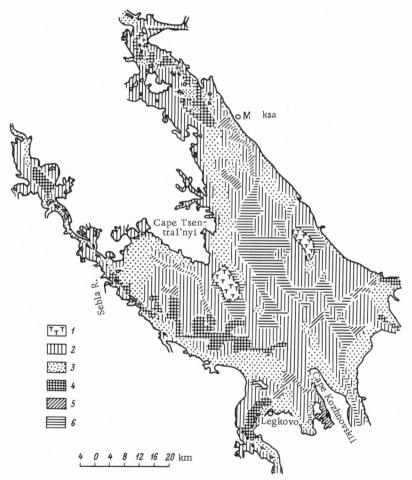

FIGURE 11. Scheme of the distribution of bottoms in the Rybinsk Artificial Reservoir:

1) floating peats; 2) former soils; 3) sands; 4) gray silts; 5) transitional silts; 6) peaty silts (after Kudrina).

Another type of artificial reservoir results from the regulation of the water level of some natural lakes. In Lake Baikal, for example, the water level was raised by 1 m. Other reservoirs of this type are Lake Onega and the lakes along the Northern Dvina and White Sea-Baltic canals.

Lakes formed in meteorite craters. This is a small but peculiar group. It includes Lake Kaalijärv on the Island of Ösel, Great Arizona Crater, Crater Lake, etc. Hutchinson describes these lakes as a separate type.

Sources of Water Supply to the Lake

The nature of the water supply is one of the major factors that determine the physical, chemical, and biological properties of the lake. The lakes are divided into four groups on the basis of their water supply: (1) undrained, closed lakes, feeding on springs and atmospheric precipitation; (2) drained or spring-type lakes, whose water supply comes entirely from springs or atmospheric precipitation and is balanced by a permanent or temporary runoff; (3) running or river-type lakes, with both inflow and outflow of water; and (4) terminal, or river-mouth lakes, which have tributaries but are not drained.

The salinity of a lake depends on its water balance and location, that is, the presence of links with the sea or a salt soil. A gradual salinization of the lake may occur if the inflow of surface or sea waters outpaces the drainage or is compensated by evaporation. Such phenomenon is especially pronounced in the lakes of the fourth group, where the water supply is balanced by evaporation.

Thermal Regime of the Lake

Before describing the thermal regime of lakes, let us outline briefly the major physical properties of water because of the great influence these factors exert on the thermal conditions.

Density of water. Many important phenomena in the lake result from fluctuations in the density of water, which in turn depends on three major factors — temperature, salinity, and pressure.

At a temperature of +4°C and atmospheric pressure, the surface water has a density of 1.0000. This figure increases to 1.0005 at a pressure of 10 atmospheres, 1.0010 at 20 atmospheres, and 1.0015 at 30 atmospheres, which corresponds to a depth of about 300 m.

Water is almost unique in that its maximal density is not at freezing temperature but at 4°C. Thus, natural water bodies have a minimal density at their maximal summer temperatures. As the water cools down in the fall, its density increases until the temperature drops to 4°C; below this temperature the density decreases until the freezing point is reached. Figure 12 shows the relationship between density and temperature in pure water.

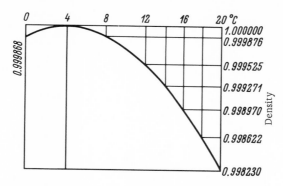

FIGURE 12. Relation between density and temperature of water.

Substances dissolved in the water exert a major influence on its density. The concentration of these substances differs from one water body to another. Their effect on the water density is especially strong in salt lakes: the greater the salinity, the higher the density of water. Evaporation and atmospheric precipitation greatly affect the water density in salt lakes.

All three factors act simultaneously in natural water bodies. Consequently, the temperature at which the water reaches its maximal density varies considerably — from 4°C in fresh waters to −3.5°C in the sea. In other words, the bottom water layers of seas and salt lakes may have a sub-zero temperature in winter. The following table shows the relationship between salinity, pressure, and the temperature of maximal density.

Salinity, g/L	Depth, m	Pressure, atm	Water temperature at maximal density, °C
0	0	1.0	4.0
0	90	8.1	+ 3.5
35	0	1.0	−3.5

Water has a limited heat transparency. Since solar radiation is the main source of energy reaching the lake, only the upper layer of water is directly warmed. Laboratory tests with optically pure water have shown that the first 10 cm retain 45% of the heat radiation entering the water, while the amounts penetrating to a depth of 10 and 100 m are respectively 18% and 1%. The absorption of heat radiation is even greater in natural water because of its color and the presence of various suspended particles.

The heat conductivity of water is extremely low. The role of this factor in lakes is in fact negligible in comparison with other factors affecting the distribution of heat. Because of the low heat conductivity, solar heat almost fails to penetrate into the water mass.

The distribution of heat in lakes depends largely on the mixing effect of wind and, to a lesser extent, on convection currents.

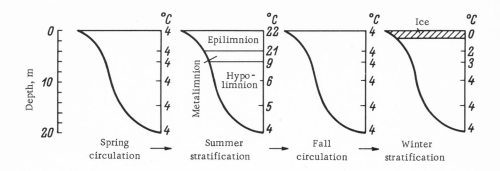

FIGURE 13. Seasonal changes of the vertical distribution of temperature in lakes.

The thermal regime of freezing lakes of the temperate zone has been thoroughly studied by L. L. Rossolimo (1932a), whose work is based on the Kosino lakes. The distribution of temperature in lakes is of particular importance in view of the fact that the rate of all microbiological processes depends on the temperature of the environment and changes roughly 2.5 times with each 10°C rise or fall in temperature.

Figure 13 shows schematically the annual cycle of temperature in lakes.

Spring circulation. Just before the ice cover of a lake thaws, the temperature of the water is almost 0°C just below the ice and gradually increases with depth (Figure 13). Although differing from one lake to another, the bottom temperatures are equal or close to the temperature of maximal water density.

In this thermal pattern, the colder and lighter water is on top, while the warmer and heavier water lies on the bottom. With the coming of spring, the rising temperature of the air melts the ice, and the surface water becomes gradually warmer. When the temperature of the surface water reaches 4°, its density becomes greater than that of the underlying water. Now a process of mixing begins, as a result of which the density becomes homogeneous throughout the water mass. Spring winds often assist in the mixing of water. Eventually a homothermy sets in, that is, the temperature and density become equal throughout from the surface to the bottom of the lake (Figure 13). At this stage, further mixing of the whole water mass is only possible by the action of winds. The period in which the mixing affects the whole water mass of the lake is known as the period of complete spring circulation or spring overturn.

After the disappearance of the ice, the temperature of the lake water can rise to 4° within a few days. However, the spring circulation may last several weeks, depending on the air temperature, the force and direction of wind, etc. During this time the lake water is usually well mixed and aerated, and the temperature may rise much above 4° at all depths (Figure 14).

In some cases, however, the spring circulation is incomplete or totally lacking. This occurs in small, deep lakes that are protected from the wind, especially when spring comes suddenly, causing a rapid rise in the air temperature. In such cases there is no complete mixing of the water, owing to the great depth of the lake and the lack of wind currents or because the surface layers suddenly become much warmer and consequently lighter than the underlying waters, which creates a stable equilibrium in that density increases with depth.

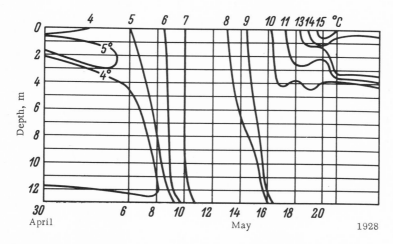

FIGURE 14. Water temperature of Lake Beloe (Kosino, Moscow Region) during the spring circulation in 1928 (after Rossolimo).

Summer stagnation and thermocline formation. The duration of the spring mixing varies considerably from one year to another, according to weather conditions. As the air temperature gradually rises, the surface water becomes warmer and lighter and remains on top. At the same time the resistance to the effect of winds, which tend to mix the surface water with the cooler and heavier deep water, increases. When the difference in temperature between surface and deep waters attains a given value, the wind circulation of water becomes confined to the surface layer (Figure 13). This is the period of thermal stratification or summer stagnation. Now the water temperature of the lake has the following vertical distribution (Figure 15). First, there is a surface layer or epilimnion with an almost uniform temperature. Next below is a layer known as metalimnion or thermocline, characterized by a drastic drop of temperature with depth. Finally, the underlying water mass or hypolimnion shows a slight decrease of temperature with depth, the temperature here being low and equal to that of the whole water mass by the end of the spring circulation.

Fall circulation. In early autumn, the cooling of the air leads to a decline in the temperature of the surface water, which consequently becomes heavier and sinks, causing convection currents. Gradually, the whole epilimnion cools down. As the temperature continues to decline, the mixing affects the deeper water, first in the metalimnion, later the hypolimnion. Winds assist to a considerable extent in this process. Finally, the temperature and salinity of the water become uniform, regardless of depth. This is the fall homothermy — a condition in which the water is freely mixed and aerated from the surface to the very bottom and its properties do not depend on depth.

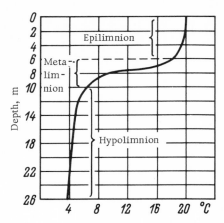

FIGURE 15. Curve showing the vertical distribution of
temperature in a lake during the summer stagnation.

If the summer temperature of the hypolimnion was above 4°, the complete
fall circulation begins at this or at a slightly higher level and lasts until a
short time before the lake freezes. During a long cool windy autumn, the
water temperature may drop to 2° throughout the depth range of the lake.
The fall circulation is essentially a repetition of the spring circulation, the
main difference being that it causes a decrease of temperature. That the
water mass at this time has a uniform composition regardless of depth is
evident from various physical, chemical, and biological analyses.

As in the spring, the fall circulation may last a considerable time, depending on the weather and the day of onset of ice cover. Delayed ice cover
usually causes a prolonged fall circulation.

Winter stagnation. The decline in air temperature in early winter lowers
the water temperature to 4°. Below this temperature the water becomes
lighter and tends to remain on the surface in the absence of wind currents.
At this stage, the thermal pattern is the reverse of that observed in summer:
now the warmer water lies at the bottom and the colder water is on top. In
terms of density, however, the same relationship prevails, namely, the lighter
water lies on the surface. Finally, the formation of ice cover isolates the
lake from atmospheric influences and the effect of winds; now the whole
lake can be compared to the hypolimnion during the summer stagnation.

Just below the ice is a thin water layer with a temperature near 0°.
Below this layer the water temperature rises rapidly to 3°; still deeper it
reaches 4°. In temperate latitudes, however, a prolonged fall circulation
often cools the water to 2 or even 1°; after the freezing, heat released from
the bottom sediments warms up the deep waters, and from this moment the
thermal stratification approximates the ideal pattern outlined above.

In tropical or subtropical regions, where the lakes do not freeze in winter,
a reversed stratification of temperatures does not set in during the winter.
By contrast, the thermal stratification of the cold polar lakes remains reversed almost throughout the year, possibly with brief intervals of homothermy and complete circulation during the summer.

Thermal stratification of lakes. Yoshimura (1936) has proposed the
following classification (terminology) for the thermal stratification of lakes.

1. *Tropical lakes.* Surface temperature between 20 and 30°; small seasonal fluctuations of temperature and moderate thermal gradient with depth. Water circulation unstable, occurring in the coldest part of the year.

2. *Subtropical lakes.* Surface temperature never below 4°; high seasonal fluctuations of temperature; large thermal gradient. Complete circulation in winter only.

3. *Temperate lakes.* Surface temperature above 4° in summer, below 4° in winter. Large thermal gradient and considerable fluctuations of temperature from one season to another. Complete circulation of water during the spring and fall.

4. *Subpolar lakes.* Surface temperature above 4° during a very brief summer period only. Small thermal gradient. Slight thermocline at the very surface of water. In the ideal case, lakes of this type show two periods of circulation: in early summer and in early fall, though the summer cooling may cause a complete summer circulation.

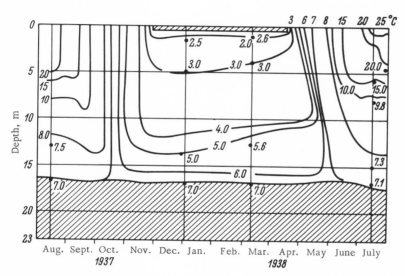

FIGURE 16. Seasonal course of temperature in the meromictic Lake Belovod'. The spring and fall circulations do not extend beyond a depth of 15 m.

The shaded area represents a layer with a higher salinity. This layer does not participate in the circulation.

5. *Polar lakes.* Surface temperature always below 4°. Ice-free period very brief; circulation possible in mid-summer only.

Hutchinson (1957) classifies the thermal stratification of lakes on the basis of the seasonal course of the water circulation. Thus, lakes with a complete circulation in the spring and fall are "dimictic"; "warm monomictic," the tropical lakes where the winter circulation occurs at a temperature above 4°; "cold monomictic," the polar lakes with summer circulation at a temperature below 4°.

In some lakes, however, the surface fresh-water layers perform complete spring and fall circulations, while saline and consequently heavier bottom waters do not circulate (Figure 16). Hutchinson proposes for such lakes the term "meromictic" instead of the early name "bioanisotropic" (as Lake Belovod' in Vladimir Region).

A particular thermal regime is observed in salt steppe lakes and those situated in salt domes.

Some mineral-rich lakes in the lower reaches of the Volga, on the north coast of Caucasus, in western Siberia, and in the Kazakhstan semideserts have a very cold brine in winter, retaining a liquid phase at a temperature as low as −21° and even below. In summer, the temperature of these salt lakes rises to 60° and higher, while the air temperature is in the 30 to 40° range.

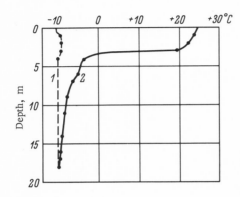

FIGURE 17. Water temperature in Lake Razval (after Dzens-Litovskii):

1) February 1, 1938; 2) July 25, 1938.

In certain conditions, abundant fresh edgewater seeping gradually in calm weather forms a thin layer over the more dense brine of the whole lake. This creates a hothouse effect with the fresh-water layer acting as a lens through which the underlying brine and bottom silts are warmed up by direct and back irradiation in the infrared light region (Dzens-Litovskii, 1953). For example, at noon on August 15, 1945, the following temperatures were determined in Lake Goryachee in the Kulundin-skaya steppe: air 37°, coastal soil 40°, fresh-water layer 35°, brine at a depth of 0.25 m 48°, dark gray bottom silts below the brine 62°.

Other thermal anomalies occur in lakes situated in karst funnels or deep excavations in salt domes.

From 1936 to 1950 measurements of temperature were made in Lake Razval, formed in 1916 in an excavation in the Iletsk salt dome (Dzens-Litovskii, 1953). Sharp seasonal fluctuations of temperature are confined to the surface layers of brine to a depth of 3 m; here the temperature varies from 38.5° in summer to −21.5° in winter. Figure 17 shows the results of measurements made in 1937—1939. During the following winters the brine became even colder than in 1939. In February 1956, for example, the surface and bottom temperatures were as low as −20.5 and −21.5°, respectively. Such supercooling of the deep brine can be the result of the following factors: (1) the high concentration of brine, which prevents freezing; (2) the cooling of the surface layers to −20° and lower in winter; and (3) the low heat conductivity of brine, because of which the brine, supercooled to a temperature of −21.5°, sinks to the bottom in winter, while the summer heat is confined to the surface layer. The lack of wind currents is a contributory factor in preserving the subzero temperature during the summer.

Optic Properties of the Water

Turbidity of lake water. The turbidity of water is due to the presence of suspended particulate matter including plankton. All natural waters contain some amount of such suspended particles. According to their behavior in water, these particles can be divided in two categories — sedimentable and non-sedimentable (living or colloidal). Particles sinking to the bottom form the bulk of the silt in lakes. The rate of sedimentation depends on time, form, and specific weight, and also on the density of water and a number of other factors.

A rough idea of the rate at which spherical particles of a specific weight of 2.65 sink in pure standing water at 10° can be obtained from the following data (Whipple, 1927).

Particle	Diameter, mm	Time of sinking 1 m
Gravel	10.0	1 sec
Coarse sand	1.0	9 sec
Fine sand	0.1	115 sec
Silt	0.01	100 min
Bacteria	0.001	165 hr
Clay	0.0001	690 days
Colloidal particles	0.00001	190 years

The turbidity of lake water may vary greatly in its intensity and other properties not only during a given season but also vertically, as a result of a drastic increase in the density of the metalimnion water.

The non-sedimentable particulate matter comprises colloidal particles, those with a specific weight less than unity and extremely fine suspensions, which settle down very slowly and may consist largely of plankton organisms; for example, a blooming lake often contains masses of Gloeotrichia, which does not settle even after centrifugation of the water.

Color of lake water. The color of lake water varies from blue in Lake Issyk-Kul to brown in peat lakes. The factors affecting the color of water have been discussed in detail by S. S. Lepneva (1950). Particulate suspensions change the natural color of water and may impart to it their own color. For example, the chocolate color of the Tashkeprinskii Artificial Reservoir is due to the clay particles brought in by the Murgab. The color of water is a reliable indicator of the distribution of water masses in the Rybinsk Artificial Reservoir (M. A. Fortunatov, 1959).

Transparency of water. The depth to which sunlight penetrates into the water mass depends mainly on the transparency of water, which in turn is a function of the turbidity and color. For example, the transparency of water is usually high in alpine lakes and low in muddy flatland lakes.

Although it is well known that light exerts a great influence on the whole complex of biological processes that take place in the water, the exact limit to which the various wave lengths of light penetrate in various lakes has not yet been established.

The transparency of water is commonly determined by the Secchi method, which consists in lowering a white plate 20 cm in diameter to a depth at which the plate becomes invisible. This depth is taken as an indicator of the transparency of water, while its double value is a measure of the penetration of light in the water, since the light traverses the distance from the water surface to the plate and back across the same layers before it reaches the observer. Direct determinations of photosynthesis have shown, however, that this value is somewhat low, that is, that light actually penetrates deeper than the double index of transparency, which may be due to the specific absorption of wave lengths responsible for photosynthesis.

TABLE 1. Annual changes in the transparency of water (in m) (after Lastochkin, 1925)

Lake	Month											
	June	July	Aug.	Sept.	Oct.	Nov.	Dec.	Jan.	Feb.	March	April	May
Pereyaslavskoe..	4.5	3.7	2.0	3.4	—	3.6	—	6.7	—	8.75	—	2.3
Beloe (Kosino, Moscow Region)	0.6	0.8	0.8	1.6	2.0	—	3.3	—	2.3	2.0	1.5	—
Baikal	26	19.2	10.1	11.1	12.5	20.8	25.1	22.0	18.9	18.9	10.3	17.5

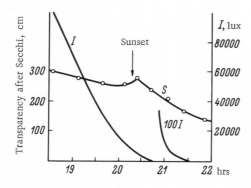

FIGURE 18. Changes in the transparency of water as a function of the intensity of illumination, measured in the air at sunset (after Aberg and Rodhe, 1942):

I) intensity of illumination; S) transparency as determined with the Secchi disk.

The transparency of lake water reaches a peak just before the ice cover goes off, in January—March. Little data have been published on the annual changes of the transparency of Russian lakes. Table 1 contains measurements made in three lakes of different types.

The highest transparency values with the Secchi disk were obtained in the Japanese crater Lake Masyuko (Hutchinson, 1957) and in Crater Lake, Oregon (Hasler, 1938) — respectively 41.6 and 40 m.

Penetration of light into the lake. There is no direct proportionality between the intensity of light reaching the water surface and the depth to which this light penetrates in the lake. This is evident from measurements of the transparency of water by the Secchi method and of the intensity of illumination in the air at Lake Erken during sunset (Aberg and Rodhe, 1942). As shown in Figure 18, the intensity of light in the air dropped within three hours, from 7 to 10 p.m., to 0.001 of the original value, while the transparency by the Secchi method decreased only to one-half, from 3.0 to 1.6 m.

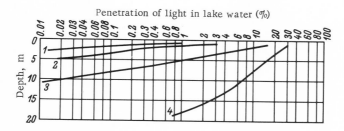

FIGURE 19. Curves showing the penetration of sunlight in four Wisconsin lakes, as percentage of the surface illumination (after Birge and Juday, 1932):

1) Lake Helmet; 2) Lake Mary; 3) Lake Nelson; 4) Lake Crystal.

Most of the light penetrating in the water is absorbed in the upper 1 m layer. This value varies greatly, as shown in some lakes in Wisconsin, USA (Birge and Juday, 1932). Thus, the illumination at a depth of 1 m corresponds to the following percentages of the surface illumination: Lake Crystal — 30%, Lake Nelson — 17%, Lake Helmet — only 1%. The corresponding values for a depth of 10 m are 7% for Lake Crystal and 0.03% for Lake Nelson; in Lake Helmet the light is completely absorbed at a depth of 3 m.

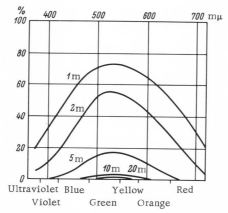

FIGURE 20. Graphs showing the penetration of different wavelengths of light in pure water. The penetration is expressed as percentage of the surface illumination.

21

Photometric determinations of light penetration in water have shown that complete darkness begins at greater depth in some sea-water areas than in fresh water. The "Michael Sars" Expedition has found, for example, that light penetrates to a depth of 1,000—1,500 m near the Azores in the Atlantic, using an exposure time of eighty minutes. Moreover, the rate of light absorption depends on the wavelength: green and blue light penetrates deepest, while the ultraviolet and red portions of the spectrum are most strongly absorbed (Figure 20).

Basic Hydrochemistry of Lakes

Salt Composition of the Water

Several factors determine the salt composition of lake water. Among them is the geographic location of the lake, whose water supply clearly depends on the climate. Of particular importance in closed lakes is the relationship between the supply of water from the water-collecting basin and the rate of evaporation. The geographic zones can be divided into five types (Figure 21): (1) tundra zone, with a probable predomination of siliceous and hydrocarbonate-siliceous lake waters; (2) forest zone, mostly with hydrocarbonate-calcium lake waters; (3) steppe zone, where lakes with a sulfate or hydrocarbonate-sodium content predominate; (4) desert and semidesert zone, where the lakes are mostly of the chloride-sodium category; and (5) zone of the tropics and subtropics, represented by hydrocarbonate-siliceous lakes. Additional factors may cause marked deviations from these types in each geographic zone.

Data on the chemistry of Soviet lakes can be found in the reports of S. G. Lepneva (1950), O. A. Alekin (1948), A. I. Dzens-Litovskii (1938), and E. V. Posokhov (1955). Chemical analyses of many Wisconsin lakes were made by Juday, Birge, and Meloche (1938). The authors have determined the vertical distribution of some ingredients in a number of lakes, though most of the studies represent statistical analyses of determinations made in samples of surface water. Some information on lakes in the German Federal Republic has been published by Ohle (1934); Yoshimura (1936b, 1938b) has investigated lakes in Japan.

The following chemical compositions were determined in lakes situated in different soil and climate zones. As shown in Table 2, the lake waters of the temperate zone represent dilute solutions of salts of alkali and alkali-earth elements in the form of bicarbonates, sulfates, or chlorides with a variable amount of silicic acid, although the concentration of the latter may exceed that of the sulfates and chlorides. In addition, there are minute quantities of trace elements, many of them of great biologic importance, together with various organic and mineral colloids and suspensions.

Drained lakes may differ greatly in their salt composition from closed ones. The mineral composition of the water supply of lakes depends on three factors (Hutchinson, 1957): (1) the composition of atmospheric precipitation, which contains a number of salts; (2) the compounds arriving

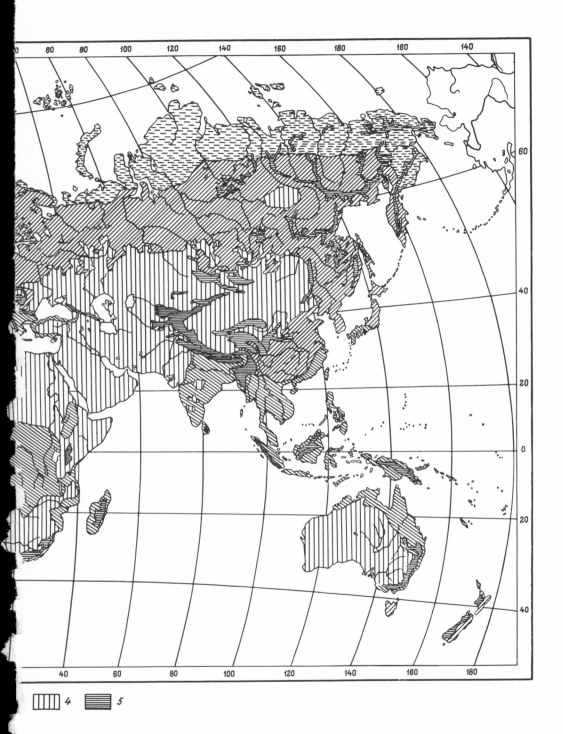

e of deserts and semideserts with salt lakes and mineral deposits; 5) vertical zone of fresh-water lakes

FIGURE 21. Geographic zonality in the distribution of lake waters and sediments:

1) tundra zone; 2) forest-belt zone; 3) zone of subtropical and tropical fresh-water lakes and sediments; 4) arid z
and sediments.

with the water from the collecting basin; and (3) the ionic equilibrium established by the exchange of ions between the water and the soils or lake silts. After a comparison of numerous analyses, Hutchinson concludes that waters with a salinity of less than 50 mg/L originate mainly from crystalline massifs. Such waters have the following average composition, based on a large number of determinations (in mg/L): Na 15.3; K 3.5; Mg 7.1; Ca 24.1. With increasing salinity the concentration of alkali ions decreases in favor of Ca and Mg ions. The salt composition of running lakes equals that of river water.

It is preferable to classify the waters of closed basins on the basis of their anion composition, which closely reflects the rate of evaporation. Evaporation of ordinary fresh water creates first a sediment of calcium carbonate. If the water contains an excess of Ca ions in relation to the CO_3 ions, calcium sulfate begins to precipitate next. The remaining water contains mostly Cl ions. As seen in Table 2, these patterns are repeated in the passage from the forest belt to the steppe and semidesert.

However, for life to develop in a lake the content of biogenous elements such as nitrogen, phosphorus, potassium and iron is more important than the degree of general mineralization of water. The content of free carbon dioxide and bicarbonates, mostly bound to calcium, is vitally important for the development of algae, in particular, phytoplankton. Within a single geographical zone the salt content of lake water during the year has no constant value since almost every element participates to some extent in the chemical cycle of the water body. However, this value fluctuates around some average resulting from inflow and outflow of salts. Salts enter the lake with the seepage of surface and ground waters, and also diffuse from silt during mineralization. Salt outflow is largely connected with the activity of living organisms; these extract salt from the water, if only at small concentrations, or precipitate such elements as calcium in the form of carbonates, thereby altering the physicochemical properties of the lake water.

During periods of stagnation, when the water is not mixed, irregular distribution of salt occurs at varying depths, but normally, the salt content evens out during the fall or spring circulation.

Meromictic lakes are the exception, particularly lakes with deep spring inflow of strongly mineralized water, for instance, Lake Belovod' in Vladimir Region or Chernoe-Kucheer Lake in Mari ASSR. The difference in specific gravity of surface and deep waters may be so great that even during fall and winter cooling, the densities of deep, relatively warmer layers remain higher than the cooled, surface waters. In this case, as was mentioned previously, the complete fall circulation does not include the entire lake but only the fresh, surface layers, while the deep layers always remain isolated from the air. The annual course of temperature fluctuation of water in meromictic Lake Belovod' is given in Figure 16.

For such lakes Egunov proposed the term "bioanisotropic," but according to Hutchinson's terminology they are called "meromictic." The content of salts in deep layers of water in lakes of this type may be much higher than in the surface layers, as observed in a number of Norwegian fjords (Strøm, 1933, 1936) and Japanese lakes (Yoshimura, 1932a) as well as in Mogil'nyi on Kildin Island (Isachenko, 1914).

TABLE 2. Chemical composition of the water of different types of lakes

Zone	Lake	mg/l				
		K· + Na·	Ca··	Mg··	HCO$_3^-$	SO$_4^-$
Tundra	Donty		7.1	2.58	45.8	0
	Vatushkiny	4.25	5.81	2.43	20.75	11.25
	Vanyuty	2.75	7.21	4.10	20.75	18.25
Temperate forest zone	Gorodnya (Kalinin Region)	—	45.2	1.8	285	—
	Volgino (Kalinin Region)	—	39.2	1.55	279	—
	Onega	1.5	5.4	1.6	20.4	1.3
	Ladoga	8.6	7.1	1.9	40.2	2.5
	Glubokoe (Moscow Region)	—	8.7	2.4	33.2	2.6
	Teletskoe	1.73	12.4	2.1	48.6	2.8
	Baikal	4.3	16.76	2.3	67.5	4.24
	Valdai	3.5	29.1	3.3	100.6	4.3
	Michigan	4.4	31.5	10.4	210.0	15.5
	Belovod', surface	59.6	161.3	72.0	250.0	539.9
	Belovod', depth 25 m	169.0	219.0	79.3	235.0	973.7
	Beloe (Kosino, Moscow Region)	7.04 + 15.18	22.44	9.48	88.48	19.40
Steppe	Utah (USA)	252	67	86	108	380
	Aidarkol' (Siberia)	1,808	7	50	130	560
	Balkhash	694	26	164	444	893
	Issyk-Kul'	1,475	114	294	240	2,115
	Gor'koe (Siberia)	2,178	7	130	100	2,170
	Caspian Sea	3,244	344	730	111	2,996
	Aral Sea	2,249	479	538	158	3,169
	Muyal'dy (near Pavlodar)	26,600	2,600	1,600	5,510	25,020
Desert and semi-desert	Great Salt Lake (USA)	96.6	0.55	7.15	—	8.5
	Dead Sea:					
	surface	25.94	9.09	25.52	—	0.49
	depth 300 m	18.7	17.26	43.4	—	0.52
	Asmantai	66.84	0.57	21.31	—	13.26
	Kosobulak (Ust'-Urt)	90.7	0.38	8.41	—	20.31
Humid tropics and subtropics	Tanganyika	24	15	36	128	15
	Albert	16.3	9.3	31.5	47.6	25
	Edward	200	12.4	47.8	601	31

mg/l			%·equivalent						Total concentration of salts, mg/L
Cl^-	SiO_2	CO_3	$K^+ + Na^+$	Ca^{++}	Mg^{++}	HCO_3^-	SO_4^-	Cl^-	
1.0	—	—							56.4
3.19	—	—	13.0	21.9	15.1	25.8	17.4	6.8	47.48
3.19	—	—	6.8	22.2	21.0	21.0	23.5	5.5	62.25
0	11.6	—	18.7	29.7	1.6	50.0	0	0	—
0	10.0	—	27.0	21.4	1.6	50.0	0	0	—
1.5	—	—	7.4	26.3	16.3	41.3	3.7	5.0	30.2
7.7	—	—	22.6	18.8	8.6	35.5	2.7	11.8	69
0.5	—	—	—	36.7	15.0	44.6	4.2	1.2	
0.8	5.0	—	4.6	35.5	9.9	45.4	3.25	1.26	68.4
0.43	2.24	—	7.8	34.5	7.65	45.6	3.7	0.5	91.4
4.2	—	—	3.8	39.0	7.3	44.4	2.4	3.2	145.0
6.2	3.1	—	3.2	30.3	16.5	40.5	6.1	3.4	
43.6	—	—	7.82	24.32	17.86	12.37	33.92	3.71	1,126.4
78.1	—	—	13.96	20.76	15.28	7.31	38.51	4.18	1,772.1
31.56			3.2 + 12.0	20.6	14.2	26.5	7.3	16.2	193.58
337	—	—	25.2	7.9	16.9	8.6	18.8	22.6	1,230
2,130	—	270	46.9	0.24	2.76	1.4	7.9	40.7	
574	—	48	33.0	1.4	15.6	10.3	21.5	18.2	2,843
1,585	—	—	33.9	3.1	13.0	2.1	23.8	24.1	5,823
1,900	—	150	49.3	0.17	0.53	0.8	22.5	26.7	6,638
5,321	—	—	32.5	3.97	13.8	0.8	14.4	34.5	12,744
3,461	—	—	29.4	7.1	13.5	0.8	19.4	29.1	10,054
27,400	—	1,040	40.7	4.58	4.95	3.4	18.4	27.2	
									g/kg
152.7	—	—	43.5	0.3	6.2	—	4.1	45.9	265.5
131.1	—	—	14.7	6.3	29.0	—	0.1	49.9	192.13
182.0	—	—	7.2	8.3	34.5	—	0.1	49.9	261.87
155.8	—	—	31.1	0.2	18.7	—	3.0	47.0	
149.7	—	—	42.6	0.2	7.2	—	4.5	45.5	269.5
34	—	—	10.6	8.0	31.4	31.3	4.6	14.1	
32	3.4	—	31.6	2.5	13.9	42.5	2.8	4.7	
36	6.5	—	30.6	2.78	16.7	43.5	2.75	4.48	

Dissolved Gases

Lake water contains greater or smaller amounts of dissolved gases such as nitrogen, oxygen, carbon dioxide, methane and hydrogen in addition to the salts. Methane, hydrogen, and to a lesser extent carbon dioxide enter water as a result of anaerobic disintegration of silt deposits, while oxygen and nitrogen, supplied by the atmosphere, are dissolved on the surface of the water. During the spring and fall circulation the content of dissolved gases comes into equilibrium with that of the atmosphere. The normal percentage of oxygen, nitrogen, and carbon dioxide in the air and the quantity of dissolved gases in water at normal pressure and temperature fluctuate within the limits indicated below.

Temperature, °C	Oxygen, mg/L	Nitrogen, mg/L	Carbon dioxide, mg/L
5	10.72	32.3	0.94
25	8.23	14.0	0.59

The concentration of oxygen fluctuates greatly during the vegetation period. The gases dissolved in the epilimnion are in equilibrium with the air. In the case of a strong water bloom, the daytime concentration of oxygen in this zone may reach supersaturation levels as high as 20 mg of O_2 per liter. In the hypolimnion, the dissolved oxygen is consumed in oxidation processes; the result may be a sharp decrease in the oxygen concentration, depending on the trophic state of the lake. Further details on the oxygen regime of lakes will be given below.

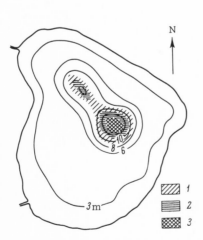

FIGURE 22. Gas production zone in Lake Beloe (Kosino) (after Rossolimo).

Amounts of gas (in liters) freezing in 1 cubic meter of ice during the winter: 1) 0—2; 2) 4—8; 3) 8—12.

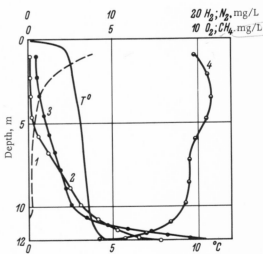

FIGURE 23. Vertical distribution of dissolved gases in the water of Lake Beloe, Kosino, at different depths on March 7, 1938:

1) O_2; 2) CH_4; 3) H_2; 4) N_2.

Free carbonic acid is formed not only in the water mass of the lake but also in the silt sediments as a result of the mineralization of organic matter. Appreciable amounts of methane and hydrogen accumulate in eutrophic waters, where the decomposition of silt (notably in the deep zone, Figure 22) yields marsh gas, which dissolves in the bottom water layers (Figure 23) and represents a source of energy for hydrogen-oxidizing and methane-oxidizing bacteria.

Free hydrogen sulfide may accumulate in lake water in some particular cases. The concentration of this gas in Big Soda Lake reaches 780 mg/L (Hutchinson, 1957). Since the formation and further oxidation of this gas are associated with the activity of microorganisms, these topics will be discussed below.

Active Acidity

The active acidity of the medium (i. e., the concentration of hydrogen ions) exerts a major influence on the composition and distribution of the aquatic population. The pH of lake water varies greatly, from 2 in Lake Kipyashchee on Kunashir Island (Ivanov and Karavaiko, 1966) and the volcanic lakes of Japan (Yoshimura, 1931) to 12 in Lake Nakuru, Kenya (Jenkin, 1932). S. N. Skadovskii (1928) has examined some theoretical aspects of this topic. Yoshimura (1931a) has classified the lakes in a series of groups on the basis of the acidity of water. The principles of this classification are outlined in Table 3.

TABLE 3. Relationship between pH and trophy of lake water

Type of lake	Buffer capacity		Development of plankton	Concentration of hydrogen ions (pH)			Annual fluctuations of pH
				circulation (overturn) period	summer stagnation period		
					epilimnion	hypolimnion	
Acidotrophic	Low	Little carbonate and humate	Very poor	2.0—4.8	2.0—4.8	2.0—4.8	Very slight
Oligotrophic			Poor	6.0—7.5	6.0—7.5	6.0—7.5	Slight
Eutrophic			Abundant		8.0—10.0		Very considerable
Dystrophic	High	Humates	Very slight	4.0—6.0	4.0—6.0	4.0—6.0	Very slight
Oligotrophic		Carbonates	Slight	7.0—8.5	7.0—8.5	7.0—8.0	Very slight
Eutrophic			Considerable		8.0—9.0		Considerable

In the USSR, systematic information on the acidity of lake water has been obtained from Lake Glubokoe (Kuznetsov and Duplakov, 1923; Shcherbakov,

1928, 1967a, etc.) and Lake Beloe in Kosino. V. I. Olifan (1928) has studied the diurnal changes of acidity in the Gigirevskii pond, where the pH fluctuates from 6.3 at night to 10.1 in the daytime during periods of peak photosynthesis.

Yoshimura (1931a, 1932a) has made a thorough study of the vertical distribution of pH. He describes a number of Japanese lakes where the lowest values of pH are found in the metalimnion.

Extremely low pH values were found in Lake Tyrrell, Australia (pH = 3.0), Lake Hawah-Taiwede on Java (pH = 2.1), and a number of Japanese lakes: Katanuma (pH = 1.4), Okamazao (pH = 1.9−3.4), Itsibisinai (2.3), Hudoki (2.9), Onumaike (2.8−3.7), etc. (Pervol'f, 1944).

A highly alkaline reaction of lake water is associated with an increased concentration of potassium and sodium. For example, several lakes in Kokchetava Region have a pH of 9.2−9.5, which results in a poorly developed plankton (Kuznetsov, 1950a).

Oxidation-Reduction Potential of Lake Water

The development of some microorganisms in water depends on the amount of dissolved oxygen. For example, many cellulose-destroying aerobes cannot grow in the absence of oxygen. Thiobacteria prefer a lower partial pressure of oxygen, while methane-producing bacteria are strict anaerobes.

The ecologic effect of aeration is only one aspect of the problem. For a better understanding of the transformation of matter in the water, it is necessary to determine the rate of environmental oxidation or reduction. This property is described by the oxidation-reduction potential.

All oxidative phenomena consist in the loss of an electron by the oxidized substance, regardless of whether the reaction is anaerobic or occurs with the participation of oxygen.

The oxidation-reduction potential is expressed generally as the potential between the environment and a normal hydrogen electrode that is conditionally taken as zero. Thus,

$$E_h = \frac{RT}{2F} \log \frac{|H^{\cdot}|^2}{|H_2|} \; .$$

In other words, the oxidation-reduction potential is a function of the concentration of hydrogen ions as oxidizing agent and the pressure of molecular hydrogen as a reducing agent.

The concentration of undissociated hydrogen, rH_2, can be expressed in atmospheres in the form of common logarithms. Thus, rH_2 is the negative logarithm of the concentration of undissociated hydrogen, which could create the given reducing properties of the medium. For example, at a hydrogen pressure of 0.01 atmospheres, the rH_2 of the solution will be $-\log 10^{-2} = 2$. The lower the value of rH_2, the greater the reducing capacity of the solution, and vice versa.

The neutral point of oxidation-reduction phenomena is $rH_2 = 28$. This value applies to water solutions; it is obtained from the equation of the dissociation of water vapor into oxygen and hydrogen. For 18° the constant $K = (H_2)^2 \times (O_2) = 10^{-85}$. By converting this equation into logarithms and substituting the respective values, we obtain $2rH_2 + rH_2$ since active hydrogen and oxygen are equimolecular. By substituting these values in the above formula, we have $3rH_2 = 85$, or $rH_2 \approx 28$. The relationship between rH_2 and E_h can be expressed as follows:

$$E_h = 0.029 \, (rH_2 - 2pH), \quad \text{or} \quad rH_2 = \frac{E_h}{0.029} + 2pH.$$

E_h, which represents the difference in potentials between the medium and the normal hydrogen electrode, depends not only on the concentration of molecular hydrogen but also on the concentration of hydrogen ions. For this reason, E_h alone cannot characterize the oxidation-reduction properties of a given environment unless the pH is specified. By contrast, rH_2 depends entirely on the concentration of the reducing agent and therefore is a direct expression of the prevailing oxidation-reduction conditions.

This distinction becomes especially evident when one examines the effect of E_h and pH on the degree of reduction of oxidation-reduction indicators.

Clark (1925) has made such a study with a number of oxidation-reduction indicators. Figure 24 shows the results obtained with methylene blue. Hence, the E_h values are plotted on the abscissa, while the ordinate indicates the reduction of methylene blue (in %). Each curve corresponds to a given value of pH. Thus, the curves show the effect of pH on the reduction of methylene blue.

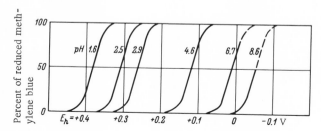

FIGURE 24. Reduction of methylene blue as a function of the oxidation-reduction potential and pH of the medium.

The organism has much in common with oxidation-reduction indicators as far as the reaction to oxidation-reduction conditions is concerned. Both actually react to the oxidation-reduction conditions; conclusions about the reaction of the living organism can be drawn from the data showing the effect of pH and rH_2 on the reduction of the indicator.

Methylene blue is 50% reduced at $rH_2 = 17$, regardless of the pH. When E_h is used as an expression of the oxidation-reduction potential, methylene blue can be 50% reduced at E_h values ranging from +0.380 to −0.05 V, depending on the pH of the stain solution.

Thus, the "conditional" symbol rH_2 accurately reflects the oxidative properties of the medium (Uspenskii, 1936, (1963)).

Since most biologic reactions occur at pH close to neutrality, even a slight absolute change of pH in the presence of stable oxidation-reduction conditions causes a major change in E_h. Because of its dependence on pH, E_h cannot provide a clear idea of the degree of aerobic conditions in the surrounding medium. Moreover, the existence of a reduction process may be overlooked if accompanied by a lowering of pH, because these two phenomena affect the E_h in opposite directions.

Chemists usually study the oxidation-reduction processes by means of strong oxidizing and reducing agents as ferric and ferrous salts in highly acidic solutions. In such conditions, even a major absolute change of acidity has little effect on pH, and E_h gives an accurate characteristic of the oxidation-reduction conditions.

The oxidation-reduction potential depends on the partial pressure of the oxygen dissolved in the water but is also associated with the transformations of nearly all biologically important compounds in the lake (Hutchinson, 1957). Oxygen dissolved in water reacts with the latter according to the equation:

$$O_2 + 2H_2O + 4e = 4\,OH^- \, .$$

Since the reaction is reversible, the equilibrium at the electrode can be expressed as follows:

$$E_h = E_0 - \frac{RT}{F} \ln \frac{\alpha OH^-}{4\sqrt{pO_2}} \, ,$$

where E_0 can be obtained by calculating the thermodynamics of the process, αOH^- is the activity of hydroxyl ions, pO_2 the partial pressure of oxygen. Now the activity of hydroxyl ions is associated with that of the hydrogen ions according to the formula

$$\log \alpha_{OH^-} = pK_w - pH.$$

Thus the above equation assumes the following form at a temperature of 18°, at which K_w equals 14.23:

$$E_h = 1.234 - 0.058\,pH + 0.0145 \log pO_2 \, ;$$

This equation shows the relationship between the oxidation-reduction potential and the partial pressure of oxygen dissolved in the water.

The same equation demonstrates also the effect of a lowering in the concentration of dissolved oxygen on the oxidation-reduction potential of lake water. Assuming that the partial pressure of oxygen at 18° is 100% and that pH=7, this relationship assumes the form shown in Figure 25. As the graph shows, the oxidation-reduction potential falls appreciably when the partial pressure of oxygen drops below 10% of the saturation level. In other words, a marked decrease in the oxidation-reduction potential can take place only if the concentration of dissolved oxygen drops below 1 mg/l, though even in such case the E_h of the solution will not fall below 0.810 V. Clearly, the decrease in the oxidation-reduction potential of the silts and deep waters of the lake must be due to the formation of active reducing agents.

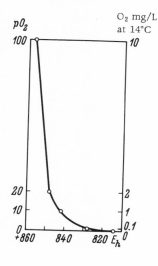

FIGURE 25. Relationship between the content of dissolved oxygen and the oxidation-reduction potential of pure water.

The scarcity of data on the oxidation-reduction potential of lake water results largely from practical difficulties, such as the necessity of carrying out electrometric measurements on the site and the prolonged period of time necessary for the establishment of the potential between the electrode and the water.

TABLE 4. Oxidation-reduction potentials of the waters of different types of lakes during the summer stagnation period

Type of lake	Epilimnion			Hypolimnion					
				upper layers			bottom layers		
	E_h	rH_2	pH	E_h	rH_2	pH	E_h	rH_2	pH
Oligotrophic	450–420	29.5	7.0, 6.4	450	28.0	6.2, 6.3	458	28.0	6.2, 6.3
Mesotrophic	460	31.0	7.5	—	—	—	330	25.0	6.8
Eutrophic	460	30.0	7.2	440	28.0	6.5	250	21.6	6.5
	410	26.5	6.2	320	22.6	5.8	120	15.6	5.8
Dystrophic	510	29.4	5.7	320	22.6	5.8	120	15.6	5.8
	480	29.1	6.3	250	19.3	5.6	260	20.0	5.6

Measurements of the oxidation-reduction potential of lake waters have been carried out in the USSR by S. I. Kuznetsov (1935) and T. I. Nekhotenova (1938), and in the USA by the group of Hutchinson (Hutchinson et al., 1939) and the Wisconsin limnological group (Allgeier et al., 1941). Table 4 shows data obtained by these authors during the summer stagnation period. Oligotrophic lakes have a high oxidation-reduction potential throughout the water mass.

In eutrophic and dystrophic lakes, the potential reaches very low values in the bottom layers of water, to $rH_2 = 15$. Thus, in these layers intensive reduction processes take place and continue at a sufficiently high rate even after the total disappearance of dissolved oxygen. The next marked drop of the oxidation-reduction potential occurs at the border between water and silt sediments.

As will be shown below (Table 17, Figure 32), the rH_2 of the surface layers of silt equals 9—12 in eutrophic lakes and 18—23 in mesotrophic lakes, depending on the presence or absence of oxygen in the bottom water.

Organic Matter in the Water Mass of Lakes

The organic matter found in lakes can be divided into three categories (Waksman, 1941).

1. Suspended organic matter, namely: (a) live phytoplankton and bacteria; (b) dead plankton, also plant and animal remains brought in by winds or currents; (c) detritus or partly degraded organic remains showing major chemical changes due to the activity of animals and bacteria and to physical-chemical processes.

2. Dissolved organic matter, including colloidal organic substances. Some authors (Krogh and Lange, 1931) place in this category organic particles that are smaller than bacteria but are retained by the existing colloid filters.

Waksman divides the dissolved organic matter into (a) substances resistant to further degradation — a group that can be broadly named "aquatic humus"; (b) intermediate decomposition products more easily assimilable by bacteria, such as amino acids, fatty acids, alcohols, hydrocarbons, and proteins.

3. Organic matter of the silt sediments. This category, like that of suspended organic matter, is subdivided into three groups: (a) substances of live organisms; (b) readily decomposable components of dead organisms, such as hydrocarbons, polyuronids, some proteins, and fats; (c) "lake humus" — substances highly resistant to further degradation, such as lignins and their transformation products, some nitrogen compounds of the melanin type, etc.

Birge and Juday (1927, 1934), who have studied the organic composition of the water of many American lakes, note that the concentration of suspended organic matter in the surface layer ranges from 0.23 to 12 mg/L, averaging 1.36 mg/L. Seasonal fluctuations in the amount of suspended organic matter are absent from a few lakes only; usually they reach a considerable magnitude. Running lakes are usually richer in suspended organic matter and consequently more productive than stagnant lakes. Indeed, running lakes receive an abundant supply of organic matter with the river inflow. Shallow lakes having a depth of 2—3 m are especially productive as a rule. The repeated complete circulation of water that often takes place in such lakes during the summer refills the water mass with biogenic elements formed by the breakdown of silt. This leads in turn to a proliferation of phytoplankton.

TABLE 5. Quantity and chemical composition of organic matter in lakes (after Birge and Juday, 1934)

Total carbon content of water, mg/L (C)	Total content of organic matter in water, mg/L		Composition of organic matter of water after removal of plankton, %		
	plankton	dissolved	proteins*	fats extracted by ether	hydrocarbons and organic acids**
1.0—1.9	0.62	3.09	24.3	2.3	73.4
5.0—5.9	1.27	10.33	19.4	1.3	79.0
10.0—10.9	1.89	20.48	14.4	0.4	85.2
15.0—15.9	2.32	31.30	12.9	0.2	86.9
20.0—25.8	2.22	48.12	9.9	0.2	89.9
Average	1.36	15.24	15.6	0.7	83.7

* Obtained by multiplying the total nitrogen by a coefficient of 6.25.
** Calculated from the carbon content, after subtracting the carbon of the proteins and the ether fraction.

The vertical distribution of suspended organic matter is not uniform. Birge and Juday give the following data for the position of the peak concentration of organic matter in lakes whose depth exceeds 18 m: at the surface in 10% of the cases, in the bottom layers in 34%, and in the meta- and hypolimnion in 54%.

Table 5 shows the relationship between dissolved and suspended organic matter in lake water.

Birge and Juday (1922, 1926) give the following average composition of organic matter in eighty-seven plankton samples from Lake Mendota: protein 44.5%, fats 7.5%, hydrocarbons 48.0%.

The figures showing the composition of dissolved organic matter as given in Table 5 are highly conditional, since only a fraction of the nitrogen is bound in proteins. Moreover, the ether fraction contains not only fats but also bituminous compounds, while a considerable part of the residual carbon participates in humin compounds and organic acids (Goryunova, 1952); naturally, Birge and Juday have only conditionally assigned the residual carbon to the group of hydrocarbons.

The presence of humic matter in lake water has been demonstrated by Ohle (1933), by direct determination of methoxyl groups, and by Fotiev (1966), who has obtained preparations of fulvic acid from the water of rivers flowing into the Rybinsk Artificial Reservoir.

In a thorough study of some organic nitrogen compounds in lake water, Peterson, Fred, and Domogalla (1925) found the existence of free amino acids and determined the concentration of tryptophan, tyrosine, histidine, arganine, and cysteine. They report a concentration of about 13 mg/m³ for each of the first three amino acids and about 4 mg/m³ for cysteine.

According to Fogg and Westlake (1955), the concentrations of amine and peptide nitrogen in nine English lakes are respectively 6—25 mg/m³ and 16—43 mg/m³. These results are in harmony with the data published by the American authors.

The degradation of dissolved organic matter by bacteria is an important factor in the chemical cycle of lakes. By determining the utilization of oxygen for the breakdown of organic matter in water kept in sealed vessels, Keys and co-authors (1935) found that only 10% of the organic matter dissolved in sea water can be assimilated by bacteria. Waksman and Renn (1936) obtained higher figures — up to 25%.

Similar tests were made for the determination of the assimilable organic matter in different types of lakes (Table 6).

TABLE 6. Relationship between assimilable and total organic matter in the surface water of different types of lakes during the summer stagnation (after Novobrantsev, 1937; Kuznetsov, 1952)

Type	Lake	Total amount of organic matter, mg O_2/L	Easily assimilable organic matter		Assimilable organic matter as percent of total
			mg O_2/L	mg glucose/L (by calculation)	
Oligotrophic	Pertozero	15.0	0.3	0.44	2.0
	Konchozero	15.3	0.5	0.67	3.3
	Gabozero	15.8	0.3	0.40	0.9
Dystrophic	Old peat bank ..	226.6	3.96	4.96	1.3
Eutrophic	Beloe (Kosino, Moscow Region) ..	32.1	3.06	4.25	9.6
	Bol'shoe Medvezh'e	33.7	5.16	7.16	15.3

As shown in Table 6, the assimilable organic matter can reach an absolute magnitude equivalent to 7 mg of glucose per liter, while its percentage of the total depends on the trophic state of the lake — 2—3% in oligotrophic lakes, about 1.5% in dystrophic lakes, and 15% in eutrophic lakes; here the total amount of organic matter is determined by the chromium method (Vinberg et al., 1934; Fatchikhina, 1948).

Lake Silts and Their Physical-Chemical Characteristics

Silt sediments are an essential component of lakes. Their quantity depends on the lake morphology, the amount of biogenic elements, and the runoff and geographic position of the lake. In many cases the silt layer is thicker than the water mass of the lake (Figure 26). Silts invariably contain some proportion of organic matter, which participates to a large extent in the chemical transformations in the lake. A brief outline of the chemical and physical properties of silt is therefore necessary before entering into a discussion of the chemical role of microorganisms in lakes.

Terminology and Classification of Lake Sediments

The term sapropel ("rotten mud"), proposed by Potonier, is commonly used in the USSR for lake silts (Solov'ev, 1932). However, this same term is commonly applied to highly mineralized silts that have little in common with "rotten mud." Even Potonier distinguished between several varieties of sapropel.

Lundquist (1927) has proposed a detailed classification based on morphologic signs. These two classifications have much in common; the terminology used by Potonier therefore appears in parentheses in the classification of Lundquist, which is outlined below.

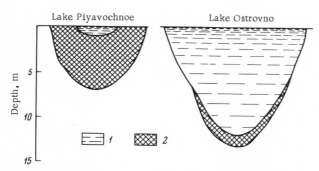

FIGURE 26. Comparative thickness of silt sediments in lakes of different types (after Stal'makova, 1941):

1) water; 2) silt.

Lundquist distinguishes between the following types of lake sediments:
    I.   Sediments rich in mineral components — clayey gyttja;
    II.   Sediments rich in lime (sapropel clay);
       A) poor in organic matter — lake marl;
       B) rich in organic matter — calcareous gyttja (calcareous sapropel);
    III.   Sediments rich in organic matter with valves of molluskan shells visible to the naked eye — shell gyttja;
    IV.   Sediments with ferruginous inclusions visible to the naked eye — lake iron ore;
    V.   Sediments rich in organic matter without mineral inclusions visible to the naked eye;
       A) rich in peat particles, does not become lighter upon drying — dy;
       B) rich in organic remnants of a gelatinous structure, becomes lighter upon drying;
          1. Microscopic structure: fine, strongly decayed elements whose origin cannot be established with certainty — fine-detritus gyttja (sapropel);
          2. Microscopic structure: less decomposed elements whose origin can be easily established;
             a) composed essentially of remains of higher plants, mosses, and some algae — coarse-detritus gyttja (sapropel);
             b) composed essentially of remains of lower plants, algae, and a transparent detritus — algal gyttja (sapropel).

The microscopic structure of lake silts was largely neglected after Lundquist. A. G. Rodina (1963a, 1963b, 1967) has started a new trend with her studies of lake detritus with the ultraviolet microscope.

The silt sediments outlined by Lundquist can be classified in the following simpler manner on the basis of their origin.

    I. Predominantly inorganic silts;

      A) composed mostly of clay particles — lake clays;

      B) composed mostly of calcium carbonate particles — lake marl;

      C) composed mostly of ferruginous inclusions visible to the naked eye — lake iron ore;

      D) composed mostly of valves of diatoms — diatom silt;

    II. Silts with low inorganic content (loss on calcination amounts to more than 15%);

      A) rich in gelatinous organic remains, become lighter upon drying: microscopic structure — mostly fine, decomposed elements whose nature and origin cannot be determined with certainty — fine-detritus silt;

        1) microscopic structure — various remnants of higher plants, mosses with some proportion of zooplankton and algae — coarse-detritus silt;

        2) microscopic structure — remains of algae and a transparent detritus — algal silt;

      B) rich in peat particles, do not become lighter upon drying — peaty silt.

Microzonal Theory of Silt Structure

The heterogeneous vertical structure of silt sediments is often apparent to the naked eye. This phenomenon reflects irregularities in the physical-chemical conditions of the environment and is therefore associated with an irregular distribution of microorganisms, whose metabolism in turn affects the vertical distribution of the different elements. The result is a regular vertical series of silt formation representing consecutive stages of the process in layers whose thickness is often measured in fractions of the milli-meter. These thin layers indicate an alternation of microbiologic processes. They are especially evident in the surface zone of silt. B. V. Perfil'ev (1932) refers to these layers as "microzones," defined as silt layers characterized by biological and physical-chemical factors that are combined into a given dynamic complex of certain duration.

B. V. Perfil'ev distinguishes between three microzonal types on the basis of their origin: (1) conversion microzones; (2) sedimentation microzones; and (3) growth microzones.

The conversion microzones develop in the silt at a short distance from its surface, that is, in places where the mechanical effect of waves is no longer evident and the silt particles settle into a resting condition. This zone of the silt usually exhibits a fine stratification of microorganisms and physical-chemical factors. Such phenomena can be easily obtained in laboratory cultures of silt, when the surface zone of the latter shows a ser-ies of fine layers, each with a specific color and microfauna.

According to B. V. Perfil'ev, the conversion microzones owe their existence to the establishment of a dynamic chemical equilibrium between two opposite diffusion currents. One of these currents consists of oxidized compounds produced by the oxidation of protoxide substances with oxygen dissolved in the water. This current flows from the water mass into the silt. The opposite current brings reduced compounds formed by the anaerobic decomposition of silt materials in deeper layers.

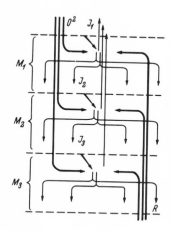

FIGURE 27. Scheme showing the formation and interrelationships of the conversion microzones (after Perfil'ev):

M_1, M_2, and M_3) successive microzones of silt; O^2) oxidizing agent; R) reducing agent; I_1, I_2, and I_3) sedimentation of different ingredients from the solution as a result of microbial activity.

The vertical gradation of oxidation-reduction conditions at the boundary between these currents creates a series of optimal conditions for different microorganisms. The rate of chemical decomposition and transformation of silt differs from one microbial species to another; hence, the conspicuous microzonal stratification of silt. B. V. Perfil'ev illustrates these relationships in the scheme shown in Figure 27.

M_1, M_2, and M_3 represent three consecutive microzones. Each microzone receives two opposite currents: oxygen (O_2) from the overlying water and reduced decomposition products (hydrogen sulfide, methane, ferrous oxide, etc.) designated collectively with the letter R.

The reactions are induced by the microorganisms I_1, I_2, and I_3, represented by oblique arrows; the vertical arrows indicate the sedimentation of products specific to the given microzone.

The sedimentation microzones reflect the considerable seasonal changes in the composition of the dust and solid materials that are brought into the lake and settle on its bottom year after year.

Biogenic sedimentation microzones are produced by the death of microflora within a short time following a summer bloom in the water mass. Such a phenomenon often occurs in small water bodies. By settling on the silt surface, the remains of plankton can give rise to sedimentation microzones.

In oligotrophic lakes, sedimentation microzones are usually formed by mineral particles of different origin. The commonest material is calcium carbonate, which precipitates in summer as a result of an uptake of carbonic acid by microflora. Clay particles usually settle in winter; they represent a reliable guide of annual layers (B. V. Perfil'ev, 1931) (Figure 28). B. V. Perfil'ev has studied the microzonal structure of silt in Lake Averno near Vesuvius in Italy. There he found microzones of Vesuvian ashes among alternating annual microzones of plankton and calcium carbonate. That the different microzones correspond to annual cycles is evident from the number of biogenic microzones between the layers of volcanic ashes. However, a chronologic conclusion based on the microzonal distribution of morphologic remains in the silt can only be regarded as reliable (when compared to laboratory experiments with similar sediments).

Conversion microzones often hamper geochronological research by masking the stratification pattern.

According to B. V. Perfil'ev, the microzones of growth are thin biologic films developing on the silt surface. These films consist of a rich microflora of algae or bacteria growing at the expense of biogenic elements from the silt. Such growths lead to a massive precipitation of salts from the water mass. In other words, the growth microzones are intermediate between the sedimentation and conversion microzones.

Geographic Zonality of Lake Sediments

Starting from the theory of geographic landscapes and climatic zones, V. V. Alabyshev (1932) established certain regularities in the zonal distribution of lake sediments. More information on this topic is available in connection with lakes situated in the European part of the USSR (Figure 29).

In the tundra and temperate forest zones, the bottoms of shallow lakes contain gelatinous sediments with a large proportion of organic material. According to V. V. Alabyshev, the southern border of the fresh-water sapropels extends from Gomel in Belorussia to Ryazan Region (through Kaluga and the Meshcherskaya Lowland) then to Vladimir Region (Murom), the Chuvash Autonomous SSR (Cheboksary), and finally to Elabuga and Ufa.

Clayey and calcareous silts are also found in lakes of the forest zone. However, sediments rich in calcium carbonate are usually associated with outcrops of calcareous bedrock.

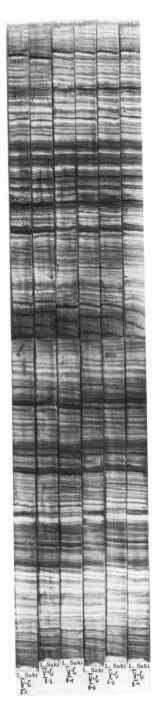

FIGURE 28. Microzonal structure of the silt of Lake Saki (after Perfil'ev).

FIGURE 29. Scheme of the zonal distribution of lake sediments in the European part of USSR (after Alabyshev).

Areas: 1) diatom silts; 2) lake chalk; 3) iron and manganese lake ores; 4) clay silts; 5) sand silts; 6) zone of brackish lakes; 7) zone of salt lakes; 8) tundra zone with fine-detritus silts; 9) mountain zone; 10) northern border of chernozems; 11) fresh-water silts; 12) lake chalk; 13) diatom silt; 14) medicinal mineral muds; 15) Glauber's salt; 16) sodium chloride; 17) magnesium salts; 18) lake iron ores.

Lake iron sediments occur mostly in the Fennoscandian crystalline shield in the north, that is, in Arkhangel'sk Region and the Karelian Autonomous SSR (Gaevskii, 1923) at outcrops of crystalline rocks, diorites, labradorites, etc.

Calcareous sapropels are known in the Baltic Silurian calcareous plateau, between Lake Onega and Lake Voldozero in an area of rendzina soils, along Kama River, and on the watershed between Vychegda and Pechora. According to V. V. Alabyshev, the moraine may have been rich in soluble salts of sodium and calcium during the retreat of the glacier, judging from the abundance of calcium salts in the lower parts of the silt sediments of many lakes, including Lake Glubokoe in Moscow Region (Rossolimo, 1961).

Brackish and salt lakes gradually replace the fresh-water ones in the south, in the arid climate of the desert and semidesert zones. V.V.Alabyshev divides these lakes in two groups on the basis of their silt sediments: (a) salt lakes with vast deposits of black and gray-black organic medicinal muds containing a large proportion of iron sulfide; (b) salt lakes in which the mineral salts may predominate at the expense of the organic compounds — polyhaline lakes.

The area of these lakes decreases considerably in summer because of the dry climate. The evaporation of water leaves snow-white surfaces of Glauber's salt (sodium sulfate), soda, or sodium chloride, and in some cases even gypsum. However, the bulk of the salts precipitates from the water in winter during the ice formation.

The bottom sediments of lakes in the desert-steppe zone can attain a thickness of several meters. The black layers of mineral muds are often interspersed with streaks of mirabilite crystals, notably in the lakes of the Kulunda Steppe.

In tropical areas, where rainfall is considerable, the silts of fresh-water lakes contain a large proportion of organic matter — up to 50%.

A similar transition from mineral muds to fresh-water sapropels is observed in a vertical sense. One example of such transition is found in Kokchetav Region, where the Kokchetav crystalline range lies amid the steppe. Here the polyhaline lakes Balpash and Orazsor are situated in the steppe, while fresh-water lakes, such as Borovoe, Svetloe, and Lebyazh'e, lie in the highlands; each category of lakes has its type of bottom sediments.

Many transitions exist between the clear-cut types of lake silts. For this reason, the classification of lake silts is largely conditional, like the division of lakes on the basis of their trophic conditions.

Thermal Relationships of Silt Sediments

The temperature of lake silt exerts a major influence on the microbiological processes in the lake by affecting the temperature of the whole water mass. The heat budget of the silt of Lake Beloe in Kosino accounts for about 24% of the total annual heat budget of the lake (Rossolimo, 1932a). In Lake Mendota, seasonal fluctuations of temperature affect the silt to a depth of more than 5 m (Birge et al., 1928) (Table 7).

As shown in Table 7, the winter temperature of silt at a depth of 0.5 m is much higher than that of the silt surface; moreover, the silt temperature in winter rises with depth. In summer, the relationship is reversed.

As a result of heat conductivity, the bottom water layer gradually warms up in winter and cools down in summer. This pattern is largely responsible for the bottom water currents and the warming of the deep masses of lake water in winter.

It is noteworthy that the temperature of the bulk of the silt of lakes of the temperate zone does not exceed 8—10°C. Higher temperatures occur only in summer and are confined to the very surface of silt. The seasonal fluctuations of the silt temperature decrease with depth in the silt, reaching a practically negligible range (1—2°C) at a depth of 0.5—1 m from the silt surface.

Chemical Composition of Silt Sediments

Silts take some part in the lake chemistry even after settling on the bottom. Their mineralization supplies the water mass with biogenic and inorganic elements and provides a substrate for mineralizing microorganisms. It is evident, therefore, that the chemical composition of silt represents an important ecological factor to the bottom microflora. The organic composition of silt is of particular interest in this connection.

Composition of organic matter. Chemical analysis after Waksman and Tenney (1927) provides comprehensive data on the composition of organic matter in terms of its availability to microorganisms (Kuznetsov, Speranskaya, and Konshin, 1939; Kazakov and Tovbin, 1939, etc.). The scheme proposed by Waksman includes the following components: waxes and bitumens, water-soluble substances and sugars, hemicelluloses and gluconic acids, celluloses and lignin-humus compounds.

Both the quality and the quantity of organic matter affect the activity of microorganisms. Table 8 shows the proportions of the organic components of silt in lakes of different types.

TABLE 7. Temperature at different levels in the silt sediments of Lake Mendota, °C (after Birge et al., 1928)

Depth of station, m	1918—1919	Depth from surface of silt, m							
		surface	0.5	1.0	1.5	2.0	3.0	4.0	5.0
8	15 Dec	2.3	5.7	8.3	9.8	11.0	11.5	11.1	10.6
	1 Aug	22.3	20.1	16.5	13.3	11.6	9.7	9.2	9.4
12	15 Dec	2.2	5.5	7.9	9.4	10.1	10.1	9.5	9.3
	15 July	15.3	12.8	11.2	9.9	9.0	8.6	8.7	8.8
18	1 Jan	1.8	4.4	6.4	7.7	8.5	8.8	8.5	8.6
	1 Oct	12.5	11.0	9.8	9.1	8.6	8.1	7.8	7.8
23	1 Jan	2.8	5.1	7.0	7.9	8.3	8.7	8.6	8.2
	1 Oct	11.5	10.5	9.6	8.9	8.5	8.0	7.8	7.8

TABLE 8. Composition of organic matter in the surface silt of lakes

Substance	% of total amount of organic matter			
			average for lakes	
	minimum	maximum	in Moscow and Kalinin regions	in Karelia
Waxes and bitumens ················	1.91	23.93	8.0	6.11
Hemicellulose ····················	3.99	22.64	14.1	9.76
Cellulose ························	3.63	12.12	7.5	7.04
Lignin-humus complex ··············	33.85	77.99	60	51.09
Total carbon ·····················	32.18	59.43	—	—
Extractable compounds that do not reduce the Fehling solution (by difference) ··	—	—	5.88	22.26
Total nitrogen ····················	1.90	5.86	4.52	3.74

Despite the considerable difference in the percentage of some organic components of silt, the composition of the organic matter varies but little from one type of lake to another (Table 8); greater deviations occur in exceptional cases only.

Organic analysis of the successive layers of silt provides data on the rate of decomposition, the origin of the sediments, and the thickness of the layer where biologic phenomena proceed at a fast rate. Table 9 shows the organic composition as a function of depth inside the silt.

The silts become denser and less moist in the course of time (Table 9). Theoretically, their ash content should increase with depth because the decomposition of the organic components of silt yields gases. In Lake Beloe, however, the ash content at a depth of 5 m is less than on the surface of the silt. This is so because the conditions of silt formation were different from the present regime; in other words, the ash content of the silt is not an indicator of the mineralization of its organic matter.

The amount of compounds extractable in the alcohol-benzene fraction usually reaches a peak at the very surface of silt and decreases with depth. The proportions of hemicellulose and cellulose sharply decrease from the silt surface to a depth of 1 m. Nevertheless, the reserves of these compounds are still sufficient for a microbiological decomposition, although at a depth of 1 m such decomposition practically stops.

It was believed until recently that the abundance of microorganisms in lake silts precludes the existence of free sugars. By means of alcohol extracts, however, Vallentyne and co-workers (1959) have found in silts a variety of sugars, including saccharose, maltose, glucose, fructose, galactose, arabinose, xylose, ribose, and an unidentified sugar, probably a trisaccharide. The total amount of sugar reached 100—300 mg per 1 kg of dry organic weight. Maltose, glucose, and saccharose occurred in greatest quantities, and only traces of pentoses were present. Extraction with cold ether or 70% boiling alcohol yielded a much greater amount of sugars than did extraction with water. This indicates that the sugars are situated inside particulate components of the silt. In the silts of Lake Opinicon, Ontario, the ash content is close to 50% (Table 10), and the amount of sugars ranges from a maximum at the silt surface to nil at a depth of 40—45 cm.

TABLE 9. Analysis of silt at different levels in lakes Beloe and Chernoe, Kosino, Moscow Region (after Kuznetsov, Speranskaya, and Konshin, 1939)

Lake	Depth from silt surface, cm	moisture, %	% of dry weight						% of organic matter					
			ash content	alcohol-benzene fraction	hemicellulose	cellulose	lignin-humus complex	total nitrogen	alcohol-benzene fraction	sugars and hemicellulose	cellulose	lignin-humus complex	total nitrogen	total carbon
Beloe	0–15	97.5	54.12	5.58	8.60	5.61	21.60	2.69	12.16	18.74	12.23	47.08	5.86	43.57
	100	94.4	58.36	3.79	5.91	3.92	19.91	2.39	9.10	14.19	9.41	47.81	5.74	45.04
	250	90.5	63.03	2.17	4.66	3.13	19.78	2.38	5.87	12.60	8.47	53.50	6.44	45.98
	500		42.18	4.45	9.65	1.85	27.69	3.09	7.20	16.69	3.20	47.89	5.34	45.52
Chernoe ...	0–15	97.0	49.26	3.74	7.34	3.91	31.48	2.34	7.37	14.47	7.71	62.04	5.40	55.83
	100	94.0	49.15	2.93	4.55	2.84	31.56	3.25	5.76	8.95	5.59	62.06	6.39	46.37
	200	93.5	47.30	2.84	3.97	2.30	35.20	2.80	5.39	7.53	4.36	66.79	5.31	45.90
	300	92.1	48.52	2.37	3.62	2.26	35.36	2.85	4.60	7.07	4.39	68.69	5.54	46.39
	500	90.9	46.57	2.63	3.36	3.57	37.72	2.43	4.92	6.29	6.61	70.60	4.55	45.72

TABLE 10. Sugar content of the silt sediments of Lake Opinicon, Ontario (sugars extractable with 70% alcohol, g per kg of organic matter of silt) (after Valentine, 1959)

Depth from silt surface, cm	Maltose	Saccharose	Glucose	Total amount of sugars	Loss in roasting of silt	Moisture of silt, %
0—5	1.6	0.2	1.3	2.9	51.9	97.8
5—10	1.0	0.1	0.9	1.9	52.1	96.8
10—15	0.95	0.00	0.46	1.4	51.5	96.2
20—25	0.81	0.00	0.57	1.4	51.5	95.9
30—35	0.34	0.00	0.17	0.5	52.5	95.9
40—45	0.04	0.00	0.04	0.08	54.8	95.9

TABLE 11. Forms of nitrogen in lake sediments, % of the total nitrogen (after Konshin, 1939)

Type of lake	Lake	Ammonia		Amide	Diamino-acids	Monoamino-acid fraction	Non-hydroly-zable
		total	volatile				
Eutrophic	Beloe (Kosino, Moscow Region)..	15.91	5.46	12.21	6.02	59.85	8.23
	Svyatoe (Kosino, Moscow Region)..	5.22	0.88	14.66	18.16	47.58	18.50
	Chernoe (Kosino, Moscow Region)..	0.72	—	17.79	9.55	60.30	17.76
Mesotrophic	Glubokoe (Moscow Region)	3.43	0.00	15.02	17.74	53.02	17.14
	Valdai	1.45	—	12.73	32.64	40.64	10.91
	Krugloe (Moscow Region)	1.96	—	16.18	19.55	50.33	11.51
Dystrophic	Kobelevo (Valdai)	0.66	—	13.75	19.78	51.20	19.49
	Mazurinskoe ..... (Moscow Region)	0.00	—	13.27	15.37	46.29	31.26

Forms of nitrogen in silt sediments. Nitrogen is one of the major organogenic elements in microbial growth. For this reason it is interesting to examine the concentrations of different forms of nitrogen in the surface layers of silt. Water extracts of silt contain only ammonia salts but no nitrogen bases or peptones. The concentration of volatile ammonia is greatest in eutrophic lakes but nil in dystrophic ones; it decreases as the carbon/nitrogen ratio of the silt rises. The rest of the nitrogen is bound in proteins and in the lignin-humus complex. Hydrolysis with strong hydrochloric acid converts the proteins into simpler components whose proportions vary according to the trophic regime of the lake (Table 11).

Most of the protein nitrogen occurs in the form of monoamino acids. The amount of nonhydrolyzable nitrogen in the form of humin compounds is lowest in the typically eutrophic Lake Beloe and increases with the degree of dystrophy.

Similar analyses were made by N. T. Shabarova (1950) for the silt of Lake Piyavochkoe (Table 12).

TABLE 12. Forms of nitrogen in the silt of Lake Piyavochnoe, % of the total nitrogen (after Shabarova, 1950)

Depth from silt surface, cm	Base nitrogen	Amide nitrogen	Monoamino-acid nitrogen	Nonhydrolyzable nitrogen
0—20	6.6	4.7	44.6	41.9
40	3.8	9.4	43.6	42.4
75	3.6	4.3	47.0	44.2
220—260	4.2	6.6	39.6	47.7
300—340	6.7	3.8	42.0	42.5
500	8.9	0.4	37.7	51.6
540—580	7.8	0.0	34.5	57.5
760	2.7	0.0	28.1	68.9

The percentage of humus nitrogen increases with depth into the silt, that is, with the age of silt; at the same time there is a decrease in the concentration of amide and monoamino-acid nitrogen.

However, only a fraction of the amide and amino-acid nitrogen of the silt is in a form that can be utilized by microorganisms. The availability of these nitrogen compounds depends largely on the bonds between the different components of the protein molecule. Since microorganisms can utilize only those organic compounds that can be enzymatically hydrolyzed, the utilizable fraction of organic matter can be determined by weak hydrolysis with 5% sulfuric acid — a process roughly comparable to enzymatic hydrolysis (I. V. Tyurin and M. M. Kononova, 1934).

We have treated in a similar manner a number of samples of the surface sediments of lakes with different trophic regimes. The data obtained (Table 13) were used for a classification of the lakes into groups according to the concentrations of readily hydrolyzable nitrogen and the total carbon — factors of particular importance to microbial physiology.

The lakes in the second column of Table 13 are mostly of the winter-kill category, characterized by a severe deficiency of oxygen in the hypolimnion. The third column comprises lakes with less pronounced reductive conditions associated with various aspects of microbial activity. In this group, some of the lakes with carbon-rich silts are markedly influenced by surrounding swamps, while those with carbon-poor silts show a transition to the meso-trophic type.

In the fourth column are listed lakes with a still lower concentration of utilizable nitrogen — between 0.59 and 0.27%. Here the lakes with carbon-rich silts are typically dystrophic (Lake Mazurinskoe). At a carbon content below 20%, the lakes of this group are typically mesotrophic, with a drastic deficiency of oxygen in the metalimnion (Seredei, Glubokoe, Valdaiskoe, Beloe, and Valdai).

Finally, the fifth column of Table 13 includes typically oligotrophic Karelian lakes with silts poor in nitrogen and carbon.

Mineral composition of silt sediments. Beside their organic components lake silts contain considerable amounts of mineral compounds. Of the latter, those participating in microbial metabolism are of particular interest to us. This category includes phosphorus, sulfur, iron, manganese, calcium,

TABLE 13. Division of lakes into groups according to the concentrations of carbon and assimilable nitrogen in the silt

Total carbon, % of dry weight	Assimilable nitrogen, % of dry weight			
	1.69—1.19	1.02—0.62	0.59—0.27	0.25—0.08
48.6—42.2	Nelyushka (Moscow Region)	Svyatoe (Kosino, Moscow Region), Dilevo (Moscow Region), Chernoe (Vyshnii Volochek)	Mazurinskoe (Moscow Region)	
37.98—28.36	Bisserovo (Moscow Region)	Zaverkhov'e (Vyshnii Volochek), Chernushka, and Golubova (Valdai)	Lepestovo and Lyubinets (Vyshnii Volochek), Koverlamba (Karelia)	Peat bank near Lake Maloe Medvezh'e (Moscow Region)
27.38—19.90	Chernoe (Kosino, Moscow Region), Maloe Medvezh'e (Moscow Region), Kolomenskoe (Vyshnii Volochek), Bol'shoe Medvezh'e (Moscow Region), Beloe (Kosino, Moscow Region)	Ovinchishche, Bol'shoe Vyskodno, and Koretskoe (Valdai)	Chernoe, Beloe, and Seredei (Valdai)	
19.9—11.4		Ostrovki, Ostrovno, Klin, and Imolozh'e (Vyshnii Volochek)	Shitovskoe (Vyshnii Volochek), Brezgovo, Glubokoe (Valdai)	Pol'lamba (Karelia)
7.3—1.9			Uzhino and El'chino (Valdai), Krugloe (Moscow Region)	Gabozero, Urozero, and Konchozero, Imanda, Ukshezero, and Pertozero (Karelia)

TABLE 14. Ash content of the silt of lakes with different trophic states (after Deksbakh, 1934; Rossolimo, 1928; Titov, 1949; Vereshchagin, 1948)

Type of lake	Lake	Nature of sediments	Ash content, % of dry weight	Composition of ash, % of dry weight								
				SiO$_2$	SO$_3$	P$_2$O$_5$	Al$_2$O$_3$	Fe$_2$O$_3$	MnO$_2$	CaO	MgO	K$_2$O
Eutrophic	Chernoe (Kosino, Moscow Region)	Algal silt	46.6	18.95	0.62	1.79	19.75		–	1.48	–	0.06
	Trostenskoe (Moscow Region)	Fine detrital silt	30.65	20.46	0.61	0.45	5.55			1.72		0.25
	Beloe (Vyshnii Volochek)	Algal silt	15.06	11.51	–	0.10	0.33	0.80	1.82	0.94	0.08	–
	Mazurinskoe (Urals)	Freshwater marl	58.69	9.84	–		2.4	0.78		23.0	0.4	–
Mesotrophic	Imolozh'e (Vyshnii Volochek)	Coarse detrital silt	62.95	41.7	–	0.48	6.59	5.58	0.22	1.27	0.16	–
	Krugloe (Myshetskoe)	Coarse detrital silt	80	66.98	0.18	0.33	9.14		–	0.66	–	0.86
Dystrophic	Gacha (Vyshnii Volochek)	Peaty silt	16.15	8.81	–	0.75	0.25	2.86	–	0.90	0.10	–
	Nekhlyudovo (Moscow Region)	Coarse detrital silt	22.17	17.84	1.22	0.29	–	1.27	–	0.72	–	0.11
Oligotrophic	Baikal	Clay silt	97	53.55	–	0.09	16.31	10.45	–	2.43	3.38	2.66
	Segozero (Karelia)	Ferruginous streak in the silt	72.9	12.72	–	–	15.63	40.47	4.17	0.66	0.09	–

47

potassium, and silicon. Some of these elements (iron, calcium) can accumulate in vast amounts on the lake floor, forming iron ore and fresh-water marl. Phosphorus is of particular biological importance; indeed, the biological productivity of the lake depends largely on the mobility and transition of phosphorus from the silt to the water. Sulfates are a substrate for sulfate-reducing bacteria, which may play a significant role in the lake chemistry.

Table 14 shows some data on the ash content and composition of silts. Clearly, the concentration of the different mineral elements in the silt varies within wide limits. Silts containing large quantities of silicate are usually poor in calcium. Phosphorus is usually associated with iron. Lake iron ores may contain up to 64% iron, and manganese ores up to 80% manganese in terms of dry weight. A considerable proportion of the silicon and calcium carbonate present in the silt of many lakes is of biogenic nature.

The ash content of silt differs not only among the silt surfaces of lakes with a different degree of trophy but also with depth inside the silt mass. Table 15 (after V. D. Konshin, 1949) shows the change in the ratio between calcium and silicic acid as a function of depth inside the silt of Lake Karas'e near Sverdlovsk.

TABLE 15. Analysis of sapropel from Lake Karas'e, Sverdlovsk Region, % of dry weight (after Konshin, 1949)

Depth from surface, m	Loss during calcination	Fe_2O_3	CaO	CO_2	SiO_2	Total nitrogen
0	43.7	4.16	1.22	0	47.6	3.23
0.5	58.5	2.24	1.63	0	—	2.39
0.75	69.3	2.51	2.91	0	48.0	2.81
1.0	66.9	3.62	6.48	5.26	—	2.73
1.35	58.3	0.96	24.22	22.02	28.0	1.60
1.75	57.8	0.64	31.42	28.66	—	1.24
2.0	56.2	0.64	31.77	27.72	—	1.20
2.3	33.7	3.20	25.60	17.60	—	0.44
2.6	41.4	—	—	28.88	—	0.58
2.8	36.5	3.84	20.05	17.60	—	0.93
2.9	7.4	4.48	5.72	1.14	—	0.14

As can be seen in the table, the nature of silt sediments varies greatly in the vertical sense; that is, it changes in the course of time. The silts formed in the early stages of the existence of the lake contain a large proportion of lime; later an increase begins in the concentration of silicic acid, mainly of biogenic nature, since organic matter accounts for nearly 50% of the silt.

Electric conductivity of the silt solution. The organic matter that settles on the lake bottom is subjected to further mineralization. The result is an increase in the ionic conductivity of the silt solution.

Measurements of the electric conductivity of the silt solution during different seasons provide, therefore, information on the exchange of electrolytes between silt and water and the rate of microbiologic processes of silt mineralization.

On the basis of these considerations, A. D. Pel'sh (1939) has proposed a method for measuring the electric conductivity of silt solutions by means of a specially built device. He tested this method in the oligotrophic lake Gabozero in Karelia. Pel'sh believed that the active mineralization of organic matter by microbial agents in the surface layers of silt should be associated with seasonal changes in the electric conductivity of the silt solution because of seasonal changes of temperature, since the latter factor exerts a lesser influence on the rate of the diffusion of electrolytes in the bottom water than on the biogenic processes of mineralization of organic matter. For this reason, electrolytes should accumulate in summer in the surface layer of silt, creating a peak of the electric conductivity of the silt solution, while in winter the conductivity should decline to a minimum.

The electric conductivity should remain constant the year round in places where the microbial activity approaches zero. As shown in Figure 30, this compensation point lies at a depth of 20 mm from the silt surface in Gabozero (A. D. Pel'sh, 1939).

A. D. Pel'sh provides the following explanation for the changes in the electric conductivity of the water and silt solution. During the fall over-turn, oxygen spreads to the bottom layer and the temperature drops by 5–6°. This immediately lowers the rate of biochemical processes. As a result, the concentration of electrolytes in the silt solution becomes equal to that in the bottom water. The dotted line shows a certain intermediate position, while the extreme minimum reached in late winter is represented by an interrupted line. An anaerobic breakdown of detritus predominates in the silt mass during the summer, owing to the cessation of water circulation and the lack of oxygen in the bottom water. This increases the concentra-tion of electrolytes in the silt solution, whose electric conductivity rises to a peak value (Figure 30, continuous line). Thus, the concentration of ions

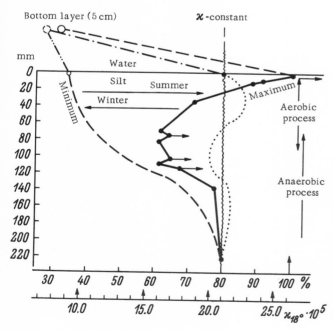

FIGURE 30. Seasonal changes of the electric conductivity of silt solutions (after Pel'sh, 1939):

1) minimal values in winter; 2) maxi-mal values in summer; 3) a certain intermediate value of electric con-ductivity, which is higher than the constant in the upper layers of silt and lower than the constant in the upper part of the anaerobic zone of silt.

in the silt solution in the surface layers varies periodically between a maximum in late summer and a minimum in late winter. In Lake Gabozero, these seasonal changes are confined to the upper 20 cm, below which lies a zone of silt conservation.

Table 16 shows the results of our measurements of the electric conductivity of the silt solution in the dystrophic Lake Piyavochnoe and the eutrophic lakes Biservo and Kolomenskoe.

It appears that the extinction point of silt decay in Lake Piyavochnoe (and probably in the eutrophic lakes) lies a little deeper, about 60 cm from the silt surface. However, the observed increase in the electric conductivity of the silt solution with depth inside sapropel sediments reflects the existence of processes of silt mineralization.

TABLE 16. Vertical distribution of electric conductivity of the silt solution, $K_{18} \times 10^{-4}$ (after Kuznetsov, 1952; Ekzertsev, 1948)

Depth of layer, cm	Biserovo	Kolomenskoe	Piyavochnoe	
			winter	summer
Bottom water	—	—	0.64	0.66
Surface silt	4.45	1.0	1.03	1.99
10 cm	4.76	1.08	1.33	1.46
30	6.85	1.36	2.04	1.84
60	7.15	1.76	—	2.04
100	7.60	1.70	—	2.14
200	7.90	2.50	—	
300	9.20	3.04	—	
400	9.70	3.72	—	2.54
500	12.90	3.78	—	2.76
600	—	—	—	3.80

Oxidation-Reduction Potential of Silt Sediments

The oxidation-reduction potential of silt is usually lower than that of the water mass. Its magnitude depends on two factors, namely the rate of the decomposition of the organic matter of silt and the penetration of oxidizing agents (dissolved oxygen) from the water mass.

Studies of the oxidation-reduction potential of silt have been made in a variety of lakes. Rather thorough observations of its seasonal changes have been reported from the lakes Esthwaite Water and Windermere in Britain (W. H. Pearsall and C. H. Mortimer, 1929; Mortimer, 1941, 1942).

Silt columns were obtained from a depth of 14 m in the marginal part of the lake and 65 m in the central part. The oxidation-reduction potentials of the bottom water and silt surface were determined by means of microelectrodes. Figure 31 shows the obtained data in volts at pH = 7.

As shown in Table 31, the potential decreases sharply with depth into the silt; during the circulation period it remains positive only in the sur-

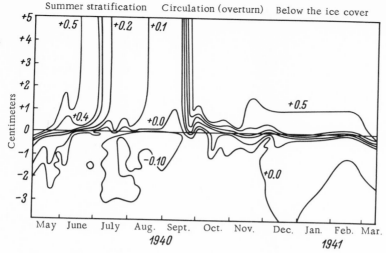

FIGURE 31. Seasonal changes in the oxidation-reduction potential of the silt of Lake Esthwaite Water at a depth of 14 m.

The figures on the isolines are E_h.

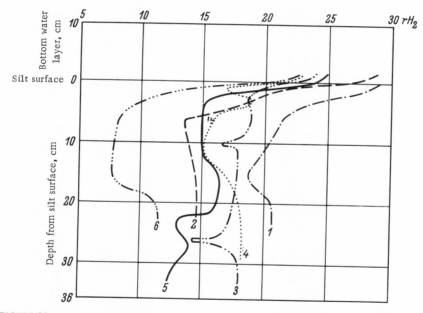

FIGURE 32. Oxidation-reduction potential of the surface silt of lakes of different types in Vologda Region:

1) Lake Onega near Kizhi; 2) Lake Onega, central part; 3) Lake Beloe, Vologda Region; 4) Lake Zaulomskoe; 5) Lake Kishemskoe; 6) Lake Siverskoe.

face layer, where oxygen penetrates. The brown oxidative microzone of iron hydroxide disappears from the silt surface during the stratification period, when the concentration of oxygen in the bottom water drops to nil. At the time of the fall overturn, when oxygen penetrates to the bottom, the oxidation-reduction potential rises again to $E_h = 0.2$ and the oxidized ferruginous microzone reappears on the silt surface of the lake.

Isolated measurements of the oxidation-reduction potential have been made in various types of lakes and artificial reservoirs (S. I. Kuznetsov and G.S. Karzinkin, 1931; V.A. Ekzertsev, 1948; S.I. Kuznetsov and V.I. Romanenko, 1963b; N.I. Semenovich, 1964, 1966).

The difference in the oxidation-reduction potentials is most pronounced in the surface sediments of lakes of various types (Figure 32).

The highest oxidation-reduction potential, $rH_2 = 28.5$, was recorded in iron-ore sediments of Lake Onega; the lowest, in the silts of Lake Siverskoe, which is rich in iron sulfide. The silts of Lake Beloe in the Vologda Region contain black streaks rich in hydrotroilite. As shown in Figure 32, the low values of the oxidation-reduction potential are associated precisely with these microzones, $rH_2 = 11.8$, while the surface silt has $rH_2 = 23$ and from a depth of 2 cm the potential fluctuates around $rH_2 = 18$.

It is also evident from Figure 32 that the oxidation-reduction potential drops sharply at the water/silt boundary, reaching a minimum at a depth of 2—3 cm from the silt surface, and then rises with depth.

TABLE 17. Oxidation-reduction potential of the silt of lakes with different trophic states (average data)

Depth from silt surface, cm	Oligotrophic		Mesotrophic		Eutrophic	
	pH	rH_2	pH	rH_2	pH	rH_2
0—1	7.0—7.2	25—30	6.8—7.0	20—24	6.0—6.5	10—14
4—5	7.1—7.3	19—23	6.5—7.0	17—20	6.5—7.0	8—12
10—15	7.0—7.3	20—23	6.8—7.0	14—20	6.5—7.0	11—13
30	6.8—7.0	20—23	6.5—7.0	17—20	6.5—6.7	10—12

TABLE 18. Magnitudes of the oxidation-reduction potential in the sapropel layer of lakes Biserovo and Piyavochnoe (after Ekzertsev, 1948)

Depth, m	Biserovo			Piyavochnoe		
	E_h	rH_2	pH	E_h	rH_2	pH
Surface	−0.106	8.5	6.1	+0.189	18.5	6.0
0.1	−0.064	11.0	6.5	+0.004	12.3	6.1
0.3	−0.139	8.3	6.5	−0.009	12.8	6.4
0.6	−0.038	12.2	6.7	—	—	—
1.0	−0.049	12.6	7.1	+0.011	13.3	6.4
2.5	—	—	—	+0.156	15.4	6.7
4.0	—	—	—	+0.044	14.6	6.6

Data from different authors on the oxidation-reduction potential of lakes with various trophic states are summarized in Table 17.

As shown in the table, rH_2 fluctuates between 9 and 17 from a depth of 5—6 cm from the silt surface. Such values of rH_2 were found in the silt of various types of water bodies. The oxidation-reduction potential is lowest in eutrophic lakes whose silts are richer in organic matter and contain iron sulfides. The conditions in such water bodies are close to the optimum for a large number of anaerobic forms. In deeper masses of silt, the oxidation-reduction potential often begins to rise a little (V. A. Ekzertsev, 1948). Table 18 (after V. A. Ekzertsev) shows the oxidation-reduction potential of the silts of lakes Piyavochnoe and Biserovo.

The oxidation-reduction potential is lowest at a depth not exceeding 30 cm from the silt surface (Table 18). It appears that the increase of the oxidation-reduction potential in the deeper layers results from the extinction of biologic phenomena. On the other hand, the rise of the potential on the silt surface is due to the penetration of oxygen from the water mass into the silt.

Classification of Lakes according to
Their Trophic Conditions

The earliest criterion used for the classification of lakes was the concentration of dissolved oxygen in the hypolimnion. Later, Thienemann pointed to the chironomid larvae as indicators for the classification of lakes. On the other hand, Naumann regarded the total amount of phytoplankton as the main criterion, assuming erroneously that the biomass of the phytoplankton depends directly and entirely on the existing amounts of mineral nitrogen and phosphorus and neglecting the supply of these elements from extraneous sources.

These two classifications were united, and the extreme types of lakes were named "oligotrophic" and "eutrophic." Thienemann added another type, named "dystrophic" and characterized by a large content of humus. The further accumulation of knowledge, however, created difficulties in the classification of lakes. It became evident, for example, that the concentration of oxygen in the hypolimnion depends largely on allochthonous organic substances, available to deeper organisms, and there is no direct relationship with the density of phytoplankton and the biogenic elements, etc.

The original concepts of Naumann were based on the assumption that there is a direct relationship between the amount of algae (standing crop) and the primary production of organic matter. This, however, applies only to limited zones of landscape and climate and is obviously untrue when tropical lakes are compared with those of the temperate zone. The indicator organisms remained longer in use in the classification of lakes. However, difficulties arose in establishing the connection between the species and the production.

Most authors agreed that lakes should be classified according to the biomass produced during a given period of time. Elster (1958) attributes particular importance to the determination of the primary production in lakes. Such an approach met however with great practical difficulties. One of the proposed solutions was to determine the potential production rather than the actual production, since a low actual production may result from insufficient utilization of all the resources.

Rodhe (1958) likewise maintains that lakes must be classified on the basis of a readily calculable magnitude, such as primary production. In his view, the other indicators can be used for the subdivision of the major types.

The term "trophic" should be applied in a general sense only, as in "oligotrophic" and "eutrophic." Obviously, the rate of biological processes in a water body depends mainly on the continual supply of nitrogen, phosphorus, and other biogenic elements to the water, not on their analytically determined concentration. Therefore, the major types of lakes can be characterized as follows.

A scarce supply of biogenic elements to the lake is usually associated with a poor development of the phytoplankton, which in turn means a low primary production of organic matter. This condition affects the whole biological cycle in the lake. The absorption of oxygen proceeds at a low rate, and even in the fall the concentration of oxygen in the hypolimnion corresponds to 60—70% of the saturation level. The water is highly transparent, with little or no humin compounds. Thienemann (1925, 1928) and Naumann (1927, 1932) place such lakes in the oligotrophic type, which is characterized by a considerable depth, a poorly developed coastal vegetation, and a sharp boundary between the coastal and deep-water zones.

At the other end of the scale is the eutrophic type, characterized by a rich supply of nutritive biogenic substances. The lakes of this type are mostly shallow, that is, the water mass of their hypolimnion is small in comparison with that of the epilimnion. Here the phytoplankton is abundant in summer and the transparency of water limited. The color of water ranges from green to brownish green. Oxygen vanishes from the hypolimnion at the beginning of the summer or winter stagnation. The silt sediments of these lakes are rich in organic matter owing to the high primary production of the phytoplankton and the higher coastal vegetation. Lakes occupying an intermediate position between these types are referred to as mesotrophic.

The third type comprises lakes whose water budget includes an inflow of swamp waters containing a large concentration of humin substances. The lakes of this dystrophic type are poor in nutritive compounds and tend to become bogged up. Their water has a low transparency and is yellow or brown colored. It is poor in mineral compounds but contains large amounts of organic matter of humin origin. Water blooms are usually absent. During any stagnation period, the concentration of oxygen in the hypolimnion decreases sharply and may even reach zero. The abundant silt consists of allochthonous particles (originating from swamps around the lake). Bogging-up converts such a water body into a peat lake. Such lakes are named dystrophic in the classification of Thienemann—Naumann; Jahrnfield (1953) designates the humified lakes by adding the prefix "chthonio" to the term indicating the lake type, for example, "chthonio-eutrophic."

Although the extreme types in the Thienemann-Naumann classification are rather clearly defined, natural lakes show an infinite variety of transitional forms (Lastochkin, 1931). For this reason, Rodhe notes quite correctly that the concepts "oligotrophy" and "eutrophy" are meaningless as a basis for classification but should be used in a general way as an expression of the population and salt composition of the lake.

Ohle (1958) approaches the problem from another direction. In his view, the lakes should be classified according to the rate of the transformation processes. As Figure 33 shows, the net production cannot be used as a measure of the rate of biological processes or trophic conditions of the

TABLE 19. Biological activity of the lakes Grosser Plöner See and Kleiner Uklei See in Schleswig-Holstein (after Ohle, 1958)

| Lake | mcg of C per cm² of surface for 24 hours in the lake as a whole | | | | | | Ratio of net to total production, % |
| | photosynthesis | | | bioactivity | | | |
	res-pir-ation	net produc-tion	total produc-tion	epi-lim-nion	hypo-lim-nion	in the whole lake	
Grosser Plöner See	81	48	129	210	50	260	37.2
Kleiner Uklei See	26	17.5	43.5	69.5	59	128.5	39.7

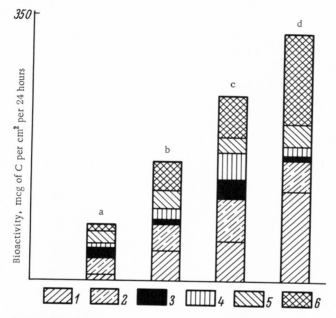

FIGURE 33. Relationships between the different elements of the production process characterizing the bioactivity (after Ohle):

1) total production; 2) net production; 3) organic matter buried in sediments; 4) decay of organic matter in the sediments; 5) decomposition in the hypolimnion; 6) decomposition in the epilimnion; a) arctic lakes; b) alpine lakes; c) lakes of the temperate zone; d) tropical lakes.

lake. Indeed, the net production cannot be used as a measure of the rate of biological processes or trophic conditions of the lake. Indeed, the net production is largely the same in arctic and tropical lakes, but the rate of destruction is far greater in tropical lakes. Clearly, such lakes have different biological activities, even if their net productions are equal. Basically similar differences exist between lakes of the temperate zone, though on a smaller scale.

According to Ohle, the lakes can be classified on the basis of their total "bioactivity." In his definition, the "specific bioactivity" of a biologic system is the sum total of kinetic energy passing into potential energy and vice versa per unit time and volume of water or below a unit of water surface.

The bioactivity can be expressed in calories or as an equivalent amount of organic carbon. It represents the total of all the processes involving the synthesis and decomposition of organic matter. To this category belong the primary production of the phytoplankton and the higher aquatic vegetation, the chemosynthesis and the secondary production of bacteria, and the zooplankton of the lake, which develop at the expense of autochthonous and allochthonous organic matter. The rate of all these processes depends on temperature, the biogenic elements, the depth of the lake, etc.

Figure 33 shows the interrelationships of the different elements that characterize the bioactivity. These magnitudes differ considerably in lakes situated in different climatic zones. Ohle divides the lakes into oligodynamic (a, b) and eudynamic (c, d).

Ohle determined the bioactivity of Grosser Plöner See on May 11 – July 12, and of Kleiner Uklei See on July 5 and 9. The average results of the analyses are given in Table 19. The bioactivity of Grosser Plöner See is twice as much as that of Kleiner Uklei See, although both lakes have roughly the same percentage of net production.

This classification has not yet been accepted in practice, although it provides a full quantitative picture of all the processes associated with the trophic regime of the lake.

We showed in this chapter that the salt composition and the concentration of biogenic elements differ greatly from one lake to another. These differences create specific ecological conditions for the development of various groups of microorganisms. Thus, some lakes provide suitable conditions for the multiplication of bacteria capable of living in the presence of small amounts of organic matter and mineral salts, while other lakes are inhabited by halophilic bacteria.

Lakes also differ from one another in the distribution of temperature. The temperature of polar lakes never rises above 4–5°, while in tropical lakes it remains above 30–35°. Such conditions lead to the proliferation of psychrophiles, on the one hand, and thermophilic or thermotolerant organisms, on the other.

The penetration of light into the water mass is of particular importance to the life of photosynthetic organisms. This factor in turn is closely associated with the presence of biogenic elements – nitrogen and phosphorus.

Finally, the aeration regime. It can be said generally that aerobic conditions prevail in the water mass, while the silt is an anaerobic environment. This distinction is reflected in the distribution of the different groups of bacteria. The silt provides favorable conditions for the multiplication of bacteria that break down organic matter into methane, hydrogen, and carbonic acid, as well as for sulfate-reducing bacteria. On the other hand, the aerobic conditions of the water mass favor the development of microorganisms that obtain energy by oxidizing organic compounds – a process involving oxygen dissolved in the water.

At least a rough classification of the lakes into different types is necessary in order to understand the effect of ecological factors on the development of the microflora.

A comprehensive classification of lakes is impossible because of their great variety in nature and the abundance of factors that can serve as the main identification. In our view, the problem can be solved by using certain gross features, and here we return to the classification of Thienemann — Naumann. Indeed, the terms oligotrophic, mesotrophic, eutrophic, and dystrophic provide a fairly accurate general picture of a lake.

In order to determine the role of microorganisms in the transformation of different compounds, it is necessary to establish not only the presence or distribution of the microbial species in the lake but also the effect of the environmental factors on their development. Such a task requires a thorough knowledge of the physiology of the microorganisms involved in the process. Moreover, an evaluation of the actual participation of micro-organisms in the transformations necessarily involves a follow-up of their activity in parallel with the annual changes of any given compound in the lake. Finally, it must be borne in mind that the rates of the different stages of the chemical transformations can be determined by the use of radioactive or stable isotopes, in addition to the conventional chemical procedures. After being introduced into the lake or in an isolated volume of water, these elements serve as markers in the following transformations and can be determined by methods far more sensitive than those used in classical chemistry.

The structure and physiology of microorganisms have much in common with those of all living cells. On the other hand, some features are specific to bacteria. Finally, some physiological groups of microorganisms have characteristic traits of their own. These aspects are the domain of the special morphology and physiology of microorganisms. The latter applies in particular to the autotrophic bacteria, which play a dominant role in the transformations of nitrogen, sulfur, and iron.

In this book, general physiology will be discussed before the transforma-tions of different compounds, and the special physiology of microorganisms will be dealt with together with the role of these microorganisms in the transformations of the respective elements.

Principles of the Morphology and Physiology
of the Living Cell

Basic Features of the Cell of the Living Organism

In 1665, Hook showed that plant tissues consist of separate cells. Much later, Schleiden (in 1838) and Schwann (in 1839) found that plant cells contain a nucleus and a nucleolus, which they regarded as the carriers of life. The next major advance came in 1858, when Virchow formulated a major biological law stating that new cells can be formed only by the division of a maternal cell. Many organisms consist of a single cell whose structure and development have much in common with those of higher plants and animals. The living cell of multicellular organisms is built of protoplasm, which consists of nucleic matter and cytoplasm. The nucleus and cytoplasm perform different functions in the cell.

There are two major types of cellular activity: metabolism and preservation of the species. Metabolism is the whole complex of chemical transformations in which food and energy serve for the synthesis of new protoplasm. Preservation of the species involves two conditions: first, the creation within the cell of a stable physical and chemical state in which the cell becomes resistant to environmental changes, second, the ability of the cell to reproduce itself. All these processes are controlled by the nucleus, although most of them take place in the cytoplasm. The modern concepts of the general cell structure of organisms will be outlined below. Later we shall deal with the specific features of the bacterial cell.

DNA and RNA

The deoxyribonucleic acid (DNA) molecule. DNA probably represents the key substance that characterizes living matter. It contains the code that determines the genetic properties and actually controls the activity of the organism. The DNA molecule is visualized as a long intertwined helix with double coils and side branches containing carbon, oxygen, and phosphorus in an order to be indicated below.

The links of the DNA helix are arranged in a strict sequence, which repeats itself thousands of times along the molecule. Each link consists of a residue of the pentose sugar deoxyribose and one of four nitrogen compounds joined with one another in the center of the double ring. These nitrogen compounds are adenine (A), thymine (T), guanine (G), and cytosine (C). Adenine of one coil of the molecule is joined by a weak (hydrogen) bond with thymine of the next coil, and a similar link exists between guanine and cytosine.

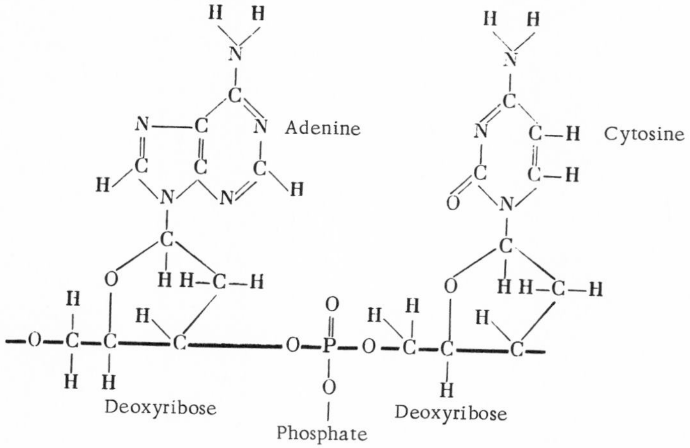

Sequence 1	Sequence 2
A— — —T	T— — —A
G— — —C	C— — —G
C— — —G	G— — —C
A— — —T	G— — —C
T— — —A	A— — —T
C— — —G	G— — —C

The genetic information is contained in a code that appears to be composed of different combinations of these pairs of nitrogen compounds. For example, sequence 1 differs from sequence 2, and each of them can control a different synthetic pathway.

Such a double residue, consisting of nitrogen bases, pentose, and phosphate, has a molecular weight of about 600. The weight of the DNA molecule is approximately 6,000,000. Thus, each molecule represents a double chain of about 10,000 links (Figure 34). The nitrogen compounds can be paired in two possible ways, namely A-T or T-A. This means that the molecule can store 20,000 "bits" of information.

Replication of DNA. DNA serves as template for the further synthesis of identical DNA. The mechanism of DNA replication can be outlined as follows on the basis of recent knowledge. The double DNA helix gradually opens (Figure 35), forming two new helices from the old one. Adenine combines with thymine only, guanidine with cytosine only. This explains why the code remains unchanged through consecutive replications of DNA during the division of the nucleus and cytoplasm.

An accident or error in the DNA replication alters the sequence and thus changes the activity of the cell, which may lose or acquire the ability to perform a given synthesis or breakdown of cell components. These changes represent mutations: if the cells survive, they transmit the change to their progeny.

The ribonucleic acid (RNA) molecule. Although DNA is usually confined to the nucleus, its influence extends throughout the cell. The synthesis of enzymes is presumably controlled by DNA by a hitherto obscure mechanism. It appears that RNA serves as a carrier that transmits the information stored in the DNA molecule. Although structurally similar to DNA, RNA is distinguished by two basic features: (1) the pentose is ribose (not deoxyribose as in DNA); (2) RNA contains the pyrimidine uracil (instead of thymine in DNA).

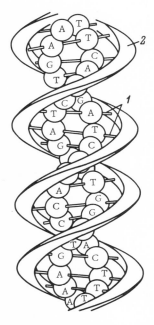

FIGURE 34. Double DNA helix. Hydrogen bonds link adenine, thymine, guanine, and cytosine into pairs, forming a solid molecule (after Carpenter, 1961).

1 — base pairs belonging to the DNA molecule; 2) chains built of sugar and phosphate molecules.

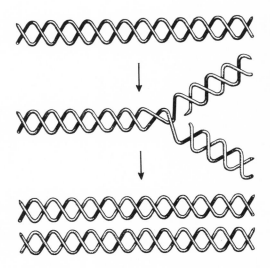

FIGURE 35. The probable method of DNA replication. As the spiral of two complementary strands opens, each strand creates a complementary partner (after Carpenter, 1961).

It appears that the RNA molecules examined so far correspond structurally to the DNA molecules. Some ribonucleic acids are soluble and diffuse readily. RNA affects the synthesis of enzymes. The information stored by DNA and transferred from one cell or generation to another can be utilized in any cell reaction proceeding under the direct control of RNA. Thus, nucleic DNA influences a large number of processes.

Distribution of DNA in cells. DNA forms only a small fraction of the large cells of most animals and plants but is quantitatively a major component of bacteria and other small cells. Some of the smallest viruses consist of DNA clad in a protein coat. It appears that RNA replaces DNA as genetic material in many small viruses. DNA of one species differs from that of another. Gross analysis of DNA cannot reveal such interspecific differences. Indeed, the nitrogen base sequence (A-T, G—C) attached to the deoxyribose-phosphate chain differs not only according to the species but also from one individual to another.

Composition of the Cytoplasm

More than thirty chemical elements have been detected in the cytoplasm of various plants and animals. Of these, only twelve are found in larger amounts. Oxygen, carbon, hydrogen, and nitrogen are the most widespread of these. The first three of these elements occur in hydrocarbons and fats; all four are constituents of proteins. Lesser quantities of sulfur appear in all of these compounds.

Water is a major constituent of living matter — it accounts for 75—90% of the weight of the protoplasm. Next are proteins (10—15%), lipids (1—3%), hydrocarbons (1—2%), nucleic acids (1%), and inorganic compounds (1—2%). The composition of protoplasm varies from one species to another. Some microorganisms contain 40% of lipids. The proportion of nucleic acid may be as high as 15%; in the tobacco mosaic virus it reaches 40%.

Nutrition of the Cell

Most unicellular organisms obtain various nutritive substances through the cell membrane by diffusion from the surrounding medium. In order to penetrate through the cell membrane, a substance must be soluble in the latter and possess a comparatively small molecule. Many inorganic salts diffuse rapidly and easily reach the interior of the cell. On the other hand, large molecules, such as polysaccharides and proteins, must be hydrolyzed or otherwise broken down to smaller units before being assimilated.

The cell activity of higher organisms depends on the availability and diffusion of nutritive compounds. Enzymes released by bacteria and fungi into the surrounding medium break down various complex foods into simpler ingredients capable of entering the cell. Such extracellular hydrolysis is far from economical since most of its products diffuse away into the environment and are therefore lost to the cell. Cultures relying on such nutrients grow slowly, especially during the early stage following the introduction of a small inoculum.

Photosynthetic plant cells need mainly water and inorganic salts. Their nitrogen supply comes in the form of nitrates, and carbon is taken up as carbon dioxide. The cells of nonphotosynthetic plants, bacteria, and fungi must receive both inorganic and organic compounds from their environment.

Structure of the Plant Cell

Cells vary greatly in size from one organism to another, though most of them measure between 5 and 15 microns. The cells of some large protozoans reach a size of 100 microns and are visible to the naked eye. Other forms have much smaller cells. Some bacteria are less than 1 micron long; rickettsiae and viruses are even smaller. Each cell consists of two major parts: cytoplasm and nucleus (Figure 36, A).

Cytoplasm. The cytoplasm contains a number of constantly occurring structures that have various biologic functions. Of particular importance to the cell metabolism are the mitochondria — highly complex formations with a triple membrane from which numerous outgrowths named cristae project into an inner cavity. The membranes and inner cavity of the mitochondria contain respiratory enzymes.

The cytoplasm also contains an intricate system of endoplasmic membranes whose surface bears granules containing RNA. These structures, also known as ribosomes, appear to be responsible for protein synthesis. Some cytoplasmic membranes do not possess ribosomes. Such structures belong to the Golgi apparatus. Here are concentrated various secretions produced by the cell. The endoplasmic network is connected and partly fused with the intracellular membrane.

Another feature of the cell are the lysosomes. These cytoplasmic organelles are morphologically similar to the mitochondria but differ from them in the absence of a fine internal structure. The lysosomes presumably contain digestive enzymes.

In addition to these cytoplasmic organelles, the cells may contain various inclusions associated with the metabolism or with specific functions of the cell. To this category belong chloroplasts (containing chlorophyll), starch granules, oil inclusions, etc.

Most cells contain a single nucleus. Some cells, however, possess two or three nuclei. In addition, some organisms (fungi, for example) are multinucleate. These organisms consist of cytoplasmic cords or filaments containing many nuclei without cell walls or membranes between them.

Nucleus. The nucleus of most organisms represents a spherical or elliptic body situated inside the cytoplasm. The nucleus of a liver cell accounts for only 10—18% of the total mass of the cell; in the thyroid gland, the nucleus occupies 60% of the cell volume. The nucleus may contain one or several nucleoli and a chromatin network, which stains strongly with such basic dyes as crystal violet or methylene blue. The rest of the nucleus is composed of nucleoplasm, which stains poorly.

Chromosomes. The chromatin network of the nucleus bears chromosomes — long threads of proteins and nucleoproteins, containing the genes. Most of the nucleic acid in the nucleoproteins is DNA; however, some proportion of RNA is also present in the majority of cases. It appears that DNA is the specific substance of which the genes are built; its complex configuration creates the structural and functional differences between the genes. Chromosomatic DNA can be detected by special staining procedures or by its specific absorption of ultraviolet rays.

Nucleolus. The nucleolus contains nucleoprotein whose only nucleic acid is RNA. The origin of the latter is obscure. Some authors maintain that

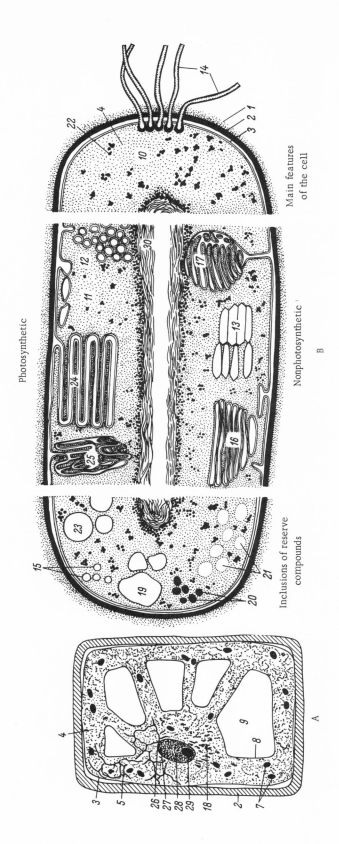

FIGURE 36. Schematic sections of cells: plant cells — eucaryote (A), and bacterial cells — procaryote, combined for photosynthetic and nonphotosynthetic microorganisms (B). The schemes are prepared after Carpenter (1963) and Schlegel (1969):

1) capsule; 2) cell wall; 3) cytoplasmic membrane; 4) cytoplasm; 5) Golgi apparatus; 7) chloroplasts; 8) vacuolar membrane; 9) vacuoles; 10) basal bodies; 11) vesicles; 12) vesicles or chromatophores; 13) gas vacuoles; 14) flagella; 15) oil droplets; 16) lamellar structures; 17) mesosomes; 18) mitochondria; 19) poly-β-hydroxybutyric acid; 20) polyphosphates; 21) polysaccharide granules; 22) ribosomes; 23) sulfur inclusions; 24) laminar thylacoids; 25) tubular thylacoids; 26) nuclear membrane; 27) nucleus; 28) chromatin; 29) nucleolus; 30) nuclear substance.

63

this RNA belongs to the chromosomes; others believe that the chromosomatic RNA originates from the nucleolus and point out that the latter is actually the site of RNA synthesis. Recent data indicate that the nucleolus plays a major role in protein synthesis.

Nuclear membrane. Electron micrographs show that the nuclear membrane of many cells is at least double. The nuclear membrane keeps the nucleus intact and controls the movement of materials in and out of the nucleus.

Locomotor organelles. Many cells of protozoans and other plankters bear cilia and flagella on their surface. These organelles are filamentous in structure; examination with the electron microscope shows that they consist of very fine fibrils. They are supported and controlled by granules situated just below the cell wall. The flagella are usually longer than the cilia; the cells of flagellates usually bear one or two flagella, while those of infusorians may possess hundreds of cilia. The flagella and cilia are locomotor organelles in unicellular organisms; in addition, they assist in the process of feeding by propelling food particles toward the mouth. Cilia perform an important function in the respiratory and genital ducts of animals.

Morphology of the Bacterial Cell

Extremely fine details of the microbial cells have been revealed by the electron microscope and by means of ultrathin sections whose thickness is measured in tenths and hundredths of the micron. Fractionation of microbial cells with a subsequent centrifugation at a speed of tens and hundreds of thousands of revolutions per minute yield a variety of structural elements. On the other hand, the biochemical approach indicates the position of the cell enzymes, the site of the hereditary properties of the cells, etc.

The taxonomy of bacteria is much less developed. Little is known on the affinities between different groups of bacteria and fungi. This explains the lack of a uniform approach in the classification of bacteria. At present, the most widely used manuals for the determination of bacteria are those by N. A. Krasil'nikov (USSR) and Bergey (Breed et al., 1957).

Chemical Composition of the Bacterial Cell

Bacteria do not differ from other organisms in their chemical composition. Their biomass contains a large percentage of water — from 75 to 85% in terms of weight. Proteins account for about 50% of the dry weight, hydrocarbons 10—30%, fats 10—15%, nucleic acids — RNA 10—20% and DNA 3—4%.

Almost all the amino acids have been detected in bacterial proteins. One of these compounds, diaminopimelic acid (DAP), has been found only in bacteria and blue-green algae, where it forms polypeptides together with mureic acid — an important component of the cell wall.

Hydrocarbons are present in the cell walls and capsules of bacteria. The capsule of some species consists entirely of polysaccharides. The cell wall of Gram-positive bacteria contains 35—60% hydrocarbons, that of Gram-negative bacteria 15—20%. The cytoplasm contains granules of glycogen and other polysaccharides.

Fats (lipids) occur in the cell wall and cytoplasmic membrane, which represents a layer of lipoproteins. Acid-fast bacteria like the tubercle bacillus produce an extraordinarily large amount of lipids — up to 40% — when grown on glycerol-containing media. The concentration of RNA in rapidly growing cells is roughly twice as great as in resting cells. One Escherichia coli cell contains about one thousand molecules of DNA.

Beside these components, bacterial cells contain a variety of organic compounds of lesser molecular weight, such as sugars, organic acids, amino acids, nucleotides, phosphoric esters, vitamins, and coenzymes. These compounds are readily metabolized. The reserve materials in the cell number more than ten million molecules. It is noteworthy that the concentration of amino acids and other compounds in the cell is hundreds of times greater in comparison with the surrounding medium.

Structure of the Bacterial Cell

The structure of the bacterial cell is shown schematically in Figures 36,B and 37. The protoplast of the cell is enveloped in a cytoplasmic membrane situated on the inner side of the cell wall. On the outside, the cell wall may be covered with fimbriae (Figure 38), a microcapsule, a capsule, or a slime layer.

Inside the protoplast lie various granular inclusions, vacuoles, and chromatin bodies or a nucleus. Motile bacteria possess one or several flagella, and spore-forming bacteria may contain endospores.

The study of the inner structure of the bacterial cell is a rather difficult task, largely because the refractive indices of the cell structures differ little from one another and from that of the surrounding medium. As a result, the conventional microscope reveals few if any details in unstained preparations.

Protoplast. The term protoplast applies to that part of the cell which lies inside the cell wall. In some species, the cell wall can be removed by treating the cells with lysozyme, which is obtained from tears or from egg protein and destroys the polysaccharide complex of the cell wall. Some microorganisms can grow even without a cell wall in the presence of penicillin. In any case it is necessary to prevent osmatic lysis by adding a stabilizing agent, such as 0.2 M of sugar. A cell treated in this manner assumes a spherical form and probably becomes more sensitive to environmental factors; it lyses readily upon dilution of the stabilizing solution with distilled water.

The protoplast performs most of the metabolic reactions of the whole cell, including the synthesis of proteins, enzymes, and nucleic acids and the energy-yielding processes of respiration. However, the protoplast apparently cannot synthesize components of the cell wall. This means that the cell wall must possess a mechanism responsible for its synthesis. The protoplast of Mycoplasma (Figure 39) can grow and reproduce without a cell wall. The protoplast of spore-forming bacteria is capable of completing the sporulation process after being removed from cells that have entered the first stage of sporulation. On the other hand, the protoplast of motile organisms may bear flagella but cannot move from one place to another.

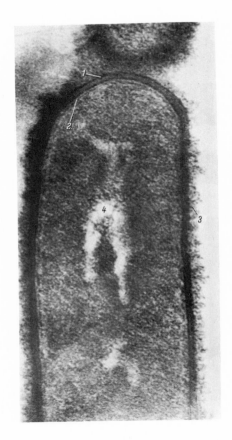

FIGURE 37. Scheme of the structure of the bacterial cell, after an electron micrograph of an ultrathin section of Bac. anthracis.

1) cell wall; 2) cytoplasmic membrane; 3) remnants of the dried capsule; 4) loose nuclear substance.

Cytoplasmic membrane. A suspension of protoplasts in 0.2 M sugar solution usually undergoes lysis when diluted in water. The lysis breaks the extremely thin cytoplasmic membrane and releases the cytoplasm and certain granules composed of fats, glycogen, or volutin.

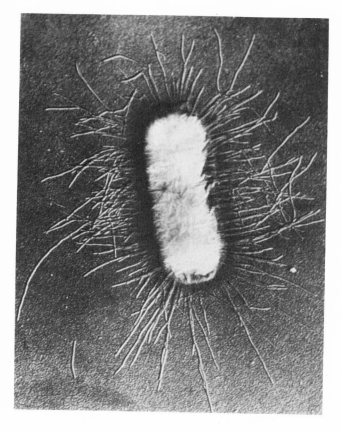

FIGURE 38. Bacterial cell covered with fimbria. Electron micrograph (after Carpenter, 1963).

The cytoplasmic membranes are 5—8 μ thick and constitute between 10 and 20% of the dry weight of the cell. They consist essentially of lipo-proteins. The cytoplasmic membrane differs from the peripheral layer of cytoplasm in being contiguous with the cell wall. It forms a variety of cytoplasmic processes — mesosomes, thylacoids, and lamellar structures, which bear different enzymes. An indirect proof of the existence of a cyto-plasmic membrane can be obtained by observing the contraction of the proto-plasm of bacteria placed in a hypertonic solution. As water leaves through the cell wall, the cytoplasm shrinks from the wall, as if covered with a membrane.

The cytoplasmic membrane regulates the passage of substances in and out of the cell. Some low molecular weight compounds, such as urea, glycin, and glycerol, readily penetrate the bacterial cell. By contrast, passage through the membrane is very difficult for such electrolytes as NaCl and KCl and for such larger organic molecules as glucose and sucrose. The cytoplasmic membrane is almost impermeable to polar organic compounds owing to its high lipid content. It is believed that a group of enzymes known as permeases facilitate the entry of certain compounds or groups of them by forming readily dissociable complexes. Synthesis or breakdown of these complexes can take place on either side of the membrane.

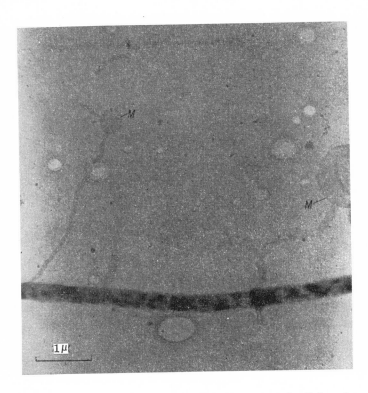

FIGURE 39. M y c o p l a s m a sp.(M), resting on a bacterial cell from the silt of Lake Glubokoe. Electron micrograph by G.A. Dubinina.

Cytoplasmic inclusions. The cells of an old culture usually contain various granules or inclusions. These cannot be regarded as living elements of the cell. Many of them represent food stores, since they accumulate in rich media and tend to disappear in a starving culture. The nature of these inclusions varies from one organism to another. The volutin granules observed in various bacterial species, but also in fungi, algae, and protozoans, react as metachromatin; they stain strongly with basic dyes and contain compounds of polymerized phosphoric acid, known as polyphosphates.

Polysaccharides can accumulate as glycogen or starch. Lipid spherules appear in various bacteria, usually Gram-positive ones. Some bacteria bear inclusions of molecular sulfur, pyrite, calcite, or other compounds.

Nucleus or chromatin body. A great controversy has persisted concerning the presence or absence of a nucleus in bacteria. The different views on this topic can be summarized as follows: (1) bacteria lack a nucleus;

(2) bacteria possess a discrete, clearly distinguishable nucleus; (3) bacteria have a diffuse nucleus. However, there is no doubt as to the presence of bacterial structures containing DNA, which is responsible for the genetic mechanisms of the cell. The experimental techniques for the detection of different structures in such small organisms as bacteria fall short of the requirements. Despite the successful application of special staining methods, phase contrast, and electron microscopy, there is much truth in a recent remark by Botner, who notes that because of the subjective nature of cytologic research it is desirable that a given conclusion be reached independently by two cytologists (cited from Carpenter, 1961, p. 130).

As we noted above, the nucleus of higher plants and animals is a discrete cell structure enveloped by a nuclear membrane and containing chromosomes; it divides mitotically, with typical structural changes.

The nuclear substance of bacteria differs in many ways from the nucleus of other organisms with the exception of such primitive forms as blue-green algae. It is a plastic body, usually without a separate membrane. It is featureless structurally and in its staining properties. These signs persist during the division cycle, which consists of direct fission and rarely involves mitosis. The bacterial chromosomes are indistinguishable, if present. These and other considerations are responsible for the frequent use of the term "chromatin body" instead of "nucleus" with respect to the part of the bacterial cytoplasm that divides together with the cell and bears the DNA.

The chromatin bodies take up basic stains, like the cytoplasm. This confirms the hypothesis of the existence of a diffuse nucleus in bacteria; it also explains the failure of previous attempts to detect chromatin bodies inside the bacterial cell, since the stains used to elicit the nucleus of higher forms react strongly with RNA of the bacterial cytoplasm and thus mask the chromatin bodies. RNA can be removed from the cytoplasm by means of the enzyme ribonuclease or by hydrolysis with 1 N HCl at 60°C for 5—15 minutes. After such treatment, staining with the Schiff aldehyde reagent (Feulgen reaction), Giemsa, or other suitable dyes reveals the intracellular structures, whose size and form vary with the age of the culture. This represents a definitive proof of the existence of nuclear matter in bacteria.

The chromatin bodies of resting cells are more or less centrally located and have a spherical, oval, or rodlike form. In actively growing cells they divide along the same axis as the cell, usually preceding the latter by a brief period. Two or four pairs of chromatin bodies can often be seen in an actively growing rodlike cell. The chromatin bodies revert to their normal condition at the end of cell division.

The chromatin can exist in two basic conditions: (1) as H-shaped bars or V-shaped rods; (2) in form of small granules linked into fine strands.

The size of the chromatin bodies varies not only from one species to another but also among individuals of the same species, according to their age. Resting S t a p h y l o c o c c u s cells have chromatin bodies about $0.4\,\mu$ in diameter, compared with $0.5-0.8\,\mu$ in growing cells of the same bacterium. These structures constitute between 5 and 16% of the cell volume. In E. c o l i, chromatin bodies occupy from 15 to 25% of the protoplasmic volume. The structure of the bacterial nucleus or chromatin bodies is still controversial. At any rate, their condition depends on the age of the organism and is also influenced by chemical and physical factors. Moreover, different conditions of chromatin can be observed in viable cells, regardless of natural or artificial factors. DNA, an essential component of the nucleus, appears to be closely associated with the spongy framework of the nucleoproteins and belongs as a whole to the cytoplasm. Although the existence of bacterial chromosomes has not been proved, the persistent experimental evidence for gene transfer from one bacterium to another in the process of conjugation suggests that bacterial DNA forms linear, chromosomelike structures.

Flagella. The bacterial flagella are flexible spirally coiled appendages, found in the majority of free-swimming bacteria. Although very thin, they can attain a considerable length. With a diameter ranging from 0.01 to 0.05μ, they can be several times longer than the cell itself. Flagella 70μ long have been described. The flagella consist of an elastic fiber of protein related to skin keratin or muscle myosin but chemically distinct from them. The flagella are analogous to muscle tissue; each flagellum consists of two or three fibers twisted around one another.

Electron photomicrographs show that the flagellum arises from a granule situated within the cytoplasmic membrane. The number of flagella per bacterial cell varies from one to several hundred. Both the number and the arrangement of the flagella are constant for each species; the same is true of the flagellar length and the number of coils, though to a lesser extent. With regard to the arrangement of their flagella, bacteria can be divided into four types:

1) monotrichous — with a single terminal or subterminal flagellum having more than two coils;

2) multitrichous — with more than one flagellum situated terminally or subterminally at one or both ends of the cell and having more than two coils;

3) lophotrichous — usually with more than one terminal or subterminal flagellum situated at one or both ends of the cell and having only one or two coils;

4) peritrichous — with flagella all around the cell.

Peritrichous bacteria can move at a speed of 25μ/sec; in monotrichous ones, like the cholera vibrio, the velocity of movement reaches 200μ/sec.

Endospores. These are highly resistant bodies formed within the cells of certain bacteria that are united in the family Bacillaceae on the basis of this feature. Bacillaceae consist of two genera: Bacillus (aerobic spore-forming bacteria) and Clostridium (anaerobic spore-forming rods). Endospore formation is also known in a few species of Spirillum, Vibrio, and Sarcina, as well as in several species of filamentous bacteria of the order Caryophanales, for example, Oscillospira guillermondii.

Normally, one bacterium produces a single endospore. For this reason, bacterial sporulation cannot be regarded as a method of reproduction comparable to that of yeasts and molds.

Physical and physiological characteristics of endospores. In a sense, endospores can be regarded as intracellular sporangia. They range in form from spherical to elliptic. Their diameter may be slightly shorter than, equal to, or longer than the diameter of the cell. The names of some bacteria reflect the position of their endospores. Thus, the term clostridium applies to a cell with a very elongated central endospore, while a cell with a large terminal spore is known as plectridium. The size of endospores differs from one species to another and serves as a taxonomic sign. Another specific feature of endospores is their fine structure (Figure 40). On the whole, an endospore consists of a central body enveloped by a coat, which in many species grows into a cell wall after germination. Around this coat is a second, thicker, and less permeable layer known as the cortex. The latter is covered in turn by one or two additional spore coats, which may be smooth, grooved, or symmetrically crested. The entire complex may be situated inside an exosporium, which surrounds the endospore at the sides only and projects beyond its ends. Endospores are highly resistant; some withstand heating to 80—90° for several minutes, and those of a few species remain viable even after heating at 100° for twenty-four hours. This striking heat resistance of endospores suggests a chemical composition or physical structure radically different from those of the maternal cell. Endospores contain RNA, DNA, and a number of proteins identical to those found in vegetative cells, as well as fats, hydrocarbons, enzymes, and inorganic compounds. Their water content is 60—80%, that is, less than in vegetative cells.

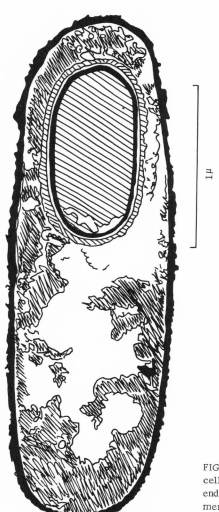

FIGURE 40. Scheme showing the structure of a cell of B a c. c e r e u s with an almost mature endospore enveloped with three clearly visible membranes. The large white formations at the lower end of the cell are vacuolelike inclusions.

All endospores contain dipicolinic acid at a concentration of 5 to 15% in terms of dry weight. This compound does not occur in vegetative cells. Dipicolinic acid is discarded together with other compounds during germination. The heat resistance of the endospore vanishes at the same time.

Endospores have a very low metabolic rate. They contain three or four active enzymes and a large number of inactive ones.

Many enzymes of the endospore are associated with dipicolinic acid and to a lesser extent with peptides and calcium. These complexes are highly heat resistant. Other factors also contribute to the resistance and low metabolic activity of the endospores. The impermeability of the endospore coat undoubtedly prevents the penetration of toxic compounds; this appears to be connected with the dehydrated state of the endospore.

Endospore formation. Under favorable conditions, endospores appear mostly in healthy, well-fed cells after a period of intensive reproduction. Sporulation takes place mostly at temperatures that favor the development of vegetative cells and in a narrow pH range close to neutrality. It is inhibited by some metabolic by-products, such as fatty acids having a straight chain of ten to fourteen carbons and resulting from peptone or other ingredients of the medium. As a rule, aerobic bacteria do not sporulate in anaerobic conditions; the same is true of anaerobes in aerobic environments. The mechanism of spore formation is associated with the protein metabolism of the cell. It involves not only the transformation of "vegetative proteins" into "endospore proteins" but also the synthesis of new endospore proteins from components of the medium.

The development of the endospore begins with the formation of a shining body at one end of the cell. The cytoplasm around this body gradually thickens into a coat. The development of the endospore proceeds in parallel with the synthesis of dipicolinic acid, apparently from diaminopimelic acid. The whole process rapidly ends with the formation of a mature endospore. Afterward the remnants of the cell undergo autolysis, and the naked endospore is released.

Germination begins a few hours after the endospore has entered an environment with suitable temperature, humidity, food supply, etc. During the germination, the nuclear material changes; the chromatin bodies divide twice, and cells appear. A brief warming to 80° stimulates the germination. The process is also favored by the presence of 1-alanine, glucose and adenosine — compounds necessary for the synthesis of cytoplasm.

General Physiology of Bacteria

Growth, Reproduction, and Death of Bacteria

The process of cell production. The growth and reproduction of the cell represent a cyclic phenomenon in which each new cell is potentially capable of reproduction and division into daughter cells having a similar physiology and capacity for further reproduction. This process proceeds as follows. The bacterial cell grows, accumulating protoplasm by a number of independent reactions. Nutritive materials penetrate through the cytoplasmic membrane. Molecules too large to penetrate the membrane, such as polysaccharides and proteins, are broken down by enzymes released by the cell; the resulting components, notably monosaccharides and amino acids, readily enter the cell and take part in the synthesis of new cytoplasm, either in their original condition or after undergoing additional transformations. The synthesis of new proteins, hydrocarbons, fats, or nucleic acids involves a large number of specific compounds supplied by the chemical mechanisms of the given type or species of bacterium.

Vegetative reproduction of bacteria. This process was first studied in stained preparations. It starts with the formation of fresh cytoplasm and the growth of the cell, which becomes longer, often several times the original length. Nuclear division begins; some authors interpret the observed changes as manifestations of mitosis. It appears that cell division starts with an inner growth of the cytoplasmic membrane, which forms a transverse plate separating the two daughter cells.

Electron photomicrographs of ultrathin sections of B. cereus have shown that cell division is accompanied by one or two divisions of the nucleus (Shapman and Hillier, cited after Carpenter, 1961). A ring of six or eight peripheral bodies 0.2μ in diameter appears within the cytoplasm close to the longitudinal axis of the cell, roughly midway between the nucleus and the end of the cell. The peripheral bodies gradually approach the ends of the cell, while the cell wall grows inward like a gradually closing iris. This inward growth of the cell wall follows the peripheral bodies step by step, suggesting that the peripheral bodies synthesize and release the material of the cell wall. The cell wall sometimes develops after the end of nuclear division; in other cases the wall appears within a single cell. The transverse wall may be incomplete, leaving a small central opening with a protoplasmic bridge or plasmodesm connecting the two cells.

Normally, the transverse wall grows thicker; its softer middle layer splits into two parts, one for each new cell. A notch appears on the cell surface at the site of the transverse wall.

In unicellular bacteria, the daughter cells become increasingly turgid in the course of growth; because of the pressure exerted on the cell wall in the area of contact between two neighboring cells, the division of the cell begins at the outer part and advances along the axis. Filamentous bacteria apparently possess a more solid cell wall, which withstands the inner pressure resulting from the growth of the daughter cell; this process leads to the formation of a bacterial filament.

The cycle begins again some time after the cell division is complete. The new cytoplasm differentiates into cell wall, cytoplasmic membrane, nuclear substance, capsule, granules, and a Gram-positive layer. The molecular orientation follows a predetermined pattern, which passes in heredity from one generation to another, provided that spontaneous or induced mutations do not occur. Little is known about the mechanism by which this genetic control of reproduction and growth operates.

Reproduction and death of bacteria. Bacterial cultures provide excellent models for the study of population problems. Sexual phenomena are not essential in bacteria. This basic fact is reflected in many bacteriological procedures, such as inoculation methods, the discovery of new species, the use of biochemical mutants, the isolation of strains resistant to chemical factors, etc. Placed in a suitable nutrient medium, a single cell divides into two daughter cells, which repeat the process many times. The period between the formation and division of the cell is known as the generation time. As will be shown below, the generation time depends on a number of factors, including the characteristics of the given strain, the medium, the temperature, the age of the culture, etc. The generation time varies considerably from one bacterial species to another. Even in optimal conditions it ranges from twenty minutes to several hours. The effect of external factors on the generation time is best determined in pure cultures. The growth rate at different temperatures or nitrogen sources depends on two factors, namely the period that must elapse before the inoculated material begins to reproduce and the generation time.

Let us return to the inoculation of a single cell in a nutrient medium.

Assuming that reproduction does take place, the number of bacteria b in each generation will be as follows:

1st generation: $b = 1 \times 2 = 2$
2nd " $b = 1 \times 2 \times 2 = 2^2 = 4,$
3rd " $b = 1 \times 2 \times 2 \times 2 = 2^3 = 8,$

or for each of the subsequent generations $b = 1 \times 2^n$, where n is the number of generations. In the case of a more massive inoculum of 100 or 100,000 cells, the formula becomes

$$b = a \times 2^n,$$

where a is the number of inoculated bacteria.

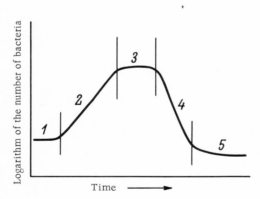

FIGURE 41. Growth curve of bacteria:

1) lag phase; 2) phase of logarithmic growth; 3) stationary phase with a maximal number of bacteria; 4) phase of logarithmic death; 5) stationary phase of surviving bacteria in the culture.

Thus, the number of bacteria in a developing culture follows an exponential expression of 2, as shown in the above formula.

In plotting the growth curve of bacteria, it is more convenient to use the logarithm of the bacterial population. This follows clearly from Figure 41 and the above formula. Since the inoculum usually contains 1,000 or more bacteria, logarithms to the base 10 can be used, but it must be borne in mind that such expression can be converted to logarithms to the base 2 ($\log_{10}$ of any number being equal to $0.3010 \times \log_2$), i. e.,

$$b = a \times 2^n.$$

By taking the logarithms to the base 2, we obtain:

$$\log_2 b = \log_2 a + n \log_2 2,$$

or with logarithms to the base 10:

$$\log_{10} b = \log_{10} a + n \log_{10} 2 = \log_{10} a + (n \times 0.3010).$$

Rearranging the formula, we have the following expression for n, which shows the number of generations between the inoculation and the sampling:

$$n = \frac{\log b - \log a}{\log 2} = \frac{\log b - \log a}{0.301}.$$

The average generation time for the same interval can be found by substituting n in the equation

$$G = \frac{\text{duration of test}}{\text{number of generations}} = \frac{t}{n}$$

$$G = \frac{t}{\dfrac{\log b - \log a}{0.301}} = \frac{0.301 \cdot t}{\log b - \log a}$$

where a is the initial number of bacteria, b the final number of bacteria, t the duration of the test, n the number of generations, and G the generation time. Figure 41 shows a hypothetical case in which the bacteria divide every thirty minutes after the moment of inoculation and the generation time becomes constant only after several divisions.

It can be shown experimentally that the typical growth curve resembles that of Figure 41. During a certain period following the inoculation, the bacteria do not reproduce and their number remains constant. Then begins a slow increase in the bacterial population at a gradually accelerating rate, which attains a constant level. The initial interval, known as the lag phase, is undoubtedly one of intensive chemical changes within the cell, despite the absence of division. Next is a period of rapid, logarithmic growth during which the generation time remains constant. Afterward the reproduction rate gradually declines, the generation time increases, and finally, the number of live cells becomes constant. This marks the beginning of the stationary phase of the growth curve. During this phase the number of live cells remains constant because the increase of the number of live cells compensates for the mortality in the population.

This equilibrium ceases when the multiplication rate drops below the death rate and the number of live cells accordingly decreases. The bacterial culture has entered the phase of decline, in which the death rate gradually increases to a given constant level. Environmental factors, however, cause various deviations from the exponential course of this phase. Ultimately, the death rate sharply decreases when the majority of cells are already dead, and a small number of live cells persist in the culture for months and even for several years, probably at the expense of moderate amounts of nutrients released in the medium by the decomposition of dead bacteria.

In some cultures, the microscopic cell count decreases during the death phase as a result of autolysis or self-digestion. In others, it remains constant although the culture has already become practically sterile. These differences result from the activity of cell enzymes. Even if autolysis does not occur, the shape of the dying cells changes considerably and involute forms appear.

However, the decline of the bacterial population is a statistical rather than individual phenomenon. A constant death rate means that a constant proportion of the surviving cells die during a given period.

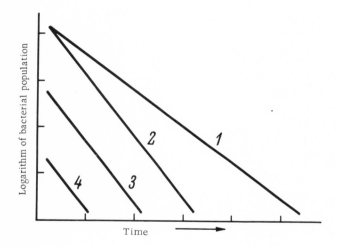

FIGURE 42. Effect of the inoculum size and the death rate on the number of live cells in a culture. Cultures 2, 3, and 4 have an equal death rate but differ in the size of the inoculum; culture 1 has a lower death rate than culture 2.

Thus, if 90% of the initial population die during the first minute, the corresponding percentages would be 99% after two minutes, 99.9% after three minutes, 99.99% after four minutes, etc. In other words, the number of surviving cells decreases at a geometric rate as a function of time. This relationship is expressed graphically in Figure 42, where the ordinate shows the logarithm of the bacterial population and the time is plotted on the abscissa. Figure 42 shows clearly that a bacterial population survives longer if it has developed from a larger inoculum.

Enzymes and Their Role as Carriers of Energy

Enzymes are involved in all aspects of the activity of living cells of bacteria, plants, and animals alike. Each cell is capable of producing a set of enzymes, but no cell possesses all its existing enzymes at the same time. Although enzymes are produced by live cells only, many of them can be extracted from the cells and studied in vitro.

Some reactions proceed slowly because the existing temperature, concentration, pressure, and other factors do not allow adequate contact between the reactants. Such contact (exchange of electrons) must take place if the reaction is to begin. An increase of temperature, concentration, and pressure can accelerate the process. This, however, is not always feasible in nature or in the laboratory.

Enzymes are organic catalysts. They accelerate a chemical reaction that can proceed very slowly in their absence. The mechanism of enzyme action involves a more or less specific adsorption of some compounds, which thus come into contact and react with one another.

The nature of enzymes. All known enzymes are proteins. In some of them, the protein moiety (apoenzyme) is combined with a coenzyme and cofactors. Coenzymes are low molecular weight organic compounds that can be easily separated from the enzyme. Cofactors are compounds containing a metal ion, such as magnesium, zinc, copper, iron, or manganese.

The enzyme protein probably possesses surface forces (i.e., positive or negative radicals) that attract some molecules or ionized parts of them. It is also apparent that enzymes have surface structures that permit the adsorption of these molecules. Almost without exception, enzymes have a rough surface whose features, notably size and disposition, depend on the nature and arrangement of the constituting atoms within the molecule. Some molecular types can interact and unite at a distance not exceeding 1 Å (i.e., 0.1 mμ). The adsorbed molecules enter into a variety of chemical reactions involving an exchange or a loss of electrons, atoms, or atomic groups (H_2, CO_2, H_2O). They can also combine with other compounds before being utilized by the cell. The regenerated enzyme can again adsorb a large amount of compounds, and the process is repeated.

Coenzymes are less specific. They can react with a variety of substrates and with different apoenzymes (protein moieties of enzymes), thus contributing to the enzymatic process. Both cofactors and coenzymes can alter the pattern of surface forces on the substrate or enzyme, creating an optimal "fit" that allows a rapid interaction.

These phenomena can be illustrated in the following scheme, taken from Carpenter (1961):

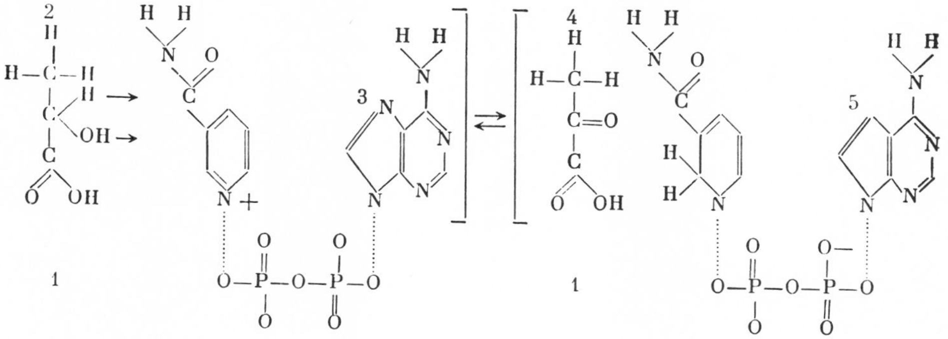

The substrate, in this case lactic acid (2) (CH_3-CHOH-COOH), is adsorbed by the enzyme protein (1), followed by the adsorption of the coenzyme (3). Two electrons and hydrogen ions move from the lactic acid to the coenzyme; the resulting pyruvic acid (4) leaves the enzyme protein in a dissociated condition. The reduced coenzyme (5) likewise dissociates and can be adsorbed by another enzyme, which has already adsorbed other substrates. Now the two electrons and hydrogen atoms can pass from the coenzyme to the new substrate.

Factors affecting the activity of enzymes. The activity of enzymes depends on physical and chemical factors that affect the properties of proteins.

Temperature. High temperature causes protein denaturation. It appears that this denaturation involves the rupture of some unstable links, which leads to rearrangements of certain atoms or radicals, changes the configuration of the protein molecule, and creates new bonds. Most enzymes are rapidly inactivated at temperatures exceeding 70°C; low temperatures considerably depress their action.

Each enzyme has a maximal activity in a given range of temperatures, below which the activity decreases and practically reaches zero at 0°C. Thus, temperature exerts a twofold effect on enzyme activity: a rise of temperature to the optimal level accelerates the process, provided that the other chemical reactions are similarly affected, while heating above this level denaturates the protein and lowers the enzyme activity.

The exact thermal characteristics differ from one enzyme to another. The enzymes of most bacteria show a maximal activity in the range of 30° to 50°C. However, some thermophilic bacteria grow best at a temperature of 60° to 75°C; their enzymes and proteins are apparently more heat resistant.

pH. Each enzyme has an optimal pH range, outside which its activity decreases. For most bacterial enzymes this optimal range lies from pH 6 to pH 8. The enzymes of various molds and yeasts have an optimum at pH 3—5. The effect of pH on enzyme activity is attributed to changes in the ionization and consequently the mutual affinity of the enzyme and its substrate.

Ultraviolet rays. Ultraviolet radiation causes denaturation of proteins and has a strong destructive effect on enzymes. Solutions containing enzymes are inactivated more rapidly when stored in light jars than in dark ones.

Chemical preparations. Heavy metals and their salts coagulate proteins; many of them also have an inactivating or "toxic" effect on enzymes. On the other hand, some inorganic compounds react with enzymes in such a manner that they increase their activity.

Compounds similar in structure to the normal substrate (e. g., $CH_2Cl \cdot CHOH \cdot COOH$ instead of $CH_3 \cdot CHOH \cdot COOH$) can be adsorbed on the enzyme, which consequently becomes unable to adsorb its normal substrate. This lowers the normal activity of the enzyme. Such compounds, which interfere with enzyme action in the live cell, are known as antimetabolites. These relationships are illustrated in the following example, taken from Carpenter (1961):

$$H_2N-\langle \rangle-COOH \qquad N_2H-\langle \rangle-SO_2-NH_2$$

p-aminobenzoic acid ———→ ┈┈┈ Sulfanilamide

$$H_2N-C \begin{matrix} N & N \\ \end{matrix} CH$$
$$N \quad C \quad C-CH_2-NH-\langle \rangle-CO-NH-\overset{H}{\underset{COOH}{C}}-CH_2-CH_2-COOH$$
$$C \quad N$$

Pteridine nucleus   p-aminobenzoic acid   Glutamic acid

Folic acid

Concentration of reactants. If an excess of substrate is present, the rate of the reaction depends on the concentration of enzymes, cofactors, and coenzymes. Naturally, the amount of substrate determines that of the final product.

Enzymes and the live cell. Although closely associated with the components of all living cells, enzymes are not regarded as living matter. Inactivation of cell enzymes can kill the cell since it deprives the latter of some functions essential to life. Compounds or conditions that inactivate enzymes (pH, for example) show an adverse and even lethal effect on bacteria.

Specificity of enzymes. Though not stressed in the preceding text, the specificity of enzymes is one of their major characteristics. One enzyme can adsorb and react with a given substrate or, at most, a group of closely related substrates. Thus, maltase hydrolyzes maltose but not sucrose or lactose. In view of the great specificity of enzymes, it is evident that an organism must possess a large variety of adequate enzymes if it is to utilize different substrates or perform a large number of reactions. One organism can possess hundreds of enzymes. Hence the now discarded concept of the bacterial cell as a "bag of enzymes."

Inductive and constitutive enzymes. Recent studies have confirmed an old hypothesis that certain enzymes are produced by the bacterial cell only if their specific substrates are present in the medium. These enzymes are known as inductive; those constantly present in the cell are named constitutive enzymes.

The formation of inductive enzymes can be demonstrated, for example, in Leuconostoc mesenteroides (Table 20). After being cultured in a medium containing glucose, or lactose, or arabinose, or lacking any sugar at all, the bacterium is transferred crosswise to a medium containing one of these sugars. Glucose was utilized in all the cases, meaning that a constitutive enzyme was involved. By contrast, the enzymes responsible for the decomposition of lactose and arabinose were inductive; they were synthesized only when the organism was previously grown in a medium containing the respective sugar. Traces of inductive enzymes exist in all cells, but the production of appreciable amounts of them requires a certain stimulation on the part of an "inductor," which may be the substrate or a closely related compound. The ability of bacterial cells to produce inductive enzymes assists in solving the problem of the number of enzymes in the cell.

Reversibility of enzyme action. Like most chemical processes, enzymatic reactions are reversible in certain conditions. In the reaction $A+B \rightleftarrows C+D$, the long arrow indicates that substances A and B participate in large amounts and the process proceeds to the right. The reaction ends when a small amount of A and B remains together with C and D. At this time, the addition of greater quantities of C and D causes a reversal of the reaction, which now proceeds to the left and yields certain amounts of the substances A and B. Clearly, the course of the reaction depends on the quantities of the initial products, A and B, in relation to the final products, C and D.

TABLE 20. Inductive formation of disaccharidases in Leuconostoc mesenteroides

	Sugars decomposed by bacterium		
	glucose	lactose	arabinose
After growth in a medium containing:			
glucose	+	−	−
lactose	+	+	−
arabinose	+	−	+
no sugar	+	−	−

Note: +presence, − absence of decomposition of the sugars.

Most enzymatic reactions in the living cell appear irreversible because the reaction products are immediately removed from the system. These products can enter other synthetic reactions, which yield insoluble compounds, undergo further enzymatic decomposition, or break down with the formation of gaseous CO_2, which leaves the cell and even escapes from the medium.

Nomenclature, classification, and activity of enzymes. The names of most enzymes are obtained by adding the suffix "ase" to the name of their specific substrate. Thus, proteinase acts on protein, lipase on lipids (fats), carbohydrase on carbohydrates; gelatinase hydrolyzes gelatin; maltase, maltose, etc.

Enzymes that split their substrates by means of hydrolysis are known as hydrolases. Those that carry out a direct oxidation are oxidases, and those that remove hydrogen from their substrates are dehydrogenases.

Extracellular enzymes. Enzymes can be classified according to their main site of action. The extracellular enzymes or exoenzymes are excreted by the cell and catalyze reactions outside the cell. Most of these enzymes are hydrolases.

Intracellular enzymes. Enzymes acting inside the cells are known as intracellular or endoenzymes. They are subdivided according to the type of the reaction or the substrate they attack. To this category belong the permeases, hydrolases, and transferases.

1. Permeases. These enzymes facilitate the penetration of some nutrients from the medium through the cell membrane into the cell. As a

result of their action, these compounds accumulate inside the cell to a much higher concentration than in the surrounding medium. The mechanism by which these enzymes act is still obscure.

2. Hydrolases. The intracellular hydrolases perform some hydrolytic reactions inside the cell. For example, disaccharides can be broken down to monosaccharides after being previously oxidized. Peptidases hydrolyze peptides inside the cell, yielding amino acids. A few enzymes carry out a dehydration.

3. Transferases. Enzymes capable of transferring phosphate radicals are of particular importance in carbohydrate metabolism and in the creation of energy-rich bonds. Beside phosphate, many other radicals can be attached or removed by specific enzymes. To this category belong the methyl, acetyl, amino, and carboxyl groups. These reactions play a major role in the transformations of amino acids and other organic compounds.

Typical extracellular enzymes will be mentioned below. The reactions involved create protoplasm from such raw materials as water, amino acids, carbohydrates, etc.

Cells possess a remarkable ability to build new cells by using a variety of substrates. Many bacteria satisfy their nitrogen requirements from a single amino acid or even from ammonia, and build all the twenty or more amino acids found in their protoplasm. Moreover, some species use the same amino acid as a combined source of nitrogen and carbon.

Oxidoreductases. The oxidoreductases or oxidation-reduction enzymes catalyze the transfer of electrons or hydrogen at the expense of energy-rich bonds analogous to those of phosphates or other compounds. Enzymes that remove hydrogen from a hydrogen donor are named dehydrogenases. Their name usually includes that of the substrate. Thus, lactic dehydrogenase removes hydrogen from lactic acid.

The apoenzyme or protein moiety of each dehydrogenase usually shows a strict specificity to its substrate. In other words, it can combine only with a given substrate (as lactic or succinic acids). The coenzymes are less specific; they react with a number of different dehydrogenases. The following three coenzymes are involved in dehydrogenation: (1) diphosphopyridine nucleotide (DPN) or coenzyme I; (2) triphosphopyridine nucleotide (TPN) or coenzyme II; (3) flavin adenine dinucleotide (FAD). Dehydrogenases unite with DPN and TPN, which are the main carriers of electrons and hydrogens from the substrate to the flavoprotein. Flavoproteins are colored proteins containing iron, molybdenum, or copper; their metal atom facilitates the transfer of electrons.

Typically, a dehydrogenation can be expressed in the following formula: $AH_2 + B \rightleftharpoons A + BH_2$, where AH_2 is the hydrogen donor and B the hydrogen acceptor. A few dehydrogenases utilize oxygen as hydrogen acceptors, yielding water or hydrogen peroxide. Most dehydrogenases transfer hydrogen from the substrate to one or several intermediate hydrogen carriers, including DPN, TPN, and FAD (Figure 43).

The enzyme transfers hydrogen from the first to the second carrier and so on. The last carrier is one of the cytochromes — iron-containing proteins. The reduced cytochrome (i. e., one that has accepted hydrogen) is oxidized back to its original condition by cytochrome oxidase, while the hydrogen unites with oxygen to form water. Cytochrome oxidase and other oxidoreductases that transfer hydrogen directly to oxygen are named oxidases.

81

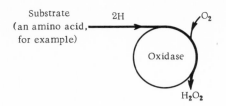

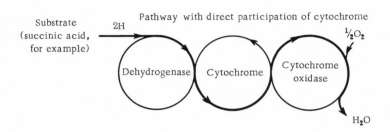

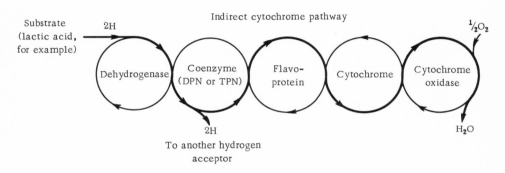

FIGURE 43. Main types of participation of enzymes in oxidizing the substrate.

Most dehydrogenases transfer hydrogen from the substrate to the coenzyme, which in this reduced state represents a specific substrate to the coenzyme dehydrogenase. The latter in turn transfers the hydrogen to the cytochrome. The fate of hydrogen depends on the enzymes or carriers produced by the cell in each particular case. Thus, aerobic bacteria usually produce cytochromes and can fully oxidize the substrate. Anaerobes, on the other hand, cannot transfer hydrogen to oxygen since they do not produce cytochromes; instead, they use other final acceptors of hydrogen and yield products that are only partly oxidized.

Two other enzymes deserve particular attention. Catalase breaks down hydrogen peroxide into water and gaseous hydrogen according to the reaction: $2H_2O \rightarrow 2H_2O + O_2$. By this mechanism the cell eliminates the hydrogen peroxide, which otherwise would accumulate and poison the organism. The anaerobic bacteria, which cannot develop in the presence of air, do not produce catalase.

Enzymes	Formula of type of reaction
Proteases	Hydrolysis of proteins to proteoses, proteins, and peptides
Gelatinase	Hydrolyzes gelatin, destroying its ability to gel, produced by many bacteria
Caseinase	Hydrolyzes case in milk; produced by many bacteria
Pepsin	Hydrolysis of proteins in the stomach of animals
Trypsin	Hydrolysis of proteins in the intestine of animals
Carbohydrases	Hydrolysis of polysaccharides, dissacharides, etc. $(C_6H_{10}O_5)n + nH_2O \rightleftarrows n\,C_6H_{12}O_6$
Cellulase	$\text{Cellulose} \rightarrow \underset{\text{cellobiose}}{C_{12}H_{22}O_{11}}$
Amylase	$\text{Starch} \rightarrow \underset{\text{maltose}}{C_{12}H_{22}O_{11}}$
Maltase	$\underset{\text{maltose}}{C_{12}H_{22}O_{11}} + H_2O \rightarrow \underset{\text{glucose}}{2\,C_6H_{12}O_6}$
Lactase (β-galactosidase)	$\underset{\text{lactose}}{C_{12}H_{22}O_{11}} + H_2O \rightarrow \underset{\text{glucose}}{C_6H_{12}O_6} + \underset{\text{galactose}}{C_6H_{12}O_6}$
Sucrase (invertase)	$\underset{\text{sucrose}}{C_{12}H_{22}O_{11}} + H_2O \rightarrow \underset{\text{glucose}}{C_6H_{12}O_6} + \underset{\text{fructose}}{C_6H_{12}O_6}$
Lipases	Hydrolysis of fats to glycerol and fatty acids $C_3H_5(O-CO-R)_3 + 3H_2O \rightarrow C_3H_5(OH)_3 + 3R-COOH$

Classification of Bacteria on the Basis of Their Nutrition and Energy Supply

The term nutrients applies to those compounds that can penetrate through the cell membrane and enter the cell either in their original state or after an extracellular digestion in order to be used as building material or a source of energy in the cell.

To this category belongs a large variety of compounds: proteins, lipids, carbohydrates, cellulose, chitin, that is, practically all the natural organic chemicals, as well as inorganic compounds, including water and gases — oxygen and carbon dioxide. However, no microorganism can utilize all these compounds at the same time. Only a few microorganisms are capable of utilizing fats. Some microorganisms cannot break down natural proteins but grow perfectly in the presence of compounds obtained by a partial decomposition of proteins. Many microorganisms utilize a variety of carbohydrates, while some cannot do so at all. Certain bacteria obtain energy by oxidizing different inorganic compounds, such as hydrogen, methane, ferrous and manganese salts, sulfur, hydrogen sulfide, thiosulfates, ammonia, nitrites, etc.

Nutrients enter into microorganisms and plants by a largely uniform mechanism involving diffusion or enzymatic transfer through the cytoplasmic membrane.

In his review of chemosynthesis and inorganic oxidation, G. A. Zavarzin (1964c) notes that the progress of knowledge on the physiology of different microorganisms makes it increasingly difficult to distinguish between autotrophs and heterotrophs. Accordingly, the term "chemoautotrophs," defined by S. N. Winogradsky in 1922 as organisms capable of inorganic oxidation and chemosynthesis, becomes less and less clear.

According to G. A. Zavarzin (1964), terms created to designate the type of metabolism should not be applied to the microorganisms themselves, since the latter can switch from one metabolic pattern to another.

In characterizing the nutrition and metabolism of microorganisms, one must take into account their ability of photosynthesis, chemosynthesis, and assimilation of organic compounds. Such classification of microorganisms on the basis of their metabolism appears in Table 21.

TABLE 21. Classification of bacteria according to the type of their metabolism

Organisms and type of metabolism	Oxidized substrate (hydrogen donor)	Source of energy	Source of carbon	Organisms
Photosynthetic autotrophs (photolithotrophy)	Mineral compounds	Light	CO_2	Green plants, Chlorobacteriaceae (green sulfur bacteria), Thiorhodaceae (purple sulfur bacteria)
Chemosynthetic autotrophs (chemolithotrophy)	Mineral compounds	Oxidation of inorganic compounds	CO_2	Hydrogenomonas, Thiobacillus, Nitrosomonas, Nitrobacter, etc.
Photosynthetic heterotrophs (photoorganotrophy)	Organic compounds	Light	CO_2 and organic compounds	Athiorhodaceae (nonsulfur purple bacteria)
Heterotrophs (chemo-organotrophy)	Organic compounds	Oxidation-reduction reactions in the oxidation of organic compounds	Organic compounds	Animals and the majority of microorganisms, excluding algae

Autotrophic bacteria utilize inorganic compounds only. They obtain carbon from carbon dioxide, while the hydrogen necessary for the reduction of the carbon into organic compounds comes from inorganic sources such as H_2O, H_2, H_2S, and NH_3. The sources of energy are light in the photoautotrophic microorganisms and oxidation-reduction reactions in the chemoautotrophic ones.

Heterotrophic bacteria require at least one source of organic matter and can also utilize small amounts of CO_2 at the same time. Even in this case, however, the energy necessary for the reduction of carbon dioxide comes from the oxidation of organic compounds. When living photoheterotrophically, the photosynthetic heterotrophic bacteria of the family

Athiorhodaceae consume CO_2 as the only source of carbon but still require organic compounds as donors of the hydrogen necessary for the reduction of CO_2.

The majority of bacteria dealt with in general or applied microbiology are heterotrophs. This group of bacteria is also referred to as chemo-organotrophs, since the energy for their general metabolism comes from the oxidation of organic compounds. Some bacteria can lead not only an autotrophic but also a heterotrophic life. The hydrogen bacteria (H y d r o - g e n o m o n a s), for example, can live chemosynthetically as autotrophs in a purely mineral medium in an atmosphere of hydrogen and carbon. In other words, the hydrogen bacteria are facultative autotrophs.

The nonsulfur purple bacteria (Athiorhodaceae) are capable of photo-synthesis in the presence of light, using as hydrogen donors not only hydro-gen sulfide but also organic compounds. In the dark they can live aero-bically only by oxidizing organic compounds. Thus, Athiorhodaceae can live not only photoheterotrophically but also as heterotrophs.

Sources and Carriers of Energy in Microorganisms

One of the main characteristics of life is the transfer of energy. Indeed, the organism remains alive by utilizing energy for the production of com-pounds that constitute its protoplasm. The conventional concept of energy as a capacity for work is largely inaccurate. Energy has various mani-festations, and one form can pass into another. Light (solar) energy can be captured as chemical energy in a photochemical process similar to photo-synthesis. In turn, chemical energy can be transformed into mechanical energy, which moves, for example, the flagella of protozoans and bacteria. The synthesis of protoplasm involves another transformation of energy. At any rate, energy is never lost or created again.

Chemically bound energy. Chemical bonds contain electrostatic energy. Electrons are held in orbit by electrostatic forces; their passage from one orbit to another involves a release of energy. Moreover, the transfer of electrons is accompanied by a transfer of energy. Some (unstable) chemical bonds are energy rich in comparison with other bonds; the transfer of their electrons causes the release of large amounts of energy.

Energy invariably tends to pass from a higher to a lower level (from the burning stove to the cold tea kettle). In a given set of conditions, such as temperature, pressure, and concentration of reactants, a chemical reaction will take place only if it involves a release of energy.

The utilization of free energy by microorganisms has been examined in detail by Thimann (1963), who defines the term "energy" as a capacity for work. Thus, the energy of a given reaction is determined by the maximal work that can be performed. This maximal work is referred to as the "free" energy of the reaction. Although the absolute amount of energy enclosed in matter cannot be measured, it is possible to determine the "maximal" work during the transition of one substance into another, that is, the change in free energy that accompanies the process. This change in free energy occurring as a result of a chemical reaction is designated ΔF.

In the reaction $A + B \leftrightarrows C + D$, the change in free energy can be expressed as follows at given concentrations of A and B and in a state of equilibrium:

$$\Delta F = RT \ln \frac{C \times D}{A \times B} - RT \ln K,$$

where $C, D, A,$ and B are the initial concentrations of the reactants, K the equilibrium constant, R the gas constant, and T the absolute temperature. This equation can be expressed more conveniently in the following form:

$$\Delta F = \Delta F° + RT \ln \frac{C \times D}{A \times B},$$

where $\Delta F° = -RT \ln K$; $\Delta F°$ is the change of the free energy in standard conditions (where all concentrations are molar and the gas pressure equals 1 atmosphere). A negative ΔF means that the reaction proceeds with the release of energy. At $\Delta F = 0$, no energy is released or absorbed. Finally, at a positive ΔF the reaction consumes energy; such reactions do not occur in the live cell.

Beside photosynthesis, chemical oxidation is the main source of energy for biologic phenomena. The synthesis of protoplasm creates compounds whose energy is more readily utilizable than that of the initial materials. The energy of one chemical reaction cannot be transferred to another, unrelated reaction. If this is so, how can the energy of oxidation be stored in the components of the protoplasm? The answer to this question lies in the existence of conjugated reactions.

Coupling of reactions. Let us consider two simultaneous reactions, one of them involving the release of energy (1), the other accompanied by a loss of energy under known conditions (2).

$$A + B \longrightarrow C + D - \Delta F, \tag{1}$$
$$E + F \longrightarrow G + H + \Delta F. \tag{2}$$

Reaction (1) can occur spontaneously, while (2) cannot. However, both reactions can take place simultaneously if one of the products, Y, reacts with $A + B$ to form the intermediate product Y_1, from which Y can be regenerated by reacting with $E + F$.

$$A + B + Y \longrightarrow C + D + Y_1 - \Delta F, \tag{3}$$
$$E + F + Y_1 \longrightarrow G + H + Y - \Delta F. \tag{4}$$

Reactions (3) and (4) proceed with the release of energy, and the process can occur simultaneously. This is the principle of the "coupling of reactions" — the probable way in which chemically bound energy can be harnessed for biological synthesis.

High-energy compounds. As we said above, some kinds of chemical bonds are richer in energy than others. Such bonds, known as high-energy, exist in some organic phosphorus compounds formed by electron rearrangements of inorganic phosphate. Energy-rich phosphate bonds are less stable than normal bonds; their rupture yields an amount of energy that is 3—5 times greater.

Phosphates serve as connecting reactants. They lead to reactions that can take place only in their presence and convert these reactions into others that proceed spontaneously since they yield energy. Phosphates transfer energy from reactions that yield large amounts of it to others that require a continuous supply of extraneous energy.

The above example can be presented in a different form in order to show the conversion of normal phosphate bonds (—P) into energy-rich phosphate bonds (~P) and the participation of the latter in the process:

$$A + B + -P \rightarrow C + D + \sim P, \tag{3a}$$
$$E + F + \sim P \rightarrow G + H + -P. \tag{4a}$$

Not all energy-rich compounds contain phosphorus. Some oxidative reactions yield "active acetate" — an energy-rich compound that takes part in other reactions. It can be said that energy-rich bonds are the principal carriers of energy in the general metabolism of the organism.

Microbial anabolism, that is, the construction of cell substance, requires free energy in the form of adenosine triphosphate (ATP) and a reducing agent, notably $DPN \cdot H_2$, capable of reducing the free carbon dioxide or the more oxidized organic compounds to the level of the cell substance.

As Zavarzin (1964c) points out in his review of inorganic oxidation and chemosynthesis, anabolism and energy metabolism are more or less independent of one another and proceed by different mechanisms. Nevertheless, the autotrophic mechanism of CO_2 assimilation via the ribulose-diphosphate cycle (Figure 48) has much in common with the pentose phosphate cycle of heterotrophic organisms. The overall equation of CO_2 fixation can be represented as follows:

$$3CO_2 + 9ATP + 5H_2O + 6DPN \cdot H_2 = COOH-CHOH-CH_2-O \cdot H_2PO_3 + \\ + 9ADP + 6DPN + 8H_3PO_4.$$

As the equation shows, anabolism (i.e., the fixation of CO_2 and the synthesis of biomass) requires a constant supply of energy in the form of ATP and a reducing agent at the DPN (diphosphopyridine nucleotide) level. It is further evident that the production of 1 molecule of phosphoglyceric acid involves the breakdown of 9 molecules of ATP. In the synthesis of bacterial biomass, as in the case of Desulfovibrio desulfuricans growing on pyruvic acid, the formation of 9.57 g of dry bacterial weight requires not 9 but 10 moles of ATP (Senez, 1962). Energy-rich compounds of phosphorus and other elements are formed in oxidative reactions in which the synthesis of 1 mole of ATP consumes about 10,000 calories. Heterotrophic organisms produce energy-rich compounds by oxidizing organic nutrients and by respiration, which breaks down reserve food in the cell.

In photosynthetic organisms, both ATP and $DPN \cdot H_2$ are produced at the expense of solar energy with the participation of chlorophyll in a process involving the photolysis of water and the addition of phosphoric acid to ADP. In chemosynthetic organisms, energy-rich compounds can be formed by the oxidation of inorganic substrates as the electrons pass from the reduced substrate to oxygen, though endogenous respiration can also take place.

Energy is stored in ATP in the following three stages of the oxidative process, which yield the largest amounts of energy: (1) the transfer of electrons or hydrogen from the reduced DPN·H$_2$ to flavoproteins; (2) the transfer of electrons from cytochrome b to cytochrome c; (3) the final transfer of hydrogen or electrons from cytochrome a to molecular oxygen.

If an inorganic oxidation process is to take place at all, the oxidation-reduction potential of the compound to be oxidized must be lower than that of the hydrogen transfer system. In other words, the hydrogen carrier, DPN for example, must be reduced by hydrogenase to DPN·H$_2$; otherwise the oxidized coenzyme cannot be reduced without an expenditure of extraneous energy. The following list shows the oxidation-reduction potentials of the main biologic systems:

Compound	E_0 mV	ΔF calories per electron
Oxygen	+810	−12,000
Cytochrome a	+290	−460
Cytochrome c	+270	−7,150
Cytochrome b	−40	−920
Flavoprotein	−80	−4,600
DPN (dipyridine nucleotide)	−280	
Hydrogen	−420	
Glucose-6-phosphate	−430	
α-Ketoglutarate	−600	
Pyruvate (pyruvic aldehyde)	−630	
Nitrate	+300	
Fe^{++}	+300	
Hydrogen sulfide	−380	

Clearly, such direct reduction of DPN can hardly occur in the nitrification and iron oxidation processes performed by Gallionella ferruginea and Thiobacillus ferrooxidans.

As will be shown below, G. A. Zavarzin (1964c) and N. N. Lyalikova (1968) assume in such cases the existence of a back phosphorylation in which DPN is reduced at the expense of ATP formed in other oxidative reactions.

Biological Oxidation as a Source of Energy in the Heterotrophic Mode of Life

Most bacteria obtain energy from oxidative reactions. Oxidation consists in the loss of an electron; it is accompanied by a removal of hydrogen or an acquisition of oxygen. If the oxidation is to take place at all, there must be a simultaneous and equivalent reduction of one or more compounds; oxidation necessarily involves the reduction of the oxidizing agent. For this reason, it would be more correct to speak of oxidation-reduction reactions instead of oxidation and reduction separately. However, the terms oxidation and reduction are often preferred in order to stress the changes occurring in a given compound. In the majority of biologic oxidative reactions, hydrogen atoms and electrons are transferred from the substrate, which serves as hydrogen donor, to another compound acting as hydrogen acceptor. Between the hydrogen donor and the final acceptor of hydrogen may be a number of intermediate carriers that readily take up and yield hydrogen.

Chemosynthetic bacteria obtain energy from oxidation-reduction reactions involving inorganic compounds; heterotrophic bacteria do so by oxidizing organic substrates.

Respiration as biological oxidation. The main function of respiration is to yield energy. There are several pathways by which energy can be obtained in a form suitable for use by the cell.

An organism capable of respiration obtains 5—10 times more energy from a given substrate when grown in the presence of air than in anaerobic conditions. This is due to the fact that the bulk of the energy is released during the final oxidation of organic matter to carbon dioxide; by contrast, the anaerobic conditions create a variety of partly oxidized products. The growth of the organism and the utilization of the substrate in aerobic and anaerobic conditions can proceed in three directions, which can be outlined as follows: (1) the Pasteur effect; (2) oxidative phosphorylation; (3) oxidative assimilation. Although these are actually three aspects of the same process, we shall discuss them separately for the sake of clarity.

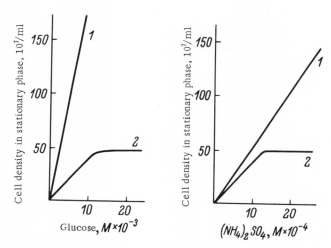

FIGURE 44. Increase in bacteria numbers in aerobic (1) and anaerobic (2) conditions (after Oginsky and Umbreit, 1959).

Pasteur effect. Many organisms produce a greater biomass per unit of utilized substrate when grown in air than in anaerobic conditions. This is the Pasteur effect. Otherwise stated, the Pasteur effect means that aerobic life requires less substrate in comparison with anaerobic life. Aerobic life is more efficient, since it yields a greater number of cells per unit of substrate; the aerobic growth of one cell requires a smaller amount of medium.

As the graph in Figure 44 shows, glucose at a concentration of 10×10^{-3}M is a limiting factor in the given conditions. Anaerobic growth here ceases at a density of 500×10^6 organisms/ml, while the aerobic culture attains a density of over $2,500 \times 10^6$ organisms/ml at the same concentration of the substrate. This difference between aerobic and anaerobic growth is much smaller when the limiting factor is the concentration of a mineral salt, which cannot be used as a source of energy (Figure 44, right). If the organism obtains energy by respiration, the aerobic process yields more energy per unit of utilized substrate. Living aerobically, the organism can grow longer and produce a greater amount of biomass.

The organisms can be divided into four types on the basis of their relation to air.

1. Obligate anaerobes. Air is toxic to these forms, which naturally do not show a Pasteur effect.

2. Indifferent organisms. These organisms do grow in the presence of oxygen but cannot obtain useful energy by the oxidation of a substrate. The organisms of this type, S t r e p t o c o c c u s   f a e c a l i s, for example, can grow equally well in a glucose peptone medium in the presence and absence of air. They lack cytochromes and virtually do not utilize oxygen even when grown in the presence of air. In a glycerol medium, the same strain can only grow aerobically, oxidizing the glycerol via triose phosphate to lactic acid. This process requires a considerable amount of oxygen and yields H_2O_2, which is toxic and must be disposed of. The organism lacks an enzymatic system for the oxidation of glucose with oxygen, which is no more than an indifferent gas to it. However, it does possess the necessary set of enzymes for the oxidation of glycerol, as shown by the utilization of oxygen. Yet the energy released by this oxidation is not utilized but accumulates in the triose phosphate, which releases it during the oxidation to lactic acid. Thus, 1 mole of glycerol consumed aerobically yields the same growth as 0.5 mole of glucose in aerobic or anaerobic conditions. Therefore, it would be incorrect to say that the indifferent organisms do not possess mechanisms for the fixation or utilization of oxygen. It is, however, true, that the utilization of oxygen by these organisms does not yield energy that can be harnessed by the cell. Most of the lactic acid bacteria belong to the indifferent group. These organisms do not show the Pasteur effect.

3. Facultative aerobes. Organisms of this type can grow both aerobically and in the absence of air. However, they give a better yield (number of cells per unit of utilized substrate) in the presence of air. This group (of which E. c o l i can be taken as an example) shows a pronounced Pasteur effect.

4. Strict aerobes. These organisms cannot grow in the absence of air. Here belong many bacterial genera, as well as a large number of molds and actinomycetes. Since these organisms cannot grow without air, many authors believe that they show a maximal Pasteur effect. Those who dispute this viewpoint out the fallacy of applying the term "optimal growth" in air (i. e., the Pasteur effect) to organisms that can grow only in the presence of air.

According to Oginsky and Umbreit (1959), only the facultative aerobes show a Pasteur effect.

Mechanism of the formation of energy-rich phosphorus compounds. Since chemical reactions involve a release or consumption of energy, it is important to distinguish between the total amount of heat produced by the reaction $(-\Delta H)$ and the free energy of the reaction $(-\Delta F)$, that is, the maximal amount of energy obtained from the reaction. Only $-\Delta F$ expresses the utilizable chemical energy. The free energy $(-\Delta F)$ obtained from a given reaction depends on temperature, gas pressure, and concentration of the key substances. In some biological reactions it may be almost 20% greater or smaller than the heat of the reaction $-\Delta H$.

$$CH_{4\,gas} + 2\,O_{2\,gas} \rightarrow CO_{2\,gas} + 2H_2O_{\text{solution}}$$
$$-\Delta H = 212,600 \text{ cal.}$$
$$-\Delta F = 194,600 \text{ cal.}$$

$$C_6H_{12}O_{6\,solid} + 6CO_{2\,gas\ 0.2\,atm.} \rightarrow 6CO_{2\,gas\ 0.0003\,atm.} + 6H_2O_{\text{solution}}$$
$$-\Delta H = 674,000 \text{ cal.}$$
$$-\Delta F = 688,000 \text{ cal.}$$

The energy is not released in the form of heat; instead, a large part of it is transformed into chemical energy or stored in other compounds. Consequently, the amount of energy released in the course of metabolism is of great significance to the cell. This can be explained by tracing the pathway of energy transfer. As noted above, the transfer of energy involves the formation of a few ester bonds, where oxygen is replaced by sulfur, and a large number of organic compounds containing phosphoric acid. Thioesters are formed in metabolic processes by the interaction of organic acids with the mercaptan complex $(E) \cdot SR$ of the enzyme:

$$CH_3COR + (E) \cdot SR \rightleftarrows CH_3CO \sim SR + (E) \cdot R.$$

Two such mercaptan compounds are known at present: a thioester with coenzyme A and a thioester with lipoic acid.

There are two kinds of organic phosphates: (1) those that actually represent esters, like glucose phosphate, where an ester bond unites the phosphate group with the hydroxyl of the alcohol group $C_6H_{12}O_5-O-H_2PO_3$, a relatively solid phosphate bond having an energy of about 3,000 calories per gram molecule; (2) those in which an ester bond unites the phosphorus with a carbon having a double bond or with a second phosphorus atom, which likewise has a double bond with oxygen. In this case the phosphate bond has an energy of 7,000 to 14,000 calories per gram molecule, and the bond is unstable. These energy-rich bonds are designated $\sim P$. Twelve such compounds are known. Six of them will be discussed below. The other six are the triphosphates of guanosine, uridine, inosine, thymidine, cytidine — all analogous to adenosine. These compounds are designated briefly as follows: GTP, UTP, ITP, TTP, and CTP. Other purines and pyrimidines form similar compounds.

Phosphorylation on substrate level. Energy-rich phosphorus compounds are formed in two ways: by fermentation and in oxidation reactions. In the former case, also known as phosphorylation on substrate level, energy is stored in thioester bonds as follows:

$$CH_3CO \cdot R + (E) \cdot SR' \rightleftarrows CH_3CO \sim SR' + (E) \cdot R.$$

This energy can afterward be transferred to phosphates. Such is the mechanism of the formation of acetyl phosphate from acetyl-coenzyme A with the participation of the enzyme transacetylase:

$$CH_3CO \sim S \cdot CoA + -HPO_3OH \rightleftarrows CH_3COO \sim PO_3H^- + HSCoA.$$

In another type of phosphorylation on substrate level during a fermentation process, the formation of a double bond in the substrate molecule converts a low-energy bond to an energy-rich one. For example, 2-phosphoglyceric acid, which usually has an ester bond with phosphate, loses a molecule of water and becomes phosphoenolpyruvic acid, whose energy-rich phosphate bond results from the proximity of phosphate to an enolpyruvate carbon atom possessing a double bond:

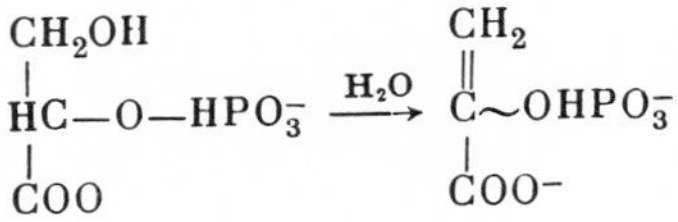

$$\begin{array}{c} CH_2OH \\ | \\ HC-O-HPO_3^- \\ | \\ COO \end{array} \xrightarrow{H_2O} \begin{array}{c} CH_2 \\ \| \\ C \sim OHPO_3^- \\ | \\ COO^- \end{array}$$

In this case, the energy of dehydratation concentrates in the phosphate bond. In the final analysis, some energy-rich phosphate bonds join such compounds as GTP, UTP, CTP, and especially ATP, which serves as carrier of energy in transphosphorylation reactions.

The energy of phosphate bonds finally passes to bonds between carbon atoms in the course of synthesis. In biological systems, the energy of phosphate bonds is used for the synthesis of protein, nucleic acids, polysaccharides, glutamines, and arginine; these phosphates also supply the energy necessary for the reduction of carboxyls to aldehyde groups. The energy of sulfate bonds serves in the transfer of acetyl groups, for example in the synthesis of citric acid in the Krebs cycle and in the synthesis and decomposition of fats.

Type	Name	Formula
$P \sim N - C -$ $\|$	Phosphocreatine	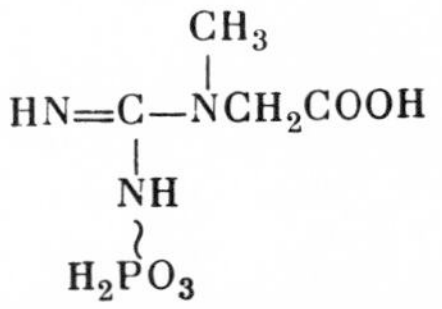 $\begin{array}{c} CH_3 \\ \| \\ HN=C-NCH_2COOH \\ \| \\ NH \\ \wr \\ H_2PO_3 \end{array}$
	Phosphoarginine	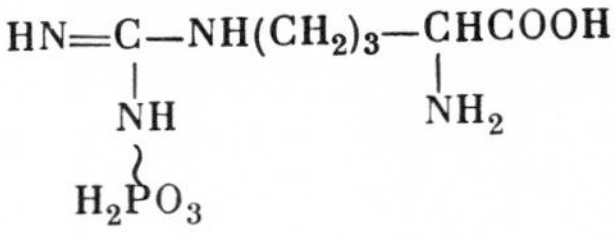 $\begin{array}{c} HN=C-NH(CH_2)_3-CHCOOH \\ \| \| \\ NH NH_2 \\ \wr \\ H_2PO_3 \end{array}$

P~O—C—   Phosphoenolpyruvic acid

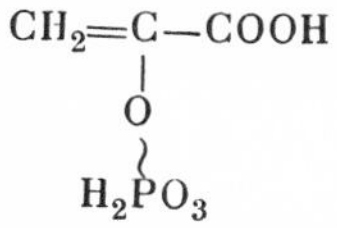

$$CH_2=C—COOH$$
$$|$$
$$O$$
$$?$$
$$H_2PO_3$$

Phosphoglyceryl phosphate

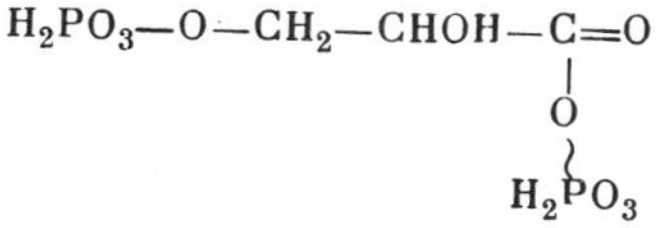

$$H_2PO_3—O—CH_2—CHOH—C=O$$
$$|$$
$$O$$
$$?$$
$$H_2PO_3$$

Acetyl phosphate

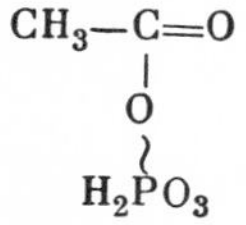

$$CH_3—C=O$$
$$|$$
$$O$$
$$?$$
$$H_2PO_3$$

P~O—P   Adenosine triphosphate

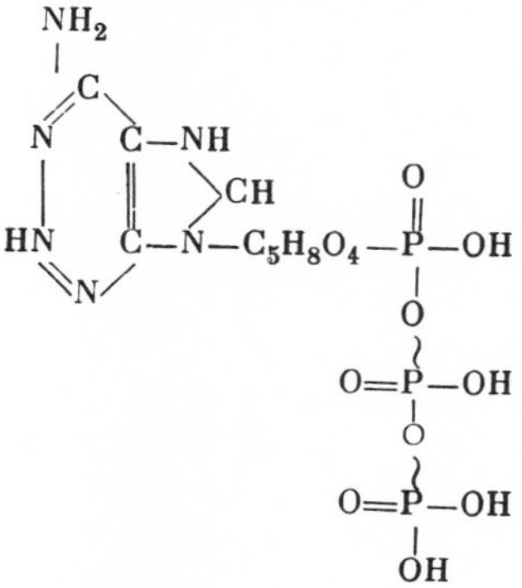

$$NH_2$$
$$|$$
$$C$$
$$N \diagdown C—NH$$
$$\diagdown CH \quad O$$
$$HN \quad C—N—C_5H_8O_4—P—OH$$
$$\diagup N \diagdown \qquad\qquad O$$
$$O=P—OH$$
$$O$$
$$O=P—OH$$
$$OH$$

Oxidative phosphorylation.

Facultative anaerobes grow much more rapidly in the presence of air than in anaerobic conditions because respiration yields a much greater amount of energy in the form of energy-rich phosphorus compounds. Thus, the oxidation of 1 g mole of glucose yields 680,000 calories, which create thirty to forty energy-rich bonds, compared with the mere four energy-rich bonds from the 58,000 or 57,000 calories produced respectively by the lactic and alcoholic fermentations.

The energy released in oxidation enters the phosphate bonds via the cytochrome system in a mechanism involving the quinone group.

It has become evident that energy-rich phosphorus compounds must be formed along the oxidation pathway from the substrate to oxygen. This process, known as "oxidative phosphorylation," consists of the transfer of 2H from the nicotinamide coenzyme via the flavoproteins, cytochromes, and cytochrome oxidase to oxygen; it converts inorganic phosphate into an energy-rich organic compound. The transfer of 2H from the reduced nicotinamide coenzyme to oxygen must produce a slightly greater amount of energy than that necessary for the creation of four energy-rich bonds per mole of 2 H. It was shown experimentally that the energy obtained is in excess of that needed for the synthesis of three bonds. Thus, the transfer of 2H to oxygen through the intermediary system yields energy that can be utilized by the cell (i. e., not in the form of heat) and can be measured not only in terms of growth but also as the amount of phosphorus in energy-rich compounds.

Oxidative assimilation. This process consists of the oxidation and assimilation of the substrate without any multiplication of organisms. It resembles the growth of facultative aerobes in the presence of air, although in this case the cell count remains constant during the experiment. When resting cells are given glucose, lactose, or any other utilizable substrate, after some period the substrate disappears and the consumption of oxygen ceases. Direct analysis shows that 30 to 60% of the glucose is oxidized to carbonic acid and water, while the rest is assimilated as building material of the cell. Every 10 moles of glucose (60 moles of C) yield only 30 moles of CO_2, while the increment of the cell biomass amounts to 30 moles of C. This synthesis consumes energy released in the oxidation of glucose. In other words, the oxidation of glucose allows the cell to assimilate part of the substrate, converting the latter into biomass.

Other hydrogen acceptors. As shown in Figure 43, the amount of useful energy released is greatest when hydrogen is directly oxidized by gaseous oxygen into water. However, gaseous oxygen is not always available. It would be surprising indeed if nature did not possess mechanisms for oxidizing substrate hydrogen in the absence of gaseous oxygen. The organisms capable of utilizing this energy in anaerobic conditions can be divided in two categories. The first category consists of strict aerobes that direct the hydrogen to bound oxygen. These organisms can grow in the absence of gaseous oxygen if compounds of this element are available. The second category is composed of organisms that cannot grow in air (being unable to utilize gaseous oxygen) but can use oxygen compounds.

Development Involving the Utilization of Bound Oxygen

Organisms capable of utilizing both free and bound oxygen. Most of these organisms are obligate aerobes that grow anaerobically only in the presence of bound oxygen. Nitrates are the commonest substrates used. Other compounds, such as iron cyanides, can also serve as hydrogen acceptors, though usually these very compounds can react with oxygen. Three groups of organisms can be assigned here.

The organisms of the first group use nitrates only as a source of nitrogen for protein synthesis. Inside the cell, the nitrates are reduced to ammonia; in this case, they do not serve as acceptors of hydrogen and do not participate in the normal transfer of hydrogen from the substrate to oxygen. This process, known as nitrate assimilation, represents a transition of NO_3^- to NO_2^- to NH_4^+.

The second group consists of organisms capable of utilizing nitrate as hydrogen acceptor, converting NO_3^- to NO_2^- in a process that represents a reduction of the nitrate. In this case, nitrates are strictly necessary to the respiration process as an alternative acceptor of hydrogen, but their function is rather limited owing to the toxicity of nitrites. This reaction enables some aerobes to grow in the absence of air. At any rate, this alternative pathway to the normal respiratory process is not of major physiological importance.

Finally, the third process — denitrification — converts NO_3^- or NO_2^- to gaseous nitrogen. Only a small group of organisms of the genera Bacillus and Pseudomonas belong to this group. This process can take place only in anaerobic conditions. The pathway leading to free nitrogen is unknown, and most (if not all) of the assumed intermediate products (hyponitrous acid, nitromide, nitroxyl, and hydroxylamine) have not been isolated.

Anaerobic respiration. Two distinct groups of organisms require bound oxygen. In one of these groups, hydrogen is transferred to sulfates, while the organisms of the other group utilize CO_2 as a major acceptor of hydrogen and produce methane.

Organisms	Reaction
	Methane fermentation
Various species	Organic compounds (anaerobically) $\rightarrow CO_2 + CH_4 + (CH_2O) +$ bacterial cells
	$2C_2H_5OH + CO_2 \rightarrow 2CH_3COOH + CH_4$
Methanobacterium omelianskii	$4H_2 + CO_2 \rightarrow CH_4 + 2H_2O$
Various species	$CH_3COOH \rightarrow CH_4 + CO_2$
Clostridium aceticum	$4H_2 + 2CO_2 \rightarrow CH_3COOH + 2H_2O$
	Sulfate reduction
Desulfovibrio desulfuricans	$2CH_3 \cdot CHOH \cdot COONa + MgSO_4 \rightarrow$ $\rightarrow 2CH_3COONa + CO_2 + MgCO_3 + H_2S + H_2O$

A strictly defined though widespread group of organisms can utilize sulfates as the main acceptor of hydrogen. This group includes Desulfovibrio desulfuricans — a Gram-negative, mesophilic anaerobe. A detailed discussion of it will be made in the chapter dealing with the chemical transformations of sulfur in lakes.

The organisms of the second group utilize CO_2 as the main acceptor of hydrogen. These organisms are likewise strict anaerobes. By reducing CO_2, these methane-producing bacteria can naturally use it for the synthesis of organic matter. The conversion of the carbon of CO_2 to methane can be outlined as follows. Carbon dioxide serves essentially as a source of oxygen. These organisms can use not only 2H of the substrate but also molecular oxygen by reducing CO_2 to CH_4 and H_2O. The energy liberated by the oxidation of hydrogen is utilized by the cell. It has been shown experimentally that some members of this group can remove hydrogen from isopropyl alcohol but are unable to utilize anabolically the acetone liberated in the process. The reaction has the following course:

$$4H\overset{\displaystyle CH_3}{\underset{\displaystyle CH_3}{\mid C \mid}} - OH + CO_2 \rightarrow 4\overset{\displaystyle CH_3}{\underset{\displaystyle CH_3}{\mid C \mid}} = O + CH_4 + 2H_2O$$

Isopropyl alcohol   Acetone   Methane
(from medium)

All the initial and final products have been determined quantitatively.

Some strains can grow in pure culture in a mixture of CO_2 and H_2, forming methane, water, and the energy necessary for the growth. This group includes species capable of growing in formates, producing CH_4, CO_2, and H_2O. In all cases, accurate measurements have shown that no compound can replace CO_2 as a hydrogen acceptor. Even CO cannot serve as substitute of CO_2. A few microorganisms, however, use CO as hydrogen acceptor according to the reaction $4\,CO + 2\,H_2O \rightarrow CH_4 + 3\,CO_2$. This process involves a complete oxidation of three molecules of CO to CO_2 with a simultaneous reduction of one molecule of CO to CH_4. It can be regarded as the simplest fermentation known.

Fermentation. Another type of energy-yielding reaction is known as fermentation. Here the organic compounds serve simultaneously as donors and acceptors of hydrogen. Usually these functions are carried out by different parts of the same molecule. Of particular significance is the fact that hydrogen and electrons leave the molecule. In such reactions, the intramolecular transfer of electrons yields only a small amount of energy. Most compounds are in a highly reduced state and therefore contain larger amounts of assimilable energy. In alcoholic fermentation, for example, only two atoms become much more reduced than in glucose.

Aerobic respiration, anaerobic respiration, and fermentation are mechanisms that yield energy by the transfer of electrons and hydrogen. They differ greatly from one another in the nature of the final electron acceptors (oxygen or inorganic and organic compounds) and in the amount of energy released. The major types of energy-yielding reactions are outlined below.

Type of reaction	Scheme of reaction	Amount of energy liberated
Respiration	$C_6H_{12}O_6 + 6O_2 \rightarrow 6CO_2 + 6H_2O$	688,000
Anaerobic respiration	$C_6H_{12}O_6 + 12KNO_3 \rightarrow 6CO_2 + 6H_2O + 12KNO_2$	429,000
Fermentation	$C_6H_{12}O_6 \rightarrow 2CO_2 + 2C_2H_5OH$	54,000

This energy-yielding mechanism is widespread in nature. It occurs in plants kept in the dark, in animals, and in many microorganisms.

Dissimilation

Dissimilation is the intracellular decomposition of nutrients. It yields compounds and energy that can be used for the synthesis of new cytoplasm.

Dissimilation of carbohydrates. Carbohydrates are the most important and available source of energy. Their dissimilation has been thoroughly studied, since it occurs widely and provides energy for animals and microorganisms.

Methods of study. The dissimilation of glucose by microorganisms is studied by culturing the microorganism in a suitable medium that contains this sugar. The amount and nature of the final metabolic products are then determined chemically, although it must be borne in mind that these products provide only an indirect idea of the mechanism of glucose breakdown.

The intermediate dissimilation products are sometimes difficult to identify because of a possible further oxidation. Therefore, the mechanism explaining the formation of different products was first postulated and then checked. It could be assumed, for example, that the decarboxylation of formic acid yields CO_2 and H_2:

$$HCOOH \rightarrow H_2 + CO_2.$$

To verify this hypothesis, the organism was grown in a medium containing formic acid. Production of the two gases constituted proof of the hypothesis. Further, the possible conversion of pyruvic into formic acid was examined by growing the microorganism in a medium containing pyruvic acid.

Radioactive elements are often used as markers. For example, pyruvic containing C^{13} in the carboxyl group can be introduced in the medium, in which case it takes part in the following reaction:

$$CH_3 - CO - C^{13}OOH + H_2O \longrightarrow CH_3COOH + HC^{13}OOH$$
$$\text{Pyruvic acid} \qquad\qquad \text{Acetic acid} \qquad \text{Formic acid}$$

These analyses have shown that formic acid is formed from the carboxyl radical of pyruvic acid.

Products of the dissimilation of carbohydrates. The dissimilation of carbohydrates by microorganisms yields a large variety of compounds, including acids, alcohols, and gases. Some microorganisms produce one or two compounds (lactic acid, for example), others produce a rich mixture of different products. The composition of these products depends on the enzymatic system of the microorganisms and on the environment. Even in the same facultative aerobe, the oxidative aerobic dissimilation differs sharply from the anaerobic fermentative dissimilation. Yeasts grown in aerobic conditions oxidize glucose to CO_2 and H_2O, but in the absence of air the breakdown of glucose yields ethyl alcohol and CO_2. A short list of the products of the microbial dissimilation of carbohydrates is given below.

Acids	Alcohols	Gases
H—COOH formic	C_2H_5OH ethyl alcohol	CO_2
CH_3COOH acetic	C_3H_7OH propyl alcohol	H_2
C_2H_5COOH propionic	CH_3—CHOH—CH_3 isopropyl alcohol	
C_3H_7COOH butyric	C_4H_9OH butyl alcohol	
CH_3—CHOH—COOH lactic	CH_3—CO—CHOH—CH_3 acetyl-methyl-carbinol	
COOH—CH_2—CH_2—COOH succinic	CH_3—CHOH—CHOH—CH_3 2, 3-butylene glycol	

Mechanism of the oxidation of organic compounds in the process of respiration. As we showed above, the endogenous or exogenous nutrients of the cell, notably glucose, are subjected to an intracellular oxidation that yields a variety of products for further use in the anabolism of the cell. The same process provides energy that can be stored in the cell in the form of energy-rich phosphorus compounds or can be used for the synthesis of cytoplasm from the products of the incomplete oxidation of the glucose.

Most oxidations of organic matter in the cell proceed simultaneously and stepwise. The further oxidation of the intermediate products follows independent pathways that are controlled by specific enzymes or coenzymes. The whole process has a very rapid course, and its successive stages can be traced only with great difficulty. Once started, this chain reaction usually proceeds to the end.

Embden-Meyerhof-Parnas pathway. The dissimilation of glucose to pyruvic acid has been thoroughly studied. This process, known as the Embden-Meyerhof-Parnas pathway, can be expressed as follows:

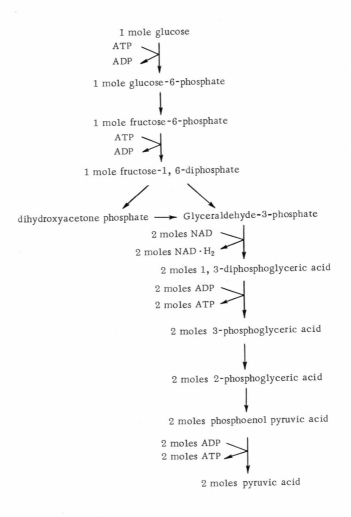

This process involves the breakdown of a hexose to two three-carbon sugars in nine stages. Part of the released energy is dissipated, while the rest is stored in energy-rich ATP. Pyruvic acid apparently plays a major role in the breakdown of glucose in almost all organisms; it is further oxidized to CO_2 in the Krebs cycle and it also takes part in anaerobic fermentations.

Aerobic oxidation of pyruvic acid (respiration process) — Krebs cycle. The aerobic oxidation of organic compounds inside the cell, also known as respiration, consists in the transfer of hydrogen (and electrons) from the substrate to molecular oxygen with the participation of one or several enzymes and usually within the framework of a system of coenzymes and pigments, as noted above (Figure 43).

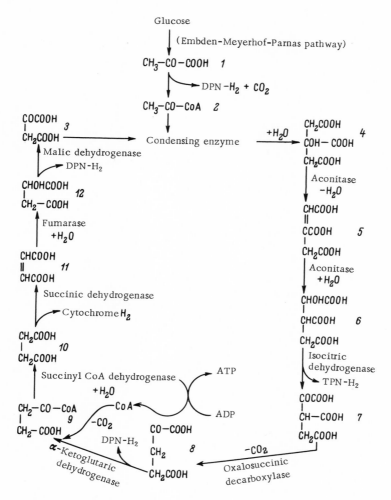

FIGURE 45. Scheme of the Krebs cycle:

1) pyruvic acid; 2) active acetate; 3) oxaloacetic acid; 4) citric acid; 5) cis-aconitic acid; 6) isocitric acid; 7) oxalosuccinic acid; 8) α-ketoglutaric acid; 9) succinyl CoA; 10) succinic acid; 11) fumaric acid; 12) malic acid.

99

The Krebs cycle of tricarboxylic acids (Figure 45) shows the oxidation of the pyruvic acid formed in the breakdown of glucose. This respiratory process has been studied in great detail. The complete oxidation of pyruvic acid yields three molecules of CO_2 and two molecules of water.

Pyruvic acid is decarboxylated and dehydrogenated while hydrogen combines with DPN. The acetyl residue joins CoA (coenzyme A), forming acetyl CoA or "active acetate." Oxaloacetic acid condenses with acetyl CoA into the tricarboxylic citric acid. This is followed by a whole series of reactions, some of which provide hydrogen atoms and CO_2, while the oxaloacetic acid is constantly regenerated. Therefore, the cycle continues as long as active acetate remains.

Hydrogen is removed from the intermediate substrates by the corresponding enzymes and passes to TPN and DPN, which possibly transfer it to atmospheric oxygen via the cytochromes.

The ten hydrogen atoms that react with oxygen form five molecules of water, three of which participate in various stages of the Krebs cycle, leaving a net yield of two water molecules. Carbon dioxide is liberated during the decarboxylation of three acids.

The dissimilation of carbohydrates leads to various intermediate products. The intracellular site of the process facilitates the transfer of electrons from one substrate to another. Such fermentation and respiration phenomena are not confined to bacteria but occur widely in many other organisms.

Anaerobic breakdown (fermentation) of pyruvic acid. The anaerobic breakdown of pyruvic acid can follow different pathways.

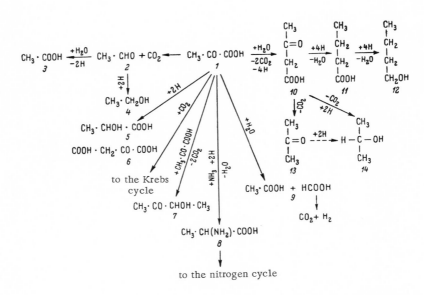

Notation: 1) pyruvic acid; 2) acetic aldehyde; 3) acetic acid; 4) ethyl alcohol; 5) lactic acid; 6) oxaloacetic acid; 7) acetylmethyl carbinol; 8) alanine; 9) acetic and formic acids; 10) acetoacetic acid; 11) butyric acid; 12) butyl alcohol; 13) acetone; 14) isopropyl alcohol.

Most of the above reactions consist of several stages, each catalyzed by a specific enzyme. Naturally, the formation of dissimilation products in a given organism depends on the availability of suitable enzymes, and the lack of a single enzyme can stop the whole series of reactions. The energy output is greatest when the compound is completely oxidized to CO_2 and H_2O. However, most of the products are only partly oxidized and therefore still contain some amount of assimilable energy. Anaerobic dissimilation (fermentation) therefore provides a small amount of energy. Many products of the anaerobic dissimilation are assimilated by the organism and become components of the protoplasm. One of the assimilation reactions — the formation of alanine from pyruvic acid and ammonia — was outlined above. The amino acids in turn are the building stones of protoplasmic proteins.

Assimilation in Microorganisms and the Role of CO_2 in the Process

Assimilation is a term covering the building activity of the organism. It covers the synthesis of proteins, carbohydrates, fats, and other compounds from simpler materials in the cell, the formation of these compounds by the breakdown of larger molecules, or their diffusion from the medium to the cell.

Among bacteria, the strict autotrophs possess the most developed mechanism for synthesis. They produce all the components of their cells from carbon dioxide and mineral salts only, using for this purpose energy obtained from light or from the oxidation of inorganic compounds.

Heterotrophic bacteria obtain carbon mainly from organic compounds. Many species can fix free nitrogen; others utilize ammonia or nitrates, while a third category requires organic nitrogen compounds like amino acids. In heterotrophs, the energy necessary for the synthesis of protoplasm comes from the oxidation of organic compounds entering the cell.

Growth factors. Many organisms use simple inorganic or organic compounds for the synthesis of vitamins, coenzymes, and other inorganic molecules needed in minute amounts for the transfer of energy. These syntheses may consist of a series of consecutive steps. Below are shown four of the consecutive reactions leading to the formation of coenzyme I (DPN).

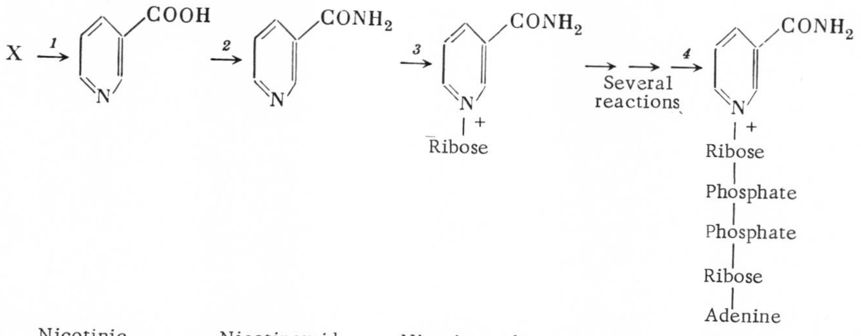

Nicotinic acid   Nicotinamide   Nicotinamide ribose   Coenzyme I (DPN)

Many organisms, including E. coli, perform all four stages and produce coenzyme I from the substrate X. On the other hand, Proteus vulgaris lacks the necessary enzymes for the conversion of X into nicotinic acid (1) but can carry out steps 2, 3, and 4. For this reason, P. vulgaris can synthesize coenzyme I only if supplied with nicotinic acid. In other words, nicotinic acid is a growth factor for P. vulgaris. Other, more fastidious bacteria can perform reactions 3 and 4 only or 4 only, which makes them dependent on nicotinamide alone or together with nicotinamide ribose. Some organisms do not require growth factors but cannot develop unless supplied with one or more amino acids.

Synthesis of polysaccharides. Many microorganisms can convert glucose into starch or glycogen or some other polysaccharides. The first intermediate product of these reactions is glucose phosphate, which polymerizes by releasing phosphate radicals. Starch (amylase) consists of a linear chain of glucose molecules, while glycogen has a branched molecule.

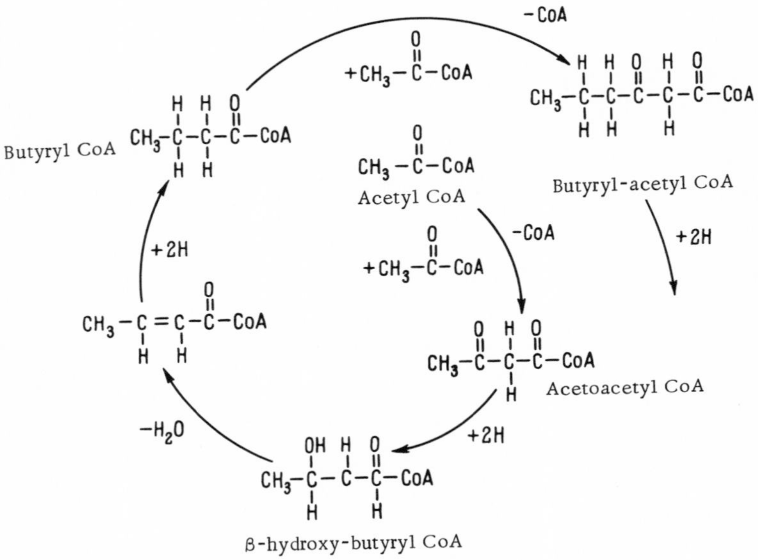

FIGURE 46. Mechanism of the synthesis of fatty acids with a paired number of carbon atoms (after Carpenter, 1961).

Disaccharides yield a large number of polysaccharides. Dextran can be formed from sucrose by the union of the glucose (units), while the fructose molecules remain free. Similarly, levans are produced by organisms that polymerize the fructose units, leaving the glucose free. Dextrans and levans have been found in the capsules of some bacteria. The synthesis of starch from glucose absorbs energy and therefore involves energy-rich phosphorus compounds. The process begins with the enzymatic conversion of glucose-6-phosphate into glucose-1-phosphate. In the presence of phosphorylase, glucose-1, 6-phosphate can react with the end of the chain of glucose units, forming starch and releasing inorganic phosphate.

Synthesis of fatty acids. Figure 46 shows the mechanism of the synthesis of fatty acids with a paired number of carbons.

The synthesis starts with acetyl CoA, obtained from pyruvic acid. Two molecules of acetyl CoA are united by the suitable enzyme into acetoacetyl CoA, which forms a derivative of butyric acid with CoA. Repetition of the same reaction with more CoA produces acids containing six, eight, or ten carbon atoms. The reaction is reversible; it permits a stepwise degradation of higher fatty acids by the loss of two carbons at each stage.

Synthesis of proteins. The detailed mechanism of protein synthesis remains a matter of speculation. It is assumed that this mechanism operates under the direct control of RNA, which makes it indirectly dependent on DNA. The sequence of purine and pyrimidine bases in the nucleic acid probably determines the amino acid sequence in the cell protein. Nucleic acid even serves as a template of protein synthesis. This process requires the necessary complement of amino acids. If a given amino acid cannot be synthesized by the organism, it must be supplied with the medium, from which it enters the cell. Bacterial cells accumulate and concentrate some amino acids in the course of metabolism. Amino acids incapable of penetrating into the cell must be synthesized. Ammonia appears to be the only form of inorganic nitrogen that can be converted to amino groups. Only two pathways of such conversion are known.

Glutamic acid is formed from ammonia and α-ketoglutaric acid. It serves as an intermediate compound in the synthesis of other amino acids by transamination, as described above. Several amino acids, including tryptophan, are produced stepwise from smaller molecules:

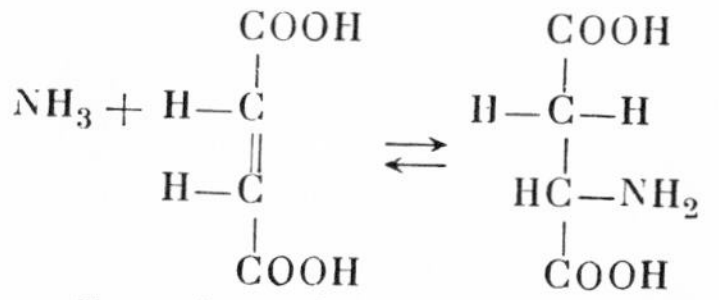

Fumaric acid → Aspartic acid

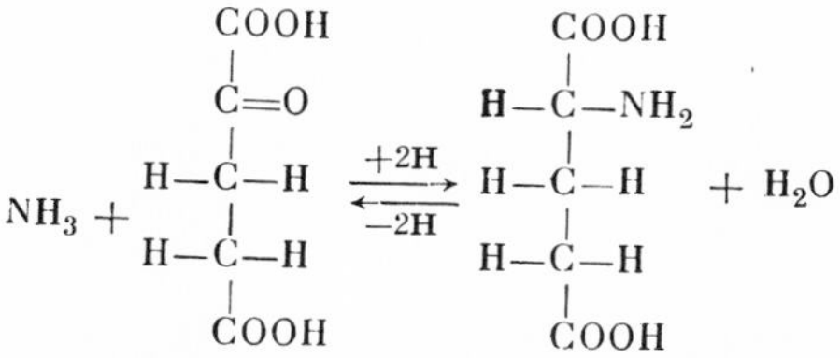

α-ketoglutaric acid → Glutamic acid

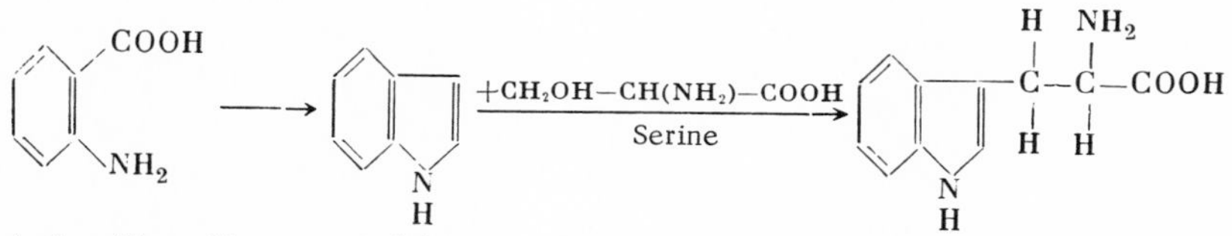

Anthranilic acid → Indole → Tryptophan

The cells of bacteria, plants, and animals perform numerous assimilation and dissimilation reactions. The same chemical reactions occur in higher organisms.

Sources of Energy in Autotrophic Bacteria

General scheme of energy transfer. According to Thimann (1963), the chemistry of autotrophic life can be outlined as follows.

1. The substance to be oxidized must be previously activated by an enzyme that is specific to the given bacterium: thiosulfate dehydrogenase in Thiobacillus thiooxidans, ammonia dehydrogenase in Nitrosomonas:

$$NH_3 + R + O_2 \longrightarrow HNO_2 + RH_2 .$$

2. The reduced enzyme, which serves as carrier, is oxidized by the cytochrome system. This is evident from the inhibition of growth by poisons that attack the cytochrome system, such as azide, cyanide, and dinitrophenols (Vogler et al., 1942). In addition, Beggiatoa and some other sulfur bacteria are killed by high concentrations of hydrogen sulfide, which is an enzyme inhibition.

3. The oxidation of the hydrogen carrier creates energy-rich chemical bonds in some highly unstable compounds of sulfur or phosphorus.

4. Carbon dioxide is converted into a carboxyl group by a very small expenditure of energy. This fully corresponds with the reactions in heterotrophic organisms.

5. The energy-rich compounds formed by the oxidation of the inorganic substrate react with carboxyls. Thimann (1963) assumes that if energy-rich phosphorus compounds are involved, these undoubtedly convert the carboxyl group into carboxyl phosphate; in the case of sulfur compounds, the product must be acetylsulfide CoA, in analogy to acetyl CoA. The syntheses of carboxyl phosphate and acetylsulfide CoA are endergonic processes. Thus, the formation of acetyl phosphate requires an energy (ΔF) of 3,000 calories. Clearly, the synthesis of acetyl phosphate must be coupled with a suitable process of hydrogen oxidation.

6. Carboxyl phosphate, which is much more reactive than carboxyl, can be reduced by the enzyme or coenzyme (1) into primary chemosynthetic products and free phosphate:

$$XCO-O \sim H_2PO_3 + RH_2 \longrightarrow XCHO + H_3PO_4 + R .$$

Carboxyl phosphate captures the bulk of the energy liberated during the oxidation of the inorganic substrate. The final regeneration of the organic acceptor of hydrogen completes the cycle. Most of the substrate hydrogen combines with oxygen via cytochrome oxidase in a process yielding energy-rich bonds; a smaller fraction of the substrate hydrogen serves for a direct reduction of bound CO_2. If the energy-rich compounds are not phosphates, stages (5) and (6) must differ from the preceding ones, but we do not yet possess reliable data as to the nature of the primary chemosynthetic products in such case.

Various details of the chemosynthetic process may be changed by future research, but this basic scheme of the autotrophic assimilation of carbonic acid very probably represents the actual relationships.

Solar radiation is the main source of energy on earth. It displaces electrons from their normal orbits in chlorophyll. This activated chlorophyll splits water by a mechanism that is still incompletely understood. Hydrogen combines temporarily with TPN (triphosphopyridine nucleotide) and enters the CO_2 reduction cycle. The light energy is captured in energy-rich bonds of ATP (adenosine triphosphate), which is the main carrier of energy in the cell. ATP participates in the reduction of carbon dioxide, yielding free phosphate. The syntheses involved lead to glucose and other organic compounds possessing a potential energy of 688,000 calories per mole.

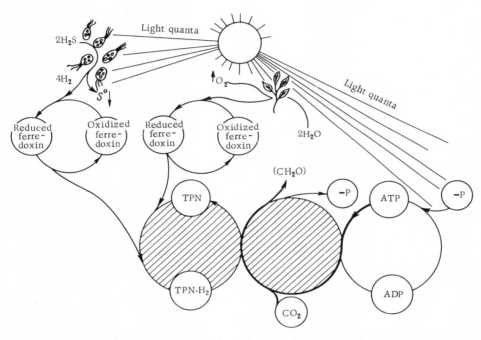

FIGURE 47. Overall scheme of the photosynthetic fixation of carbonic acid in green plants and pigmented sulfur bacteria. The dark reactions are shaded.

Figure 47 shows the overall scheme of the photosynthetic cycle. Hydrogen formed by the photolysis of water reduces CO_2 at the expense of energy-rich phosphate bonds. The thick line indicates the pathway of energy utilization.

Bacterial photosynthesis. Bacterial photosynthesis resembles its counterpart in green plants. The pigments involved are varieties of chlorophyll — bacteriochlorophyll a in purple bacteria, bacteriochlorophyll b in Rhodopseudomonas viridis, and bacteriochlorophylls a, c, and d in green bacteria. Some bacteria contain also red or yellow pigments composed of carotenoids.

Oxygen is never liberated, since organic or inorganic compounds other than water serve as hydrogen donors. For example, the purple and green sulfur bacteria can utilize hydrogen sulfide, while the nonsulfur purple bacteria use organic sources of hydrogen for this purpose.

Primary light reactions. As we showed above, photosynthesis can be outlined by the following overall equation, which applies to all photosynthetic species, bacteria and plants alike:

$$2H_2A + CO_2 \xrightarrow[\text{chlorophyll}]{\text{light}} 2A + (CH_2O) + H_2O .$$

In other words, all photosynthetic processes are essentially similar, while the initial reactions induced by light and catalyzed by chlorophyll are probably identical in all photosynthetic organisms.

In green plants, the photolysis of water yields ATP and reduced ferridoxin, which differs from hemoprotein and flavoprotein in having a reducing capacity not inferior to that of molecular hydrogen (Arnon, 1965). In the case of photosynthetic purple sulfur bacteria H_2S is subject to photolysis, and reduced ferrodoxin are also formed. The photosynthesis of pigmented sulfur bacteria yields molecular sulfur instead of the oxygen liberated by green plants.

The dark phase of photosynthesis is uniform in all photosynthetic organisms. Ferridoxin reduces the TPN, which participates in the chain transfer of electrons from the hydrogen donor to the hydrogen acceptors via the cytochrome system. Here the acceptors belong to the Calvin cycle in which carbonic acid is reduced to primary photosynthetic products.

Photosynthetic phosphorylation. In addition to the reducing agent necessary for the conversion of CO_2 to cell substance, photosynthetic organisms must obtain from the primary photochemical reaction a certain amount of chemically bound energy in the form of ATP. This energy feeds the endergonic processes of biosynthesis. Energy-rich phosphorus compounds are formed in a process named photosynthetic phosphorylation. Bacterial chromatophores and plant chloroplasts can produce ATP from inorganic phosphorus and ADP anaerobically in the presence of light. This process can take place without a simultaneous reduction of CO_2. Although the details of photosynthetic phosphorylation remain unknown, it is assumed that ATP arises during the recombination of H- and OH-radicals formed by the photolysis of water.

It must be borne in mind that a process known as "oxidative" phosphorylation is the main mechanism of ATP synthesis in aerobic organisms. In respiration, hydrogen atoms from the oxidized compounds unite with molecular oxygen via a sequence of carriers; part of the energy liberated by the oxidation is captured in the energy-rich bonds of ATP. Photosynthetic phosphorylation can be interpreted as an analogous capture of energy in which the hydrogen atom is oxidized not by molecular oxygen but by the OH-radical.

Relationship between photosynthesis and other cell processes. Photosynthesis, a process of major physiological significance, leaves its imprint on the metabolism and growth of the cell. Although the basic mechanism of photosynthesis is more or less satisfactorily understood, many gaps remain in our knowledge of the effect that photosynthesis exerts on the cell metabolism. It is hoped that further research will shed more light on the mechanisms by which the cell controls different stages of the photosynthesis.

Illumination of Chlorella cells inhibits the oxidation of triose phosphate, probably because of competition between the effects of triose phosphate dehydrogenase and photophosphorylation (Kandler, 1964). It was also found that light increases the respiratory consumption of oxygen by algae and also stimulates respiration in higher plants (Hoch et al., 1963). Although much concerning the "light respiration" remains to be discovered, these data show that the consumption of oxygen is related with respiratory pathways other than the respiratory enzymes of the mitochondria. This assumption finds support in the fact that the respiration of green plants is largely insensitive to carbon monoxide — a potent inhibitor of cytochrome systems. Clearly, photosynthesis affects the respiration phenomena both quantitatively and qualitatively. Recent experiments have shown that the assimilation of carbon dioxide is not the only function of photosynthesis. Thus, ATP and NADP·H (coenzyme II, or nicotinamide adenine dinucleotide phosphate) produced by the absorption of solar energy can be utilized in a number of endergonic metabolic processes, including the reduction of fatty acids (Stumpf et al., 1963), the consumption and transfer of ions and molecules into cells and tissues, the reduction of nitrites (Marre et al., 1963; Santarius et al., 1964), etc. It is well known that the intracellular synthesis of glucose requires ATP and cannot occur outside the chloroplast.

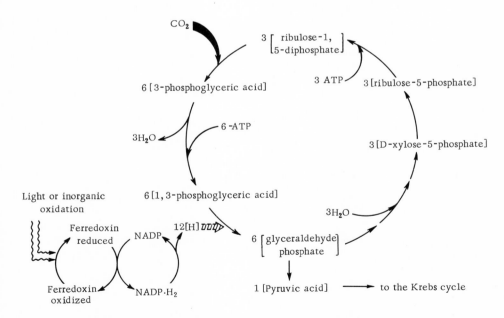

FIGURE 48. Mechanism of the assimilation of carbon dioxide in autotrophic microorganisms (simplified, after Calvin).

All this indicates that ATP formed by cyclic phosphorylation inside the chloroplast can serve for biosynthesis elsewhere in the cell. Although the research in this field has not yet passed its initial stage, it is evident that photosynthesis should not be regarded merely as a mechanism for carbohydrate synthesis, since it exerts a profound influence on all aspects of the intracellular metabolism.

Mechanism of CO_2 fixation. Photosynthetic organisms are not the only ones capable of reducing and utilizing carbon dioxide. Chemolithotrophs (autotrophs) can utilize CO_2 as the only source of carbon. Moreover, most chemoorganotrophs (heterotrophs) fix a certain amount of CO_2. However, the mechanism of CO_2 fixation in chemoorganotrophs differs from that of the autotrophs and does not represent the main anabolic pathway. By contrast, green plants, photosynthetic bacteria, and at least some chemolithotrophs possess a special mechanism for CO_2 fixation. This mechanism consists of a complex of cyclic processes involving phosphorylated sugars.

Mechanism of CO_2 fixation in autotrophic organisms. Figure 48 represents a simplified scheme of the process.

One of the main features of CO_2 fixation is the binding of CO_2 with a phosphorylated pentose (ribulose-diphosphate), which splits afterward into two molecules of phosphoglyceric acid. Each molecule of phosphoglyceric acid is reduced by two H-radicals, which originate from the photolysis of water in photosynthetic organisms and from NAD·H_2 in the chemolithotrophs. The product of this reaction is again a triose, glyceraldehyde phosphate. By a series of reactions, this compound regenerates a molecule of ribulose diphosphate, which participates in the first phase of CO_2 fixation. In all, five molecules of glyceraldehyde phosphate yield three molecules of ribulose diphosphate, while each three molecules of ribulose diphosphate produce six molecules of glyceraldehyde phosphate. Thus, one extra molecule of glyceraldehyde phosphate appears from each three molecules of fixed CO_2 in one complete cycle. This molecule serves for biosynthesis. A total of twelve H-radicals are utilized for the reduction of three CO_2 molecules to cell substance. This means that all six molecules of phosphoglyceric acid must be reduced in each cycle. These relationships correspond with the overall equation of CO_2 fixation:

$$CO_2 + 4\,[H] \longrightarrow (CH_2O) + H_2O\,.$$

Several intermediate products of this cycle must be phosphorylated. The ATP necessary for this purpose is formed by photosynthetic or oxidative phosphorylation.

As shown in Figure 48, the union of CO_2 and ribulose-1,5-diphosphate requires an enzyme named carboxydismutase. The presence of this enzyme in a given organism speaks for the occurrence of CO_2 fixation by the ribulose cycle and also indicates that the organism is capable of autotrophic life.

The photolithotrophic (photosynthetic) microorganism C h l o r o b i u m t h i o s u l f a t o p h i l u m has a different mechanism for CO_2 fixation (Evans et al., 1966). This new cycle, known as the reductive cycle of carbonic acids, is shown by the ellipse in Figure 49. It begins with a reversible enzymatic breakdown of citric acid to acetate and oxaloacetic acid. The acetate combines with a CO_2 molecule to form pyruvic acid, which takes up another CO_2 molecule and yields another molecule of oxaloacetic acid.

A shorter cycle of carbonic acids is represented by the circle in Figure 49. Both reductive cycles — the complete one, shown by the ellipse, and the short one, represented by the circle — have in common the pathway from oxaloacetic to citric acid. These processes can be regarded as a Krebs cycle in reverse. In the presence of CoA and ATP, succinic acid forms succinic CoA, which takes up a molecule of CO_2 to form α-ketoglutaric acid; the latter in the presence of $NADP \cdot H_2$ combines with another CO_2 molecule and becomes isocitric acid, which later undergoes a transformation into aconitic and citric acid.

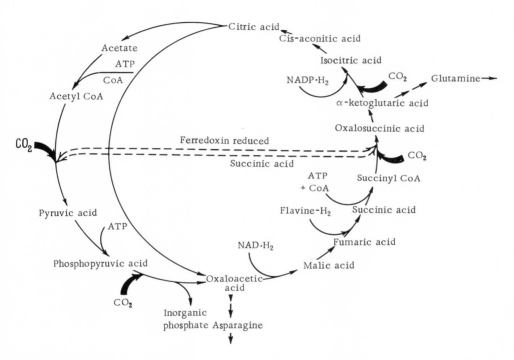

FIGURE 49. Simplified scheme of the fixation of CO_2 by the reductive cycle of carbonic acids (after Evans, Buchanan, and Arnon, 1966).

The oxalocetic and α-ketoglutaric acids formed in the reductive cycle of carbonic acids can be transaminated to aspartic and glutamic acids, which serve as starting products for further anabolic processes.

Thus, four CO_2 molecules are fixed in the complete reductive cycle of carbonic acids, and only two such molecules in the short cycle. The direct and the reductive Krebs cycles differ from one another mainly in that the reductive cycle leads to CO_2 fixation, while the direct cycle generates CO_2 and free energy (Figure 45), which is captured in ATP. Clearly, the reductive cycle requires the presence of enzymes that catalyze reversibly the fixation of CO_2.

Among the necessary agents are CoA and enzymes leading to the formation of pyruvic and α-ketoglutaric acids.

In addition, the synthesis of these acids requires reduced ferredoxin:

$$\text{Acetyl CoA} + CO_2 + \text{ferredoxin red} \rightarrow \text{pyruvic acid} + \text{CoA} + \text{ferredoxin oxid.} \quad (1)$$

$$\text{Succinyl CoA} + CO_2 + \text{ferredoxin red} \rightarrow \alpha\text{-ketoglutaric acid} + \text{CoA} + $$
$$+ \text{ferredoxin oxid.} \quad (2)$$

These two reactions of the Krebs reductive cycle depend on the presence of ferredoxin. In the cell of aerobic bacteria they probably proceed irreversibly because of the high oxidation-reduction potential inside the cell. Reduced ferredoxin has been found so far in some anaerobes only — in pigmented sulfur bacteria, where it arises from the photolysis of water, and in C l o s t r i d i u m   t h e r m o a c e t i c u m (Wilder et al., 1963).

Two other carboxylation reactions in the reductive cycle are quite possible from a thermodynamical viewpoint. One of these reactions is catalyzed by isocitrate dehydrogenase — an enzyme specific to NADP, which reversibly catalyzes the carboxylation of α-ketoglutaric acid to isocitric acid. The other enzyme — phosphoenolpyruvate carboxylase — catalyzes the carboxylation of phosphoenolpyruvic acid to oxaloacetic acid.

The presence of this and other enzymes of the Krebs cycle in C h l o r o b i u m   t h i o s u l f a t o p h i l u m was demonstrated by Buchanan, Evans, and Arnon (1967), who also observed a fixation of labeled carbon dioxide ($C^{14}O_2$) in the acids of the Krebs cycle in this species.

We do not know yet whether chemosynthesis in autotrophic bacteria can proceed according to the reductive cycle of carbonic acids. In order to perform a chemosynthesis, the organism must be able to produce reduced ferredoxin.

Assimilation of CO by heterotrophic organisms. As long ago as the 1920's, several authors found that B a c.   s u b t i l i s,   S t a p h y - l o c o c c u s,   C l o s t r i d i u m   w e l c h i i, and some other organisms cannot grow in the absence of CO_2. However, Lebedev's view that all organisms fix CO_2 did not have sufficient experimental support at the time, and with respect to heterotrophic organisms, CO_2 was regarded as an inert product of respiration and fermentation.

Wood found in 1936 a decrease in the concentration of bicarbonate in the culture medium of P r o p i o n o b a c t e r i u m   p e n t o s a c e u m during the fermentation of glycerol. In terms of the amount of carbon, the CO_2 loss was compensated by an increase in the amount of succinic acid. This reaction can be expressed by the following equation:

$$CH_2OH - CHOH - CH_2OH + CO_2 \rightarrow COOH - CH_2 - CH_2 - COOH.$$

Here a three-carbon alcohol is converted into a four-carbon acid. Since it was possible to isolate pyruvic acid from the medium, Wood concluded that this compound is an intermediate fermentation product whose carboxylation yields oxaloacetic acid. This is the Wood-Werkman reaction:

$$CH_2 = \underset{\underset{\displaystyle O - PO_3H_2}{|}}{C} - COOH + CO_2 + P_{\text{inorg}} \longrightarrow COOH - CH_2 - \underset{\underset{\displaystyle O}{\|}}{C} - COOH + PP$$

Phosphoenolpyruvic
acid

Oxaloacetic acid

Pyrophos-
phate

TABLE 22. Oxidation-reduction potential and free energy of the reactions of the Krebs cycle (after Thimann, 1963)

Reaction of Krebs cycle	Hydrogen donor	E_h, volts	Potential with respect to O_2, volts	$-\Delta F°$ per electron pair (calories)	Maximal number of energy-rich bonds formed
CH₃COCOOH $\}$ → $\{$ CoA CH₂CO DPN + 2₂ $\}$ → $\{$ DPN·H + H	Pyruvic acid	−0.78	1.58	72,500	4.5
Isocitric → oxalosuccinic	Isocitric acid	−0.30	1.10	51,000	3.2
α-ketoglutaric → succinic	α-ketoglutaric	−0.78	1.58	72,000	4.5
Succinic → fumaric	Succinic	0.00	0.80	36,500	2.3
Malic → oxaloacetic	Malic	−0.18	0.98	45,000	2.8
Complete oxidation of 1 mole of pyruvic acid				277,500	17.3

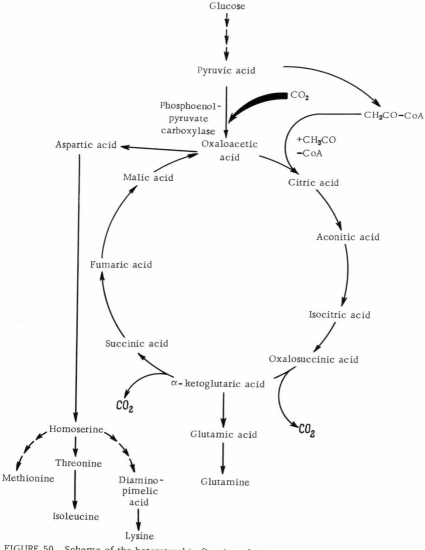

FIGURE 50. Scheme of the heterotrophic fixation of CO_2.

This reaction is catalyzed by phosphoenol-pyruvate-carboxytransphos-phorylase — an enzyme not associated with biotin.

Figure 50 shows schematically the overall process of heterotrophic fixation of CO_2 in the anabolism of the cell.

As a result of oxidative and reductive reactions, carbohydrates and other organic compounds are broken down to pyruvic acid, which enters the Wood-Werkman reaction, combining with CO_2 to form oxaloacetic acid.

Oxaloacetic acid is a key compound in the Krebs tricarboxylic acid cycle. By combining with the acetyl group of active acetate (acetyl CoA), it forms citric acid; its further transformations, via aconitic, isocitric, and oxalo-succinic acids, lead to α-ketoglutaric acid. Part of the α-ketoglutaric acid is aminated to glutamic acid, which enters the cell anabolism. The rest of the α-ketoglutaric acid loses CO_2 to become succinic acid, which is trans-formed successively to fumaric and malic acids before being converted to oxaloacetic acid. Part of the latter is aminated to aspartic acid, which like-wise participates in anabolic processes. The Krebs cycle also generates energy and reducing agents that take part in the anabolism (Table 22).

The above pathways of heterotrophic fixation of CO_2 involve a direct assimilation of CO_2 carbon into organic acids or amino acids. In other words, most of the carbon fixed in these reactions serves for the construc-tion of cell substance.

There are, however, several other reactions in which CO_2 serves largely as a catalyst in the transformation or activation of some compounds. All these enzymatic conversions usually comprise biotin and CoA (Schlegel, 1963). The energy necessary for carboxylation comes from ATP. It was known, for example, that the addition of fatty acids to the medium improves the growth of some biotin-requiring bacteria, and that the presence of free CO_2 stimulates the synthesis of fatty acids in yeasts. These phenomena were later interpreted as follows. In the presence of biotin, acetyl CoA is carboxylated to malonyl CoA, which undergoes decarboxylation, losing CO_2, while the fatty acid chain grows (Figure 46):

$$CH_3 - CO - CoA + CO_2 + ATP + H_2O \underset{}{\overset{Biotin}{\rightleftarrows}}$$

Acetyl CoA

$$\overset{COOH}{\underset{}{\rightleftarrows} \overset{|}{C}H_2 - CO - S - CoA + ADP + H_3PO_4}$$

Malonyl CoA

General scheme of anabolism in chemosynthetic organisms. Lis (1958) points out that Tracy in his review shows that the chemical composition of or-ganic matter is largely uniform in the majority of the examined organisms. This illustrates a basic concept of biochemistry, namely that all forms of life are built after the same pattern. Indeed, the cells consist of polymers of the same twenty amino acids, together with a small number of polysac-charides (hexose polymers) and fats, which represent glycerides of fatty acids possessing a more or less linear carbon chain. One concludes that no major difference can be expected between autotrophic and heterotrophic organisms. These categories differ from one another in that autotrophs can synthesize all the simple organic compounds from CO_2 and mineral substances and build their cells without an external supply of organic matter.

However, this process cannot proceed spontaneously even in the presence of all the necessary enzymes. The cell needs a source of reducing agents for the reduction of CO_2 to the "cell level" as well as a source of energy, since the reduction of CO_2 is an endergonic process. Moreover, the synthesis of proteins, fats, and polysaccharides from simpler compounds also requires a supply of energy.

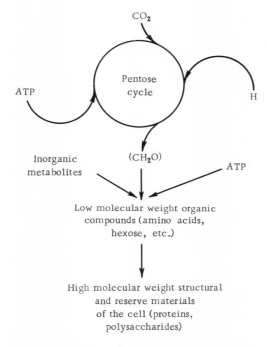

FIGURE 51. Scheme of biosynthesis in autotrophic bacteria (after Lis).

The scheme shown in Figure 51 is highly conditional. The arrows indicate the direction of the reactions, which consist of numerous steps. [H] symbolizes reducing agents, notably hydrogen carriers as $DPN \cdot H_2$ and $TPN \cdot H_2$.

Autotrophic bacteria can live, grow, and multiply with CO_2 as the only source of carbon. Since the breakdown of CO_2 does not yield energy, autotrophic organisms require the energy of light or that liberated from inorganic reactions. Thus, autotrophs can be characterized as "organisms that do not utilize organic compounds as a primary source of energy" (Lis, 1958, p. 18). By contrast, heterotrophs require one or several organic compounds, since they cannot synthesize growth factors or essential amino acids and can obtain energy for biosynthesis only by oxidizing preformed organic compounds. The growth of these organisms depends on the amount of energy they obtain by degrading a given organic compound.

Autotrophic bacteria obtain energy from the oxidation of inorganic compounds. The following reactions are known to yield energy that can be utilized by microorganisms (Rabinovich, 1951; Thimann, 1955; Larsen, 1960; Schlegel, 1960):

1. $H_2 + \frac{1}{2} O_2 = H_2O + 56,000$ calories
2. $CH_4 + 2O_2 = CO_2 + 2H_2O + 195,000$ calories
3. $NH_3 + 1\frac{1}{2} O_2 = HNO_2 + H_2O + 73,000$ calories
4. $HNO_2 + \frac{1}{2} O_2 = HNO_3 + 17,000$ calories
5. $H_2S + \frac{1}{2} O_2 = S + H_2O + 41,000$ calories
6. $S + H_2O + 1\frac{1}{2} O_2 = H_2SO_4 + 118,000$ calories
7. $2FeSO_4 + H_2SO_4 + \frac{1}{2} O_2 = Fe_2(SO_4)_3 + H_2O + 19,000$ calories
   $4FeCO_3 + O_2 + 6H_2O = 4Fe(OH)_3 + 4CO_2 + 40,000$ calories
8. $4H_2 + CO_2 = CH_4 + 2H_2O + 62,000$ calories
9. $4H_2 + 2CO_2 = CH_3-COOH + 2H_2O + 18,600$ calories
10. Quantum (energy of red light) $= 40,000$ calories.

Heterotrophic bacteria obtain energy from the oxidation of organic compounds. For example, the complete oxidation of glucose to CO_2 and water in aerobic conditions yields 690,000 calories when the partial pressures of oxygen and carbon dioxide equal those in air.

$$C_6H_{12}O_6 + 6O_2 = 6CO_2 + 6H_2O + 690,000 \text{ calories.}$$

The energy released by the breakdown of organic compounds is not dissipated as heat but accumulates in energy-rich phosphate bonds. Later this energy serves in various stages of biosynthesis.

The oxidation of inorganic compounds by autotrophs is likewise accompanied by a synthesis of energy-rich phosphate compounds whose energy can be used not only for the fixation of CO_2 but also for the subsequent reactions of biosynthesis. The creation of energy-rich phosphate bonds was demonstrated in Thiobac. thiooxidans (Vogler, LePage and Umbreit, 1942) and in hydrogen bacteria (M. I. Belyaeva, 1954; Doman, 1963).

As shown in Figure 48, CO_2 fixation by autotrophs requires the presence of reducing agents. In heterotrophs, the oxidation of organic compounds is accompanied by a reduction of DPN^+ and TPN^+ to $DPN \cdot H_2$ and $TPN \cdot H_2$ (Figure 45), which revert to their oxidized states by reducing other compounds. These or related hydrogen carriers are also found in autotrophic bacteria. If A is the hydrogen carrier, its reduced form AH_2 will be oxidized with CO_2 oxygen during the fixation of CO_2 by autotrophic bacteria:

$$CO_2 + 2 \ H_2 = (CH_2O) + H_2O + 2A.$$

A continued fixation of CO_2 requires repeated reduction of the oxidized hydrogen carrier. Theoretically, the reducing agents necessary for the regeneration of AH_2 from A can be obtained from the substrate that is subjected to oxidation.

1. In hydrogen-oxidizing and methane-producing bacteria, the reducing agent can be molecular hydrogen:

$$H_2 \longrightarrow 2H^+ + 2e; \ \Delta F = 0,$$

or

$$2H^{\cdot} + 2e + A = AH_2$$

2. In methane-oxidizing bacteria:

$$\frac{1}{2}CH_4 + \frac{1}{2}O_2 \rightarrow \frac{1}{2}CO_2 + 2H^{\cdot} + 2e; \quad \Delta F = -40,700 \text{ cal.}$$
$$2H^{\cdot} + 2e + A = AH_2$$

3. In nitrite bacteria:

$$NH_4 + \frac{3}{2}O_2 \rightarrow NO_2 + H_2O + 2H^{\cdot} + 2e; \quad \Delta F = -46,900 \text{ cal.}$$
$$2H^{\cdot} + 2e + A = AH_2$$

4. In sulfur bacteria:

$$H_2S \rightarrow S + 2H^{\cdot} + 2e; \quad \Delta F = -23,400 \text{ cal.}$$
$$2H^{\cdot} + 2e + A = AH_2$$

5. In thiobacilli (oxidizers of elemental sulfur):

$$S + 2H_2O + O_2 \rightarrow H_2SO_4 + 2H^{\cdot} + 2e; \quad \Delta F = -120,000 \text{ cal.}$$
$$2H^{\cdot} + 2e + A = AH_2.$$

These equations show that the process usually yields free energy, that is, the reducing agents must be formed spontaneously. However, the reactions listed are still hypothetical and require suitable enzyme systems.

The regeneration of the reducing agent is believed to occur as follows. First, the substrate is oxidized with the participation of the cytochrome system:

$$NO_2 + H_2O + 2(Fe^{+++} \text{ cytochrome}) = NO_3 + 2H^{+} + 2(Fe^{++} \text{ cytochrome}).$$
$$\text{oxidized} \qquad\qquad\qquad \text{reduced}$$

The subsequent oxidation of the reduced cytochrome by molecular oxygen creates an energy-rich phosphate bond:

$$2(Fe^{++} \text{ cytochrome}) + 2H^{+} + \frac{1}{2}O_2 = H_2O + 2(Fe^{+++} \text{ cytochrome}) + \text{energy.}$$

The energy of phosphate bonds is available for the regeneration of the reducing agent. Clearly, the regeneration of AH_2 can occur only if rH_2 of the reducing agent [H] is low enough to allow a coupled reaction with the existing mechanisms in the cell.

Now a few words about inorganic nutrition (Figure 51). Autotrophic bacteria obtain all the necessary inorganic elements from inorganic salts, except in those cases where the element participates in a growth factor that is not synthesized by the given organism. Beside such biogenic elements as nitrogen, phosphorus, and sulfur, microorganisms require small amounts of trace elements — iron, copper, molybdenum, zinc, cobalt, manganese, etc., which are a part of the molecules of various enzymes.

The further synthesis of low-molecular and high-molecular weight organic components of the cell appears to follow the same pathways in autotrophic and heterotrophic organisms.

115

Distribution of Bacteria in Lakes

Specific Composition and Density of Aquatic Bacteria

One of the earliest publications dealing with the bacterial population of lakes was written by V. V. Voronin (1897), entitled *Bacteriological Studies of the Plankton.* In this work, Voronin describes his own investigations made at the Lake Glubokoe Hydrobiological Station. In its concept and approach, Voronin's work was far ahead of its time. Voronin tried to compare the biomass of lake bacteria with the planktonic biomass. Although his specific conclusions were wrong, owing to the lack of direct bacterial counts in lake water, his clear-cut formulations of many problems are of major interest even today. Following Voronin's publication, the microbial population of lake water has attracted increasing attention and has become one of the standard objects of most fresh-water biological stations.

Soon after, several other works were published in other countries. These dealt mostly with the specific composition of the saprophyte microflora of lakes. Studying the water of the lake of Zürich in connection with the outbreak of typhus epidemics in Zürich, Kleiber (1894) described forty-two strains of typical aquatic bacteria. He acknowledged the appearance of new forms by their presence in spots of contaminated water at the site of the water tributaries. Using gelatin plates, Pfenniger (1902) made a thorough study of the distribution of bacteria in the Lake of Zürich not only in the stagnation period but also during overturns. He showed that the bacterial flora has an irregular distribution, being concentrated around polluted tributaries and fluctuating in density from 82 to 20,000 per ml during the season. The observations of Pfenniger were later confirmed by Minder (1918) and supplemented with chemical analyses of the water.

The second stage in the study of lake microflora began in 1925—1930 with the introduction of various microscopical methods of quantitative determination, notably those of Snow and Fred (1928), Karzinkin and Kuznetsov (1931), Razumov (1931), and Isachenko (cited from Gurfein, 1930). It was found that the actual density of bacteria in lake water is almost a thousand times greater than the figure obtained by inoculation of media. However, the microscopical method met several difficulties. Owing to the limited resolving power of the light microscope, it was impossible to distinguish any details of bacterial morphology. Moreover, this method cannot differentiate between live and dead bacteria. Finally, some fine particles of detritus might appear to be bacteria. All these drawbacks were gradually eliminated by various improvements of the method, although it is still impossible to obtain an accurate idea of the morphology of aquatic bacteria by direct microscopic techniques.

The application of the electron microscope, whose resolving power exceeds by far that of the light microscope, marks the third stage in the study of the natural microflora of lakes. Electron microscope studies of soil microorganisms (Nikitin et al., 1966) and aquatic ones of the genus Caulobacter (Poindexter, 1964; Belyaev, 1967) have created a uniform approach to the microflora of lakes of different types. One of the first studies was made at Lake Beloe in Kosino. Here Nikitin and Kuznetsov (1967) observed several extraordinary forms of bacteria whose structural details were clearly distinguishable under the electron microscope.

Specific Composition of the Bacterial Population of Lakes

Detailed lists of saprophyte bacterial species have been published for Lake Geneva (Marca, 1927), Lake Mendota (Snow and Fred, 1926), and others.

Baier (1935) has isolated and determined a number of microorganisms from small ponds in the Kiel area. A. G. Rodina and N. K. Kuz'mitskaya (1964) have determined the specific composition of the saprophyte bacterial flora of Lake Ladoga. A. A. Egorova, Z. P. Deryugina, and S. I. Kuznetsov (1952) have isolated 119 microbial species from thirty lakes in the temperate zone of the European part of the USSR, Siberia, and Kazakhstan. Although their material is not enough for statistical analysis and contains some chance findings, it allows a number of conclusions. According to this work, the commonest bacterial inhabitants of the examined lakes are Mycobacterium globiforme, M. luteum, M. phlei, Micrococcus albus, M. cinebareus, M. radiatus, M. viticulosus, Bacterium album, B. liquefaciens, B. nitrificans, Pseudomonas fluorescens, Bacterium brevis, and Bac. mycoides. Most of these forms are equally frequent in oligotrophic and eutrophic waters. The limited amount of the material prevents any conclusions as to the relationship of these species to different trophic types of lakes.

Table 23 shows the frequency of different bacterial families in lake water. The composition of the microflora of different types of lakes is best known with respect to the saprophyte bacteria; most of the isolated species belong to the category of sporeless rods. The following list shows the number of species of some of the encountered genera.

Genus	Lake Geneva (after Marca, 1927)	Siberian lakes (after Egorova et al., 1952)
Bacillus	23	11
Bacterium	25	38
Pseudomonas	17	5
Chromobacterium	—	5
Sarcina	9	9
Micrococcus	3	29
Mycobacterium	—	16
Actinomyces	—	3
Others	3	

TABLE 23. Frequency of different bacteria in lakes

Physiological group	Main family	Frequency	Physiological group	Main family	Frequency
Ammonifying bacteria	Bacillaceae	+++	Sulfur bacteria	Chromothiceae	++
	Bacteriaceae	++		Achromathiceae	+
	Pseudomonadaceae	++		Thiobacillaceae	++
	Micrococcaceae	+++	Sulfate-reducing bacteria	Desulfovibrio sulfuricans	++
	Mycobacteriaceae	+++	Hydrogen-sulfur bacteria	Hydrogenbacctriaceae	+
	Micromonosporaceae	++	Iron bacteria	Chlamydobacteriaceae	+
	Actinomycetales	+		Gallionella	+
	Chromobacteriaceae	++		Siderocapsaceae	++
	Caulobacteriaceae	++		Hyphomicrobiales	++
	Chlamydobacteriaceae	+	Bacteria decomposing organic compounds of the carbohydrate type	Spirochaetaceae	++
Denitrifying bacteria	Pseudomonadaceae	++		Bacillaceae	+
Nitrifying bacteria	Nitrobacteriaceae	+		Mycobacteriaceae	+
Nitrogen-fixing bacteria	Azotobacteriaceae	+		Actinomycetales	+
	Clostridium	++	Carbohydrate-decomposing bacteria	Bacteriaceae	+
				Pseudomonadaceae	+
				Mycobacteriaceae	++

The early authors did not devote sufficient attention to the presence of mycobacteria and actinomycetes. Indeed, the microorganisms were isolated on the third day of incubation at 37°C, while the development of visible colonies of mycobacteria requires at least ten days of growth at the optimal temperature of 20 to 22°. The large majority (95%) of the aquatic bacterial species isolated by Taylor and Lockhead (1938) were Gram-negative. Different results were obtained with bacteria from Siberian lakes (A. A. Egorova, Z. P. Deryugina, and S. I. Kuznetsov, 1952) (Table 24).

TABLE 24. Relationship of saprophyte aquatic bacteria to the Gram stain, % of the cultures examined

Type of bacteria		After Taylor and Lockhead (1938)		After Egorova et al. (1952)
		lake water	sea	Siberian lakes
Rods { Gram-negative		95.5	94.6	19.3
{ Gram-positive		3.8	2.0	47.4
Cocci		0.7	2.8	33.3
Others		—	0.5	—

However, the proportion between spore-bearing and sporeless forms is more important than the percentages of the different bacterial species isolated from the lake. Thus, the proportion between spore-bearing and sporeless saprophyte bacteria depends on the trophic properties of the lake (S. I. Kuznetsov, 1949b).

Eutrophic lakes have a greater number of sporeless forms, both absolutely and in relation to the spore-bearing forms, whose proportion here does not exceed 10%.

In mesotrophic lakes, where primary production is smaller and the rate of organic transformations lower, there are fewer sporeless forms, and the proportion of spore-bearing ones is accordingly greater.

The number of spore-bearing forms is greater, both relatively and absolutely, in dystrophic lakes, which contain large amounts of poorly assimilable dissolved organic matter. These relationships are illustrated in Table 25.

Actinomycetes remain a comparatively little known group that appears to play an important role in the transformations of organic matter in lakes. Many actinomycetes are oligocarbophiles that can mineralize complex, highly stable organic compounds.

Micromonospora species constitute about 20% of the total amount of saprophytes in Lake Mendota (Umbreit and McCoy, 1941).

Fungi perform an important function in the biology of lakes (Weston, 1941). Weston has found numerous parasitic forms of Saprolegnia on protozoans, fungi, rotifers, and fishes.

However, we do not know yet the species that constitute the bulk of the bacterial population of pure waters. As will be shown below, only about 0.1% of the microscopically visible bacteria of lake water grow on media, even in the case of eutrophic lakes.

TABLE 25. Microbiological characteristics of the surface water of lakes belonging to different trophic categories (after Kuznetsov, 1950a)

Type of lake	Lake	Total number of saprophytes per ml	Spore-bearing saprophytes per ml	Percentage of spore-bearing forms in total number of saprophytes
Eutrophic	Chernoe (Kosino, Moscow Region)	124	9	7.3
	Beloe (Kosino, Moscow Region)	154	15	9.7
	Svyatoe (Kosino, Moscow Region)	800	21	2.7
	Bel'skoe (Kalinin Region)	190	5	2.4
Mesotrophic	Shitovskoe (Kalinin Region)	46	11	24
	Kolomenskoe (Kalinin Region)	31	7	22.6
Oligotrophic	Baikal	7	0.5	7
Dystrophic	Piyavochnoe (Kalinin Region)	61	20	33
	Chernoe (Kalinin Region)	13	11	85
Bitter salt lakes	Balpashsor (Kokchetav Region)	2,200	9	0.4
	Orazsor (Kokchetav Region)	582	4	0.8
	Bol'shoe Gor'koe (Kokchetav Region)	1,200	9	0.7

It can be assumed that many of the bacteria that fail to grow in the laboratory belong to oligocarbophilic species that require only minute amounts of organic compounds.

In the Klyazma artificial reservoir, saprophytes and iron bacteria of the Blastocaulis type account respectively for 0.1 and about 3% of the total number of bacteria determined by a direct count.

In comparing the type of lake with the composition of its microflora, it must be borne in mind that ecological factors exert a definite influence on the distribution of bacteria. A rise in the salinity or pollution of lake water leads to an increase in the total amount of saprophytes; at the same time the total number of species usually decreases.

As an example, let us examine the microflora of lakes in North Kazakhstan and Western Siberia in relation to their salinity (Table 26).

Clearly, the specific composition of the microflora is intimately linked with the saprobic properties and the mineralization of organic matter in the lake.

Kolkwitz and Marsson (1902) have prepared a list of indicator organisms whose presence reflects the saprobic conditions of the lake. The essence of these works was reviewed by S.M. Visloukh (1915).

Filamentous bacteria can serve as reliable indicators in this respect (A.S. Razumov, 1961a, 1961b, 1961c). Thus, the presence of Sphaerotilus indicates a nitrogenous pollution, while Cladothrix proliferates in waters containing greater amounts of carbohydrate-type compounds, and Leptothrix lives in oligosaprobic waters.

The proportion between sporeless and spore-forming bacteria reflects the state of the mineralization of organic matter. Thus, larger amounts of spore-forming bacteria appear when the breakdown process begins to affect humus-type materials, whose mineralization proceeds with difficulty

(Bylinkina, 1940; Krasil'nikov and Nikitina, 1945; Mishustin, 1948; Kuznetsov, 1949b).

TABLE 26. Effect of salinity on the specific composition of saprophyte bacteria in lakes in Kokchetav and Kurgan regions (after Kuznetsov, 1950a)

Lake	Electric conductivity, $K_{18} \times 10^{-4}$	Number of saprophyte bacteria, thousands per ml	Number of saprophyte bacterial species	Number of species of mycobacteria
Svetloe	0.74	254	8	2
Gornoe	0.75	268	5	0
Borovoe	0.96	241	11	2
Pustynnoe	2.52	660	5	1
Bol'shoe Chebach'e	6.01	174	3	1
Terenkul'	6.56	792	4	2
Presnoe	10.0	720	8	2
Mogil'noe	29.4	3,250	5	1
Maloe Umreshevo	29.9	1,000	3	0
Bol'shoe Krivoe ..	48.0	475	45	0
Maibalyk	112.2	94	10	5
Balpash	395	2,200	2	0
Orazsor	408	582	4	3
Bol'shoe Gor'koe .	555	1,200	2	2

In determining the possible biochemical changes in a lake, it is necessary to consider not only the specific composition but also the density of each species per unit of lake water. Only a comparison of these values with the amount of organic matter subjected to mineralization can yield an estimate of the rate of these processes in the lake.

However, the general biochemical properties of the saprophyte microflora must also be considered. Many aquatic saprophyte bacteria can hydrolyze starch and gelatin, grow on protein-free media at the expense of inorganic nitrogen, and reduce nitrates to nitrites (A. A. Egorova, Z. P. Deryugina, and S. I. Kuznetsov, 1952). According to these authors, the ability to liquefy gelatin speaks for the presence of a proteolytic enzyme in a group of saprophyte bacteria, while the hydrolysis of starch is due to the action of amylase.

The reduction of nitrates proves that the bacteria in question can utilize chemically bound oxygen.

The Total Amount of Microorganisms in Lake Water

After the discovery by S.N. Winogradsky that the actual number of soil microorganisms exceeds by far the counts obtained on meat peptone agar, efforts were made to determine the true density of microorganisms in natural water bodies. These attempts were spurred by an interest in the

121

TABLE 27. Comparison between total bacterial counts by the direct method and by inoculation on agar (after Razumov, 1932)

Water body	Total number of microorganisms		Ratio of number of bacteria determined by direct method to those growing on agar
	by direct method	by inoculation	
Lake Mauzly (pure water, Southern Urals)	256,000	13	18,200
Lake Sabakty (Southern Urals)	801,000	25	32,000
Lake Bol'shoi Bogodak (Southern Urals)	2,240,000	125	17,900
Rybinsk Artificial Reservoir	1,541,000	274	5,620
Lake Glubokoe (mesotrophic, Moscow Region)..	1,300,000	50	26,000
Lake Beloe (eutrophic, Kosino, Moscow Region)	2,220,000	300	7,400
Artesian well	8,200	1	8,200
Spring	6,200	46	112
Village well	24,100	2,040	12
Liquid from a sewage canal	307,000,000	3,400,000	93

TABLE 28. Density of bacteria in the surface water of lakes of different trophic categories during the summer stagnation (after Kuznetsov, 1952; Romanenko, 1965; Dymchishina, 1964; Belyatskaya-Potaenko, 1964; Akimov, 1967a, b)

Type of water body	Name	Number of bacteria, in 10^3 per ml
Oligotrophic	Baikal	50—200
	Lake Onega	240—340
	Lake Ladoga	100—300
	Pertozero (Karelian Autonomous SSR)	130
	Konchozero (Karelian Autonomous SSR)	170
	Dal'nee (Kamchatka Region)	120
Mesotrophic	Glubokoe (Moscow Region)	1,000—1,400
	Imolozh'e (Vyshnii Volochek)	450
	Kolomenskoe (Vyshnii Volochek)................	1,000
	Pertozero (Karelian Autonomous SSR)	650
Eutrophic	Beloe (Kosino, Moscow Region)	2,200
	Chernoe (Kosino, Moscow Region)...............	4,000
	Baturin (Belorussia)	3,500—8,000
	Bol'shoe Medvezh'e (Moscow Region)	3,700
	Bol'shoe Krivoe (brackish, Petropavlovsk Region) ..	12,300
	Maloe Umreshevo (brackish, Petropavlovsk Region)	12,300
Eutrophic artificial water bodies	Fish ponds	1,000—40,000
	Dubossary artificial reservoir	3,000—16,000
	Kakhovka artificial reservoir..................	Up to 40,000
	Kashkorenskoe	7,800—57,900
Dystrophic	Peat bank	2,300
	Piyavochnoe (Vyshnii Volochek)	1,070
	Chernoe (Vyshnii Volochek)	430

relationship between the activity of microorganisms and the physical-chemical dynamics of the water.

The maximal density of bacteria in lake water as determined by the Koch method does not exceed 200—300 cells per ml. The activity of such small amounts of bacteria cannot explain the dynamics of oxygen, nitrates, or phosphorus in the water. It is hardly surprising, therefore, that several authors (N. G. Kholodnyi, S. I. Kuznetsov and G. S. Karzinkin, A. S. Razumov, and others) have proposed almost simultaneously various microscopical methods for determining the density of bacteria in lake water.

A. S. Razumov (1932, 1947) has proposed a thoroughly developed procedure for a direct count of microorganisms. He has also discussed the whole complex of problems connected with the microbial plankton (Razumov, 1962). Even at the beginning of his work, it became clear that the purer the water, the greater the difference between the results obtained by the direct method and by inoculation on agar (Figure 27). Conversely, the difference is minimal in water from sewage or polluted wells. This can be explained as follows. Sewage water is rich in organic compounds whose carbon and nitrogen are readily assimilated by saprophyte bacteria; this creates a suitable medium for the growth of saprophyte forms detectable on meat peptone agar, but which is unfavorable for the development of oligocarbophilic organisms, which consequently can be determined by the microscopical method only.

Many authors have determined the total number of bacteria in lakes, artificial reservoirs, and ponds. It was found that the density of bacteria in different types of water bodies varies not only with depth but also from one season to another. These changes follow certain basic principles.

Table 28 shows the density of bacteria in the surface layer of different types of water bodies during the summer stagnation.

It is evident from Table 28 that the density of bacteria per ml is about 150,000 in oligotrophic lakes, from 500,000 to 1,500,000 in mesotrophic lakes, and usually from 2,000,000 to 4,000,000 in eutrophic lakes, although some lakes of the latter type contain more than 10,000,000 bacteria per ml (as is the case with some brackish lakes in North Kazakhstan Region, fish ponds, and southern artificial reservoirs).

In some cases, the number of bacteria reached 7,000,000 per ml in the deeper layers of the eutrophic Lake Beloe in Kosino (S. I. Kuznetsov, 1934a,b). In dystrophic lakes the density of bacteria ranges from 430,000 (Lake Chernoe, Vyshnii Volochek) to 2,300,000 cells per ml (in a peat quarry situated in a lowland lake), depending on whether the lake lies in highland or lowland peat bogs (Novobrantsev, 1937).

The vertical distribution of bacteria in lakes is most distinct during the summer in lakes with clearly defined thermocline and hypolimnion. Figures 52—54 show three typical cases of an oligotrophic (Baikal), a mesotrophic (Glubokoe), and a eutrophic lake (Beloe).

In deep, oligotrophic lakes, of which Baikal serves as an example (Figure 52, A), the density of bacteria is greatest in the epilimnion and declines sharply with depth (Kuznetsov, 1956; Romanova, 1958b).

Figure 52, B represents the vertical distribution of bacteria in the oligotrophic Lake Dal'noe on Kamchatka. Also shown in the figure are the distribution of live and dead diatoms and the concentrations of nitrates

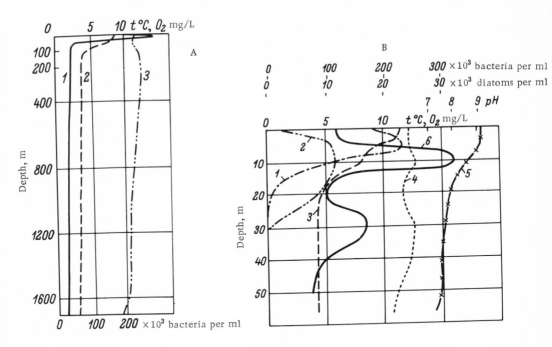

FIGURE 52. Vertical distribution of bacteria in oligotrophic lakes:

A — Lake Baikal, central depression opposite Cape Ukhan: 1) total density of bacteria; 2) temperature (°C); 3) oxygen, mg/L; B) Lake Dal'nee: 1) live phytoplankton; 2) dead diatoms; 3) temperature (°C); 4) oxygen, mg/L; 5) pH; 6) total density of bacteria.

and inorganic phosphorus. The bacterial density reaches a peak in the thermocline layer at a depth of 10 m, where the largest amounts of dead algae are found.

In mesotrophic and eutrophic lakes, which rarely attain a considerable depth, the vertical distribution of bacteria remains more or less uniform, though of magnitudes far greater than those observed in oligotrophic lakes. A typical case of this category is Lake Glubokoe (Figure 53). However, the density of bacteria in the thermocline zone or in the bottom layers may increase considerably during periods of a mass mortality of plankton and a replacement of certain forms by others (S. I. Kuznetsov, 1939).

A similar pattern of the distribution of bacteria was observed on August 1(1932, in the eutrophic Lake Beloe in Kosino (Figure 54).

The seasonal changes in the density of bacteria have been thoroughly studied in Lakes Beloe and Chernoe in Kosino (Kuznetsov, 1934a), Lake Glubokoe in the Ruza District of the Moscow Region (Kuznetsov, 1937; Sokolova, 1961; Shcherbakov, 1967a), the alpine Lake Sevan (Gambaryan, 1957), Lake Punnus-Yarvi on the Karelian isthmus (Drabkova, 1965), Lakes Naroch' and Baturin in Belorussia (Belyatskaya-Potaenko, 1964; Potaenko, 1968), and Lake Baikal (Romanova, 1958a, 1958b).

Table 29 shows the changes of bacterial density in Lake Glubokoe, Moscov Region. The density of bacteria is usually greatest at the end of the summe

124

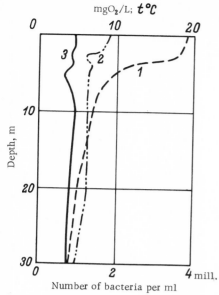

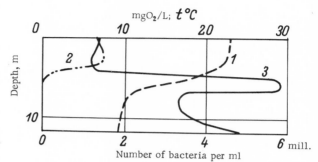

FIGURE 53. Vertical distribution of bacteria in the mesotrophic Lake Glubokoe:

1) temperature (°C); 2) oxygen, mg/L; 3) total density of bacteria.

FIGURE 54. Vertical distribution of bacteria in the eutrophic Lake Beloe in Kosino:

1) temperature (°C); 2) oxygen, mg/L; 3) total density of bacteria.

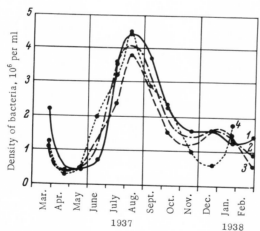

FIGURE 55. Seasonal changes in the density of bacteria in the water of Lake Chernoe, Kosino, during 1937:

1) at a depth of 0−1 m; 2) 2 m; 3) 3 m; 4) 4 m.

stagnation and lowest in winter. The bacterial densities in eutrophic and mesotrophic lakes become roughly equal in winter at an average of about 500,000 cells per ml.

TABLE 29. Seasonal fluctuations in the density of bacteria (in 10^3 cells per ml) in the water of Lake Glubokoe (Ruza District, Moscow Region) (after Kuznetsov, 1934a)

Depth, m	1932					1933
	Feb. 26	Apr. 1	July 25	Aug. 30	Sep. 7	Jan. 12
Surface	405	519	436	1,730	1,751	946
5	340	418	849	134	3,240	676
10	700	382	826	357	2,017	657
20	620	—	754	620	1,302	628
30	575	—	348	894	1,609	666

The vertical distribution of bacteria varies considerably according to the characteristic features of the lake and also from one season to another. Table 30 shows the corresponding data for Lake Beloe.

TABLE 30. Seasonal changes in the density of bacteria in the water of Lake Beloe, Kosino (in 10^3 cells per ml) (after Kuznetsov, 1934a)

Depth, m	1932						1933
	Feb. 6	Apr. 11	May 11	July 12	Sep. 13	Sep. 14	Feb. 26
Surface	379	621	880	2,672	706	1,495	156
3	801	435	858	833	1,850	1,397	351
7	446	621	1,534	1,782	—	—	537
10	—	—	1,280	—	5,320	3,140	1,968
12	773	2,045	3,230	4,678	3,225	7,421	1,854

In this lake, the vertical distribution of bacteria can be more or less uniform throughout the depth range, or a peak of bacterial density can develop in the epilimnion or thermocline zone. The density of bacteria in the bottom waters is usually higher, regardless of the density in the intermediate water mass.

Figure 55 contains data on the seasonal changes of the density of bacteria in the shallow eutrophic Lake Chernoe, where a thorough mixing of water prevails during the whole ice-free period. Figure 56 shows the average density of bacteria in the mesotrophic Lake Punnus-Yarvi (Drabkova, 1965), and Figure 57 shows the average density in the oligotrophic Lake Baikal.

In Lake Baikal (Figure 57), the fluctuations of bacterial density are confined to the trophic surface layer, and the highest figures are obtained in late July. Here the density of bacteria remains practically constant throughout the year at a depth of 200 m. It appears that the decomposition of the organic matter of dead plankters ends before the detritus particles sink to this depth.

The bacterial population of some water bodies can attain a very high density. To this category belong fish-rearing ponds, where the fish are fed organic materials and inorganic fertilizers are also introduced. Here the density of bacteria can be as high as 40,000,000 per ml (V. A. Akimov, 1967a, 1967b).

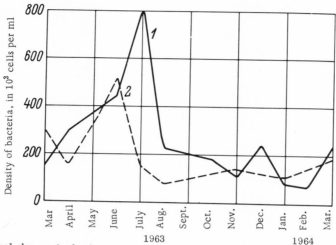

FIGURE 56. Seasonal changes in the density of bacteria in the water of the mesotrophic Lake Punnus-Yarvi (according to Drabkova, 1965):

1) at a depth of 0.2 m; 2) at a depth of 10 m.

Of particular interest is the proliferation of the blue-green alga S i n e - c h o c o c c u s   p l a n c t o n i c u s. In contrast to the green sulfur bacteria, this organism contains chlorophyll and phycocyanin, which enable it to live photosynthetically by releasing free oxygen and using water as a hydrogen donor. Because of its minute size — 0.9 by 1.5 microns — S. p l a n c t o - n i c u s was regarded as a bacterium until Drews, Prauser, and Ulman (Arch. Microbiol., 1961) proved that it represents a blue-green alga.

Masses of "green" bacteria were regularly observed in purification ponds on the Lublin sewage disposal works (Zakharov and Konstantinova, 1929). The water became emerald green in color, while the density of bacteria ranged from 49 million to 366 million per ml of water. At the same time, the pond water contained small protococcal algae at a density of 50,000—2,600,000 per ml. A similar organism was found in a stagnant pond of the Minsk city sewage disposal works (Godnev and Vinberg, 1951; Vinberg and Sivko, 1952). In late August, the density of this organism reached 11 billion cells per ml, while the rate of photosynthesis fluctuated from 5 to 10 mg O_2 per liter per hour, though in some cases it was as high as 34 mg O_2/L/hour. Another interesting case was observed in evaporation fields of the salt industry, where the bacterial plankton consisted practically of a single species (S. I. Kuznetsov and V. I. Romanenko, 1968).

The pink color of salt lakes and the sedimentation of a pink salt are widespread phenomena in arid regions, both in the USSR and elsewhere. Earlier, this color was attributed to the mass growth of the flagellated alga D u n a l i e l l a   s a l i n a. It was shown, however, that the responsible organism is a pink bacterium that grows optimally in the saturated solution (Larsen, 1962). This was confirmed by S. I. Kuznetsov and V. I. Romanenko (1968), who described the appearance of a pink color in evaporation basins of salt enterprises in the Sivash area and on Lake Sasyk in Crimea. Filtration of the water through membrane filters of $3-5\mu$ pore size produced colorless water, and the filter membrane became pink. The density of bacteria in this water reached 65 million cells per ml in some cases. The rate of heterotrophic fixation of CO_2 in this water was found to be several times greater than in fresh waters. Dunaliella salina is evidently a photosynthetic organism, while the pink bacteria consume allochthonous organic compounds and the products of photosynthesis.

The density of bacteria in artificial reservoirs varies considerably from year to year.

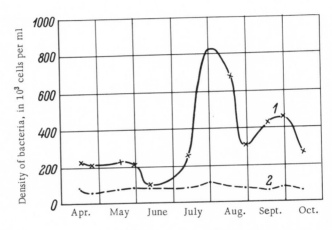

FIGURE 57. Seasonal changes of the density of bacteria in the oligotrophic Lake Baikal opposite Cape Sytyi (after Romanova):

1) average density of bacteria in the 0—25 m layer; 2) average density of bacteria at a depth of 200 m.

Artificial reservoirs differ from lakes in two main features, namely their high rate of water exchange and the considerable seasonal fluctuations of the water level. A rich supply of organic matter from the flooded soil enters the artificial reservoirs during the first years after damming. This allochthonous organic material leads to a proliferation of bacteria. As the reservoir becomes more "mature" these processes gradually decline.

A thorough follow-up of the density of bacteria has been carried out for a number of years by regular trips to standard stations in the Rybinsk Artificial Reservoir (Novozhilova, 1955; Kuznetsov, 1962; Kuznetsov and Karpova, 1966; Kuznetsov, Romanenko, and Karpova, 1967). Similar studies are being made in the Kuibyshev Artificial Reservoir during the maturation of this water body in the first years after the flooding (Salmanov, 1958) and ten years later (Mikheeva, 1966; Ivatin, 1968).

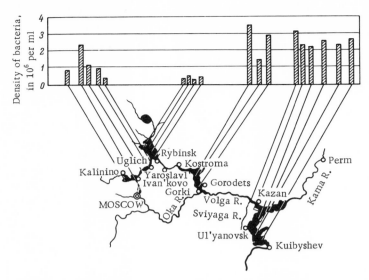

FIGURE 58. Density of bacteria in the Volga artificial reservoirs in June 1956 (after the high water).

A simultaneous determination of bacterial density in all the artificial reservoirs of the Volga system was carried out in June 1956 in field conditions (Kuznetsov, 1959a). At that time the Ivan'kovo and Rybinsk artificial reservoirs were already mature; the Gorki and Kuibyshev reservoirs were filled up to capacity in 1954 and 1955.

The Ivan'kovo Artificial Reservoir has a comparatively high bacterial count, which reaches 2 million cells per ml (Figure 58). As the water passes through the Uglich Artificial Reservoir, the density of bacteria decreases to 900,000 per ml. The lowest densities, from 300,000 to 500,000 per ml, are found in the Rybinsk Artificial Reservoir. Then the density increases to about 3 million cells per ml or more in the river bed zone of the Gorki and Kuibyshev reservoirs. By 1966, when the latter two reservoirs became more mature, the density of bacteria in them decreased to the level observed in the Rybinsk Reservoir, 1—2 million cells per ml.

In a study of the density of bacteria in different types of artificial reservoirs, V. I. Romanenko (1965) stresses the great influence of the water supply, as in the case of lakes. Thus, the lowest density was found in the Svir and Irkutsk artificial reservoirs, which receive pure waters from Lake Onega and Lake Baikal, respectively. On the other hand, the muddy waters of the Syroyaz and Chiryurt artificial reservoirs (on the rivers Murgab and Sulak, respectively) showed the highest counts — from 10 to 12 million cells per ml. As the water flows along, the suspended particles settle down, the transparency increases from 5—10 cm to 1—2 m, and the bacterial density drops to 1—2 million cells per ml.

The biomass of bacteria can be calculated on the basis of their density. Only a few attempts have been made so far in this direction. In determining the bacterial biomass in the water, some authors have assumed that bacterial cells have a volume of 0.5—1.5 cubic microns, while the specific weight of bacteria and plankton is close to unity (V. S. Butkevich, 1938b, 1939; A. S. Razumov, 1948a, 1948b; S. I. Kuznetsov, 1951).

The following list shows the biomasses of bacteria and phytoplankton in some lakes and seas (after Butkevich, 1938; Kuznetsov, 1954):

Name of lake or sea	Density of bacteria, in 10^3 cells per ml	Bacterial biomass, mg/L	Phytoplanktic biomass, mg/L
Lakes:			
Beloe (Kosino)	2,000	1.8	9.0
Glubokoe (Moscow Region)	1,000	0.97	1.85
Dolgoe (Moscow Region)..	1,500	1.43	1.26
Baikal	90	0.13	0.36
Seas:			
Barents	40—80	0.05—0.25	0.1—2.0
Azov	180—300	0.1	
Caspian	2,000	1.0	

It is evident from these data that seas and oligotrophic lakes have a roughly similar bacterial biomass. On the other hand, the bacterial biomass of eutrophic lakes is much greater in absolute terms but smaller in relation to the quantities of phytoplankton and dissolved organic matter.

The Total Amount of Microorganisms in Lake Silts

The pioneering studies of V. L. Omelyansky (1917—1925) have shown long ago that only the superficial layers of silt participate in the transformations of organic and inorganic matter. Deeper inside the silt, organic matter breaks down much more slowly because of the scarcity of microbial life. Hence the particular interest in the microbiology of the surface silt in connection with the chemical transformations that occur in lakes. Depending on the type of lake, the silt or bottom sediments can consist of sapropel (eutrophic lakes) or a more mineralized material (mesotrophic and oligotrophic lakes).

The density of microorganisms in the surface layers of lake sediments is of the order of hundreds of millions of cells per gram of moist silt. This was established by workers of the Kosino Limnological Station (Karzinkin and Kuznetsov, 1931; Khartulari, 1939) and confirmed elsewhere (Drabkova, 1966; Aliverdieva, 1965; Daukshta, 1967).

Silt sediments have a rich microbial population (Table 31) that can play a significant part in the mineralization of the organic matter of silt. However, the density of microorganisms decreases sharply with depth into the silt (V. L. Omelyansky, 1917). It was even assumed that the breakdown of organic matter of silt ceases at a depth of about 25 cm because of the accumulation of bacterial metabolic products (Omelyansky, 1925).

TABLE 31. Density of bacteria in the surface sapropel layers (microscopical analyses after Khartulari, 1939)

Lake	Ash content, %	Number of bacteria per gram of moist silt	Number of bacteria per gram of dry silt	Organic substance of bacteria as % of organic substance of silt
Beloe (Kosino, Moscow Region) ..	54.1	2,326	54,219	7.8
Medvezh'e (Moscow Region)	58.3	1,905	38,253	6.0
Chernoe (Kosino)	49.3	1,285	35,109	4.5
Maloe Medvezh'e (Moscow Region)	47.3	1,624	32,032	4.0
Svyatoe (Kosino)	18.6	922	29,790	2.3
Krugloe (Moscow Region)	79.2	1,110	7,991	2.5
Gabozero (Karelia)	81.9	1,883	15,680	5.8

In a study of this problem, V. A. Ekzertsev isolated pure cultures of saprophyte organisms (Sarcina flava) taken from the surface layer and inoculated them on meat peptone agar together with lumps of silt obtained from a depth of more than 0.5 m from the silt surface. Detecting no inhibition of growth in the vicinity of the silt particles, Ekzertsev concluded that the accumulation of microbial metabolic products cannot be regarded as an adverse factor. It was later found that the addition of glucose to silt samples from greater depths stimulates gas formation in comparison with the controls (S. I. Kuznetsov, 1950b). This suggests that microbial growth stops inside the silt owing to the absence of easily assimilable carbohydrates.

Now we possess a considerable amount of evidence on the vertical distribution of bacteria in the sapropel layer of many water bodies, mainly of the eutrophic type (Williams and McCoy, 1935; Stark and McCoy, 1938; Shturm and Kanunnikova, 1945; Kuznetsov, 1950b; Ekzertsev, 1948; Zavarzina, 1955b; etc.). These data were obtained by two basically different methods — microscopically and by inoculation of nutrient media.

Table 32 shows the results obtained by direct microscopic observations. The surface layer is richest in bacteria, with 1—2 billion cells per gram of moist silt. The density of bacteria decreases sharply in the upper one-meter layer to 200—300 million cells per gram of moist silt at a depth of 1 m. The decrease continues deeper, but even the bedrock clays of Lake Piyavochnoe do not contain less than 130 million bacteria per gram of moist silt.

The question of the viability of these bacteria arises in connection with such high microscopic counts. To solve this problem, N. B. Zavarzina (1955b) compared the microscopic results with preparations made from the same material and stained with Giemsa and light green strains after Peshkov-Pekarskii. Then she determined the percentage of the cells that took up the blue stain — an indication that they possessed an intact nuclear apparatus and could be regarded as viable. The results obtained by Zavarzina with the silts of Lake Biserovo are shown on p. 132, top.

The percentage of live bacteria decreases from 66% at the silt surface to 56% at a depth of 2—3 m.

Depth from silt surface, m	Total density of bacteria, millions of cells per gram of moist silt	Density of "live" bacteria, millions of cells per gram of moist silt	Dead bacteria, %
0	612	404	34
1.0	359	219	39
2.0	279	155	44
3.0	366	114	69
4.0	213	64	70

TABLE 32. Vertical distribution of bacteria in the silt (direct microscopical counts), in millions of bacteria per gram of moist silt (after Kuznetsov, 1934a, 1950b; Khartulari, 1939; Ekzertsev, 1948; Zavarzina, 1955b)

Depth of sediment, m	Lake Beloe (Kosino, Moscow Region)	Lake Chernoe (Kosino, Moscow Region)	Lake Biserovo (Moscow Region)	Lake Piyavochnoe (Kalinin Region)	Lake Kolomenskoe (Kalinin Region)	Lake Pustynnoe (Kurgan Region)	Maibalyk, a salt lake (Kurgan Region)	Balpashsor, a bitter salt lake (Kurgan Region)
0.0	2,326	1,285	740	515	516	810	907	324
0.1	—	—	603	425	425	—	—	—
0.3	—	—	520	347	415	—	464	237
0.6	—	—	402	279	402	—	345	236
1.0	992	449	347	256	310	648	216	—
1.5	—	—	—	201	—	—	119	—
2.0	—	336	347	—	261	626	—	—
2.5	279	—	—	178	—	—	—	—
3.0	—	279	283	—	229	475	—	—
4.0	—	—	288	164	192	453	—	—
5.0	—	—	192	160	156	334	—	—
6.0	—	—	—	133	—	302	—	—
7.0	—	—	—	—	—	280	—	—
8.0	—	—	—	—	—	205	—	—

Inoculation in bacteriological media produces totally different results. Naturally, bacterial densities determined by inoculation on meat peptone agar cannot be expected to correspond with those obtained by direct count, since only saprophytes grow on meat peptone agar. At any rate, saprophytes can be regarded as a guide group that indicates an intensive breakdown of organic matter. The amounts of saprophytes and anaerobes decrease sharply with depth. This was established by V. E. Ekzertsev (1948) with the saprophytes of several lakes (Table 33); similar results were obtained by L. D. Shturm and Kanunnikova (1945), and Henrici and McCoy (1938).

Comparison of Tables 32 and 33 shows that the inoculation method fails to detect bacteria deep inside the silt, in contrast to the direct microscopical method.

TABLE 33. Vertical distribution of saprophytes in the sapropel sediments of lakes in the Kalinin Region. (thousands of cells per gram of moist soil) (after Ekzertsev, 1948)

Depth, m	Biserovo		Piyavochnoe		Kolomenskoe	
	aerobes	anaerobes	aerobes	anaerobes	aerobes	anaerobes
0	42	1.9	220		100	16
0.1	12	1.2	50	14	60	8
0.3	7	0.8	10	8	12	7
0.6	7	0.8	—	1.2	—	4
1.0	5	1.2	—	0.5	2	0.07
1.5	—	—	0.6	0.3	—	—
2.0	1.2	—	—	—	0.3	0.06
2.5	—	—	0.2	0.3	—	—
3.0	1.1	—	—	—	0.6	0.05
4.0	0.5	—	—	0.2	0.8	0.04
5.0	0.2	—	—	0.1	—	0.01

TABLE 34. Vertical distribution of different physiological groups of bacteria in the sapropel of lakes in Kalinin Region (after Shturm and Kanunnikova, 1945)

Depth from silt surface, m	Piyavochnoe					Shitovskoe					Kolomno		
	ammonifiers	denitrifiers	nitrifiers	Clostridium pasteurianum	cellulose-digesting bacteria	ammonifiers	denitrifiers	nitrifiers	Clostridium pasteurianum	cellulose-digesting bacteria	ammonifiers	denitrifiers	cellulose-digesting bacteria
0	200	0	4	200	200	300	0	0	200	20	94	500	20
0.5	370	3	0	37	20	300	0	0	80	80	200	1	27
1	550	0	0	5	3	40	0	0	0	80	16	1	1
3	300	0	0	3	4	20	0	0	0	0	1	1	1
6	37	0	0	3	—	—	—	—	—	—	1	1	1

Most analyses of the vertical distribution of different physiological groups of microorganisms in sapropel were largely qualitative in approach. Only the work of L. D. Shturm and Z. A. Kanunnikova (1945) contains some quantitative information (Table 34).

To sum up, the inoculation of silt samples on universal or selective media shows that starting from a depth of 60 cm from the silt surface there is a drastic decrease in the density of bacteria capable of growth on bacteriological media. In other words, the rate of biological processes decreases with depth. Measurements of the oxidation-reduction potential of the deep sapropel layers confirm this conclusion, if this potential can be considered as an index of the rate of microbiologic processes.

Characteristics of the Aquatic Microflora That Can
Be Detected Only at Very High Magnification

The electron microscope allows a magnification of 30,000 times and has a resolving power on the order of 10 Å.

Electron microscopy was used by M. P. Volarovich in the examination of peat suspensions and by D. I. Nikitin (1964) for the detection of soil

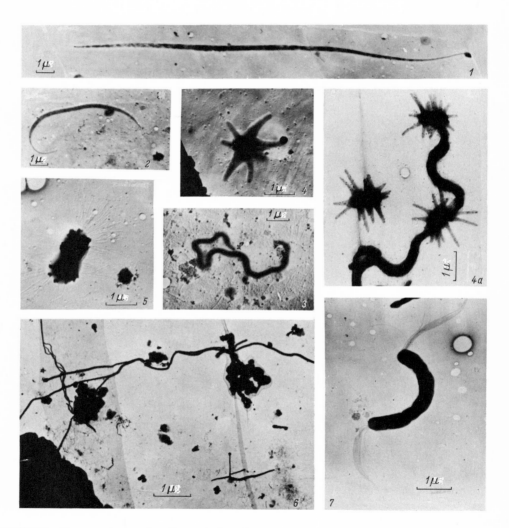

FIGURE 59. Electron micrographs of bacteria from the water and silt of Lakes Beloe and Glubokoe:

1) long filamentous form; 2) very thin forms with sharp ends; 3) coiled filamentous forms; 4, 4a) P r o s t h e - c o m i c r o b i u m; 5) fimbriate bacteria; 6) G a l l i o n e l l a, a membraneous bag containing reniform cells; 7) a vibrio with a horsetail-shaped group of flagella.

microorganisms.   Later, D. I. Nikitin, L. V. Vasil'eva, and R. A. Lokhmacheva (1966) described several new morphologic types of soil microorganisms.   Similar procedures were used in the study of aquatic microorganisms.

The first electron photomicrographs of microorganisms from the water
and silt of Lakes Beloe and Chernoe in Kosino (Nikitin and Kuznetsov, 1967)
revealed a great variety of forms that remain invisible under the light
microscope.

As seen by the electron microscope, the microbial population of lakes
Beloe and Chernoe and the mesotrophic Lake Glubokoe consists mainly of
bacteria, with small rods as the predominant element; there are large
amounts of Caulobacteriales.   Some cells do not exceed 0.3 microns in
diameter, while the stem, which is even thinner, attains a length of 27 microns
(Figure 79).   Among the frequent morphologic types are cells with pointed
ends, 0.075 microns thick and 0.25 microns in diameter.   Clearly, such
microorganisms cannot easily be seen under the light microscope.

Another frequent type in the examined water samples consisted of long
filiform organisms with a cell diameter of 0.6 microns (Figure 59).   Filamentous bacteria 0.31 microns in diameter were also found. The separate
cells of this organism are enclosed in a common envelope that is transparent to the electron beam.   The envelope has an outer diameter of
0.41 microns.   Also visible are separate cells with fimbria whose thickness ranges from 0.2 to 0.025 microns, as well as bacterial cells with filamentous appendages thinner than fimbria (less than 0.012 microns thick).

In addition, the water contained organisms similar to S p i r u l i n a but
much thinner (Figure 59); such forms are not found in soil.   There were
considerable numbers of an unknown bacteriumlike organism, probably
P r o s t h e c o m i c r o b i u m, with outgrowths comparable to the pseudopodia
of amebae.   These cells are 1.4—1.6 microns long and about 0.6 microns
wide, with 15—18 outgrowths having a length of 0.15 to 1.6 microns and
slightly tapering ends.

Another extraordinary form discovered in silt suspensions is a spiral
microorganism similar to S e l i b e r i a.   Silts often contain bacterialike organisms possessing fimbria and numerous knobs on the cell surface; each knob
has a diameter of about 0.06 microns (Figure 59).

Thus, the application of electron microscopy to the study of the aquatic
microflora has revealed a number of new forms that cannot grow on conventional media and are invisible under the light microscope. Rodlike forms
predominate in the water; cocci are less frequent.

Factors Affecting the Growth of Bacteria

The Effect of Organic Compounds

Many authors have studied the influence that the concentration of organic
nutrients exerts on the development of microorganisms.   However, most of
the experiments were made at concentrations far greater than those occurring

in natural conditions or in the silt solution. The scarcity of nutrients begins to exert a limiting effect on bacterial growth only at a nutrient concentration below 0.01—0.1% (Rahn, 1932). It was found that the minimal concentration of organic nutrients necessary for the reproduction of saprophytes ranges from 0.001 to 0.01%, that is, from 10 to 100 mg per liter (ZoBell and Grant, 1942, 1943).

The abundance of bacteria in lake and sea water proves their ability to live and reproduce in very dilute solutions (Sorokin, 1964b).

The concentration of organic matter in sea water is usually less than 5 mg/L. Nevertheless, even saprophyte bacteria can multiply from a few hundred to several millions of cells per ml of sea water after a prolonged storage of the latter in laboratory conditions (Waksman and Carey, 1935). The reproduction of bacteria is accompanied by consumption of oxygen, production of CO_2 and ammonia, reduction of nitrates, and other biochemical changes of the environment (ZoBell and Anderson, 1936). Similar phenomena were found in lake water. Thus, G. G. Vinberg and L. I. Yarovitsina (1946) have observed by direct microscopic method an increase in the number of bacteria during the storage of jars containing water from lakes Beloe and Svyatoe; at the same time there was a corresponding decrease in the oxygen content of the jars. Similar results were reported elsewhere, notably by ZoBell (1940a, b), who worked with water from Lake Mendota (USA), which contains less than 10 mg of organic matter per liter. After a protracted lag phase, Aerobacter aerogenes rapidly multiplies in solutions containing both glucose and peptone at a concentration as low as 0.5 mg/L each (Butterfield, 1929). In the presence of glass beads added to increase the contact surface between the liquid and solid phases, Escherichia coli can develop in a solution containing peptone and glucose at a concentration of 0.5 mg/l (Heukelekian and Heller, 1940).

Marine bacteria can grow in mineral media where the concentration of organic nutrients is less than 0.1 mg/L (ZoBell and Grant, 1942, 1943). Moreover, there are indications that even lower concentrations can bring about the multiplication of bacteria.

According to Waksman and Carey (1935), nitrogen is a limiting factor in the development of bacteria. On these grounds, Jannasch (1958c) examined the effect of threshold concentrations of ammonia, nitrite, and organic nitrogen on the growth of Flavobacterium aquatile, Aerobacter aerogenes, and Bac. subtilis. These organisms were isolated on minimal media composed of natural waters and were then inoculated in an artificial medium containing glucose at a concentration of 10 mg/L together with various amounts of nitrogen. The threshold concentrations of nitrogen that still permitted bacterial reproduction ranged from 1 to 500 μg/L, depending on the organism and the form of nitrogen used. Aerobacter aerogenes required high concentrations of nitrate nitrogen but grew in low threshold concentrations of ammonia nitrogen and peptone hydrolysate.

All these results were obtained with stationary cultures. Theoretically, however, the threshold concentration of the substrate is associated with the density and growth rate of the population. In an attempt to examine these relationships in continuous cultures, Jannasch (1963) found that the cells can compensate for adverse or suboptimal growth conditions by increasing their metabolism and growth rate. This intrinsic factor becomes evident

only in those cases in which the population density and the substrate concentration in the continuous culture decrease below the threshold value.
It is also known that the threshold level of substrate concentration (i. e., the concentration that still allows bacterial growth) depends on the oxidation-reduction potential. Thus, lower threshold concentrations of the substrate are required in cultures with a lower oxidation-reduction potential. Jannasch found also that the threshold concentrations of substrate in continuous cultures can be lower than those in stationary cultures.

Aquatic bacteria actively assimilate organic compounds at a concentration of 1 to 10 mg per liter (Wright and Hobbie, 1965).

Summing up all these results, it can be said that even a very low concentration of nutrient compounds allows bacterial growth, although differences do exist from one species to another. Organisms isolated from pure waters can grow in the presence of carbohydrates and ammonia nitrogen at a concentration of 1 to 10 mg/per liter each.

In natural conditions, however, bacterial growth depends less on the total amount of organic matter than on the concentration of that part of it which can be assimilated. The effect of organic substances on bacterial growth becomes especially evident when a sufficiently large amount of sewage water enters a lake.

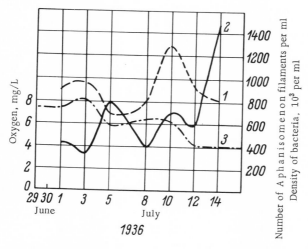

FIGURE 60. A sharp increase in bacterial density in the thermocline in Lake Glubokoe following the death of the dominant form of the phytoplankton:

1) phytoplankton; 2) bacteria; 3) oxygen.

Bere (1933) studied the relationship between the density of bacteria and the chemical properties of lake water, notably the concentration of organic matter. After an analysis of more than fifty American lakes of different organic content, hardness, dry residue, and electric conductivity, Bere concluded that the bacterial density is proportional to the concentrations of organic and inorganic compounds in one-half of the examined lakes but depends on the organic content alone in one-third of them. In a more thorough treatment of this problem, P. V. Novobrantsev (1937) and S. I. Kuznetsov (1949b) found that the bacterial count of lake water depends not on the total quantity of dissolved organic matter but only on the assimilable part of it (Table 35).

TABLE 35. Density of bacteria and concentration of dissolved organic substances in the surface layer of some lakes and artificial reservoirs (after Kuznetsov, 1949b; Novobrantsev, 1937; etc.)

Type of water body	Name	Total concentration of organic substances (bichromate oxidability), $mg\,O_2/l$	Assimilable organic substances, $mg\,O_2/l$	Total density of bacteria, thousands per ml
Oligotrophic	Konchozero (Karelia)	15.0	0.3	170
	Pertozero (Karelia)	15.3	0.5	130
	Lake Onega	19.4	1.4	260
Mesotrophic	Lake Elovoe (Urals)	—	1.43	342
	Lake Il'menskoe (Southern Urals)	—	3.03	1,640
	Rybinsk Artificial Reservoir	30	1.7	1,300
Eutrophic	Lake Beloe (Kosino, Moscow Region)	32.1	3.06	2,230
	Lake Medvezh'e (Moscow Region)	33.7	5.16	3,420
Dystrophic	Peat bank	226.6	3.96	2,320
	Ivina broadening of the Svir Artificial Reservoir	73	2.90	2,300

Assimilable organic matter is not necessarily exogenous. It can arise within the lake as a result of a mass mortality of plankton, for example, when one organism responsible for water bloom is replaced by another. Such increase in the supply of assimilable organic compounds leads to luxuriant bacterial growth, as in the case of Lake Glubokoe (Figure 60).

The observations were made in the metalimnion of the lake (Kuznetsov, 1939). Owing to the calm warm weather, the wind-induced movements of water did not go beyond a depth of 3–4 m. A drastic decrease in the oxygen content of the water at a depth of 3 m occurred twice during the observations; later the oxygen concentration remained unchanged. These two decreases in the oxygen concentration corresponded with a sharp decline in the density of planktonic algae and an increase in the density of bacteria.

A similar relationship was found at a depth of 4 m, where these changes appeared one day later at a depth of 3 m, and the phytoplankton reached a peak at a time when the lowest levels of cells are recorded at a depth of 3 m. In other words, a rapid multiplication of bacteria begins when the surface plankton dies and sinks.

The Effect of Sunlight on the Distribution of Bacteria in Lakes

Many authors have tried to prove that sunlight is responsible for the irregular vertical distribution of bacteria in lakes. Minder (1918), for example, explains in this manner the decrease of bacterial density in the surface water of Lake of Zürich during the summer, while Zich and Rutner (1932) attribute to the same factor the winter peak of bacteria in the Lunzersee in Austria. Fischer (1894) and other authors speak of a lethal effect of sunlight on bacteria in sea water.

On the other hand, Fred and co-workers (1924) were unable to detect any direct influence of sunlight on bacteria during their studies of the distribution of bacteria in Lake Mendota. Similar results are reported by Lloyd (1930), Reuser (1933), ZoBell and Feltham (1934), and others with marine bacteria.

Clearly, the ultraviolet component of sunlight with a wavelength of 2,100–2,960 Å shows the greatest bactericidal effect. However, 50% of the active radiation is absorbed in the uppermost 10 cm of water. Sunlight cannot be expected to exert a great bactericidal effect in view of this fact.

Studies of the seasonal variations in the bacterial count of lake water have shown that ultraviolet radiation does not reduce the density of bacteria in the water. Such is the view of Taylor (1940, 1941) after an eleven-month observation of Lake Windermere in England. In this lake, the density of bacteria at the surface was the same as at a depth of 1 m, and the count obtained at a depth of 10 m was even lower.

The sedimentation of bacteria in sewage waters has been ascribed to the lethal effect of sunlight (Prescott and Winslow, 1931).

At any rate, if solar radiation does cause a certain mortality of bacteria in the surface layers of lake water, it remains a minor factor among those adversely affecting the growth of bacteria in lakes.

The Effect of Temperature

The metabolic rate of bacteria varies directly with temperature up to a certain limit, which is about 20–25°C for most bacterial species. At first, the rise of temperature accelerates the reproduction of bacteria until the population becomes stable because of an increase in mortality.

Within a certain range of temperature, cooling slows down the successive phases of bacterial development. However, the final density of bacteria grown in a sufficiently rich medium at a lower temperature can be equal to or even greater than that obtained with a similar culture at a higher temperature.

These phenomena become more pronounced in media containing scant amounts of nutrients. Thus, Waksman and Renn (1936) examined the bacterial count and oxygen consumption in jars containing sea water with a low concentration of organic compounds (Figure 61). The peaks of bacterial density were obtained on the second day at 22°C and on the seventh day at 4°, as determined by inoculation in meat peptone broth. The consumption of oxygen at the peak points was the same in both cases, 0.45–0.47 mg/L.

It is far more difficult to determine the effect of temperature on bacteria living in a natural water body, since various additional factors are involved in succession during the different seasons of the year. At any rate, the effect of temperature can be traced by determining one of the factors that influence the bacterial density, notably the reproduction rate.

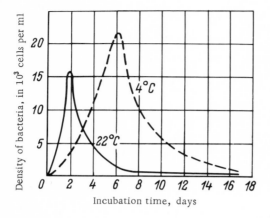

FIGURE 61. Effect of temperature on bacterial development (after Waksman and Reen).

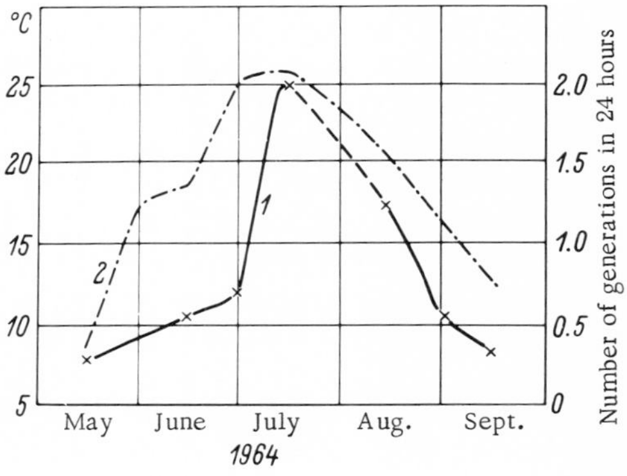

FIGURE 62. Reproduction rate of bacteria in the Rybinsk Artificial Reservoir during the vegetative period of 1964:

1) number of bacterial generations per 24 hours;
2) water temperature.

Such a study was made by S. I. Kuznetsov and V. I. Romanenko (1967) at the Rybinsk Artificial Reservoir. The generation time was determined by the radioactive carbon method during the summer of 1964. Samples were taken at two-week intervals at six standard stations situated in different parts of the reservoir. The number of bacterial generations occurring in twenty-four hours was determined for each interval at all stations on the basis of these anlayses (after Kuznetsov, Romanenko, and Karpova, 1966).

Date	Temperature, °C	Generation time, hours	Number of generations in 24 hours
May 12	8.5	82	0.29
June 1	17.3	68	0.35
June 15	18.7	43	0.56
July 1	25.3	36	0.70
July 15	25.9	12	2.0
August 3	23.0	22	1.1
August 16	20.0	19	1.26
September 2	16.0	42	0.57
September 17	12.5	67	0.35
October 2	10.0	42	0.57

Figure 62 shows the obtained results together with the average temperatures for each date of analysis. During the cool month of May, one generation took eighty-two hours, which corresponds to 0.29 generations per twenty-four hours. In July at a water temperature of 25.9°C there were two generations per twenty-four hours or one generation every twelve hours. Finally, the generation time increased to sixty-seven hours in the fall at a water temperature of 10°C. In view of the relatively stable composition and concentration of organic matter in the Rybinsk Artificial Reservoir, it can be said that temperature exerts a pronounced effect on the reproduction rate of the existing bacteria.

Temperature is undoubtedly a major ecological factor. Its influence on the density of bacteria, however, may be masked by other processes.

On the whole, temperature exerts a twofold effect — it accelerates the growth and phytosynthetic activity of phytoplankton. The latter process enriches the water with organic compounds, which in turn increase the density of bacteria. In this chain of events, the direct influence of temperature may be much smaller than the effect of the increased organic content. Thus, the density of bacteria in the epilimnion of Lake Beloe (Kosino), the Rybinsk Artificial Reservoir, and other lakes often attains a peak in November at a temperature of about 9°, that is, at a time of a mass death of phytoplankton and a water temperature far below the optimal range for bacteria.

The Effect of the Zooplankton on the Density of Bacteria in Lakes

Many authors have stressed the role of bacteria as food for the zooplankton. Thus, bacteria are an important component of the diet of protozoans, some crustaceans, mollusks, and rotifers, especially during the self-purification of polluted waters. This view, first proposed by Emmerich (1904), was later developed by Zuelzer (1908) with respect to planktonic crustaceans and rotifers.

This problem is reviewed by Prescott and Winslow (1931), Ya. Ya. Nikitinsky (1938), and in a somewhat wider context by Baier (1935). On the basis of the literature and his own observations, Baier examined the role of bacteria in the food of the zooplankton of different types of lakes (Table 36).

TABLE 36. Role of bacteria in the diet of different groups of plankters (after Baier, 1935)

Type of lake	Type of animals		
	protozoans	filter feeders	sediment feeders
Eutrophic	Very important	Very important	Moderately important
Dystrophic	Of minor importance	Of minor importance	Of minor importance
Oligotrophic	Important	Important	Moderately important

Laboratory experiments with bacteria-free cultures of Daphnia have shown that aquatic bacteria together with phytoplankton are the normal food of many filtering zooplankters (N. S. Gaevskaya, 1948; A. G. Rodina, 1946, 1948; MacGinitie, 1932). However, the food selectivity of some zooplankters and the assimilation of food in the specific conditions of the given lake remained unknown or incompletely understood. Progress in this field was achieved by means of radioactive isotopes, namely, the application of radioactive P^{32} and C^{14}, respectively, for the study of food selectivity and the assimilation of different types of food.

Thus, A. G. Rodina (1957) used radioactive phosphorus isotopes in a study of the food selectivity of Daphnia pulex, Chironomus plumosus, Procladius sp., Sphaerium corneum, and Limnaea stagnalis.

Different bacterial species were tagged with radioactive phosphorus by cultivation in media containing $KH_2P^{32}O_4$. Then each tagged species was mixed with equal numbers of cells of other bacteria in such a manner that each mixture contained a single and different tagged species.

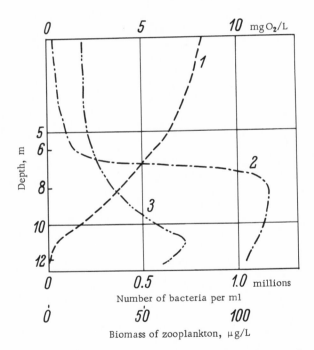

FIGURE 63. Relationship between the aggregation of zooplankton and the magnitude of bacterial chemosynthesis in the Rybinsk Artificial Reservoir over the former bed of the Mologa during the winter:

1) oxygen; 2) zooplankton; 3) bacteria.

If the consumer shows a preference for a given bacterial species, it absorbs radioactivity in the mixture where this species is tagged. The experiments, which lasted two hours, showed that Daphnia pulex,

Limnaea stagnalis, and Bithynia prefer Azotobacter, while Coretus corneus selects Bac. subtilis.

In food selectivity studies, the radioactivity of the consumer must be determined by a brief experiment and immediately after its removal from the test vessels. This is required in order to measure the radioactivity of the food in the intestine before the tagged material has passed into the body of the consumer.

Several publications deal with the assimilability of different foods. Sorokin (1963, 1966; Sorokin et al., 1965) has developed procedures for introducing radioactive carbon into algae and bacteria and a method for determining the assimilability of food by consumer organisms.

Thus, the feeding of cladocerans was studied with natural water, and that of chironomid larvae in Petri dishes containing silt with tagged bacteria or algae. At the end of the experiment, the consumers were transferred to pure water containing natural (nontagged) food until their intestines became free of radioactive food. Afterward their radioactivity was determined by means of a Geiger counter. The quantity of carbon per unit of radioactivity could be easily calculated from the initial radioactivity of the food. This equivalent, multiplied by the radioactivity of the consumer, yields the amount of food carbon consumed.

Sorokin expressed the daily amount of consumed food as a percentage of the consumer weight in order to show the nutritive value of the different foods. He found that chironomid larvae readily eat bacteria and blue-green algae present in the aquarium together with natural silt, while Daphnia consumes bacteria and protococcal algae.

A. V. Monakov and Yu. I. Sorokin (1959) examined the assimilation of protococcal algae by different cyclopid species. Although the algae were found in the intestines of all the cyclopid species, one of the latter, namely, Diaptomus graciloides did not utilize them at all, while Acanthocyclops viridis and Mesocyclops leuckartii consumed only negligible amounts of them. By means of this method Sorokin and workers of the Institute of Biology of Inland Waters studied the consumption of bacteria by infusorians, rotifers, predatory and filtering cladocerans, copepods, oligochetes, mollusks, and fish larvae (Sorokin, 1963, 1966). The radioactive carbon method is undoubtedly of great value in determinations of the secondary productivity of water bodies.

Using the isotope method, Sorokin (1957) was able to demonstrate a mass accumulation of zooplankton over the former bed of the Mologa in the Rybinsk Artificial Reservoir at a depth of 8—12 m, in a zone of active chemosynthesis involving the oxidation of methane produced in the bottom sediments (Figure 63).

A similar phenomenon was reported by Sorokin in the Cheremshan inlet of the Kuibyshev Artifical Reservoir, where an oxidation of hydrogen sulfide took place and the chemosynthesis was accompanied by a luxuriant development of hydrogen sulfide-oxidizing bacteria (Figure 104).

Finally, E. F. Manuilova (1953) observed a decrease in the density of bacteria in water samples from the Rybinsk Artificial Reservoir after the introduction of zooplankters at a concentration corresponding to that in the reservoir. Similar results were obtained by Yu. S. Belyatskaya-Potaenko (1964) with the zooplankton of Lakes Naroch' and Baturin, and by

M. E. Gambaryan (1964) with the zooplankton of Lake Sevan. According to A. G. Rodina, D a p h n i a requires a minimal concentration of 50,000 bacteria per ml.

Oligotrophic lakes have a scant bacterial population whose food value is still open to question. In eutrophic lakes, on the other hand, filtering organisms can appreciably decrease the bacterial density in view of the vast volume of filtered water.

Relationships between the Phytoplankton and the Aquatic Microflora

The literature contains contradictory information about the effect of the phytoplankton and aquatic vegetation on the aquatic bacteria. Some authors believe that the bacteria feed on organic products of the metabolism and decomposition of the phytoplankton. Others regard algae as a source of toxic substances that inhibit the growth of the aquatic microflora.

In an attempt to solve this problem, A. S. Razumov (1962) tried to determine the distribution of bacteria on phytoplankton organisms, the effect of algae on the reproduction rate of bacteria in cultures, and the specific circumstances under which bacteria can utilize organic compounds produced by algae.

Inoculation of plankton from several lakes on dishes containing meat peptone agar showed that many live phytoplankters have a sterile surface (A. S. Razumov, 1948a, 1962). To this category belong various species of M e l o s i r a, F r a g i l l a r i a, T a b e l l a r i a, A s t e r i o n e l l a, N a v i - c u l a, S y n e d r a, A p h a n i z o m e n o n, A n a b a e n a, M i c r o c y s t i s, O s c i l l a t o r i a, C h l a m i d o m o n a s, E u d o r i n a, P a n d o r i n a, S c e n e d e s m u s, P e d i a s t r u m, A n k i s t r o d e s m u s, etc. Thus, Razumov was able to prove that the surface of live plankters is free of saprophyte microflora.

Similar results are obtained by microscopic examination of phytoplankters in preparations of membrane filters. The cell surface of these organisms is usually clean, with only a rare bacterial cell attached to a diatom valve or resting on the surface of a blue-green alga.

It can be said, as a rule, that live phytoplankters lack a bacterial microflora. Exceptions are some filamentous algae, such as V a u c h e r i a, C l a d o p h o r a, which possess solid cell walls without mucus. These forms are usually fouled up by numerous plant and animal epiphytes.

The effect of the phytoplankton on bacterial growth can be determined only in laboratory conditions. Afterward, the obtained results can be applied to the lake.

A. S. Razumov (1962) attributes the sterility of the surface of planktic organisms to the secretion of bactericidal substances.

Filtrates of S c e n e d e s m u s q u a d r i c a u d a cultures inhibit the growth of C h l o r e l l a p y r e n o i d o s a (N. B. Zavarzina, 1955, 1959). The metabolic products of pure cultures of C h l o r e l l a v i r i d i s are toxic to some Gram-positive and Gram-negative bacteria (Pratt et al., 1944).

Conversely, it is also difficult to obtain a bacteriologically pure culture of the same Chlorella species or to purify an algal culture from Caulobacter vibrioides, to mention only two examples.

In order to determine the effect of the phytoplankton on lake bacteria in natural conditions, A. S. Razumov calculated the generation time of saprophytes and the total density of bacteria in natural water from the Klyazma Artificial Reservoir with and without a previous removal of the phytoplankton by filtration through a cotton filter. The following figures show the effect of the phytoplankton on the density of bacteria as expressed in thousands of cells per ml (after A. S. Razumov, 1962):

Conditions of test	Initial number of bacteria	Number after 24 hours	Generation time, hours
Nonfiltered water	8,222	14,522	26.4
Filtered water	6,576	83,433	5.1

On the basis of numerous experiments after the above scheme, Razumov concludes that the removal of phytoplankton from the water increases the density of bacteria and shortens their generation time. In other words, it was found that water bloom adversely affects the density of bacteria. A similar relationship was reported by V. G. Drabkova (1965) for Lake Punnus-Yarvi in Leningrad Region.

Let us now discuss the conditions in which organic substances produced by algae can be utilized by bacteria.

The decrease of the density of bacteria in the Ucha Artificial Reservoir during periods of luxuriant algal growth has been attributed to a depletion of the organic resources of water (K. A. Guseva, 1941).

Munro and Brock (1968) examined the consumption of low concentrations of organic compounds dissolved in sea water in the presence of a mixed culture of algae and bacteria. They used for this purpose C^{14}-labeled acetate at concentrations ranging from 10 to 5,000 $\mu g/L$.

By means of radioautography they were able to demonstrate that only the bacteria assimilated the labeled acetate. On these grounds they concluded that algae do not utilize more than negligible amounts of organic matter in the sea.

In fresh waters, where the concentration of assimilable organic substances does not exceed 1–2 mg/L, the algae probably live as photoautotrophs and do not compete with bacteria for organic matter.

The density of bacteria in lake water increases considerably during storage of the water in the laboratory. This fact has been explained as follows.

In laboratory conditions, the introduction of dead phytoplankton into the water causes a luxuriant growth of saprophyte bacteria (Waksman et al., 1937) (Table 37). However, the density of saprophyte bacteria decreases even below the control level following the introduction of a live culture of Nitzschia closterium.

The nature of the substances released by algae into the surrounding medium was first established by Ya. Ya. Nikitinskii (1930). His conclusion that the release of organic compounds into the medium results from the autolysis of old dying cells was later confirmed by B. S. Aleev (1933, 1936). These products are largely nitrogenous and can be utilized by bacteria.

TABLE 37. Effect of diatoms on the reproduction of saprophyte bacteria and the consumption of oxygen in sea water

Time from beginning of test, hours	Sea water		Sea water + 10 mg of dried diatoms	
	consumption of oxygen, mg/L	density of bacteria, thousands per ml	consumption of oxygen, mg/L	density of bacteria, thousands per ml
0	0.0	10.4	0.0	10.4
12	0.057	690	1.12	2,000
24	0.21	770	1.93	1,290
36	0.27	850	2.20	1,310
48	0.47	—	2.46	—
60	0.54	600	2.80	750
96	0.71	—	3.66	142
132	1.12	6.1	3.80	109

Microscopic examination of dying plankton collected during a shift from one dominant form to another in the lake reveals an intensive development of bacteria on dead and decaying fragments of algae. Some coenobia of Anabaena collected from the Tsymlyanskii Artificial Reservoir during such a period were found to be densely strewn with Caulobacter cells (S. S. Belyaev, 1967).

Fogg and co-workers (1965) used isotopes in their study of the ability of algae to release organic substances into the environment. Lake water with phytoplankton was placed in jars containing a solution of $Na_2C^{14}O_3$. The jars were incubated in the lake. The radioactivity of the plankton was determined at the end of the test, and the same was done with the filtrate after removal of the labeled carbonates. It was found that between 7 and 50% of the organic products of photosynthesis leave the algal cells. According to laboratory experiments, the release of organic substances is greater at poor illumination (1,000 lux) and at very strong illumination; moreover, it varies directly with the density of the population and the duration of exposure to $Na_2C^{14}O_3$ and increases if the plankton consists of different algal species. The authors believe that the released organic substances can be used by bacteria and exert a strong influence on the trophic relationships of the lake bacteria.

One of the crucial factors affecting the development of bacteria in lakes and artificial reservoirs is the supply of allochthonous dissolved organic compounds arriving with tributaries and surface waters.

Such is the conclusion of S. I. Kutnetsov, V. I. Romanenko, and N. S. Karpov (1966), who have studied the heterotrophic assimilation of CO_2 in the Rybinsk Artificial Reservoir. Their observations in 1964 and 1965 have shown that the annual production of bacterial biomass exceeds the photosynthesis of organic matter by the phytoplankton. This can occur only if the majority of the bacteria determined by direct microscopic counts live heterotrophically as oligocarbophiles that feed on organic compounds dissolved in the water.

The methods for the study of the lake microflora have steadily improved during the last fifty years. Today we know that lake water contains hundreds of thousands and even millions of bacteria per ml, while the bacterial count of raw silt is of the order of billions per gram in eutrophic lakes. The density of bacteria in water depends on their reproduction rate and their consumption by the zooplankton and zoobenthos. The generation time of bacteria normally ranges from several hours to a number of days; it depends largely on the water temperature and the presence of assimilable organic substances, of which a concentration as low as a few mg per liter can support bacterial growth.

The application of electron microscopy to the study of the aquatic microflora will possibly reveal a whole world of minute forms that remain invisible under the light microscope.

After about forty years of research in the distribution of lake bacteria, the following major conclusions can be made.

Microscopic procedures for counting bacteria in lake water have shown that the density of bacteria varies from hundreds of thousands to several millions per ml, according to the trophic conditions in the lake. The actual figure, however, may be even higher, since the electron microscope detects forms invisible under the light microscope.

Only a fraction of the microscopically visible microorganisms grow in conventional media. The specific composition of the bacterial population of lakes remains therefore only partly known. Isotope procedures (C^{14}) lead to the conclusion that the unknown microorganisms are heterotrophs capable of utilizing minimal concentrations of allochthonous and autochthonous organic substances dissolved in water. The biomass produced by these bacteria is considerable and corresponds to the primary production of the phytoplankton.

In view of the vast production of bacterial biomass and the negligible fluctuations of bacterial density as a function of time, it can be assumed that invertebrates consume a considerable part of the bacteria. In other words, it can be said that bacteria constitute an important component of the diet of the zooplankton and zoobenthos. Bacteria are especially numerous in lake silts (see above). The density of saprophyte bacteria varies inversely with depth into the silt, reaching nil at a depth of 2—3 m.

The microbial mineralization of organic matter is most intensive at the silt surface; it vanishes at a depth of about 20 cm in oligotrophic lakes and 60—100 cm in eutrophic lakes.

Transformations of Organic Matter in Lakes

The transformations of organic matter represent one of the most important phenomena that take place in a body of water. They are closely associated with the transformations of different biogenic elements, notably nitrogen. Since the transformations of nitrogen will be discussed separately, here we shall deal mainly with the synthesis of organic matter from CO_2 and the breakdown of organic compounds to mineral components. The decomposition of proteins is described in the chapter on the transformations of nitrogen.

The Origin of Organic Matter in Lakes

The organic matter of lakes has a twofold origin. Part of it is allochthonous, that is, it enters the lake in a preformed state. The other part is autochthonous, which means that it results from the photosynthetic activity of plants in the lake. Both categories of organic matter enter a variety of transformations in the lake and provide food for all the heterotrophic organisms, either directly or by means of other organisms. In the final analysis, these transformations involve a gradual breakdown of organic matter. Even the autotrophic organisms participate in this breakdown, since part of the organic matter synthesized by them is utilized by the same organisms as a source of energy. However, most of the breakdown of organic matter is due to the activity of heterotrophs — animals and especially bacteria. Indeed, bacteria are responsible for the decomposition and mineralization of the remains of dead animals and plants.

Like other products of the breakdown and mineralization of organic matter, carbon reenters the cycle of transformations in the form of CO_2, which can be utilized by autotrophic organisms.

Not all the allochthonous or autochthonous organic matter in lakes undergoes destruction and mineralization. Part of the organic matter leaves the lakes in a variety of forms and ways — dissolved or suspended in water flowing out of the lake, or in the bodies of animals and plants leaving the lake (the emergence of the imagines of aquatic insects, fishing, consumption of aquatic animals and plants by birds, etc.), or as gaseous products of the anaerobic decomposition of silt (methane, CO_2).

In the vast majority of lakes, an unchanged fraction of the organic matter settles on the bottom in the form of organic sediments. A variable part of these sediments undergoes a subsequent breakdown and mineralization, depending on the specific conditions in the lake. The rest of the sediments are subjected to extremely slow geochemical transformations that lead to a variety of fossil rocks containing a large proportion of organic matter.

Microorganisms are responsible for a major part of the organic transformations in lakes. After a brief outline of the role of the phytoplankton and bacteria in the synthesis of organic matter, particular attention will be devoted to various aspects of the bacterial decomposition of organic compounds.

The primary production of organic matter in lakes is due mainly to the phytoplankton and higher aquatic vegetation. To determine the role of the higher vegetation in the production of organic matter in lakes is a comparatively easy task. Matters are different with the phytoplankton and bacteria. Indeed, the conventional methods of quantitative hydrobiology cannot reveal the magnitude of organic production by phytoplankton and bacteria; at best, they show only the existing biomass and its changes in the course of time.

The same is true of most hydrochemical methods. These can show only the existing quantity of a chemical or biological component at a given moment, without reference to the rate or magnitude of the simultaneous processes involving the synthesis and breakdown of this component.

Hydrobiologists are now trying to develop new methods for determining the rate and volume of the synthesis and breakdown of organic matter, both generally and with respect to its different components.

G. G. Vinberg has proposed a method for the determination of the overall synthesis and destruction of organic matter in the lake on the basis of the formation and utilization of free oxygen (Vinberg, 1934, 1937a, 1937b, 1960; Vinberg and Ivanova, 1935).

The application of microbiological procedures sheds light on the mechanism of destruction of organic matter in lakes. By determining the amount of microorganisms, it is possible to find the rate of the utilization of oxygen for the oxidation of organic matter in the water mass of the lake. Further, similar quantitative studies of different groups of microorganisms provide information on the breakdown pathways of different organic constituents of aquatic animals, phytoplankton, and higher aquatic vegetation.

On the basis of these considerations, all the processes that constitute the transformations of carbon in the lake will be divided broadly and conditionally into two groups: 1) processes leading to synthesis of organic compounds, that is, production of biomass in the lake; 2) processes involving the breakdown of autochthonous and allochthonous organic compounds.

It must be borne in mind that the formation of organic matter by photosynthesis is largely confined to the upper photic layers of the water mass, while the breakdown occurs throughout the depth range of the lake, including part of the silt.

Before entering into a detailed discussion of the synthesis of organic matter in the lake, it must be noted that the approach to this problem differs widely from one author to another. Writing on the classification of lakes, Thienemann (1925) determines the productivity as the degree of the development of life in the lake. Ström (1932) introduced a more precise terminology in connection with the productivity of lakes. He defined the production of organic matter in terms of its synthesis from inorganic compounds by the biological activity of organisms. In his view, the net production of the lake is represented by its silt sediments, while the gross production can be defined as the total amount of algae, live and dead, developed during a year and expressed as number of organisms, amount of organic nitrogen, etc.

Both Thienemann and Ström treat the productivity of lakes in close connection with the chemical transformations that take place there. This concept was later developed by several authors. G. G. Vinberg (1960) formulates it as follows: the "primary" or "gross" production is the amount of newly formed organic matter in the process of photosynthesis by the phytoplankton, while the "effective primary production" equals the quantity of photoautotrophic organisms produced during a given period. The latter value is smaller than the gross production because of the organic matter broken down in the course of the daily algal metabolism. In Vinberg's terminology, the "net production" is the difference between the gross primary production of plankton and the total amount of organic matter destroyed in the lake, regardless of its origin.

Some authors, notably G. S. Karzinkin, hold a different position. In their view (Karzinkin, 1952), the study of biological productivity in water bodies must be aimed at the growing of commercially important animals and plants. From this viewpoint, the productivity of a water body is defined in terms of its capacity to satisfy the requirements of its commercially valuable inhabitants (Karzinkin, 1952). In other words, the productivity of a water body is reflected in the yield of commercial items, for example, the annual catch of fish.

Thus, the very concept of productivity in water bodies has been the object of many discussions, with the participation of L. A. Zenkevich (1953), Ström (1932), L. L. Rossolimo (1934, 1964), G. G. Vinberg (1936a), G. S. Karzinkin (1952), S. D. Muraveiskii (1936), V. S. Ivlev (1945), G. V. Nikol'skii (1950), and others. In the final analysis, each of these authors retained his own position.

Since the following discussion will deal mainly with the role of microorganisms in the synthesis and breakdown of organic matter in lakes, such terms as gross, effective, and net production will be applied as defined by G. G. Vinberg (1960).

Photosynthesis by the Phytoplankton

The accumulation of dissolved organic compounds in lakes depends largely on the flow rate of the water entering and leaving. In lakes having a small catchment area and no tributaries, most of the organic matter is produced by the plankton and higher aquatic vegetation. Lakes with a greater flowage receive larger amounts of organic compounds via tributaries and surface and underground waters from the catchment area. Finally, most of the organic matter dissolved in artificial reservoirs, especially those with a higher rate of water exchange, is allochthonous.

The photosynthetic production of organic matter can be expressed by the following scheme:

$$CO_2 + H_2O \longrightarrow CH_2O + O_2 .$$

Clearly, one molecule of gaseous oxygen arises for each carbon atom that takes part in photosynthesis in the form of CO_2. Side by side with the liberation of oxygen in the course of photosynthesis, however, another process takes place, namely a consumption of oxygen in the respiration of the phytoplankton and the oxidative breakdown of organic matter by bacteria:

$$CH_2O + O_2 \longrightarrow CO_2 + H_2O .$$

This is the theoretical foundation of the methods for determining the production and breakdown of organic matter in water bodies. Oxygen change and radioactive carbon procedures are used for the determination of organic production, while the amount of destroyed organic matter is calculated from the consumption of oxygen.

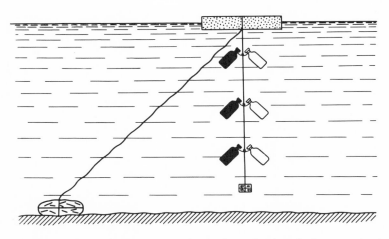

FIGURE 64. Scheme of an experiment for the determination of primary production of organic matter by the jar method (after Vinberg).

Briefly, the procedure is as follows. The water to be tested is placed in dark and light jars, which are incubated in the water body for a number of days at the same depth from which the water was collected for the analysis (Figure 64). The rate of breakdown of organic matter is determined from the decrease in the amount of oxygen dissolved in the water of the dark jar, while the difference in the oxygen content of the dark and light jars at the end of the incubation period shows the total magnitude of photosynthesis, which also represents the "primary" or "gross" production. The difference between the "gross" production and the "destruction" is the "net" production, which equals the net gain of photosynthesis. The latter magnitude is often negative.

The "oxygen jar" method has been thoroughly developed and introduced into practice by G. G. Vinberg (1934—1939, 1960).

The radioactive carbon method differs radically from the oxygen method. Indeed, by the oxygen method one can determine the rate of algal photosynthesis, the gross and net production, and the overall breakdown of organic matter, while the radioactive carbon method shows the summary amount of organic matter formed during the experiment by such processes as photosynthesis, chemosynthesis, and heterotrophic fixation of CO_2. The latter magnitude corresponds more or less to the "effective primary production" in the terminology of G.G. Vinberg.

However, the oxygen method faces two difficulties when applied to the primary production of seas and oligotrophic lakes, which possess a scant phytoplankton. First, photosynthesis is practically undetectable in such water bodies owing to the negligible increment of oxygen in light jars exposed for twenty-four hours. Second, the procedure requires that isolated samples of water be placed directly in the water for twenty-four-hour periods, which is obviously time-consuming for a research vessel that must cover great distances with a large number of stations.

To overcome these obstacles, Steemann-Nielsen (1952) proposed a method involving the use of radioactive carbon. This method can be outlined as follows. Water samples from different depths are distributed in jars of clear glass. Labeled carbon in the form of $Na_2C^{14}O_3$ is added to the water, and all jars are placed in a luminostat with a daylight lamp of given intensity. The CO_2 fixed in the course of photosynthesis enters the organic matter of the phytoplankton. The latter is removed by means of a membrane filter, and its radioactivity is determined in a Geiger counter. After making the necessary corrections for the intensity of illumination and the penetration of light into the water, the author calculates the organic production by photosynthesis per square meter of water surface.

In the USSR, this method has been modified by Yu. I. Sorokin (1956, 1959b) in that the photosynthetic activity of the phytoplankton is tested in water samples under natural illumination (see also Kuznetsov and Romanenko, 1963b). This procedure was later used, with some modifications by Saunders and co-workers (1962) at the Great Lakes.

TABLE 38. Scheme of an experiment for the determination of photosynthesis and chemosynthesis

Treatment of water	Conditions of the experiment	Processes determined
Not filtered	Light jar	Photosynthesis by bacteria and phytoplankton, chemosynthesis and heterotrophic assimilation of CO_2
	Dark jar	Chemosynthesis and heterotrophic assimilation of CO_2
Filtered through membrane filters of 5 microns porosity	Light jar	Photosynthesis and chemosynthesis by bacteria and heterotrophic assimilation of CO_2
	Dark jar	Chemosynthesis and heterotrophic assimilation of CO_2

In a somewhat more complex form (Table 38), this method can be used for determining the photosynthetic activity of green and purple bacteria, as well as the magnitude and rate of chemosynthesis and heterotrophic fixation of CO_2.

The production of organic matter as determined by the isotope method is necessarily smaller than the "gross" production, since the isotope method does not detect the secondary release of CO_2 during the respiration of the algae, which involves a partial oxidation of organic compounds produced photosynthetically during the experiment. On the other hand, this same magnitude must be more than the "net" production because the isotope method does not reveal the breakdown of allochthonous organic matter in the examined water sample. Further, if the organic production determined by the isotope method is less than the "net" production, we conclude that the cells of live or dead algae released soluble organic compounds, which readily passed the membrane filter used for removing the phytoplankton at the end of the test, and that the radioactivity of these compounds was not considered. Fogg et al. (1965) mention the possibility of such liberation of organic compounds from live algal cells.

The annual production of organic matter in the whole lake can easily be calculated on the basis of the lake morphometry and the results of periodic determinations of the organic production during the entire vegetation period at different depths.

Such determinations were made in the lakes Beloe and Chernoe in Kosino (G. G. Vinberg, 1934, 1948), Lake Sevan (M. E. Gambaryan, 1961, 1964), several American lakes (Goldman, 1960, 1964), the Rybinsk Artificial Reservoir (Yu. I. Sorokin, 1958a; V. I. Romanenko, 1966), and other water bodies.

Naturally, this method does not detect the entry of preformed organic matter from the catchment basin into the lake. The determination of the allochthonous organic matter requires a chemical analysis of the total amount of organic matter present in the surface and underground waters that enter the lake. In bogged-up water bodies it is also necessary to consider the erosion of the peaty shores.

The rate of the photosynthetic production of organic matter in lakes depends on the season and the type of lake. The daily rate of photosynthesis is greatest in eutrophic and lowest in dystrophic lakes (G. G. Vinberg, 1934, 1937). Table 39 shows the daily magnitudes of photosynthesis and respiration in the upper water layers of some lakes in the temperate zone of the European part of the USSR as determined by the oxygen method.

It is evident from the table that the summer value of diurnal photosynthesis in the trophogenous layer of the lake is usually twice as great as the overall destruction of organic matter in the same water layer. Clearly, photosynthesis attains such levels only in summer, when the phytoplankton finds optimal conditions for development. In some dystrophic lakes the breakdown of organic matter may exceed the daily rate of photosynthesis, especially when the lake receives a considerable inflow of allochthonous organic compounds from the catchment basin.

Various modifications of the radioactive carbon method are being widely used for determining the magnitude of photosynthesis by the plankton (Saunders et al., 1962; Goldman, 1960, 1963).

Steeman-Nielsen (1952) has made numerous measurements of photo-planktic photosynthesis during a trip around the world on board the Danish research vessel Galatea. According to his results, photosynthesis in the Pacific and Atlantic oceans attains a peak in areas where deep-sea waters containing a high concentration of biogenic elements ascend to the surface. These studies were expanded and confirmed by Yu. I. Sorokin (1959a, 1959b) and Sorokin and L. B. Klyashtorin (1961).

TABLE 39. Daily rate of photosynthesis and respiration (breakdown of organic matter) in the surface layer of the water of some lakes during the summer, mg O_2/L (after Vinberg, 1934, 1937; Romanenko, 1967)

Type of lake	Name of lake	Photosynthesis	Respiration in water mass	Daily balance
Eutrophic	Chernoe (Kosino, Moscow Region)	18.8	9.8	+9.0
	Beloe (Kosino, Moscow Region)	3.45	1.8	+1.65
	Dotka (Latvian SSR)	30.6	6.60	24.0
	Shingeide (Latvian SSR)	13.3	1.79	11.51
Mesotrophic	Glubokoe (Moscow Region)	1.2—1.8	1.1—0.8	+0.1—+1.1
	Glubokoe (of the Petrovo lake group in Kalinin Region)	2.5—3.5	1—2	+1.5
	Beloe (as above)	1—2	1	+1.0
	Svetloe (as above)	0.8—1.6	0.1—0.6	0.7—10
Dystrophic	Tatnoe (as above)	0.10	0.05	+0.05
	Chernoe (as above)	0.05	0.20	—0.15
	Melnezers (Latvian SSR)	0.55	0.68	—0.13

The vertical distribution of the phytoplankton must be taken into account in determining its photosynthetic activity. In highly transparent waters the marine phytoplankton often attains maximal density in the upper part of the thermocline, where a current of deep-sea water delivers biogenic elements. In such cases, sampling from standard horizons often misses the most trophogenous layer and yields too low values of phytoplanktic photosynthesis.

The main advantage of the radioactive carbon method is its high sensitivity. Indeed, the levels of photosynthesis in seas and oligotrophic lakes lie within the experimental error of the oxygen method. This is illustrated in Table 40, which shows the results of analyses by the radioactive carbon method with a theoretical conversion to oxygen values.

It can be seen in the table that the daily quantity of organic products of photosynthesis in seas and oligotrophic lakes is expressed in hundredths and thousandths of a milligram of carbon per liter. Such values can be accurately determined by the radioactive carbon method. Conversion to oxygen equivalents yields a magnitude of the order of hundredths of a milligram of oxygen per liter, since 1 mg of C corresponds to 2.7 mg O_2 (Table 40). In view of the fact that the sensitivity of the oxygen method does not exceed 0.05 mg O_2/L, it follows that this method cannot be used for determining the primary production of organic matter in seas or oligotrophic lakes.

Observations in the oligotrophic Lake Sevan (Kuznetsov and Gambaryan, 1960) have shown that the isotope method can be used for determining the magnitude of photosynthesis even when a twenty-four-hour exposure of isolated water samples in the lake does not cause an increment of oxygen. Although the maximal rate of photosynthesis in the surface water did not exceed 0.05 mg C/L (Table 40), the photosynthesis per unit area reached 100—150 mg C/m^2 in some places. This was due to the high transparency of the water, which allowed a penetration of light (and consequently, photosynthesis) to a depth of 20—30 m.

TABLE 40. Production of organic matter as a result of photosynthesis by the phytoplankton in the sea and some oligotrophic lakes

Origin of sample	Production of organic matter			References
	mg C per liter surface water per day	mg C per m² water surface per day	mg O₂ per day per liter	
Sea of Japan .... {	0.00013	0.0025	0.00035	Sorokin, 1959b
	0.12	1.9	0.324	
Pacific Ocean	0.003	0.11	0.0081	
Pacific Ocean, coastal zone of Hokkaido Island	0.013	0.18	0.035	
Atlantic Ocean, Canaries Current	0.0027	0.11	0.0073	Sorokin and Klyashtorin, 1961
Atlantic Ocean, South Equatorial Current	0.00083	0.189	0.00216	
Sargasso Sea	0.000109	0.0099	0.00022	
Naknek Lake, Alaska .... {	0.0103	0.164	0.028	
	0.0038	0.170	0.010	Goldman, 1960
Lake Brooks, Alaska	0.0019	0.088	0.005	
Lunzer Untersee	0.02	0.110	0 054	Rodhe, 1958
Lakes in Lapland .... {	0.022	0.025	0.0054	
	0.005	0.035	0.0135	
Erken, Sweden .... {	0.0019	0.040	0.0051	
	0.060	0.300	0.1620	
	0.200	0.560	0.540	
Lake Zürich	0.050	0.410	0.135	
Lesser Sevan	0.004	0.109	0.0108	Kuznetsov and Gambaryan, 1960
Greater Sevan .... {	0.0026	0.442	0.007	
	0.0048	0.099	0.013	
Baikal .... {	0.013	0.028	0.035	
	0.0206	0.046	0.056	Romanenko, 1965
	0.0184	0.041	0.050	
Lake Onega .... {	0.018	0.072	0.049	
	0.025	0.073	0.067	

In the Rybinsk Artificial Reservoir, which has an area of about 4,500 square kilometers, the phytoplanktic photosynthesis during the summer of 1956 ranged from 0.01 to 0.9 g C/m²/day, depending on the place (Yu. I. Sorokin, 1958a) (Figure 65). In order to determine more or less accurately the magnitude of photosynthesis for the whole reservoir within two or three days it was necessary to examine samples from about forty stations — clearly an impossible task by the oxygen method (Sorokin, 1958a).

Because of its advantages, the radioactive carbon method was widely used in the determination of the photosynthetic activity of the phytoplankton of Lake Baikal (Figure 66) (Kuznetsov, Romanenko, and Glazunov, 1964), the Gor'kii, Kuibyshev, and Mingechaur artificial reservoirs (Salmanov, 1959), and other bodies of water characterized by a large area and an irregular distribution of phytoplankton.

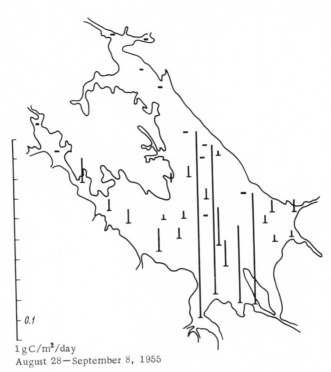

1 g C/m²/day
August 28—September 8, 1955

FIGURE 65. Daily production of organic matter as a result of photo-synthesis by the phytoplankton in the Rybinsk Artificial Reservoir during August 1956 (after Sorokin, 1958).

Observations of several artificial reservoirs by means of the isotope method during the entire vegetation period have revealed the average annual yield of organic matter as a result of photosynthesis (Table 41).

TABLE 41. Photosynthetic production of organic matter in artificial reservoirs in 1957

Artificial reservoir	In July, mg of C/m²/day	Year of filling	Year of analysis	Annual production, mg of C/m²	References
Rybinsk	296	1941	1956	51.2	Sorokin, 1958a
Gorki	510	1956	1958	73.2	Sorokin, Rozanova, and Sokolova, 1959
Kuibyshev . .	479	1957	1959	143.0	Salmanov, 1959
Mingechaur.	1,700	1957	1960	217.5	Salmanov, 1959

As shown in Table 41, the photosynthetic activity of the phytoplankton reaches a peak during the first and second years after the flooding of the artificial reservoir. In the Rybinsk and other "old" artificial reservoirs, the magnitude of photosynthesis approximates that observed in mesotrophic lakes.

Goldman and Wetzel (1963) have examined the primary production in Clear Lake, California, from May 1959 through July 1960. This large eutrophic subtropical lake has an area of more than 16,000 hectares and an average depth of 6.5 m. Its water is highly turbid throughout the year. Despite the high water temperature, thermal stratification develops rarely and only for brief periods.

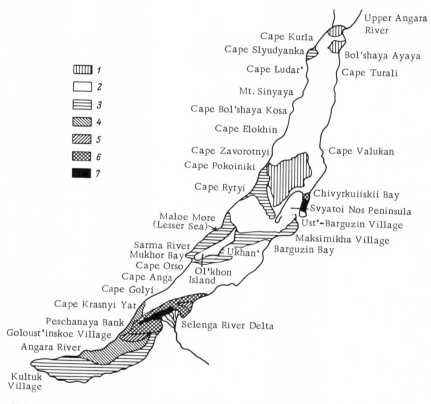

FIGURE 66. Photosynthetic activity of the phytoplankton in different parts of Lake Baikal during August 1964 (after Kuznetsov, Romanenko, and Glazunov).

In mg C fixed daily per m²: 1) 20—40; 2) 40—60; 3) 60—80; 4) 80—100; 5) 100—150; 6) 150—200; 7) 200—260.

The primary production was measured by the isotope method once a month in the central deepest part of the lake; similar measurements were made at some other stations for comparison. Determined were not only the total fixation of carbon by the large forms but also the share that the ultraplankton (<5—10 microns) of different depths has in this process.

The curves of the primary production typically showed two peaks. The production was low in winter and early spring but rose slightly later during the spring. In summer the production increased considerably to a peak in the fall before the sudden cooling that occurred in winter. It appears that the seasonal fluctuations of the production are not determined solely by illumination and temperature but depend also on turbidity, which increases during the winter rains. In the winter and spring, the size of the primary production varied considerably from one area to another owing to the great turbidity of water. Production was lowest in the vicinity of river mouths. The summer production was more uniform throughout the lake because of the greater transparency of the water.

TABLE 42. Comparison of the production of organic matter in the Tsimlyanskii Artificial Reservoir as determined by the oxygen and isotope methods (July 1965)

Site of sampling	mg O_2/L/day			mg C/L/day			
	primary production		break-down	primary production			photo-synthesis from C^{14} minus net production
	"gross" production	"net" production		"gross" production	"net" production	"photo-synthesis" from C^{14}	
June 1965							
Gorki at Yur'evets	2.34	1.95	0.39	0.878	0.731	0.517	−0.214
Kuibyshev:							
at Tetyushi	0.62	0.09	0.53	0.233	0.034	0.188	0.154
at Tol'yatti	1.52	0.42	1.10	0.570	0.158	0.341	0.183
at Shelanga	1.77	0.76	1.01	0.664	0.258	0.362	0.104
July 1965							
Tsimlyanskii Artificial Reservoir:							
at Verkhnaya Chirskaya	5.55	4.46	1.09	2.086	1.676	0.724	−0.952
at Popov	9.24	5.10	4.14	3.473	1.917	2.940	+1.023
at coast off Zhukovskaya	2.61	1.73	0.88	0.979	0.649	0.846	0.197
the center of Zhukovskii	1.53	0.90	0.63	0.574	0.336	0.220	−0.116
at the Ternovskaya Ravine	1.80	0.70	1.10	0.675	0.263	0.391	0.128
at Krasnoyarskaya	3.04	2.43	0.61	1.140	0.911	0.660	−0.251
opposite Popov	5.10	3.93	1.17	1.913	1.474	1.170	−0.304
at Nizhne-Chirskaya	3.44	2.51	0.93	1.290	0.941	0.355	−0.586
at Nizhne-Yablochnaya	4.26	2.57	1.69	1.589	0.964	0.145	0.181

The annual average daily primary production of Clear Lake was 0.4 g C/m² ranging from 0.002 g in February to 2.44 g in October. Calculated per hectare of water surface, this corresponds to 1,597.8 kg of carbon.

Other important determinations of the primary production of organic matter were made by Rodhe (1958) in Swedish lakes, notably Erken, in the Great Lakes (Saunders et al., 1962), and African lakes (Talling, 1965).

However, the primary production was determined in each case either by the oxygen method or by the isotope method. For this reason, a simultaneous measurement by both methods would be of particular interest, since it provides a better idea of the ecological circumstances under which photosynthesis takes place in different bodies of water. Such determinations of the primary production and destruction of organic matter were made by V. I. Romanenko, who used both methods in various parts of the Gorki, Kuibyshev, and Tsimlyanskii artificial reservoirs. Water for analysis was taken from the surface layer of the reservoirs (Kuznetsov and Romanenko, 1967). Table 42 shows the results obtained.

The daily primary production of organic matter reaches a very high level in many parts of the Tsimlyansk Artificial Reservoir, which shows distinct signs of eutrophy (Table 42). The rate of photosynthesis as determined by the isotope method was generally close to that of the net production, though in some places it was even above the latter, notably in areas of phytoplanktic death and autolysis. This suggests that some of the organic compounds synthesized during the experiment are released to the water as a result of the autolysis. Being in a dissolved state, these compounds passed through the membrane filter and could not be detected by the isotope method.

Photosynthesis by Pigmented Sulfur Bacteria

The photosynthetic production of organic matter by pigmented sulfur bacteria occurs in anaerobic conditions and does not yield molecular oxygen. Clearly, the oxygen method cannot be used for the determination of the organic production in such cases. The only alternative is the radioactive carbon method, whose setup is shown schematically in Table 38.

One of the best-studied water bodies with a large population of purple sulfur bacteria in the hypolimnion is the meromictic or bioanisotropic Lake Belovod' in Vladimir Region. Determinations of the photosynthesis of the phytoplankton and sulfur purple bacteria were made here by several authors (N. N. Lyalikova, 1957; G. A. Dubinina, 1958; Yu. I. Sorokin, 1966b).

As shown in Figure 67, during the summer of 1954 the surface layers of the lake contained dissolved oxygen to a depth of 13 m; the 13—24 m depth range was polluted with hydrogen sulfide, whose concentration attained 25 mg/L at the lake bottom. In July 1954, the water at the upper border of the H_2S layer had a pink color owing to the luxuriant growth of purple sulfur bacteria. Light penetrated to a depth of 16.5 m in the lake, that is, deeper than the peak zone of purple sulfur bacteria.

The photosynthetic activity of the purple sulfur bacteria was concentrated in a very narrow layer from 13.5 to 14 m, where the daily photosynthetic production of organic matter attained 0.42 mg C/L — nearly six times the production of phytoplankton in the surface water layer.

Further studies of the photosynthetic activity of purple sulfur bacteria in Lake Belovod' were made in 1964 by Yu. I. Sorokin (1966b), who showed that in 1964 the halocline descended to a depth of 15 m, while the layer of mass development of purple sulfur bacteria occupied a depth range of about 2 m, contrary to the observations of S. I. Kuznetsov (1942) and A. A. Egorova (1951), and performed vertical diurnal movements depending on the intensity of illumination (Table 43). Yu. I. Sorokin found that in late July 1964 the purple sulfur bacteria of the lake photosynthesized about $60 \mu g$ C/L/day, which is far lower than the $420 \mu g$ C/L/day determined by N. N. Lyalikova (1957) at a depth of 13.5 m in July 1954. According to Yu. I. Sorokin, the total daily photosynthetic production of purple sulfur bacteria in late July 1964 was 110 mg C per m^2, compared with an algal photosynthetic production of 500 mg C per m^2. Hydrogen sulfide diffuses at night from the lower layers and rises by dawn to a depth of 10 m (Table 43, Figure 68). The purple sulfur bacteria, notably C h r o m a t i u m, follow the H_2S and form a peak at a depth of 10 m by 05 00 hours (Yu. I. Sorokin). Thus, Sorokin maintains that the purple sulfur bacteria of Lake Belovod' perform diurnal vertical migrations of an amplitude of 3 m. These data contradict the findings of earlier authors and raise some doubts. A possible explanation is that the layer of maximal density of C h r o m a t i u m occupied a depth range of 2 m where the density did not exceed 46,000 bacteria per ml, while the density reported by N. N. Lyalikova (Figure 26) at a depth of 13 m exceeded 450,000 bacteria per ml; in other words, it appears that conditions for the development of purple sulfur bacteria in Lake Belovod' were unfavorable in 1964.

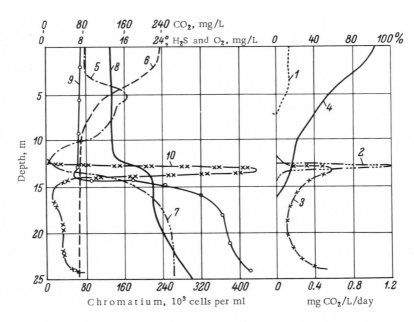

FIGURE 67. Photosynthesis by phytoplankton and purple sulfur bacteria in Lake Belovod' (after Lyalikova):

1) photosynthesis by the phytoplankton; 2) photosynthesis by purple sulfur bacteria; 3) chemosynthesis by thiobacilli; 4) penetration of light, % of the surface intensity; 5) oxygen; 6) temperature; 7) H_2S; 8) total CO_2; 9) electric conductivity; 10) density of C h r o m a t i u m.

TABLE 43. Concentration of H₂S and distribution of Chromatium during the 24-hour-period at the contact zone between the oxygen and H₂S layers (after Sorokin, 1966b)

Depth, m	July 29, 1964, a fine day										
	6 h			14 h			19 h		22 h		
	O_2, mg/L	H_2S, mg/L	Chromatium, thousands per ml	H_2S, mg/L	O_2, mg/L	Chromatium, thousands per ml	H_2S, mg/L	Chromatium, thousands per ml	H_2S, mg/L	H_2S, mg/L [sic]	Chromatium, thousands per ml
9	0.05	0	6	0.0	0.2	0	0	0	0	0	3
10	0.0	0.1	46	0	0.05	12	0	2	0	0.1	34
10.5	—	0.15	32	0	—	—	0	0	0	0.15	—
11	—	0.25	32	0.01	0.02	25	0	18	0.01	0.20	33
11.5	—	0.35	—	0.01	—	—	0	—	0.05	0.25	—
12	—	0.45	21	0.02	—	33	0.01	23	0.12	0.40	29
12.5	—	0.75	—	0.04	—	—	0.3	—	0.5	0.60	—
13	—	1.8	10	1.4	—	38	1.1	36	1.2	1.30	21
14	—	2.6	7	2.4	—	12	2.2	21	2.7	2.5	8
15	—	6.2	5	6.1	—	7	6.1	10	6.4	6.3	4
19	—	34	0.6	—	—	0.8	—	0.8	—	—	0.6
20	—	45	0.9	—	—	0.4	—	0.4	—	—	0.4
21	—	95	1.3	—	—	1.3	—	1.4	—	—	1.5
23	—	152	—	—	—	—	—	—	—	—	—

On sunny days, when light penetrates to a depth of 15 m, Chromatium consumes photosynthetically the hydrogen sulfide dissolved at a depth of 9—12.5 m; after the exhaustion of this compound it sinks to deeper waters. Between 13 00 and 19 00 hours the greatest density of Chromatium was observed at a depth of 13 m, where the H_2S concentration remains practically unchanged. On cloudy days, when light does not reach a depth of 10 m, photosynthesis does not occur at the indicated depth range; accordingly, the concentration of H_2S does not decrease and Chromatium does not migrate to deeper layers.

The variation in the penetration of light during the twenty-four-hour period caused vertical migrations of the purple sulfur bacteria and influenced accordingly the production of organic matter by the photosynthetic activity of Chromatium. At noon, for example, the layer of peak photosynthesis descended from a depth of 11 m to 12 m, while the absolute production per liter decreased.

Thus, the radioisotope method has assisted in determining the optimal conditions for the growth of purple sulfur bacteria in this lake.

Clearly, the luxuriant growth and peak photosynthetic activity of these bacteria in the upper layer of the H_2S zone of the lake could take place only in the presence of a sufficient supply of H_2S, which serves as hydrogen donor in the photosynthesis. The purple sulfur bacteria do not rise above this layer, where the presence of oxygen and the lack of H_2S make life impossible for them. On the other hand, photosynthesis in deeper water is inhibited by the scarcity of light.

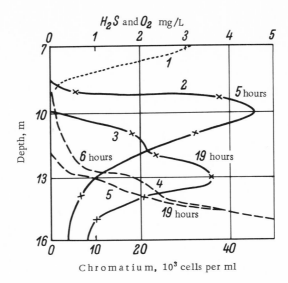

FIGURE 68. Diurnal migration of Chromatium in Lake Belovod' in connection with the photosynthetic oxidation of H_2S (after Sorokin).

1) oxygen; 2, 3) Chromatium; 4, 5) H_2S.

Chemosynthetic Production of Organic Matter in Lakes

Organic matter in lakes can also be produced by various processes of chemosynthesis, which derives energy by the oxidation of methane, hydrogen, hydrogen sulfide, ammonia, ferrous compounds, and other molecules formed by the anaerobic breakdown of organic components of silt.

Thus, the chemoautotrophic processes that take place in most water bodies complete the cycle of the transformation of organic matter with a fresh synthesis of bacterial protein from CO_2 and mineral salts. Chemosynthesis in water bodies can be regarded as a secondary process that, in the final analysis, utilizes the solar energy captured in organic compounds as a result of photosynthesis (G. G. Vinberg, 1934).

The main sources of energy available to chemosynthetic bacteria in lakes are the oxidation of methane, hydrogen, and reduced sulfur compounds.

$$CH_4 + 2O_2 = CO_2 + 2H_2O; \quad \Delta F = -195,000 \text{ cal.}$$
$$2H_2 + O_2 = 2H_2O; \quad \Delta F = -112,000 \text{ cal.}$$
$$H_2S + \tfrac{1}{2}O_2 = S° + H_2O; \quad \Delta F = -41,600 \text{ cal.}$$
$$S° + H_2O + 1\tfrac{1}{2}O_2 = H_2SO_4; \quad \Delta F = -118,500 \text{ cal.}$$

The free energy liberated in the process is utilized by the methane-oxidizing, hydrogen-oxidizing, and sulfur-oxidizing bacteria for the synthesis of organic matter. Thus, hydrogen bacteria consume 1,700 calories for the fixation of one CO_2 molecule (Sorokin, 1956), if molecular hydrogen

162

serves as reducing agent, or 112 calories if the reducing agent is water (Baas-Becking and Parks, 1927).

$$CO_2 + 2H_2 = (CH_2O) + H_2O; \quad \Delta F = +1,700 \text{ cal.}$$

The utilization of the obtained free energy can be more or less efficient; in Nitrosomonas (G. Lis, 1958) and Thiobacillus ferrooxidans (N. N. Lyalikova, 1958) this depends on the age of the culture.

Like the bacterial photosynthesis, the chemosynthesis of organic matter does not yield free oxygen. Such processes can be determined only by the radioactive carbon method. As already shown (Table 38), the analysis consists of incubating water with added $Na_2C^{14}O_3$ for twenty-four hours in the dark in a closed vessel at the natural temperature of the lake; afterward the bacteria are removed by means of a membrane filter and their radioactivity is determined by means of a Geiger counter.

In such conditions, however, heterotrophic organisms can also produce organic matter from CO_2. Indeed, the heterotrophic fixation of CO_2 involves this compound in anabolic processes via the Krebs cycle, though the energy necessary for these processes comes from the oxidation of organic compounds.

Yu. I. Sorokin (1961a) has determined the amount of CO_2 participating in the anabolism of about forty bacterial strains. For various species of heterotrophic bacteria this magnitude ranges from 1.5 to 18% of the bacterial biomass; for mixotrophic organisms it is 10—30% in the presence of carbohydrates. Hydrogen bacteria grown in the absence of organic matter (i. e., in conditions of chemosynthesis) produce all of their biomass from bicarbonate carbon.

In his studies of the heterotrophic fixation of CO_2 by the microflora of water samples from the Rybinsk Artificial Reservoir, V. I. Romanenko (1964a, 1964b) determined the proportion of bacterial biomass formed by a heterotrophic fixation of CO_2 during growth in natural water only or with added glucose or peptone. In experiments lasting a few hours, the proportion of heterotrophically assimilated carbon in the bacterial biomass reached a stable value of 6—7%.

Yu. I. Sorokin (1963) and V. I. Romanenko (1964a, 1964b) conclude on the basis of their results that the above method reveals the summary value of the chemosynthesis and the heterotrophic assimilation of carbon dioxide in natural waters.

In order to determine the contribution of chemosynthesis to the synthesis of organic matter, the magnitude of the heterotrophic assimilation must be subtracted from the total fixation of CO_2 by bacteria. The heterotrophic assimilation can be easily calculated by taking from 2 to 6% of the carbon of the bacterial biomass in the water sample where the magnitude of chemosynthesis is to be determined. The bacterial biomass is calculated from the average size of the cells in the given preparation and the total density of the bacteria as determined by the direct microscopic method. Table 44 shows the rate of chemosynthesis in different water bodies; the heterotrophic assimilation is taken here as equal to 6% of the bacterial biomass.

It is evident from these data that the chemosynthetic production of organic matter requires strictly defined conditions in order to attain an appreciable level. Thus, chemosynthesis accompanies the decomposition

TABLE 44. Chemosynthesis and heterotrophic assimilation of CO_2 by the natural microflora of different water bodies (after Sorokin, 1958b; Romanenko, 1965)

Water body	Water layer sampled	Depth, m	Gases in water	Chemosynthetic bacteria	C, mg/L/day		
					chemosynthesis + heterotrophic assimilation	heterotrophic assimilation (calculated)	chemosynthesis (from the difference)
Rybinsk Artificial Reservoir	Bottom	7	O_2	Absent	0.003	0.0007	0.0023
				Absent	0.0015	0.0048	0.0033
Rybinsk Artificial Reservoir over the Mologa bed (winter)	Surface	0	O_2	Absent	0.0044	0.0017	0.0027
	Bottom	17	O_2, CH_4, H_2	Hydrogen- and methane-oxidizing	0.0231	0.0015	0.0216
Kuibyshev Artificial Reservoir, Cheremshan inlet	Surface	0	O_2	Absent	0.004	0.006	−0.002
	Bottom	10	O_2, H_2S and CH_4	Sulfur- and methane-oxidizing	0.033	0.009	+ 0.024
		13	CH_4, H_2S	Sulfur-oxidizing	0.005	0.010	−0.005
Lake Belovod' (Vladimir Region)	Midwater	13	O_2, H_2S	Sulfur-oxidizing	0.150	0.003	+ 0.147
					0.0003	0.00039	−0.00009
Lake Onega, center	Bottom	63	O_2	Absent	0.00045	0.00029	+ 0.00016
					0.00021	0.00064	−0.00043

of silt into methane and hydrogen, as is the case in the Rybinsk Artificial Reservoir over the Mologa bed, or occurs in the presence of hydrogen sulfide formed by the bacterial reduction of sulfates. Several examples of intensive chemosynthesis are given below.

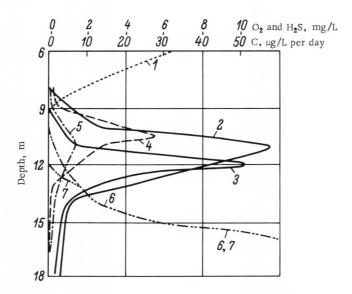

FIGURE 69. Decrease at the end of the day in rate of photosynthesis by purple sulfur bacteria and chemosynthesis by sulfur-oxidizing bacteria as a result of the exhaustion of H_2S in the border layer of water (after Sorokin):

1) O_2; 2, 3) photosynthesis by purple sulfur bacteria; 4, 5) chemosynthesis by sulfur-oxidizing bacteria; 6, 7) H_2S.

Yu. I. Sorokin has observed chemosynthesis by the oxidation of methane and H_2S in the Cheremshan inlet of the Kuibyshev Artificial Reservoir. At a depth of 11 m, where O_2, H_2S, and methane were present simultaneously, the daily rate of chemosynthesis reached $25 \mu g\,C/L$. The process was undoubtedly due to the oxidation of these gases by a biocenosis of methane-oxidizing bacteria and T h i o b a c . t h i o p a r u s.

Yu. I. Sorokin (1966b, 1966c) reports an interesting biocenosis of thiobacilli and purple sulfur bacteria in Lake Belovod'. Here the rate of chemosynthesis at a depth of $10-12$ m reached $20-27\ \mu g\,C/L$ per day, depending on the time of day (Figure 69). In the zone of peak chemosynthesis there was a competition for H_2S between the chemosynthetic and photosynthetic bacteria. During the second half of the day, the purple bacteria of this layer oxidized almost completely the H_2S supplied at night from deeper waters. This explains why the daily rate of chemosynthesis did not exceed $10 \mu g\,C/L$ in samples taken during the second half of the day. At night the photosynthetic activity of the purple bacteria of this layer ceased, the H_2S diffused to the lower boundary of the oxygen zone, and the chemosynthesis of T h i o b a c . t h i o p a r u s increased.

Production of Bacterial Biomass from Organic Compounds Dissolved in the Water

The attempts of A. S. Razumov (1962) and other authors to identify the food resources of the bacterial population as determined by the direct microscopic method have shown that this population consists essentially of heterotrophic bacteria capable of utilizing dissolved organic compounds.

In his study of the nutrition of the aquatic microflora, V. I. Romanenko (1964a, 1965) found that heterotrophic bacteria consume preformed organic compounds and at the same time fix about 6% of free CO_2. The biomass of heterotrophic bacteria in the Rybinsk Artificial Reservoir was determined on the basis of these data (S. I. Kuznetsov, V. I. Romanenko, and N. S. Karpova, 1966).

TABLE 45. Production of bacterial biomass in the total water mass of the Rybinsk Artificial Reservoir in 1964

	May 15	June 1	June 15	July 1	July 15	August 3	August 16	September 2	September 17	October 2
Volume of the reservoir, km³	17.5	18.9	20.3	19.5	18.7	17.7	16.7	16.2	15.7	14.8
Assimilation of CO_2, mg of C/m³/day	0.86	2.32	2.71	2.55	—	3.80	5.75	2.53	1.11	2.09
Assimilation of CO_2, tons/day in the whole reservoir	17.05	43.85	55.00	49.73	—	67.26	96.03	40.99	17.43	30.90
Production of bacterial biomass in the whole reservoir, tons/day	249.8	727.9	913.0	825.5	—	1,117	1,594	680.4	289.3	512.9

To find the daily increment of bacterial biomass in the Rybinsk Artificial Reservoir, these authors determined the heterotrophic assimilation of CO_2 by the isotope method (Table 45). The value obtained, expressed as carbon, was taken as 6% of the bacterial biomass (Romanenko, 1966). Thus, the biomass of the total number of bacteria (x) could be calculated from the equation:

$$x = \frac{a \cdot 100}{6} \ \mu g \ C \ \text{per liter per day},$$

where a represents the heterotrophic assimilation in μg C per liter per day.

S. I. Kuznetsov, V. I. Romanenko, and N. S. Karpova (1966) calculated by this method the production of bacterial biomass under 1 m² of water surface in the Rybinsk Artificial Reservoir during the vegetation period of 1964. The figure obtained easily led to the production of bacterial biomass in the whole reservoir. Table 45 shows the results of the analyses.

In addition to the biomass of heterotrophic bacteria (Table 45), which consume allochthonous and autochthonous organic compounds, these authors also calculated the production of organic matter as a result of photosynthesis by the phytoplankton. The values obtained are compared in Figure 70. It can be shown graphically that the production of bacterial biomass in the Rybinsk Artificial Reservoir during the entire vegetation period of 1964 amounted to 117,000 tons of carbon, which corresponds to 33 grams per m², while the photosynthetic activity yielded 102,000 tons of organic carbon in the whole reservoir or 29 g per m².

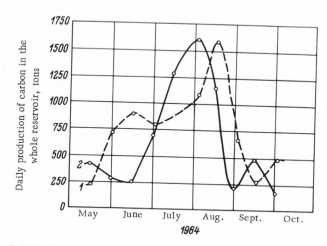

FIGURE 70. Production of bacterial biomass (1) and photosynthetic production of organic matter by the phytoplankton (2) in the Rybinsk Artificial Reservoir in 1964.

In other words, the biomass of bacteria that consume allochthonous and autochthonous organic compounds is roughly similar to the primary production of organic matter by the photosynthetic activity of the phytoplankton.

Since bacteria are an important food item for the zooplankton, it follows that they consume dissolved organic compounds that are unassimilable by the zooplankton and convert them into a readily assimilable biomass.

Mineralization of Organic Matter in Lakes

Organic matter can be formed within the lake by the photosynthetic activity of the phytoplankton and higher aquatic vegetation; in addition, it arrives from the outside with the surface waters of the catchment basin. Consequently, the mineralization affects not only remnants of phytoplankton and higher plants but also the dissolved or colloidal allochthonous organic compounds. The microflora that attack the different components of the plant remnants is more or less satisfactorily known and can be divided into several physiologic groups. However, less is known about microflora that breaks down the allochthonous dissolved and colloidal compounds. These materials are still poorly known and can be roughly classified in two groups:

colored humic substances and colorless substances. Some of the latter appear to be more easily assimilated by microorganisms. The bacteria that can utilize these substances are probably oligocarbophiles. They constitute the bulk of the microflora as seen under the microscope in the direct method. Morphologically, they represent sporeless rods and cocci. Much remains to be discovered about this microflora. Below we shall deal with species that participate in the mineralization of different organic compounds.

Microbiology of Cellulose

Cellulose is one of the most widespread compounds found in phytoplankton and higher aquatic plants. After the death of these organisms, cellulose undergoes decomposition, which can proceed both in the presence of air and anaerobically.

Chemically, cellulose is a carbohydrate whose molecule consists of 1,400–10,000 glucose units combined into a chain. Its molecular weight ranges from 200,000 to 2,000,000.

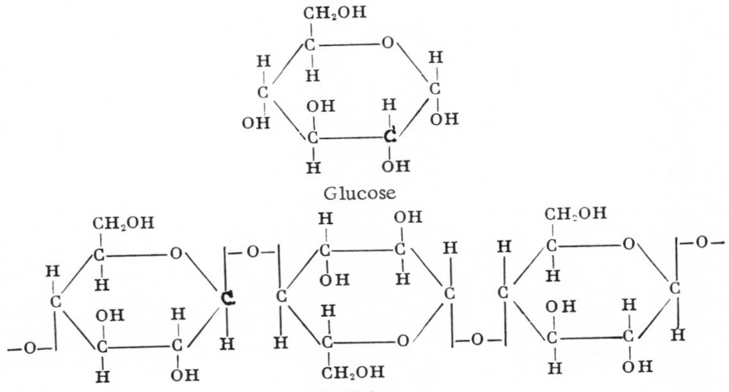

Glucose

Cellulose

Cellulose rarely occurs in a pure form in nature. In plants, it often forms complexes with lignin or other polysaccharides, which affects the rate of its decomposition by microorganisms.

Aerobic mesophilic organisms that attack cellulose. Hutchinson and Clayton (1919) gave the name of Spirochaeta cytophaga to a long, rodlike microorganism that they isolated from soil. Further studies by S. N. Vinogradsky (1929) showed that the aerobic bacteria that attack cellulose can be divided into three genera: Cytophaga, Cellvibrio, and Cellfallicula. Cytophaga is a long rod with pointed ends; Cellvibrio is a thin long slightly curved rod (Figure 71); Cellfallicula is a fusiform rod. All three are pigmented. As Vinogradsky correctly pointed out, they live strictly on cellulose and cannot break down glucose.

Cellvibrio develops best in a neutral or slightly alkaline environment, while Cytophaga prefers a slightly more acid reaction. Below pH=5.5, the decomposition of cellulose is carried out mainly by fungi.

Further investigation into the decomposition of cellulose has shown, however, that the aerobic bacteria that attack this compound belong to different taxonomic groups and can be divided among three orders of microorganisms (Imshenetsky, 1953):

Order	Genus
Myxobacteriales	Promyxobacterium, Cytophaga, Sporocytophaga, Sorangium
Eubacteriales	Micrococcus, Streptococcus, Bacterium, Achromobacter, Chromobacter, Pseudomonas, Vibrio, Bacillus
Actinomycetales	Mycobacterium, Proactinomyces, Micromonospora, Actinomyces

FIGURE 71. Bacteria that attack cellulose.

Cellvibrio.

Myxobacteriales, which include four genera capable of destroying cellulose (Table 46), are distinguished by the following signs. The unstained cells are somewhat dull under the microscope and lack distinct boundaries. A differentiated nucleus is absent. Cell division begins with a constriction rather than a formation of a partition. Although devoid of flagella, the cells can move by secreting a slime. The cells contain a pigment and perform bends and other creeping movements on the surface of a solid substrate. In the "swarming" stage, the cells gather into a compact mass that moves on solid substrates.

With the exception of Cytophaga and the family Promyxobacteriaceae, Myxobacteriales form fruiting bodies that consist of cysts united into a common slime and filled with contracted rods (Figure 72).

This group has been studied by A.A. Imshenetsky (1953); Dworkin (1966) has published a review of the biology of Myxobacteriales.

TABLE 46. Order Myxobacteriales

Genus	Fruiting bodies	Microcysts	Cell form
Promyxobacterium	Absent	Absent	Rod with rounded end
Cytophaga	Absent	Absent	Long, thin, with pointed ends
Sporocytophaga	Absent	Round or oval	Long, thin, with pointed ends
Sorangium, Archangium	Present	Angular	Thick rods, up to 8 microns long, with rounded ends

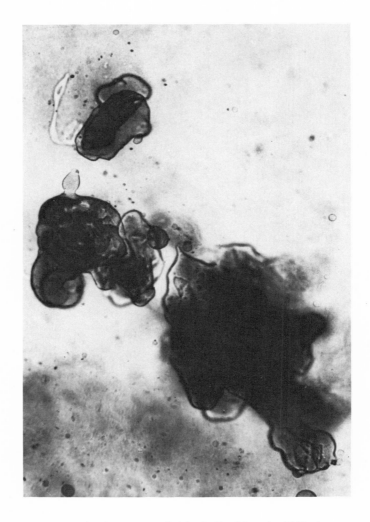

FIGURE 72. Archangium, fruiting bodies (photo by Zhilina).

The order Eubacteriales comprises a large number of cellulose-attacking species. According to A. A. Imshenetsky (1953), it is still poorly known. At any rate, the species of this group are not strictly specialized and destroy cellulose at a comparatively slow rate. As a rule, these organisms grow on meat peptone agar and stain Gram-negative. Many of them are pigmented and decompose glucose, while for the destruction of cellulose they require a medium containing casein hydrolysate, peptone, and yeast extract.

Some species of A c h r o m o b a c t e r and P s e u d o m o n a s also attack cellulose, though in laboratory conditions they develop better on glucose and other sugars than on cellulose. The breakdown of cellulose is usually more rapid in mixed cultures than in pure ones, possibly because the satellite microflora utilizes the products of the primary breakdown of cellulose. Further research has shown that a considerable number of microorganisms can attack cellulose. S. N. Vinogradsky has established the genus C e l l - v i b r i o for the typical vibrios that can destroy cellulose, while A. A. Imshenetsky maintains that these organisms should be placed in the genus V i b r i o. The commonest of these forms are V. v u l g a r i s and V. f u l v a. These species grow rapidly in tubes containing Hutchinson's medium with cellulose; turbidity appears within twenty-four hours at 28°. In contrast to C y t o p h a g a, the cultures of V. v u l g a r i s produce little or no slime; another distinction from Myxobacteriales is the appearance of numerous fine fibers of cellulose in the culture fluid after the tube is shaken.

Some species of Actinomycetales and spore-forming aerobic bacteria do attack cellulose but at a far slower rate in comparison with the cellulose bacteria; moreover, these do not comprise highly specialized forms.

Several fungi can utilize cellulose as a source of carbon and energy. To this category belong some species of A s p e r g i l l u s, C h a e t o n i u m, C u r v u l a r i a, F u s a r i u m, P h o m a, and T r i c h o d e r m a.

S p o r o c y t o p h a g a m y x o c o c c o i d e s was initially regarded as requiring cellulose (Dubos, 1928; S. N. Vinogradsky, 1929; A. A. Imshenetsky and L. I. Solntsevaya, 1936, 1937). Later it became clear, however, that the sterilization of glucose yields products that are toxic to a number of cellulose bacteria (Stanier, 1942). According to A. A. Imshenetsky (1953), it appears that all the aerobic cellulose-digesting bacteria can utilize such products of the hydrolysis of cellulose as cellobiose and glucose, and some of them, notably S o r a n g i u m, P r o m y x o b a c t e r i u m, and P s e u d o - m o n a s sp., assimilate starch, mono-, and disaccharides.

The typical cellulose bacteria readily assimilate inorganic nitrogen and cannot utilize some amino acids. The less typical forms, such as the sporulating and nonsporulating rods, require organic nitrogen.

The thermal range of cellulose bacteria extends from 10 to 37°, with 22–30° as optimum for most of them.

The breakdown of cellulose begins with enzymatic hydrolysis. The exoenzyme or group of exoenzymes produced by the cellulose-digesting microorganisms is known as cellulase. It catalyzes the breakdown of the insoluble cellulose to simpler, water-soluble products, that is, polysaccharides. These penetrate through the cell membrane; in anaerobic bacteria they are oxidized to CO_2, and the energy released in the process serves for biosynthesis.

Cellulase is an adaptive enzyme in most microorganisms. According to the Levinson group (Levinson et al., 1951), the hydrolysis of cellulose involves two enzymes, C_1 and C_x. These act in such a manner that the comparatively long chains left by C_1 are broken down further with the participation of C_x:

$$\text{Native cellulose} \xrightarrow{\text{Enzyme } C_1} \text{Compounds containing several glucose units} \xrightarrow{\text{Enzyme } C_x} \text{Cellobiose}$$

This follows from the fact that some microorganisms can grow only on the primary products of the decomposition and do not utilize cellulose.

Anaerobic mesophilic microflora that attack cellulose. As long ago as 1894, V. L. Omelyansky, following a suggestion by S. N. Vinogradsky, used selective media for the isolation of anaerobic cellulose-digesting bacteria. Thus he obtained enrichment cultures of two sporulating bacteria that break down cellulose into CO_2, hydrogen or methane, and fatty acids (Omelyansky, 1899, 1902). Later experiments with pure cultures (Clausen, 1931) revealed a picture somewhat different from that obtained by Omelyansky, namely that the only gaseous product of this fermentation is hydrogen and that methane does not appear.

The organisms in question were very similar morphologically to the form established by Omelyansky. They were given a variety of names, including Clostridium cellobioparus and Bac. celluloseae fermentans — actually synonyms of the species known as Bac. omelianskii. This microorganism is a motile rod measuring 0.2 × 4—12 microns. Its vegetative form produces terminal spores measuring 2 × 2.5 microns. It ferments cellulose and its hydrolysis products to form CO_2, H_2, ethyl alcohol, and acetic, formic, butyric, and lactic acids. Starch is not digested. Pure cultures of this species use peptone or a set of amino acids as sources of nitrogen, and only the enrichment cultures can grow on mineral nitrogen. This probably results from the vitamin requirements of Bac. omelianskii. This species is unanimously regarded as a strict anaerobe (A. A. Imshenetsky, 1953). It produces cellulase and cellobiase. However, saccharification of cellulose with enzymes isolated from this culture has not yet been demonstrated.

The gas released in the hydrogen fermentation of cellulose consists of H_2 and CO_2 (V. L. Omelyansky, 1899). Hydrogen predominates during the first days of fermentation, reaching 85% of the volume of the released gas. The fermentation products consist largely of acetic and butyric acids with an admixture of valeric acid and, possibly, formic acid. The proportion between acetic acid and all other acids varied greatly from one experiment to another — between 1:4 and 3:1. Sugars, proteins, or succinic acid were not found. In an experiment made by Omelyansky, the fermentation of 3.5 grams of cellulose for thirteen months yielded the following products: fatty acids 2.241 grams, CO_2, 0.972 gram, H_2 0.013 gram. On the whole, 3.347 grams of cellulose were actually broken down, yielding a total of 3.226 grams of fermentation products.

Thus, the anaerobic fermentation of cellulose produces a large amount of fatty acids that can be assimilated by other anaerobic microorganisms with the formation of methane in the silt.

Methane-producing bacteria. Higher aquatic vegetation often grows luxuriantly in shallow lakes. Its dead remnants sink to the bottom, where they undergo an anaerobic breakdown to fatty acids and gases. The gas escaping from the lake sediments invariably contains a high proportion of methane. Studies of the mechanism of methane production in the anaerobic breakdown of organic matter began as long ago as the nineteenth century. Although the biological nature of the process was demonstrated at an early stage (Omelyansky, 1906), pure cultures of methane-producing bacteria were not obtained before 1936 (by Barker).

Because of the great difficulties in isolating and maintaining the pure cultures, many of the forms obtained were lost (Barker, 1956), and only Methanobacterium omelianskii could be kept for years in pure culture.

All the methane-producing bacteria are strict anaerobes. They grow better in semisolid media with added reducing agents.

A number of observations have shown that the methane-producing bacteria represent a highly specialized group that uses certain specific compounds as substrate but cannot assimilate carbohydrates or amino acids. Many of the utilized substrates are products of fermentations carried out by other bacterial species. To this category belong lower fatty acids containing 1 to 6 carbons, normal and isoalcohols with 1 to 5 carbons, and inorganic gases, notably hydrogen, carbon monoxide, and carbon dioxide. Some compounds that can be assimilated by methane-producing bacteria are listed below.

Acids	Alcohols	Gases
Formic	Methyl	Hydrogen
Acetic	Ethyl	Carbon monoxide
Propionic	n-propyl	Carbon dioxide
n-butyric	Isopropyl	
n-valeric	n-butyl	
n-caproic	Isobutyl	
	n-valeric	

In enrichment cultures, methane appears when the organic substrate is one of the following acids: caprylic, isobutylic, stearic, oleic, benzoic, phenylacetic, oxalic, or succinic; the same result is obtained with acetone or 2,3-butylene glycol. The decomposition of these compounds with the formation of methane can be explained as follows: the accompanying bacteria first destroy cellulose, proteins, and hemicellulose to short-chain fatty acids or alcohols, which are then broken down by the methane-producing bacteria.

Although the group of methane-producing bacteria comprises a number of species, some organisms are highly specific with respect to the substrate.

The classification of these bacteria is based on their morphology and physiology (Barker, 1956).

According to Barker, all these species should be united into a single family because of their physiologic traits.

Classification of the Methane Bacteria
Family Methanobacteriaceae
A. Rods
    I. Non-spore-forming Methanobacterium
       1. M. formiricum. Produces methane from formates or carbon monoxide and hydrogen
       2. M. propionicum. Produces methane from salts of propionic acid
       3. M. söhngenii. Produces methane from acetates and butyrates
    II. Heat-resistant sporelike bodies formed
       M. omelianskii. Produces methane from hydrogen and carbon dioxide
B. Cocci
    I. Cells not collected in packets — Methanococcus
       1. M. mazei. Produces methane from acetates and butyrates
       2. M. vannielii. Produces methane from formic acid and also from hydrogen and carbon
         dioxide
    II. Cells collected in packets — Methanosarcina
       1. M. barkerii. Produces methane from methanol, carbon monoxide, and hydrogen
       2. M. methanica. Produces methane from acetates and butyrates

Barker and co-workers have studied in detail the mechanism of the production of methane from the above-mentioned substrates. They have shown (Barker, 1956) that Methanobacterium omelianskii oxidizes ethyl alcohol to acetic acid, in which process the carbon dioxide is quantitatively reduced to methane:

$$2CH_3CH_2OH + CO_2 \rightarrow 2CH_3COOH + CH_4 .$$

The oxidation of the alcohol ceases when all the CO_2 is exhausted. Sulfates or nitrates cannot replace CO_2.

The fermentation of butyrate by Methanobacterium suboxydans proceeds in a similar manner. Stadtman and Barker (1951) have shown that the process can be represented by the following reaction in which CO_2 is similarly reduced to methane:

$$2CH_3CH_2CH_2COOH + 2H_2O + CO_2 \rightarrow 4CH_3COOH + CH_4 .$$

Scheller has found that the methyl alcohol is easily broken down by Methanosarcina according to the equation:

$$4CH_3OH - 3CH_4 + CO_2 + 2H_2O ,$$

where methane originates directly from the reduction of methyl alcohol and does not arise from the reduction of CO_2.

Using methyl-labeled acetate, Stadtman and Barker (1949, 1951) have demonstrated that several cultures convert the methyl carbon of acetate into methane.

Finally, Methanobacterium omelianskii reduces CO_2 to CH_4 in the presence of hydrogen but cannot do so when only the carbon compound is present (Kluyver and Schnellen, 1947).

Anaerobic cultures of Methanobacterium omelianskii in alcohol-containing media invariably consist of long thin rods and short thick ones (Bryant et al., 1967). Cultivation in a mineral medium in an atmosphere of hydrogen and CO_2 deprived the culture of the ability to grow in alcohol-containing media. Using a solid medium, Bryant and co-workers have divided the culture into two forms.

The long rods developed in an atmosphere of hydrogen and CO_2 but not in alcohol-containing media. The short thick rods grew on a medium containing ethyl alcohol and produced only small quantities of acetate and hydrogen. The latter inhibited its growth. Inoculation of both strains in a medium with ethyl alcohol resulted in an abundant production of methane. Bryant and co-workers believe that one of the strains utilizes alcohol and liberates hydrogen, which is used by the second strain for the reduction of CO_2 to methane.

Evidently, the production of methane in nature involves a whole biocenosis of different bacterial species.

Methanosarcina barkerii reduces carbon monoxide to methane in two stages:

$$CO + H_2O \rightarrow CO_2 + H_2 ,$$
$$CO_2 + 4H_2 \rightarrow CH_4 + 2H_2O$$

All these studies suggest that monocarbon compounds are not present among the intermediate products along the pathway leading to methane.

Barker (1956) has suggested a scheme of the formation of methane from acids and alcohols on the basis of a comparative study of the acetate and methanol fermentations and Van Niel's theory of the reduction of CO_2 (Figure 73).

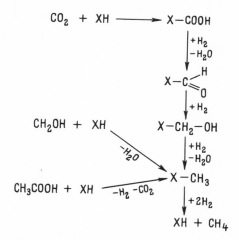

FIGURE 73. Scheme of the production of methane from fatty acids and alcohols (after Barker).

According to this scheme, CO_2 combines with a certain organic compound, XH, forming a carboxylated derivative, which later undergoes three successive stages of reduction to a methyl compound. The latter is further reduced to methane, and the CO_2 acceptor, namely XH, is regenerated. It is assumed that the methanol and acetate formed along the CO_2 reduction pathway can also react with XH and form the intermediate product X-CH₃. According to Barker, ATP can supply the necessary energy for these endergonic reactions, and a coenzyme can function as the intermediate compound XH.

175

E. S. Pantskhava (1967) has investigated the synthesis of methane from H_2 and CO_2. He has proposed the following scheme of the process (Figure 74) on the basis of his own data and those published in the literature.

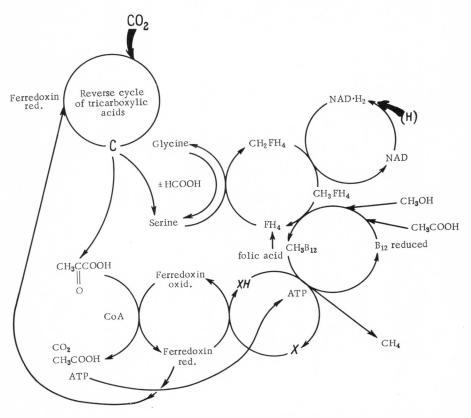

FIGURE 74. Modified scheme of the production of methane from carbon dioxide and hydrogen (after Pantskhava).

According to this scheme, Methanobacterium omelianskii assimilates CO_2 via the ribulose diphosphate cycle with the formation of phosphoglyceric acid, which is later converted to serine or pyruvic acid. The serine carbon then probably undergoes reduction through the folate cycle to 5-methyl-tetrahydrofolic acid (methyl $N^5 FH_4$). As in the synthesis of methionine, $NAD \cdot H_2$ probably serves as reducing agent in this reaction. Further, methyl $N^5 FH_4$ transfers the methyl group to reduced B_{12}, converting the latter to CH_3-B_{12}. At this stage, preformed methyl groups of methanol and acetic acid can join the process. At any rate, this is only a hypothetical scheme, since the agent that carries methyl groups between these substrates and B_{12} has not yet been established, although an enzymatic synthesis of CH_3-B_{12} from methanol has been demonstrated in Methanosarcina barkerii.

In the presence of ATP, H^+, and e, methyl-B_{12} decomposes into CH_4 and reduced B_{12}. This reaction was observed in cell-free extracts of M. barkerii and Methanobacterium omelianskii.

The hydrogen for the production of methane from methyl groups and for the reduction of B_{12} apparently comes from pyruvic acid, which reacts with oxidized ferredoxin, CoA, and inorganic phosphate to form reduced ferredoxin, acetate, CO_2, and ATP. The methyl is reduced to methane while the reduced ferredoxin is converted to the oxidized form either directly or by means of some intermediate compounds.

Since ferredoxin has been demonstrated in these bacteria, it can be assumed that the assimilation of CO_2 follows the reverse Krebs cycle and does not proceed along the ribulose cycle.

Hydrogen Bacteria

Like the methane-oxidizing bacteria, the bacteria that oxidize hydrogen exert a great influence on the oxygen regime of autrophic lakes. As we showed previously, the anaerobic breakdown of organic matter yields hydrogen and methane, which escape from the lake sediments and are oxidized by bacteria in the presence of dissolved oxygen as they traverse the aerated water mass of the lake.

The oxidation of hydrogen yields free energy, which can be utilized in the metabolism of many bacteria:

$$H_2 + \tfrac{1}{2}O_2 = H_2O; \ \Delta F = -57,000 \text{ calories.}$$

However, all the bacteria of this group are mixotrophs. They can grow not only in autotrophic conditions by using the energy derived from the oxidation of hydrogen but also heterotrophically on conventional media. Morphologically they closely resemble one another, the differences between them being of a secondary nature only. All of them are solitary Gramnegative rods with round ends. They vary greatly in size and often contain deposits of poly-β-oxybutyric acid. With the exception of the spore-forming rod Bacillus pantotrophus (Kaserer, 1906), all of them can be placed in the genus Pseudomonas because of their ability to grow in conventional media with an organic ingredient.

The group of hydrogen bacteria comprises the following species: Bac. pantotrophus (Kaserer, 1906), Bac. hydrogenes (Lebedev, 1910), Hydrogenomonas flava (Niklewski, 1908, 1910), Hydrogenomonas vitrea (Niklewski, 1908), Bac. pycnoticus (Ruhland, 1924; Grohmann, 1924), Hydrogenomonas facilis (Schatz and Bovell, 1952), a Hydrogenomanas species related to the former (Schlegel, 1954a, 1954b) (Figure 75), and others.

All these bacteria can grow in a mineral medium, assimilating CO_2 with the energy obtained from the oxidation of hydrogen. It was shown, however, that many saprophyte bacteria consume gaseous hydrogen though not as a source of energy for the fixation of CO_2 (M. I. Belyaeva, 1954).

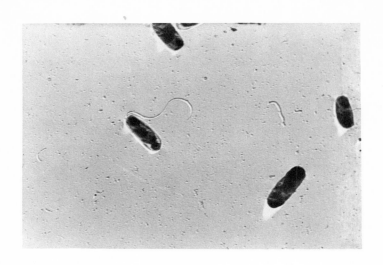

FIGURE 75. Hydrogenomonas sp.

Hydrogenomonas facilis is probably the best known member of the group from a physiological and biochemical viewpoint. This obligate aerobe is rodshaped, 0.3×2.5 microns, with one or two polar flagella. It grows well in autotrophic and heterotrophic conditions. Although incapable of nitrification, it reduces nitrates to nitrites. It grows in an atmosphere of hydrogen where the concentration of oxygen should not exceed 30%. When grown autotrophically in the presence of excess hydrogen, however, this bacterium avidly consumes all the available oxygen. The concentration of phosphates in the medium exerts a major influence on the growth of hydrogen bacteria. The absorption of hydrogen by the bacterial suspensions is most intensive at pH 7−9, the extremes being pH 4.0 and 10.5. Bacterial growth, however, takes place in the narrower pH range of 5.5 to 8.6. For optimal growth, the culture medium must be well saturated with the gas mixture. The oxidation of the hydrogen proceeds very rapidly, the amounts of hydrogen and oxygen consumed within one hour being respectively $\frac{1}{16}$ and $\frac{1}{2}$ of the dry weight of the cells. When grown anaerobically, Hydrogenomonas facilis cannot take up hydrogen from any acid of the Krebs cycle, while in aerobic conditions it oxidizes a number of acids except oxalic, formic, and citric acids. It can be assumed, therefore, that the heterotrophic metabolism of this species involves only some parts of the Krebs cycle. There are indications in the literature that hydrogen bacteria possess a complete set of enzymes participating in the electron transfer chain (G. A. Zavarzin, 1964c). The oxidation of hydrogen is catalyzed by hydrogenase, which reduces the pyridine nucleotide; later the process continues with the participation of flavins, cytochromes b and c, and cytochrome oxidase, which carries out the final transfer of hydrogen to oxygen.

The oxidations of hydrogen and lactate proceed independently of one another (Kluyver and Manten, 1942). The high rate of CO_2 fixation in the heterotrophic growth of Hydrogenomonas facilis can be interpreted as an indication that this bacterium can utilize the energy obtained from the oxidation of organic compounds for an "autotrophic" assimilation of CO_2 (Lis, 1958).

The chemosynthetic activity of hydrogen bacteria produces intracellular reserve food in the form of poly-β-oxybutyric acid (Hirsch and Schlegel, 1962). Carbon dioxide is assimilated via the ribulose diphosphate cycle.

One of the major aspects of chemosynthesis is the pathway of the reduction of CO_2 to the cellular level.

In the case of hydrogen bacteria, the substrate that is being oxidized can serve as reducing agent. This process does not consume energy; the reduction of CO_2 can be catalyzed by hydrogenase, which activates TPN^+ according to the following scheme:

$$TPN^+ + H_2 \xrightarrow{\text{hydrogenase system}} TPN-H + H^+ .$$

The reduction of CO_2 by this pathway requires a very small amount of energy (Sorokin, 1956):

$$CO_2 + 2H_2 \rightarrow CH_2O + H_2O; \quad \Delta F = +1,700 \text{ calories}.$$

This probably explains the high percentage of free energy utilized by hydrogen bacteria.

Another scheme for the fixation of CO_2 involves water. Though less economical, it answers satisfactorily the balance of reaction products obtained by Schatz (1952):

$$6H_2 + 3O_2 \xrightarrow{\text{cytochrome}} 6H_2O + 210,000 \text{ calories}; \quad \text{(A)}$$

Of this energy, 70% is used for the decomposition of water:

$$160,000 \text{ calories (from reaction A)} + 4H_2O \rightarrow 4[H] + 4[OH];$$
$$CO_2 + 4[H] \rightarrow (CH_2O) + H_2O; \quad \text{(B)}$$
$$4[OH] \text{ (from reaction B)} \rightarrow 2H_2O + O_2 .$$

The overall reaction is

$$6H_2 + 2O_2 + CO_2 = (CH_2O) + 5H_2O .$$

According to Ruhland (1924), the development of hydrogen bacteria comprises two reactions: oxidation of hydrogen by oxygen and reduction of CO_2 with substrate hydrogen. In cultures of Bac. pycnoticus growing in the presence of CO_2, the ratio of absorbed hydrogen to oxygen (H_2/O_2) ranges from 2.3 to 2.6, the excess of hydrogen consumed above the 2.0 level being equal to one half of the assimilated CO_2.

The H_2/O_2 ratio was found to be equal to 2.0 when suitably washed bacteria were placed in an atmosphere of H_2-O_2 without CO_2. This indicates that hydrogen bacteria perform two unrelated reactions and confirms the view that substrate hydrogen serves for the reduction of CO_2 to cell level.

According to Kluyver (1953), Micrococcus denitrificans is the only hydrogen bacterium capable of anaerobic growth using nitrate oxygen for the oxidation of hydrogen:

$$Ca(NO_3)_2 + 5H_2 \rightarrow 4H_2O + Ca(OH)_2 + N_2,$$
$$Ca(OH)_2 + CO_2 \rightarrow CaCO_3 + H_2O.$$

Hydrogen bacteria utilize about 30—40% of the free energy released.

Methane-Oxidizing Bacteria

The gas escaping from lake silts contains up to 80% methane. It results from the anaerobic breakdown of remnants of aquatic plants and phytoplankton. The oxidation of methane is carried out entirely by biological systems that utilize dissolved oxygen, often causing mortalities in lakes.

The biologic nature of methane oxidation has been demonstrated simultaneously by Söhngen (1906) and Kaserer (1906), while S. I. Kuznetsov (1934a, 1934b), L. L. Rossolimo and Z. I. Kuznetsova (1934), Ohle (1958), Overbeck and Ohle (1964) and others have studied the effect of this process on the oxygen regime of lakes.

Most methane-oxidizing bacteria belong to the genera Pseudomonas and Mycobacterium. Their characteristics are given in Table 47.

Almost all methane-oxidizing bacteria can grow on nutrient media. In such conditions, however, some of them lose the ability to assimilate methane (Leadbetter and Foster, 1958; Overbeck and Ohle, 1964). Only the organism described by Hutton and ZoBell (1949) cannot develop on standard nutrient media.

As shown by the quantitative experiments of Söhngen, the oxidation of methane proceeds in the following manner:

$$CH_4 + 2O_2 \rightarrow CO_2 + 2H_2O; \quad \Delta F = -195,000 \text{ calories.}$$

The final products are CO_2 and water, plus a large amount of free energy (Thimann, 1963).

There are numerous indications that many bacteria can utilize carbohydrates as the only source of carbon and energy. Despite the wide distribution of methane in nature, however, there are only a few reports of its utilization by bacteria. There is no reliable proof that Bac. methanicus (Söhngen, 1906) has been encountered again since its original discovery more than sixty years ago.

Referring to this problem, Dworkin and Foster (1956) reported the isolation of an organism identical to Bac. methanicus in every detail. Following the rules of modern classification, they named it Pseudomonas methanica (Söhngen) comb. nov. These authors found that P. methanica requires growth factors present in agar and that these factors can be partly replaced by calcium pantothenate. Out of a large variety of organic compounds tested, P. methanica utilized only methane and methyl alcohc

Growth in the presence of methane was inhibited by yeast extract, corn extract, peptone, meat extract, and alanine at concentrations ranging from 0.01 to 0.3%.

Measurements of the carbon balance of the culture have shown that during seven days of incubation of 31.5 mM methane utilized, 16 mM O_2 were assimilated and 7.5 mM CO_2 produced, whereas the total carbon dissolved in the medium amounted to 22.6 mM. In other words, a very high percentage of the methane (72%) was converted into biomass. An attempt to determine the intracellular enzymes failed.

Davis and co-workers (Davis et al., 1964) have isolated the methane-oxidizing bacterium P. methanitrificans, which can assimilate atmospheric nitrogen. After two months of growth in a nitrogen-free medium, the microorganism fixed 46.3 mg of nitrogen per liter of medium; four months after the beginning of the experiment, the amount of fixed nitrogen reached 257 mg per 2 liters of medium. Nitrogen was determined by the Kjeldahl method, and precaution was taken to eliminate any penetration of atmospheric ammonia into the medium. The authors stress the necessity of carrying out the experiment with heavy nitrogen (N^{15}). So far, however, this has not been done. Leadbetter and Foster (1958) have made important experiments with a number of strains of P. methanica and Mycobacterium methanica. Two of the strains did not grow in organic media. After the introduction of labeled CO_2 in the medium it became evident that the fixation of CO_2 accounts for up to 70% of the bacterial biomass in cultures growing in an atmosphere of methane and air.

It is still unknown whether this group of microorganisms is capable of autotrophic life. Some facts speak in favor of this assumption. The oxidation of methane yields a large amount of free energy, which is quite sufficient for the creation of energy-rich compounds of phosphorus or other active carriers of energy. Furthermore, the microorganisms of this group can grow in a strictly inorganic medium in an atmosphere of methane and oxygen and readily fix CO_2. Cultivated on membrane filters on a solid medium containing $Na_2C^{14}O_3$ in an atmosphere of nonradioactive methane and air, they become radioactive and produce radioautographs (Romanenko, 1959). Finally, the colonies of methane-oxidizing bacteria do not give radioautographs when grown in similar conditions in an atmosphere of radioactive methane and air (V. I. Romanenko). The latter result indicates that there is no direct assimilation of methane or its oxidation products and consequently, speaks for an autotrophic way of life.

G. A. Zavarzin (1964c) holds a different position. In his view, the formation of 40% of the bacterial biomass from CO_2 cannot be regarded as proof of an autotrophic metabolism, since some heterotrophs assimilate large amounts of free CO_2. The bacteria in question utilize methanol and some monocarbon compounds that probably represent intermediate products of the oxidation of methane.

Pseudomonas AMI and Pseudomonas PRLW4 — microorganisms incapable of oxidizing methane but closely related to the methane-oxidizing bacteria — contain the enzyme carboxydismutase, which is also present in autotrophs. When $Na_2C^{14}O_3$ is added to the medium of these microorganisms, the amino acids glycine and serine appear to be the primary labeled products,

TABLE 47. Main species of methane-oxidizing bacteria

Bacterium	Size, microns	Flagella	Requirement for methane	Utilization of other organic compounds	References
Bac. methanicus	1.5–2 × 2–3	1	–	–	Söhngen, 1906
Bact. methanicum	0.3–0.4 × 0.9–2.2	Immotile	Facultative	Yes	Münz, 1915
Without name	0.6–1 × 2.2–3.3	1 or more, polar	Obligate	No	Hutton and ZoBell, 1949
Mycobact. flavum var. methanicum	0.6 × 2–3(6)	None	Facultative	Yes	Nechaeva, 1949
Mycobact. methanicum	0.6 × 3–5	None	Facultative	Yes	Nechaeva, 1949
Methanomonas methanica	0.6 × 1	1 polar	Obligate	Only in the presence of methane	Dworkin and Foster, 1956;
Pseudomonas methanica	0.4 × 1.5	1 polar	Obligate	No	Leadbetter and Foster, 1958

although the existence of the ribulose diphosphate cycle here has not been demonstrated. Quayle (1961) concludes on these grounds that the methane-oxidizing bacteria cannot be regarded as autotrophs.

Much remains to be discovered about the physiology of methane-oxidizing bacteria. Nevertheless, the existing data on the distribution and ecology of these microorganisms show that they can utilize the energy liberated in the oxidation of methane to carbon dioxide and water. It appears that the methane-oxidizing bacteria can lead a mixotrophic life.

Bacterial Oxidation of Hydrocarbons

Hydrocarbons and analogous bituminous compounds enter into lakes together with plant remnants and in the form of oil or other industrial contaminants. Their breakdown in the water mass and silt sediments of the lake can take place only in the presence of microorganisms.

Various amounts of hydrocarbons occur in all plant tissues (Chibnall, 1934). Among other proofs, this is evident from analyses of the surface silt, where up to 10% of the dry organic matter can be extracted with alcohol-benzene (Kuznetsov et al., 1939).

Large quantities of hydrocarbons enter into lakes, especially in the vicinity of oil enterprises and river ports.

Hydrocarbons belong mostly to the paraffin series of compounds having a linear open chain, or to naphthene series, characterized by hydrogen-saturated rings that usually contain 6 carbons and bear side chains of different lengths:

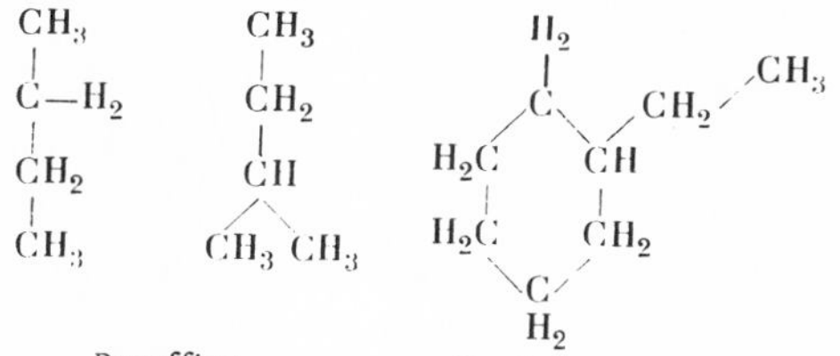

Paraffins   Naphthenes

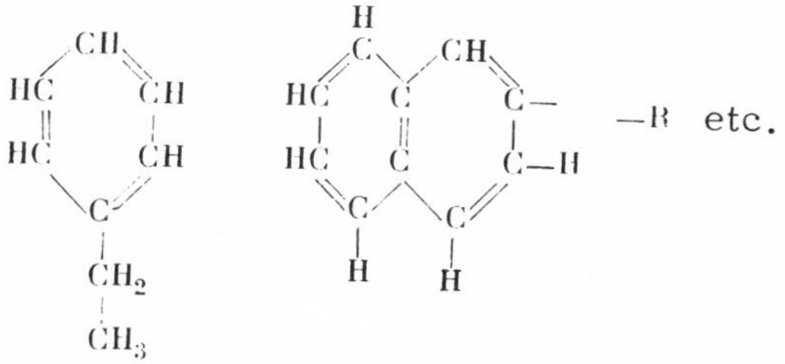

Benzene series   Naphthalene series

Aromatic hydrocarbons are much less abundant in some oils and in nature generally.

183

In his review of the literature, Fuhs (1961) lists about one hundred species of bacteria, yeasts, fungi, and actinomycetes capable of assimilating hydrocarbons.

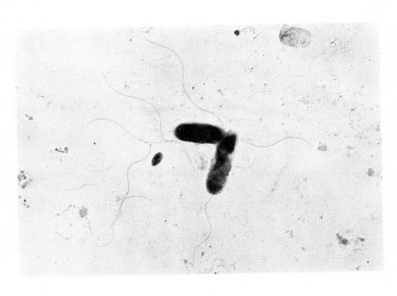

FIGURE 76. Pseudomonas aeruginosa.

Isolation of these organisms on mineral agar media in Petri dishes usually revealed a greater number of species in comparison with liquid media. The isolated microorganisms have been assigned more or less accurately to the genera Streptomyces, Nocardia, Mycobacterium, Corinebacterium, Brevibacterium, and Pseudomonas. According to Foster (1962), these groups of bacteria play a major role in the breakdown of hydrocarbons; the genus Pseudomonas is especially widespread. Bushnell and Haas (1941) have tested the ability of collection cultures to grow in mineral media containing hydrocarbons as the only carbon source, after being previously cultivated in hydrocarbon-free media. A total of seventy species belonging to thirty genera were examined. Of these species, 17% did oxidize hydrocarbons, while 21% of the examined fungal species grew on n-tridecane. These observations explain the fast multiplication of Pseudomonas aeruginosa (Figure 76) and other Pseudomonas species in the presence of hydrocarbons.

The most readily assimilated hydrocarbons are paraffins with a linear chain. Of twenty-one examined strains belonging to nine Mycobacterium species, all assimilated linear hydrocarbons containing eleven carbon atoms and only four were also able to utilize propane (Lukins, 1962). Similar data have been published by R. Lopatik (1964). All the mycobacteria isolated from the Volga artificial reservoirs rapidly oxidized oil. The assimilation of isoalkanes — that is, hydrocarbons with a branched chain — is much more difficult. Of all the hydrocarbons tested, methane is assimilated by the smallest number of species (E. N. Bokova, 1954; N. B. Nechaeva, 1949; Dostalek, 1954; Davis, Chase, and Raymond, 1956).

However, the methane-oxidizing bacteria are widespread in nature (Leadbetter and Foster, 1958; Romanenko, 1963; Overbeck and Ohle, 1964; Kuznetsov, 1947).

The main factors affecting the availability of hydrocarbons to bacterial attack can be summed up as follows: (1) the presence of a suitable enzyme system in the organism; (2) the relative solubility of the hydrocarbon in the environment; (3) the capacity of the hydrocarbon for active transport through the cell membrane; (4) the lack of a specific toxic effect of the hydrocarbon or its oxidation products on the cytoplasm.

Many authors have examined the mechanism of the oxidation of hydrocarbons. Several reviews of this topic have been published (Leadbetter and Foster, 1960; Foster, 1962; McKenna and Kallio, 1965; E. P. Rozanova, 1967). In abiotic conditions, that is, in strictly chemical systems, oxidizing agents attack mainly the second carbon atom. The oxidation of hydrocarbons can be represented by the following scheme:

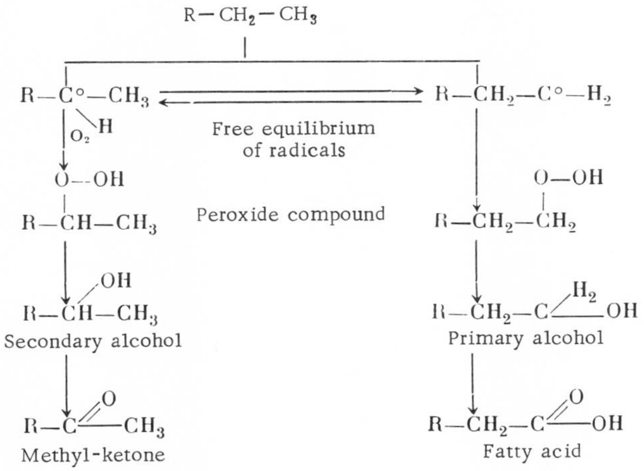

$$R-CH_2-CH_3$$

$$R-\overset{|}{C}{}^{\circ}-CH_3 \rightleftharpoons \text{Free equilibrium of radicals} \rightarrow R-CH_2-\overset{|}{C}{}^{\circ}-H_2$$

$$\overset{O_2}{\searrow}H \qquad\qquad\qquad\qquad$$

$$\overset{O--OH}{\underset{|}{R-CH-CH_3}} \qquad \text{Peroxide compound} \qquad \overset{O-OH}{\underset{|}{R-CH_2-CH_2}}$$

$$R-\overset{OH}{\underset{|}{CH}}-CH_3 \qquad\qquad R-CH_2-C\overset{H_2}{\diagup}OH$$

Secondary alcohol | Primary alcohol

$$R-C\overset{O}{\diagup}-CH_3 \qquad\qquad R-CH_2-C\overset{O}{\diagup}-OH$$

Methyl-ketone | Fatty acid

The electron transfer that creates the initial free radicals increases the reactivity of the second carbon atom. An equilibrium develops between hydrocarbons with activated free radicals, namely, between the activated second carbon of one molecule and the neighboring terminal carbon atom of another molecule. Bacterial oxidation must involve the activated carbon of the free radical. The formation of the intermediate and final oxidation products is but a logical conclusion of the above scheme.

On the basis of the work of several authors, Foster (1962) proposed the following scheme for a rather frequent type of decomposition of long-chain hydrocarbons, namely, into acetic acid and a fatty acid having a shorter carbon chain than the original hydrocarbon:

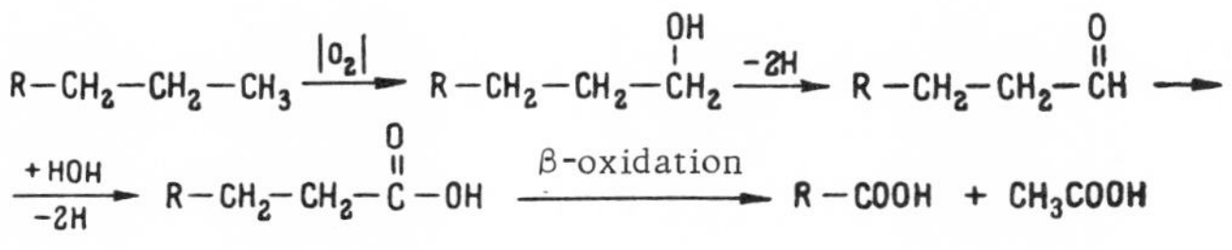

$$R-CH_2-CH_2-CH_3 \xrightarrow{|O_2|} R-CH_2-CH_2-\overset{OH}{\underset{|}{CH_2}} \xrightarrow{-2H} R-CH_2-CH_2-\overset{O}{\overset{\|}{CH}} \longrightarrow$$

$$\xrightarrow[-2H]{+HOH} R-CH_2-CH_2-\overset{O}{\overset{\|}{C}}-OH \xrightarrow{\beta\text{-oxidation}} R-COOH + CH_3COOH$$

185

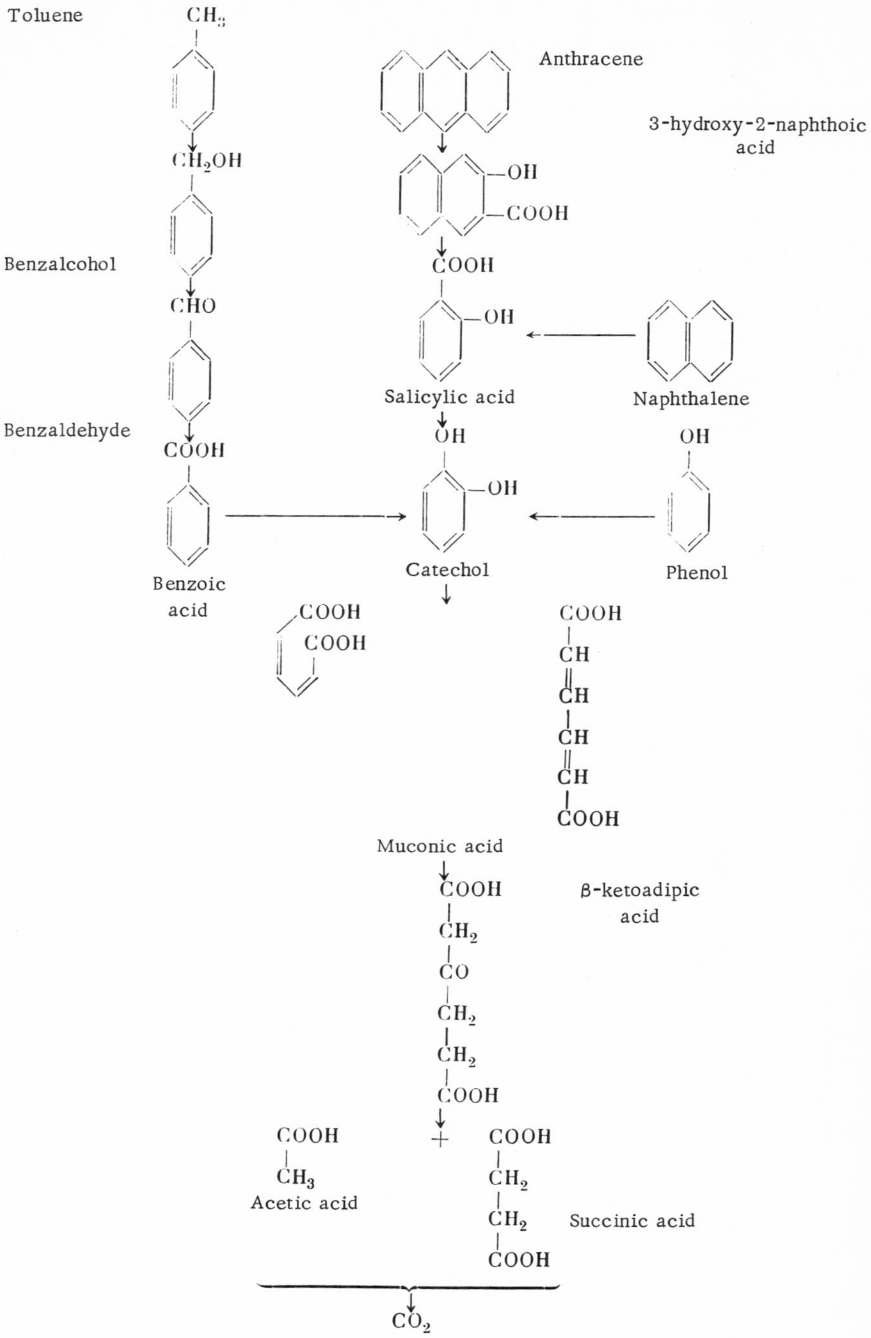

Toluene CH_3

Anthracene

3-hydroxy-2-naphthoic
acid

    CH_2OH

—OH

—COOH

Benzalcohol

COOH

CHO

—OH   ←

Benzaldehyde

Salicylic acid   Naphthalene

$COOH$

OH   OH

—OH   ←

Benzoic
acid   Catechol   Phenol

COOH
COOH

COOH
|
CH
‖
CH
|
CH
‖
CH
|
COOH

Muconic acid

COOH
|
CH₂
|
CO
|
CH₂
|
CH₂
|
COOH

β-ketoadipic
acid

COOH   +   COOH
| |
CH₃   CH₂
Acetic acid |
          CH₂   Succinic acid
          |
          COOH

CO_2

Scheme of the oxidation of cyclic hydrocarbons (after Ooyama and Foster, 1965)

186

He assumes that DPN participates in the transfer of hydrogen to oxygen:

$$R-CH_2-CH_3 + O_2 + DPNH^+ \xrightarrow{+ H^+} R-CH_2-\overset{\overset{\displaystyle OH}{|}}{CH_2} + DPN + H_2O.$$

The oxidation of cyclic or naphthene hydrocarbons similarly occurs with the participation of a large number of microorganisms.

In their study of the oxidation of cyclopropane, Ooyama and Foster (1965) used a culture 10B5, which apparently belongs to the genus Pseudo-monas. This microorganism is a Gram-negative rod that produces a yellow pigment and grows in standard media. The authors showed that the oxidation of naphthene hydrocarbons begins at the side chain and proceeds as in the aliphatic hydrocarbons.

The oxidation of the ring involves the addition of water and the formation of an aliphatic aldehyde, which can be oxidized later to a fatty acid and finally to CO_2 and H_2O.

There is no experimental evidence on the rupture of cycloparaffins with rings containing a large number of carbons.

The growth of bacteria on benzene and other aromatic hydrocarbons has been studied by Tauson (1950), who has isolated a number of microorganisms capable of oxidizing benzene, toluene, xylene, naphthalene, anthracene, phthalic, and benzoic acids. To this category belong Pseudomonas aeruginosa, Mycobacterium rhodochrous, and other bacteria, isolated by different authors.

The oxidation of aromatic hydrocarbons begins at the double bond with the formation of a diphenol; afterward the ring opens and a dicarboxylic fatty acid appears.

Microbiology of Hemicellulose

Hemicelluloses are widespread in plant tissues. Semisubmerged and submerged aquatic vegetation grows abundantly in the shallow areas of many lakes. When this vegetation dies in the fall, its remnants undergo further breakdown in the lake. Polysaccharides of the hemicellulose group are among the major components of plant tissues and consequently an important source of energy and food for the aquatic microflora.

The chemical hydrolysis of hemicelluloses yields simple sugars; in fact, many hemicelluloses are named after the particular sugar that builds them. Some hemicelluloses contain not only sugar but also uronic acids, which can be released by treating the hemicellulose with weak alkali. On these grounds, Norman divides the hemicelluloses into two classes: polyuronides

COOH H OH COOH

—O— C O H H C C —O— C O H

H H OH H H

C C C C C

H OH H H OH H H OH H

C C —O— C —O— C C —O

H OH COOH H OH

Polyuronide

and cellulosans or glucosides.

CH_2OH H OH CH_2OH

C O —O— C C H H C O OH

H H OH H H

C C C C C

OH OH H H OH H H

C C H H C —O— —O— C C H

H OH CH_2OH H OH

Cellulosan

Polyuronides can be regarded as polysaccharides containing various amounts of uronic acid units in the molecule. However, not all polyuronides are hemicelluloses; certain water-soluble polyuronides and compounds related to pectins, plant humus, and mucilages are usually not assigned to this group. The polyuronide hemicelluloses rarely occur in a pure form in plants; usually they appear as lignin-polysaccharide complexes.

The hydrolysis of polyuronide hemicelluloses by weak acids at high temperature yields sugars and uronic acids. According to the products of the hydrolysis, the polysaccharides can be divided into two major types. One of them consists of xylose and gluconic acid, which alternate in such a manner that one molecule of the acid corresponds to 1—19 molecules of xylose. The polysaccharides of the second type are composed of arabinose and galacturonic acid.

Xylans are natural polymers of xylose with the empirical formula $C_5H_8O_4$. Usually, they do not contain gluconic acid. Some xylans contain small amounts of D-xylose, or arabinose and D-gluconic acid.

Mannan — a polymer containing from 50 to 500 mannose molecules — is a glucoside, that is, a hemicellulose without uronic acid. Araban is a polysaccharide of arabinose; it occurs in pectin.

Algae contain alginic acid at a concentration reaching 30% of the dry weight. Alginic acid is a complex of hydrocarbons of the polyuronide group; hydrolysis of the purified compound yields molecules of mannuronic acid.

Many microorganisms utilize hemicelluloses as a source of food and energy. However, the microflora that attacks hemicelluloses varies greatly according to the sugars that participate in these compounds.

Fungi are largely responsible for the initial stages of the breakdown. This can be demonstrated with overgrowth plates after the method of Rossi-Kholodnyi. The breakdown of hemicelluloses can proceed both aerobically and in anaerobic conditions (Waksman, 1935). The following list contains microorganisms that attack various hemicelluloses (after Alexander, 1961).

Composition of hemicellulose	Organisms	References
Galactan and mannan	Anaerobes	Waksman and Diehm, 1931
Xylan	Bacillus sp.	Inaoka and Soda, 1956
Hemicellulose from oats	Bacillus sp., Achromobacter ubiquitum	Norman, 1934
Pentosans of wheat	Bacillus sp., Pseudomonas sp	Simpson, 1954
Hemicellulose	Cytophaga, Sporocytophaga	Fuller and Norman, 1943
Xylan	Lactobacillus	Fred, Peterson, and Davenport, 1920
Mannan and xylan	Vibrio andoi	Aoi and Orikura, 1928
Alginic acid	Bact. alginovorum	Waksman, Carey, and Allen, 1934
Galactan, mannan, pentosan	Actinomyces sp., Aspergillus sp., Rhizopus sp.	Waksman and Diehm, 1931
Polyuronide	Alternaria sp., Fusarium sp., Trichoderma lignorum	Fuller and Norman, 1945

Since hemicelluloses are insoluble in water, their hydrolysis requires the presence of an extracellular enzyme, namely hemicellulase. Similarly, the enzyme xylanase breaks down the long chain of the polysaccharide xylan. Further research will probably reveal other enzymes that catalyze the degradation of different polysaccharides.

The final oxidation of the products of this hydrolysis proceeds more rapidly in the presence of a mixed microflora. This is so because only some microorganisms can hydrolyze hemicellulose, while the resulting sugars are utilized by a large number of species.

Microbiology of Chitin

Chitin is one of the commonest polysaccharides. It consists of amino sugars and is insoluble in water, organic solvents, strong alkalies, or dilute acids. However, it can be degraded enzymatically or by treatment with strong inorganic acids. The chitin molecule represents a long chain of normal acetylglucosamine units with the empirical formula $(C_6H_9O_4-NHCOCH_3)_n$, which corresponds to a nitrogen content of 6.9%. The structural formula of chitin is given below:

189

In water bodies, chitin is a major component of crustacean shells; it is also found in the cell membrane of many fungi, where its concentration may attain 26% in terms of dry weight (Alexander, 1961). Although its breakdown rate in soil is lower than that of proteins, from 30 to 60% of it is mineralized within two months.

As Alexander points out, many microorganisms can degrade chitin in aerobic conditions. To this group belong many Streptomyces species, some strains of Nocardia and Micromonospora, which can produce the corresponding enzyme, and many bacteria of the genera Achromobacter, Bacillus, Chromobacterium, Cytophaga, Flavobacterium, Micrococcus, and Pseudomonas. Fusarium, Mucor, Trichoderma, and other fungi show a similar property.

The products of the hydrolysis of chitin have been analyzed in the case of Pseudomonas chitinovorum and Cytophaga johnsonae. These include N-acetyl-D-glucosamine, glucosamine, acetic acid, and ammonia The microorganisms oxidize these compounds to CO_2 or use them for the synthesis of protoplasm. Because of the insolubility and large molecular weight of chitin, its utilization requires the presence of an exoenzyme. Chitinase occurs usually as an adaptive enzyme, but in some Streptomyces it is constitutional.

The degradation of chitin probably proceeds according to the following scheme:

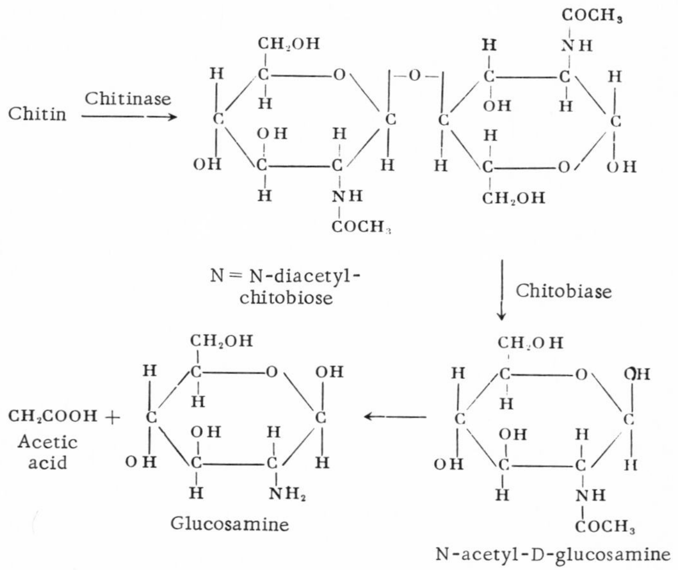

As with all polysaccharides, the most important and difficult stage of this process is the breakdown of chitin to N-acetyl-D-glucosamine fragments, which requires the presence of chitinase. The further degradation proceeds easily. The obtained products enter the cell and serve as source of energy and building material.

Seki and Taga (1963) have isolated thirty-nine strains of chitin-attacking bacteria from Aburatsu Bay on the Pacific coast of Japan. These bacteria were assigned to five species, which were determined as related to B e n e c - k e a i n d o l t h e t i c a, B. l i p o p h a g a, B. h y p e r o p t i c a, B. c h i t i - n o v o r a, and B. l a b r a.

These authors tested the enzymatic activity of the bacteria by adding 0.2 grams of finely dispersed chitin to 10 ml of medium and inoculating with the corresponding microorganism at a concentration of 100 cells per ml of medium. The amount of degraded chitin after seven days of incubation at 25°C varied from 113 to 129 mg. In other words, the rate of chitin break-down was largely uniform.

Further experiments showed that in suitable conditions, 30 mg of chitin are degraded daily out of an initial amount of 200 mg when 10 billion bac- teria are present in the medium. The degradation rate depends largely on the state of dispersion of the chitin. In the case of chitin bands measuring less than 0.3 mm, as in cladoceran shells, a bacterial population of about 0.9 billion cells destroys approximately 27 mg of chitin daily. The authors assume that the breakdown of chitin in the ocean proceeds at a similar rate. Because of the great depths existing in the ocean, all the chitin is probably degraded while the remnants of the crustacean shells are sinking to the ocean floor.

Okarof (1966) has studied microscopically the degradation of chitin by soil microorganisms in laboratory conditions. In his experiments, frag- ments of purified chitin were placed on slides and were incubated in soil at a temperature of 29 and 16°C.

In tropical soils and at high temperatures, chitin was attacked mainly by actinomycetes, nematodes, and protozoans. Fungi and bacteria performed a major role at 10°C. It appears that bacteria are largely responsible for the mineralization of chitinous remains of zooplankton in the surface layers of silt sediments.

The anaerobic breakdown of chitin in silt is much slower, if it takes place at all. Indeed, cladoceran shells are often found in large amounts even at a considerable depth from the silt surface. Sulfate-reducing bacteria parti- cipate in the anaerobic degradation of chitin (V. I. Aleshina, 1938).

Microbiology of Lignin

Lignin accounts for about one-third of all plant tissues. Its degradation is much more difficult than that of hemicellulose or cellulose. Consequently, the proportion of lignin in the organic matter of silt may be as high as 60%. Lignin resists hydrolysis even in the presence of concentrated mineral acids. It has the following elementary composition: carbon 64%, hydrogen 6%, methoxy groups ($-OCH_3$) 14%. The lignin molecule is a polymer of aromatic rings composed of two recurring structural units. It appears that the main building unit is phenyl propane (C_6-C_3), which contains one methoxy carbon; C_6 is a benzene ring bearing a linear chain of three carbons. There is one aromatic ring for every ten carbon atoms. In addition to the methoxy group, the benzene ring bears a hydroxyl group. The concentration of methoxy groups varies from 15 to 21%, depending on the plant from which the lignin originates. The extent of lignin degradation can be gauged from the amount of liberated methoxy groups. The hypothetical building units of lignin are shown below:

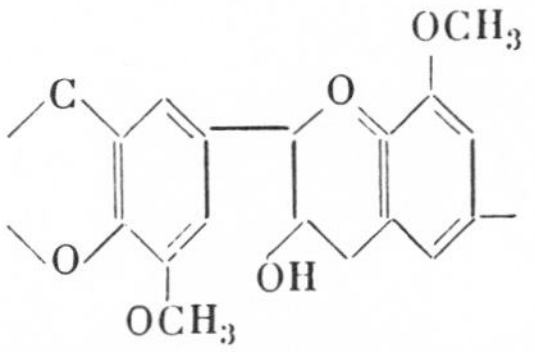

Derivative of guaiacylpropane

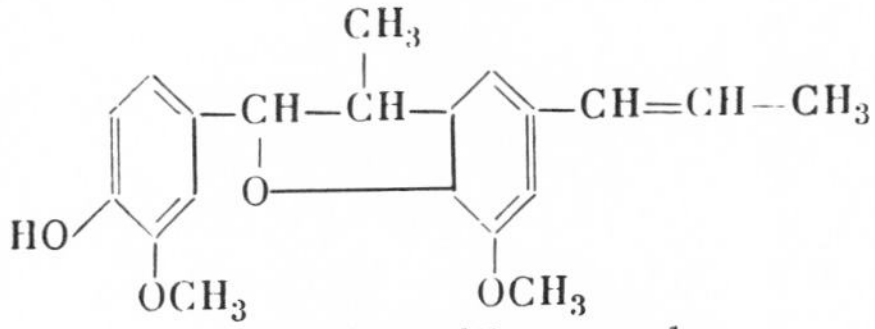

Dehydrodiisoeugenol

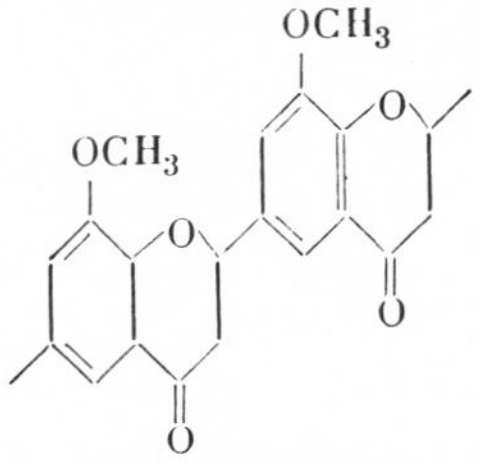

Structure of the polyflavone type

As noted above, lignin is the most resistant component of the organic matter found in higher aquatic plants.

Waksman and Hutchins (1935) have found in soil a number of bacteria and roughly identified fungi of the genera F u s a r i u m and A l t e r n a r i a, capable of destroying plant lignin in aerobic conditions. To obtain a degradation of lignin, the authors prepared it in a finely dispersed state in water. The degradation process was very slow in pure cultures and much faster in enrichment cultures of bacteria and fungi.

Waksman and Hutchins were unable to identify the degradation products of lignin. However, they report a considerable growth of bacteria in the cultures. It appears that lignin cannot be broken down in anaerobic conditions.

Microbiological Breakdown of Humic Compounds

The composition of the humic compounds is still poorly known. This results in part from the uncertainty concerning their origin, although the topic has been studied by many soil scientists.

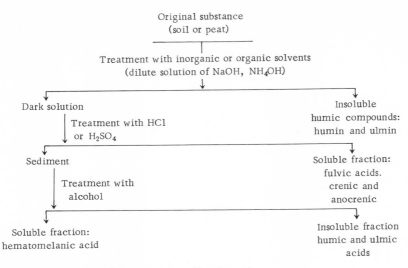

Original substance
(soil or peat)

Treatment with inorganic or organic solvents
(dilute solution of NaOH, NH₄OH)

Dark solution

Treatment with HCl
or H₂SO₄

Insoluble
humic compounds:
humin and ulmin

Soluble fraction:
fulvic acids.
crenic and
anocrenic

Sediment

Treatment with
alcohol

Soluble fraction:
hematomelanic acid

Insoluble fraction
humic and ulmic
acids

FIGURE 77. Scheme of the separation of humic acids.

Figure 77 shows schematically the existing classification of humic compounds, which is based entirely on color and solubility.

Many authors have studied the nature and structure of humic acids. A review of this topic was published by M. M. Kononova (1951). It was established that humic acids are products of the condensation of polyphenols and amino acids.

Undoubtedly, the availability of humic acids to microorganisms depends on the position of the nitrogen.

According to recent knowledge, the molecule of humic acid contains: (a) an aromatic nucleus; (b) nitrogenous organic in cyclic form and as side chains; (c) carbohydrate-type compounds. Dragunov et al. (1948) have proposed the following structure for humic acid:

The crenic, apocrenic, and fulvic acids are even less known than the humic acids. They similarly possess large molecules; however, their formation results from microbial activity. These compounds contain nitrogen and polyuronic acids. The presence of aromatic rings in their molecule has not been established; it is known, however, that they contain four carboxylic groups, like humic acid. Phenolic hydroxyls have not been demonstrated. These acids form soluble complexes with iron, manganese, and aluminum.

The hematomelanic acids represent simpler varieties of humic acids (Kukharenko, 1948). It appears, therefore, that the different humic substances are not individual compounds in the chemical sense but possess a number of common features, notably the size of the molecule and the arrangement of its components.

Microorganisms undoubtedly perform an important function in the formation and breakdown of humus (M. M. Kononova, 1951). The proportion between these processes apparently determines the humic content of soil (Kononova). This applies also to water bodies, although it must be borne in mind that a considerable amount of humic compounds can enter the water body together with swamp waters.

The formation of humus appears to be an enzymatic process in which different bacterial species participate (Mishustin et al., 1965). According to luminescent and chromatographic determinations, the dark substances formed in mold cultures are humic acids (Kononova, Aleksandrova, and Bel'chikova, 1960).

Little is known about the role of different microbial groups in the breakdown of humus. A degradation of soil humus under the influence of soil bacteria, notably A c t i n o m y c e s, has been demonstrated (E. S. Kudrina, 1951). In experiments made by E. N. Mishustin and D. I. Nikitin (1961), the process was found to be most intensive in the presence of bacteria of the genus P s e u d o m o n a s and could be attributed to the action of peroxidase on the humus.

In the experiments of D. I. Nikitin, however, the decoloration of solutions of humic acid required the presence of about 2% glucose in the culture fluid. Thus, it is still unknown whether the decomposition of humic acids results directly from the action of P s e u d o m o n a s or is a side effect due to the interaction of the humic acids with the products of the breakdown of glucose.

A decomposition of natural fulvic acids has been observed in several pure cultures of mycobacteria (S. I. Kuznetsov and I. N. Dzyuban, 1960a). After twenty-two days of culture in deeply colored natural water, the density of these bacteria rose from 0.2—0.4 million to 20—120 millions per ml. The color paled more intensively in the presence of light than in the dark, reaching respectively 100—140° and 40—80° in the chromium-cobalt scale. The process was most rapid in the presence of M y c o b a c t e r i u m p h l e i, M. c i t r e u m, and M. v a d o s u m.

In a study of the role of microorganisms in the accumulation of iron in the soil, T. V. Aristovskaya (1961) isolated an organism that she named P e d o m i c r o b i u m f e r r u g i n e u m. This species satisfies its requirements for organic matter with fulvic acid from complexes of the latter with iron or manganese oxides.

Less Known Organisms Participating in the Mineralization of Organic Matter in Water Bodies

A great difference exists between the bacterial counts of water as determined microscopically and by culturing on nutrient media. It appears that most aquatic microorganisms are oligocarbophiles, which cannot survive or grow in the presence of such concentrations of organic compounds as are

usually found in nutrient media. These microorganisms probably utilize
the low amount of organic matter dissolved in natural water. Their
specific composition is virtually unknown. Stalked bacteria are probably
an important factor in the mineralization of organic matter.

Perfil'ev and Gabe (1961) have described a third group of bacteria that
do not grow in standard media. Here belong the predatory bacteria, which
were discovered in silt by the application of capillary methods of microbiological research. These organisms will be dealt with below, although
they cannot be characterized in terms of fermented organic compounds.

FIGURE 78. Developmental cycle of Caulobacter
(after Zavarzin).

Stalked microorganisms of the order Caulobacteriales. Henrici and
Johnson (1935) have described several forms of attached bacteria that were
isolated as periphytes on glass slides submerged for various periods in
Lake Alexander. The bacteria developed stalks that adhered to the substrate. Some of them divided by budding.

Later this group of bacteria was subdivided into two orders: Caulobacteriales and Hyphomicrobiales.

The family Caulobacteriaceae has been studied in detail by Poindexter
(1964). These bacteria adhere to planktonic algae and other substrates by
means of stalks that represent protoplasmic outgrowths. In their developmental cycle they form rosettes and motile forms. Caulobacteriaceae
occur frequently in algal cultures and grow luxuriantly after the death
of the algae.

Poindexter distinguishes between several species that differ in the form
of the cells, the color of the colonies, and in relation to riboflavin. Thus
Caulobacter henrici and C. vibrioides (Figure 79, a) are vibrioid
cells, C. vibrioides limonus (Figure 79, d) lemon-shaped cells,
C. subvibrioides and C. fusiformis, respectively, subvibrioid and
fusiform ones, C. bacterioides sporeless rods (Figure 79, b), and
Asticocaulis excentricus asymmetric cells with excentric stalks
(Figure 79, c). A rosettelike stage of the development of C. bacterioides is shown in Figure 80.

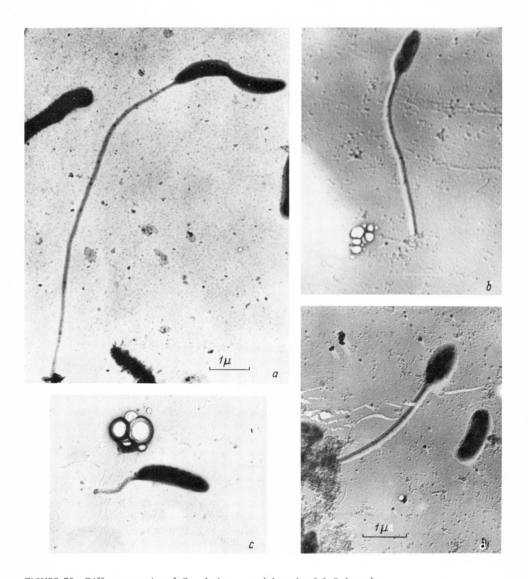

FIGURE 79. Different species of Caulobacter (photo by S.S. Belyaev):

a) C. vibrioides; b) C. bacterioides; c) Asticocaulis excentricus; d) C. vibrioides limonus.

The developmental cycle of C. vibrioides has been described by G. A. Zavarzin (1961a).   Figure 78 shows the different stages of this cycle.
The cells of C. vibrioides produce a stalk that adheres to the substrate.   This is followed by transverse fission.   The daughter cell is motile owing to the presence of a polar flagellum.   It moves until it meets

a rosette of Caulobacter cells or some other substrate to which it adheres. In this process, the flagellum develops a sheath and becomes a stalk. Afterward the cycle is repeated.

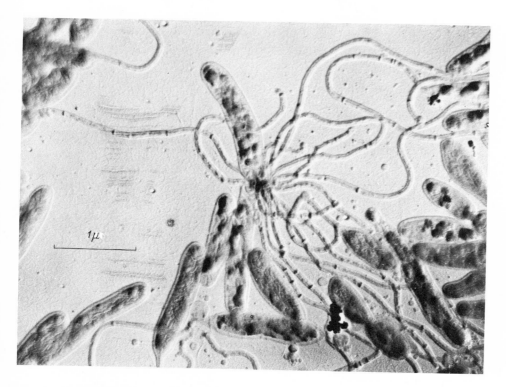

FIGURE 80. Rosette formed by the attachment of Caulobacter bacterioides to a common center (photo by S.S. Belyaev).

The order of budding bacteria — Hyphomicrobiales. The distribution of budding bacteria in fresh waters has been studied by Hirsch (1968), who noted that the following three characteristic features of the group must be taken into account if a successful isolation and enrichment culture is to be made: (1) the budding bacteria grow in highly dilute media; (2) most of the cells are attached to the substrate; (3) prolonged storage of the water helps increase the density of budding bacteria.

Hyphomicrobiales have been found in the mucus of Gloeocapsa and other algae. It appears that the mucus or substances adsorbed on its surface serve as food for these bacteria.

Hyphomicrobiales attain a high density in many oligotrophic lakes. The rapidly growing heterotrophic bacteria compete successfully with them in eutrophic conditions. Preliminary tests have shown that even small concentrations of carbohydrates and amino acids exert a pronounced inhibiting effect on these bacteria. On the other hand, many of them withstand high concentrations of nitrites and mineral salts and can be regarded as typical aquatic bacteria.

In addition to the bacteria listed in Bergey's manual, the genera Blasto-caulis, Pedomicrobium, Blastobacter, and Ancalomicro-bium can be assigned to this order.

Hyphomicrobiales reproduce by budding. Their vegetative body consists of cells with outgrowths or filiform appendages. The buds develop on the cells proper or on their filiform appendages.

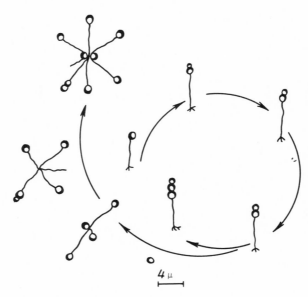

FIGURE 81. Developmental cycle of Blastocaulis.

Family I. Blastobacteriaceae, fam. nov. Unicellular microorganisms. Reproduction by budding. Cells piriform, sometimes stalked. Rosettes frequent. Buds developing on the maternal cell.

Genera. 1. Nitrobacter. For a detailed description see the chapter on the nitrogen cycle.

2. Blastobacter and Blastocaulis occur frequently in lakes; they deposit iron hydrates around their coenobium. Figure 81 shows the developmental cycle of Blastobacter.

3. Ancalomicrobium adetum was described by Staley (1968) as a new species (from the Greek: ancalo, "hand"; adetum, "not attached") Unicellular Gram-negative bacteria. Each cell bearing from two to eight outgrowths up to three microns long. The outgrowths can bifurcate but do not bud. Buds are formed on the cell, which accordingly develops two or

more outgrowths. The buds break loose upon reaching the size of the maternal cell. The cells are immotile and lack stalks for attachment, but they may possess gas vacuoles.

Family II. Hyphomicrobiaceae. Unicellular organisms reproducing by budding. Buds develop at the end of a hypha that arises terminally from the cell. The motile stage has one flagellum.

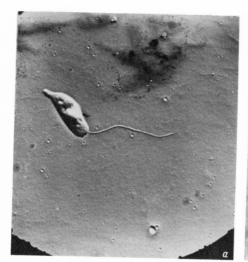
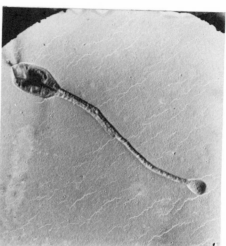

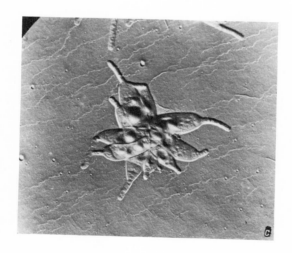

FIGURE 82. Hyphomicrobium vulgare:

a) motile cell; b) growth of a bud on the hypha; c) rosette.

Genera 1. Hyphomicrobium. The developmental cycle of the type form, H. vulgare, has been studied by G. A. Zavarzin (1960) and Hirsch (1968). Figure 82 shows the stages and developmental cycle of this bacterium. The cells of Hyphomicrobium are elongate fusiform rods measuring 0.5 to 1 by 2 microns. From one of their poles arises a hypha that represents a protoplasmic outgrowth about 0.2 microns in diameter and up to 100 microns long. The cell contains a nucleus. Reproduction begins with division of the nucleus and terminal budding on the hypha. One of the nuclei moves along the hypha and enters the bud, which breaks away upon reaching the size of the cell. The liberated cell is motile and bears a polar flagellum. In some species, the cells fuse into rosettes at the flagellated ends. The hyphal rudiment, situated at the opposite end of the cell, begins to grow longer and develops into a hypha. Then the nucleus divides again, one of the new nuclei enters the hypha at the end of the cell, and a new cycle begins.

This family comprises several budding bacteria that participate in the chemical transformations of iron and manganese. The characteristics of these bacteria will be discussed below in the description of the microorganisms that participate in the cycles of the respective elements.

2. Prosthecomicrobium is a generic name derived from the Greek word prosthecos, "appendage" (Staley, 1968). Unicellular Gram-negative bacterium with processes departing in different directions from the cell. The processes are about one micron long, which roughly corresponds to the size of the cell. The cells divide by binary fission. Obligate aerobes, sometimes with gas vacuoles. Motile, with polar flagellum. Some species are pigmented. These bacteria can use humic compounds and secretions of planktonic algae, ranging from compounds of glycolic and oxalic acids to some polysaccharides. Frequent in freshwaters (Figure 59, 4).

Predatory bacteria. S. N. Vinogradsky pointed out that the study of natural populations of microorganisms must begin with a microscopical examination of them in their original habitats. B. V. Perfil'ev (1964) followed this concept in his analysis of the silt microflora. After years of research and improvement, he proposed a capillary method for the study of the microbial panorama.

A silt sample taken from a natural water body and placed in the laboratory rapidly shows a sharp vertical differentiation of oxidation-reduction conditions. This causes corresponding differentiations in the chemical properties of the silt solution and in the distribution of the silt microflora. In view of these facts, Perfil'ev (1964) placed capillaries with plane-parallel walls in different zones of silt, which enabled him to observe the microflora in natural conditions. The opening of the capillary is only 70—200 microns deep and 200—500 microns wide. The upper wall is only 0.17 mm thick, which allows a microscopic examination of the silt microflora with an immersion system. After a certain period, the silt solution inside the capillary becomes identical to that located outside, and a similar relationship develops with respect to the microflora.

Using this procedure, B. V. Perfil'ev (1954) found a new type of predatory bacteria in the silt of the Kistatelevyi pond near Leningrad.

Besides their interest from the viewpoint of general biology, representative of this group have significance in microstratigraphic studies (Perfil'ev and

Gabe, 1961). One of the first predatory bacteria discovered in silt by means of peloscopic capillaries was Dictyobacter rapax (Figure 83). This species forms round or elongate motile colonies that measure 10—40 by 20—60 microns and divide by fission. Each colony consists of 100—200 separate cells measuring 0.7—1.2 by 2—6 microns. The cells occupy the periphery of the colony and are joined by plasmodesmata. They are capable of a slow movement comparable to that of blue-green algae and are immersed in a transparent homogeneous slime. The central cavity of the colony is filled with a homogeneous liquid. Dictyobacter selectively envelop live microbes into the central cavity of the colony via an opening that opens and closes accordingly. Digestion of the prey is followed by the ejection of a lump of fecal substance. In addition to its predatory habits, this species can feed on organic substances from the silt solution.

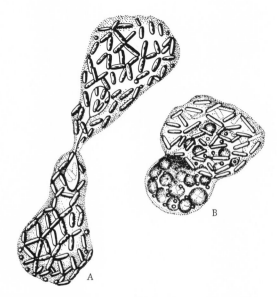

FIGURE 83. The predatory bacterium Dictyobacter rapax (after Perfil'ev):

A) bacterial network; B) a giant cell of Achromatium being swallowed by a predatory network of D. rapax.

The second microorganism of this group, Cyclobacter constrictor, gen. nov., sp. nov. (Figure 84), forms multicellular colonies of colorless cylindrical cells measuring about 1.5 by 6 microns, arranged in filaments and linked by plasmodesmata. The developmental cycle of this species consists of three stages (Figure 85).

The first stage is a motile filament that lives as a saprophyte. The second stage, which has the combined characteristics of a net and a lasso ("net-lasso stage"), lives both as a saprophyte and as a predator. Its lasso captures live filamentous microorganisms and coils around them, forming

a "digestive cocoon." The third stage develops from the filamentous or
lasso-shaped forms and consists of round saprophytes. All stages show
a motility comparable to that of sulfur bacteria. In the microzonal profile,
this species forms a microzone at the border of the oxidative horizon.

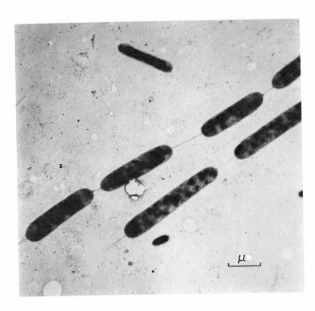

FIGURE 84. Cyclobacter. The cells are joined by plasmodesmata.
Preparation from the silt of a swamp near Lake Glubokoe (photo by
G.A. Dubinina).

Trigonobacter, another predatory bacterium, forms slender spherical microcolonies of thin rods measuring 1×7 microns, of which about
twenty are joined radially at one end around a common center. The spherical stage can open into slightly branched chains that develop into a network
with a triangular mesh (Figure 86).

The new genera Streptobacter, Desmobacter, and Teratobacter (Figure 87) similarly belong to the group of predatory bacteria
(Perfil'ev and Gabe, 1961).

Observations of these bacteria in peloscopic capillaries have revealed
three different mechanisms for the capture of prey: (1) the tightening of a
loop or lasso around filamentous bacteria (in Cyclobacter, Teratobacter); (2) swallowing in a cavity from which there is no escape (Dictyobacter); (3) the formation of a weblike network that secretes a sticky
slime, the capture being followed by a curling of the colony into a spherical
mass (Trigonobacter, Desmobacter, Streptobacter).

All these predatory bacteria have a motile ring-shaped stage. On these
grounds, they can be placed in a separate taxonomic group (together with
Lieskella and Trichonema) for which Perfil'ev proposes the new
order Cyclobacteriales.

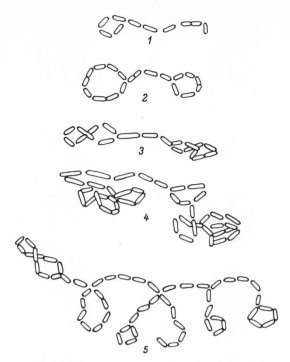

FIGURE 85. C y c l o b a c t e r   c o n s t r i c t u s. Developmental
cycle (after Perfil'ev):

1) motile filamentous stage; 2) net-lasso stage; 3—5) lasso stage.

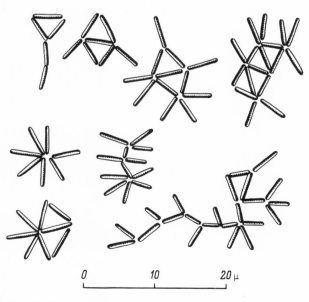

0   10   20 μ

FIGURE 86. T r i g o n o b a c t e r (after Perfil'ev).

Another predatory bacterium is B d e l l o v i b r i o (Figure 88) — a vib-rioid form with a thick flagellum (Starr and Baigent, 1966). This predator penetrates into a bacterium, feeds on it, and reproduces, forming sphero-blasts; when the cell wall of the host dissolves, the progeny escape.

Degradation of Organic Matter in Lakes

In most cases, the mineralization of organic matter in the water mass of lakes was determined in an overall manner by the consumption of oxygen in an isolated volume of water kept as close to natural conditions as pos-sible. Clearly, this method cannot be applied in anaerobic conditions. In the latter case, the production of CO_2 provides some information on the rate of the process. However, chemical analysis alone does not give an accurate answer as to the details of the decomposition process. Microbiological procedures must also be applied for this purpose. The following list shows the budget of organic matter in the trophogenic zone of Lakes Beloe and Chernoe in Kosino during the vegetation period (in tons of glucose for the whole lake). The figures are taken from Vinberg (1934, 1948).

Lake	Area of lake, hectares	Primary production	Destruction	Organic matter destroyed, %
Beloe	26.0	126.0	99.5	75.4
Chernoe	2.6	25.8	20.2	78.3

Degradation of Organic Matter in the Water Mass of Lakes

The total amount of organic matter that is being mineralized in the water mass of lakes can be determined by the jar method. Analyses in Lakes Beloe and Chernoe in Kosino have shown that about 80% of the organic matter formed in the lake is degraded while still in the water mass before sinking to the lake bottom. The amount of organic matter destroyed daily in the surface waters varies greatly from one lake to another, not only in absolute terms but also in relation to the quantity produced by photosynthesis. Lakes receiving large amounts of allochthonous organic substances show a break-down rate equal to or greater than the rate of photosynthetic production of organic matter.

Table 48 shows the relation between the production and degradation of organic matter in Lake Chernoe (in Kosino) on the basis of a detailed study by G. G. Vinberg (1948). The transformations of organic matter evidently proceed most intensively during the summer and involve mainly the water mass of the lake.

Comparative studies of the planktonic biomass and the production and breakdown of organic matter in the water mass of several Belorussian lakes

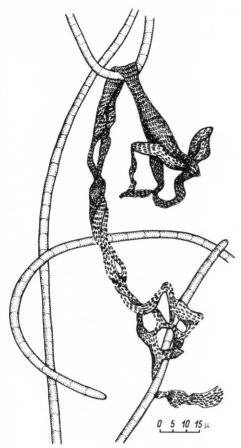

FIGURE 87. Teratobacter (after Perfil'ev).

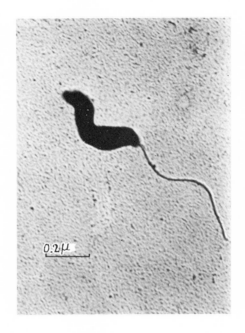

FIGURE 88. Bdellovibrio. Lake Glubokoe, depth 15 m (photo by G.A. Dubinina).

TABLE 48. Budget of organic matter in Lake Chernoe, kilocalories/m²/year (after Vinberg, 1948)

Item	Primary production	Destruction	Net production of organic matter
I. Water mass: bacteria, phytoplankton, and zooplankton	3,104	2,303	+711
II. Macrophyte growths	207	83	+124
III. Bottom region:			
(a) phytobenthos	3	1	+2
(b) zoobenthos	0	25	−25
(c) summer destruction in the bottom sediments (bacteria)	0	176*	−176
IV. Winter destruction	0	98	−98
V. Fishes	0	20	−20
Total	3,224	2,706	+518

* According to our own calculations based on the total amount of bacteria and the hydrologic regime of the lake; the active silt layer was taken as 1 mm.

have shown that the daily production by the phytoplankton in midsummer corresponds to 41—89% of the existing biomass (G. G. Vinberg and I. S. Zakharenkov, 1950). During the same period, 30—57% of the existing biomass is destroyed daily. These figures reflect the high rate of the transformations of organic matter in the upper water layers during the summer.

The water-soluble organic compounds formed by the autolysis of phytoplankton comprise proteins, amino acids, uronic acids, pectins, and humic substances. These are utilized by various microorganisms as building material or as general metabolites, which are finally degraded to carbon dioxide and water. To this category belong many bacteria capable of growing on pure agar in the presence of such extremely low concentrations of organic compounds as occur in natural waters (A. S. Razumov, 1962; M. F. Lazareva, 1953). Since the microorganisms in question account for about 30% of the total bacterial count (Razumov, 1948b, 1962), there can be no doubt about their role in the mineralization of dissolved organic substances.

TABLE 49. Proportions of various groups of microorganisms in different types of water bodies (after Razumov, 1948)

Water body	Total number of bacteria, direct count	Oligocarbophiles	Saprophytes		
			total number	sporeless, %	sporeforming, %
Klyazma Artificial Reservoir:					
near Ostashkov	926,000	88,600	280	—	—
near Chiverev	533,000	9,300	355	—	—
Baikal, oligotrophic	200,000	—	7	93	7
Shitovskoe, mesotrophic (Vyshnii Volochok)	—	—	46	76	24
Beloe, eutrophic (Kosino, Moscow Region)	2,000,000	—	154	90	10
Chernoe, dystrophic (Vyshnii Volochok)	—	—	13	15	85

Gram-negative bacteria are responsible for the initial stages of the decomposition of dissolved organic matter (A. S. Razumov, 1962). The following stages of the decomposition require the participation of sporeforming bacteria and Gram-positive rods and cocci. Pectins and humic substances, which are the most resistant of all, are attacked by mycobacteria (Kuznetsov and Dzyuban, 1960b). Table 49 shows the relationship between these bacterial groups.

In her studies of the destruction of organic matter in laboratory conditions, G. L. Margolina (1965) calculated the amount of readily assimilable organic substances from the magnitude of the biochemical consumption of oxygen. In these experiments, water from the Rybinsk Artificial Reservoir was distributed in bottles that were divided into two groups. One group was incubated at 18—20°, the other was kept in the refrigerator at 4°C.

Samples were taken periodically for determination of total biochemical oxygen demand, the total number of bacteria, the number of colonies of spore-forming saprophytes, and change in species composition. The myco-bacteria were counted separately.

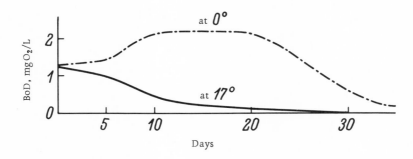

FIGURE 89. Change in the concentration of readily oxidizable substances in water from the Rybinsk Artificial Reservoir during storage in laboratory conditions (after Margolina, 1965).

The amount of readily assimilable organic compounds steadily decreased at room temperature (Figure 89). This was accompanied by a change in the composition of the microflora — namely, the percentage of sporeless forms decreased in favor of mycobacteria and spore-bearing ones. The destruction of organic matter took a different course at 4°. Here the amount of readily assimilable organic substances decreased during the first 2—3 days but began to rise afterward. It appears that the inhibitory effect of low tem-perature is less pronounced in the case of microorganisms that attack resis-tant organic substances and more so with those that feed on readily assimi-lable materials. The changes in the specific composition and the densities of the different groups of saprophyte bacteria confirm this view.

Judging from the amount of total nitrogen, the concentration of proteins in lake water is about 2—3 mg/L. These compounds are most readily attacked by organisms that possess proteolytic enzymes, notably some Pseudomonas species that commonly occur in lakes. Also readily assimilable are the amino acids, whose concentration is usually measured in hundredths of a milligram per liter.

Among the nonnitrogenous compounds are several hydroxyacids, whose concentrations in Lake Glubokoe (in mg/L) is as follows (S. V. Goryunova, 1952): malic acid 0.5—1.5, citric acid 1.1—1.9, tartaric acid 0.1—0.2; volatile acids have not been detected in this lake. These acids possibly result from the oxidation of sugars by the phytoplankton, which liberates them into the environment as part of its metabolic activity. Their salts are assimilated by microorganisms with comparative ease. Free sugars have not been found in lake water, probably because they occur at concen-trations that permit their utilization by oligocarbophilic organisms.

Other more or less readily decomposable compounds are liquid and gaseous hydrocarbons that enter the water from the outside as a result of the breakdown of silt. The solubility of these compounds is of the order of several mg per liter. Of eighty-seven strains of mycobacteria isolated from the water of the Volga Artificial Reservoirs, thirty-three proved capable of oxidizing kerosene and mineral oil. In addition to mycobacteria, some Pseudomonas species can oxidize liquid hydrocarbons. The oxidation of mineral oil often yields dark products.

Finally, some of the most resistant products are the humic acids, whose concentration attains 11.5 mg/L (A. V. Fotiev, 1966).

We found that the introduction of a pure culture of Mycobacterium to artificial reservoir water having a color of 200° according to the platinum-cobalt standard decreases the color to 100—110° within twenty days. Mycobacterium lacticolum, M. phlei, M. hyalinum, and M. album showed the most active destruction of humic acids. Glucose accelerates the oxidation of humic acids isolated from soil (D. I. Nikitin, 1960). Several Pseudomonas species take part in this process. Thus, a quantitative analysis of dissolved organic compounds made in parallel with a study of the distribution of different microbial species reveals the role of saprophytic microorganisms in the breakdown of different categories of organic matter.

Breakdown of Organic Matter Suspended in the Water Mass of Lakes

As we noted previously, the primary production of organic matter in water bodies depends mainly on the development of the phytoplankton. In lakes, the phytoplankton usually represents the main form of suspended organic matter exposed to bacterial attack.

However, microscopical analysis of various phytoplankters reveals a virtually bacteria-free surface. Inoculation of samples of net plankton on Petri dishes containing meat peptone agar shows that the colonies of saprophytic microorganisms that develop during an incubation period of 3—5 days appear invariably in the spaces between the planktic organisms. In other words, live plankters inoculated on meat peptone agar never serve as foci for colonies of saprophytic bacteria. The breakdown of phytoplankton in the water mass evidently begins only after its death.

The absence of bacteria from the surface of live phytoplankters is attributed to the secretion of bactericidal compounds (A. S. Razumov, 1948a, 1962).

Before sinking to the bottom, all the components of the silt traverse the water mass. A considerable part of the less resistant organic constituents of silt undergoes an aerobic breakdown during this traverse.

Figure 90 shows the changes in the composition of suspended particles at different depths in Lake Beloe as determined in midsummer in the presence of a luxuriant growth of phytoplankton (Kuznetsov, 1949b).

During the bloom period, the matter suspended in the surface water consisted largely of planktonic organisms, while the formless organic detritus accounted for a negligible fraction of it. Comparison of these data with the composition of suspended particles at a depth of 7 m shows that the particles descending to such depth are more than 90% decomposed. An even smaller proportion reaches a depth of 12 m. On the other hand, the proportion of the formless organic detritus increases slightly with depth.

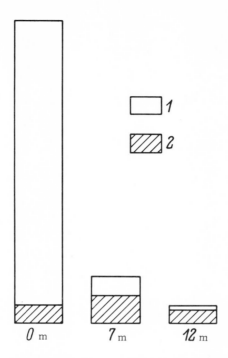

FIGURE 90. Composition of suspended organic particles in the water of Lake
Beloe (Kosino) on August 8, 1940 (after Kuznetsov):

1) plankton and bacteria, relative units of turbidity; 2) formless organic detritus.

These observations are in agreement with the results obtained by
M. A. Kastal'skaya-Karzinkina (1937) in Lake Glubokoe, where the majority
of the dead plankters undergo decomposition before sinking to the bottom.
On the basis of comparative chemical determinations of the composition
of the plankton and surface silt layers at a depth of 12 m in Lake Beloe
(Speranskaya, 1935), it is estimated that 90% of the dead plankton undergoes
decomposition while still in the water mass of the lake (Kuznetsov, 1952).
Ohle (1958, 1962) has reached a similar conclusion with respect to Gr. Plöner
See and other lakes in Schleswig-Holstein. The decomposition of plankton
begins with autolysis of the dead cells, which release readily assimilable
compounds into the surrounding water (Gaevskaya, 1948). These compounds
are then mineralized by the bacterial population of the water. The mineralization process affects first and foremost the organic compounds containing
readily assimilable nitrogen. The nature of this process depends largely
on the concentration of organic matter. At low concentrations, the reactions
are largely carried out by that fraction of the microflora which can be determined only under the microscope and does not grow on meat peptone agar.
This probably explains the commonly observed relationship between the
total bacterial count and the trophic regime of the lake (Khartulari and
Kuznetsov, 1936; Novobrantsev, 1937; Kuznetsov, 1949b). What remains
intact is the aquatic humus, whose concentration varies greatly from one
lake to another according to the trophic conditions (P.V. Novobrantsev, 1937)
(Table 50).

TABLE 50. Concentration of assimilable organic matter in different types of water bodies (after Novobrantsev, 1937)

Water body	Total organic matter, mg of O_2/L	Assimilable organic matter, mg of O_2/L	Aquatic humus, % of total organic matter	Total density of bacteria per ml by direct method
Peat quarry	276.5	8.1	97.0	2,320,000
Eutrophic lakes:				
Bol'shoe Medvezh'e				
(Moscow Region)..	33.7	7.6	77.4	3,720,000
Beloe (Kosino,				
Moscow Region)..	32.1	4.5	83.1	2,230,000

The lysis does not affect the debris of the cell walls of the phytoplankton. These fragments, which consist essentially of alginic acids and cellulose, undergo further aerobic degradation in the water mass of the lake.

Z. I. Kuznetsova (1937) has examined the saprophytic microflora that develop on dead plankton in Lake Glubokoe. Water for analysis was collected in sterile flasks, and the plankton was separated by filtration through sterile membrane filters, which were then placed in Petri dishes containing glucose peptone agar. Bacterial colonies developed in the vicinity of dead plankters, around Anabaena, for example, while the dead filaments of Aphanisomenon became surrounded with colonies of large cocci. Kuznetsova isolated seventeen saprophytic species from detritus and planktic debris in Lake Glubokoe. This microflora consisted largely of spore-forming bacteria. Among the identified microorganisms were Bac. subflavus, Bac. agnatilis graveolens, Bac. devorens, Bac. liodermus, and Serratia rutilescens.

Bac. corrugatus was encountered almost throughout the vegetation period; Bact. subflavus occurred mostly in the spring during the bloom of diatoms, and Bact. liodermus occurred mainly in the fall.

According to the studies of S. I. Kuznetsov (1934a) in Lakes Beloe and Glubokoe (Moscow Region), the density of cellulose-destroying aerobic bacteria in the lake water remains rather low except in summer, when it may attain several hundreds per ml (Table 51). Most of these bacteria belong to the genera Cytophaga and Cellvibrio.

TABLE 51. Density of cellulose-destroying bacteria in the water of the Lakes Beloe and Glubokoe (per ml)

Lake	Layer	Time of analysis					
		April	June	August	September	November	February
Beloe (Kosino,	Epilimnion	10	40	—	100	0.1	0.1
Moscow Region)..	Hypolimnion	1	2	—	100	0.4	0.2
Glubokoe (Moscow	Epilimnion	9	—	600	10	2	0.2
Region)	Hypolimnion	2	—	40	40	8	0.4

It appears, however, that the conventional method of dilution counting by inoculation of tenfold dilutions yields too low figures, since the bacteria appear on the detritus as aggregates that are counted as single cells.

A. G. Rodina (1963a, 1963b, 1967) used luminescent microscopy in her studies of bacterial aggregates on detritus from a number of lakes. She observed large aggregates of different forms of bacteria. This method, however, does not reveal the physiologic properties of the bacteria.

Among the allochthonous organic substances found in lakes are hydrocarbons, which constitute the bituminous fraction of the plant debris, and various polluting agents, such as oil and bitumen hydrocarbons. All these compounds are more or less readily oxidized by bacteria; they occur in lakes and especially in artificial reservoirs.

The work of S. I. Kuznetsov (1947) on the distribution of hydrocarbon-oxidizing bacteria in freshwaters and the corresponding studies of ZoBell (1943) in marine environments have shown the existence of bacteria that oxidize methane, hexane, heptane, and similar compounds, especially in the bottom water. In addition, bacteria-utilizing naphthalene and phthalic acid were found to be widespread in some water bodies. The latter bacterial groups appear to be involved in the decomposition of humus (V. E. Pontovich, 1938). Paraffin-oxidizing bacteria are even more common in various water bodies.

TABLE 52. Occurrence of hydrocarbon-oxidizing bacteria in different types of lakes (% of number of examined lakes) (after Kuznetsov, 1947, 1959b; Dzyuban, 1959)

Type of lake	Bacteria that oxidize					
	methane	propane	hexane	solar oil	naphthalene	phthalic acid
Eutrophic	100	10	50	—	100	50
Mesotrophic	40	0	0	—		50
Oligotrophic	10	0	0	—	0	0
Dystrophic	100	0	100	—	50	0
Artificial reservoirs	100	—	—	100	—	—

Decay of the Higher Aquatic Vegetation

In shallow lakes with extensive macrophyte growths, the role of the higher aquatic vegetation in the formation of bottom sediments is fully comparable to that of the plankton.

After a detailed study of the decay of macrophytes and the participation of their debris in the formation of lake silts, M. A. Messineva and A. M. Gorbunova (1946) concluded that the decay starts at the moment of death and is accompanied by the growth of a large bacterial population that develops on the debris and comprises forms attacking sugar, starch, and cellulose. The bacterial count attains hundreds of millions per gram of dry plant. The concentrations of water-soluble compounds, hemicelluloses, pentosans and cellulose decrease during the process, while that of lignin-humus substances increase. Regrettably, the authors do not report on the ash content of the initial and final materials, which makes it impossible to calculate the proportion of the destroyed organic matter.

Messineva and Gorbunova conclude on the basis of these results that the decaying fragments enrich the water with soluble nitrogen compounds, salts, gases, etc., while the silt sediments receive such substances as lignin, cellulose, hemicelluloses, bitumens, and proteins of the microflora that participate in the breakdown of the plant debris. The decay of reed and pond weeds follows a similar course. In contrast to pond lilies, these plants supply large amounts of bituminous substances to the lake silt.

Other authors report a similar increase in the number of bacteria living on cut-down and decaying aquatic vegetation.

An anaerobic zone with a rich bacterial population develops around masses of cut-down, decaying reed in empondment water bodies along the Volga. Here the boundary between the aerobic and anaerobic zones attracts masses of zooplankton that apparently feed on the bacteria (S.I.Kuznetsov, G.S. Karzinkin, 1955).

S. A. Krasheninnikova (1958) studied the effect of live and cut-down vegetation on the bacterial population of the littoral of the Rybinsk Artificial Reservoir. Determinations of the saprophyte microflora living on green vegetating plants showed that the density of saprophyte bacteria on reed and water smartweed reaches in mid-August a peak of more than 100 million cells per gram of raw scrapings from the surface of the plants. Much lower figures are obtained in October. The density of saprophytic bacteria in the water around the higher aquatic vegetation attained several thousands per ml, compared with only a few cells in the open part of the artificial reservoir.

The density of saprophytic bacteria on bundles of cut-down plants increased considerably with the decay of the vegetation. As shown in Figure 91, the population of saprophytic bacteria reached a peak of 940 million cells per gram of raw scrapings from reed stems twenty-five days after the beginning of the experiment. Thus, the decay of higher aquatic vegetation proceeds rather quickly at a temperature of about 20°C and is accompanied by a luxuriant growth of saprophytic bacteria, not only on the dead plants but also in the surrounding water.

Decomposition of Organic Matter in Silt

Silts largely reflect the nature of the water body in which they develop. In eutrophic lakes, where the primary production reaches a high magnitude in the surface layers, about 50% of the silt consists of organic remnants of phytoplankton and higher aquatic vegetation. Conversely, the ash content of silt can exceed 90% in oligotrophic waters.

A considerable proportion of the organic remnants undergoes further decay after sinking to the lake bottom. V. A. Ekzertsev (1948) and N. B. Zavarzina determined the vertical range of microbiological decay phenomena in silt from the microbial growth that develops on a glass slide

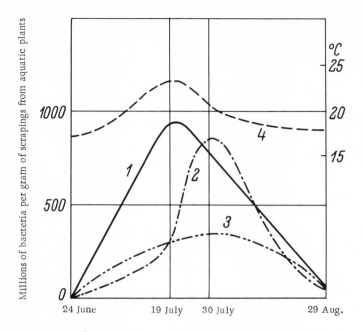

FIGURE 91. Density of saprophytic bacteria on scrapings from cut-down plants: 1) reed; 2) sedge; 3) water smartweed (after Krasheninnikova); 4) water temperature, °C.

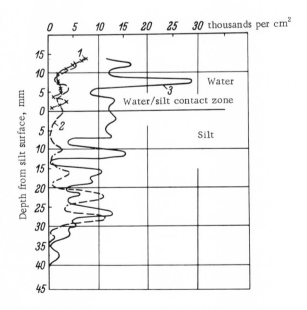

FIGURE 92. Development of microbial growths on glass slides immersed in the water and silt of Lake Piyavochnoe:

1) blue-green algae; 2) iron bacteria; 3) bacterial organisms.

placed in the lake for a period of five days in such a manner that the water/ silt boundary passed along the middle of the glass.

In the dystrophic Lake Piyavochnoe (Figure 92), filamentous iron bacteria developed only on the glass surface exposed to water, while S i d e r o c a p s a t r e u b i i grew in contact with the silt to a depth of 1.7 cm. In addition, there were thick filaments of blue-green algae, probably L y n g b y a, mostly above the silt surface. Fungal hyphae formed masses of fine filaments on the glass at a depth of 1.5—3 cm from the silt surface, that is, below the area occupied by live algal cells. Bacterial organisms, rods as well as cocci, showed a more uniform distribution, though their greatest density corresponded to the bottom water layer. Beyond a depth of 3—3.5 cm from the silt surface there were only isolated bacteria. Glasses placed at a depth of more than 40 mm remained practically sterile.

Clearly, the rapid decay of organic matter in the silt of Lake Piyavochnoe covers a vertical range of only 4 cm.

Similar results were obtained by N. B. Zavarzina, who placed glass slides in silt monoliths extracted from lakes and kept in glass tubes.

The nature of the decomposition of silt in the pelogenic zone depends largely on the absolute quantity of "readily assimilable nitrogen," that is, the total nitrogen that passes into solution after a hydrolysis of the silt with 5% sulfuric acid; another important factor is the ratio between the "readily assimilable" forms of nitrogen and carbon.

Large amounts of such readily assimilable organic compounds usually occur in the silts of eutrophic lakes. Their further breakdown proceeds anaerobically with the production of methane and CO_2. The silts of oligotrophic lakes are so poor in organic matter that anaerobic conditions can develop only at some depth inside the silt; aerobic conditions prevail in the bottom water of such lakes.

After a thorough analysis of the organic matter at different depths inside the silts of Lakes Beloe and Chernoe (in Kosino), Kuznetsov, Speranskaya, and Konshin (1939) conclude that the breakdown of hemicelluloses, cellulose, and compounds extractable with alcohol-benzene proceeds most rapidly in the surface layer of silt. The organic composition of silt remains largely unchanged from a depth of 1 m (see Table 9).

These results agree with the vertical distribution of the overall bacterial count in silt. The density of bacteria in silt is of the order of billions of cells per gram of raw silt (G. S. Karzinkin and S. I. Kuznetsov, 1931; S. I. Kuznetsov, 1950b, 1952; E. M. Khartulari, 1939; V. A. Ekzertsev, 1948). This magnitude decreases rapidly with depth and levels off at about 100—200 million cells per gram of raw silt from a depth of 1 m; at the same time the proportion of live bacteria drops to 30% (N. B. Zavarzina, 1955b).

Numerous works deal with the vertical distribution of different physiologic groups of microorganisms, including cellulose-destroying ones, in the silt. Most of these publications have a largely qualitative approach (Omelyansky, 1917; Shturm, 1928b; Salimovskaya-Rodina, 1932). Table 53 contains some quantitative data from L. D. Shturm and Z. A. Kanunnikova (1945), and S. I. Kuznetsov (1950).

Despite the presence of considerable amounts of hemicelluloses, cellulose, and bitumens deep inside the silt mass, the microorganisms that attack these compounds are concentrated in the surface layer of silt. This applies to aerobes and anaerobes alike.

TABLE 53. Vertical distribution of different groups of bacteria in lake silts (thousands of cells per gram of raw silt)

Depth, m	Piyavochnoe (Vyshnii Volochok)				Western Siberia			
					Andreevskoe		Lipovoe	
	ammonifying bacteria		cellulose-attacking anaerobes	Clostridium pasteurianum	cellulose-attacking bacteria	bacteria that decompose fatty acids	cellulose-attacking bacteria	bacteria that decompose fatty acids
	aerobes	anaerobes						
0	220	35	0.2	0.2	10	0.1	1	0
0.5	7	1.3	0.02	0.04	1	0.1	0.1	0
1	—	—	0.003	0.005	0.3	0.01	0.1	0
3	0.2	0.3	0.004	0.003	0	0	0.1	0
6	—	0.3	—	0.003	—	—	—	—

Anaerobic breakdown of hydrocarbons with the production of gases. The methane-yielding anaerobic destruction of organic matter is a widespread phenomenon in nature (V. L. Omelyansky, 1906). For example, an anaerobic breakdown of lake silt with the formation of gaseous products was observed in Lake Beloe in Kosino (S. I. Kuznetsov and Z. I. Kuznetsova, 1935), and V. I. Romanenko (1966) has examined the distribution of methane-producing bacteria in the Rybinsk Artificial Reservoir. Figure 93 shows the results of his work.

The organic matter of lake silts contains a large proportion of such highly resistant compounds as lignin and humus, besides various components that are more or less readily attacked by microorganisms (S.I. Kuznetsov, T. A. Speranskaya, and V. D. Konshin, 1939). The average concentrations of some ingredients are as follows: sugars and hemicelluloses 14%, cellulose 7%, bitumens 8%, lignin-humus complex 60%, and total nitrogen 4.52%, which corresponds to a "raw protein" content of 28.3%. The "raw protein" is not identical with protein, since part of the nitrogen belongs to the humus complex. Nevertheless, some silts contain a high percentage of proteins, especially those of eutrophic lakes. Moreover, salts of fatty acids are constantly present in the silts of all the lakes and artificial reservoirs examined by T. A. Speranskaya (1935), V. I. Romanenko (1965), Vallentyne (1959), and others. In Lake Beloe (Kosino), for example, the concentration of acetic acid reached 2.3% of the organic matter of silt. Butyric and formic acids were present in smaller amounts.

Comparing the chemical composition of silt with the theoretically possible pathways of anaerobic fermentation of this substance, S. I. Kuznetsov and E. M. Khartulari (1941) list the following sources of lake gas (a mixture of methane, hydrogen, carbon dioxide, and nitrogen):

1. Sugars and hemicelluloses are broken down to carbon dioxide and fatty acids, which are further degraded to carbon dioxide and methane or hydrogen.

2. Cellulose is decomposed to carbon dioxide, fatty acids, and hydrogen (V. L. Omelyansky, 1899, 1902; Clausen, 1931).

3. Fatty acids are decomposed to methane and carbon dioxide.

4. The anaerobic breakdown of proteins can yield hydrogen, carbon dioxide, and free nitrogen (without such stages as nitrification or denitrification) (Bach and Sierp, 1923—1924; Korol'kov, 1926).

5. Another conceivable mechanism of methane formation involves condensation of hydrogen and carbon dioxide (Barker, 1956) — a process first postulated by Söhngen (1906).

6. Citric acid may be formed from hydrogen and carbon dioxide (Wieringa, 1940).

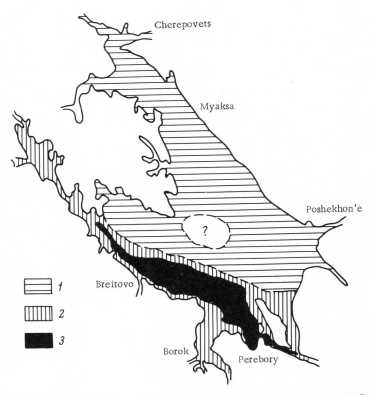

FIGURE 93. Distribution of methane-producing bacteria in the Rybinsk Artificial Reservoir (after Romanenko).

Numbers of methane-producing bacteria per gram of raw silt: 1) less than 30,000; 2) 30,000—100,000; 3) 100,000—200,000.

Anaerobic breakdown of hemicelluloses and sugars. In order to isolate the corresponding group of bacteria, S. I. Kuznetsov and E. M. Khartulari (1941) prepared an acid hydrolysate of silt from Lake Beloe. After being neutralized with alkali, the hydrolysate was converted to a solid medium by the addition of 2% agar. Clearly, the silt hydrolysate contains the products of readily hydrolyzable proteins, sugars, and hemicelluloses. After inoculating this medium with a suitable dilution of fresh silt, Kuznetsov and

Khartulari distributed it (while it was still in a liquid state) in sterile glass tubes. Bacterial colonies appeared in the agar after an incubation of 3—4 days at 30°. The agar was cracked around some colonies owing to the production of gas. The tubes were cut at the suitable places, and bacteria from each colony were transferred to tubes containing meat peptone broth with glucose. In this manner five cultures were selected that produced abundant gas in meat peptone broth with glucose. After suitable tests for purity and further inoculations in glucose broth and peptone broth, it became evident that the gas results from the breakdown of glucose and does not originate from peptone or other proteins.

All five cultures showed identical traits, the only difference between them being the rate of gas production. They were determined as closely related to Clostridium tertium, although they differed from the latter in the lack of growth on agar slants and the wide variation in the size of the bacterial cells.

Silt from Lake Beloe was sterilized in test tubes and was inoculated with Clostridium tertium. The inoculation resulted in a partial decomposition of the silt, accompanied by gas formation and a liquefaction of the upper part of the silt column. This picture closely resembles the rupture and liquefaction of the silt column in a stratometric cylinder from the deep-water areas of Lake Beloe. Further tests showed that the gas formed in the fermentation of the sugar consists of carbon dioxide and hydrogen. Since pure cultures of C. tertium also produce acids when grown in a sugar-containing synthetic medium, we assume that in silt this microorganism attacks mainly sugars and hemicelluloses, oxidizing them by a dehydrogenation pathway that leads to molecular hydrogen.

Anaerobic breakdown of cellulose. In view of the fact that cellulose is a major component of the organic matter of silt, Kuznetsov and Khartulari tried to isolate an anaerobic cellulose-attacking bacterium and obtain a breakdown of sterile lake silt to gaseous products under the influence of this bacterium.

An enrichment culture was obtained on the Omelyansky medium for anaerobic cellulose-destroying bacteria. The next step was the preparation of a pure culture on the Omelyansky inorganic medium with added agar and cellulose that was previously ground in a mortar to fine fibers. The molten agar was inoculated with a suitable dilution of the enrichment culture of cellulose bacteria and was distributed in thin sterile glass tubes as in the case of hemicellulose-attacking bacteria. Several colonies and gas bubbles were found in the tubes after an incubation for 5—6 days at 30—32°. Colonies could not be seen with the naked eye in the vicinity of the gas bubbles. However, microscopic examination of slides with imprints from sites of agar breaks revealed the presence of rods of different sizes. The largest rods had a terminal spore. For the preparation of a pure culture, a piece of agar taken from a suitable part of the tube was placed in the Omelyansky medium in small bulbs 1—1.5 cm in diameter, made by blowing glass tubes 5 mm in diameter. After the cellulose bacteria were allowed sufficient time for development and gas production, the content of the small bulbs was transferred to normal test tubes. Such abundant inoculum led to a satisfactory growth of the cellulose bacteria in the test tubes. The culture was passed three times in the small glass tubes. It was highly uniform morphologically.

The gas produced in the decomposition of cellulose was found to consist of hydrogen and carbon dioxide. On these grounds the authors identified the microorganism as Bac. omelianskii.

Microscopic examinations showed the presence of large numbers of cellulose bacteria on the fibers of the filter paper, on the asbestos, and in the culture fluid during the production of gas. The test tubes containing sterilized silt were inoculated with culture fluid and asbestos — a cellulose-free material. However, a breakdown of silt under the influence of cellulose bacteria could not be detected in this case. Such breakdown occurred only in those experiments in which the inoculum was introduced together with cellulose in the form of filter paper. This result can be explained in two ways. One possibility is that the silt does not contain cellulose and the observed reduction of Fehling's solution results from the presence of products of the hydrolysis of proteins. According to the other explanation, the cellulose present in silt becomes available to cellulose bacteria after being acted upon by a satellite microorganism. At any rate, the conditions for the development of cellulose bacteria were quite satisfactory in the cultures and natural silt alike. In fact, gas production ensued rapidly even when the filter paper was introduced long after the inoculation of the sterile silt with cellulose bacteria.

Since the cellulose bacteria are a constant component of the bacterial cenosis of natural silt, one could assume that the fermentation of silt cellulose results from the combined activity of different bacteria. To test this hypothesis, silt from Lake Beloe was inoculated in a medium composed of an acid hydrolysate of silt with 2% agar. After six days of incubation at 30°, bacterial colonies accompanied by agar cracks were found. One of the numerous isolated strains from the silt hydrolysate cultures caused little or no decomposition of silt; when inoculated together with a culture of cellulose bacteria in tubes with sterile silt, however, this same strain produced large quantities of gas. This strain was later determined as closely related to Achromobacter rathonis (G. and T.), although it differs from the latter in being unable to utilize phenol as a source of organic matter.

The isolate related to Achromobacter rathonis does not cause a gas-yielding decomposition of silt when inoculated alone in sterile silt. Together with cellulose bacteria, however, it produces gas bubbles at a rate comparable to that observed in Clostridium tertium.

According to S. I. Kuznetsov and E. M. Khartulari (1941), further and more precise chemical analyses are necessary in order to determine the state of cellulose in silt; a microbiological breakdown of silt to gaseous products can be carried out by a number of combined cultures, including one composed of Bac. omelianskii and an organism related to Achromobacter rathonis.

Anaerobic breakdown of fatty acids. As we noted above, salts of fatty acids are among the constant components of lake silts. The distribution of microorganisms capable of decomposing these salts in anaerobic conditions was determined in a number of lakes and artificial reservoirs. It was found that the water of artificial reservoirs usually contains microorganisms that utilize salts of formic, acetic, and butyric acids; in lakes, these microorganisms penetrate to a considerable depth in the silt (E. M. Khartulari, 1939; V. I. Romanenko, 1964c, 1966).

A breakdown of fatty acids undoubtedly does occur in lake silt at a rate depending on the oxidation-reduction potential of the surrounding medium.

Bacteria capable of destroying formic acid were isolated from the silt of Lake Beloe in Kosino (N. N. Krasina, 1936). This organism is related to Bact. formicicum (Omelianskii). Without particular difficulties, Krasina obtained an enrichment culture that performed an anaerobic breakdown of acetate in a liquid Omelyansky medium containing 2% calcium acetate and 0.2% peptone. A series of inocula in a liquid medium with added fibrous asbestos resulted in a highly active culture, especially when the bacteria were inoculated by means of the asbestos.

S. I. Kuznetsov and E. M. Khartulari (1941) obtained analogous bacterial cultures from silt and demonstrated that sterile silt can be partly decomposed to gaseous products under the influence of bacteria that ferment fatty acids.

Fermentation of silt by pure bacterial cultures. Having obtained pure cultures of the main groups of bacteria that attack the organic ingredients of silt, S. I. Kuznetsov and E. M. Khartulari (1941) tested the activity of these microorganisms in the fermentation of silt sterilized in the autoclave.

The experiments showed that sterile silt invariably ferments after being inoculated with fresh silt. Bac. omelianskii never produces gas in silt. Cultures that attack fatty acids cause fermentation only in some cases. This probably depends on the activity of the culture and the composition of the silt, which may vary from one season to another. Combined cultures of Bac. omelianskii and Achromobacter rathonis invariably produce gas. A. rathonis appears to accompany cellulose bacteria, like Clostridium tertium.

S. I. Kuznetsov and E. M. Khartulari (1941) analyzed the gas produced in sterilized silt following an inoculation with pure cultures of Achromobacter rathonis and Clostridium tertium. Table 54 shows the results of this analysis.

TABLE 54. Composition of the gas obtained by the fermentation of silt from Lake Beloe (Kosino), in vol. % (after Kuznetsov and Khartulari, 1941)

Conditions of test	Duration of test, days	CO_2	H_2	CH_4	N_2
Fresh silt from Lake Beloe	2	7.2	12.5	55.2	25.1
	9	14.0	9.5	76.0	0.5
Sterile silt inoculated with Achromobacter rathonis	3	0	78.8	0	21.2
Sterile silt inoculated with Clostridium tertium	2	0	77.0	0	23.0
Sterile silt inoculated with Bac. omelianskii + Achromobacter rathonis	4	2.3	80.0	9.6	8

It is evident from Table 54 that most of the microorganisms produce hydrogen from the decomposition of silt. Kuznetsov and Khartulari assumed on these grounds that the synthesis of methane in silt consists of two stages:

TABLE 55. Biological reduction of CO_2 to CH_4 over silt

Conditions of test	Days of incubation	Pressure, mm of Hg	Composition of gas mixture, %				Composition of gas mixture in cm³, calculated for 100 ml initial volume				
			CO_2	H_2	CH_4	N_2	CO_2	H_2	CH_4	N_2	total at 760 mm of Hg
Fermented silt	1	760	12.39	80.76	0	6.85	12.4	80.8	0	6.8	100
	10		0.27	48.28	0	51.46	0.2	4.8	0	5.0	10
Over the same silt without contact with the air, filled with new gas mixture	1	760	16.14	83.86	0	0	16.1	83.9	0	0	100
	10	360	24.86	67.81	0	7.33	11.8	32.2	0	3.5	47.5
	26	120	36.22	9.51	24.12	38.15	5.7	1.5	3.8	4.8	15.8
Fresh surface silt from a depth of 12m in Lake Beloe	1	760	13.06	86.94	0	0	13.1	86.9	0	0	100
	140	490	11.25	4.65	76.15	7.95	8.05	3.0	49.1	5.15	65.3

(1) fermentation of silt with the production of carbon dioxide and hydrogen by the above-mentioned microorganisms; (2) synthesis of methane according to the equation $CO_2 + 4H_2O = CH_4 + 2H_2O$.

To test this hypothesis, it was necessary to establish the existence of the following reactions: (1) a production of methane from hydrogen and carbon dioxide in the presence of lake silt; (2) a formation of hydrogen side by side with methane during the fermentation of lake silt.

The production of methane from carbon dioxide and of hydrogen was tested after the method of Fischer, Licke, and Winzer (1932). A mixture of one part CO_2 and four parts H_2 was placed in a jar of a capacity of 500—700 ml over 50 ml of silt. Then the jar was hermetically sealed off. The experiments were made in parallel with fresh and fermented silt; the latter produced not more than 0.1 ml of methane for thirty days, which means that practically all the methane was obtained from hydrogen and carbon dioxide.

As shown in Table 55, the volume of the gas mixture decreases considerably during the first ten days of the experiment, while methane begins to appear after 20—30 days from the beginning of the experiment. Fischer and co-workers (Fischer, Licke, and Winzer, 1932) observed a similar decrease of the volume of the gas mixture owing to the formation of acetic acid as an intermediate product of the reaction.

Methane appears in laboratory conditions from the interaction of hydrogen and carbon dioxide in the presence of silt. On the other hand, M e t h a -
n o b a c t e r i u m   o m e l i a n s k i i is invariably present in silt. It is almost certain, therefore, that a similar process occurs very intensively in natural lake-type environments, especially in view of the fact that in laboratory conditions the reaction is much faster over fresh silt than over fermented silt (Table 55).

To answer the second question, namely, whether the anaerobic breakdown of the organic matter of silt yields molecular oxygen, Kuznetsov and Khartulari made the following experiment. They took fresh surface silt from a depth of 12.5 m in Lake Beloe and placed it in a fermentation jar. The gas produced in the course of fermentation was removed daily from the jar as quantitatively as possible for a period of nine days and was analyzed. The changes in the course and nature of the fermentation could thus be determined from the composition of the released gas. Indeed, the percentage of hydrogen was much higher during the early days of the fermentation but later decreased in favor of methane. This can be explained as follows. The higher temperature prevailing in the laboratory accelerated the breakdown of the fresh silt. First affected by this change were the primary processes of organic breakdown to hydrogen and other products, whereas the secondary processes involving the reduction of carbon dioxide with hydrogen into methane were intensified some time later. The following figures (in percentage) show the changes in the composition of the gas released during the fermentation of silt in laboratory conditions:

Duration of incubation of silt, days	CO_2	H_2	CH_4	N_2
1	7.2	12.5	55.2	25.1
2—3	7.2	11.6	76.4	4.8
4—5	7.6	8.5	79.0	4.9
6—9	8.7	2.3	86.2	2.8

TABLE 56. Distribution of hydrocarbon-oxidizing bacteria in silt (% occurrence from number of lakes tested)

Depth from silt surface, m	Number of samples	Bacteria that oxidize			
		hydrogen	methane	propane	hexane
Surface	15	53	73	0	7
0.5	8	50	38	25	12
1.0	6	17	17	0	17
1.5	2	0	0	0	0
2.0	3	0	0	0	0
2.5	1	0	0	0	0

Clearly, the reduction of carbon dioxide to methane does occur on a considerable scale in nature.

Breakdown of the bituminous fraction of organic matter. The hydrocarbons and bituminous fraction of the organic matter of silt were largely regarded as resistant to bacterial attack. This view must be revised in the light of recent evidence (Osnitskaya, 1953; Hutton and ZoBell, 1949). Indeed, bacteria that oxidize liquid and gaseous hydrocarbons are widespread in sapropels. Such is the conclusion of S. I. Kuznetsov (1950b) with respect to lakes in Western Siberia and Northern Kazakhstan. The data obtained by this author show also the vertical distribution of bacteria in the silt mass (Table 56). Bacteria that oxidize gaseous and liquid hydrocarbons are widespread in sapropels, and a breakdown of these hydrocarbons is possible to a depth of 1 m (Table 56).

Bacteria that oxidize naphthalene and phthalic acid appear to be even more widespread in silt (Kuznetsov, 1947). Bacteria that oxidize paraffin, wax, and fats are also commonly found in sapropels (L. D. Shturm and S. I. Orlova, 1937; L. D. Shturm and N. P. Fedorovskaya, 1941; L. D. Shturm, M. A. Messineva, and N. P. Fedorovskaya, 1941). Bituminous compounds undergo a comparatively rapid anaerobic breakdown in parallel with the reduction of sulfates (Tauson and Aleshina, 1932). At any rate, the lignin-humus complex remains the most resistant in anaerobic conditions.

Vertical range of active breakdown of organic matter in silt. By comparing the chemical analyses with the above-mentioned data on the vertical distribution of different physiologic groups of bacteria, S. I. Kuznetsov (1949a) concludes that the further breakdown of the organic matter of sapropels becomes negligible or absent at a depth of about 1 m. This was somewhat puzzling in view of the constant presence of hemicelluloses, cellulose, and nitrogenous organic compounds at even greater depths. Moreover, deep-lying sapropels often contain a greater proportion of organic matter in comparison with shallow-water ones. The observed extinction of the further decomposition of organic matter might be due to the accumulation of microbial metabolic products that inhibit the further activity of the microorganisms (Omelyansky, 1925). Another possible cause is the scarcity of organic substrate. To solve this problem, Kuznetsov tested the combined and individual effect of glucose and peptone on silt samples placed in Dunbar vessel the amount of gas produced by the anaerobic breakdown of organic matter was determined (Kuznetsov, 1950b).

TABLE 57. Effect of glucose and peptone on the production of gas from the fermentation in laboratory conditions of silt taken from several lakes in Western Siberia and Northern Kazakhstan (% of tested samples) (after Kuznetsov, 1950b)

Depth from silt surface, m	Number of samples examined	Production of gas (average of 3 tests)				
		silt only	with added glucose	with added peptone	with added glucose and peptone	with added glucose, peptone, and yeasts
Surface	18	1	80	19	100	100
0.5	10	0.2	68	11	100	100
1.0	8	0	75	5	100	100
2.0	5	0	44	5	100	100
3.0	2	0	45	4	100	100
4.0	1	0	45	3	100	100
5.0	1	0	45	1	100	100
6.0	1	0	40	1	100	100
7.0	1	0	30	5	100	100
8.0	1	0	30	0	100	100

Table 57 shows the results obtained with silt samples taken from different depths.

The high figures of gas production in the presence of glucose and peptone reflect the possibility of a rapid activation of the silt microflora. On the other hand, the lack of gas in the absence of glucose or peptone indicates that carbohydrates and proteins assimilable by microorganisms do not occur at a depth of more than 0.5 m in silt. It appears that the whole reserve of carbohydrates and readily assimilable proteins is already exhausted by fermentation at greater depths, which prevents the further breakdown of silt.

The results obtained separately with glucose and peptone indicate that the slowing-down of the decomposition of silt is due primarily to the exhaustion of assimilable carbohydrates.

Causes of the Localization of the Gas-Yielding Breakdown of Organic Matter in the Deep Part of the Basin of Eutrophic Lakes

Observations in many lakes show that gas production is maximal over the deep part of the lake basin (Rossolimo, 1932b).

Why is the production of gas largely confined to the deep part of the lake basin? S. I. Kuznetsov and E. M. Khartulari (1941) approached this problem from a biological standpoint.

Silt samples from the surface and from a depth of 10—15 cm were taken from several sites of different water depth in Lake Beloe. The silt samples were placed in sealed vessels, and the quantity of gas formed was measured in the laboratory after an incubation of eleven days at 28—30°. The results obtained appear in Table 58.

223

TABLE 58. Gas production during the breakdown of silt taken from different depths in Lake Beloe (after Kuznetsov and Khartulari, 1941)

Depth of station, m	Silt layer, cm (depth from silt surface)	Raw weight of silt, grams	Moisture, %	Gas produced, cm^3		
				in whole experiment	per gram of dry silt	
					in each duplicate	average
4	0—1	251.60 253.20	96.55	22.8 29.0	2.63 3.32	2.98
	10—15	250.15	96.75	2.0	0.25	0.25
5.5	0—1	247.15 248.35	95.52	53.5 37.5	3.93 3.37	3.65
	10—15	251.80 265.67	92.43	4.0 6.5	0.21 0.31	0.26
10	0—1	275.30 225.90	94.29	61.0 52.2	4.49 4.05	4.27
	10—15	254.1 273.75	93.46	66.5 50.0	4.00 2.79	3.39
12	0—1	215.68 246.30	94.82	58.5 54.0	5.24 4.62	4.93
	10—15	243.30	93.72	55.5	3.63	3.63

As the table shows, the fermentation of silt taken from the deep part of the lake basin yields large quantities of gas, regardless of whether the silt originates from the surface or from a depth of 10—15 cm. Conversely, a considerable difference was observed in this respect with silt samples from shallow stations. In other words, the gas-yielding decomposition of silt occupies a greater vertical range in the deeper central part of the lake basin than in the shallower peripheral areas.

The presence of a thicker layer of gas-producing silt in the deep-water part of lakes is due to the fact that the dead plankton participates in further movements after settling on the bottom and forming the surface layer of silt. Indeed, observations in Lake Glubokoe (Karzinkin, Kuznetsov, and Kuznetsova, 1930) and Lake Beloe (Rossolimo, 1932b, 1935) have shown that the summer temperature of silt is lower than that of the bottom water; by giving up part of its heat to the bottom proper, the lowermost water cools down and descends to the deepest part of the lake, sweeping along the surface silt (Rossolimo, 1932a).

Scheme of Carbon Cycle in Lakes

Figure 94 shows the overall cycle of carbon in lakes. In the process of photosynthesis, free CO_2 and bicarbonates become part of the phytoplankton and higher aquatic vegetation. Moreover, the chemosynthetic activity of many autotrophic bacteria involves a direct fixation of carbon dioxide (1). Heterotrophic bacteria develop mainly at the expense of allochthonous organic matter and remnants of phytoplankton (5).

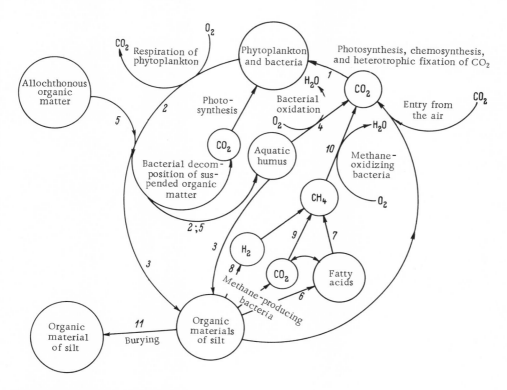

FIGURE 94. Scheme of the carbon cycle in lakes.

Explanation in the text.

The remains of the dead plankton, aquatic plants, and bacteria undergo an extensive aerobic decomposition while still in the water mass (2). This process leads to carbon dioxide and "aquatic humus." The latter is highly resistant; together with other unchanged remnants of plant and animal organisms it settles on the bottom (3), where it becomes a part of the organic matter of silt (3), although a fraction of it undergoes bacterial decomposition with the formation of carbon dioxide (4).

Depending on the nature of the water body, a varying proportion of the plant remnants undergoes further anaerobic decomposition in the silt.

Fatty acids (6) are among the main intermediate products of this anaerobic breakdown; they do not accumulate in appreciable amounts but are immediately degraded to methane and carbon dioxide (7). The anaerobic breakdown of cellulose and carbohydrates of plant origin yields fatty acids, carbon dioxide, and hydrogen (8). M e t h a n o b a c t e r i u m o m e l i a n s k i i uses these gases for the synthesis of methane (9); the latter, a major component of lake gas, enters the water and is oxidized there again to carbon dioxide (10).

A large proportion of the pelogenic organic matter is buried (11) in the silt and leaves the cycle at a depth of 0.5—1 m inside the silt.

Concerning the transformation of carbon in the lake, it must be noted that the bulk of the organic matter is synthesized and broken down again to mineral components in the water mass, the mineralization being along aerobic pathways. However, a certain proportion of the organic matter — smaller in oligotrophic lakes, larger in eutrophic ones — is buried as organic component of the silt and thus leaves the cycle. On the other hand, part of the carbon of the organic fractions of the silt is converted into methane, which escapes into the atmosphere, while another part leaves the lake with the bodies of live organisms.

Clearly, the maintenance of the carbon budget of lakes requires a constant supply of this element, which arrives in the form of atmospheric carbon dioxide and to a lesser extent as organic substances from the catchment basin.

Microbiological Processes Associated with Oxygen Dynamics in Water Bodies

The oxygen regime of a lake consists of a series of oxidation-reduction processes that occur not only in the water mass but also in the silt. Reductive phenomena predominate in the silt, while the water of the lake contains a certain oxidative capacity, hence the steep gradient of oxidation-reduction potential at the border between water and silt. The position of this gradient varies according to the season and the nature of the lake — inside the silt or, as is more often the case, in the bottom water layer, or even higher as in some eutrophic lakes during the stagnation period. The reductive and oxidative processes in the water and silt are due to the activity of microorganisms. Not surprisingly, a definite relationship exists between the oxygen content and the oxidation-reduction potential of water. As noted above, the rH_2 of the water mass ranges from 30 to 12, while that of silt is usually below 16.

The extent and rate of biological processes depend not only on the supply and concentration of oxygen but also on the oxidation-reduction potential. Consequently, the magnitude of rH_2 can be regarded as an ecological factor. An rH_2 value of 20 provides optimal conditions for a number of facultative anaerobic processes, such as denitrification, biological oxidation of methane and hydrogen, etc. Higher values of rH_2 are necessary for the aerobic processes of nitrification and nitrogen fixation by Azotobacter.

The zooplankton and benthos react sharply to a decrease in the oxygen content of the lake. There is a definite relationship between the migrations of zooplankton and the lowering of the oxygen content of the bottom water. Fish are even more sensitive to a deficiency of oxygen. At an oxygen content as low as 2 mg/L, most fish die of asphyxia (A. N. Eleonskii, 1932). Clearly, knowledge of the budget and dynamics of oxygen in a lake is of great value for the solution of various theoretical and practical problems.

Characteristic Types of the Vertical Distribution of Oxygen in Lakes during the Summer and Their Nomenclature

A vast literature deals with the vertical distribution of oxygen in lakes. For a better understanding of the following text, we shall indicate here the main types of oxygen regime in lakes, illustrating their characteristic features with curves of the vertical distribution of oxygen during the summer stagnation.

The water of oligotrophic lakes, including the hypolimnion, contains considerable amounts of oxygen the year round. Such lakes receive very small amounts of organic matter from the catchment basin; moreover, the limited development of their phytoplankton allows only a low production of autochthonous organic matter. Consequently, only a negligible fraction of the oxygen dissolved in the water of such lakes is consumed for the oxidation of organic matter even in the bottom water layers (Figure 95). Typical oligotrophic lakes in the USSR are Baikal (Vereshchagin, 1927a, 1927b, 1948), Teletskoye (Dukel'skii, 1930; Lepneva, 1950), and the Karelian lakes — Konchozero, Pertozero, Urozero, etc. (Zelenkova-Perfil'eva, 1927). Juday and Birge (1932) have described several oligotrophic lakes in the USA. Thus, Crystal Lake, Great Carr Lake, Fence Lake, and Trout Lake belong at least in part to this category. Ström (1930, 1933, 1934) has described a large number of oligotrophic lakes in Norway (Flakevatn, Strynsvatn, Lyngavatn, Oldevatn, Hornindalsvatn, etc.). A typical Swiss oligotrophic lake is Bodensee (Auerbach et al., 1924). Finally, Yoshimura (1938b) has described many typical oligotrophic lakes in Japan.

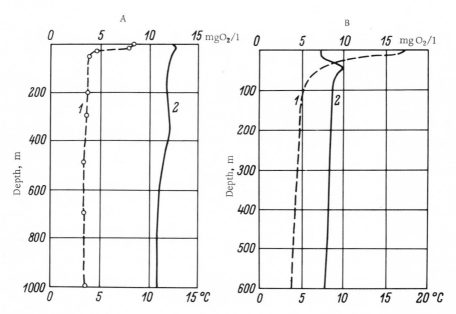

FIGURE 95. Vertical distribution of oxygen (2) and temperature (1) in oligotrophic lakes:

A) Lake Baikal, August 2, 1925; B) Issyk-Kul Lake, July 9, 1927.

The eutrophication of a lake exerts a twofold effect on its oxygen regime. On the one hand, there is an increase in the quantity of organic matter — dissolved, suspended in the water, and sedimented on the bottom. The oxidation of these substances causes a more or less pronounced depletion of the oxygen in the hypolimnion. On the other hand, there is an increased growth of phytoplankton, whose photosynthetic activity enriches the oxygen content of water to a depth determined by the penetration of light. The former process decreases the quantity of oxygen throughout the depth range of water but mostly in the bottom layers, while the latter process supplies oxygen to the epilimnion and the upper part of the metalimnion. The amount of oxygen in excess of the saturation level at the given temperature goes from the epilimnion into the atmosphere. Under such circumstances, an oxygen maximum develops in the metalimnion. Thus, the eutrophication of the lake involves at first a metalimnial oxygen maximum, in addition to which a progressive depletion of this element develops later in the hypolimnion.

In contrast to European and American lakes, the metalimnion of many Japanese lakes shows an oxygen maximum. According to Yoshimura, such a maximum occurs in 98 of a total of 209 examined lakes. Examples are the lakes Hongetsuku (Figure 96, B), Tazava-ko, Moke, Shikarabetsu-ko, etc., where the metalimnial maximum of oxygen increases in parallel with the eutrophication of the lake.

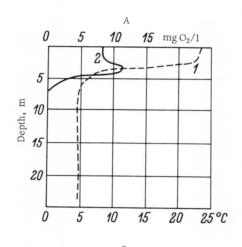

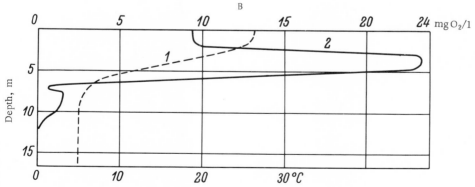

FIGURE 96. Vertical distribution of oxygen (2) in mesotrophic lakes. Metalimnial maximum of oxygen (2) in Lake Beloe (Pokrov district of Moscow Region) (A) and Lake Hongetsuku, Japan (B):

1) water temperature, °C.

A sharp oxygen maximum was observed in the metalimnion of Lake Beloe near the town of Pokrov in the Orekhovo-Zuyevo district of Moscow Region (Figure 96) and in that of Lake Belovod' in Vladimir Region (S.I. Kuznetsov, 1942). These lakes are rather deep, although their area does not exceed 2—3 hectares, and they are situated in a forested area. In Lake Beloe, the thermocline begins at a depth of 2 m, while the concentration of oxygen reaches a peak at a depth of 3 m and decreases sharply below this level (Figure 96). Comparison of the oxygen and temperature curves suggests that the scarcity of oxygen from a depth of 7 m can be attributed to the absence of spring circulation from this depth downward. In view of the fact that the lake has a transparency of 2.4 m, which indicates a low degree of eutrophy, one can hardly assume such a depletion of the oxygen in the hypolimnion within two months.

In Lake Belovod', where the transparency of water reaches 6 m, there is a sharp maximum of oxygen at a depth of 5 m. This lake shows marked signs of oligotrophy. The lack of oxygen in its bottom layers results from a particular phenomenon, namely, the reduction of sulfates, which causes an accumulation of hydrogen sulfide in the hypolimnion (Kuznetsov, 1942; Ivanov, 1956; Lyalikova, 1957).

An oxygen maximum was also observed in Lake Valdai, Kalinin Region (D. A. Lastochkin, N. V. Korde et al., 1942) and in Beloe and Glukhoe lakes in the Meshchera Lowland (L. L. Rossolimo, 1928); other examples of this category are American lakes — Black Oak, Pallet, Blue, Weber, etc. (Juday and Birge, 1932) and Plöner See in West Germany (Thienemann, 1928).

The consumption of oxygen is much more pronounced in the hypolimnion of mesotrophic lakes, which show a lower transparency, a higher concen-

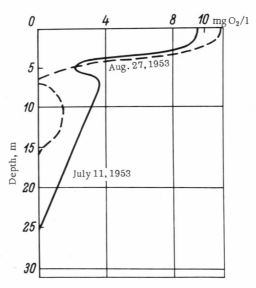

FIGURE 97. Metalimnial minimum of oxygen in Lake Glubokoe, Moscow Region.

tration of nutrient salts, and a greater production of organic matter. This applies in particular to the bottom layers, though an oxygen minimum appears even in the metalimnion of deep mesotrophic lakes during late summer. The process was studied in detail in Lake Glubokoe in the Ruzskii District of Moscow Region (Figure 97) (Voronkov, 1913; Kuznetsov, 1937; Shcherbakov, 1967a). An oxygen minimum was also observed in the metalimnion of several Valdai lakes, such as Uzhino, Beloe near the village of Polosa, and Seredei (Kuznetsov, Speranskaya, and Konshin, 1939).

A similar distribution of oxygen with a minimum in the metalimnion is also known in many lakes outside the USSR, such as Little Long Lake in Wisconsin, USA (Juday and Birge, 1932) and a number of lakes in Western Europe (Thienemann, 1928). Examples of the latter are Plöner See, Tollense-See, Lubbe-See* of Lower Pomerania, Enzig-See,* and Uklei-See in Germany; Lake Vigriberg in Poland; Lake Skårhilt in Sweden; and Lake Bisu in Japan (Yoshimura, 1932). In Switzerland, a moderate minimum of oxygen appears in the metalimnion of Lake Zürich, which is more eutrophic than Bodensee (Minder, 1923). Sometimes, as in Plöner See, a metalimnial maximum of oxygen in a given lake can develop into a minimum. The latter fact is explained in Ruttner's (1962) theory of the development of the oxygen minimum in the metalimnion.

Finally, true eutrophic lakes are characterized by an almost total absence of dissolved oxygen in the deep waters during the late summer and a severe deficiency of this element below the ice cover in winter. The physical-chemical conditions prevailing in lakes of this category allow the development of large quantities of organic matter in the form of phytoplankton and higher coastal vegetation. The oxidative decomposition of this organic matter and the oxidation of the products of its anaerobic breakdown consume practically all the oxygen dissolved in the hypolimnion.

The abundance of biogenic elements in the water of such lakes leads to a rich growth of phytoplankton. Here the water has a very low transparency. The silt contains a large proportion of organic matter and undergoes a rapid anaerobic microbial breakdown with the production of gases. In winter, the concentration of oxygen drops sharply below the ice cover and may even reach zero, as in Lake Chernoe (Kosino). The consumption of oxygen in the water of eutrophic lakes during the winter is closely associated with the release of gases from the lake bottom. This was shown first in Lake Beloe (L. L. Rossolimo, 1932b, 1935) and later in other lakes in Moscow Region (L. L. Rossolimo and Z. I. Kuznetsova, 1934).

A large number of eutrophic lakes are situated in the temperate zone of the USSR. The most typical and best known of them is Lake Beloe in Kosino (Figure 98). Here the depletion of the oxygen content of the hypolimnion at times reached 2 mg/L/day (S. I. Kuznetsov, 1934a, 1934b). Some eutrophic lakes have considerable depths. Examples are the thoroughly studied lakes Mendota, Garvin (Figure 98, B), Presque Isle, Adelaide, Mary, etc., in the USA (Juday and Birge, 1932). A total absence of oxygen develops in late August just below the thermocline of these lakes to a depth of 20 m or more.

* [The Lubbe-See and Enzig-See lakes are now in Poland.]

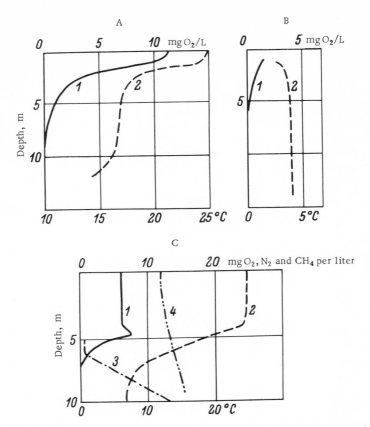

FIGURE 98. Vertical distribution of oxygen and temperature in eutrophic lakes:

A) Lake Beloe (in Kosino), August 15, 1935; B) Lake Beloe, April 1, 1936;
C) Garvin Lake, July 27, 1906; 1) oxygen; 2) temperature, °C; 3) methane;
4) nitrogen.

As is usually the case in the formative stage of any science, there was a certain confusion concerning the terminology of oxygen stratification in lakes. Aberg and Rodhe (1942) tried to introduce more clarity in this field.

The vertical distribution of oxygen depends entirely on physical factors, as we explained above in the case of oligotrophic lakes. On the other hand, the distribution of oxygen is more or less uniform not only in the epilimnion but also in the hypolimnion. An irregularity in the distribution of oxygen in these zones can result only from factors existing during the circulation period. Aberg and Rodhe name such an oxygen curve "orthograde" or ascending. This term can be used in a broader sense to include other cases of a nearly uniform distribution of oxygen without any marked lowering of its concentration in the deep waters. Such a pattern of oxygen concentration is named "oligotrophic" in Thienemann's terminology. However, it can also occur in eutrophic lakes during a complete summer overturn of the water.

The orthograde curve shows no sharp bends. It may be linear or with a steady rise or descent from surface to bottom. In eutrophic lakes, orthograde curves can be obtained only during the period of complete overturn, while oligotrophic lakes show such curves also during the period of thermal stratification.

However, processes that consume various amounts of oxygen occur in the hypolimnion of the majority of examined lakes. Such depletion of oxygen usually begins in the metalimnion and becomes most pronounced in the bottom water of the lake. With the establishment of the thermal stratification in the spring, the oxygen curve tends to reach zero even in the upper layers of the hypolimnion (Figure 98). Aberg and Rodhe refer to such an oxygen curve as clinograde or broken. According to Thienemann, such a pattern of oxygen distribution occurs in eutrophic lakes. As Hutchinson (1957) points out, however, the above term should not be associated with the trophic regime of the lake.

Clinograde curves characteristically show a sharp decline of the oxygen content with depth. In typical clinograde curves, the steep part coincides with the thermocline layer. However, a clinograde distribution of oxygen is by no means confined to eutrophic lakes. Indeed, it often occurs in dystrophic and sometimes even in oligotrophic lakes.

As we saw previously, oxygen can vanish from the metalimnion or reach a maximum there. This phenomenon will be discussed later in detail. Aberg and Rodhe apply the term "heterograde" or irregular to a distribution of oxygen showing a minimum or maximum in the metalimnion (Figures 96, 97).

The heterograde oxygen curves are divided into "minus heterograde" and "plus heterograde," depending on the presence of a minimum or maximum. As a rule, the curve bends within the thermocline or close to it. Minus heterograde curves are not observed in oligotrophic lakes, while dystrophic lakes with humus-containing waters never show plus heterograde curves. This terminology is being widely used in the foreign literature. However, it has not been accepted in the USSR.

The described curves apply only to the macrostratification of oxygen in the water mass of lakes; they do not refer to the bottom water layer. A depletion of the oxygen of the bottom water occurs frequently even in oligotrophic lakes. This feature, however, is not reflected in the above oxygen curves.

Oxygen Dynamics of Lakes and Associated Factors

Entry of Oxygen into Lakes

A large proportion of the lake oxygen originates from the atmosphere. The rate at which this oxygen dissolves in lake water depends on a number of factors, such as water temperature, the rate of water mixing, the rate of oxygen consumption in the water mass, and the saturation of water with oxygen. The entry of atmospheric oxygen may be close to zero in lakes with a negligible consumption of this element for oxidative processes.

The exchange of oxygen with the atmosphere (P) is directly proportional to the difference (D) between the actual concentration of oxygen in the surface water and the concentration corresponding to 100% saturation at the given temperature and pressure. For a period of time t this relationship is expressed by the equation

$$P = -2.3 \times K^e \times D \times t,$$

where K^e is the reaeration factor — a magnitude unrelated to the saturation of water with oxygen but depending on the units of t (days) and the conditions of water mixing. In stagnant waters, K^e varies from 0.05 to 0.15. K^e bears a negative sign, since the difference between the oxygen pressures in the water and air tends to diminish. Unsaturated waters have a negative D and a positive P (atmospheric reaeration), while the opposite condition characterizes supersaturated waters.

The role of atmospheric reaeration becomes especially important during the spring and fall circulations in lakes where the ascending water masses are poor in oxygen. Conversely, an intensive photosynthesis supersaturates the surface water with oxygen, which consequently escapes to the atmosphere. According to G. G. Vinberg, the upper 60 cm of water lose daily 1.61 grams of oxygen per square meter of water surface at a supersaturation of 120%.

The photosynthetic activity of the phytoplankton and submerged aquatic vegetation provides another route of oxygen supply to lakes. In lakes of the temperate zone, photosynthesis begins beneath the ice cover. In Lake Beloe (in Kosino), for example, the thaw is often preceded by a luxuriant growth of M a l l o m o n a s and a supersaturation of the surface water with oxygen beneath the ice sheet. The supply of oxygen to lake water by the phytoplankton is especially abundant during the summer stagnation.

Some information on the quantitative aspect of the photosynthetic reaeration by the plankton can be obtained from direct measurements of photosynthesis by the jar method. The daily rate of photosynthesis exceeds 10 mg of O_2/liter in practically pure eutrophic waters with a rich phytoplankton (Vinberg, 1960). In such cases the photosynthetic reaeration contributes up to 10—15 grams of O_2 daily per square meter of lake surface.

G. G. Vinberg examined the relations of oxygen in thirty-eight lakes. In the mesotrophic lakes, the daily increment of oxygen in the epilimnion was about 1 mg per liter, which corresponds to about 2 grams of oxygen daily per square meter of water surface in the presence of a trophic layer 2 m thick.

Not surprisingly, the magnitude of photosynthesis depends on the development of the phytoplankton. However, the relationship is rather complex. Thus, the rate of photosynthesis in the epilimnion often remains relatively constant during the vegetation period, despite the considerable fluctuations in the quantity of phytoplankton. The following figures show the quantities of oxygen produced daily by photosynthesis in lakes (Vinberg, 1960):

Summer rate of photosynthesis in the epilimnion (daily production of oxygen, mg/liter)	Number of lakes
0—0.03	0
0.03—0.1	1
0.1—0.33	3
0.33—1.00	9
1.00—3.3	16
3.3—10	7
More than 10.1*	1

* Chernoe in Kosino — 22.0; Lyublino ponds [Lyublino near Moscow] — 40.6.

Stationary observations at frequent intervals are necessary for an understanding of the causes of the consumption of dissolved oxygen in the water mass of the lake. Such observations were made in the lakes Beloe (Kosino) and Glubokoe (Moscow Region). The first of these lakes is characterized by a total disappearance of oxygen from the hypolimnion during the summer and dome-shaped isooxygen curves in winter. The second lake is mesotrophic and shows an oxygen minimum in the metalimnion during the summer, and its winter isooxygen curves are not dome-shaped.

According to extensive studies made by several authors, the main processes involving a decrease in the oxygen content of water bodies can be classified as follows: (1) strictly chemical oxidation of organic compounds dissolved in the water; (2) consumption of oxygen for biological and chemical oxidation of formed and dissolved organic ingredients of silt; (3) respiration of algae and zooplankton; (4) respiration of bacteria; (5) biological oxidation of the gases H_2 and CH_4, which escape from the lake bottom; (6) oxidation of hydrogen sulfide, ferrous salts, etc., along biological pathways; (7) abiogenic oxidation of inorganic protoxides.

We shall discuss in greater detail each of these processes and its role in the consumption of oxygen in lakes.

Consumption of oxygen for the oxidation of organic compounds dissolved in the water. The organic matter dissolved in eutrophic lakes results mainly from the decomposition of remnants of plankton and higher aquatic vegetation. In Lake Beloe (Kosino), the concentration of these substances reaches a peak in late summer (G. G. Vinberg and T. P. Platova, 1951; P. V. Novobrantseva, 1951).

Krogh and Lange (1931) reported comparatively small seasonal changes in the concentration of organic matter in the Furesee. Their analyses of the concentration of different forms of organic matter in the surface layer in 1929 show that the quantity of dissolved organic matter is seven to eight times greater than that of the suspended particulate organic matter:

	kcal/L	mg/L
Plankton	6.9	0.09
Colloidal organic matter	4.1	0.06
Dissolved organic matter	43.1	0.52
Total	54.0	0.66

Similar results were obtained with respect to the organic matter in American lakes, where the plankton corresponds to about $1/10$ of the total amount of organic matter (Birge and Juday, 1926).

Lönnerblad (1931c) stressed the possibility of a chemical utilization of oxygen for the oxidation of humin substances. He reported the following results in support of this view. Water samples were collected from the surface and bottom layers of Lake Rusken. The bottom water contained large quantities of humin substances. In sealed vessels, the oxygen consumption was greater in bottom water than in surface water. Although the experiment was made in nonsterile conditions and was not accompanied by bacteriological analysis, the author interpreted the results as evidence for a chemical consumption of oxygen for the oxidation of humin substances.

TABLE 59. Effect of aeration and light on the bleaching of humic substances in dystrophic waters (after Aberg and Rodhe, 1942)

Water body	Conditions of experiment	Duration of experiment, days	Color of water according to platinum-cobalt standard		
			initial	final	decrease
Fiolen, a brook, Sweden	Without sterilization: In light				
	without aeration	30	98	23	75
	with aeration		98	12	86
	In darkness				
	without aeration		98	83	15
	with aeration		98	74	24
Lake Stråken, Sweden	In light, not sterile	43	56	10	46
	In darkness, not sterile		56	45	11
	In light, sterile	56	56	11	45
	In darkness, sterile	56	56	60	0

Aberg and Rodhe (1942) made similar experiments with water from different Swedish lakes containing various amounts of dissolved humic compounds. Table 59 shows the results of these analyses.

As shown in the table, the color of water from Lake Stråken dropped from 56° to 11° by the platinum-cobalt standards within fifty-six days in sterile conditions in the presence of light. This corresponds to a bleaching of 45°. However, no bleaching occurred in the dark. Aeration exerts some influence on the rate of bleaching, which indicates that the process involves a consumption of oxygen.

The bleaching is due to a chemical destruction of colored organic compounds belonging to the group of humic acids. This abiogenic process is slow and requires the presence of light. Bacteria accelerate the oxidation of humic compounds (Table 59). This was shown by the experiments of Aberg and Rodhe with unsterilized natural water.

S. I. Kuznetsov tested the possibility of oxygen consumption for a strictly chemical oxidation of colorless dissolved organic matter formed by the decomposition of the phytoplankton and aquatic vegetation. Water from the eutrophic Lake Beloe (in Kosino) was filtered through a Seitz filter and was distributed in sterile oxygen vessels. To eliminate any air bubbles under the ground joint stopper, the vessels were sealed with mercury. The experiment was made at 35°C. Sterility was tested by inoculation of 1 ml of water on nutrient agar at the beginning and end of the experiment; water for this purpose was taken from the same vessel that later served for the determination of oxygen. The analysis showed the following quantities of oxygen (mg/L) in sterile water from Lake Beloe:

Initial content	After 48 hours	Parallel determination (after 144 hours)	Consumption of oxygen during experiment
5.1	5.15	5.17	0.0

Clearly, there was no consumption of oxygen in sterile water from Lake Beloe during an incubation period of six days at 35°. Even in a eutrophic lake like Beloe, oxygen serves mainly for a biological oxidation of organic matter. Such experiments require a careful set-up with sterility checks.

To sum up, consumption of oxygen by purely chemical oxidation of organic matter is practically absent in lakes that do not contain humic acids, even if the lakes belong to the eutrophic group; such a process is virtually non-existent in oligotrophic lakes.

Consumption of oxygen by silt and its effect on the overall dynamics of oxygen in lakes. Mixing of lake silt with oxygen-containing water causes a rapid absorption of this element by the silt (Alsterberg, 1927; Lönnerblad, 1930; Miyadi, 1934; Berval'd, 1939; ZoBell, 1934).

To determine the causes of this absorption of oxygen, ZoBell examined the effects of sublimate, which eliminates the activity of enzymes and bacteria, and toluene, which suppresses the bacteria but leaves the enzymes intact. The results of his experiments appear in Table 60.

TABLE 60. Rates of oxygen consumption by chemical and biological processes, mg of O_2 per gram of silt (after ZoBell, 1939)

Time from beginning of test	Treatment of material			Biological consumption of oxygen	
	no treatment	addition of toluene	addition of sublimate	enzymatic	bacterial respiration
2 hours	0.19	0.16	0.18	0	0
6 hours	0.18	0.15	0.19	0	0
24 hours	0.22	0.20	0.17	0.03	0.05
2 days	0.28	0.21	0.15	0.04	0.07
4 days	0.42	0.24	0.18	0.07	0.16
7 days	0.76	0.30	0.17	0.13	0.46
10 days	1.09	0.39	0.19	0.22	0.70
21 days	1.64	0.44	0.16	0.27	1.20
35 days	1.73	0.47	0.19	0.30	1.26

Evidently, some of the consumed oxygen serves for a chemical oxidation of reduced products of the decomposition of silt, but the bulk of it is used by the microflora.

Ruhle (1966) studied the rate of oxygen absorption by the silt of three artificial reservoirs. Her work contains a review of the pertinent literature with comments on the methods used. The experiments were made by the bottle method and the magnitudes of the biological consumption of oxygen were presented in relation to the total content of organic matter in silt (Table 61).

TABLE 61. Biological consumption of oxygen in reservoirs of drinking water (after Ruhle, 1966)

Reservoir	Type of reservoir	BOD, mg O_2/g dry material	Total content of organic matter, mg of O_2 per gram of dry material	Ratio of BOD to organic matter
Neuzeinhan	Eutrophic	0.56	49.3	1:88
Saidenbach	Mesotrophic	0.58	69.3	1:119
Karlsfeld	Dystrophic	2.46	358.0	1:146

Organic matter from dystrophic lakes is most resistant to biological oxidation. Consequently, the bottom of such lakes consumes smaller amounts of dissolved oxygen.

A reduction of the oxygen content of the bottom water in comparison with the overlying waters can be interpreted as direct evidence for oxygen consumption by the silt. G. S. Karzinkin, S. I. Kuznetsov, and Z. I. Kuznetsova (1930) examined from this viewpoint the oxygen content of the bottom water of Lake Glubokoe. Samples of silt and bottom water were taken by means of a corer in a glass tube of a diameter of 4 cm. Water from the layer adjacent to the silt and that situated at a distance of 5—6 cm from the silt surface was collected with a pipette immediately after the sample was hauled up. The water was transferred to small vessels with ground joint stoppers, and the amount of dissolved oxygen was determined after Winkler (Table 62). The experiment showed that lake silt consumes oxygen in natural and experimental conditions; however, it did not reveal the rate of the process in nature.

TABLE 62. Oxygen content of microlayers of bottom water from Lake Glubokoe during the summer stagnation

Depth of station in east-west profile of lake, m	Oxygen content in water layer in contact with silt, mg/L	Oxygen content in water layer 5—6 cm from silt surface, mg/L	Difference
6	7.28	7.86	0.58
8	3.35	3.56	0.21
18	2.53	2.86	0.33
30	0.72	1.17	0.45
25	1.21	1.80	0.59
18	2.30	2.41	0.41
9	2.48	2.86	0.38
5	7.40	7.92	0.52

The rate of the process was determined by analyzing the oxygen content of a given volume of water situated on the silt and isolated by means of a plastic or metal hood.

Such experiments were made by N. I. Semenovich (Lake Punnus-Yarvi), N. A. Trifonova (Rybinsk Artificial Reservoir), G. G. Vinberg (Ivan'kovo Artificial Reservoir), and V. A. Akimov (fishponds). Their results appear in Table 63.

TABLE 63. Rate of consumption of dissolved oxygen by silt in artificial reservoirs and fishponds

Water body	Nature of silt	Date	Duration of test, days	Consumption of O_2, mg/m^2/day	Daily average, mg of O_2/m^2
Rybinsk Artificial Reservoir					
Former bed of the Mologa	Grey	February 13—18, 1960	5	224	
		May 19—27	7.9	115	
		July 15—19	4	229	200
		July 16—19	2.5	232	
Former bed of the Sheksna	Peaty	May 26—31	4.7	153	
Open part of the reservoir	Peat	May 19—27	1.5	84	
At the former village of Novolok	Peat	February 16—22	6.1	58	
		March 4—22	18.3	79	
Former left floodplain of the Sheksna	Flooded soil	February 24 — March 5	9.2	25	59
	Flooded soil	July 22—27	3.8	74	
Former right floodplain of the Mologa	Sand	February 21— March 2	9	100	
		July 16—19	2.5	258	179
Ivan'kovo Artificial Reservoir					
Fedorovskii inlet	Silted sand	August 1939	4.5 hours	1,680	
				6,960	4,320
Fishponds	Clayey silt covered with detritus and remnants of fish feeds	August 1966	3	1,200	
			3	3,600	2,400

Note. The data on the Rybinsk Artificial Reservoir are taken from the communication of N.A.Trifonova; on the Ivan'kovo Artificial Reservoir from G.G.Vinberg (1960); on the fishponds from V.A.Akimov (1967a).

The rate of oxygen consumption ranges from 0.025 to 3 grams/m²/day in artificial reservoirs; in thoroughly fertilized fishponds it reaches 3—5 grams/m²/day (Table 63). Evidently, the consumption of oxygen by bottom sediments can exert a profound effect on the oxygen regime of shallow water bodies.

Most lake silts tend to absorb large quantities of oxygen. Among other proofs, this is evident from the oxygen content of bottom water. However, the oxygen dynamics of a water body cannot be explained merely by a diffusion of this element from the water to the silt or by a diffusion of readily oxidizable materials from the silt to the water mass.

On the basis of Fick's law and the Graham-Fick formula and taking the diffusion coefficient of oxygen in water as equal to 1.62, Alsterberg (1928) calculated the time that elapses before the consumption of oxygen by the silt affects the concentration of this element at different distances from the bottom. It became evident that the consumption of oxygen by the silt is an extremely slow process. If the only compensatory factor is the diffusion of oxygen from the neighboring water layer, this consumption can deplete the oxygen content of water to a height of only a few millimeters from the bottom. Alsterberg assumed on these grounds that wind-induced currents create a horizontal flow of oxygen-poor water to the center of the lake. Such continuous flows deplete the oxygen content of the water as a whole and lead to a macrostratification of the lake oxygen.

Later studies by G. S. Karzinkin, S. I. Kuznetsov, and Z. I. Kuznetsova (1931) demonstrated, however, that wind-induced currents are confined to the epilimnion, while the only water movements that can take place in the hypolimnion are bottom currents resulting from thermal gradients between the silt and the bottom water. In other words, a complete absorption of oxygen is possible only in the deepest part of the lake, which receives descending masses of oxygen-poor bottom water from the whole lake basin.

Density currents of bottom water occur in all lakes. Such currents are observed at a water temperature of 2—3° in winter, when the temperature of the bottom water is about 4°. In summer, at a water temperature above 4°, such bottom currents can result from a transfer of heat from the water to the bottom sediments, which are then colder than the water.

After a study of the thermal relations of the bottom sediments of Lake Beloe (in Kosino), L. L. Rossolimo (1932) published a detailed scheme of the heat exchange between the lake bottom and the bottom water during different stages of the heat regime.

There can be no doubt that the surface silt can absorb large quantities of oxygen. This is evident not only from laboratory tests with silt samples but also from direct observations of freshly flooded soils in the Ivan'kovo Artificial Reservoir, where the oxygen absorption reached 7—8 g/m²/day (Vinberg, 1960).

This process, however, cannot reduce appreciably the oxygen content of the entire water mass of the lake in the absence of a thorough circulation of water and an intensive exchange of the bottom layer. These conditions exist in shallow lakes, where a complete circulation persists throughout the summer, or in the epilimnion of deep lakes (Glubokoe). In most cases, however, the absorption of oxygen by the bottom exerts little effect on its total content in the lake, since any losses are easily compensated with atmospheric oxygen.

In deep lakes with a well-developed hypolimnion, the bottom absorption of oxygen can be only of minor importance. Here the bottom water does not mix with the bulk of lake water, and the only existing bottom currents flow toward the deepest part of the lake basin. Consequently, the absorption of oxygen by the bottom can affect only the lowermost layers of the hypolimnion in such lakes.

It follows that a loss of oxygen in the intermediate layers of the lake — the metalimnion and the upper part of the hypolimnion — can result only from consumption of this element in the water mass of the lake. This applies in particular to the formation of an oxygen minimum in the metalimnion.

Consumption of oxygen in the water mass of the lake for respiration of the zooplankton and phytoplankton. In the 1930s, several authors tried to determine the role of the zooplankton in the destruction of organic matter according to the consumption of oxygen. A. P. Shcherbakov (1935) made such measurements in Lake Beloe (in Kosino).

On the basis of his own determinations of the respiration of planktonic crustaceans and the detailed data of S. N. Duplakov on the density of these animals in the lake plankton, Shcherbakov concluded that the quantities of oxygen consumed daily by the zooplankton (in mg/L/day) reach 0.086 in the epilimnion and 0.065 in the metalimnion during the summer. The winter values are even lower. According to Shcherbakov, the daily consumption of oxygen by the zooplankton at a depth of 2 m beneath the ice cover amounts to only 0.0078 mg/L, which corresponds to about 2% of the overall daily consumption of this element in the lake water.

The literature dealing with this topic contains contradictory conclusions (A. P. Shcherbakov, 1967b). Some authors believe that the zooplankton plays a very modest role in the consumption of oxygen, while others regard it as responsible for the entire consumption. The controversy stems from the fact that calculations of this sort require data on the stratified distribution of the different zooplanktic species, the density of each age group, and the respiration rate as a function of temperature.

TABLE 64. Consumption of oxygen by different zooplankters according to laboratory tests (after Vinberg, 1948; Shcherbakov, 1967b)

Organisms	Consumption of O_2 (mg per organism per day)	Q_{O_2} (mm^3 of O_2 per mg of dry weight per hour)
Crustaceans (average data)	$0.41-5.86 \times 16^{-3}$	—
Cyclops sp.	$0.41- 10^{-3}$	—
Diaptomus longispina	9.36×10^{-3}	—
Bosmina sp.	1.19×10^{-3}	—
Daphnia sp.	8.2×10^{-3}	—
Polyphemus sp.	5.9×10^{-3}	—
Anurea aculeta	0.017×10^{-3}	—
Paramecium caudatum	0.048 mm^3	—
Amoeba proteus	—	1.6
Pelomyxa corolinensis	—	2.4
Anabaena scheremetievi ...	0.0384×10^{-6}	11.3
Dinobrion sp.	0.146×10^{-6}	4.4
Microcystis sp.	0.117×10^{-6}	3.4
Ceratium sp.	31.2×10^{-6}	24.8

G. G. Vinberg (1950) proposed a method for the determination of the respiration rate on the basis of the weight of the organism. Using a sedimentation procedure with a suitable fixative, A. P. Shcherbakov (1967b) determined over a period of several years the density of various zooplankters (crustaceans, rotifers, protozoans) in Lake Glubokoe with reference to the different age groups. On the basis of Vinberg's formula and his own average figures of the density of zooplankton (covering a period of several years), he gave the following data on the consumption of oxygen in the different layers of the lake (Table 64).

Thus, the Lake Glubokoe zooplankton daily consumes the following quantities of oxygen during the ice-free period: 0.07 mg/L in the epilimnion, 0.11 mg/L in the metalimnion, and 0.002 mg/L in the hypolimnion. For the metalimnion and hypolimnion, these figures correspond respectively to 15.8% and 6% of the total consumption of oxygen in the indicated zones.

A table showing the consumption of oxygen by different phytoplankters and zooplankters will be given below (after data from G. G. Vinberg and A. P. Shcherbakov).

The respiration of phytoplankton is a much more important factor in the oxygen dynamics, especially during the summer and in the surface waters of blooming lakes. Indeed, oxygen consumption by the phytoplankton may lead to a sharp deficit of this element at night and a mortality of fish.

An example is Lake Chernoe (in Kosino), where the density of algae in the plankton reaches 3.6 million colonies per liter and photosynthesis proceeds at a daily rate of 17.5 mg of O_2/L, while the combined respiratory activities of algae and bacteria consume 8.5 mg of O_2/L. A n a b a e n a cells are responsible for a considerable part of the consumed oxygen (G.G.Vinberg, 1948). According to Lomeiko, one cell of A. s c h e r e m e t i e v i from Lake Chernoe utilizes 16×10^{-10} mg of O_2 per hour. On the basis of these data and the known density of A. s c h e r e m e t i e v i cells in the Lake Chernoe plankton, Vinberg estimated that the respiration of the phytoplankton consumed daily 3.2 mg of O_2 at the time of the measurements. Such intensive consumption of oxygen can occur only in the epilimnion, which contains the bulk of the phytoplankton. Below this zone the density of phytoplankton decreases sharply, and the rate of oxygen consumption falls accordingly with depth to a negligible level in the hypolimnion.

The contribution of bacterial respiration to the total consumption of oxygen in the water mass of the lake. The first attempt to determine the role of bacteria in the consumption of oxygen from the water mass was made in Lake Glubokoe (Kuznetsov, 1925). The microscopical method of bacterial count was not yet developed at the time, and the density of bacteria was determined on agar and gelatin plates. By this procedure, no relationship could be found between the distribution of bacteria and the oxygen regime of Lake Glubokoe.

After the work of S.N.Winogradsky (1924) on the direct microscopical count of soil bacteria, it became clear that agar plates reveal only a fraction of the whole bacterial population. Many authors reached the conclusion that direct bacterial counts must be made in order to determine the relationship between the distribution of bacteria and the oxygen regime, since agar and gelatin plates are unsuitable for this purpose. The only procedure for a direct count of lake bacteria existing at the time involved adsorption of the bacteria on aluminum hydroxide (Snow and Fred, 1926). This method proved unsatisfactory, and others were unknown. This state of affairs stimulated S. I. Kuznetsov and G. S. Karzinkin (1930) to work out a new microscopic method for counting the total density of bacteria in water. The first counts of Lake Glubokoe bacteria by this method in 1928 revealed the presence of a rich bacterial population whose respiration represents a

TABLE 65. Bacterial respiration rates (after Vinberg, 1946)

Physiologic state of bacteria	mm^3 of O_2/hour/mg of dry weight (Q_{O_2})		mm^3 of O_2/hour/cell (volume 1 μ^3)		mg of O_2/hour/cell (volume 1 μ^3)	
	20°	37°	20°	37°	20°	37°
Well-fed on a complete medium	580–1,120	2,500–5,000	$110\text{–}210 \times 10^{-9}$	$50\text{–}1,000 \times 10^{-9}$	$156\text{–}298 \times 10^{-12}$	$0.71\text{–}1.42 \times 10^{-9}$
Resting cells in the presence of substrate ...	11–33	50–150	$2\text{–}6 \times 10^{-9}$	$10\text{–}30 \times 10^{-9}$	$2.8\text{–}8.4 \times 10^{-12}$	$14.2\text{–}42.6 \times 10^{-12}$
Endogenous respiration, i.e., without substrate	2–20	10–100	$0.4\text{–}4 \times 10^{-9}$	$2\text{–}20 \times 10^{-9}$	$0.56\text{–}5.6 \times 10^{-12}$	$2.8\text{–}28.4 \times 10^{-12}$

major factor in the oxygen regime of the lake (Kuznetsov and Karzinkin, 1930).

Later it became evident that the anaerobic breakdown of organic matter in the bottom of some lakes creates large quantities of methane and hydrogen whose biological oxidation consumes dissolved oxygen.

Consumption of dissolved oxygen for bacterial respiration. The vast majority of the bacteria determined by a direct count consume dissolved and suspended organic substances, even if these are present in negligible amounts. The respiration rate of aerobic bacteria is an accurate index of their metabolism, quantitatively as well as energetically. The effect of bacteria on the oxygen regime of the lake can be evaluated on the basis of their respiration rate and density.

G. G. Vinberg (1946) has reviewed the pertinent information from various published sources. He divided the published measurements of bacterial respiration rates into three groups: (1) respiration rate of bacteria cultured in rich media; (2) respiration rate of bacteria in the presence of a respiratory substrate but without any sources of nitrogen — a state known as resting cells; (3) endogenous respiration of bacteria washed free of medium and living in the absence of a respiratory substrate. The respiration of bacteria depends on temperature, the size of the bacterial cell, and particularly the concentration of nutrients in the medium. Consequently, the respiration rates of bacteria are usually given in relation to the dry weight of the cells or to the total nitrogen of the bacterial biomass. Table 65 shows the observed fluctuations of the respiration rate of bacteria.

According to G. G. Vinberg, the peak rates of aerobic metabolism during the logarithmic growth stage are rather uniform among different aerobic bacteria. Q_{O_2}, that is, maximal rate of oxygen consumption per unit dry weight, equals 2,500 – 5,000 mm^3/mg/hour. The same applies to the respiration of resting cells in the presence of the respiratory substrate; the values obtained in this case, however, are tens of times smaller than the peak metabolic rates of young cultures. Finally, the endogenous respiration, or the respiration of starving cells, is only one-fifth the value observed in resting cells.

Thus, the consumption of oxygen in the respiration process depends largely on the nature and quantity of dissolved organic compounds.

243

ZoBell and Stadler (1940) reached a similar conclusion about the effect of dissolved organic matter on the respiration rate of aquatic bacteria. They determined the daily bacterial count and oxygen consumption in Lake Mendota water kept in jars with ground joint stoppers and incubated at 25°. Using the formula of Buchanan and Fulmer (1930),

$$m = \frac{2 \cdot 303 \times S \times \log \frac{b}{B}}{t \times (b - B)},$$

where m is the quantity of oxygen consumed by one cell during one hour, S the total amount of oxygen consumed during the period t, B the initial bacterial count, and b the bacterial count at the end of the experiment, ZoBell and Stadler found that the respiration rate of bacteria is highest during the first day of incubation, when the development of the bacteria is in the logarithmic stage.

The amount of consumed oxygen ranges from 51×10^{-12} to 93×10^{-12} mg/cell/hour at 25°C. However, the concentration of the organic substrate rapidly drops to a negligible level, and by the third day the rate of oxygen consumption becomes as low as $0.2-0.7 \times 10^{-12}$ mg/cell/hour. ZoBell and Stadler note that their absolute figures of the oxygen uptake per cell are too conservative because the bacteria were counted on agar plates.

In a more thorough approach to this problem, S. I. Kuznetsov and Z. I. Kuznetsova determined the respiration rate of some bacterial strains isolated from lake water and grown in media containing different concentrations of organic nutrients. It was found that a scarcity of nutrients in the medium exerts a considerable effect on the respiration rate of bacteria washed free of the medium. Thus, the oxygen uptake per cell at 15°C was 6×10^{-12} mg per hour in previously starved bacteria and 58×10^{-12} mg per hour in bacteria previously grown in media rich in organic matter.

On the basis of these and similar experiments, an attempt was made to calculate the bacterial uptake of oxygen in the metalimnion and hypolimnion of Lake Glubokoe (Table 66). Assuming that the bacterial respiration rate in the lake is the same as in the laboratory, the individual uptake multiplied by the total number of bacteria in the lake water at the time of the observations yields the estimated total uptake of oxygen by the lake bacteria. This value is close to the observed magnitude of oxygen uptake in the lake. Therefore, bacteria are responsible for nearly all of the oxygen uptake in the metalimnion and hypolimnion of Lake Glubokoe and other mesotrophic water bodies without a bottom production of gases.

The exhaustion of the oxygen content of the metalimnion occurs rapidly, especially during a mass mortality of plankton. S. I. Kuznetsov (1939) determined the oxygen content, bacterial count, and phytoplanktic density in Lake Glubokoe during the summer of 1936. His observations lasted throughout the summer, and particular attention was devoted to the analysis of samples collected during shifts of leading algal species in the plankton or on days of a sharp decrease in the concentration of dissolved oxygen.

The death of the leading algal species reduces sharply the density of phytoplankton. At the same time the density of bacteria increases, while the oxygen content of water drops sharply (Figure 60). This sequence of events occurred at a depth of 3 m, and twenty-four hours later at a depth

TABLE 66. Oxygen consumption in Lake Glubokoe for bacterial respiration (after Kuznetsov, 1939, 1952)

Conditions of test	Date in 1936	Depth, m	Temperature, °C	Average density of cells in lake water (millions per liter)		Experimentally determined oxygen uptake per cell (10^{-12} mg of O_2/hour)		Depletion of oxygen content of water between analyses	
				rods	cocci	rods	cocci	calculated	experimentally determined
Cases of low oxygen uptake (in calculating the oxygen uptake, the bacterial respiration rate is taken as corresponding to a low content of organic matter in the water)	July 10–12	10	5.00	166	119	5.07	2.08	0.04	0.03
	July 8–10	8	5.90	125	68	5.23	2.31	0.03	0.02
	July 6–8	6	7.50	141	71	5.52	2.67	0.03	0.02
	July 3–5	4	13.50	135	2.43	6.62	5.07	0.11	0.26
Cases of high oxygen uptake (in calculating the oxygen uptake, the bacterial respiration rate is taken as corresponding to a high content of organic matter in the water)	July 5–6	10	5.0	137	81	42.64	16.19	0.20	0.21
	July 3–5	8	5.9	95	84	44.02	18.52	0.29	0.26
	July 8–10	6	7.55	125	83	46.96	22.78	0.42	0.43
		4	13.5	252	156	55.69	48.76	1.26	0.90

of 4 m, where the observed changes were less pronounced, since the peak density of phytoplankton at a depth of 4 m was comparable to the minimal density at a depth of 3 m. This indicates that a mass mortality and sinking of plankton in the surface layers enriches the water with readily assimilable organic matter that stimulates the reproduction and respiration of bacteria and thus causes a severe depletion of the oxygen content of water.

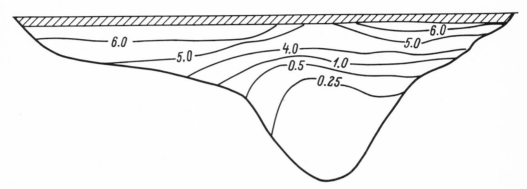

FIGURE 99. Dome-shaped winter pattern of isooxygen curves in Lake Beloe (Kosino) (after L.L.Rossolimo, 1932b, 1935).

Consumption of oxygen for the **biological oxidation of methane and hydrogen liberated from the lake bottom.** L. L. Rossolimo (1932b, 1935) first drew attention to the dome shape of isooxygen curves in Lake Beloe (Kosino) during the existence of the ice cover. Later studies of the distribution of oxygen in lakes during the winter stressed the importance of this phenomenon in the oxygen regime of the lakes. Dome-shaped isooxygen curves were obtained in many lakes in the USSR (Rossolimo and Kuznetsova, 1934) and other countries (Alsterberg, 1927, 1928; Yoshimura, 1930). Alsterberg (1928) tried to explain this phenomenon on the basis of the theory of Birge and Juday (1922) of the existence of descending above-bottom currents and a compensatory ascending current in the lake center. According to Birge and Juday, such currents appear during certain periods of the year as a result of a heat exchange between the bottom and water mass of the lake.

However, the Alsterberg theory arouses some doubt in view of the fact that dome-shaped winter isooxygen curves occur in some lakes only. On the other hand, the production of gas by the bottom of Lake Beloe (in Kosino) may be associated with this pattern of the isooxygen curves (L.L.Rossolimo, 1932b) (Figure 99).

Direct analyses of the concentrations of methane and hydrogen in the water of eutrophic lakes were made by Birge and Juday (1911) in the lakes Mendota and Garvin during the summer stagnation period, L. L. Rossolimo (1932b) in Lake Beloe in Kosino, Ohle (1958) in Plöner See, and S. I. Kuznetsov in Lake Beloe (Kosino) during the spring before the thaw. Table 67 shows the results obtained by S. I. Kuznetsov.

The above authors note that the concentration of methane in lake gas varies from 65 to 85%.

TABLE 67. Quantity of gases dissolved at different depths in the water of Lake Beloe, April 7—11, 1938, mg/L (after Kuznetsov and Khartulari, 1941; Kuznetsov, 1952)

Depth, m	Temperature, °C	O_2	CH_4	H_2	N_2
1	2.4	3.6	0.1	1.0	19.4
3	2.7	0.84	0.17	1.39	21.5
5	3.1	0.38	0.1	2.1	21.0
7	—	0.27	1.3	3.1	13.0
10	3.5	0.17	3.1	5.0	18.5
12	4.3	0.0	7.1	20.2	7.6

The quantities of dissolved methane and hydrogen are especially large in the bottom water, which lacks oxygen (Table 67). At a greater distance from the bottom, the water contains oxygen in addition to methane and hydrogen. This creates optimal conditions for the growth and activity of bacteria that oxidize methane and hydrogen. Undoubtedly, even these early studies point to the existence of a satisfactory environment for the growth of methane and hydrogen bacteria in eutrophic lakes.

Attempts were made to isolate methane and hydrogen bacteria from the water of these lakes.

The distribution of methane- and hydrogen-oxidizing bacteria in lake waters of different trophic categories was studied by Kuznetsov (1934b, 1939), Rossolimo and Kuznetsova (1934), Overbeck and Ohle (1964), Ohle (1958, 1965), Romanenko (1959, 1966), Krasheninnikova (1959), Osnitskaya (1953), and others.

Various procedures were used for the isolation of these bacteria: (1) inoculation of lake water or silt in a mineral medium and subsequent incubation in an atmosphere of air mixed with methane or hydrogen; (2) incubation of lake water in glass containers with bubbled methane or hydrogen and with periodic checks of the concentration of dissolved oxygen as a measure of the activity of methane- or hydrogen-oxidizing bacteria; (3) radioautography of bacterial colonies grown on membrane filters on an agar-containing medium with added $Na_2C^{14}O_3$ in an atmosphere of air and methane.

Methane- and hydrogen-oxidizing bacteria are widespread in lakes, especially in eutrophic ones. Thus, the water of Plussee contains up to 3 million cells of methane-oxidizing bacteria per ml (Overbeck and Ohle, 1964). More detailed data are available on the distribution of methane-oxidizing bacteria in the Rybinsk Artificial Reservoir. S. A. Krasheninnikova (1959) determined the density of these bacteria by inoculation of silt and water samples from different parts of the reservoir; she also measured their capacity for oxygen consumption (Figure 100). The consumption of oxygen for the oxidation of methane was greatest in water samples collected above former river beds or above flooded peat bogs, that is, in areas where the silt undergoes an intensive decomposition with gas production.

Later this topic was examined in greater detail by V. I. Romanenko (1959, 1964c, 1966c), who counted the methane-oxidizing bacteria by the radioisotope method. He found that the density of methane- and hydrogen-oxidizing bacteria in the reservoir water is of the order of 100 cells per ml (Figure 101), while the corresponding figure in the top silt is 1 million cells or more per gram of raw silt. The following list shows the distribution of methane-oxidizing bacteria in the surface layer of the silt of the Rybinsk Artificial Reservoir as determined in January 1959 by Romanenko (1966) (thousands of cells per gram of raw silt):

Silt layer, cm	At flooded town of Mologa	At Navolok in center of reservoir	Former bed of Mologa near Breitovo	Former bed of Sheksna near Yagorba
0—1	1	550	1,200	140
4—5	0	57	120	15

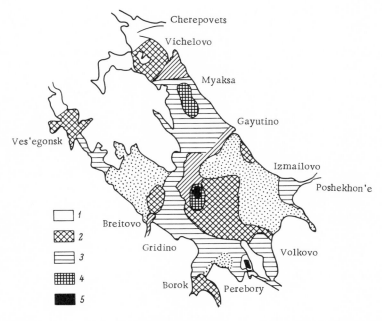

FIGURE 100. Capacity of methane-oxidizing bacteria to consume oxygen in the water mass of the Rybinsk Artificial Reservoir.

Consumption of oxygen in mg/L/day: 1) up to 0.5; 2) from 0.5 to 1.0; 3) from 1.0 to 2.0; 4) from 2.0 to 3.0; 5) more than 3.0.

S. I. Kuznetsov (1934) demonstrated long ago that the methane-oxidizing bacteria of Lake Beloe can utilize large quantities of dissolved oxygen. Later, Ohle (1958) examined more thoroughly the bacterial consumption of dissolved oxygen for the oxidation of lake gas. He placed surface water from the Plöner See in vessels with ground joint stoppers, together with 20 or 5 ml of lake gas from the Grosser Plöner See. Water samples without gas served as controls. The samples were incubated at 5° and 20°; the quantity of dissolved oxygen was determined at given intervals. Figure 102 shows the results of the analysis.

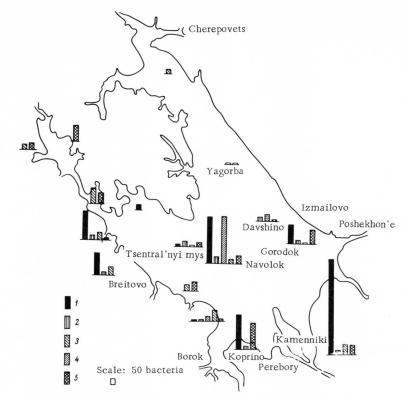

FIGURE 101. Density of methane-oxidizing bacteria in the bottom water layer of the Rybinsk Artificial Reservoir in 1959 (cells per ml) (after Romanenko, 1966):

1) in January; 2) in March; 3) in May; 4) in July; 5) in August.

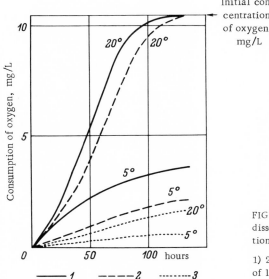

FIGURE 102. Consumption of dissolved oxygen for the oxidation of methane (after Ohle):

1) 20 ml of lake gas; 2) 5 ml of lake gas; 3) without lake gas.

249

All the oxygen was used up within five days at 20° (Figure 102). The oxidation rate was slightly higher in the presence of a greater quantity of lake gas. The process was much slower at 5°, especially in the vessels that contained only 5 ml of lake gas. Finally, the consumption of oxygen was even smaller in the absence of lake gas. This experiment illustrates the great influence that the biological oxidation of methane and hydrogen exerts on the oxygen regime of lakes whose silt produces lake gas.

The experiments of S. I. Kuznetsov (1939) and Ohle (1958) showed that the oxygen dissolved in lake water is used for bacterial respiration and for the oxidation of methane. In order to distinguish between these processes, S. I. Kuznetsov (1939) analyzed the relation between the production of carbon dioxide and the oxygen uptake in different water layers of Lake Beloe in Kosino.

The production of carbon dioxide and the consumption of oxygen during a given period can be determined by suitable analyses at the beginning and end of this period for each layer, notably the hypolimnion, metalimnion, or beneath the ice cover. Further, the respiratory quotient can be easily calculated from the obtained values.

As shown long ago by the elementary analyses of Boussingault, the loss of weight during the respiration of germinating seeds results from the escape of carbon, hydrogen, and oxygen; plants never lose nitrogen. As S. P. Kostychev (1924) indicated, sugars are the normal substrates of respiration, which can be expressed by the equation:

$$C_6H_{12}O_6 + 6O_2 = 6CO_2 + 6H_2O.$$

The respiration rate of plants depends largely on the developmental stage of the organism and the quantity of active protoplasm. It follows from the above basic equation that for each volume of consumed oxygen there is an equal volume of carbon dioxide released. However, various deviations from this rule can occur: (1) the respiratory quotient becomes lower than unity when the plant accumulates organic acids in parallel with the respiration process; (2) the respiratory quotient can be greater than unity when the respiration is accompanied by the release of additional amounts of carbon dioxide, as is the case with the respiration of yeasts, which simultaneously carry out an alcoholic fermentation; (3) the respiratory quotient differs from unity in the presence of a nonsugar substrate. Having exhausted its carbohydrate stocks, the plant may oxidize its own proteins, in which case the respiratory quotient usually varies between 0.70 and 0.80. This type of respiration, however, is obviously abnormal; it yields large amounts of free ammonia and decreases the bacterial count as a result of autolysis — a sequence of events hardly ever observed in nature. It can be said that the respiratory quotient of aquatic bacteria approximates unity in natural conditions. In their studies of the organic matter found in sea water, Keys, Christensen, and Krogh (1935) take the respiratory quotient of marine bacteria as equal to 0.85.

According to S. I. Kuznetsov (1939), carbohydrates produced by the photosynthetic activity of green algae are the main respiratory substrates of lake bacteria; thus, if the consumption of oxygen in lake water were due entirely to respiration, the ratio between the accumulated CO_2 and the consumed oxygen during a given period in the hypolimnion of Lake Beloe would be equal to unity. In his further considerations, however, he took a respiratory quotient of 0.9 in view of the fact that algae release nitrogenous compounds into the water (B. S. Aleev, 1936).

The oxidation of methane proceeds according to the formula

$$CH_4 + 2O_2 = CO_2 + H_2O,$$

where the ratio between the produced CO_2 and the consumed O_2 is 0.5. The oxidation of hydrogen can be represented by the equation $2H_2 + O_2 = 2H_2O$. Since it does not yield carbon dioxide, the corresponding ratio here equals zero. Thus, Kuznetsov intended to determine separately the quantities of oxygen used for respiration and for the oxidation of lake gas by calculating the ratio between the released CO_2 and the consumed O_2.

Direct measurements of temperature were made in the lake and samples were collected for the determination of the dissolved oxygen, carbon dioxide, bicarbonates, and the pH. The samples were taken from the deepest part of the lake at short intervals, 3—5 days apart, with some interruptions. A total of forty-two series of analyses were made in Lakes Beloe, Glubokoe, and Chernoe.

Observations were made in Lake Beloe during the summer when wind-induced circulations caused a supersaturation of the water with atmospheric oxygen, as well as during later periods of calm weather. These spells of calm weather were especially valuable since they allowed a follow-up of the oxygen uptake in the hypolimnion at different temperatures. Table 68 shows the results of these observations.

TABLE 68. Daily consumption of oxygen in the water of Lake Beloe during different periods (mg/L/day) (after Kuznetsov, 1939)

Depth, m	26—29 May	13—16 June	16—19 June	19—22 June	10—15 Aug.	19—23 Nov.	23—28 Nov.	28 Oct.— 5 Dec.	5—20 Dec.	20—25 Dec.
1	—	—	—	—	—	—	—	0.13	0.10	0.21
3	—	—	—	—	0.82	—	—	0.15	0.10	0.11
5	0.19	—	1.59	0.95	0.76	—	0.16	0.11	0.18	0.06
7	0.61	1.06	0.65	0.06	0.86	0.40	0.19	0.14	0.15	0.15
9	0.93	1.0	0.25	—	0.85	0.50	0.47	0.46	0.06	0.05
12	1.27	0.34	—	—	—	1.14	0.67	0.05	—	—

It is evident from Table 68 that the daily consumption of oxygen reaches a peak of 1—1.5 mg/L in June. The lowest values were recorded in winter at a water temperature of about 3°C.

The ratios between the produced CO_2 and the consumed O_2 in Lake Beloe during the same period appear in Table 69. In the bottom layers, the indicated ratio is excessively high owing to the presence of dissolved carbon dioxide produced by the silt. In most cases, however, the ratio between carbon dioxide and oxygen is less than unity — an indication that methane and hydrogen are being oxidized. These processes proceed at a faster rate beneath the ice cover, since the gases produced by the silt are more soluble in cold water. On the other hand, respiratory processes predominate at the beginning of the summer stagnation, immediately after the fall overturn. The absolute values of the oxygen uptake in the autotrophic oxidation of methane and hydrogen can be easily calculated from the CO_2/O_2 ratio (Table 69) and the absolute consumption of oxygen.

TABLE 69. Ratio between produced CO_2 and consumed O_2 in the water of Lake Beloe in 1935 (in ml) (after Kuznetsov, 1939)

Depth, m	13—16 June	16—19 June	19—22 June	10—15 Aug.	19—23 Nov.	23—28 Nov.	28 Nov.— 5 Dec.	5—20 Dec.	20—25 Dec.
1	—	—	—	—	—	—	0.63	0.38	0.59
2	—	—	—	0.53	—	—	0.34	1.00	0.53
5	—	0.93	—	0.52	—	1.41	0.27	0.78	1.22
7	0.82	0.38	0.8	0.71	0.72	0.58	0.77	0.65	0.81
9	0.49	0.33	—	0.75	0.84	0.23	0.73	1.43	1.25
12	1.34	—	—	—	1.22	1.15	0.50	—	—

The CO_2/O_2 ratio of the hypolimnion of Lake Beloe averages 0.65 during the summer stagnation and 0.68 during the winter stagnation, except in the bottom layer, which contains an excess of carbon dioxide released from the silt. Assuming that respiratory processes occur side by side with an oxidation of methane and hydrogen, S. I. Kuznetsov (1939) found that respiration consumes from 40 to 60% of the oxygen uptake, while the rest serves for the oxidation of the lake gas. Similar results were obtained from Lake Chernoe in Kosino. Calculations were also made on the basis of the ratio between the produced CO_2 and the consumed O_2.

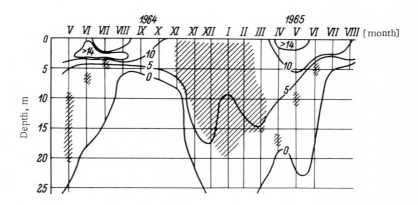

FIGURE 103. Consumption of dissolved oxygen for the oxidation of methane in Lake Plussee. The shaded areas show that the oxidation of methane consumes more than 40% of the dissolved oxygen (after Anagnostidis and Overbeck).

In a study of the effect of bacteria on the consumption of oxygen in Lake Plussee in eastern Holstein, West Germany, Anagnostidis and Overbeck (1966) found that the oxidation of methane in this eutrophic water body accounts for up to 70% of the oxygen uptake. They published a scheme of the distribution of oxygen in connection with the activity of methane-oxidizing bacteria in the lake (Figure 103); as shown by the shaded areas in the scheme, the bacterial oxidation of methane consumes more than 40% of the dissolved oxygen.

Effect of the Biological Oxidation of Ferrous Salts on the Oxygen Regime of Lakes

During the summer and winter stagnations, ferrous compounds can accumulate in the bottom layers of lakes with more or less evident signs of eutrophy. After a detailed study of this process in Lake Beloe (Kosino), V. S. Ivlev notes that the migration of iron from the bottom to the water mass begins when the bottom water becomes very poor in oxygen and develops an acid reaction. Because of this, the oxidation of ferrous to ferric compounds at the expense of dissolved oxygen never reaches considerable proportions during a stagnation. This process assumes an appreciable magnitude only at the beginning of the fall overturn, when the ferrous salts become oxidized and precipitate in the form of ferric hydrate. An oxygen deficit cannot develop in such periods, since any losses are covered from the atmosphere.

At least part of the oxidation of ferrous compounds follows purely chemical pathways. Iron bacteria, however, are responsible for a large proportion of it. Such is the conclusion of G. A. Sokolova (1959, 1961) after a study of the dynamics of iron bacteria in Lake Glubokoe. In addition, masses of O c h r o b i u m   t e c t u m were found in the plankton of Lake Chernoe (in Kosino) during the spring overturn of 1937. Iron bacteria were abundant in the plankton of Lake Chainoe at the edge of the oxygen zone (A. G. Salimovskaya-Rodina, 1936). Finally, a rich growth of O. t e c t u m was reported in Lake Lunzersee (Ruttner, 1962).

Effect of the Biological Oxidation of Hydrogen Sulfide on the Oxygen Regime of Lakes

Freshwater lakes of glacial origin usually contain only small quantities of sulfates; accordingly, the concentration of hydrogen sulfide rarely rises above a negligible level. S. I. Kuznetsov (1942) did not detect hydrogen sulfide in the water of about fifty lakes of largely glacial origin and belonging to different trophic categories in Moscow, Kalinin, and Leningrad regions, in Karelia, and on the Kola Peninsula. Hydrogen sulfide was lacking in the water of these lakes, although many of them had oxygen-free bottom layers. By contrast, silt sediments usually contain hydrogen sulfide either in the form of sulfides or free, sometimes even in considerable amounts. For example, hydrogen sulfide was found even in the highly oligotrophic Lake Gabozero (M. V. Zelenkova-Perfil'eva, 1927). On the other hand, Lake Beloe

TABLE 70. Vertical distribution of oxygen and hydrogen sulfide in the water of the eutrophic Lake Beloe during different seasons (after Kuznetsov, 1942)

Depth, m	30 December 1937			23 February 1938			1 April 1938			27 August 1939		
	tempera-ture, °C	O_2, mg/L	H_2S, mg/L	tempera-ture, °C	O_2, mg/L	H_2S, mg/L	tempera-ture, °C	O_2, mg/L	H_2S, mg/L	tempera-ture, °C	O_2, mg/L	H_2S, mg/L
0	—	—	—	—	—	—	—	—	—	20.6	8.57	—
1	0.4	11.8	—	0.8	2.6	—	1.25	4.75	—	—	—	—
2	—	—	—	—	—	—	—	—	—	20.4	—	—
3	1.2	10.4	—	2.2	1.7	—	2.25	2.41	—	—	—	—
4	—	—	—	—	—	—	—	—	—	19.9	8.47	—
5	—	7.9	—	—	0.95	—	—	0.38	0.0	15.8	7.12	0.0
6	—	—	—	—	—	—	—	—	—	—	0.0	0.126
7	2.0	6.6	—	3.0	0.68	—	—	0.31	0.0	10.4	—	0.22
8	—	—	—	—	—	—	—	—	—	—	—	0.46
9	—	4.6	—	3.2	0.37	—	3.3	0.18	0.0	—	—	0.41
10	2.4	1.9	0.0	—	0.32	0.0	—	0.06	0.03	—	—	—
11	—	0.7	0.0	3.6	0.0	0.0	—	0.00	0.05	8.65	—	0.63
12	—	0.2	0.0	4.2	0.0	0.14	4.2	0.00	0.18	—	—	—

in Kosino is poor in sulfates. Table 70 shows the annual relationship between the distributions of oxygen and hydrogen sulfide, notably by the end of the summer stagnation and in late winter.

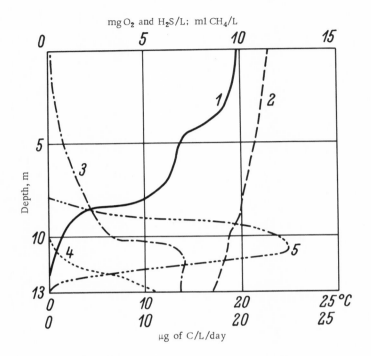

FIGURE 104. Consumption of oxygen for the oxidation of methane and hydrogen sulfide in the Cheremshan inlet of the Kuibyshev Artificial Reservoir:

1) oxygen; 2) temperature (°C); 3) methane; 4) hydrogen sulfide; 5) chemosynthesis, µg of C/L/day.

As in the case of iron, hydrogen sulfide migrates from the bottom to the water mass only after other factors have exhausted the oxygen content of water. When greater amounts of sulfates are present in the lake water, the production of methane in the top silt is often accompanied by a reduction of sulfates to hydrogen sulfide. This phenomenon was observed by Yu. I. Sorokin (1961b) in the Cheremshan inlet of the Kuibyshev Artificial Reservoir (Figure 104).

Water layers with dissolved oxygen border on layers containing dissolved hydrogen sulfide (Figure 104), while methane is present throughout the water mass. Chemosynthesis reaches a peak at the lower edge of the oxygen zone, since oxygen serves for the oxidation of methane and hydrogen sulfide. According to Yu. I. Sorokin, the presence of methane-oxidizing bacteria and Thiobacillaceae is evident from the pronounced capacity of the lake water to oxidize methane and thiosulfate.

255

Obviously, at first the oxygen is consumed largely for the oxidation of methane. Then hydrogen sulfide begins to diffuse from the silt throughout the anaerobic zone to the border of the oxygen zone, where it undergoes oxidation by the dissolved oxygen in microaerophilic conditions. This oxidation is due largely to bacteria of the family Thiobacillaceae. As a result, the contact zone between hydrogen sulfide and oxygen steadily rises. This state of affairs persists until the thermal or wind-induced overturn in the fall.

Matters are different in lakes containing large amounts of sulfates. Regardless of salinity, such water bodies can possess considerable quantities of hydrogen sulfide. In the Big Soda Lake, USA, for example, the concentration of hydrogen sulfide was found to be 780 mg/L (Hutchinson, 1957).

If the water is transparent enough to let light through beyond the thermocline as deep as the edge of the hydrogen sulfide zone, as is often the case in meromictic lakes, masses of sulfur purple or green bacteria develop during the summer at the upper edge of the hydrogen sulfide zone. Lake Belovod' in Vladimir Region can be taken as an example. Table 71 shows the distribution of oxygen and hydrogen sulfide in this lake during the summer, in early winter, and before the thaw. Hydrogen sulfide is produced here by the reduction of sulfates in the silt, and its concentration in the deep waters increases year after year (Dolgov, 1955).

The deep waters of Lake Belovod' have a greater specific weight and contain a higher concentration of sulfates. As a result, the fall overturn affects the water mass from the surface to a depth of 14 m but does not extend deeper into the hydrogen sulfide zone. The double transparency of water as measured with Secchi disks exceeds 15 m. This creates favorable conditions for the development of Chromatium okenii and other purple sulfur bacteria at the edge of the illuminated zone at a depth of about 14—15 m. The thickness of the Chromatium layer varies from one year to another. Similar phenomena are known in many lakes in Japan and Western Europe.

The purple sulfur bacteria are anaerobes. They use solar energy for the fixation of carbon dioxide; hydrogen sulfide serves as a hydrogen donor whose oxidation consumes CO_2 oxygen. Thus, the purple sulfur bacteria can exert only a positive effect on the oxygen regime of the lake since they prevent the rise of hydrogen sulfide from the deep waters to the surface layers during the summer. In winter, the density of these bacteria in the upper layer of the hydrogen sulfide zone falls from one million or several hundred thousand cells to only 1,000—15,000 cells per ml. During this season the photosynthetic activity of the purple sulfur bacteria ceases beneath the ice cover, and the upper border of the hydrogen sulfide zone rises from a depth of 15 m to 11 m, which depletes the oxygen content of water at a depth of 13—15 m.

In addition to the pigmented sulfur bacteria, the water of Lake Belovod' contains Thiobacillus thioparus (G. A. Dubinina). Chemosynthesis is especially rapid in the border layer, where both oxygen and hydrogen sulfide are present; here the oxidation of hydrogen sulfide results mainly from the activity of Thiobacillaceae and follows a strictly chemical pathway. The oxygen regime of the lake deteriorates under these circumstances, since the layer in question is situated beneath the thermocline and losses cannot be covered with atmospheric oxygen during the stagnation period.

TABLE 71. Distribution of oxygen, hydrogen sulfide, and sulfur bacteria in the water of Lake Belovod' during different seasons (after Kuznetsov, 1942)

Depth, m	August 17, 1937				December 9, 1937				March 11, 1938				July 30, 1938			
	temperature, °C	O_2, mg/L	H_2S, mg/L	Chromatium, thousands of cells per ml	temperature, °C	O_2, mg/L	H_2S, mg/L	Chromatium, thousands of cells per ml	temperature, °C	O_2, mg/L	H_2S, mg/L	Chromatium, thousands of cells per ml	temperature, °C	O_2, mg/L	H_2S, mg/L	Chromatium, thousands of cells per ml
0	22.6	9.18	0.0	0	—	—	—	—	2	—	—	—	25.7	7.79	—	—
1.5	—	—	—	—	1.2	12.6	0	0	2.1	7.45	0	—	—	—	—	—
2	—	—	—	—	2.5	—	—	—	—	—	—	—	—	—	—	—
3	—	—	—	—	—	—	—	—	3.5	—	—	—	23.8	8.58	—	—
4	22.6	9.14	—	—	3.2	10.58	—	—	—	—	—	—	19.0	14.22	—	—
5	20.2	9.68	—	—	—	—	—	—	—	—	—	—	14.6	21.52	—	—
6	14.9	10.37	—	—	3.2	12.2	—	—	—	—	—	—	11.5	8.78	—	—
7	11.9	9.3	0.0	0	—	—	0.0	—	—	—	—	—	9.8	7.78	—	—
8	10.0	—	—	—	3.2	8.4	—	0.04	4.0	7.12	—	0.09	8.4	6.0	—	—
10	8.25	2.39	0.0	—	—	—	—	—	—	3.21	0.34	3.4	—	—	—	—
11	—	—	—	—	3.6	—	—	—	5.0	0.63	0.40	7.9	—	—	—	—
12	7.5	—	—	—	3.6	—	—	—	—	0.00	1.97	15.8	—	1.48	—	—
13	7.3	0.31	0.0	4.7	5.4	3.4	0.45	1.0	6.3	0.00	2.36	—	7.6	—	0.00	0.1
14	—	—	0.69	160	—	0.05	2.65	3	—	—	—	—	—	—	0.0	0.05
14.5	—	—	—	293	—	—	—	—	—	—	—	—	—	—	—	66
14.8	—	—	—	254.5	—	—	—	—	—	—	—	—	—	—	0.0	1,004
15	7.2	0.11	1.0	—	6.7	0.0	3.86	5.04	6.8	0.00	3.65	7.2	7.3	—	1.98	382
17	—	0.00	5.48	—	6.7	0.0	5.4	2.7	7.0	—	4.93	—	—	0.00	4.86	28
20	7.0	0.00	7.24	4	7.0	0.0	8.94	0.92	7.1	0.00	8.58	11.0	7.1	—	7.68	8.5

257

Thiobacillaceae can exert a considerable influence on the oxygen regime of lakes with such characteristics.

Finally, Thiobacillaceae can utilize nearly all the dissolved oxygen for the oxidation of hydrogen sulfide during the winter in shallow eutrophic lakes whose silt produces large amounts of hydrogen sulfide by the reduction of sulfates (as in Lake Karas'e, Vladimir Region). Just before the thaw, the water of such lakes lacks oxygen and contains various amounts of dissolved hydrogen sulfide.

The Nitrogen Cycle in Lakes

Nitrogen is the main biogenic element. The quantity and nature of its compounds often determine the total productivity of the lake. Hence the need for a thorough understanding of the nitrogen cycle with all its stages, such as ammonification, nitrification, denitrification, fixation of free nitrogen, etc. Regrettably, many aspects of the nitrogen cycle are still obscure.

There is no general agreement on such important topics as the ways by which nitrogen enters into lakes. Some authors believe that nitrogen penetrates into lakes mainly from the catchment basin, while others maintain that the main sources of nitrogen are fixation from the atmosphere and regeneration of mineral nitrogen in the breakdown of nitrogenous organic compounds inside the lake.

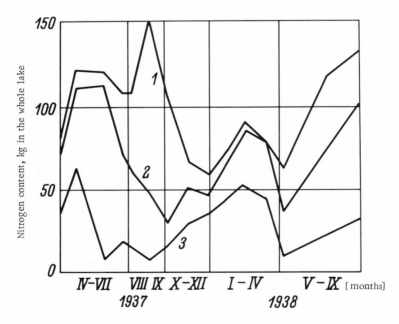

FIGURE 105. Seasonal dynamics of the total and fractional nitrogen content of the water of Lake Chernoe in Kosino:

1) total amount of nitrogen in dissolved and suspended form; 2) dissolved nitrogen; 3) ammonia nitrogen.

In our view, the only way of establishing the relative importance of the different stages of the nitrogen cycle (and the cycles of other elements in the lake) is by determining the nitrogen budget (L. L. Rossolimo, 1934, 1964, 1967). Such tasks involve a thorough study of the microorganisms that participate in the cycle.

The nitrogen cycle is best studied in bodies of freshwater, especially lakes and artificial reservoirs, where the elements of the water budget are more easily accounted for and all microbiological processes occur faster than in the sea.

The concentration of different forms of nitrogen in lake water varies considerably from one season to another, depending on such factors as the development of plankton, the extent and nature of water circulation (which affects the supply of nitrogen from the bottom), the entry of nitrogen from the catchment basin, etc. Nevertheless, the average value of the total nitrogen content and often that of its different compounds remain constant over a period of many years in each lake. Such is the case with Lake Chernoe in Kosino (Konshin, 1949) (Figure 105).

This constancy in the nitrogen content of each particular lake and the great variations in this respect from one lake to another explain the prominent place of this element as an index of the trophic properties of lakes (Birge and Juday, 1911, etc.; Naumann, 1927, 1932; Yoshimura, 1932b, 1932c).

TABLE 72. Concentration of nitrogen and other organogenic elements in water of lakes of different trophic categories (mg/L)

Type of lake	After Yoshimura (1932b, c)				After Naumann (1927)		
	ammonia nitrogen	nitrate nitrogen	protein nitrogen	total nitrogen	P_2O_5	CaO	humus
Eutrophic	0.015–1.0	0.0–0.5	0.2–0.7	>1	0.5	25–100	25–50
Mesotrophic	0.0–0.1	0.0–0.03	0.1–0.2	–	–	–	–
Oligotrophic	0.0–0.003	0.0–0.02	0.005–0.03	<1	<0.5	<25–100	<25–50
Dystrophic	–	–	–	<1	<0.5	<25	>50

Table 72 (after Yoshimura and Naumann) shows the concentrations of nitrogen and some other biogenic elements in lakes of different trophic categories.

Despite the somewhat arbitrary classification of lakes into trophic categories, Table 72 helps to introduce some order into the infinite variety of natural water bodies. Water samples for determining the trophy of the lake must be collected in winter, when there is no mass growth of phytoplankton. The concentration of nitrogen in lakes is closely associated with the development of phytoplankton and the photosynthesis of organic matter. Using the biological method of A. V. Frantsev (1932), S. I. Kuznetsov (1945) tried to determine the biogenic elements whose concentration limits the growth of phytoplankton in a number of lakes (Table 73).

TABLE 73. Requirement of the phytoplankton for biogenic elements in different lakes (the control, lake water without additives, considered as 100%)

Lake	Date of analysis (1935)	Increment of Scenedesmus quadricauda as percentage of control after addition of			
		N	P	K	Fe NPK
Syvatoe (Kosino, Moscow Region)	April 27	115	127	161	156
	September 7	214	233	157	220
Chernoe (Kosino, Moscow Region)	April 28	119	132	201	164
	June 17	215	116	105	241
	September 7	145	105	107	190
Krugloe (Myshchetskoe)	September 7	156	106	114	140
Nerskoe (Myshchetskoe)	November 7	160	175	117	185
Beloe (Kosino, Moscow Region)	September 7	101	86	93	190
Glubkoe (Ruza District)	September 29	116	98	108	144

The protococcal alga Scenedesmus quadricauda served as indicator organism. Potassium sulfate, sodium phosphate, and ammonium nitrate were added separately and together to samples of lake water. The alga was cultured in the presence of light, and the increment in the number of Scenedesmus cells was determined after incubation for three days. The results of these experiments appear in Table 73, which show that nitrogen deficiency is the main limiting factor in the development of the phytoplankton of the examined lakes.

Except for the recruitment or loss of nitrogen by the flow of surface or underground waters in or out of the lake, all the transformations of this element result from the activity of microorganisms. Consequently, these transformations must be studied by microbiological methods.

All the processes of the nitrogen cycle in lakes can be divided into three main groups: (1) fixation of free nitrogen, which increases the quantity of bound nitrogen in the lake; (2) conversion of one form of nitrogen to another; (3) escape of bound nitrogen from the lake. Before discussing these phenomena we shall deal briefly with the morphology and physiology of the most important microorganisms that take part in the nitrogen cycle.

Morphology and Special Physiology of Microorganisms
Participating in the Nitrogen Cycle

Nitrogen Fixation

Azotobacter. Beijerinck (1901) obtained enrichment cultures of bacteria capable of fixing atmospheric nitrogen. The isolated forms were named Azotobacter agilis and A. chroococcum (Figure 106).

Several other species were isolated later (see the monograph by Mishustin and Shil'nikova, 1968). Table 74 shows the characteristics of the commonest Azotobacter species.

TABLE 74. Main species of Azotobacter

Species	Cell morphology in a 24-hour culture	Colonial morphology on glucose agar
Azotobacter chroococcum	Oval, 2μ long	Large, slimy, dark brown to black
A. agilis	Round, to 3.5μ, solitary or in pairs	Minute, yellowish, producing a green fluorescent pigment
A. vinelandii	Small, oval, 1.5μ, solitary or in pairs	Large, slimy, light brown, in some cases with fluorescent pigment
A. beijerincki	Long, 2μ wide, forming chains	Large, slimy, usually colorless
A. indicum	Oval, paired; each end of the cell bears a body which takes up stains	Large, slimy, cream-colored, slightly brown at the margins

Morphologically, the Azotobacter cells resemble blue-green algae. Their mucous capsule keeps the cells in pairs or tetrads. Azotobacter forms cysts in certain conditions. In contrast to algae, however, all Azotobacter species are motile and peritrichous.

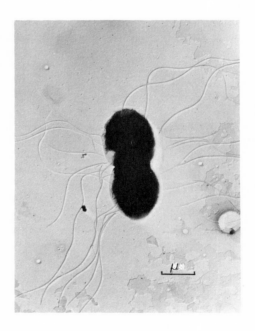

FIGURE 106. Morphology of Azotobacter (A. chroococcum).

To quote S. N. Vinogradsky (1938), "the morphology of each bacterial species must be studied during its developmental cycle in normal conditions." Starting from this ecologic principle, Vinogradsky examined the developmental cycle of Azotobacter in media poor in organic ingredients

262

As sources of organic matter he took not mannitol or glucose but compounds that occur in soil and rank far lower in nutritive value, namely, the salts of benzoic, acetic, propionic, and butyric acids, ethanol, and normal butanol. Vinogradsky observed the following sequence of developmental forms of the green Azotobacter in media containing 0.2% of the above compounds. When freshly inoculated in a liquid medium, the young Azotobacter culture usually consists of large motile rods measuring 2.0—2.5 by 1.2—1.5μ. On the third day, Azotobacter forms oval and round adult cells, and the liquid becomes fluorescent. On the fourth or fifth day the cells become smaller and coccoid. Characteristic capsules develop afterward around the cells.

Azotobacter meets its requirements for organic matter with a variety of compounds, including sugars, dextrins, lower alcohols, organic acids, some hydrocarbons, etc. It can also assimilate low concentrations of bound nitrogen.

A nitrogen-fixing microorganism related to Azotobacter was assigned to a separate genus, Beijerinckia, of the family Azotobacteriaceae (Mishustin and Shil'nikova, 1968). This acid-tolerant bacterium produces large amounts of slime; in sugar-containing media it fixes nitrogen at a rate comparable to that of Azotobacter.

Clostridium pasteurianum. S.N. Vinogradsky (1893, 1894) started his famous studies of the fixation of free nitrogen in 1893. By using selective media and pasteurizing the inoculum, he was able to isolate an anaerobic spore-forming rod, which he named Clostridium pasteurianum. This species fixes about 2 mg of nitrogen per 1 mg of utilized sugar in a liquid medium. Its cytology and morphology was later studied in detail by V. L. Omelyansky (1923).

The young cells of Clostridium pasteurianum are straight, cylindrical, motile, 1.2—1.3 by 1.5—2.0μ, with round ends. They have a homogeneous protoplasm that becomes yellow under the influence of iodine. With the exhaustion of the medium, growth slows down and sporulation begins; the rods become thick and fusiform, and their central diameter becomes nearly twice as long. The spores germinate after being transferred to a fresh medium. The germination begins with a swelling of the spore, whose envelope splits open to make way for the germ cell, which begins to divide.

V. L. Omelyansky (1923) examined the capacity of C. pasteurianum to grow in media containing different organic compounds. He obtained satisfactory growths with the following carbon sources: dextrose, levulose, sucrose, galactose, maltose, raffinose, dextrin, inulin, glycerol, and mannitol. On the other hand, starch, lactose, arabinose, and the salts of formic acid and hydroxy acids proved unsuitable. The presence of nitrogen salts inhibits the fixation of nitrogen.

Blue-green algae as nitrogen-fixing agents. Beijerinck (1901) obtained cultures of Anabaena catenula and Anabaena sp. in nitrogen-free media inoculated with soil. This led him to the conclusion that blue-green algae can fix nitrogen. Pringsheim (1914) and co-workers, however, were unable to detect any fixation of free nitrogen in pure cultures of several blue-green algae and suggested that such fixation can take place only in mixed cultures with Azotobacter. Later, Drewes (1928) proved that cultures of Nostoc punctiforme and Anabaena variabilis fix free nitrogen.

The literature dealing with this topic was reviewed by Fogg and Wolfe (1954). In addition to the Kjeldahl method, the fixation of nitrogen was determined by the use of isotopes, namely heavy nitrogen, N^{15}. The latter procedure eliminated various errors, notably the penetration of bound nitrogen into the culture in the form of NH_4 or NO_3^- from the air or other extraneous sources.

TABLE 75. Nitrogen-fixing capacity of some blue-green algae (after Fogg and Wolfe, 1954)

Order and family	Species capable of fixing nitrogen	Species incapable of fixing nitrogen
Chroococcales		Chroococcus turgidus, Gloeothece linearis, Microcystis aeruginosa, Gloeocapsa membranina: Synechococcus cedrorum
Oscillatoriaceae		Lyngbya aestuarii, Oscillatoria spp., Phormidium foveolarum, Aphanizomenon flosaquae
Nostocaceae	Anabaena ambigua A. cylindrica A. fertilissima A. gelatinosa A. humicola A. naviculoides A. variabilis Aulosira fertilissima Cylindrospermum gorakporense C. licheniforme C. maius Nostoc paludosum N. punctiforme	
Rivulariaceae	Calothrix brevissima C. parietina	
Scytonemataceae	Tolypothrix tenuis	Plectonema notatum, P. nostocorum
Stigonematales	Mastigocladus laminosus	

A list of blue-green algae capable of fixing nitrogen in pure culture appears in Table 75.

In the absence of organic matter, blue-green algae fix atmospheric nitrogen at approximately the same rate as does Azotobacter. However, they do so only in the presence of light. A culture of Anabaena cylindrica growing in a normal medium without bound nitrogen fixed at least 0.2 mg of nitrogen per liter during eighteen days (Wolfe, 1953). It was shown experimentally that some species can fix nitrogen also in the dark, but only in the presence of glucose or fructose. Moreover, the growth and nitrogen-fixing activity of A. cylindrica require the presence of molybdenum salts in the medium; the growth of this species practically ceases in the absence of such salts. Blue-green algae are widespread in nature; their rich growths in some lakes fix large quantities of atmospheric oxygen.

Other organisms capable of fixing atmospheric nitrogen. A slight fixation of nitrogen was observed in many microorganisms, which were accordingly placed in the category of oligonitrophiles (Mishustina, 1955). More accurate experiments with heavy nitrogen (N^{15}), however, gave negative results (N. P. L'vov, 1964).

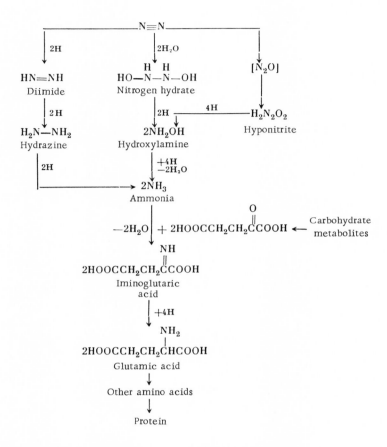

Scheme of the bacterial fixation of molecular nitrogen.

The ability of a microorganism to fix free nitrogen is largely associated with two other properties, namely the presence of the enzyme hydrogenase and the capacity for photosynthesis or chemosynthesis.

Among the chemosynthetic microorganisms, this group includes the hydrogen-oxidizing bacteria and Methanobacterium omelianskii (Barker, 1956), while the photosynthetic forms are represented by blue-green algae and such photosynthetic bacteria as Chlorobium, Chromatium, Rhodomicrobium, Rhodopseudomonas, and Rhodospirillum.

Mechanism of nitrogen fixation. Studies of the enzymatic system of different nitrogen-fixing organisms and their ability to assimilate some intermediate products point at ammonia as the basic product of the fixation (Vinogradsky, 1930; Alexander, 1961). The possible pathways of the process are shown on p. 265.

According to Wilson and Burris (1948), the fixation of nitrogen proceeds as follows. A specific respiratory enzyme, A, is reduced to AH_2, which reacts with hydrogen peroxide (a product of the respiratory reactions) and forms AH — a free radical that reacts with nitrogen. This process yields first diimide, N_2H_2, which is reduced to ammonia:

$$2AH_2 + H_2O_2 \rightarrow 2AH + 2H_2O,$$
$$N_2 + 2AH \rightarrow N_2H_2 + 2A,$$
$$N_2H_2 + 4(H) \rightarrow 2NH_3 .$$

Some workers assume that a N_2H_2-type intermediate product reacts with an organic acid in the presence of a hydrogen donor, yielding directly glutamic or aspartic acid.

Mineralization of Organic Nitrogen

Decomposition of proteins. The microbial breakdown of proteins begins as an extracellular process. It occurs only in species that possess proteolytic enzymes and can secrete them into the environment. Under such circumstances, proteins are broken down to smaller molecules that can enter the cell. Here the protein subunits undergo hydrolysis to simple peptides or amino acids, which become components of the cell proteins or are degraded with the release of ammonia. Organisms that cannot utilize natural proteins satisfy their nitrogen requirements with peptones, amino acids, inorganic salts, or other compounds small enough to diffuse through the cell membrane.

The category of microorganisms that can mineralize proteins includes aerobic and anaerobic bacteria, fungi, and actinomycetes.

The anaerobic decay of proteins, also known as putrefaction, yields carbon dioxide, organic acids, indole, scatole, mercaptanes, hydrogen sulfide, and ammonia.

The ability of bacteria to mineralize proteins serves as a taxonomic trait determined by the liquefaction of gelatin or the peptonization of casein.

Molds release slightly smaller quantities of ammonia because they immediately utilize this compound as a building unit, especially in the presence of assimilable nitrogen-free organic compounds. Many actinomycetes secrete proteolytic enzymes during their life span; others do so after the autolysis of dead mycelium cells.

The protein molecule consists of a chain of amino acids joined by a peptide bond. Pure proteins are readily mineralized by various bacteria of the genera Pseudomonas, Bacillus, Clostridium, and Micrococcus

An enzyme named protease hydrolyzes the protein molecule at the peptide bond, yielding peptides or separate amino acids and purine or pyrimidine bases, as shown in the following scheme:

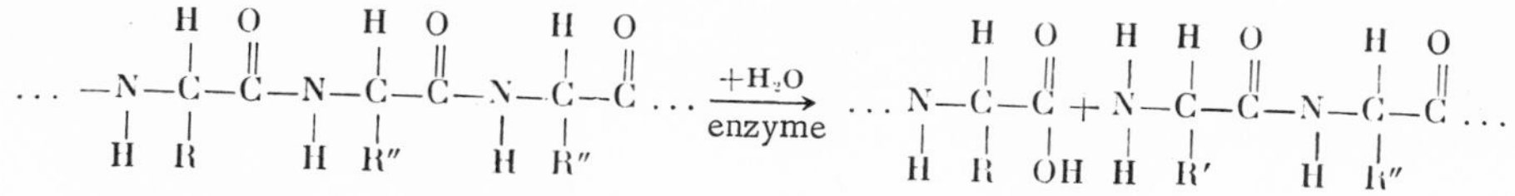

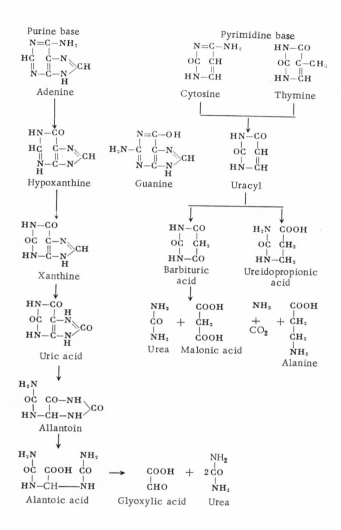

The breakdown of purine and pyrimidine bases similarly leads to amino acids, urea, ammonia, and carbon dioxide:

The decarboxylation yields amines, many of which have an unpleasant smell. Putrescine appears from the amino acid ornithine, and cadaverine from lysine. These and other amines were previously regarded as ptomaines, that is, as food poisons occurring in stale meat and fish. It is now established that food poisoning actually results from toxins produced by some bacteria. The deamination of amino acids produces organic acids and ammonia, the nature of the organic acid being dependent on the circumstances of the deamination of the process — aerobic, anaerobic, etc.

267

The breakdown of amino acids usually proceeds along one of the following pathways:

(1) Direct deamination

$$R-CH_2-\underset{\underset{NH_2}{|}}{CH}-COOH \longrightarrow R-CH=CH-COOH + NH_3$$

(2) Oxidative deamination

$$R-\underset{\underset{NH_2}{|}}{CH}-COOH + {}^1/_2O_2 \longrightarrow R-\underset{\underset{O}{\|}}{C}-COOH + NH_3$$

(3) Reductive deamination

$$R-\underset{\underset{NH_2}{|}}{CH}-COOH + 2H \longrightarrow R-CH_2-COOH + NH_3$$

(4) Decarboxylation

$$R-\underset{\underset{NH_2}{|}}{CH}-COOH \longrightarrow R-\underset{\underset{NH_2}{|}}{CH_2} + CO_2$$

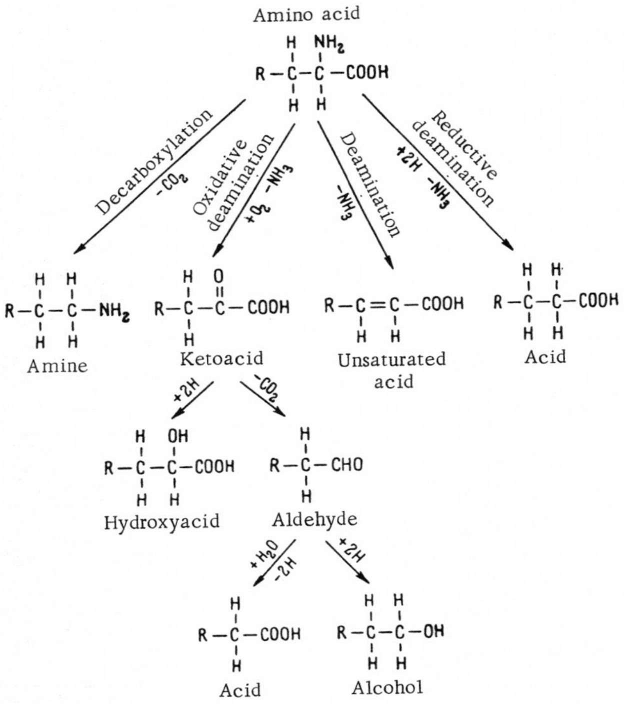

Amino acid

$$R-\overset{\overset{H}{|}}{\underset{\underset{H}{|}}{C}}-\overset{\overset{NH_2}{|}}{\underset{\underset{H}{|}}{C}}-COOH$$

Decarboxylation −CO₂

Oxidative deamination +O₂ −NH₃

Deamination −NH₃

Reductive deamination +2H −NH₃

$$R-\overset{\overset{H}{|}}{\underset{\underset{H}{|}}{C}}-\overset{\overset{H}{|}}{\underset{\underset{H}{|}}{C}}-NH_2$$

Amine

$$R-\overset{\overset{H}{|}}{\underset{\underset{H}{|}}{C}}-\overset{\overset{O}{\|}}{C}-COOH$$

Ketoacid

$$R-\overset{\overset{H}{|}}{C}=\overset{\overset{H}{|}}{C}-COOH$$

Unsaturated acid

$$R-\overset{\overset{H}{|}}{\underset{\underset{H}{|}}{C}}-\overset{\overset{H}{|}}{\underset{\underset{H}{|}}{C}}-COOH$$

Acid

+2H

−CO₂

$$R-\overset{\overset{H}{|}}{\underset{\underset{H}{|}}{C}}-\overset{\overset{OH}{|}}{\underset{\underset{H}{|}}{C}}-COOH$$

Hydroxyacid

$$R-\overset{\overset{H}{|}}{\underset{\underset{H}{|}}{C}}-CHO$$

Aldehyde

+H₂O −2H

+2H

$$R-\overset{\overset{H}{|}}{\underset{\underset{H}{|}}{C}}-COOH$$

Acid

$$R-\overset{\overset{H}{|}}{\underset{\underset{H}{|}}{C}}-\overset{\overset{H}{|}}{\underset{\underset{H}{|}}{C}}-OH$$

Alcohol

Dissimilation of amino acids. The intracellular dissimilation of amino acids usually consists in their deamination or decarboxylation, which sometimes proceed simultaneously; at any rate, there is invariably a partial degradation of the amino acid.

Arginine and tryptophane are readily deaminated. The process is more difficult with other amino acids. The acid residue undergoes further breakdown in aerobic or anaerobic conditions.

Amino acids provide nitrogen and carbon to many heterotrophs, which first remove the amino group in the form of ammonia and then utilize the acid residue.

Transamination is a particular type of deamination in which the amino group migrates to an α-ketoacid:

$$
\begin{array}{ccccc}
\text{COOH} & \text{COOH} & & \text{COOH} & \\
| & | & & | & \\
\text{H}-\text{C}-\text{NH}_2 + & \text{C}=\text{O} & \text{COOH} & \text{H}-\text{C}-\text{NH}_2 \\
| & | & | & | \\
\text{CH}_3 & \text{CH}_2 \rightarrow & \text{C}=\text{O} + & \text{CH}_2 \\
\text{Alanine} & \text{CH}_2 & \text{CH}_3 & \text{CH}_2 \\
& | & & | \\
& \text{COOH} & & \text{COOH} \\
& \alpha\text{-Ketoglutaric} & \text{Pyruvic} & \text{Glutamic} \\
& \text{acid} & \text{acid} & \text{acid}
\end{array}
$$

It represents an important mechanism for the synthesis of new amino acids in the cell.

Mechanism of mineralization of organic nitrogen. The means by which amino acids are degraded inside the organism depend partly on the pH of the medium. An acid environment stimulates the synthesis of decarboxylases, while deaminases are produced in alkaline media. Organisms living in acid media can therefore decarboxylate amino acids to amines, which are more alkaline than the respective amino acids from which they originate. This causes a shift of pH to the alkaline side. The same organisms in an alkaline environment deaminate amino acids to organic acids, which lower the pH (see scheme). In short, deamination and decarboxylation represent a fine and important mechanism for controlling the acidity of the environment.

$$
\begin{array}{c}
\qquad\qquad \xrightarrow[\text{Alkaline medium}]{\text{Deamination}} \quad \text{NH}_3 + \text{R}-\overset{\overset{\displaystyle H}{|}}{\underset{\underset{\displaystyle H}{|}}{\text{C}}}-\text{COOH} \quad \text{(acid)} \\
\overset{\displaystyle \text{NH}_2}{\underset{\displaystyle H}{\overset{|}{\underset{|}{\text{R}-\text{C}---\text{COOH}}}}} \\
\qquad\qquad \xrightarrow[\text{Decarboxylation}]{\text{Acid medium}} \quad \text{CO}_2 + \text{R}-\overset{\overset{\displaystyle H}{|}}{\underset{\underset{\displaystyle H}{|}}{\text{C}}}-\text{NH}_2 \quad \text{(amine)}
\end{array}
$$

Acidification

Alkalinization

Nitrifying Bacteria

A pure culture of nitrifying bacteria was first obtained by S. N. Vinogradsky (1890), who demonstrated that these microorganisms fix carbon dioxide at the expense of energy obtained from the oxidation of ammonia to nitrites and further on to nitrates. He described two autotrophic microorganisms: Nitrosomonas, which oxidizes ammonium salts to nitrites, and Nitrobacter, responsible for the further oxidation of nitrites to nitrates.

Nitrosomonas. This genus, a rod measuring 0.6—1.0 by 0.9—2μ, reproduces by binary fission and shows a number of developmental stages in a liquid medium. A motile form appears 3—4 days after the inoculation of a fresh medium. S. N. Vinogradsky (1890) believed that N. europea has a single flagellum. According to E. L. Ruban (1961), however, the motile cells can possess a bundle of flagella and are fringed with fine fimbria that are visible under the electron microscope.

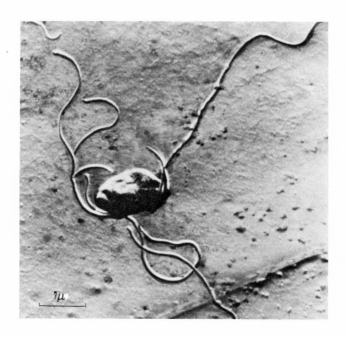

FIGURE 107. Nitrosomonas europea (electron micrograph by Ruban).

Nitrosomonas reproduces by binary fission of the motile stage. The final stage of the development of the Nitrosomonas cell forms dense zoogloea, which glue together the calcium carbonate sediment on the bottom of the vessel. The zoogloea usually appear after the oxidation of ammonia is completed. It appears that the form described by Vinogradsk as Nitrosocystis is actually the zoogloea stage of Nitrosomonas.

This genus contains all the essential components of the electron transfer chain — pyridine nucleotide, flavin, and cytochromes a, b, and c; all
these compounds can be reduced by the addition of ammonium salts
(E. L. Ruban and G. A. Zavarzin, 1958; A. B. Lozinov and V. A. Ermachenko,
1960; Aleem and Lees, 1963).

The nitrification begins with the oxidation of ammonia:

$$NH_4^+ + 1\tfrac{1}{2}O_2 = 2H^+ + NO_2^- + H_2O + 66,000 \text{ cal.}$$

This process occurs in three stages. At first the ammonium ion is
oxidized to hydroxylamine, the energy being probably carried by DPN^+.

According to Engel (1941), ammonia is oxidized on the cell surface:
$NH_3 + O = NH_2(OH)$.

The hydroxylamine formed in this reaction readily penetrates the cell.
Its oxidation yields an amount of energy comparable to that contained in the
ammonium ion. This energy is harnessed by suitable mechanisms in the cell.

The oxidation of hydroxylamine to nitrites can follow three possible pathways (G. Lis, 1958).

1. Via dioxyammonia:

$$NH_2OH + H_2O = NH(OH)_2 + 2(H),$$

$$NH(OH)_2 = HNO_2 + 2(H).$$

Though highly probable, this reaction has not been demonstrated, perhaps
because of the instability of dioxyammonia.

2. Via nitroxyl:

$$NH_2OH = NOH + 2(H),$$

$$NOH \cdot H_2O = HNO_2 + 2(H).$$

Here again, the instability of this intermediate compound makes a demon-
stration of the reaction rather difficult.

3. Via hyponitrous acid:

$$2NH_2OH \longrightarrow HO-\underset{|}{\overset{H}{N}}-\underset{|}{\overset{H}{N}}-OH + 2H$$

$$HO-\underset{|}{\overset{H}{N}}-\underset{|}{\overset{H}{N}}-OH \longrightarrow HO-N{=}N-OH + 2H.$$

$$HO-N{=}N-OH + O_2 = 2HNO_2.$$

This pathway is regarded as the most probable of the three, although it
still awaits proof.

Nitrobacter. G. A. Zavarzin (1958a, b, 1961a) places Nitrobacter
winogradskii in the new family Blastobacteriaceae of the order Hyphomicrobiales. Its developmental cycle was studied under the electron
microscope. The cell of Nitrobacter is pyriform, 0.45 by 1 micron.
It reproduces by budding. The bud develops as a small swelling at the
pointed end of the cell; it bears a long flagellum by the time it has reached

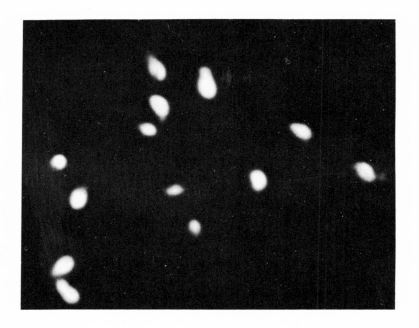

FIGURE 108. Nitrobacter (phase contrast micrograph; × 2,000). (Photo by G.A. Zavarzin.)

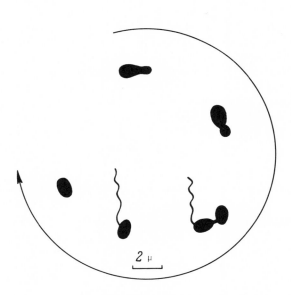

2 μ

FIGURE 109. Developmental cycle of Nitrobacter (after G.A. Zavarzin).

the size of the maternal cell. Afterward the bud breaks away and develops into a motile stage, which persists only during the phase of logarithmic growth. Then the cell settles down, loses the flagellum, and, in adverse conditions, forms a mucous capsule. The developmental cycle is shown in Figure 109.

Wimmer (1904) and Nelson (1931) described a new motile species, which Nelson named Nitrobacter agile; according to an electron micrograph published by Watson (1963), this species has the appearance of a typical Pseudomonas. Cultures of N. agile do not glue the sediment and do not cause turbidity of the medium.

It was established that cytochrome c and cytochrome oxidase take part in the oxidation of nitrite by N. winogradskii; there are indications (Zavarzin, 1958a,b, 1965) that this process involves a reduction of flavin and pyridine nucleotide.

Cultural characteristics of nitrifying bacteria. The pH tolerance and optimum of Nitrosomonas and Nitrobacter vary from one strain to another. On the average, the optimal pH is 8.0 for Nitrosomonas and 7.7 for Nitrobacter, while the pH range extends from approximately 6.5 to 9.5.

Both genera can grow on solid substrates. In cultures, the most viable cells rest on the sediment of calcium carbonate or magnesium ammonium phosphate.

Accordingly, nitrification phenomena are most pronounced in the surface silt layer and very slight in the surface water layer. The nitrifying bacteria do not assimilate organic compounds. Moreover, peptone and glucose inhibit their growth (Vinogradsky and Omelyansky, 1899), and Nitrosomonas are also inhibited by mannose and various amino acids, notably cystein (Jensen, cited from Lees, 1958).

The nitrifying bacteria assimilate carbon dioxide at the expense of energy obtained from the oxidation of ammonia and nitrites.

However, this reaction has a low probability since the oxidation-reduction potential of the $TPN^+ \rightleftarrows TPN\text{-}H$ system is close to $rH_2 = 4$, while the $NO_2^- \rightleftarrows NO_3^-$ system has $rH_2 = 30$. In other words, the equilibrium between the oxidized and the reduced form of tripyridine nucleotide will be shifted to the left unless the system is supplied with extraneous energy. It appears that the energy required for the regeneration of the hydrogen carrier comes from energy-rich phosphorus compounds formed with the participation of the cytochrome system:

$$NO_2^- + H_2O + 2(Fe^{+++} \text{ cytochrome}) \rightarrow 2(Fe^{++} \text{ cytochrome}) + 2H^+ + NO_3^-.$$

The reduced cytochrome is then oxidized directly with atmospheric oxygen:

$$2(Fe^{++} \text{ cytochrome}) + 2H^+ + \tfrac{1}{2}O_2 + P + ADP \rightarrow H_2O + 2(Fe^{+++} \text{ cytochrome}) + ATP.$$

This mechanism produces energy-rich phosphate bonds whose energy can be used for regenerating the reduced form of tripyridine nucleotide ($TPN\text{-}H_2$). However, this theory has not yet been proven.

The possibility of such utilization of ATP energy has been demonstrated in animal mitochondria. Here, the addition of ATP caused a reduction of TPN^+. In the presence of ATP, mitochondria incapable of phosphorylation caused a reduction of TPN^+ with succinic acid, which cannot do so directly. The ability of N i t r o b a c t e r to convert ATP energy to $TPN \cdot H_2$ can be represented in the following scheme (Zavarzin, 1958a, 1958b, 1965):

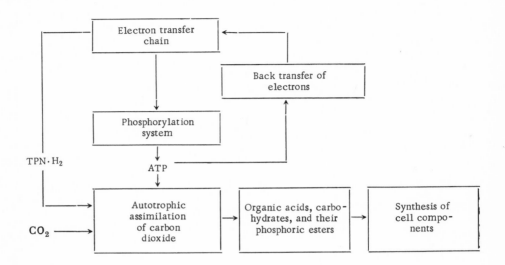

Thus, nitrification yields free energy, which is utilized for growth. There is still no accurate method of calculating the efficiency of the utilization of free energy by autotrophic organisms. Baas-Becking and Parks (1927) have proposed the formula:

$$E = \frac{A}{M} \cdot \frac{C}{F} \cdot 100\%,$$

where A represents the number of CO_2 carbon atoms assimilated, M the molecules of oxidized substrate, C the number of calories necessary for the reduction of 1 mole of CO_2 to the cell level, equal to 120,000 calories, F the amount of free energy released in the microbial oxidation of the given substrate, and E the efficiency of the utilization of the free energy.

The magnitude of C is not clear. According to Baas-Becking, C equals 120,000 calories. Yu. I. Sorokin believes that this figure must be much lower if the reduced substrate itself participates in the reduction of carbon dioxide and this in view of the fact that the oxidation of glucose to carbon dioxide yields 690,000 calories.

In the case of N i t r o s o m o n a s, the substrate is NH_4^+ and the reaction consumes a much smaller amount of energy:

$$NH_4^+ + CO_2 + O_2 = CH_2O + NO_2^- + H_2O; \quad \Delta F = +12,300 \text{ cal.}$$

Applying the Baas-Becking formula to the oxidation of NH_4^+ to NO_2^-, Meyerhof (1916) found an efficiency of 7.9%; in Lees (1958) the correspondir figures range from 6.0% to 60% according to the age of the culture. For Nitrobacter, the oxidation of NO_2^- to NO_3^- has an efficiency of 5.9% (Meyerhof, 1917).

If the ammonium ion serves as hydrogen donor, as Sorokin believes, it follows from Meyerhof's data that C equals 12,300 calories (instead of the 120,000 calories postulated by Baas-Becking), which corresponds to an efficiency of 77%. A similar modification of the data of Lees on the basis of Sorokin's hypothesis leads to an efficiency of more than 100%, since Lees speaks of an efficiency as high as 60% according to the Baas-Becking formula. Therefore, the efficiency of chemosynthesis is calculated after Baas-Becking.

Bacteria That Produce Free Nitrogen

Denitrifying bacteria. The nitrogen cycle in nature involves a variety of reactions in which nitrogen is converted from one form to another. The transition of nitrogen from nitrates to gaseous nitrogen is known as denitrification.

Many saprophytic bacteria can reduce nitrate to nitrite only. In the presence of ammonium salts or amino acids, however, nitrite yields free nitrogen by a chemical reaction:

$$2KNO_2 + (NH_4)_2SO_4 \rightarrow 2NH_4NO_2 + K_2SO_4$$
$$NH_4NO_2 \rightarrow N_2 + 2H_2O.$$

This process is referred to as indirect denitrification.

The direct denitrification converts nitrate to free nitrogen, causing an alkalinization of the medium:

$$4KNO_3 + 5"CH_2O" \rightarrow 2K_2CO_3 + 3CO_2 + 5H_2O + 2N_2.$$

Only a small number of bacteria can perform such a reaction. This group includes some species of Pseudomonas, Achromobacter, Bacillus, Micrococcus, and a few other genera. All of them are aerobes. They use nitrate as electron acceptor only in the absence of oxygen or, according to M. P. Korsakova (1941a, 1941b), in the presence of a great excess of readily assimilable organic compounds. Among the more widespread and known species of this group are Pseudomonas denitrificans, P. fluorescens (Figure 110), P. aeruginosa, Micrococcus denitrificans, and Achromobacter siccum.

The reduction of nitrate to free nitrogen occurs in the absence of oxygen. In addition, it depends on pH and the concentration of organic compounds in the medium. Pseudomonas stutzeri and P. denitrificans do not produce free nitrogen at pH lower than 5.5 in the presence of calcium tartarate and citrate (T. M. Zakharova, 1925). Denitrification is most intensive at pH 7—8. A more alkaline reaction inhibits the process; accordingly, denitrification can proceed with $Ca(NO_3)_2$, which is physiologically less alkaline than KNO_3.

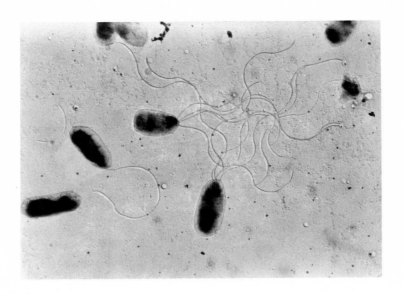

FIGURE 110. Pseudomonas fluorescens (electron micrograph).

The denitrifying bacteria can be divided into two groups on the basis of their ability to use nitrate as the only source of nitrogen. These bacteria can utilize nitrate only after reducing it to ammonia. They possess simultaneously two enzymatic systems — one that reduces nitrate to free nitrogen and another responsible for the reduction of nitrate to ammonia. In laboratory conditions, some denitrifying bacteria lose the second enzymatic system and become unable to assimilate nitrate.

The denitrifying bacteria are equipped with two oxidation-reduction mechanisms — respiratory, with atmospheric oxygen as hydrogen acceptor, and nitrate-reduction, where nitrate serves as hydrogen acceptor.

On the basis of her own results and information in the published literature, M. P. Korsakova (1953) notes that denitrifying bacteria utilize a variety of carbon compounds, such as carbohydrates, alcohols, acids, etc.; however, each species can use certain strictly defined organic compounds as hydrogen donors, especially in the case of complex hydrocarbons and aromatic alcohols and acids.

Nitrates can be reduced to free nitrogen even in the presence of air. Under such circumstances, however, the process depends largely on the nature of the organic compound present and requires that such a compound be available in large excess and in a readily assimilable form (M. P. Korsakova, 1941a, b; Meiklejohn, 1940; G. S. Rusakova and V. S. Butkevich, 1941).

In the presence of a given amount of organic matter, even not in very large excess, the reduction of nitrates to free nitrogen proceeds much faster in anaerobic conditions. On the other hand, the rate of bacterial growth is much higher in the presence of air.

Saks and Barker (1949) distinguish between two stages of denitrification: (1) reduction of nitrate to nitrite; (2) reduction of nitrite to free nitrogen.

Each stage of denitrification has its separate enzymatic system. The effect that the partial pressure of oxygen exerts on the process is less evident in the reduction of nitrate to nitrite than in the further reduction of nitrite to free nitrogen.

However, the effect of aeration differs from one species to another. Free access to air causes only a slight decrease in the rate of denitrification in Bact. fluorescens and Bact. pyocyanea in comparison with anaerobic conditions but totally inhibits the reduction of nitrate by Achromobacter arcticum (Rusakova and Butkevich, 1941).

The mechanism of denitrification. In aerobic conditions, the oxidation of carbohydrates yields carbon dioxide and water as final products. For example, the oxidation of glucose can be expressed as follows:

$$C_6H_{12}O_6 + 6O_2 \longrightarrow 6CO_2 + 6H_2O.$$

In aerobic conditions, heterotrophs obtain energy by the oxidation of carbohydrates with molecular oxygen. In the case of anaerobic life, the oxygen required for the oxidation of carbohydrates can be obtained from oxidized nitrogen compounds. This is shown in the following equations, where H denotes the reductive capacity of the carbohydrates:

$$2NO_3 + 10H \rightarrow N_2 + 4H_2O + 2OH^-$$
$$2NO_2 + 6H \rightarrow N_2 + 2H_2O + 2OH^-$$
$$N_2O + 2H \rightarrow N_2 + H_2O.$$

In this process, every two molecules of nitrate or nitrite yield one molecule of N_2. Though normally associated with oxygen, the energy-producing reactions of Thiobacillus thiooxidans can be coupled with nitrate as oxygen donor, while the oxidation of molecular sulfur becomes a source of energy:

$$5S + 6KNO_3 + 2H_2O \rightarrow 3N_2 + K_2SO_4 + 4KHSO_4.$$

The respiration of heterotrophs is linked throughout the Krebs cycle with their constructive metabolism (multiplication). Most true denitrifying organisms are also heterotrophs and strict aerobes, which means that they do not reproduce in the absence of oxygen, even if nitrate is present. Thus, denitrification should not be regarded as a respiratory process. The nitrate oxygen serves merely as acceptor of electrons or of hydrogen, and the energy released in the process goes solely for the maintenance of life without taking part in anabolic reactions.

In view of the presence of two enzymatic reductive systems in denitrifying organisms, namely one system responsible for the reduction of nitrate to free nitrogen and another that converts nitrate to ammonia, Alexander (1961) proposes the following scheme for the denitrification process:

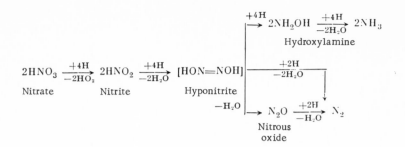

$$2HNO_3 \xrightarrow[-2HO_2]{+4H} 2HNO_2 \xrightarrow[-2H_2O]{+4H} [HON{=}NOH]$$

Nitrate   Nitrite   Hyponitrite

$$\xrightarrow[-2H_2O]{+4H} 2NH_2OH \xrightarrow[-2H_2O]{+4H} 2NH_3$$

Hydroxylamine

$$\xrightarrow{+2H}_{-2H_2O}$$

$$\xrightarrow{-H_2O} N_2O \xrightarrow[-H_2O]{+2H} N_2$$

Nitrous
oxide

Numerous experiments have shown that nitrite appears in both cases as an intermediate product of the reaction. It appears that hyponitrite can be directly reduced to free nitrogen. On the other hand, nitrous oxide (N_2O) is usually detected by analytical methods in cultures of denitrifying microorganisms and in soil air; moreover, P s e u d o m o n a s   s t u t z e r i contains an enzyme that can reduce nitrous oxide to N_2. All this suggests that nitrous oxide can also be an intermediate product of the denitrification.

Microbiological Processes of the Nitrogen Cycle in Lakes

In the preceding pages we noted the characteristic features of the different types of lakes in terms of their mineral and total nitrogen content, after which we discussed the morphology and physiology of the main microbial groups that participate in the nitrogen cycle. This makes it possible to examine the geochemical role of microorganisms in the nitrogen cycle of lakes.

Fixation of Free Nitrogen

Losses of bound nitrogen in lakes can be covered by the fixation of atmospheric nitrogen. This process is performed by free-living nitrogen-fixing microorganisms, namely different species of A z o t o b a c t e r, C l o s t r i - d i u m   p a s t e u r i a n u m, and some blue-green algae. A z o t o b a c t e r was first isolated from the water canals of the city of Delft; later studies showed that it occurs in pure freshwater bodies and not only in the water but also on submerged aquatic vegetation.

The early attempts to detect A z o t o b a c t e r in lake water failed. The first successful isolation of this genus from lake water is due to Baier (1936), who added trace elements to the medium. Satisfactory growths of A z o t o b a c t e r can be obtained by the addition of silt extract to the medium (A. G. Salimovskaya-Rodina, 1939).

The first systematic study of the distribution of C l o s t r i d i u m   p a s - t e u r i a n u m and A z o t o b a c t e r was made in our laboratory by M. Titova with samples of Moscow Region lakes having different degrees of peat content. Table 76 shows the distribution of nitrogen-fixing microorganisms in different types of lakes.

TABLE 76. Distribution of nitrogen-fixing bacteria in the water and surface silt layer of different lakes

Type of lake	Number of lakes examined	Density in the water, per ml		Density in the silt, per gram		References
		Azotobacter	Clostridium pasteurianum	Azotobacter	Clostridium pasteurianum	
Oligotrophic	5	0	0	0—10	0—10	Gambaryan (1957), Nechaeva and Salimovskaya-Rodina (1935), Kuznetsov (1956)
Mesotrophic	5	0—10	0—10	0—10	0—1,000	Aliverdieva (1964), Drabkova (1965, 1966), Kuznetsov, Shturm, and Kanunnikova (1945)
Eutrophic	10	0—10	1—20	0—10	100—10,000	Kuznetsov (1934a), Omelyansky (1917), Shturm and Kanunnikova (1945), Zavarzina (1959)
Eutrophic with an undercurrent of humic waters	2	10	1	—	—	Titova (after Kuznetsov, 1952)
Dystrophic	3	1—10	0—1	—	—	Omelyansky (1917)
Artificial reservoir		5—10	1—5	10—1,000	1,000—10,000	T. Vinberg, Dymchishina-Kriventsova (1964)

Azotobacter is scant in lake waters. Even dystrophic lakes with a large humin content have only small numbers, although some authors (Omelyansky, 1923; Kaserer, 1911; Prazmowski, 1912) maintain that humin substances stimulate its growth.

Clostridium pasteurianum often occurs in greater numbers than Azotobacter. In Lake Chernoe, which is better known in this respect, the density of C. pasteurianum shows some fluctuations and increases during the spring and fall overturns (Figure 111). This is probably due to movement of the bacteria from the silt to the water.

Azotobacter lives also on submerged aquatic vegetation in lakes. P. S. Kossovich (1894) and B. L. Isachenko (1914) speculated long ago about a possible symbiosis between Azotobacter and the submerged aquatic vegetation, namely that Azotobacter consumes carbohydrates supplied by the plants. The distribution of Azotobacter on aquatic vegetation was studied by A. G. Salimovskaya-Rodina (1939), who invariably obtained cultures of this bacterium by inoculating Beijerinck's medium with a piece of submerged aquatic vegetation.

M. G. Alipova (1955) examined more thoroughly the distribution of Azotobacter in water bodies of the Volga delta. She was unable to isolate this genus from such plants as M a r s i l e a, water lily (N y m p h a e a a l b a), L i m n a n t h e m u m n y m p h a e o i d e s, and burreed (S p a r g a n i u m t r i e d r u m), which occupy a considerable area in these waters. Only small numbers of A z o t o b a c t e r were found in slime collected from the surface of leaves and stems of arrowhead (S a g i t t a r i a s a g i t t i f o l i a), pond weeds (P o t a m o g e t o n), and reed (P h r a g m i t e s c o m m u n i s). A z o t o b a c - t e r was comparatively abundant in slime from the surface of leaves of com- mon cattail (T y p h a l a t i f o l i a), where its concentration reached 500 cells per gram of slime; however, this bacterium could not be isolated from the copious transparent slime of the sheath of this plant. Alipova notes that the inoculation of diluted or undiluted slime on Ashby's nitrogen-free medium for A z o t o b a c t e r led invariably to the development of numerous colonies of a small slime-forming rod and A z o t o b a c t e r-like organisms, which, according to E. V. Dianova and A. A. Voroshilova (1930), could be easily con- fused with A z o t o b a c t e r. Alipova obtained enrichment cultures of A z o t o b a c t e r c h r o o c o c c u s from slime collected from the surface of reed.

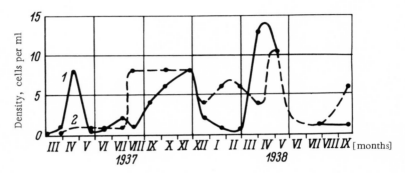

FIGURE 111. Seasonal changes in the density of C l o s t r i d i u m p a s - t e u r i a n u m in the water of Lake Chernoe, Kosino:

1) in the surface water layer; 2) in the bottom water layer.

A z o t o b a c t e r and C l o s t r i d i u m p a s t e u r i a n u m live also in the lake bottom. The density of C. p a s t e u r i a n u m cells in the surface layers of lake silt averages 300—500 cells per gram of raw silt, depending on the trophic properties of the lake (Table 76). This figure is much higher than the density of A z o t o b a c t e r.

More detailed investigations of the seasonal changes of the density of C. p a s t e u r i a n u m in silt were made by our co-worker E. M. Khartulari in the eutrophic Lake Chernoe in Kosino, by V. G. Drabkova in the meso- trophic Lake Punnus-Yarvi on the Karelian Isthmus, and by M. E. Gambaryan in the oligotrophic Lake Sevan.

The density of C. p a s t e u r i a n u m in the silt of Lake Chernoe (in Kosino varies considerably from one season to another (Figure 112); in the fall it attains 10,000 cells per gram of raw silt from the pelogenic layer. This figure decreases sharply with depth, and 30 cm beneath the silt surface there are only 1,000 cells per gram of raw silt, regardless of the season.

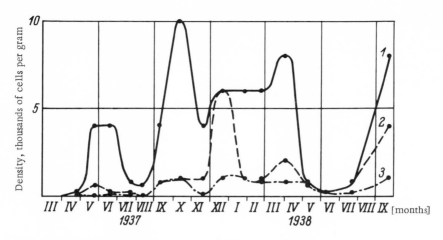

FIGURE 112. Seasonal changes in the density of C l o s t r i d i u m   p a s t e u r i a n u m
in the silt of Lake Chernoe in Kosino.

Depth inside the silt: 1) 0—2 cm; 2) 15—20 cm; 3) 30—35 cm.

In the pelogene of Lake Punnus-Yarvi, the density of C. p a s t e u r i a n u m
fluctuates throughout the year within a limit of 1,000 cells per gram of raw
silt; here too, it reaches a peak in the fall. In the oligotrophic Lake Sevan,
the density of this species is lowest in sand and highest in silt, though it
always remains below 10 cells per gram of raw silt.

There is no general agreement concerning the distribution of A z o t o -
b a c t e r in silt. Authors using cultural counting methods conclude that
this genus is scarce or lacking in silt (Omelyansky, 1917; Shturm, 1931,
1939b; Drabkova, 1965; Gambaryan, 1958; Kuznetsov, 1934a, etc.). On the
other hand, those who look for A z o t o b a c t e r by means of luminescent
microscopy of pelogene and detritus fragments are convinced of its abundance. However, a definite identification of A z o t o b a c t e r requires a
cultural procedure (E. V. Dianova and A. A. Voroshilova, 1930). At any rate,
there is as yet no proof of a wide distribution of A z o t o b a c t e r in lakes,
and the contribution of bottom-living nitrogen-fixing agents to the nitrogen
balance of lakes appears to be small.

As we noted above, some pigmented sulfur bacteria can fix atmospheric
nitrogen, and the same ability is observed in some methane-producing and
sulfate-reducing bacteria. All these microorganisms possess an active
hydrogenase and are capable of autotrophic life. Their optimal growth,
however, requires certain specific conditions. As to their role in the nitrogen budget of lakes, it appears to be modest, although much remains to be
learned on this topic.

A. G. Rodina (1956) described a new active nitrogen-fixing microorganism,
S p i r i l l u m   a z o t o c o l l i g e n s, whose occurrence in freshwaters was
later confirmed by several authors. The contribution of this microorganism
as a nitrogen-fixing agent is probably small and comparable to that of
A z o t o b a c t e r. There is still no adequate method for determining the
rate of the bacterial fixation of free nitrogen in the natural conditions of
the lake.

Particular attention is being devoted currently to the nitrogen-fixing activity of blue-green algae. Of the freshwater forms that cause water bloom, this category includes only some species of the family Nostocaceae (see above). The first determinations of the rate of nitrogen fixation by the phytoplankton in close-to-natural conditions were made by Dugdale et al. (1959) and Nees et al. (1962) in Sanctuary Lake, Pennsylvania. The fixation was determined by the use of the isotope N^{15}.

These authors poured lake water into a flask and removed the dissolved nitrogen ($N_2{}^{14}$) by bubbling a mixture of oxygen and helium. Afterward they introduced gaseous nitrogen containing a given proportion of the stable isotope N_2^{15}. The flask was placed in the lake at the same depth from which the water was taken, and was kept there for one to two days. Then the contents were evaporated and the dry residue treated after Kjeldahl. The ammonium sulfate formed in the latter process was decomposed, yielding free nitrogen, whose N^{15} content was determined in the mass spectrometer. The quantity of fixed nitrogen was calculated on the basis of the N^{15}/N^{14} ratio in the atmosphere and in the burned residue according to the formula

$$N_j = \frac{A_f \cdot N_i}{A_i},$$

where N_j is the amount of fixed nitrogen in mg, A_f the excess N^{15} in atompercent in the enriched nitrogen added at the beginning of the test, N_i the total reduced nitrogen at the end of the test in mg as determined after Kjeldahl, and A_i the excess N^{15} in atom-percent of the total nitrogen at the end of the test.

The authors found a direct relationship between the amount of fixed nitrogen and the overall growth of A n a b a e n a   f l o s - a q u a e, A. c i r c i n a l i s, and A. s p i r o i d e s in the plankton. Moreover, there was a close connection between photosynthesis and nitrogen fixation. The fixation of atmospheric nitrogen was greatest in the surface water layer. The daily amount of nitrogen fixed from the surface to a depth of 1 m was 0.13 mg/L, which corresponded to 3% of all the nitrogen present in this layer (Figure 113), while the daily increment of nitrogen averaged only 0.03 mg/L, or less than 1% of the total nitrogen.

In the Alaskan lakes, this value varies from 0 to 0.0047 mg/L daily. No fixation of nitrogen was detected in the water of the eutrophic Lake Mendota during October. Finally, the rate of nitrogen fixation in the presence of light is ten times greater than in the dark.

Thus, direct determinations of the rate of the biological fixation of nitrogen have already been made in lakes. However, the significance of this process can be evaluated only in terms of the nitrogen budget, that is, by comparing the entry and loss of this element in the lake.

An attempt to determine the nitrogen budget was made in the Rybinsk Artificial Reservoir by calculating the inflow of water from all the rivers and the outflow through the dam. Analyses of different forms of nitrogen were carried out at many stations in the reservoir and in the inflowing and outflowing waters (by F.I.Bezler). Table 77 shows the nitrogen budget of the reservoir for three years and the summer of 1960.

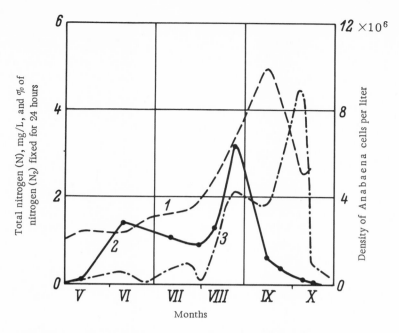

FIGURE 113. Fixation of free nitrogen by blue-green algae in the surface water layer of Sanctuary Lake:

1) total nitrogen, mg/L; 2) amount of nitrogen fixed for 24 hours, % of the total nitrogen; 3) density of A n a b a e n a per liter of water.

TABLE 77. Nitrogen balance of the Rybinsk Artificial Reservoir (tons of nitrogen in the whole reservoir)

Item	Index	June 1, 1960 — June 1, 1961	April 1, 1961 — April 1, 1962	June 1, 1962 — June 1, 1963
Actual nitrogen content of the water mass	A	+12,519	+5,399	−12,170
Difference between the inflow and outflow	B	−180	−7,329	+1,565
Nitrogen present in the water mass	A−B = C	+12,699	+12,728	−10,604
Nitrogen accumulated in the silt (on the basis of analyses of silt sedimented over a period of 20 years)	D	12,500	12,500	12,500
Theoretical balance of the water mass minus the silt nitrogen	C−D = E	199	228	−23,104
Nitrogen supplied from the air and by shore erosion minus the loss of gaseous nitrogen from the water and silt	A−E = F	12,320	5,171	10,934

The annual nitrogen budget of the Rybinsk Artificial Reservoir was calculated on the basis of the following considerations.

The total nitrogen content of the reservoir in June 1960, 1961, 1962, and 1963 was determined after analyses of water from 20–30 stations, the obtained values being applied to the whole water mass of the reservoir by taking into account the total area and actual depths.

The obtained value for a given year was subtracted from that of the following year. The result is the annual nitrogen budget, designated here by the letter A. Thus, the nitrogen budget was positive in 1960–1961 and negative in 1962–1963.

The total nitrogen entering the reservoir with river water and that leaving through the dam can be determined from the respective quantities of water that flow in and out of the reservoir. The difference between the annual inflow and outflow of total nitrogen is represented by the letter B. As shown in Table 77, B was negative in 1960–1961–1962 and positive in 1962–1963. Thus, the nitrogen gain of the water mass, excluding the nitrogen entering and leaving the reservoir, must be equal to the budget of the water mass minus the difference between the inflow and outflow of nitrogen, that is, $C = A - B$.

The thickness of the sediments accumulated during the twenty years since the creation of the reservoir was determined at a number of sites by coring. In addition, the nitrogen content of the sediments was determined. This revealed the total amount of nitrogen accumulated on the bottom during the existence of the reservoir throughout its area. This magnitude, divided by the age of the reservoir (in years), yields the value D, which equals the amount of nitrogen migrating from the water mass to the silt during the year.

Thus, A represents the actual annual budget of the water mass by June 1. By subtracting from this budget the values of B and D, which equal respectively the net inflow of river nitrogen and the amount of nitrogen passing from the water to the silt, we obtain E, which expresses the theoretical annual budget of nitrogen in the water mass:

$$E = A - B - D, \text{ or } E = C - D.$$

The theoretical budget of the water mass (E) minus the actual budget (A) yields the total amount of nitrogen supplied to the reservoir with precipitations, by biological fixation from the air, and by shore erosion (F).

It is evident from Table 77 that the total amount of nitrogen in the reservoir decreased in 1962 as a result of the low water level, but the supply of atmospheric nitrogen remained about 10,000 tons, as in the preceding years. Of this amount, rain and snow account for about 1,300 tons, while the rest can be attributed to biological fixation of atmospheric nitrogen.

Detailed analyses made in 1960 according to the above scheme provided data on the fixation of atmospheric nitrogen during each month of the vegetative period.

Despite all losses, the June and July balances of the reservoir as a whole were positive, with an average increment of 0.1 mg of nitrogen per liter per month (Table 78). At that time, the plankton contained large quantities of the blue-green alga A n a b a e n a.

TABLE 78. Total nitrogen budget of the Rybinsk Artificial Reservoir in 1960

Month	Present on first day of month	River inflow	Total at end of month	Outflow through dam	Balance	Difference from first day of next month
June	13,359	772	14,131	1,911	13,220	+1,730
July	14,950	535	15,485	2,415	13,070	+2,377
August...	15,447	748	16,195	1,945	14,250	−658
September	13,592	1,783	15,375	1,127	14,248	−838
October ..	13,410	1,866	15,276	1,508	13,768	−1,768
November	12,000					

Conversions of One Form of Nitrogen to Another

Assimilation of inorganic nitrogen. Most lakes contain very small amounts of inorganic nitrogen, rarely more than a fraction of a milligram per liter.

Inorganic nitrogen is used mainly by algae, especially in the plankton. Thus, the phytoplankton of fishponds consumes within three days practically all the inorganic nitrogen added as fertilizer at an initial concentration of 3—5 mg/L (V.A.Akimov, 1967a, 1967b).

TABLE 79. Requirements of some algae for inorganic nitrogen (after Uspenskii, 1932; Guseva, 1941)

Species	Concentration of nitrate nitrogen, mg/L		
	minimal growth	satisfactory growth	optimal growth
Spirogyra varians	0.5	20	—
S. neglecta	0.1	1	—
S. protecta	0.1	1	—
S. elongata	0.003	1	—
Mougeotia genuflexa	0.002	0.16	—
Zygnema stellinum	0.005	4	—
Scenedesmus quadricauda..	0.004	20	—
Melosira varians	0.006	1	—
Cladophora fracta	0.015	—	—
Anabaena lemmermannii...	0.1	—	0.8
Nostoc verrucosum	0.009	10	—
Coelosphaerium nägelianum	0.009	—	4.0
Oscillatoria agardhii	—	—	2.4
Asterionella formosa	0.004	—	0.2

Some species of the filamentous alga Spirogyra grow satisfactorily in the presence of about 0.015 mg of nitrate per liter, the lowest concentration supporting growth being of the order of a few milligrams per liter

(E. E. Uspenskii, 1932). Table 79 shows the requirements of some algae for inorganic nitrogen.

Many saprophyte bacteria can utilize ammonium salts and nitrates as a source of nitrogen (Egorova et al., 1952).

Since bacteria and planktonic algae are important food objects for many aquatic animals (Rodina, 1946, 1948, 1951; Gaevskaya, 1948; Sorokin, 1966c), they can be regarded as biological agents that concentrate the highly dilute inorganic and organic nitrogen of lake water and convert it to forms that can be utilized by higher organisms.

One gram of raw bacteria contains about 500 billion cells (S. P. Kostychev and O. G. Shul'gina, 1927). Since the total nitrogen content of saprophyte microflora is about 10% in terms of dry weight (Porter, 1946) and the water content of bacteria ranges from 75 to 85%, it follows that a bacterial population of one million cells per ml corresponds to about 0.04 mg of total bacterial nitrogen per liter of water.

In summer, the water of Lake Chernoe (in Kosino) has a total nitrogen content of 1.65 mg/L, distributed as follows: bioseston and abioseston 0.75 mg/L, bacteria 0.1 mg/L, and dissolved nitrogen 0.8 mg/L. The concentration of bacterial nitrogen is lowest during the spring and fall overturns: 0.01—0.02 mg/L.

Ammonification. The proteins of dead organisms undergo a process of mineralization that yields nitrogen mainly in the form of ammonia. Depending on the depth and other properties of the lake, a different proportion of the available nitrogen is mineralized in the water mass, while the settling remnants of dead plankton and aquatic vegetation undergo similar changes in the upper layers of silt.

In the presence of small quantities of assimilable nitrogen-free organic compounds, the breakdown of proteins leads to free ammonia (Waksman and Tenney, 1927). On the other hand, the liberated nitrogen serves again for the synthesis of fresh bacterial protein if the water contains larger amounts of carbohydrates.

The early stages of the mineralization of organic matter are carried out largely by a nonsporogenous microflora, as shown by S. N. Vinogradsky (1930) for soil and V. A. Akimov (1967a, b) with respect to the water mass. Spore-forming bacteria become dominant later, after the exhaustion of the readily assimilable proteins. This explains the distribution of bacteria in lake silt, where the proportion of the spore-forming microflora increases with depth (V. A. Ekzertsev, 1948).

Several authors have studied the specific composition of the saprophyte microflora of lake water (A. A. Egorova, Z. P. Deryugina, and S. I. Kuznetsov, 1952; A. G. Rodina and N. Kuz'minskaya, 1964, etc.).

On the whole, the saprophyte microflora that grow on meat peptone agar are largely identical with the group of ammonifying organisms. According to the above authors, the following saprophyte bacteria occur most commonly in lake water and produce large quantities of ammonia when grown in meat peptone broth: Pseudomonas fluorescens, Bact. agile, Micrococcus albidus, Bac. filaris, Bac. mycoides, Bac. brevis, Bac. oligonitrophilus, Bac. subtilis, Mycobacterium globiforme, Mycobacterium filiforme. Of the spore-forming bacteria that attack dead plankton, the water of Lake Glubokoe contains

Bac. mesentericus, Bac. corrugatus, and Bac. subflavus
(Z.I. Kuznetsova, 1937).

TABLE 80. Distribution of saprophyte bacteria in the water of lakes of different trophic types during the summer stagnation

Type of lake	Lake	Number of cells per ml		Percentage of spore-forming bacteria	Species of spore-forming bacteria
		saprophyte	spore-forming		
Eutrophic	Beloe (Kosino, Moscow Region)	154	15	9.7	Bac. mesentericus
	Chernoe (Kosino, Moscow Region)	124	9	7.3	Bac. megaterium
	Bisserovo (Moscow Region)	39	1		
Mesotrophic	Borovoe (Kokchetav Region)	241	30	12.4	Bac. megaterium
	Lebyazh'e (Kokchetav Region)	461	7	1.5	Bac. agglomeratus
	Ucha Artificial Reservoir	390	13	3.3	Bac. subtilis
	Krugloe (Moscow Region)	10	1	10	
	Punnus-Yarvi	150	15	10	
Oligotrophic	Baikal	7	0.5	7	
	Onega	10	—	—	
Dystrophic	Piyavochnoe (Vyshnii Volochek)	61	20	33	Bac. megaterium
	Chernoe (Vyshnii Volochek)	13	11	85	Bac. mesentericus
	Dolgoe (Moscow Region)	9	7	77	
Brackish lakes	Bol'shoe Krivoe (Kurgan Region)	450	119	25.0	
	Maloe Umreshevo (Kurgan Region)	1,000	260	26.0	
Bitter-salt lakes	Balkhash	2,200	9	0.4	
	Bol'shoe Gor'koe (Tyumen Region)	1,200	9	0.7	
	Orazsor (Kokchetav Region)	582	4	0.8	

The density of ammonifying bacteria in lake water depends largely on the season and the properties of the lake. Table 80 contains pertinent data on a number of lakes and artificial reservoirs.

The seasonal changes in the density of ammonifying bacteria was studied in different types of water bodies including the eutrophic lakes of Kosino, the mesotrophic Lake Glubokoe, and the Rybinsk Artificial Reservoir

(S. I. Kuznetsov, 1934a, 1958a); the lakes of Dagestan (L. A. Aliverdieva, 1964); the Karelian isthmus (V. G. Drabkova, 1966); and a number of lakes outside the USSR (Minder, 1918; Duggeli, 1924).

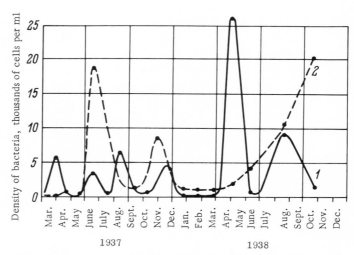

FIGURE 114. Seasonal changes in the density of saprophyte bacteria in the water of Lake Chernoe in Kosino:

1) in the surface layer; 2) in the bottom layer.

This question was examined more thoroughly in the eutrophic Lake Chernoe in Kosino (Figure 114). Here the density of saprophyte bacteria is lowest in winter; it rises in summer owing to the growth and death of plankton, and is also high during the spring and fall overturns. In addition to the summer peak, the bottom water shows a distinct autumnal peak that corresponds to the mixing of water and the stirring-up of bacteria and silt.

In order to understand the transformations of a given element, it is necessary to determine not only the direction of the different stages of the cycle but also their rates. V. A. Akimov (1967a) developed an original method for the determination of the rates of the different stages of the mineralization of organic nitrogen in fishponds (phytoplankton and dissolved nitrogen). A large dark vessel containing natural nonfiltered water was placed for 3—4 days in the pond in order to bring the conditions of the mineralization of organic nitrogen as close as possible to those that prevail in nature. The total nitrogen and the concentrations of the different forms of this element were determined at the start of the experiment. Afterward, samples were taken daily from the dark vessel. One half of the water sample was passed through a membrane filter, and similar determinations of nitrogen were made in both halves of each sample. This revealed the changes in the nitrogen content of the solution and the suspended particles. It became clear that the mineralization begins with a breakdown of the phytoplankton and seston, which increases the nitrogen content of the filtered water. Later begins a mineralization of the dissolved organic nitrogen with the production of free ammonia.

In fishponds with rich phytoplankton and abundant organic matter in the form of fish feeds, the daily rate of mineralization to ammonia during the summer was found to be about 4% of the total nitrogen content.

The density of ammonifying bacteria is much greater in the surface layers of silt than in the water mass. In Lake Chernoe, this magnitude reaches a peak in the surface layer of silt during the autumnal overturn in connection with the decay of dead plankton (Figure 115).

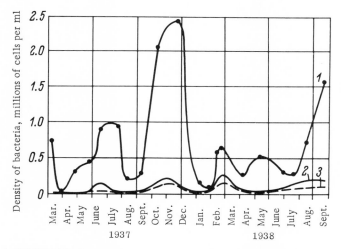

FIGURE 115. Seasonal changes of the density of saprophyte bacteria in the surface silt of Lake Chernoe in Kosino.

Depths inside the silt: 1) 0—2 cm, 2) 15—20 cm, 3) 30—35 cm.

At depths of 20 and 35 cm from the silt surface, the bacterial density shows generally the same seasonal changes as in the surface silt, though the counts of saprophyte bacteria are much lower here.

The percentage of spore-forming bacteria in the total saprophyte population of silt differs from the corresponding ratio in the water mass. Using the procedure of E. N. Mishustin and M. I. Pertsovskaya (1954), N.B. Zavarzina examined in our laboratory a number of samples from the surface silt layer of lakes belonging to different trophic categories (Table 81). Although the inoculations were made with pasteurized material, it is evident from the table that the saprophyte microflora differ but little from one type of lake to another.

The percentage of spore-forming bacteria in the silt is much greater than in the water mass. The only exception is oligotrophic lakes, where the spore-forming bacteria account for only a small fraction of the total population of saprophyte bacteria (Table 81).

The concentration of ammonia nitrogen in water shows considerable seasonal fluctuations. The entire water mass of the lake becomes free of ammonia nitrogen during the spring and fall overturns. On the other hand, ammonia accumulates during the stagnation periods, especially in the bottom water as shown in the case of Lake Chernoe (Figure 116). This indicates that the mineralization of organic nitrogen in comparatively shallow eutrophic lakes takes place mainly in the top silt, whence the ammonia enters the water mass to be nitrified and consumed by the phytoplankton.

TABLE 81. Distribution of saprophyte bacteria in the surface silt layer of lakes of different trophic categories during the summer stagnation

Type of lake	Lake	Density of bacteria, thousands of cells per gram of raw silt	% of spore-forming bacteria	Species of spore-forming bacteria
Eutrophic	Bol'shoe Medvezh'e (Moscow Region)	280	70	Bac. megaterium, Bac. mesentericus, Bac. mycoides, Bac. idosus, Bac. cereus, Bac. agglomeratus, Bac. arachnoideus
	Maloe Medvezh'e (Moscow Region)	1,200	25	
	Bisserovo (Moscow Region)	570	48	
	Bel'skoe (Vyshnii Volochek)	194	75	
	Beloe (Kosino, Moscow Region)	502	35	
Mesotrophic	Pereslavskoe (Yaroslav Region)	1,570	5.1	Bac. mesentericus, Bac. cereus, Bac. agglomeratus, Bac. mycoides
	Nikulino (Vyshnii Volochek)	873	13	
	Imalozh'e (Vyshnii Volochek)	321	21	
	Kolomno (Vyshnii Volochek)	294	28	
	Glubokoe (Moscow Region)	472	3.6	
Oligotrophic	Baikal	512	1.5	Bac. mycoides, Bac. cereus, Bac. arachnoideus, Bac. mesentericus, Bac. idosus
	Dal'nee (Kamchatka)	415	4.3	
Dystrophic	Nero (Moscow Region)	164	50	Bac. megaterium, Bac. mesentericus, Bac. mycoides, Bac. cereus, Bac. agglomeratus, Bac. arachnoideus

The relation between the density of ammonifying bacteria and the concentration of ammonium salts in the water is more evident in deep lakes, where a summer overturn does not exist. This was first noted by Minder (1918) in Lake Zürich.

TABLE 82. Exchange of nitrogen between the bottom and bottom water of the Rybinsk Artificial Reservoir (average figures, mg of nitrogen per day) (after Trifonova, 1963)

Type of bottom	N/NO$_3$	N/NH$_3$	Protein nitrogen	Organic nitrogen	Total nitrogen
Sand	+0.14	+ 1.14	+0.52	− 6.00	− 4.72
Nonflooded soils	−0.44	+ 0.36	+0.41	+ 2.13	+ 2.03
Gray silt of river bed area	−1.20	+21.43	+3.19	+10.98	+31.28
Peat overlays	−4.3	+ 1.2	+1.3	+ 7.1	+ 4.0

Note: The symbol + indicates release of nitrogen from the silt, while − means adsorption of bound nitrogen by the silt.

N. A. Trifonova (1961, 1963) undertook a direct study of the production of ammonia in the mineralization of silt in the Rybinsk Artificial Reservoir. She determined the exchange of nitrogen between the silt and the bottom water by sealing off a given volume of water under a metal hood that covered 50 dm² of bottom area. The experiment lasted from three to six days. Analyses of the different forms of nitrogen at the start and end of the experiment revealed certain regularities (Table 82).

Nearly all silts of the Rybinsk Artificial Reservoir liberate nitrogen. Most productive in this respect are the gray silts of the former Mologa bed, with 30 mg of nitrogen daily. Conversely, denitrification takes place over all but the sandy silts, especially over the peat layers, where the daily rate of this process reaches 4 mg of nitrogen per square meter of bottom area. The liberation of ammonia nitrogen from the bottom becomes particularly intensive during periods of rich phytoplankton, when masses of dead algae settle on the bottom and undergo further breakdown. Table 83 shows the results of these analyses.

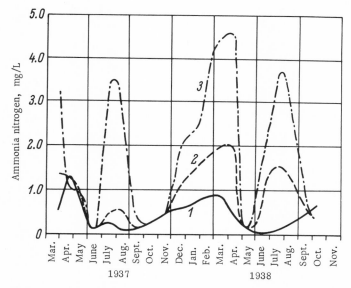

FIGURE 116. Seasonal changes in the concentration of ammonia nitrogen at different depths in the water of the eutrophic Lake Chernoe in Kosino:

1) 1 m, 2) 3 m, 3) 4 m.

In the sandy area off Shumorovskii Island, the liberation of nitrogen from the silt reached 50 mg of total nitrogen per day per square meter in August, when the reservoir bloomed with algae; this included a large proportion of protein nitrogen and ammonia nitrogen. In the fall (October) the mineralization of organic nitrogen of algal origin was already complete, and the daily liberation of nitrogen from the silt was as low as 1.4 mg per square meter.

291

TABLE 83. Liberation of nitrogen from the bottom of the Rybinsk Artificial Reservoir in August—October 1960 (after Trifonova, 1961)

Duration of test	Liberation of nitrogen, mg/m²/day						Note
	NO_2	NO_3	NH_4	protein nitrogen	organic NH_4^+	total nitrogen (sum of all forms)	
August 6 — August 11	—	−0.4	+10.4	+37.7	+51.4	+51.0	Strong bloom of blue-green algae
August 19 — August 26	−0.2	−2.2	+16.8	−2.4	+28.0	+25.6	Bloom diminishes
October 2 — October 4	0	−1.1	+ 4.2	0	0	−1.1	No bloom
October 25 — October 30	0	0	0	+ 0.4	+ 1.9	+ 1.4	

TABLE 84. Relationship between the assimilable carbon/assimilable nitrogen ratio and the percentage of ammonia nitrogen in silt (after Konshin, 1939)

Lake	Assimilable carbon/ assimilable nitrogen ratio	Ammonia nitrogen, % of total nitrogen
Beloe (Kosino, Moscow Region)	5.66	15.91
Chernoe (Kosino, Moscow Region)	6.70	5.22
Glubokoe (Moscow Region)	7.88	3.43
Krugloe (Moscow Region)	9.65	1.96
Valdai (Kalinin Region)	10.80	1.45
Svyatoe (Kosino, Moscow Region)	13.00	0.72
Kobelevo (Kalinin Region)	12.30	0.66
Mazurinskoe (Moscow Region)	15.00	0.00

The course of the breakdown of nitrogenous components of silt depends largely on the proportion between assimilable carbon and assimilable nitrogen. The lower this ratio, the greater the percentage of ammonia nitrogen of silt origin (V. D. Konshin, 1939) (Table 84).

To sum up, it is evident that a considerable part of the organic nitrogen undergoes mineralization to ammonia while still in the water mass of lakes whose depth is 10 m or more. The mineralization of the easily assimilable nitrogen becomes complete in the top layers of the silt. Ammonia liberated from the silt enters the bottom water in the form of ammonium carbonate, which rises in the water mass as a result of partial summer circulation of water or during overturns. Moreover, considerable amounts of nitrogen serve for the synthesis of bacterial protein. In summer, the rate of protein breakdown to inorganic nitrogen can reach 4% of the total nitrogen.

Nitrification. Being an exergonic reaction (59,400 calories/mole at 25°), the oxidation of ammonia to nitrate proceeds readily in the presence of suitable physical (light), chemical, and biological activators. Purely chemical agents capable of activating this reaction in natural conditions are unknown; the photochemical and biological oxidations will be discussed below.

Testing the oxidation of ammonia under the influence of ultraviolet rays, Rakestraw and Hallender (1936) found that a sample containing 970 mg of nitrogen lost 370 mg of this element during two hours of irradiation, the loss being partly accounted for by the oxidation of 270 mg to nitrite.

However, photochemical nitrification is only a minor factor in the nitrogen cycle in lakes. Owing to the intensive absorption of ultraviolet rays,
photochemical oxidation of ammonia is possible only in the top 2—10 cm of
water, which hardly affects the ammonia content of a lake several meters
deep.

Nitrification in lakes obviously depends on the presence of nitrifying
bacteria, dissolved oxygen, and ammonium salts. Consequently, an adequate
evaluation of the process requires data on the vertical distribution of ammonia, nitrate, and nitrogen during the summer stagnation in lakes of different trophic categories. Such analyses were made by Ohle (1964) in four
Holstein lakes during July, August, and September 1962. Let us examine
the results obtained in the Schluensee and Plussee. The mesotrophic
Schluensee is 45 m deep. Its metalimnion lies at a depth of 12—18 m, while
the hypolimnion contains oxygen throughout the summer, except in the bottom
layers at the end of the stagnation period. As shown in Figure 117, the vertical distribution of ammonia nitrogen was rather uniform in July and August
at about $50 \mu g/L$ but rose to $250 \mu g/L$ in the bottom layers during the fall,
when the dissolved oxygen vanished. Nitrates were present in the hypolimnion throughout the vegetative period, though their concentration gradually
decreased from 400 to $200 \mu g/L$. The phytoplankton consumed all the available nitrate in the epilimnion. The concentration of nitrite did not exceed
$1-5 \mu g/L$.

The eutrophic lake Plussee is 30 m deep, with a metalimnion situated at
a depth of 4—6 m. Oxygen was absent from the hypolimnion even in July
(Figure 117). Here the peak concentration of ammonium salts was much
higher than in Schluensee and attained $1,700-2,600 \mu g/L$ in the bottom water.
Nitrates could be detected only in the upper part of the hypolimnion with a
peak at 10—14 m; their concentration did not exceed $200 \mu g$ of nitrate nitrogen per liter. Moreover, the vertical range of nitrates dwindled steadily;
these compounds were absent from the epilimnion and lower hypolimnion.

Ohle (1964) believes that the water mass receives biogenic elements from
the silt and that such enrichment occurs not only in the profundal but also in
the sublittoral and littoral. Mineralization proceeds faster in the latter two
zones owing to the higher temperature. Wind-induced currents prevent the
establishment of a microstratification in the bottom water and accelerate
the migration of biogenic elements from the silt.

Although chemical analyses reveal only the sum total of two opposite processes concerning the biogenic elements, namely supply from the silt and
consumption by phytoplankton and bacteria, a mere comparison of the distributions of oxygen, ammonium salts, and nitrates shows that nitrification is
confined to the oxygen-bearing zone in lakes.

Many authors have examined the distribution of nitrifying bacteria and
their ability to oxidize ammonium salts. The first steps in this direction
were made by V. L. Omelyansky (1917), who tried to isolate nitrifying agents
from the silt of the Vyshnii Volochek lakes. Further experiments in this
field were carried out in the USSR and elsewhere. Nitrosomonas and
Nitrobacter were isolated in Vinogradsky's liquid selective medium. It
became clear that nitrifying bacteria exist in nearly every lake, regardless
of its type, though at a density of only one cell per 1—10 ml of lake water
(A. G. Salimovskaya-Rodina, 1932, 1938; S. I. Kuznetsov, 1934a; V. G. Drabkova,
1966; A. Romanova, 1961). In view of the fairly high rate of the oxidation of

ammonia in lake water, it appears that the selective medium of Vinogradsky does not allow an optimal growth of nitrifying bacteria and reveals only a fraction of these microorganisms.

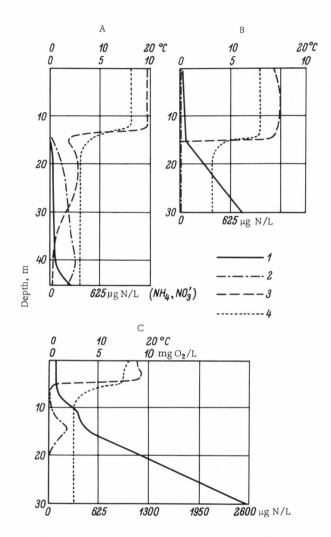

FIGURE 117. Vertical distribution of nitrogen — NH_4^+ and NO_3^- — in Holstein lakes of different trophic categories in September 1962 (after Ohle):

A) Schleinsee; B) Schöhsee; C) Plussee. 1) NH_4; 2) NO_3; 3) oxygen; 4) temperature (°C).

Probably the best procedure for determining the site of nitrification is by measuring the "nitrification capacity" of water. Such an experiment can be made as follows. About 50 mg of magnesium ammonium phosphate is added to 50 ml of lake water. Two to three weeks later, analyses are made to determine the quantity of nitrate and nitrite resulting from the oxidation of ammonia by the nitrifying bacteria present in the examined sample of water or silt.

Similar experiments by S. I. Kuznetsov (1950a) with water from several lakes in Kokchetava Region showed that the amount of NO_2^- accumulated within thirty days in the conditions of the test was 10—30 mg/L in brackish lakes and 0.01—0.03 mg/L in freshwater and bitter-salt lakes.

In lakes and artificial reservoirs, nitrification reaches a peak during the summer in the surface silt and bottom water (Table 85) (L. A. Aliverdieva, 1964; V. G. Drabkova, 1966; G. A. Sokolova). This is probably due to the fact that ammonification processes in the silt cause a constant release of ammonia, which is immediately oxidized by the nitrifying bacteria.

N i t r o s o m o n a s was also found in the silt of Lakes Beloe in Kosino and Glubokoe in Moscow Region (V. I. Lyubimov, 1937). The presence of nitrifying bacteria in the top silt of the deepest part of Lake Beloe is of particular interest in view of the anaerobic conditions that prevail there almost throughout the year, except during the fall overturn. Nitrification can hardly take place in this environment. It can be assumed, therefore, that the nitrifying bacteria have reached the top silt together with settling particles of detritus from the water mass.

TABLE 85. Rate of nitrification in the Gorki Artificial Reservoir (synthesis of nitrate nitrogen, mg/L, within 30 days; after G.A. Sokolova)

Origin of sample for analysis	Time of sampling			
	May	June	July	August
Surface water layer	18.5	36	65	40
Bottom water layer	—	—	106	38
Surface silt layer	—	—	13,000	2,600

Some saprophyte bacteria can also oxidize ammonia to nitrite (Kalinenko, 1948; Nechaeva, 1947). However, these microorganisms do not utilize the energy released by this process for the assimilation of carbon dioxide. Some saprophytic bacteria from Siberian lakes indeed produce small quantities of nitrite in media containing calcium citrate and ammonium sulfate (Kuznetsov, 1950a). However, this process is of minor importance and occurs only in bacteria that contain peroxidase; moreover, its rate is far below that observed in autotrophic nitrification. To sum up, nitrification in lakes is due mainly to the activity of autotrophic nitrifying bacteria.

Losses of Molecular Nitrogen

A third category of processes belonging to the nitrogen cycle involves the loss of this element in gaseous form.

In the water mass and pelogene (top silt) of lakes, nitrogen escapes by denitrification. Deeper inside the silt, the extensive breakdown of protein yields free gaseous nitrogen together with methane, hydrogen, and carbon dioxide. The production of these gases was first demonstrated in the methane tanks of Bach and Sierp (1923—1924).

TABLE 86. Density of denitrifying bacteria in the water and pelogene of lakes belonging to different trophic categories

Type of lake	Density of denitrifying bacteria	
	in 1 ml of water	in 1 gram of raw pelogene
Eutrophic	100—10,000	to 3,000,000
Mesotrophic	10—800	to 60,000
Oligotrophic	0—100	to 10,000
Dystrophic	10—800	—

Many saprophyte bacteria can reduce nitrate to nitrite. By reacting with ammonium salts or with the amino group of organic compounds, the nitrite undergoes an indirect denitrification. The water of some lakes, however, contains true denitrifying bacteria, which reduce nitrate to free nitrogen (see p. 275). An idea of the distribution of denitrifying bacteria in lakes can be obtained from Table 86, which is based on data from several authors (Omelyansky, 1917; Salimovskaya-Rodina, 1932; Kuznetsov, 1934a; Drabkova 1966; Romanova, 1961).

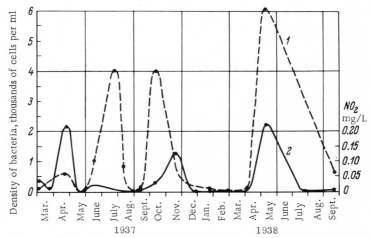

FIGURE 118. Seasonal changes in the concentration of nitrate and the density of denitrifying bacteria in the bottom water of Lake Chernoe (in Kosino):

1) bacteria; 2) nitrate.

Figure 118 shows the seasonal changes of the density of denitrifying bacteria in comparison with the concentration of nitrates in the bottom water layer of Lake Chernoe in Kosino.

296

The following conclusions can be drawn from the data that appear in Table 86 and Figure 118. A definite relationship exists between the concentration of nitrate and the density of denitrifying bacteria in lake water. The concentration of nitrate rises to a peak during the spring and fall overturns, when the density of denitrifying bacteria is at its lowest level. In summer, the surface water is poor in nitrate although it contains only small numbers of denitrifying bacteria. This is due to the utilization of nitrate by the rich phytoplankton. At the same time, the low concentration of nitrate in the bottom water results from the abundance of denitrifying bacteria during the summer.

The density of denitrifying bacteria is much greater in the silt than in the water mass. Nitrification and denitrification probably occur simultaneously in the pelogene, the overall result depending on the microzonal distribution of oxygen and on associated conditions of aeration. This topic requires further investigation.

However, the mere presence of denitrifying bacteria does not prove the existence of denitrification processes. The latter can occur at an appreciable rate only in the presence of nitrate and adequate quantities of readily assimilable organic matter; they also require anaerobic conditions and a neutral or slightly alkaline pH.

The indirect study of the role of denitrification consists of a comparative analysis of two lakes that differ from one another in a number of factors affecting the process. Such analyses were made in Lakes Beloe and Glubokoe, (S. I. Kuznetsov, 1934a). The results obtained appear in Table 87.

TABLE 87. Comparison between the concentration of nitrate and the density of denitrifying bacteria in the water of the Lakes Beloe and Glubokoe

Lake	Depth from which sample was taken, m	Spring overturn		Summer stagnation		Winter stagnation	
		nitrate nitrogen, mg/L	density of denitrifying bacteria per ml	nitrate nitrogen, mg/L	density of denitrifying bacteria per ml	nitrate nitrogen, mg/L	density of denitrifying bacteria per ml
Beloe ⋯	0—3	0.01	100	0.0	1,000	0.3—0.5	100
	7—12	0.01	100	0.0	10,000—100,000	0.1—0.2	100
Glubokoe.	0—3	—	—	0.0	60	0.3	40
	10—30	—	—	0.3	30	0.3	100

As shown in Table 87, the phytoplankton exhausts almost all the nitrate present in the epilimnion during the summer. In the hypolimnion of Lake Beloe, the disappearance of nitrate results from the activity of denitrifying bacteria, which find here the necessary anaerobic environment with readily assimilable suspended and dissolved organic matter. S. I. Kuznetsov (1934a) attributes the lack of denitrification in Lake Glubokoe to the abundance of humin and the lesser availability of assimilable dissolved and suspended organic matter.

TABLE 88. Composition of the gases liberated during the anaerobic breakdown of silt (after Rossolimo, 1932b; Sorokin, 1960)

Origin of gas	Lake or artificial reservoir	Composition of gas, vol. percent			
		N_2	CH_4	H_2	CO_2
Natural gas from lake	Lake Beloe (Kosino, Moscow Region)	5.2	80.4	11.7	1.5
		10.7	83.3	4.2	0.8
Gas obtained during experimental breakdown of silt	Lake Beloe (Kosino)	11.8	78.5	7.3	1.5
		28.8	62.8	6.4	2.95
Decay of blue-green algae	Rybinsk Artificial Reservoir	25.4	55.2	12.5	7.2
		17.39	0.96	8.15	73.5

The second cause of the escape of free nitrogen from the lake lies in the anaerobic breakdown of silt. This decomposition is rather fast in the fermentation of a sediment of sewage water (Korol'kov, 1926). Moreover, free nitrogen is constantly present among the gases produced during the anaerobic breakdown of silt, notably in the Rybinsk Artificial Reservoir (Table 88).

As shown by Yu. I. Sorokin, free nitrogen escapes also during the anaerobic decay of blue-green algae collected during their peak in the Rybinsk Artificial Reservoir.

Nitrogen accounts for up to 28% of the volume of the released gas (Table 88). The escape of gaseous nitrogen is especially great in eutrophic lakes and fish ponds, which contain inorganic fertilizers and organic fish feeds.

The annual release of free nitrogen in the lake gas amounts to 56 kg in Lake Chernoe (Kosino), which has an area of two hectares (S. I. Kuznetsov, 1952). The significance of this phenomenon becomes quite clear if one takes into account that the total nitrogen content of the lake varied from 90 to 150 kg during the year (Konshin, 1949). The escape of free nitrogen is also a major occurrence in fish ponds (V. A. Akimov, 1967a).

Scheme of the Nitrogen Cycle in Lakes

In concluding this chapter, let us outline briefly the microbiological processes associated with the transformations of nitrogen in lakes (Figure 119).

The bulk of the nitrogen enters the lake in the form of inorganic compounds — ammonium salts and nitrates (1) — and as organic compounds, namely humates. These compounds are readily assimilated by the phytoplankton and bacteria, which produce protein nitrogen. Another pathway leading to protein nitrogen is the fixation of atmospheric nitrogen (2) by some blue-green algae, Azotobacter, C. pasteurianum, and probably a number of other bacteria, including autotrophs, which possess active hydrogenase.

The protein nitrogen of the dead phytoplankton is largely mineralized while still in the water mass (3) and reenters the phytoplankton. The more resistant remnants of dead organisms sink to the bottom (4) and become part of the sediment, where the protein undergoes further mineralization (5) in anaerobic conditions, mainly with the participation of spore-forming ammonifying bacteria. Depending on the proportion between the readily hydrolyzable carbon-containing and nitrogenous organic compounds, a varying amount of protein nitrogen escapes as ammonia, while the rest becomes part of bacterial bodies or remains in the silt. Ammonia nitrogen passes from the silt to the water, where it reenters the cycle by undergoing nitrification (6) or by being assimilated (3) into the microflora of the water mass.

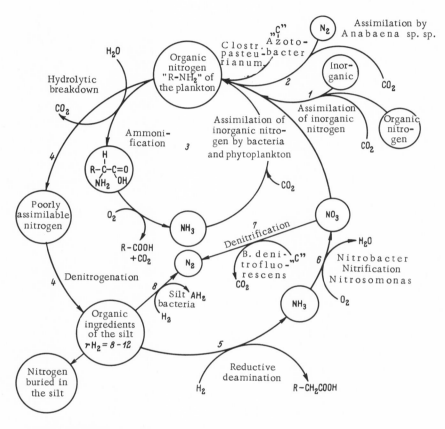

FIGURE 119. Scheme of the nitrogen cycle in lakes.

Explanations in the text.

The hypolimnion of eutrophic lakes lacks oxygen but contains readily assimilable organic compounds in a solute form. Such conditions permit a denitrification (7), which causes an escape of gaseous nitrogen from the lake. In the silt (8), the release of molecular nitrogen follows a different course: protein is broken down directly by a destruction of the amino groups, without a nitrification stage.

The specific importance of each process of the nitrogen cycle depends more or less closely on the properties of the lake.

The Sulfur Cycle in Lakes

The processes that constitute the sulfur cycle in lakes can be classified in two major groups: reduction of sulfate to hydrogen sulfide and oxidation of reduced sulfur compounds to molecular sulfur and sulfate. Many lakes are rich in sulfate and consequently can possess high concentrations of hydrogen sulfide. Clearly, such lakes deserve particular attention in a study of the sulfur cycle.

Table 89 contains data on lakes of this category.

TABLE 89. Lakes rich in hydrogen sulfide

Lake	Salinity	Sulfate sulfur in bottom layer, mg/L	Depth of the H_2S zone, m	Maximal concentration of H_2S, mg/L	I eference
Big Soda Lake (Nevada, USA)	Salt	—	—	786	son (1957)
Harutori-ko (Hokkaido, Japan)	"	—	4—9	670	Yoshimura (1936)
Hemmelsdorfer (northern part of West Germany)	"	—	33—43	304	Grinzel (after Halbfass, 1923)
Veisovo (Ukrainian SSR)	"	—	16—19	282	Nadson (1903)
Helle Fjord (Norway)	"	833	15—70	63.6	Ström (1936)
Chernoe-Kucheer (Mari Autonomous SSR, RSFSR)	Fresh	88	5—9	57.1	Kuznetsov (1942)
Suigetsu-ko (Hukai, Japan)	Salt	84	12—32	53.5	Yoshimura (1932)
Mogil'noe (Russian SFSR, Kil'din Island)	"	80	13—15.7	35.2	Isachenko (1914)
Kaiiko (Koshiki Island, Japan)	"	—	9—11	25.8	Yoshimura and Miyadi (1936)
Lago Ritom (Switzerland)	Fresh	552	13—45	30.5	Duggeli (1924)
Wakuike (Nagano, Japan)	"	—	3—7	18.9	Yoshimura and Miyadi (1936)
Rotsee (Switzerland)	"	3—12	10—16	16.1	Bachmann (1931)
Isefierfjord (Norway)	Salt	780	12—20	12.2	Ström (1936)
Hilvigefjord (Norway)	"	781	20—30	10.0	Ström (1936)
Belovod' (Ivanovo Region, Russian SFSR)	Fresh	278	11—23	152	Sorokin (1966b)
Edelberg (West Germany)	"	8.6	8.5—9.5	7.97	Ohle (1934)
Trisfjord (Norway)	Salt	840	30—87	7.75	Ström (1936)
Bol'shoi Kucheer (Mari Autonomous SSR, RSFSR)	Fresh	—	5—15	7.61	Kuznetsov (1942)
Lenefjord (Norway)	Salt	810	45—215	6.65	Ström (1936)
Kipyashchee (Kunashir Island)	Fresh	238	0—22.5	30.6	Ivanov and Karavai (1966)

Before describing the microbiological processes, it is necessary to deal with the distribution of different sulfur compounds in lakes as a function of the concentration of sulfate, organic compounds, and dissolved oxygen in the water mass and silt. Indeed, these ingredients largely determine the rate of the transformations of sulfur in lakes.

Hydrochemical and Hydrographical Characteristics of Lakes in Terms of Their Sulfate and Sulfide Content

Freshwater Homomictic Lakes

Lakes poor in sulfate. The concentration of sulfate rarely exceeds 3—4 mg/l in lakes of glacial origin. Accordingly, the hydrogen sulfide content of such lakes remains rather low in the vast majority of cases. Kuznetsov, Speranskaya, and Konshin (1939) examined this topic in about fifty lakes that are of predominantly glacial origin and show great differences in terms of salinity and the development of plankton. These lakes lie in Moscow, Kalinin, and Leningrad regions, in Karelia, and on the Kola Peninsula. Hydrogen sulfide could not be detected in these lakes, although many of them lacked oxygen in the bottom layers. The presence of hydrogen sulfide could be expected, at any rate, in the hypolimnion of glacial lakes during periods of mass mortality of a formerly rich phytoplankton and zooplankton. In fact, a faint smell of hydrogen sulfide was detected during such periods, but only in deep bottom waters at the end of a prolonged stagnation.

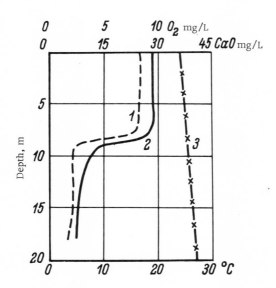

FIGURE 120. Vertical stratification of temperature and oxygen in Lake Yal'chevskoe, September 14, 1938:

1) oxygen; 2) temperature, °C; 3) CaO.

Appreciable quantities of hydrogen sulfide in the presence of a low sulfate content were found in two of the lakes listed in Table 89, namely Rotsee (Switzerland) and Edelberg (West Germany). Here the concentration of sulfate was 8—12 mg/L. Both lakes are eutrophic, especially Rotsee, which receives sewage waters from the city of Luzern. During the summer of 1922, from April 15 (spring overturn) to September 22, the production of hydrogen sulfide in the bottom water reached 12.75 mg/L (Bachmann, 1931). In most cases, however, the concentration of hydrogen sulfide in waters with a low sulfate content does not exceed 1—5 mg/L even in eutrophic lakes (Ohle, 1934; Salimovskaya-Rodina, 1938; Kuznetsov, 1942).

The relations of sulfur were studied in a number of mesotrophic lakes, of which Yal'chevskoe (Mari Autonomous SSR) and Schaalsee (West Germany) can be taken as examples. These two lakes are poor in sulfate and have a comparatively low primary production of organic matter. In summer, they show a distinct thermocline.

Oxygen persists to the very bottom of Lake Yal'chevskoe, although its concentration in the hypolimnion drops to 2 mg/L (Figure 120). The uniform distribution of calcium salts from the surface to the bottom of this lake speaks of the existence of spring and fall overturns. In other words, this lake has the hydrochemical features of an ordinary glacial lake, although it developed from a sink. Hydrogen sulfide was not found here.

Schaalsee is 65 m deep. Its bottom water contains dissolved oxygen until the fall overturn. Hydrogen sulfide is lacking, even in the bottom water (Figure 121).

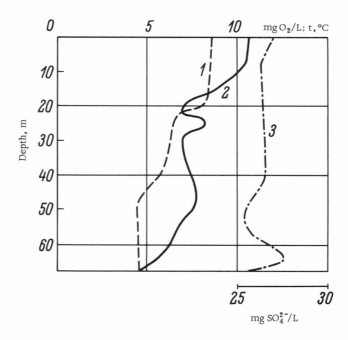

FIGURE 121. Vertical stratification of temperature, oxygen, and sulfates in the Schaalsee (after Ohle, 1954):

1) temperature, °C; 2) oxygen; 3) SO_4.

In contrast to the water mass, the silt usually contains hydrogen sulfide in the form of sulfides but sometimes also in a free state and in considerable amounts. For example, Zelenkova-Perfil'eva found hydrogen sulfide in the silt of the markedly oligotrophic Lake Gabozero, and Ohle reported H_2S in the mesotrophic Schaalsee (in Schleswig-Holstein).

Although Schaal-see shows many of the characteristics of an oligotrophic lake, the formation of hydrogen sulfide in its silt exerts a considerable influence on the chemistry of the bottom water (Ohle, 1954).

The eutrophic lakes with a high primary production can be represented by Lake Beloe (in Kosino). Here the concentration of sulfate is low—about 3 mg/L. The hypolimnion lacks oxygen during the summer. A fall overturn occurs every year, but the spring overturn may be absent (as in 1935). In late summer, a rich plankton develops in the surface water, as a result of which the transparency drops to 0.25 m. The concentration of hydrogen sulfide attains a peak at the end of the summer and winter stagnations. However, in late March and early April 1938, at a time of a distinct winter stratification, hydrogen sulfide was found only in the bottom water and in concentrations not exceeding 0.18 mg/L (S. I. Kuznetsov, 1942). Lake Beloe and other eutrophic water bodies of this type show low summer levels of hydrogen sulfide.

Comparison of the distributions of hydrogen sulfide and oxygen in the lake on August 27, (Figure 122) shows that the oxygen content drops sharply to zero in the thermocline, while hydrogen sulfide appears in the bottom water only; moreover, the two curves do not meet. A similar pattern is observed in late winter.

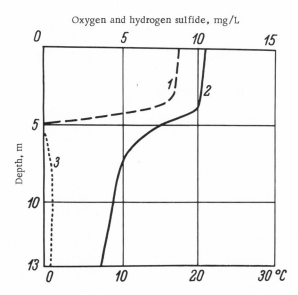

FIGURE 122. Vertical stratification of temperature, oxygen, and hydrogen sulfide in Lake Beloe (Kosino) on August 27, 1939:

1) oxygen; 2) temperature, °C; 3) hydrogen sulfide.

Anagnostidis and Overbeck (1966) reported such phenomenon from Plussee. In their view, all the oxygen of the hypolimnion is used for the oxidation of methane before the hydrogen sulfide begins to migrate from the silt and diffuse in the water mass of the lake (Figure 123).

The water of Lake Beloe in Kosino had a low hydrogen sulfide content, which reached the modest maximum of 0.63 mg/L in late summer. The eutrophication of the lake in the intervening years is responsible for an increase in the concentration of hydrogen sulfide, which reached 13 mg/L at the end of the summer stagnation in 1967.

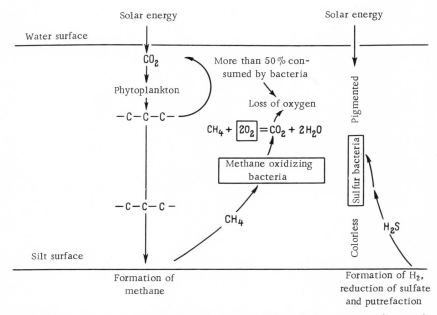

FIGURE 123. Scheme of the distribution of hydrogen sulfide in the hypolimnion of a eutrophic lake in relation to the exhaustion of the dissolved oxygen for the oxidation of methane.

Grosser Plöner See similarly belongs to the eutrophic category. Ohle (1954) examined in detail the seasonal dynamics of sulfates and hydrogen sulfide in this lake during 1952. As in the case of Lake Beloe, hydrogen sulfide began to appear here in the second half of the summer stagnation, when the hypolimnion no longer contained any oxygen. Figure 124 shows the analyses made in this lake on September 30.

The sulfate content of the hypolimnion decreases with depth in favor of the hydrogen sulfide content. It must be borne in mind that sulfate is reduce mainly in the silt, while hydrogen sulfide spreads in the hypolimnion by diffusing into the bottom water, from which it is carried by turbulent current into the upper water mass of the lake. As indicated above, the oxidation of sulfide in the eutrophic Plöner See took place in the thermocline at a depth of 22 m and in the zone of contact between oxygen-rich and hydrogen sulfide containing waters. The concentration of sulfate at this depth rose from 12 to 25 mg/L. The intensification of the fall overturn caused a sinking of the thermocline and, consequently, of the sulfate-rich layer. These data prove the active role of microorganisms in the transformations of sulfur in eutrophic lakes, although Ohle did not make microbiological analyses in the Plöner See.

Lakes with a high sulfate content. Lake Yugdem can be taken as an example of the category of freshwater lakes with a high concentration of sulfate. This lake represents a flat basin with a sharply defined funnel 15 m deep. Its water is highly transparent to 6 m.

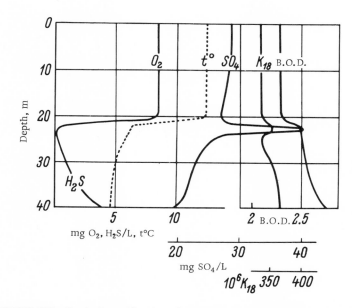

FIGURE 124. Vertical stratification of temperature, oxygen, hydrogen sulfide, and sulfate in the water of Grosser Plöner See on September 30, 1952 (after Ohle).

The plankton attains modest proportions; in the shallow part, a carpet of charophytes covers the bottom. Owing to the uniform density of water, the spring overturn affects the whole water mass of the depression. The oxygen content at a depth of 15 m does not drop below 2 mg/L at any time of the year (Figure 125). Despite the high sulfate content, hydrogen sulfide is absent from the deep zone and occurs only in the littoral, where decay of dead aquatic vegetation takes place.

As shown in the case of Lake Yugdem, the abundance of sulfate in a lake with a couple overturn and a poor primary production does not necessarily lead to a formation of hydrogen sulfide in the deep zone.

Another combination of factors — namely a high primary production, a large concentration of sulfate, and a thorough overturn in the spring and fall — exists in Lake Bol'shoi Kucheer in the Mari Autonomous SSR.

Comparison with Lake Beloe (in Kosino) shows that the presence of large amounts of sulfate allows the accumulation of hydrogen sulfide to a concentration of 7 mg/L or more in the water mass during the stagnation period.

In contrast to the pattern observed in eutrophic lakes with a low sulfate content, the oxygen-containing layer borders on the hydrogen sulfide zone in Lake Kucheer (Figure 126).

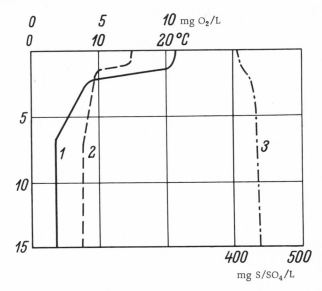

FIGURE 125. Vertical distribution of temperature and oxygen in Lake Yugdem (Mari Autonomous SSR):

1) oxygen; 2) temperature, °C; 3) SO_4.

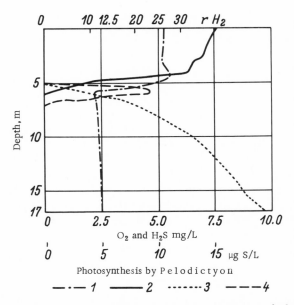

FIGURE 126. Vertical distribution of temperature, oxygen, hydrogen sulfide, and bacteria in Lake Kucheer in the Mari Autonomous SSR (after Gorlenko):

1) SO_4; 2) oxygen; 3) hydrogen sulfide; 4) Pelodictyon.

306

The deep waters of Lake Kucheer are rather cold, with a low concentration of hydrogen sulfide and a pH of 6.8. Moreover, light barely penetrates to such a depth. Such environment favors the growth of green sulfur bacteria, namely Pelodictyon clathratiforme (Pfennig and Cohen-Bazire, 1967), whose density at a depth of 6 m reaches 6 million cells per ml of water (Gorlenko, 1968).

The eutrophic Lake Solenoe is 5 m deep and has an area of one hectare. This thoroughly studied lake (Ivanov and Terebkova, 1959a, 1959b) lies in a terrace above the flood plain of the Vychegda within the boundaries of the city of Sol'vychegodsk. It receives abundant organic matter from the catchment basin and has a well-developed phytoplankton. Lake Solenoe is of karst origin. It was formed in the seventeenth century as a result of the dissolution of salts and the removal of sand during the exploitation of deep-lying sodium chloride brine, which still flows into the lake. The water contains sulfate and chloride at a concentration of 4 and 12 g/L, respectively. In the spring, the lake receives the flood waters of the Vychegda, and a complete spring overturn takes place. During the summer, there is a stratification of water and hydrogen sulfide at a depth of 3 m, reaching a concentration of 150 mg/L in late summer. The concentration of hydrogen sulfide drops sharply during the fall overturn and rises again to 40—50 mg/L in late winter.

Freshwater Meromictic Lakes with a High Sulfate Content

Karst lakes owe their existence to the erosion of gypsiferous rocks by ground waters. Sulfate is often present in high concentrations in their deep waters, while their surface layers originate from rainfall and have a low salinity. The difference in the specific weight of the surface and deep waters explains the nonparticipation of the latter in the spring and fall overturns. Such lakes usually contain less sulfate than deep lakes of marine origin. In the flood-plain lakes of the Tesha, the concentration of sulfate sulfur ranges from 28 to 300 mg/L (V. P. Grichuk, 1937). To the same category belong Lake Girotte [Lac Girotte] in France (Halbfass, 1923), the Swiss Lago Ritom, which was thoroughly studied and described by Duggeli (1924), and other lakes. Earlier, the deep waters of the Lago Ritom had a higher specific weight and contained up to 300 mg of hydrogen sulfide per liter. With the construction of an electric power station in 1913, a gallery was dug and the deep waters of the lake were drained off. As a result, the waters of the Lago Ritom have now a roughly uniform specific weight; they perform complete overturns in the spring and fall and no longer possess a hydrogen sulfide zone.

The meromictic Lake Belovod' belongs to the same category. Here oxygen extends to a depth of 12—15 m. The underlying zone is rich in hydrogen sulfide, whose concentration increases year after year (Dolgov, 1955; Sorokin, 1966b), having reached 100 mg/L in the bottom water in 1958 (Figure 127). In contrast to Lake Beloe (in Kosino), where no contact exists between the oxygen and hydrogen sulfide zones, both gases are found here at the upper boundary of the layer with a higher mineral content (Figure 127).

The upper 15 m of water become saturated with oxygen during the fall overturn. The December distribution of oxygen resembles the summer pattern; in 1938, oxygen formed a maximum in the surface layers and was totally absent at a depth of 15 m. The distribution of hydrogen sulfide in winter was generally similar to that observed during the summer.

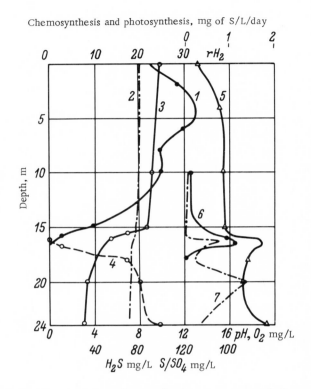

FIGURE 127. Vertical distribution of temperature, oxygen, hydrogen sulfide, and sulfate in the water of Lake Belovod '(Vladimir Region) in July 1958 (analyses made by G. A. Dubinina):

1) oxygen; 2) pH; 3) rH_2; 4) H_2S; 5) SO_4-sulfur; 6) photosynthesis of purple sulfur bacteria; 7) overall chemosynthesis.

Afterward the oxygen content of the upper layers fell during the winter from 10—12 to 7.5 mg/L, and the lower border of oxygen rose in 1938 from 14 to 12 m. The upper boundary of hydrogen sulfide rose accordingly to 10 m, in contrast to the pattern observed during the summer stagnation. The water temperature at a depth of 15 m remained constant throughout. The results of these analyses are summarized in Figure 16.

The concentration of sulfate in the water of Lake Belovod' increases with depth. In July 1958, G. A. Sokolova found an increase in the concentration of sulfate sulfur from 160 to 190 mg/L (Figure 127) at a depth of 16 m, that is, in the zone of contact between waters containing oxygen and hydrogen sulfide. As noted above, Ohle observed a similar phenomenon in the Grosser Plöner See (Figure 124).

The profundal (deep zone) silts of Lake Belovod' contain much more hydrogen sulfide — up to 0.714 g per kg of raw silt. They are therefore distinguished not only by their color but also by their microzonal structure. The profundal silts are black owing to their high iron sulfide content, in sharp contrast to the grayish white silts of the marginal zone. Treatment of the profundal silts with hydrochloric acid causes a violent bubbling owing to the release of hydrogen sulfide and carbon dioxide (Table 90).

The sink lake Chernoe-Kucheer has an abundant primary production, a high sulfate content, and no overturn (Figure 128; Table 91). Hydrogen sulfide can accumulate to considerable concentrations in the hypolimnion of such lakes.

TABLE 90. Concentration of hydrogen sulfide in the surface layer of the silt of the profundal and littoral of Lake Belovod' on August 17, 1937

Depth of station, m	Moisture, %	Total H_2S, mg/L moist silt	Total nitrogen, mg/L moist silt	Total hydrogen sulfide, % dry weight	Total nitrogen, % dry weight
4	83.14	365	764	0.216	0.45
11	95.12	506	652	1.037	1.33
15	91.02	678	799	0.755	0.89
20	90.00	714	893	0.714	0.89

TABLE 91. Analysis of the water of Lake Chernoe-Kucheer on September 13, 1938 (after Kuznetsov, 1942)

Depth, m	Temperature, °C	pH	O_2, mg/L	H_2S, mg/L	Sulfate sulfur, mg/L
0	19.8	8.8	9.01	—	2.9
3	18.7	7.4	3.16	—	2.9
4	14.0	6.8	0.06	Traces	4.3
4.5	—	6.9	—	—	14.6
5	8.5	6.9	0.00	10.48	19.6
5.5	—	6.9	0.00	34.16	33.9
6	5.7	6.9	—	—	—
7	—	6.9	—	55.78	60.2
9	5.0	6.9	—	57.10	88.8

It follows from all these examples that the nature of the sulfur cycle depends on the presence of sulfate, the synthesis or arrival of organic organic matter in the lake, the depth to which light penetrates in the water mass, and the existence of spring and fall overturns, which saturate the water mass with oxygen.

The formation of hydrogen sulfide requires a high level of organic production and a sufficient concentration of sulfate. This was shown experimentally by L. I. Rubenchik (1948), who observed a rise in the concentration of hydrogen sulfide from 136 to 334 mg/L in the meromictic Lake Repnoe within nine months after the introduction of 0.5 ton of molasses over an area of 100 m² in the deep part of the lake basin. At the same time there was a considerable rise in the sulfide content of the silt.

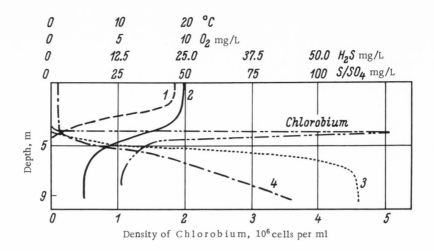

FIGURE 128. Vertical distribution of temperature, oxygen, hydrogen sulfide, and sulfate in the water of Lake Chernoe-Kucheer in July 1938:

1) oxygen; 2) temperature, °C; 3) hydrogen sulfide; 4) sulfate sulfur; 5) sulfur green bacteria.

Salt Lakes Situated in Humid Regions and Connected with the Sea

To this category belong water bodies situated in regions with a humid climate and having a past or recent connection with the sea. Examples are Lake Mogil'noe on Kil'din Island, described from a microbiological viewpoint by B. L. Isachenko (1914); many Norwegian fjords, isolated from the sea by strips of elevated land (Ström, 1936, 1962); several Japanese lakes (Yoshimura, 1932a; Jimbo, 1938a, 1938b, 1940); and the Hemmelsdorfer See in West Germany (Halbfass, 1923). Most of these lakes are meromictic. Their upper layers contain rather fresh waters, while the salinity of the lower layers approximates marine levels and includes up to 3 grams of sulfate per liter. The great difference between the specific weights of the upper and lower layers impedes a vertical mixing of the water; hence the accumulation of considerable amounts of hydrogen sulfide in the depths.

One of the best known lakes of this category is Mogil'noe, situated on Kil'din Island at the entrance to Murmansk Bay (Isachenko, 1914). The direct link that existed between this lake and the sea was severed by the elevation of a strip of land; now the lake is isolated from the sea by a low strip of sand, which, however, does not prevent the entry of sea water into the lake in stormy weather. Moreover, it appears that sea water seeps into the lake through the barrier strip. The upper waters of the lake have a low salinity (Figure 129). Oxygen spreads to a depth of 7 m and is absent from 8 m to the bottom. The concentration of hydrogen sulfide gradually increases from a depth of 8 m, reaching 194 mg/L at a depth of 16 m in the bottom waters (I. A. Khmel', 1958). A layer with abundant growth of purple sulfur bacteria was found at a depth of 9 m. Owing to the constant link with the sea, the bottom waters of the lake have a salinity of 32.0‰, which approximates the oceanic level (34.3‰). Similar conditions exist in a number of Japanese lakes that have lost their connection with the sea in historic times.

Ström (1962) described several Norwegian lakes that originally represented marine fjords but became isolated from the sea by land rises in postglacial time.

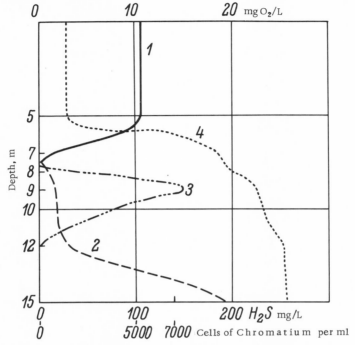

FIGURE 129. Vertical distribution of temperature, oxygen, hydrogen sulfide, and salinity in Lake Mogil'noe on Kil'din Island in 1958 (after Khmel'; salinity after data of Deryugin from 1921):

1) oxygen; 2) hydrogen sulfide; 3) density of purple sulfur bacteria; 4) salinity.

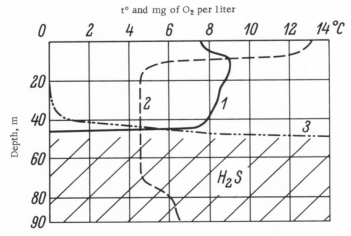

FIGURE 130. Vertical distribution of temperature (2), oxygen (1), and salinity (3) in Lake Rorhopvatn (after Ström).

One of these lakes is Rorhopvatn, which was cut off from the sea some six thousand years ago and lies at an altitude of more than 100 m. This meromictic lake is more than 90 m deep (Figure 130). It contains trapped sea water that is cut off from the sea by a stretch of land and is covered by a layer of freshwater. In six thousand years, the salinity of the lower water decreased from 34 to 20 ‰. The hypolimnion does not contain sulfate, the latter having been fully reduced to hydrogen sulfide, which is partly bound with silt iron. The microbiology of these lakes is poorly known; they certainly deserve further research.

Lakes Situated in Arid Regions and Directly Linked with the Sea

Examples of such water bodies are Kara-Bogaz-Gol Bay, which is joined by a narrow strait with the Caspian Sea, and Lake Sivash, which has a length of 117 km and is isolated from the sea by a narrow sandbar. Salinity in Lake Sivash increases sharply with the distance from the strait that links it with the Sea of Azov (Figure 10, p. 10) (Strashchuk et al., 1964). The freshened part of Lake Sivash contains rich growths of algae that are swept onshore by the wind. The abundance of sulfate and organic matter leads to an intensive reduction of sulfate, and the hydrogen sulfide resulting from this process undergoes biogenic oxidation (Kuznetsov and Romanenko, 1968).

Salinity in Kara-Bogaz-Gol Bay (Figure 9, p. 9) is much greater than in Lake Sivash. Hence the formation of calcite in the strait, where the bay waters mix with those of the sea. Then the high concentration of sodium chloride causes a precipitation of gypsum, while the intensive evaporation increases the concentration of sodium chloride and the sulfate of sodium and magnesium. Phytoplankton and higher plants are practically absent. The bottom sediments of Kara-Bogaz-Gol Bay consist of alternating layers of sodium chloride and magnesium sulfate, which settles in winter from the supercooled brine. Sulfides occur in the sediment only, and the reduction of sulfate proceeds at a slow rate owing to the high salinity. Viable sulfate-reducing bacteria were not found.

Morphology and Special Physiology of Microorganisms that Participate in the Sulfur Cycle

Sulfur is an ingredient of the proteins of all organisms and enzymes. It takes part in oxidation-reduction reactions that create transitions between hydrosulfides and disulfides. Finally, many vitamins, antibiotics, and intracellular microbial food inclusions contain sulfur.

Sulfur has several valences. It bears two negative charges as sulfides and four or six positive ones as sulfurous acid and sulfates. Consequently, sulfur is readily oxidized and reduced. Microorganisms take part in many reactions involving the reduction or oxidation of sulfur; they chemosynthetically utilize the energy liberated in the oxidation of the elementary and bound forms of sulfur.

On the whole, the organisms that participate in the sulfur cycle are rather thoroughly known. The available evidence on this subject sheds light on the role performed by different microbial groups in the specific conditions that prevail in each type of lake. All this creates a rather detailed picture of the sulfur cycle from a limnological viewpoint.

In recent years, electron microscopy has contributed much to the progress of bacterial morphology, and various sensitive analytical procedures have been developed for the detection of metabolic products of different microbial species. The data concerning the bacteria of the sulfur cycle are scattered in separate articles and monographs, and a review of the literature has not yet been published. For a better understanding of the different stages of the sulfur cycle in lakes, we shall begin with an outline of the morphology and physiology of the major bacterial groups involved.

Assimilation of Sulfur Compounds

Microorganisms assimilate sulfates with comparative ease. The reduced sulfur obtained from this reaction becomes an ingredient of protein, mainly in the form of three amino acids — lysine, methionine, and tryptophane, which constitute respectively 6.5—7.2, 1.2—1.7, and 0.3—0.8 percent of protein in terms of raw weight.

Many publications deal with the effect of different organic sulfur compounds on microbial growth. In a study of the growth of thirteen cultures under the influence of eleven such compounds, Dooren de Jong (1926, cited from Starkey, 1964) found that several sulfur-containing amino acids can be used simultaneously as sources of sulfur and nitrogen. Thioacetic, thioglycollic, and thiolactic acids and diethylthiourea are not assimilated.

Most of the sulfur liberated from organic compounds comes from cystine, cysteine, methionine, and other sulfur-containing amino acids. The sulfur is released in the form of hydrogen sulfide as a result of a rather extensive mineralization of these organic compounds. Many saprophyte bacteria can perform such reactions. Thus, all ninety species examined by Pachero and Costa (1940) proved capable of producing hydrogen sulfide in a medium containing liver extract. About 30 % of bacteria isolated from various lakes in Moscow, Kalinin, Kurgan, Petropavlovsk, and Irkutsk regions produced hydrogen sulfide in meat peptone broth (A. A. Egorova, Z. P. Deryugina, and S. I. Kuznetsov, 1952).

This group of bacteria was thoroughly studied in salt lakes in limans (L. I. Rubenchik, 1948; Rubenchik and Goikherman, 1935, 1939, 1941).

The following list contains the main putrefying bacteria that occur in different types of lakes and form hydrogen sulfide from the decomposition of proteins:

Type of Lake	Bacteria
Oligotrophic	Mycobacterium phlei, Mycobact. filiforme
Mesotrophic	Bacterium nitrificans. Pseudomonas liquefaciens, Chromobacter aurantiacum
Eutrophic	Pseudomonas liquefaciens, Bact. delicatum
Dystrophic	Pseudomonas fluorescens, Bac. pituitans
Salt lakes and limans	Mycobact. luteum, Micrococcus nitrificans, Achromobacter halophilum, Flavobacterium halophilum, Bact. albo-luteum, Vibrio hydrosulfureus

Nearly 80% of the putrefying bacteria break down proteins with the production of hydrogen sulfide. Nevertheless, only a limited number of publications deal with the decomposition of individual sulfur-containing organic compounds.

Starkey (1964) notes in his review that many molds use taurine and cysteic acid as nitrogen sources. Though highly toxic for nitrifying microorganisms, thiourea serves as source of nitrogen for many molds, and a degradation of sulfur-containing amino acids to hydrogen sulfide is observed in many fluorescent bacteria: Proteus vulgaris, E. coli, Streptococcus lactis aerogenes, Propionobacterium pentosaceum, Clostridium sporogenes, and C. perfringens. Among the decomposition products Smith identified pyruvic aldehyde, ammonia, and hydrogen sulfide. However, the breakdown of such hexavalent sulfur compounds as taurine and cysteic acid yields sulfuric acid (Stapley and Starkey, 1959). A scheme of the breakdown of these compounds is given below:

$$
\begin{array}{c}
\text{COONa} \\
| \\
\text{CH(NH}_2) \\
| \\
\text{CH}_2 \\
| \\
\text{SO}_2\text{OH}
\end{array}
\rightarrow
\begin{array}{c}
\text{COONa} \\
| \\
\text{CO} \\
| \\
\text{CH}_2 \\
| \\
\text{SO}_2\text{OH}
\end{array}
+ \text{NH}_3 \rightarrow
\begin{array}{c}
\text{COONa} \\
| \\
\text{CO} \\
| \\
\text{CH}_3 \\
\downarrow
\end{array}
+ \text{SO}_3^= \nearrow \text{SO}_4^=
$$

Cysteic acid Sulfopyruvic acid Pyruvic acid

Bacterial cells $+ \text{CO}_2 + \text{H}_2\text{O} + \text{Na}^+$

$$
\begin{array}{c}
\text{CH}_2(\text{NH})_2 \\
| \\
\text{CH}_2 \\
| \\
\text{SO}_2\text{OH}
\end{array}
\rightarrow
\begin{array}{c}
\text{R} \\
| \\
\text{SO}_2\text{OH}
\end{array}
+ \text{NH}_3 \rightarrow \text{R}' + \text{SO}_3^= \longrightarrow \text{SO}_4^=
$$

Taurine

$\downarrow$ — $+ \text{CO}_2 + \text{H}_2\text{O}$

Bacterial cells

Starkey (1964) isolated soil bacteria that can grow in a mineral medium with cystine as the only source of carbon. The breakdown of this compound led to different forms of sulfur:

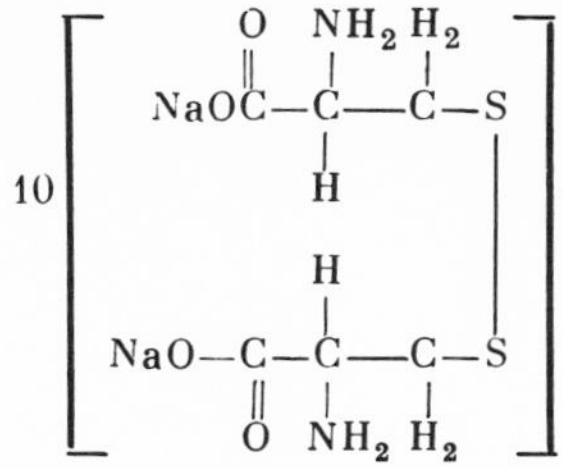

$$10\left[\begin{array}{c}\text{O NH}_2\text{ H}_2\\ \text{NaOC}-\text{C}-\text{C}-\text{S}\\ \text{H}\\ \text{H}\\ \text{NaO}-\text{C}-\text{C}-\text{C}-\text{S}\\ \text{O NH}_2\text{ H}_2\end{array}\right]+65O_2\longrightarrow 4Na_2S_4O_6+4S^0+20(NH_4OH)+6Na_2CO_3+54CO_2$$

Only a few cultures of Gram-negative sporeless rods isolated by Starkey and his group could attack methionine:

$$(HOOC-CH-CH_2-CH_2-S-CH_3).$$
$$\underset{NH_2}{|}$$

This reaction led to two sulfur-containing volatile products: methanethiol and methyl disulfide. Starkey suggested the following pathway for the breakdown of methionine by a mixed microflora:

$$HOOC-\underset{\underset{NH_2}{|}}{C}H-CH_2-CH_2-CH_3+O \rightarrow HOOC-CO-CH_2-CH_2-S-CH_3+NH_3;$$

Methionine   α-keto-γ-methylmercaptobutyric acid

$$HOOC-CO-CH_2-CH_2-S-CH_3+2H \rightarrow HOOC-CO-CH_2-CH_3+CH_3SH;$$

α-ketobutyric acid   Methanethiol

$$HOOC-CO-CH_2-CH_3+O \rightarrow HOOC-CH_2-CH_3+CO_2;$$

Propionic acid

$$HOOC-CH_2-CH_3+3^1/_2O_2 \rightarrow 3CO_2+3H_2O;$$

$$2CH_3-SH-2H \rightarrow CH_3-S-S-CH_3.$$

Dimethyl disulfide

Reduction of Sulfate

Microorganisms that reduce sulfate. In 1893, N. D. Zelinskii and E. M. Brusinlovskii (1898) demonstrated the ability of bacteria to produce hydrogen sulfide by the reduction of sulfate.

Further contributions in this field were made by Beijerinck (1895), van Delden (1904), B. L. Isachenko (1927), Baars (1930), L. I. Rubenchik (1946, 1947, 1948), L. D. Shturm and Z. A. Kanunnikova (1945), ZoBell and Rittenberg (1948), Butlin and Postgate (1953, 1954), and many others. It became clear from these studies that the sulfate-reducing bacteria are responsible for a large proportion of the hydrogen sulfide produced in nature.

In the presence of sodium lactate, these bacteria reduce sulfate to hydrogen sulfide according to the equation:

$$2C_3H_5O_3Na + MgSO_4 \rightarrow 2CH_3COONa + CO_2 + MgCO_3 + H_2S + H_2O.$$

Contrary to an early view that many bacteria can reduce sulfate, Baars (1930) proved that this property is confined to a few species — namely, thermophilic and halophilic sulfate-reducing bacteria, all of them variants of a freshwater species that he named V i b r i o   d e s u l f u r i c a n s. Baars assumed that this species adapts readily to salinity and high temperatures. Littlewood and Postgate (1957) adhered to this view, which was opposed by ZoBell and Rittenberg (1948).

D e s u l f o v i b r i o   d e s u l f u r i c a n s cannot utilize lower fatty acids as organic substrates, with the exception of formic acid. It produces acetate as a final product from carbon sources containing more than two carbon atoms in their molecule.

In the course of his studies of the reduction of sulfate in the presence of acetate, L. I. Rubenchik obtained a bacterium that grows in media containing acetate, propionate, and butyrate. This bacterium was later named V i b r i o   r u b e n t s c h i k i i.

Later attempts to isolate D. r u b e n t s c h i k i i failed. According to Postgate (1959), the original culture of this microorganism was contaminated with obligate anaerobic bacteria, which explains its ability to grow on acetate

Campbell and co-workers (1957) obtained a pure culture of a thermophilic spore-forming strain. After comparing this bacterium with several other strains, including S p o r o v i b r i o described by Starkey, they described it as a new sulfate-reducing species — C l o s t r i d i u m   n i g r i f i c a n s. Finally, Adams and Postgate (1961) described another mesophilic species that reduces sulfate, namely D e s u l f o v i b r i o   o r i e n t i s.

Postgate and Campbell (1966) compared all the known species of sulfate-reducing bacteria and revised the taxonomy of the genus. They divide the sulfate-reducing bacteria in two genera on the basis of spore formation. The spore-forming genus D e s u l f o t o m a c u l u m comprises (1) D. n i g r i - f i c a n s (synonym: C l o s t r i d i u m   n i g r i f i c a n s), (2) D. o r i e n t i s (synonym: D e s u l f o v i b r i o   o r i e n t i s), and (3) D. r u m i n i s. The non spore-forming genus D e s u l f o v i b r i o includes the following species: (1) D. d e s u l f u r i c a n s (Figure 131) (synonyms: S p i r i l l u m after Beijerinck, M i c r o s p i r a after Migula, V i b r i o after Baars, S p o r o v i b r i o after Starkey) with the varieties D. d e s u l f u r i c a n s var. a e s t u a r i i — halophilic but adaptable to fresh water, and D. d e s u l f u r i c a n s   v a r. a z o t o v o r a n s, which can utilize gaseous nitrogen); (2) D. v u l g a r i s; (3) D. s a l e x i g e n e s (synonym: M i c r o s p i r a   a e s t u a r i i) — an obligate halophile that develops in the presence of 2.5 — 5% NaCl; (4) D. g i g a s — spirals; (5) D. a f r i c a n s — long curved rods, lophotrichous, tolerating a high concentration of salt in the medium.

A simplified version of the classification proposed by Postgate and Campbell (1966) appears in Table 92.

D e s u l f o b r i o   d e s u l f u r i c a n s does not reduce nitrate; in fact, nitrate inhibits its growth. This species can fix small quantities of free nitrogen (Sisler and ZoBell, 1951). The ability of D. d e s u l f u r i c a n s to fix limited amounts of atmospheric oxygen was confirmed by Senez and co-workers, who used the heavy nitrogen isotope N^{15} (cited from Postgate, 1959). On these grounds Postgate and Campbell (1966) proposed the name of D. d e s u l f u r i c a n s var. a z o t o v o r a n s for the strain of Sisler and ZoBell

Mechanism of sulfate reduction. The reduction of sulfate to hydrogen sulfide was studied in cell-free preparations. In isotope experiments with

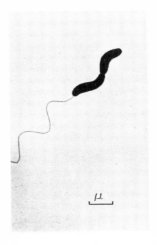

FIGURE 131. Desulfovibrio desulfuricans
(electron migrograph by V.A. Kuznetsova).

$S^{35}O_4$ and $S^{35}O_3$, sulfite appeared as the first intermediate product (Postgate, 1959; Peck, 1959; Wilson, 1962). It was also found that the first stage of the reduction requires hydrogen, hydrogenase, ATP sulfurylase, and adenosine phosphosulfate reductase (APS reductase) (Peck, 1959, 1962a). These enzymes were found in cells of Desulfovibrio desulfuricans. The reaction proceeds as follows:

$$ATP + SO_4^= \rightarrow APS + \text{pyrophosphate}$$

ATP sulfurylase

$$APS + 2H \rightarrow AMP + SO_3^= + H_2O$$

APS reductase

Such mechanism of sulfate reduction with the participation of APS is unique and occurs only in the sulfate-reducing bacteria. In eleven species of normal heterotrophic bacteria, the assimilation of sulfate proceeds via phosphoadenosine phosphosulfate (PAPS) (Peck, 1962b).

The sulfate-reducing bacteria grow at a low oxidation-reduction potential. Their growth does not begin unless E_h is below -200 mV or $rH_2 \leq 7$, (Postgate, 1959). Clearly, the addition of cysteine or Na_2S to the medium, as recommended by Grossman and Postgate (1953), stimulates the growth of these bacteria by lowering the oxidation-reduction potential. Ferrous salts and ascorbic acid exert a slightly lesser stimulatory effect on the early growth of sulfate-reducing bacteria because of their relatively higher oxidation-reduction potential.

It was originally believed (Tauson and Aleshina, 1932) that Desulfovibrio desulfuricans can utilize a variety of organic compounds, including carbohydrates, petroleum hydrocarbons, nonvolatile fatty acids,

TABLE 92. Classification of sulfate-reducing bacteria (after Postgate and Campbell, 1966)

	Desulfotamaculum			Desulfovibrio				
	nigrificans	orientis	ruminis	desulfuricans	vulgaris	salexigenes	africanus	gigas
Cell form	Rods	Curved rods	Rods	Vibrios	Vibrios	Vibrios	Curved rods	Spirals
Flagella	Peritrichous	Peritrichous	Peritrichous	One polar	One polar	One polar	Lophotrichous	Lophotrichous
Spore formation	+	+	+	−	−	−	−	−
Type of cytochrome	b	b	b	C_3	C_3	C_3	C_3	C_3
Desulfoviridine	−	−	−	+	+	+	+	+
DNA base ratio, % mole GC content	44.7	41.7	45.6	53.3	61.2	46.1	61.2	60.2
Growth in:								
Pyruvate without $SO_4^=$	+	−	+	+	−	−	−	−
Choline without $SO_4^=$	−	−	−	+	−	−	−	−
Malate + $SO_4^=$	−	−	−	+	−	+	+	−
Formate + $SO_4^=$	−	−	+	−	−	−	−	−
Acetates + $SO_4^=$	−	−	−	−	−	−	−	−
Halophily	−	−	−	−	−	+	−	+
Resistance to hibitane, mg/L	0.25	0.25	1	10—25	2.5	1000	2.5	2.5
Thermophily	+	−	−	−	−	−	−	−

alcohols, etc. Later studies showed, however, that these compounds are consumed only by enrichment cultures of this species or by cultures containing accompanying bacteria (Gorlenko and Kuznetsova, 1966).

Pure cultures of D. desulfuricans and D. desulfuricans var. aestuarii can use lactate as organic substrate. They oxidize lactate to acetate via pyruvic aldehyde. The latter can also serve as source of carbon; it is degraded to alcohol or acetate, carbon dioxide, and hydrogen. D. desulfuricans var. aestuarii oxidizes malate to succinate via fumarate. In the presence of sulfite, succinate is oxidized to acetate. All these observations show that the sulfate-reducing bacteria can perform the terminal stages of the tricarboxylic acid cycle; whether they possess a complete Krebs cycle remains unknown.

The ability of D. desulfuricans to live as an autotroph was first demonstrated by Wight and Starkey (1954), who obtained an enrichment culture of this species under a hydrogen atmosphere in a strictly mineral medium containing sulfate and bicarbonate. These authors summarize the process as follows:

$$4H_2 + H_2SO_4 \rightarrow H_2S + 4H_2O, \quad \Delta F = -60,000 \text{ calories.}$$

Later, Butlin and Adams (Butlin et al., 1949) confirmed these observations in pure cultures.

By the use of labeled carbon dioxide ($C^{14}O_2$), Yu. I. Sorokin proved the ability of D. desulfuricans to fix carbon dioxide at the expense of energy obtained from the oxidation of hydrogen with the oxygen of sulfate. He found that one mole of carbon dioxide is assimilated for every 10—20 gram-equivalents of reduced sulfate. Thus, the fixation of one mole of carbon dioxide consumes roughly the same amount of energy as in other autotrophs. D. desulfuricans, which obtains energy from the anaerobic oxidation of hydrogen with sulfate oxygen, consumes more hydrogen than is necessary for the reduction of sulfate to H_2S (Yu. I. Sorokin, 1956). Sorokin believes on these grounds that the excess hydrogen serves for a direct chemosynthetic reduction of CO_2.

Indeed, the excess H_2/assimilated CO_2 ratio was 1.9—2.3. This means that the reducing agent in chemosynthesis is molecular hydrogen rather than the hydrogen of water, especially in view of the fact that the chemosynthetic reaction

$$CO_2 + 2H_2 \rightarrow CH_2O + H_2O, \quad \Delta F = +1,700 \text{ calories}$$

consumes less energy than the reaction

$$CO_2 + H_2O \rightarrow CH_2O + O_2, \quad \Delta F = +115,000 \text{ calories.}$$

The ability of pure cultures of D. desulfuricans to grow in strictly autotrophic conditions was recently disputed by Senez, Postgate, and other workers, who note that this species requires yeast autolysate. Yu. I. Sorokin found that D. desulfuricans indeed cannot grow in a purely mineral medium, but normal development begins after the addition of only a few milligrams of sodium acetate. According to Sorokin, this minimal concentration of acetate is necessary for the synthesis and normal function of acetyl

CoA in the fixation of carbon dioxide, although acetate does not serve as organic substrate for this species in the absence of hydrogen.

D. desulfuricans is very rich in flavin proteins, which have a high proportion of flavinadenine nucleotide to mononucleotide. It also contains cytochrome C_3, which acts in an alkaline medium at pH 10.5 and has a dual function as hematohemin, with a low oxidation-reduction potential $E_0 = = -204mV$, a molecular weight of 13,000, and an iron content of 0.9%. The protein is water soluble and resistant to heating and acids; it contains thio-ether linkages between the hematin and the apoprotein. It has not yet been demonstrated that preparations of this enzyme can reduce sulfate; conse-quently, there is no direct evidence that this enzyme takes part in the reduc-tion of sulfate. Postgate (1959) believes, nevertheless, that C_3 is the final carrier of electrons in the live organism, as in the cytochrome systems of aerobic organisms.

Experiments were made to determine the capacity of D. desulfuricans to reduce various sulfur compounds and other molecules that could serve as electron acceptors.

According to Postgate (1959), the sulfate-reducing bacteria can reduce sulfate, sulfite, various polythionates, colloidal sulfur, and formic and malic acids but cannot do so with crystalline sulfur, taurine, cysteine, cysteic acid, chromates, phosphates, perchlorates, nitrates, and some other compounds. Contradictory evidence exists about the ability of sulfate-reducing bacteria to utilize the oxygen of salts of selenonic acid for the oxidation of organic compounds.

Oxidation of Reduced Sulfur Compounds

The oxidation of sulfur and reduced sulfur compounds yields a consider-able amount of free energy. Moreover, these compounds can serve simul-taneously as hydrogen donors, replacing water in photosynthesis.

Many microorganisms perform such reactions and thus participate in the sulfur cycle of nature. These microorganisms can be divided into five major groups.

1. Family Thiobacillaceae. Colorless microorganisms; autotrophs or mixotrophs. Derive energy from the oxidation of sulfur for the assimilation of carbon dioxide. Sulfur not deposited inside the cells.

2. Family Thiobacteriaceae. Colorless sulfur bacteria; autotrophs or myxotrophs. Deposit sulfur inside the cell and utilize the energy of its oxidation for chemosynthesis.

3. Family Thiorhodaceae. Purple sulfur bacteria. Autotrophs, photo-synthetic. Utilize sulfur compounds as hydrogen donors and deposit sulfur inside the cell.

4. Family Chlorobacteriaceae. Green sulfur bacteria. Autotrophs, photosynthetic. Utilize sulfur compounds as hydrogen donors and deposit sulfur outside the cell.

5. Family Athiorhodaceae. Purple nonsulfur bacteria. Do not deposit sulfur. In the presence of light, they live photosynthetically, using reduced sulfur compounds as hydrogen donors. In the dark, they revert to a hetero-trophic mode of life in the presence of organic compounds and oxygen.

Thiobacillaceae.   This family belongs to the order Pseudomonadales. It consists of Gram-negative rods with one polar flagellum or a bundle of flagella, without endospores.   The division into species is based on the source of energy and the acidity of the medium.   Thiobacillaceae oxidize sulfur compounds and use the energy derived therefrom for the fixation of carbon dioxide.   All the typical species of this family are strict autotrophs.

· Thiobacillus thioparus (synonyms: T. neapolitanus, halophilic form of Thiobacterium issatchenkoii).   Descriptions of its morphology vary among the authors (Figure 132).   According to the recent data of G. A. Sokolova and G. I. Karavaiko (1964), the cells range in width from 0.5 to 0.8μ and from 0.9 to 1.4μ in length.   They reproduce by fission.   Young cultures are highly motile, having one polar flagellum; motility ceases after four or five days.

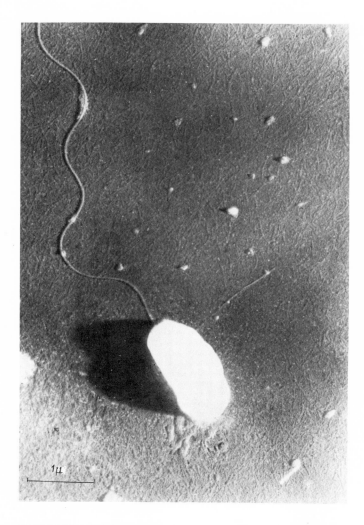

FIGURE 132. Thiobacillus thioparus (electron micrograph by G. A. Dubinina).

The ability of T. thioparus to grow in mineral media with thiosulfate and bicarbonate as the only source of carbon was first reported by Nathanson in 1902. This type of metabolism, later confirmed by many workers, represents an oxidation of thiosulfate and hydrogen sulfide according to the following scheme:

$$2Na_2S_2O_3 + O_2 \rightarrow 2S° + 2Na_2SO_4;$$

$$H_2S + \tfrac{1}{2}O_2 \rightarrow S° + H_2O; \quad \Delta F = -41,000 \text{ calories.}$$

In the absence of thiosulfate, sulfur is oxidized further to sulfuric acid:

$$S° + 1\tfrac{1}{2}O_2 + H_2O \rightarrow H_2SO_4; \quad \Delta F = -118,000 \text{ calories.}$$

Thiobacillus x, isolated by Parker (1947), is closely related to Thiobacillus thioparus. Later it was given the name of Thiobacillus neapolitanus.

B. L. Isachenko and A. G. Salimovskaya (1928) isolated several halophilic forms, which A. S. Zaslavskii (1952) united in a single species, Thiobacterium issatchenkoii. However, Zaslavskii did not observe any adaptation to different concentrations of NaCl. This form should be regarded as a variety of Thiobacillus thioparus. The ability of Thiobacillus thioparus to utilize different reduced sulfur compounds is discussed in detail by G. A. Sokolova and G. I. Karavaiko (1964).

Comparing the published data with their own observations, these authors concluded that Thiobacillus thioparus can use the following reduced sulfur compounds as a source of energy: hydrogen sulfide, calcium sulfide, molecular sulfur, thiosulfate, tetrathionate, hydrosulfide, and, to a lesser extent, di- and trithionates.

Thiobacillus thioparus requires an alkaline reaction for optimal growth. Some of its strains can develop at pH = 9.8 as an optimal level (Sokolova and Karavaiko, 1964). According to Vishniac and Santer (1957), the optimal value is pH = 7. By oxidizing sulfur, Thiobacillus thioparus can lower the pH to 3.4.

Low concentrations of organic compounds can stimulate growth. In the absence of reduced sulfur compounds, however, Thiobacillus thiooxidans does not grow on organic substrates. Ammonium salts serve as nitrogen source. This species was regarded as a strict aerobe. However it was found in nature living anaerobically in waters rich in hydrogen sulfide.

In the presence of thiosulfate, Thiobacillus thioparus consumes oxygen and lowers the oxidation-reduction potential to $rH_2 = 10-16$, which is the optimal range for this species (Sokolova and Karavaiko, 1964). Growth slows down at higher rH_2 values obtained by intensive aeration of the culture.

Given a moderate oxygen supply, these bacteria can oxidize thiosulfite even at low oxidation-reduction potentials, that is, at $rH_2 = 6-10$. Therefore, Thiobacillus thioparus is a microaerophile.

In their studies of sulfur oxidation, Skarzynski, Ostrowski, and Krawszyk (1957) used two thiosulfates — one of them with labeled sulfide group ($NaS^{35} - SO_3 - Na$), the other with labeled sulfate group ($Na - S - S^{35}O_3 - Na$). It became evident that the reaction involves only the sulfide sulfur, which is converted to organic compounds and molecular sulfur, while the sulfate group remains unchanged. Whether polythionates appear as intermediate products is still unknown.

It appears that molecular sulfur undergoes chemical reduction to hydrogen sulfide in the presence of reduced glutathione. Then the sulfur compounds enter the cell in the form of HS-groups and are oxidized there. This oxidation involves phosphates and sulfur-containing nucleotides, with the possible formation of mixed anhydrides of the —S—O—PO$_3$ type. The cells of Thiobacillus thioparus contain adenosine phosphate sulfurylase (ATP-sulfurylase) and adenosine phosphosulfate reductase (APS-reductase).

A close relationship exists between the oxidation of the substrate and the formation of energy-rich phosphorus compounds that take part in the subsequent fixation of carbon dioxide.

The Polish group found that Thiobacillaceae contain cytochrome c and demonstrated a direct participation of cytochromes in the oxidation of thiosulfate by these bacteria. This confirms the ability of Thiobacillaceae to derive energy from oxidative phosphorylation even on substrate level by means of energy-rich phosphosulfate compounds, as shown in the scheme of Peck (1962a, 1962b):

1) $2S_2O_3^= + 4H^+ + 4e \xrightarrow[\text{reductase}]{\text{thiosulfate}} 2SO_3^= + 2H_2S$;

2) $2SO_3^= + 2AMP \xleftrightarrow[\text{reductase}]{\text{APS}} 2APS + 4e$; (Adenosine phosphosulfate)

3) $APS + 2PO_4 \xleftrightarrow[\text{reductase}]{\text{ADP}} 2ADP + 2SO_4^=$;

4) $2ADP \xrightarrow[\text{kinase}]{\text{adenyl}} AMP + ATP$;

5) $2H_2S \xrightarrow[\text{H}_2\text{S}-\text{oxidase}]{\text{O}_2} 2S° + 2H_2O$.

The overall reaction is:

$$2S_2O_2^= + 2O_2 + AMP + 2PO_4 + 4H^+ + 4e \rightarrow 2S° + 2SO_4^= + ATP + 2H_2O.$$

The results obtained by Santer and Peck indicate that energy-rich sulfate compounds are directly involved in the oxidation of reduced sulfur compounds — a phenomenon unique to this family (Sokolova and Karavaiko, 1964).

The pathways of the chemosynthetic assimilation of carbon dioxide are comparatively well known in this family. Experimenting with cell extracts of Thiobacillus thioparus, Santer and Vishniac (1955) found that $C^{14}O_2$ is fixed only in the presence of ribulose-1,5-diphosphate and enters the carboxyl group of 3-phosphoglyceric acid. Trudinger (1955, 1956) and the Aubert group (Aubert et al., 1956, 1957) later confirmed these results with cell suspensions. They concluded that the assimilation of carbon dioxide in these bacteria involves the ribulose cycle. The specific enzymes that take part in this cycle in photosynthetic organisms were also found in chemoautotrophic bacteria.

Figure 133 shows the mechanism of CO_2 fixation in the autotrophic metabolism according to Vishniac et al. (1957). The energy necessary for this process originates from the oxidation of reduced sulfur compounds and is supplied in the form of ATP after the Peck scheme.

G. A. Sokolova (Sokolova and Karavaiko, 1964) calculated the efficiency of the utilization of energy by a T. thioparus culture after the Baas-Becking formula in brief experiments with $C^{14}O_2$. She obtained an efficiency of 26% in young, two-day-old cultures, whereas after seven days, the bacteria utilized only 1.5—2% of the energy liberated in the oxidation of thiosulfate.

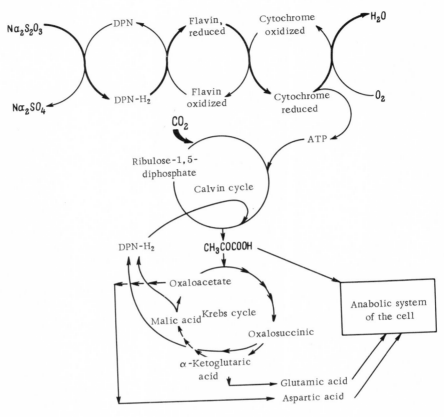

FIGURE 133. Scheme of the assimilation of CO_2 in the autotrophic metabolism of Thiobacillus thioparus (after Vishniac et al.).

Thiobacillus thiooxidans. This species was first isolated in pure culture and studied by Waksman and Joffe (1922). Further investigations of it were published by Umbreit and Anderson (1942), Knaysi (1943), and others.

This species is a rod measuring 0.5—0.8 by 1.0—1.2 μ, with one polar spiral flagellum. It remains motile for seven days in liquid media. The protoplasm is Gram-negative, but the cell vacuole contains Gram-positive matter. The protoplasm is clad in a thin cell membrane, and a dense slime covers the cell on the outside (Figure 134).

The cells of Thiobacillus thiooxidans contain terminal fatty inclusions that apparently participate in the oxidation of sulfur. Endogenous respiration is at the expense of reserve polysaccharides.

The bacteria described as Thiobacillus thermitanus, T. umbo-natus, T. lobatus, and T. crenatus differ from T. thiooxidans in the form of the colonies on agar-containing Emoto medium. However, they probably represent ecologic variants of T. thiooxidans. Another speci that can be assigned to this group is T. c o n c r e t i v o r u s, which differs from T. t h i o o x i d a n s in being able to utilize not only ammonia but also nitrate as source of nitrogen.

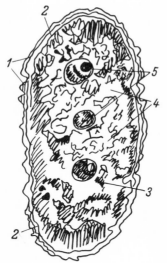

FIGURE 134. T h i o b a c i l l u s t h i o o x i d a n s. Schematic drawing after an ultrathin section (from a photograph by Mahoney and Mercedes, 1966):

1) cell wall; 2) cytoplasmic membrane; 3) ribosomes; 4) nuclear substance; 5) granule.

· T h i o b a c i l l u s t h i o o x i d a n s derives energy from the oxidation of molecular sulfur:

$$S° + 1 \tfrac{1}{2} O_2 + H_2O = H_2SO_4; \quad \Delta F = -118,000 \text{ calories}.$$

It also develops in media containing thiosulfate and sulfide. Whether it can utilize these compounds as such, however, is unknown, since the acid reaction of the culture causes their breakdown to molecular sulfur in the presence of air. A characteristic feature of this species is its ability to grow at a very low pH. Most authors agree that the optimal pH value is about 2.5, but the extreme values are a matter of controversy. After a thorough examination of this topic, G. I. Karavaiko (Sokolova and Karavaiko, 1964) concluded that T h i o b a c i l l u s t h i o o x i d a n s can grow and oxidize sulfur in a liquid inorganic medium at pH from 0.6 to 5.5. This species does not assimilate organic compounds. Peptone, urea, and a number of amino acids are unsuitable as sources of nitrogen.

T h i o b a c i l l u s t h i o o x i d a n s is a strict aerobe. Its optimal rH_2 range is 24 to 26, while the lower limit lies at $rH_2 = 17$. This explains its great sensitivity to a deficiency of oxygen in the medium. According to Karavaiko (Sokolova and Karavaiko, 1964), the culture dies quickly in anaerobic conditions.

Vogler and Umbreit (1941) made the first investigations into the mechanism of sulfur oxidation in this species. In their view, the sulfur enters a fat globule upon contact with the cell. Further studies of Suzuki and

325

Berkman (cited from Sokolova and Karavaiko, 1964) showed that glutathione and the enzyme glutathione reductase take part in the reaction. The sulfur penetrates into the cell in the form of SHS-groups and undergoes oxidation there with the participation of phosphates, probably by the formation of —S—O—PO$_3$ groups. Peck (1962) assumes that the intracellular oxidation proceeds in a uniform manner throughout the family after the scheme given in connection with T. thioparus.

It is generally accepted that Thiobacillus thiooxidans oxidizes elemental sulfur and stores the obtained energy in phosphate bonds. Vogler and Umbreit believed that the oxidation of sulfur in the absence of CO$_2$ creates energy-rich phosphate bonds that can store the energy and give it up for the fixation of CO$_2$ in the absence of sulfur. Later studies, however, did not confirm this assumption. Now the prevailing view is that both processes must take place simultaneously.

The generation of a reducing agent for the reduction of carbon dioxide to the cell level appears to be a spontaneous process in Thiobacillaceae:

$$S + 2H_2O + O_2 \rightarrow H_2SO_4 + 2H^+ + 2e; \; \Delta F = -120,000 \text{ calories.}$$

As in Thiobacillus thioparus, the fixation of CO$_2$ in T. thiooxidans is linked with the ribulose cycle. Besides this major pathway of CO$_2$ fixation, the bacteria of this family possess an additional mechanism of heterotrophic assimilation that involves carboxylation and lengthening of the carbon chain of the acids participating in the Krebs cycle, instead of reduction of CO$_2$ to the level of the cell contents. This process was studied in detail by Aubert and co-workers (Aubert et al., 1957) in T. denitrificans and by Suzuki and Werkman (1957, 1958a, 1958b) in Thiobacillus thiooxidans. In brief experiments with C^{14}O$_2$, these authors detected the radioactive tracer in aspartic and glutamic acids, which were formed by β-carboxylation of phosphoenolpyruvic acid. They also found a β-carboxylating enzyme — phosphoenolpyruvate carboxylase. The process is explained as follows. The fixation of CO$_2$ converts 3-phosphoglyceric acid to phosphoenolpyruvic acid, which is further carboxylated and transformed to oxaloacetic acid. Being a component of the Krebs cycle, oxaloacetic acid turns into glutamic and aspartic acids.

This mechanism accounts for less than 8% of the fixation of CO$_2$.

The efficiency of the utilization of energy in the chemosynthesis of Thiobacillus thiooxidans is reported to be 17% (Baalsrud and Baalsrud, 1952).

Thiobacillus denitrificans. This microorganism was first isolated by Beijerinck (1904). Further studies of it were published by Lieske (1912b) and the Baalsruds (Baalsrud and Baalsrud, 1954), who have contributed much to our knowledge on this species. Thiobacillus denitrificans differs from the closely related Thiobacillus thioparus in its ability to grow anaerobically by utilizing the oxygen of nitrate for the oxidation of sulfur or thiosulfate:

$$5S + 6KNO_3 + 4NaHCO_3 = 3K_2SO_4 + 2Na_2SO_4 + 4CO_2 + 3N_2 + 2N_2O;$$

$$5Na_2S_2O_3 + 8KNO_3 + 2NaHCO_3 = 6Na_2SO_4 + 4K_2SO_4 + 4N_2 + 2CO_2 + H_2O;$$

$$\Delta F = -179,000 \text{ calories.}$$

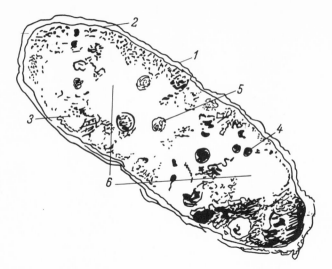

FIGURE 135. Thiobacillus ferrooxidans. Schematic morphology of the cell after an ultrathin section (after Lundgren et al., 1964):

1) cell wall; 2) cytoplasmic membrane; 3) ribosomes; 4) polyribosomes; 5) lysosomes; 6) nuclear substance.

It appears that two different microorganisms have been described under this specific name. The Thiobacillus denitrificans strain described by Lieske and the Baalsruds is a strict autotroph, a small Gram-negative rod, $0.4-0.5 \times 1\mu$, with a single flagellum. According to the Baalsruds, this microorganism is highly sensitive to nitrite and can use only ammonium salts as source of nitrogen. To prevent an accumulation of nitrite in the medium during the denitrification, the molar ratio between nitrate and sulfur compounds (N/S) should not be greater than 0.4. The bacterium develops best in a mineral medium at pH 6—8, but does not grow at all in organic media.

The reduction of nitrate to gaseous nitrogen during the oxidation of the substrate can be represented as follows:

$$NO_3 \rightarrow NO_2 \rightarrow NO \rightarrow N_2O \rightarrow N_2.$$

The enzymatic system for the reduction of nitrate is highly sensitive to nitrite. The presence of 0.003% KNO_2 in the medium causes an inhibition of 40%, and the process stops altogether when the concentration of nitrite reaches 0.03%. In the presence of air the bacteria develop satisfactorily but lose the ability of denitrification.

According to Senez (1962), this strain utilizes 25% of the free energy (Zavarzin, 1964). This strain does not develop in organic media; moreover, its growth is inhibited by 0.2% acetate, butyrate, succinate, sugars, or amino acids.

The strains of Thiobacillus denitrificans isolated by Beijerinck (1904, 1920) and Tyul'panova-Mosevich (1930) are mesotrophs. They reduce nitrate in mineral media in the presence of sulfur and can also develop satisfactorily in standard meat peptone agar, although in such an environment they lose partly or completely the capacity for denitrification in mineral media. These microorganisms can utilize molecular sulfur and thiosulfate as sources of energy in the autotrophic metabolism. Beijerinck's strain is a rod with 6—8 flagella.

Little is known on the relationships between the different strains of Thiobacillus denitrificans. To regard them as different species would be premature, especially in view of the Baalsruds' conclusion, no less extreme in itself, that all three Thiobacillus species are actually varieties of a single species.

The autotrophic assimilation of CO_2 at the expense of energy derived from the oxidation of sulfur compounds was studied by Trudinger (1955, 1956) and the Aubert group (Aubert et al., 1956, 1957) with cell suspensions of Thiobacillus denitrificans. As noted above, these authors showed that the fixation of CO_2 is coupled with the oxidation of thiosulfate. They assumed that ribulose diphosphate and triphosphoglyceric acid participates in a single cycle, as in photosynthesis. Later, Vishniac et al. (1957) gave a complete scheme of the fixation of CO_2 in the autotrophic metabolism of Thiobacillaceae (Figure 133).

Thiobacillus thiocyanoxidans. Beijerinck (1904) found that bacteria can decompose rhodanates. Happold and Key (1937) obtained a pure culture of this microorganism and name it Thiobacillus thiocyanoxidans. The latter represents a minute motile rod measuring 0.3 by 0.5—1μ, a strict autotroph. Its physiology was studied by Youatt (1954). The oxidation begins with an enzymatic hydrolysis of rhodanate to sulfide, which is further oxidized to sulfuric acid. The overall reaction is as follows:

$$KCNS + 2O_2 + 2H_2O \rightarrow NH_4KSO_4 + CO_2; \Delta F = -220,000 \text{ calories.}$$

Beside rhodanate, these bacteria can oxidize thiosulfate, sulfur, and hydrogen sulfide. Their optimal pH is close to neutrality.

Thiobacillus ferrooxidans. Colmer and Hinkle (1947; see also Temple, 1949) isolated a short rod measuring 0.4 by 0.8—1.0μ and bearing a single flagellum (Figure 135). This bacterium can oxidize thiosulfate to sulfur and sulfuric acid, but its main feature is the oxidation of ferrous to ferric ion in an acid environment:

$$4FeSO_4 + 2H_2SO_4 + O_2 \rightarrow 2Fe_2(SO_4)_3 + 2H_2O;$$

$$Fe^{++} - Fe^{+++} + e; \Delta F = -11,000 \text{ calories.}$$

Leathen and co-workers (Leathen et al., 1956) questioned the ability of this bacterium to oxidize sulfur compounds and proposed to name it Ferrobacillus ferrooxidans. However, the manometric experiments of Beck (1960) and the studies of V. I. Ivanov and N. N. Lyalikova (1962) confirm Colmer's data and the original name was retained. Thiobacillus ferrooxidans is a strict autotroph. Its optimal pH is about 2.5; growth stops above pH 4.5. This species resists the toxic effect of heavy metals. Its growth requires the presence of $CuSO_4$ in the medium at a concentration of up to 6%. Young cultures utilize up to 37% of the energy liberated in the oxidation of ferrous ions.

Mixotrophic strains of Thiobacillaceae. Better known of these are Thiobacillus novellus and T. trautweinii.

T. novellus is a strict aerobe. Its cells are short immotile almost coccoid rods measuring 0.4—0.6 by 0.6—1.8μ. Cultures in inorganic media grow slowly and do not oxidize thiosulfate completely. The product of oxidation is sulfate. The optimal pH range is from 8 to 9, the lower limit between 5 and 6. On thiosulfate agar this species forms small colonies with sulfur inclusions (Starkey, 1935; Parker and Prisk, 1953).

T. novellus grows much better on meat peptone agar, especially in the presence of glutamate and aspartate; it does not assimilate sugar.

Thiobacillus trautweinii was first isolated in pure culture by Trautwein (1921, 1924) and was later studied by Starkey (1935) and Parker and Prisk (1953). It represents a small motile rod, 0.5 by 1–2μ, with 6—8 flagella; its morphology and physiology resemble those of Beijerinck's myxotrophic strain of T. denitrificans. This bacterium can live anaerobically by reducing nitrate to gaseous nitrogen.

T. trautweinii differs from T. denitrificans in the very slow oxidation of thiosulfate to tetrathionate. Elemental sulfur is not formed in this process:

$$3Na_2S_2O_3 + 2\frac{1}{2}O_2 = Na_2S_4O_6 + 2Na_2SO_4.$$

The optimal pH is 7.8—8.5, the extremes being pH 6 and pH 10. This species grows well on organic media, forming slimy colonies.

Colorless sulfur bacteria. The colorless sulfur bacteria are microaerophilic organisms. They oxidize hydrogen sulfide and deposit intracellular elemental sulfur. The phenomenon of autotrophism was discovered and described in 1887 by Vinogradsky, who observed under the microscope an intracellular accumulation of sulfur in Beggiatoa alba and a further oxidation of this element to sulfuric acid.

The process can be summarized as follows:

$$H_2S + \frac{1}{2}O_2 \rightarrow H_2O + S; \; \Delta F = -41,000 \text{ calories};$$

then in the absence of hydrogen sulfide from the medium:

$$S + H_2O + 1\frac{1}{2}O_2 \rightarrow H_2SO_4; \; \Delta F = -118,000 \text{ calories}.$$

Filamentous sulfur bacteria. Many microorganisms derive energy from the oxidation of hydrogen sulfide to sulfur. In Bergey's manual, the filamentous forms are characterized as "alga-like bacteria" belonging to four genera of the family Beggiatoaceae, order Chlamydobacteriales. Their common feature is the formation of unbranched filaments that may contain sulfur droplets in media containing sulfide (Figure 136).

Beggiatoa and Thioploca are closely similar. Their filaments attain a length of 10 mm in favorable conditions. The filaments of Thioploca occur in bundles, enclosed by a slime sheath. In both genera, the filaments consist of numerous symmetrical cells; the terminal cells of each filament are rounded. The structure of the cells is reminiscent of the blue-green alga Oscillatoria and differs from that of filamentous bacteria, as shown in the electron micrographs of Beggiatoa, made by Johnson and Baker (1947). Beggiatoa moves in exactly the same manner as Oscillatoria. Owing to the morphologic similarity to blue-green algae, some species of Beggiatoa and Thioploca were originally assigned to the genus Oscillatoria. Thus, Beggiatoa alba was described by Vaucher in 1803 under the name of Oscillatoria alba, which caused some confusion. Beggiatoa and Thioploca differ from algae in two main features, namely in being colorless and incapable of photosynthesis. Even these signs, however, cannot be regarded as crucial criteria since some algae are colorless, and certain Oscillatoria species can accumulate intracellular droplets of sulfur when growing in waters with a high hydrogen sulfide content (Hinze, 1903b; Nakamura, 1937). The electron microscope studies of Morita and Stave (1963) showed that Beggiatoa possesses a cell wall and a cell membrane; however, these authors could not detect discrete nuclear bodies, these being probably masked by cytoplasmic ribonucleoproteins.

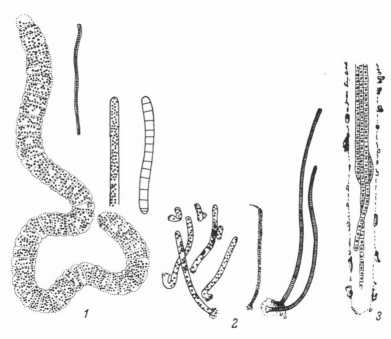

FIGURE 136. Main forms of filamentous sulfur bacteria (after Vinogradsky):

1) Beggiatoa; 2) Thiothrix; 3) Thioploca.

Thiothrix (Figure 136) resembles more closely a true filamentous bacterium. Its immotile multicellular filaments are enclosed in a delicate sheath and bear a slimy pad that adheres to a hard substrate. This genus reproduces by liberating terminal cells or short chains of cells that move t another place, adhere to a substrate, and produce young filaments.

Thiospirillopsis, the fourth genus of the group, represents a multi-cellular spiral filament that can creep on the substrate. It resembles the blue-green alga Spirulina.

330

Unicellular colorless sulfur bacteria. The colorless unicellular bacteria that accumulate sulfur inside the cells are placed in the family Achromatiaceae. Here belong microorganisms with and without flagella (Figure 137).

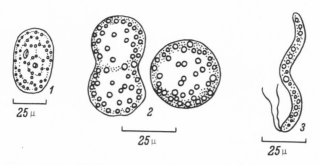

FIGURE 137. Main forms of unicellular colorless sulfur bacteria (after Bavendam):

1) Achromatium; 2) Thiovolum; 3) Thiospira.

Schewiakoff (1897) described Achromatium as large spherical or ellipsoidal organisms containing numerous sulfur droplets. This genus appears to be synonymous with Thiophysa, Thiovolum, and Thiosphaerella, which were described later. The morphology and the readily visible movements of Achromatium are regarded by some authors as contrary to a bacterial nature (Bisset and Grace, 1954). This genus closely resembles the blue-green alga Synechococcus. It can be characterized as a chlorophyll-less chemosynthetic representative of a closely related genus, just as Beggiatoa resembles the alga Oscillatoria.

Monas warmingii differs considerably from the other sulfur bacteria. Its cells are very large, 5 to 20μ in diameter, spherical, oval, or joined in pairs. They contain an excentric nucleus that stains with iron hematoxylin. The sulfur granules lie at one pole. Hinze (1903a) regards this species as morphologically similar to flagellates.

The genus Macromonas was described by Utermöhl and Koppe (1923). It has slightly curved, ellipsoidal, or cylindrical cells that move by means of a polar flagellum and contain inclusions of sulfur and calcium carbonate.

Little is known on the physiology of the colorless sulfur bacteria and the mechanism by which they oxidize sulfur. Vinogradsky demonstrated in 1887 that the ability to oxidize hydrogen sulfide, deposit intracellular sulfur, and oxidize the latter to sulfate in the absence of hydrogen sulfide is an inherent feature of the metabolism of Beggiatoa alba.

Having concluded that a pure culture of Beggiatoa cannot be obtained on a solid medium by the Koch method, Vinogradsky tried the ecological approach. He placed filaments of Beggiatoa or Thiothrix in a drop of water on a slide, which he covered with a cover glass. He examined microscopically the condition of the filaments and the presence of sulfur inclusions in cultures with or without hydrogen sulfide. In the presence of hydrogen sulfide the filaments grew rather slowly, their length doubling every twenty-four hours. Moreover, the culture consumed considerable amounts of sulfur during the growth. Cells washed during the day with a solution of hydrogen sulfide became packed with sulfur by the evening. However, nearly all the sulfur was oxidized during the night. In the absence of hydrogen sulfide, cells that do not contain sulfur die within 2 days and undergo lysis.

Vinogradsky (1887) concluded that the sulfur bacteria represent a new physiological type whose metabolism differs from that of all other bacteria. The sulfur bacteria derive energy by oxidizing sulfur and do not utilize organic compounds.

Pure cultures of Beggiatoa and Thiothrix were obtained in mineral media by Keil (1912) twenty-five years after the work of Vinogradsky. Keil confirmed Vinogradsky's view that these bacteria assimilate carbon dioxide with energy obtained from the oxidation of hydrogen sulfide. Keil isolated and cultivated these bacteria in purely inorganic media in an atmosphere of H_2S, CO_2 and O_2 at a partial pressure of 12 mm mercury.

Cataldi (1940) isolated Beggiatoa in media containing hay infusion and obtained strains requiring organic media. Such strains were later isolated by Scotten and Stokes (1962). Faust and Wolfe (1961) noted that the use of hay infusion for the isolation of Beggiatoa leads only naturally to heterotrophic strains rather than autotrophic ones. On these grounds, Faust and Wolfe doubt the autotrophy of Beggiatoa.

Burton and Morita (1964) used a Beggiatoa culture isolated by Meyer from the silt of Lake Erie. They cultivated this bacterium in a medium containing yeast extract (2 g/L). Growth was better in the presence of an accompanying microorganism than in pure culture. A two-day-old culture was able to oxidize hydrogen sulfide and accumulate sulfur granules in the filaments. In other words, this strain was capable of heterotrophic and autotrophic growth. Examination of the absorption spectrum of a cell-free extract showed the absence of a cytochrome system. According to Burton and Morita, the oxidation of hydrogen sulfide by the colorless sulfur bacteria probably involves flavin systems, as in the lactic acid bacteria. These authors showed the formation of hydrogen peroxide in microaerophilic cultures and observed a stimulatory effect of catalase, possibly because they worked with a heterotrophic strain, in contrast to the autotrophic strains of Vinogradsky and Keil. The mixotrophy of Beggiatoa is also stressed by Pringsheim (1967).

Thus, the colorless sulfur bacteria cannot be regarded as obligate autotrophs. Some Oscillatoriaceae may be confused with Beggiatoaceae because of the close similarity between the two families.

At any rate, it is established that the autotrophic and mixotrophic forms of Beggiatoa rapidly lose their sulfur inclusions and undergo lysis when placed in mineral media without hydrogen sulfide.

In view of this fact, one can hardly accept the luminescence method for the determination of Beggiatoaceae by the emission of light from the sulfur globules in their filaments, as proposed by A. G. Rodina (1963a, 1963b). In Lake Ladoga, for example, where hydrogen sulfide is lacking and the water is nearly saturated with oxygen, one cannot expect to find sulfur inclusions in the filaments of these bacteria. It appears that Rodina has erroneously taken some Oscillatoria species for Beggiatoaceae.

Purple sulfur bacteria, Thiorhodaceae. This family consists of anaerobi bacteria capable of photosynthesis by means of a pigment system composed of bacteriochlorophyll a with an absorption peak between 8,000 and 9,000 Å, and yellow and red carotenoids with a peak between 4,000 and 6,000 Å.

The reduction of carbon dioxide to the cell level involves hydrogen donors in the form of hydrogen sulfide or other sulfides, in which case sulfur is deposited inside the cells. Many purple sulfur bacteria can use other hydrogen donors, notably some organic compounds like malate or molecular hydrogen; these pathways lead to poly-β-oxybutyric acid as reserve intracellular food.

The first step in the classification of these bacteria was made by Vinogradsky (1888), who regarded them as chemosynthetic organisms. The classification and ecology of this group were later studied by Bavendam (1924) and Van Niel (1931). Van Niel obtained the first pure cultures of purple sulfur bacteria and established the following principles concerning their growth:

1. The purple sulfur bacteria can grow in mineral media in the presence of H_2S and $NaHCO_3$, but only anaerobically and in the presence of light.

2. Bacterial growth and CO_2 fixation in the presence of light proceed until the exhaustion of all the hydrogen sulfide.

3. The purple sulfur bacteria never yield oxygen as a product of photosynthesis.

4. The relationship between reduced carbon dioxide and oxidized hydrogen sulfide can be expressed roughly by the following equations:

$$CO_2 + 2H_2S \rightarrow (CH_2O) + H_2O + 2S;$$

$$2CO_2 + 2H_2O + H_2S \rightarrow 2(CH_2O) + H_2SO_4.$$

These equations prove that the assimilation of carbon dioxide is a photosynthetic rather than chemosynthetic process, since in the latter case it would be necessary to oxidize much greater quantities of hydrogen sulfide per mole of assimilated carbon dioxide.

At present, the family Thiorhodaceae comprises thirteen genera, of which the following colonial forms are more frequent.

T h i o p e d i a (Figure 138, 1). Colony shaped as flat sheet of cells arranged in regular rows.

T h i o c a p s a (Figure 138, 2). Immotile spherical cells 1.5—3.0μ in diameter, forming irregular aggregates in a common slime capsule.

L a m p r o c y s t i s (Figure 138, 3). Cell division in three directions. Cell aggregates large, flat, later broken up into smaller parts; enclosed in common slime capsule.

Of the unicellular forms, the genus T h i o s p i r i l l u m (Figure 138, 4) occurs as separate spiral cells, 2.5—4μ thick and from 30 to 100μ long, with a polar flagellum.

C h r o m a t i u m (Figure 138, 5), the commonest genus, has solitary ellipsoid cells measuring 1—4 by 2—10μ, with a polar bundle of flagella. The type species is C h r o m a t i u m o k e n i i.

P e l o c h r o m a t i u m r o s e u m, described by Anagnostidis and Overbeck (1966), is commonly found in European lakes.

The fine structure of the cell of the purple sulfur bacteria has been studied in detail by many authors. For a review of this subject, see Pfennig (1967). The structure and physiology of the family were investigated by the simultaneous application of physiological procedures and observations of fine morphology.

It was established that the cytoplasmic membrane controls the passage of various substances in and out of the cell, while electron transfer and respiration are concentrated in the mitochondria, and the chloroplasts contain the enzymes and pigments involved in the photosynthetic transfer of electrons. The different cytologic forms of the photosynthetic system of the purple sulfur bacteria and the purple nonsulfur bacteria can be regarded as varieties of the same elements of the cytoplasmic membrane.

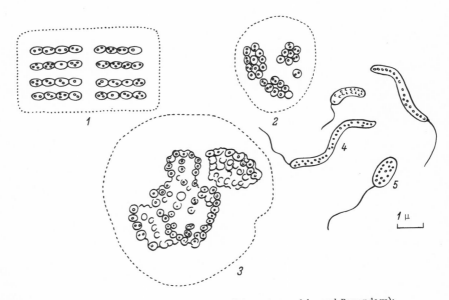

FIGURE 138. Main forms of purple sulfur bacteria (after Vinogradsky and Bavendam):

1) Thiopedia; 2) Thiocystis; 3) Lamprocystis; 4) Thiospirillum; 5) Chromatium.

Schlegel (Kran, Schlote, and Schlegel, 1963) gives a scheme of the arrangement of the inner structures of the Chromatium cell (Figure 139). The scheme shows the following structural elements: a many-layered cell wall, chromatophores adjoining the cytoplasmic membrane, sulfur droplets surrounded by a dark fringe and situated among chromatophores and small vacuoles containing polysaccharides, and inclusions of poly-β-hydroxybutyric acid. In the presence of acetate as hydrogen donor, there appear light zones with chromosome filaments, between which lie rodlike formations whose nature is unknown.

The main physiologic feature of this bacterial group is the ability to grow as a strict anaerobe in a purely inorganic medium, using light as the only source of energy; in the dark, all other conditions being equal, there is no growth whatsoever.

As in the case of algae and higher plants, photosynthetic bacteria require a hydrogen donor. The purple sulfur bacteria can grow in inorganic media, using as hydrogen donors not only reduced sulfur compounds but even some organic substances. In the presence of organic compounds as hydrogen donors, their oxidation-reduction potential affects the general metabolic pathways of these bacteria. If the hydrogen donor is more reduced than a carbohydrate (butyrate, for example), free carbon dioxide or bicarbonate must be added to the medium, which contains ammonium salts as nitrogen source. On the other hand, if the hydrogen donor is more oxidized (malate, for example) the addition of carbon dioxide becomes unnecessary, since bacterial growth in such conditions involves the liberation of large quantities of this gas.

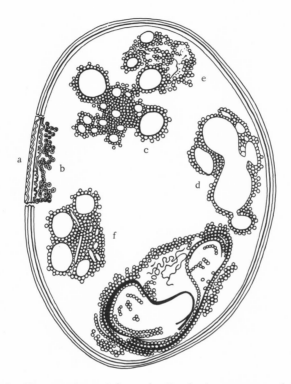

FIGURE 139. C h r o m a t i u m. Scheme showing the inner structure of the cell:

a) many-layered cell wall; b) chromatophores adjoining the cell membrane; c) small vacuoles containing polysaccharides and large vacuoles containing sulfur; d) inclusions of poly-β-hydroxybutyric acid; e) light zones with chromosome filaments (ribosomes between the chromatophores and the light zones); f) rodlike formations of unknown nature, situated between the chromatophores.

In the presence of hydrogen sulfide, the purple sulfur bacteria vary in their pH requirements (Van Niel, 1931). The Chlorobium group grows at pH values from 8.4 to 10.5, while the pH range of the Chromatium group extends from 5.5 to 9.5. Both the optimal and the extreme values depend largely on the concentration of sulfide and organic compounds in the environment.

The purple sulfur bacteria are strict anaerobes. Nevertheless, they remain viable in contact with air (Roelofsen, 1935; E. N. Kondrat'eva and E. V. Ramenskii, 1961).

The literature contains contradictory data about the effect of the oxidation-reduction potential on the growth of the purple sulfur bacteria, notably

Chromatium. E. N. Kondrat'eva (1963) maintains that only molecular oxygen inhibits growth and that these bacteria can develop at $rH_2 = 27-30$ if all traces of oxygen are removed from the medium. This can be achieved by the addition of 0.02—0.005% sodium sulfide to the medium (Kondrat'eva and Ramenskii, 1961). How to maintain the rH_2 at 27—30 in such conditions remains to be explained.

The purple sulfur bacteria use ammonium salts as nitrogen source; nitrate and amino acids are unsuitable for this purpose.

The purple sulfur bacteria can fix considerable amounts of molecular nitrogen. This process requires light; in Chromatium, it is stimulated by the addition of oxaloacetic acid (Arnon et al., 1960) (Figure 140).

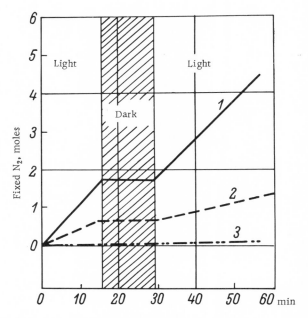

FIGURE 140. Fixation of molecular nitrogen by Chromatium (after Arnon et al., 1960):

1) medium with $Na_2S_2O_3$ and oxaloacetate; 2) medium containing $Na_2S_2O_3$ or oxaloacetate; 3) control, without any of these compounds.

In green plants, the photolysis of water yields ATP and reduced ferredoxi which differs from both hemoprotein and flavoprotein and has a reductive power comparable to that of molecular hydrogen (Arnon, 1965). Thus, the ATP and ferredoxin generated in the process perform the photosynthetic assimilation of carbon.

The photosynthetic purple sulfur bacteria photolyze the hydrogen sulfide molecule. Here the light phase yields molecular sulfur instead of oxygen, as is the case with green plants, and reduced ferredoxin appears. During the dark phase, this ferredoxin reduces the TPN, which participates in the transfer of electrons via the cytochrome system in the reduction of carbon dioxide to the cell level:

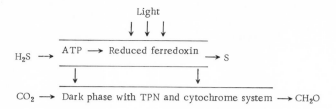

The first stable products of photosynthesis — ATP, ferredoxin, and reduced TPN — ensure the further synthesis of cell materials and the deposition of intracellular reserve materials (Kondrat'eva, 1963).

The purple sulfur bacteria can utilize some organic acids and alcohols as hydrogen donors in photosynthesis. First assumed by Müller (1933) and Van Niel (1936), this property was demonstrated by Foster (1942), who found that the photosynthetic activity of purple nonsulfur bacteria converts isopropanol to acetone without making further use of the latter.

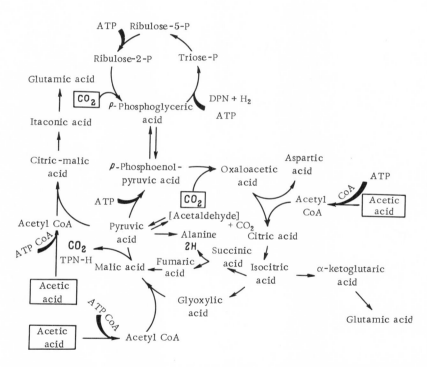

FIGURE 141. Scheme of the assimilation of carbon dioxide and acetate in the process of photosynthesis (after Losada et al., 1960).

Purple sulfur bacteria require carbon dioxide when growing in the presence of organic acids (Kondrat'eva, 1963). This proves indirectly that organic compounds serve as hydrogen donors. It is also established, however, especially by means of carbon-labeled organic compounds, that acetate can participate directly in anabolic reactions. This process does not occur in the dark, the light being required for the formation of ATP and ferredoxin as reducing agent.

Figure 141 (after Losada et al., 1960) shows the pathways of the assimilation of carbon dioxide and acetate in the photosynthesis and general metabolism of Chromatium.

As demonstrated by Roelofsen (1935) and other authors (see Kondrat'eva, 1963), the reduction of one mole of carbon dioxide requires four to twelve quanta of light.

Green sulfur bacteria, Chlorobacteriaceae. The green sulfur bacteria are anaerobes. They possess the green pigment bacteriochlorophyll a, but some species are also equipped with bacteriochlorophylls c and d. These pigments have an absorption peak between 7,000 and 8,000 Å and also absorb light in the shorter wavelengths of the spectrum. Chlorobacteriaceae are capable of photosynthesis in the presence of such hydrogen donors as hydrogen sulfide, thiosulfate, other reduced sulfur compounds, or molecular hydrogen. This process does not yield oxygen, and organic compounds do not serve as hydrogen donors in the photosynthesis.

The photosynthetic apparatus of the green sulfur bacteria lies in vesicles situated just beneath the cytoplasmic membrane. The photosynthetic pigments are borne on fibrillar structures in this family.

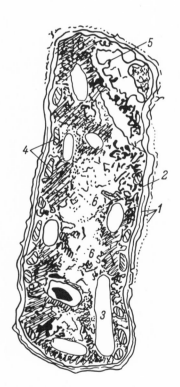

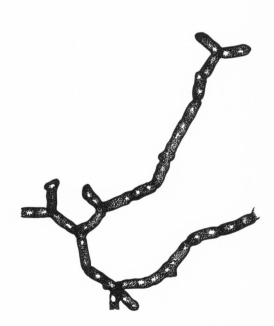

FIGURE 142. Scheme of the structure of a cell of Pelodictyon clathratiforme (from an electron micrograph by Pfennig, 1967):

1) cell wall; 2) cytoplasmic membrane; 3) gas vacuoles; 4) vesicles; 5) ribosomes; 6) nuclear substance.

FIGURE 143. Scheme of the branching of Pelodictyon clathratiforme (after a micrograph by Pfennig, 1967

Many species of green and purple sulfur bacteria contain intracellular inclusions that are clearly visible under the light microscope and were known to the early authors, starting from Vinogradsky. Identical inclusions occur in blue-green algae. These inclusions were found to be gas vacuoles. Recent studies of ultrathin sections under the electron microscope proved that the corresponding inclusions in bacteria and blue-green algae are identical.

The photosynthetic assimilation of carbon dioxide follows the same equations as in purple sulfur bacteria. However, the sulfur formed in the process is deposited outside the cells or undergoes oxidation to sulfuric acid:

$$CO_2 + 2H_2S \xrightarrow{\text{Light}} (CH_2O) + H_2O + 2S;$$

$$2CO_2 + 2H_2O + H_2S \xrightarrow{\text{Light}} 2(CH_2O) + H_2SO_4.$$

Research in this group of bacteria started with the work of Nadson (1912), who described C h l o r o b i u m   l i m i c o l a. Later, other authors established four genera of green sulfur bacteria. The main species of the family are the following.

1. C h l o r o b i u m   l i m i c o l a and C. t h i o s u l f a t o p h i l u m. Solitary cells measuring 0.7 by 0.9—1.5μ, or chains, usually enclosed in a common slime capsule. C h l o r o b i u m   t h i o s u l f a t o p h i l u m differs from C. l i m i c o l a in being able to oxidize thiosulfate and tetrathionate (Figure 142).

2. P e l o d i c t y o n   c l a t h r a t i f o r m e was isolated and described by B. V. Perfil'ev (1914a, 1914b). Two strains of it were later isolated by Pfennig (1967), who published a detailed description of the morphology and cytology of this bacterium. The cells of P e l o d i c t y o n   c l a t h r a t i - f o r m e branch and form a network, in contrast to all other sulfur bacteria (Figure 143). The intracellular gas vacuoles enable the bacterium to swim even at low temperature. The closely related P e l o d i c t y o n   a g g r e g a t u m forms cell aggregates and similarly bears gas vacuoles.

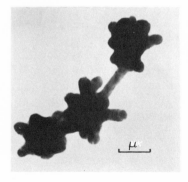

FIGURE 144. P r o s t h e c o c h l o r i s   a e s t u a r i i n. sp. Garl. (photograph by V.M. Gorlenko).

Some green sulfur bacteria, notably C h l o r o c h r o m a t i u m a g g r e -
g a t u m , often appear surrounded by motile colorless bacteria in cultures
(Pfennig, 1967).

3. C y l i n d r o g l o e a b a c t e r i f e r a Perfil'ev (1914a, 1914b) is capable
of photosynthesis in the presence of hydrogen sulfide and does not accumulate sulfur. It grows in combination with a colorless filiform bacterium.

4. P r o s t h e c o c h l o r i s a e s t u a r i i, a new species of green sulfur
bacteria, was isolated by V. M. Gorlenko (1968; Gorlenko and Zhilina, 1968)
from salt waters in Crimea. The cells measure 1 by 2μ. It can be seen
under the electron microscope that each cell bears several outgrowths
(Figure 144). Division is by constriction of the cell; the daughter cells
move away from one another while still connected by a bridge, which eventually breaks apart, leaving two separate cells. Sometimes the division is
retarded, creating a chain of cells with characteristic outgrowths.

Like other green bacteria, this organism contains bacteriochlorophyll a
and develops only in the presence of light, by photosynthesis. Sulfide and
thiosulfate serve as hydrogen donors. In its inner structure (Figure 145),
the cell has much in common with C h l o r o b i u m and P e l o d i c t y o n.

The cell wall consists of three layers. Beneath them lies the cytoplasmic membrane, which is adjoined by vesicles, each having a membrane of
its own. The cytoplasm contains a distinct nuclear zone with DNA filaments and ribosomes. Marginally, the section shows cavities surrounded
by projections of the outer layer of the cell wall. Simultaneous examination of the cell under the light microscope shows that normally these cavities are filled with molecular sulfur.

5. C h l o r o p s e u d o m o n a s e t h y l i c u m. This species belongs to
the family Pseudomonadaceae, in contrast to the other green sulfur bacteria.
It consists of a short rod, 0.5—0.7 by 1.2—1.7μ, with one long flagellum,
situated asymmetrically at one end of the cell. C h l o r o p s e u d o m o n a s
differs from the other green bacteria in being motile and by the absence of
cell chains.

Physiologically, the green sulfur bacteria have much in common with the
purple sulfur bacteria. Their growth requires light at an intensity of no
less than 600 erg/cm^2/sec, the upper limit being about 10,000 erg/cm^2/sec,
above which a light saturation develops. Thiosulfate, sulfide, and hydrogen
can serve as hydrogen donors. The wavelengths at which photosynthesis
takes place are about 3,500 Å, 7,000—8,000 Å, and 8,000—9,000 Å.

The optimal pH of green sulfur bacteria is between 7.0 and 7.5, the
extremes being 6.0 and 9.8. The green sulfur bacteria are strict anaerobes
The data about the effect of the oxidation-reduction potential on their growth
are highly contradictory. Being autotrophs, these bacteria grow satisfactorily in mineral media containing iron and cobalt salts; halophilic strains
are also known. Ammonium salts serve as nitrogen sources. In anaerobic
conditions, the green sulfur bacteria fix molecular nitrogen in the presence
of light.

C h l o r o b i u m t h i o s u l f a t o p h i l u m oxidizes hydrogen sulfide successively to sulfur and sulfate (Larsen, 1952, 1954; Shaposhnikov,
Kondrat'eva, and Fedorov, 1958):

$$CO_2 + 2H_2S \longrightarrow (CH_2O) + 2S + H_2O;$$
$$2CO_2 + H_2S + 2H_2O \longrightarrow 2(CH_2O) + H_2SO_4.$$

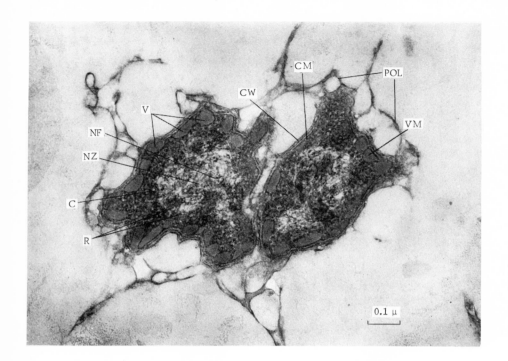

FIGURE 145. Ultrathin section of Prostheochloris aestuarii (electron micrograph by V.M.Gorlenko):

CW— cell wall; CM — cytoplasmic membrane; V — vesicles; VM — vesicular membrane; C — cytoplasm; NZ — nuclear zone; NF — nuclear filament (DNA); R — ribosomes; POL — projections of the outer layer of the cell wall.

Chlorobium thiosulfatophilum and C. limicola can utilize molecular hydrogen as hydrogen donor:

$$CO_2 + 2H_2 \xrightarrow{\text{Light}} (CH_2O) + H_2O.$$

Some species of green sulfur bacteria can grow only in mineral media containing bicarbonate and hydrogen sulfide. This feature was earlier regarded as the main distinction between the green sulfur bacteria and their purple counterparts.

Working with another strain of C. limicola, Stanier (1961) found that the addition of some organic compounds to the mineral medium with $NaHCO_3$ and Na_2S improves growth.

Chlorochromatium aggregatum grows anaerobically in the presence of light and Na_2S but without CO_2 in media containing malic acid; of the latter, 28% is converted to CO_2, while the rest enters anabolic reactions.

Chloropseudomonas ethylicum, isolated by Shaposhnikov, Kondrat'eva, and Fedorov (1958), utilizes ethanol as hydrogen donor, oxidizing it photosynthetically to acetic acid:

$$CO_2 + CH_3CH_2OH \xrightarrow{\text{Light}} (CH_2O) + CH_3COOH.$$

Part of the acetic acid obtained in the process enters the anabolic pathways. This evidence partly bridges the gap between green and purple sulfur bacteria with respect to the utilization of carbon sources.

Little is known on the mechanism of CO_2 assimilation in green sulfur bacteria. Apparently, this process does not differ from the pathways established in the purple sulfur bacteria.

Purple nonsulfur bacteria, Athiorhodaceae. Nearly all the species of this family require light for growth. Exceptions are a few species that can utilize oxygen. Athiorhodaceae can use a variety of hydrogen donors in photosynthesis, including reduced sulfur compounds, organic acids, alcohols, some other organic compounds, and molecular hydrogen. They never deposit intracellular sulfur. Athiorhodaceae require organic compounds for growth; herein lies the main difference between this family and the purple sulfur bacteria.

The purple nonsulfur bacteria belong to the following three genera.

1. R h o d o p s e u d o m o n a s . Rods measuring 0.6—0.8 by 1.2—2μ, 10μ long in old cultures. The cells secrete slime; in young cultures they are motile and bear several polar flagella.

2. R h o d o s p i r i l l u m r u b r u m . Cells more or less curved. The size varies according to the composition of the medium, from 0.5 to 1.5μ wide and from 2—10 to 50μ long.

3. The purple nonsulfur bacterium R h o d o m i c r o b i u m v a n n i e l i i has been placed in the order Hyphomicrobiales because of its particular manner of reproduction. This species has oval cells measuring an average of 1.2 by 2.8μ and joined by filaments 0.3μ in diameter.

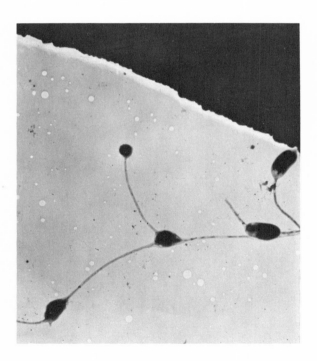

FIGURE 146. R h o d o m i c r o b i u m v a n n i e l i i (electron micrograph by V.M. Gorlenko).

Reproduction is by budding (Figure 146). From the pole of the maternal cell or from the filament between two cells departs a new filament whose end thickens to form a young daughter cell. In young cultures, the new cells bear bundles of flagella and are motile. This organism can produce spores (V. M. Gorlenko, 1968).

The purple nonsulfur bacteria can grow anaerobically in mineral media by fixing CO_2 in the presence of light at a wavelength of 7,700—8,700 Å and 4,000—5,000 Å, the absorption peaks of bacteriochlorophyll a and carotenoids:

$$2CO_2 + Na_2S_2O_3 + 3H_2O \xrightarrow{\text{Light}} 2(CH_2O) + Na_2SO_4 + H_2SO_4 .$$

R h o d o p s e u d o m o n a s v i r i d i s contains bacteriochlorophyll b with an absorption peak at almost 10,000 Å, beyond the visible range.

In the dark, the purple nonsulfur bacteria grow anaerobically in organic media containing peptone, amino acids, sugars, alcohols, and ketones. However, they grow best in the presence of lower fatty acids, some hydroxy-, keto-, or dicarboxylic acids. These compounds serve largely as hydrogen donors. For example, R h o d o p s e u d o m o n a s g e l a t i n o s a converts quantitatively isopropanol to acetone (Foster, 1944):

$$2CH_3CHOHCH_3 + CO_2 \longrightarrow 2CH_3COCH_3 + (CH_2O) + H_2O .$$

R h o d o p s e u d o m o n a s grows normally in the presence of light in an anaerobic environment without bicarbonate, but in the presence of acetic acid together with another organic acid (Kondrat'eva, 1959). Satisfactory growth is observed also in bicarbonate-free media but in the presence of Na_2S and $Na_2S_2O_3$ and a fatty or hydroxy acid.

Experiments with carbon-labeled CO_2 and acetic acid showed that R h o d o s p i r i l l u m r u b r u m assimilates these compounds photosynthetically by the ribulose and tricarboxylic cycles, as in C h r o m a t i u m (Figure 141).

Poly-β-oxybutyric acid can serve as reserve food in R h o d o s p i r i l l u m r u b r u m and probably in some other purple nonsulfur bacteria. This compound is synthesized from acetic acid in the absence of carbon dioxide (Figure 147).

In the presence of carbon dioxide, both acetate and poly-β-oxybutyric acid are converted into carbohydrates.

In addition to poly-β-oxybutyric acid, the photosynthetic activity of the purple bacteria can yield another reserve compound, namely a glycogen-type polysaccharide, which enables these bacteria to live in the dark.

Kondrat'eva (1963) believes that these data confirm the ability of the nonsulfur purple bacteria to utilize organic compounds photosynthetically as direct sources of carbon rather than as hydrogen donors.

A characteristic feature of the purple nonsulfur bacteria is their ability to liberate molecular hydrogen by the decomposition of some organic and amino acids:

$$COOH—CH_2—CHOH—COOH + 3H_2O \xrightarrow{\text{Light}} 4CO_2 + 6H_2 .$$

This phenomenon reflects the activity of hydrogenase in the purple nonsulfur bacteria.

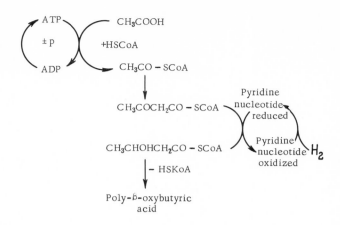

FIGURE 147. Scheme of the synthesis of poly-β-oxybutyric acid by Rhodospirillum rubrum (after Stanier, 1965).

Some strains of Rhodopseudomonas and Rhodospirillum rubrum can grow in the dark in the presence of oxygen. Purple nonsulfur bacteria growing in the dark can oxidize a variety of organic compounds, including different organic acids, amino acids, sugars, and acetone. As Kondrat'eva notes in her review (1963), cultures living in the dark utilize these compounds largely for energetic processes, bacterial growth being sluggish in such conditions.

Numerous studies were made of the development of purple nonsulfur bacteria in the dark at the expense of organic acids in the presence of oxygen. These experiments show that at least some species utilize various organic acids via the tricarboxylic cycle.

Determinations of the absorption spectrum of R. rubrum cells have shown that anaerobic photosynthesis and oxidative metabolism in the dark with the participation of oxygen involve several different cytochrome systems, especially cytochromes c_2 and b.

The optimal pH range of most purple nonsulfur bacteria is from 7.0 to 7.5 (Kondrat'eva, 1963), the extreme values being 6.5 and 8.5.

Many species of purple nonsulfur bacteria can fix molecular nitrogen in normal conditions in the presence of light. Elsden (1954) assumes, therefore, that the purple nonsulfur bacteria occupy an intermediary position between autotrophs and heterotrophs. In the presence of light, organic compounds are oxidized by the same mechanism that operates in autotrophic bacteria, the light energy serving to create hydrogen acceptors necessary for these reactions. Moreover, the fixation of carbon dioxide follows the same pathways as in green plants.

Regrettably, most of the experiments were made with a single species, Rhodospirillum rubrum, and far-reaching conclusions require comparative studies of other purple nonsulfur bacteria.

Microbiological Processes of the Sulfur Cycle in Lakes

Microorganisms play a crucial role in the transformations of sulfur in lakes. For example, the reduction of sulfate to hydrogen sulfide in the hydrosphere can proceed only in biological systems.

The oxidation of reduced sulfur compounds liberates various amounts of energy, which promotes the growth of autotrophic bacteria in suitable ecological conditions.

In the preceding pages we discussed the environmental conditions in lakes and the physiology of their microbial inhabitants. The rest of this chapter deals with the actual processes of the sulfur cycle.

Putrefaction of Organic Materials

Putrefaction yields hydrogen sulfide in anaerobic conditions. As indicated above, a lack of oxygen in the water mass develops during the stagnation period in the hypolimnion of eutrophic lakes or in the silt. Most of the material that undergoes anaerobic decomposition represents remnants of dead plankton. In view of these considerations, determinations were made of the putrefying microflora of different types of lakes.

Table 93 shows the distribution of putrefying bacteria in the water and silt of lakes belonging to different types.

It is evident from the table that hydrogen sulfide-producing putrefying bacteria occur mainly in the silt of eutrophic lakes, such as Beloe in Kosino and Chernoe-Kucheer. Such bacteria are almost absent from the water of the nearly oligotrophic Lake Yugdem. Clearly, putrefaction can be regarded as an important factor in the sulfur cycle in lakes only in special cases.

TABLE 93. Vertical distribution of hydrogen sulfide-producing putrefying bacteria in lake water and silt (number of bacterial cells per ml of water or silt)

Depth, m	Lake				
	Beloe in Kosino	Bol'shoi Kucheer	Chernoe-Kucheer	Belovod'	Yugdem
0	39	227	227	128	15
4	—	145	—	—	—
4.5	—	—	323	—	—
5.0	4,060	34	—	—	—
7.0	—	18	53	—	—
9.0	3,550	—	18	—	7
12.0	1,860	12	—	—	—
15.0	—	15	—	2	—
22.0	—	—	—	50	7
				0	—
Silt	3,000–115,000	—	14,000	100	1,200

The Role of Microorganisms in the Reduction of Sulfate

The reduction of sulfate was regarded at first as a strictly chemical process that occurs in the presence of organic substances. Experiments with radioactive sulfur isotopes ($Na_2S^{35}O_4$) showed, however, that the reduction of sulfate takes place in biological systems and stops in the presence of antiseptic agents (M. V. Ivanov, 1957).

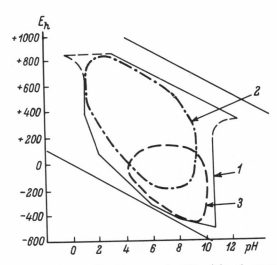

FIGURE 148. Area of stable state of sulfides (1) and occurrence of sulfate-reducing bacteria as a function of the oxidation-reduction potential and pH of the environment:

2 — area of bacteria that oxidize reduced sulfur compounds;
3 — area of bacteria that reduce sulfate.

On the basis of chemical data, Baas-Becking and co-workers (1963) plotted the stable state of sulfides as a function of the oxidation-reduction potential and pH. In addition, they indicated in the same graph the results of the numerous data on the distribution of sulfate-reducing bacteria in nature. This revealed the relationship between the distribution of sulfate-reducing bacteria, on the one hand, and the pH and oxidation-reduction potential (E_h) of the environment, on the other. Briefly, the distribution of these bacteria falls within the area representing the stable state of sulfides (Figure 148).

Distribution of sulfate-reducing bacteria in different biotopes. Many workers have examined the occurrence of these bacteria in different types of lakes. At any rate, the quantitative procedures that are used differ from one author to another, and the methods based on the agar-containing medium of Kravtsov-Sorokin (1959) or the Shturm medium (Kuznetsov and Romanenko 1963b) are far from perfect. Therefore, the results given in Table 94 must be regarded as approximate. Even with this reservation, certain regularities emerge.

Measuring bacteria in the water and silt of different types of lakes

Type of lake	Name	Number of bacteria per ml of water		Number of bacteria per gram of silt	Reference
		epilimnion	hypolimnion		
Oligotrophic	Onega	0	0	10	Romanenko, 1942
	Baikal	0	0	0	Kuznetsov, 1956
	Dridza (Latvian SSR)	0	0	0	Daukshta, 1967
	Sevan (Armenia)	—	—	0–10	Gambaryan, 1962
	Dolgoe (Latvian SSR)	—	—	0–100	Daukshta, 1968
Mesotrophic	Belovod' (meromictic)	0	1	500	Kuznetsov, 1942
	Borovoe (fresh-water)	0	0	0	Kuznetsov, 1950b
	Maibalyk (salt)	—	—	500	Kuznetsov, 1950b
	Bol'shoi Kucheer (fresh-water)	0	2	470,000	Kuznetsov, 1942
	Punnus-Yarvi (fresh-water)	0	1	100	Sokolova-Dubinina and Deryugina, 1967
	Vishki (fresh-water, Latvian SSR)	—	0	400–1,200	Daukshta, 1968
Eutrophic	Beloe (in Kosino; fresh-water)	0	0	0–1	Kuznetsov, 1942
	Chernoe-Kucheer (meromictic)	0	4.0–7.5	2,000	
	Umreshevo (brackish)	—	—	1,000	
	Mogil'noe (meromictic)	—	—	300	Isachenko, 1914
	Shengeida (Latvian SSR)	—	—	100	Daukshta, 1968
	Dotka (Latvian SSR)	—	—	100–500	Daukshta, 1968
	Tsimlyansk Artificial Reservoir	0	0	Up to 2,000,000	Kuznetsov and Romanenko, 1967
Dystrophic	Melnezers (Latvian SSR)	0	—	1,000	Daukshta, 1968
Salt lakes and limans	Balpashsor (Kokchetav Region)	—	—	300	Kuznetsov, 1950b
	Sivash (Crimea)	—	—	30,000	
	Sol'prom Basins (Crimea)	—	—	20,000	Romanenko, 1968
	Repnoe (Ukraine)	—	—	1,000,000	
	Molochnyi liman (Ukraine)	—	—	100,000	
	Kuyal'nitskii liman (Ukraine)	—	—	Up to 1,000,000	Rubenchik, 1948
	Solenoe (Arkhangel'sk Region)	10	10–100	1,000–100,000	Ivanov and Terebkova, 1959a, 1959b;
	Sventes (Latvian SSR)	0	0	10	Daukshta, 1968
	Turali (Dagestan)	0	0	200	
	Ak Gel' (Dagestan)	—	—	3,000,000	Aliverdieva, 1964

Lake Beloe in Kosino can be taken as an example of the category of eutrophic lakes with a low sulfate content.

The water of Lake Beloe is almost free of sulfate-reducing bacteria (Table 94). Direct inoculation of silt does not reveal such bacteria, though positive results can be obtained after composting the silt in the laboratory in the presence of sulfate. This reflects the presence and low activity of sulfate-reducing bacteria in the natural silt of the eutrophic Lake Beloe. Indeed, such bacteria occur only in the black silt at a depth of 5—7 cm from the surface, in a zone where the extraction of the silt sample liberates numerous gas bubbles, indicating a simultaneous anaerobic breakdown of silt with the production of methane.

Small quantities of sulfate-reducing bacteria occur in the silt of the eutrophic Lake Kolomenskoe (L. D. Shturm and T. L. Simakova, 1929) and in Lake Beloe (Pokrovskii District). Clearly, the reduction of sulfate is of minor importance in lakes with a low sulfate content.

Matters are quite different in Lakes Belovod', Chernoe-Kucheer, and Bol'shoi Kucheer. Sulfate-reducing bacteria occur here not only in the silt but also in the water mass, especially in Lake Chernoe-Kucheer, which is also richer in hydrogen sulfide. These bacteria are absent from the surface layers, where the water is saturated with oxygen. In the hypolimnion of Lake Chernoe-Kucheer, the density of sulfate-reducing bacteria did not exceed seven cells per ml; it was much greater in the silt, though only in the surface zone, which contained large amounts of freshly sedimented plankton showing still no evidence of decay.

The density of sulfate-reducing bacteria is lowest in oligotrophic lakes. The water mass of such lakes is practically free of such bacteria. In Lake Onega, for example, counts of up to ten bacteria per gram of silt occur in some cases only (V. I. Romanenko, 1965). Higher densities are obtained in the silt of the alpine Lake Sevan, where these bacteria show a microzonal distribution. Microscopic examination of the top silt of this lake reveals separate black crystals of pyrite inside valves of diatoms; treatment of the silt with hydrochloric acid yields free hydrogen sulfide.

Little is known on the distribution of sulfate-reducing bacteria in the silt of dystrophic lakes. The silt of Lake Melnezers (Latvia) contains a small amount of sulfate-reducing bacteria (Daukshta, 1968).

Sulfate-reducing bacteria are widespread in the surface silt layers of salt lakes and limans.

The activity of these bacteria was studied in detail in Lake Tambukansko (B. L. Isachenko, 1927). Sulfate-reducing bacteria attain a density of 10 mil lion cells per gram of silt in the Slavyanskie lakes and the Kuyal'nitskii liman (L. I. Rubenchik, 1948). This density decreases with depth into the silt.

Summing up the available data on the distribution of sulfate-reducing bacteria, it can be said that these microorganisms are practically absent from the water mass of lakes, except in the hydrogen sulfide zone of mero-mictic lakes. In contrast to the water mass, the silt invariably contains a certain number of sulfate-reducing bacteria even in oligotrophic lakes, whose water is poor in sulfate; in the latter case, these bacteria occur in microzones containing a large proportion of organic matter.

Rate of sulfate reduction. The application of radioactive sulfur compounds can solve various problems concerning the rate of the generation of hydrogen sulfide in lakes or the oxidation of hydrogen sulfide to sulfur and sulfuric acid (Kuznetsov, 1965).

In principle, the use of radioactive sulfur isotopes for this purpose does not differ from the experiments with labeled carbon dioxide in studies of the carbon cycle (Ivanov, 1957, 1959; Kuznetsov and Romanenko, 1963).

The rate of sulfate reduction can be determined as follows. A certain quantity of $Na_2S^{35}O_4$ is added to a dark vessel containing a sample of water and silt. The vessel is then incubated in conditions as close as possible to those prevailing in the lake itself. After a certain period of incubation, the hydrogen sulfide is distilled off into a solution containing cadmium acetate. The amount of hydrogen sulfide generated per unit time can be calculated from the total radioactivity of sulfate at the start of the experiment, the radioactivity of the cadmium sulfide produced, and the total amount of sulfate in the sample.

A parallel sample containing an antiseptic agent, such as chloroform or formalin, serves as control. Here the formation of hydrogen sulfide can proceed only by purely chemical ways.

TABLE 95. Rate of the generation of hydrogen sulfide in the water and silt of Lake Solenoe in March 1957 (after Ivanov and Terebkova, 1959b)

Sample	Depth of sample, m	Depth inside the silt, cm	Rate of generation of hydrogen sulfide, mg/L/day
Water	1	—	0.0187
	3	—	0.0173
	4.5	—	0.0202
Silt	—	0—10	0.932
	—	10—20	0.127
	—	20—30	0.017

Studies of the reduction of sulfate in the mesotrophic Lake Belovod' (Ivanov, 1956; Sorokin, 1966b) showed that this process occurs only in the silt and generates 0.067—0.127 mg of hydrogen sulfide per liter per day (Ivanov, 1956). The same process was studied more thoroughly in the eutrophic Lake Solenoe near Sol'vychegodsk (M. V. Ivanov and Terebkova, 1959a, 1959b). Analyses of water and silt carried out in March 1957 (Table 95) showed that the generation of hydrogen sulfide by the reduction of sulfate in the water mass did not exceed 0.01—0.05 mg per liter of water per day, compared with 1.0—1.4 mg per liter of surface silt. The rate of sulfate reduction was two or three times lower at a depth of 10 cm from the silt surface.

Repeated measurements of the reduction of sulfate in the surface silt layer during June 1958 revealed a far greater rate of H_2S generation; in an area rich in organic matter, this rate was nearly 19 mg per liter of silt per day (Figure 149).

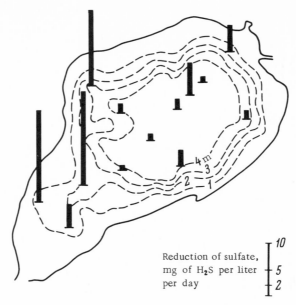

Reduction of sulfate,
mg of H_2S per liter
per day

⌉ 10
⊦ 5
⌊ 2

FIGURE 149. Rate of the reduction of sulfate in the surface silt
layer of Lake Solenoe in Arkhangel'sk Region (after Ivanov and
Terebkova, 1959b).

The numbers indicate depth in meters.

A high rate of H_2S generation does not necessarily coincide with a high
density of sulfate-reducing bacteria. Indeed, the density of D e s u l f o v i -
b r i o   d e s u l f u r i c a n s reaches a peak at a depth of 10—20 cm from the
silt surface, while the rate of sulfate reduction is highest at the silt surface.

The rate of sulfate reduction in lake sediments depends largely on the
presence of assimilable organic compounds. Such relationship was observed
in the sediments of the Rybinsk and Gorki artificial reservoirs, where the
rate of H_2S formation amounted to 0.4—1.2 mg per kg of silt per day
(G. A. Sokolova and Yu. I. Sorokin, 1957, 1958). It is manifested in a more
pronounced form in the littoral of Krasnovodsk Gulf in the Caspian Sea.
Here the hydrogen sulfide content of the sandy clay bottom reached 550 mg
per kg of sediment in areas with decaying organic matter from the sea, and
the rate of H_2S generation was 8 mg per kg of bottom per day. No reduction
of sulfate was observed in sediments where organic matter was lacking or
still undecayed.

The reduction of sulfate proceeds under similar circumstances in Sivash
Lagoon, which represents a deep bay of the Sea of Azov (see p. 10). The rate of
sulfate reduction and the density of sulfate-reducing bacteria were determined in the littoral silt of the bay, in an area strewn with wind-swept remnants of algae and higher plants. As shown in Table 96, the salinity of
Genichesk inlet and other evaporation basins of the Sol'prom (Salt Enterprises) reaches 146—193 g of Cl per liter. Even at such high salinity, which
leads to a precipitation of NaCl, the reduction of sulfate yields 33—75 mg of
H_2S per liter per day.

A more detailed study of the distribution of sulfate-reducing bacteria in relation to the rate of sulfate reduction was made by Yu. I. Sorokin (1961) in the Cheremshan inlet of the Kuibyshev Artificial Reservoir.

The calm hot weather in August 1958 created a sharp thermal stratification of the bay water. Over the former bed of the Cheremshan, oxygen disappeared and hydrogen sulfide accumulated instead. Owing to the abundant supply of organic matter from the masses of dead phytoplankton on the bottom (Figure 150), the H_2S content of the bottom water rose to 5 mg/L, and the density of Desulfovibrio desulfuricans in this layer reached 450 cells/ml, although the reduction of sulfate in the water mass did not generate more than 0.1 mg of H_2S per liter per day. At the same time the surface silt produced 1.7 mg of H_2S per liter per day.

In some cases, hydrogen sulfide can be generated in the water mass of the lake. Lake Suigets-uko (Japan) can be taken as an example. Although microbiological studies were not performed there, Yoshimura (1932) cites chemical evidence that hydrogen sulfide is generated here by sulfate-reducing bacteria.

Suigets-uko was at first a freshwater lake. After the digging of two canals that joined this lake with the sea via Lake Hiruga, the salinity of the profundal waters rose owing to the inflow of sea water. Lake Suigets-uko has a maximal depth of 32 m; the fall overturn does not extend deeper than 10—13 m.

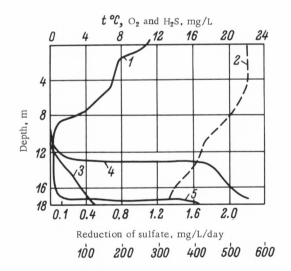

Cells of Desulfovibrio desulfuricans
per ml of water

FIGURE 150. Vertical distribution of temperature (1), oxygen (2), hydrogen sulfide (3), and sulfate-reducing bacteria (4) in Cheremshan inlet of the Kuibyshev Artificial Reservoir; (5) rate of sulfate reduction (after Sorokin, 1961).

TABLE 96. Rate of sulfate reduction in the silt of different parts of Sivash Lagoon (after Kuznetsov and Romanenko, 1968)

Origin of sample	Cl, g/L	Sulfate sulfur, mg/L	Rate of sulfate reduction, mg of H_2S per liter per day	Density of sulfate-reducing bacteria, thousands of cells per gram of raw silt
Sivash Lagoon: at Genichesk inlet · · · · ·	11.6	57	2.6	30
at Papanin Island · · · · · · · · · · · · · · · · · ·	24.9	260	5.1	—
at the Valka settlement · · · · · · · · · · ·	50.8	233	4.2	96
south of the Valka settlement · · · · · · ·	70.2	2.25	25.0	—
southern fringe · · · · · · · · · · · · · · · · · · ·	71.9	1,070	40	6
Chokrak inlet ·	154	3,400	15	—
Genichesk inlet · · · · · · · · · · · · · · · · · ·	193	2,620	33	40
Sol'prom (Salt enterprises) Basin:				
(Arabatskaya strelka) = Arbat Tongue	163	2,630	75	15
at Sivash Station · · · · · · · · · · · · · · · · ·	146	2,630	74	—

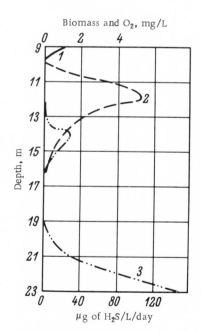

FIGURE 151. Rate of sulfate reduction in the water mass of Lake Belovod' (after Sorokin, 1966b):

1) vertical distribution of oxygen; 2) production of organic matter by purple sulfur bacteria, µg of C/L/day; 3) rate of H_2S production, µg of S^{2-}/L/day.

Analyzing the concentrations of sulfate and hydrogen sulfide in Lake Suigets-uko, Yoshimura found that below a depth of 15 m the sulfate content decreases in favor of hydrogen sulfide. Moreover, the chloride content also increases with depth.

Since sulfate could arrive here only with sea water in which the sulfate/chloride ratio is rather constant, Yoshimura estimated the sulfate content of the lake on the basis of the amount of chloride. From the difference between the calculated and actual amounts of sulfate, he determined the quantity reduced to hydrogen sulfide. These magnitudes are rather similar, indicating that the reduction of sulfate takes place in the water mass of this lake (Table 97).

TABLE 97. Actual and estimated concentrations of sulfate and hydrogen sulfide in Lake Suigetsu-uko on November 12, 1927 (after Yoshimura, 1932d)

Depth, m	Tempera-ture, °C	Oxygen, mg/L	Cl', mg/L	SO_4^{2-}, mg/L			Hydrogen sulfide, mg/L	
				actual	estimated	difference	actual	estimated from reduction of sulfate
0	13.2	8.7	920	67	107	40	0	—
5	15.3	8.57	920	56	107	51	0	—
10	16.7	1.56	1,580	167	183	17	0	—
13	15.7	1.45	2,350	250	272	22	0	—
14	15.3	0.00	—	300	274	−26	0.37	—
15	14.7	0.00	2,400	308	278	−36	1.6	0.0
20	12.3	0.00	2,960	296	343	47	23.8	20.5
25	12.6	0.00	(3,280)	268	370	100	47.5	42.5
30	12.9	0.00	—	208	380	172	54.5	72
32	12.7	0.00	(3,280)	210	380	170	53.8	72

Using radioactive isotopes, Yu. I. Sorokin (1966b) made direct observations of the bacterial reduction of sulfate in Lake Belovod' (Figure 151). Here the reduction of sulfate takes place in two layers. One of these layers is situated at a depth of 13.5—16 m, just below a zone of rich biological production due to the photosynthetic and chemosynthetic activities of purple bacteria and Thiobacillaceae, respectively. According to Yu. I. Sorokin, this layer owes its existence to the bacterial biosynthesis of assimilable organic matter in the overlying zone. In July 1964 the daily rate of sulfate reduction corresponded to almost $30 \mu g$ of H_2S per liter. The second layer of sulfate reduction is situated in the bottom water, where the daily rate of H_2S formation amounted to $160 \mu g$ per liter of water. The generation of H_2S here is probably due to the accumulation of organic matter from the water mass of the lake. This magnitude of H_2S production corresponds with the data of M. V. Ivanov (1956) on the rate of sulfate reduction in the surface silt of the lake.

TABLE 98. Growth conditions of the different groups of bacteria that participate in the oxidation of reduced sulfur compounds

Group	Oxygen requirements	Light requirements	Necessary hydrogen donors	Sources of carbon
Colorless sulfur bacteria	Require minimal quantities of oxygen	Chemosynthetic; light energy not utilized	Hydrogen sulfide	Carbon dioxide
Purple and green sulfur bacteria (Thiorhodaceae)	Anaerobes	Photosynthetic; do not reproduce without light	Sulfide, thiosulfate, and some organic compounds, especially fatty acids and hydroxy acids	Carbon dioxide, probably also fatty acids
Purple nonsulfur bacteria (Athiorhodaceae)	Grow with and without oxygen	Photosynthetic, but can also develop in the dark in the presence of oxygen and organic matter	Organic compounds, hydrogen sulfide; some species utilize molecular hydrogen; hydrogen sulfide not required in heterotrophic growth	Organic compounds, carbon dioxide, and growth factors
Thiobacillaceae (Thiobacillus thioparus, T. thiooxidans)	Grow better at a lower concentration of oxygen	Chemosynthetic; light energy not utilized	Sulfide, thiosulfates, and molecular sulfur; some species, such as Thiobacillus trautveinii, are heterotrophs	Carbon dioxide
Denitrifying Thiobacillaceae (Thiobacillus denitrificans)	Anaerobes, but grow also at a low concentration of oxygen	Chemosynthetic; light energy not utilized	Sulfur and thiosulfate (some species are heterotrophs)	Carbon dioxide

The Role of Microorganisms in the Oxidation of Reduced Sulfur Compounds

Another stage of the sulfur cycle involves the oxidation of reduced sulfur compounds. Most of these oxidative processes yield free energy, which can be utilized by chemosynthetic bacteria; on the other hand, reduced sulfur compounds serve as hydrogen donors for photosynthetic bacteria. Thus, most of the microorganisms participating in the oxidation of sulfur compounds are capable of autotrophic life.

To this category belong various groups of sulfur bacteria. Great advances were made in recent years in the physiology of these bacteria, whose basic features were indicated above. Table 98 shows the growth requirements of the main groups of these bacteria.

Distribution of sulfur bacteria in natural waters. The distribution of sulfur bacteria in lakes is closely associated with the nature of the lake and the generation or accumulation of reduced sulfur compounds.

In eutrophic lakes of glacial origin, hydrogen sulfide develops largely from putrefaction in the silt and diffuses in small quantities into the water. Filamentous colorless sulfur bacteria, such as Beggiatoa and Thiothrix, may be found on the silt surface of such lakes. Experiments with glass slides immersed in the silt of Lake Beloe in Kosino (Sorokin, 1938) showed that in the upper 0.5 cm of silt the slide becomes overgrown mainly with filamentous sulfur bacteria, whose density attains 6,000 filaments per cm² within a period of six days.

Ohle (1959, 1960) observed fine white weblike growths of Beggiatoa and Thiothrix on the silt surface of the Grosser Plöner See by means of television and photographic devices.

Thus, hydrogen sulfide is oxidized by bacteria in the bottom water to sulfur and sulfates. Anagnostidis and Overbeck (1966) examined in greater detail the distribution of sulfur bacteria in the water mass of eutrophic lakes during the summer stagnation. Figure 152 shows the results obtained by these authors in the Plussee. A distinct thermal stratification develops here during the summer. The oxygen of the hypolimnion rapidly disappears owing to the activity of methane-oxidizing bacteria. By August hydrogen sulfide accumulates throughout the hypolimnion to a concentration of 2.8 mg/L at a depth of 25 m and about 1 mg/L at a depth of 5 m in the upper part of the hypolimnion. The latter zone still receives some amount of light, which allows the development of pigmented (mostly green) sulfur bacteria. In October these organisms reached a density of one million cells per ml of water, although the latter was not visibly colored. Anagnostidis and Overbeck report the presence of various species of sulfur bacteria, notably Lamprocystis roseopersicina, Chlorobium limicola, and Rhodothece. The colorless sulfur bacteria Rhodothece conspicula and Peloploca pulchra grew luxuriantly in the lower hypolimnion at a depth of 20—25 m.

Green and purple sulfur bacteria find better conditions in mesotrophic meromictic lakes, where the denser waters contain considerable amounts of hydrogen sulfide and light penetrates to the upper part of the hydrogen sulfide zone. Masses of these bacteria often impart a pink or green color to the upper edge of the hydrogen sulfide zone.

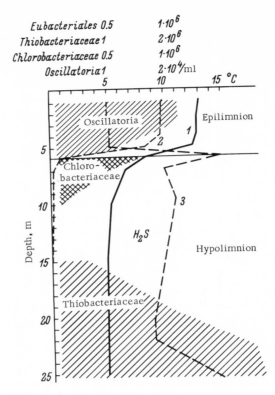

FIGURE 152. Vertical distribution of sulfur bacteria in the Plussee on October 7, 1964 (after Anagnostidis and Overbeck, 1966):

1) temperature, °C; 2) oxygen; 3) bacteria.

Such a phenomenon was first reported by Isachenko (1914) in Lake Mogil'noe on Kil'din Island. Later, it was described by other workers (Figure 100). Duggeli (1924) found masses of Chromatium at a depth of 13 m in the Swiss Lago Ritom. Jimbo (1938) cites references on the development of purple and colorless sulfur bacteria at the edge of the hydrogen sulfide zone in several Japanese lakes. Jimbo investigated this problem in three Japanese lakes — Harutori, Shigetsu, and Hamana.

Lake Harutori is 9.5 m deep and covers an area of 0.5 km². It was originally fresh, until a violent storm flooded it with sea water, raising its level by 8 m. According to Jimbo, the maximal concentration of hydrogen sulfide is 621 mg/L. The surface layers of the lake contain freshwater. Yoshimura and Hoda note the red tinge at the edge of the hydrogen sulfide zone, owing to the development of Chromatium.

Lake Shigetsu has an area of 5 km² and a depth of 31 m. Here the concentration of hydrogen sulfide attains a peak of 61 mg/L, and the boundary between the oxygen and hydrogen sulfide zones lies at a depth of 6.5—7.0 m. The author reports a distinct if slight red color of water at a depth of 7 m. A clearly distinguishable though much paler color was found at depths of 6.0, 6.5, 7.5, and 8.0 m. The water was colorless above and below these depths. The color was due to the growth of Chromatium minus and C. minutissimum.

The third of the examined lakes, Hamana, differed from the other two by the presence of spring and fall overturns. Consequently, the maximal concentration of hydrogen sulfide did not exceed 14 mg/L, and that only by the end of the summer stagnation. The water of this lake has a reddish tinge at the upper boundary of the hydrogen sulfide zone.

More detailed quantitative information on the vertical distribution of sulfur bacteria was obtained in the meromictic lakes Belovod' and Chernoe-Kucheer (see above). The observations of S. I. Kuznetsov (1942) in Lake Belovod' during the winter and summer are summarized in Table 71.

In the summer of 1937, the Chromatium layer was sharply defined and about 0.2 m thick (from 14.8 to 15.0 m). It appears that this layer was affected by the fall overturn prior to the formation of the ice cover, since it could not be detected in December. Sulfur bacteria showed a uniform distribution from December to mid-March, without a distinct peak at the boundary between the oxygen and hydrogen sulfide layers. The development of a layer rich in pigmented sulfur bacteria was probably prevented by the scarcity of light.

Observations made on July 30, 1938, similarly revealed a layer with a high density of Chromatium. The density of bacteria here reached one million cells per ml, which was much higher than the 1937 level. The water of this layer was distinctly pink. The Chromatium layer extended at a depth of 14.8 m, as in 1937, which corresponded with the limit of the pene-tration of light. Masses of sulfur bacteria were also found in the surface silt at a depth of 15 m. Here the surface film of silt was lilac colored, and microscopic examination showed the presence of Beggiatoa, Chroma-tium, and Lamprocystis.

Chromatium populations could be readily determined by means of membrane filters. Thus, A. A. Egorova (1951) observed in August 1948 large masses of Chromatium at a depth of 13.9—14.0 m, reaching a density of over one million cells per ml (Figure 153). The existence of dense populations of pigmented sulfur bacteria at the upper edge of the hydrogen sulfide zone was later confirmed by N. N. Lyalikova (1957), M. V. Ivanov (1956), Yu. I. Sorokin (1966b), etc.

TABLE 99. Vertical distribution of sulfur bacteria in Lake Chernoe-Kucheer on September 13, 1938

Depth, m	Chlorobium limicola, thousands of cells per ml	Purple sulfur bacteria		
		total density	including	
			Chromatium	Thiocystis
0	0	0	—	—
3	0.5	0	—	—
4	4,930	15.4	—	—
4.5	2,040	8.0	1.7	6.3
5.0	1,417	6.9	0.6	6.3
5.5	2,310	—	—	—
6	2,480	4.0	1.7	2.3
7	1,180	2.3		2.3
9	1,377	2.3	0.6	5.7

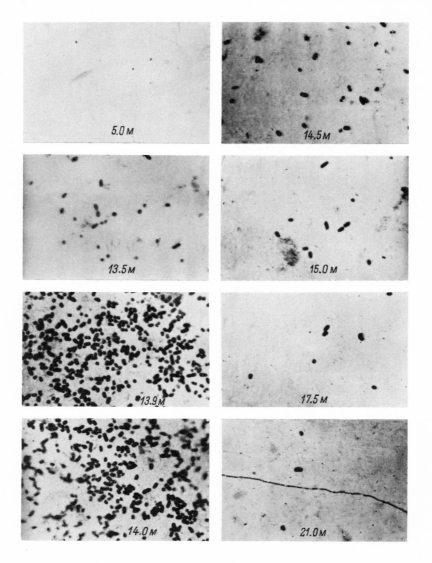

FIGURE 153. Micrographs of membrane filters, showing the vertical distribution of Chromatium in the water of Lake Belovod' in August 1948. Samples of 3 ml of water collected at different depths in the lake were passed through membrane filters 1 cm in diameter. Staining with phenolated erythrosine.

Lake Chernoe-Kucheer has water of a lower pH (pH = 6.8) and a higher concentration of hydrogen sulfide in the hypolimnion. According to Van Niel such environment favors the growth of green sulfur bacteria. Indeed, the density of Chlorobium limicola at the upper border of the hydrogen sulfide zone reached 5 million cells per ml by the end of the summer stagnation of 1938, which represents a sharp peak in comparison with the waters above and below this zone (Figure 128; Table 99). In 1967, V.M.Gorlenko (1968) found masses of Pelodictyon clathratiforme in this lake.

B. L. Isachenko (1927) has studied in detail the populations of green and other pigmented sulfur bacteria in mud lakes, where these bacteria often grow in masses owing to the rich supply of hydrogen sulfide from the silt, especially in the littoral.

Distribution of Thiobacillaceae in natural waters. This topic was largely neglected until recent years. Some of the existing evidence is summarized in Table 100. The existence of Thiobacillaceae in natural waters depends closely on ecological factors. In the water mass of lakes, the density of these bacteria reaches a peak in the upper part of the hydrogen sulfide zone of meromictic lakes or in salt lakes and limans — briefly, in water bodies where H_2S is generated. The surface layer of silt is much richer in these bacteria than the water mass. Thiobacillus thioparus is commonly found under these circumstances.

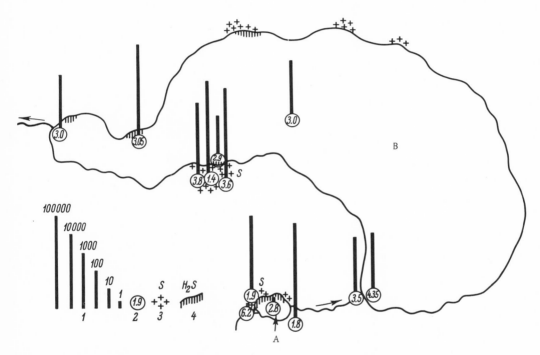

FIGURE 154. Scheme of Lakes Kipyashchee (A) and Goryachee (B) in the caldera of the Golovnin volcano on Kunashir Island:

1) density of Thiobacillus thiooxidans; 2) pH; 3) solfataras; 4) zones of H_2S oxidation.

The water of many volcanic lakes in Japan and the Kurile Islands has a very acid reaction. Two lakes of this category, Kipyashchee and Goryachee, lie in the caldera of the Golovnin volcano on Kunashir Island. A detailed study of these water bodies was published by Ivanov and Karavaiko (1966).

The small Lake Kipyashchee feeds on surface waters. However, the presence of underwater solfataras on the bottom and shores of this lake makes the water turbid with colloidal sulfur. Moreover, the water of

TABLE 100. Distribution of Thiobacillaceae in lakes of different types (number of bacteria per ml of water or gram of silt)

Type of lake	Name	T. thioparus water surface layer	T. thioparus water bottom layer	T. thioparus surface layer of silt	T. thiooxidans water surface layer	T. thiooxidans water bottom layer	T. thiooxidans surface layer of silt	Reference
Oligotrophic	Dolgoe (Latvian)	–	–	216	–	–	–	Daukshta, 1968
Mesotrophic	Punnus-Yarvi (Karelia)	–	100	2,000	–	–	–	Drabkova, 1965
Eutrophic	Shengeida (Latvia)	–	–	2,400	–	–	–	Daukshta, 1968
	Dotka (Latvia)	–	–	98,000	–	–	–	Daukshta, 1968
	Tsimlyansk Artificial Reservoir	–	–	300,000	–	–	–	Kuznetsov and Romanenko, 1966
	Volgograd Artificial Reservoir	–	–	0–10,000	–	–	–	Kudryavtsev, 1966
Meromictic	Belovod' (Vladimir Region)	0	200	1,500	–	–	–	Sokolova and Karavaiko, 1964
Salt	Caspian Sea	–	–	1,000–3,000	–	–	–	Ivanov, 1964
Volcanic	Kipyashchee (Kunashir Island)	0	0	0	1–2	0	1–2	Ivanov and Karavaiko, 1966
	Goryachee (Kunashir Island)	0	0	0	100,000	100,000	1–2	Ivanov and Karavaiko, 1966

TABLE 101. Rate of the oxidation of sulfide in the water of Lake Semoe (mg of S/L/day; after Ivanov, 1957)

Analyzed ingredient	Original water	Concentration after 1 day, mg/L — control with antiseptic agent	Concentration after 1 day, mg/L — dark jar	Concentration after 1 day, mg/L — light jar	Amount of H_2S oxidized for 1 day to S^0 and S^{6+} — chemically	Amount of H_2S oxidized for 1 day to S^0 and S^{6+} — thiobacilli	Amount of H_2S oxidized for 1 day to S^0 and S^{6+} — pigmented sulfur bacteria
H_2S	86	82.5	54.2	50.0	3.5	28.3	4.2
S^0	–	2.6	30.2	29.3	2.6	27.6	–0.9
SO_4''	–	0.9	1.7	6.9	0.9	0.7	5.2

Lake Kipyashchee is highly acid, having a pH of 2.8–3.0; it lacks dissolved oxygen and has a hydrogen sulfide content of 12.1–32.8 mg/L. The only thiobacilli found here is T. thiooxidans, at a low density. Via the Sernaya rivulet, the Kipyashchee water flows into the large Lake Goryachee (Figure 154), which has an area of about 3 km² and a maximal depth of 62.3 m (Pervol'f, 1944). The water of this lake is saturated with oxygen, except in the bottom layers, which lack this gas. The profundal waters are rich in hydrogen sulfide (Ivanov and Karavaiko, 1966). Thiobacillus thioparus is almost absent here, but the density of T. thiooxidans ranges from 1,000 to 100,000 cells per ml of water (Table 100).

After a study of the physical-chemical properties of the lake water, Ivanov and Karavaiko conclude that the acidity of Lake Kipyashchee results from the presence of fumarole gases in the water. In their view, the oxidation of hydrogen sulfide to sulfur proceeds mainly by chemical mechanisms, while T. thiooxidans is responsible for the oxidation of sulfur to sulfuric acid and causes the acid reaction of the Lake Goryachee water. According to these authors, the oxidation of sulfur in Lake Goryachee yields 7.7 tons of sulfuric acid daily. Similar factors cause the acid reaction of some Japanese lakes (Yoshimura, 1932d; Ueno, 1934; Pervol'f, 1944; Suzuki, 1961).

Little is known on the distribution of Thiobacillus denitrificans in lakes, although it appears that this bacterium can play an important role in the sulfur cycle of some lakes.

Rate of the oxidation of hydrogen sulfide by Thiobacillaceae and pigmented sulfur bacteria. Growth and photosynthesis of pigmented sulfur bacteria can take place anaerobically only in the presence of light. This process is most intensive in the littoral of sulfate lakes, where the reduction of sulfate yields large amounts of hydrogen sulfide, or in the upper part of the H_2S zone of meromictic lakes. Here the oxidation proceeds at low concentrations of sulfate in the water. By the application of radioactive sulfur compounds (S^{35}), it became possible to determine the rate of this process with bacteria as oxidizing agents (Ivanov, 1959).

The rate of the chemical and biological oxidation of sulfide was first determined in Lake Sernoe, Kuibyshev Region (M. V. Ivanov, 1957). Samples of water with added Na_2S^{35} were placed in a clear and a dark jar, in order to distinguish between the activities of thiobacilli and pigmented sulfur bacteria. A third jar containing a similar water sample together with Na_2S^{35} and an antiseptic agent served as control. This allowed a determination of the rate of the chemical oxidation of hydrogen sulfide at high concentrations of the latter. Table 101 shows the results of these experiments.

It is evident from Table 101 that only 3.5 mg of H_2S were chemically oxidized per liter of water within twenty-four hours in the conditions of the test, that is, in the presence of oxygen and at a high concentration of H_2S. Under the same circumstances, the thiobacilli oxidized 28.3 mg of H_2S to molecular sulfur only, while the pigmented sulfur bacteria produced sulfate from 4.2 mg of H_2S and from 0.9 mg of the molecular sulfur liberated by the thiobacilli, but formed little or no molecular sulfur.

The process has a different course at the upper border of the H_2S zone of the meromictic Lake Belovod'. Here the concentration of H_2S is low,

TABLE 102. Rate of the oxidation of sulfide in the water of Lake Belovod' during July 1964 (in μg of S/L/day; after Sorokin, 1966b)

Depth from which water sample was taken, m	Form of sulfur	Original	Content after 24 hours			S^{--} oxidized within 24 hours to S^0 and S^{++}		
			control with antiseptic agent	dark container	light container	chemically	by Thio-bacillaceae	by purple sulfur bacteria
11	S^{2-}	650	403	364	195	247	92	117
	S^0	—	7	7	13	7	0	7
	S/S_2O_3	—	123	104	130	123	-19	26
	S/SO_4	—	117	228	312	117	111	84
12	S^{2-}	700	540	476	426	161	64	70
	S^0	—	7	7	14	7	0	7
	S/S_2O_3	—	84	56	84	84	-28	28
	S/SO_4	—	70	140	175	70	70	35

but a constant supply of it arrives from the underlying waters. Yu. I. Sorokin (1966b) examined in detail the oxidation of hydrogen sulfide in these conditions. The rate of the chemical and biochemical oxidations of hydrogen sulfide can be calculated on the basis of his results (Table 102).

The oxidation of hydrogen sulfide at the edge of the photic zone proceeds at a slow rate owing to the low concentrations of oxygen and hydrogen sulfide (Table 102). Most of the hydrogen sulfide is oxidized by chemical reactions. In July 1964 the rate of this process at a depth of 11 m was equal to 247 μg of H_2S/L/day and according to Yu. I. Sorokin, the oxidation yielded thiosulfate and sulfate. At a depth of 12 m, the amount of H_2S oxidized daily per liter was 161 μg.

At that time, the sulfur purple bacteria had a density of 34,000 cells/ml. At a depth of 11 m, they oxidized daily 117 μg of H_2S per liter, yielding mainly sulfuric acid together with a certain amount of thiosulfate. Molecular sulfur accumulated in only slight quantities. At a depth of 12 m the oxidation of sulfide proceeded in the same direction but at a lower rate, probably because of the scarcity of light.

Thus, the rate of the oxidation of sulfide by purple sulfur bacteria depends largely on the illumination rate, the concentration of hydrogen sulfide, and the density of the bacteria. This process mainly yields sulfuric acid without appreciable amounts of molecular sulfur. Thiobacillaceae oxidized hydrogen sulfide to sulfate at a daily rate of 0.092 mg/L; within the same period, they also oxidized 0.019 mg/L of thiosulfate produced by chemical reactions. At a depth of 12 m, the process was even slower, though the proportion of the oxidation products was the same.

These early determinations of the rate of the biological oxidation of hydrogen sulfide clearly show the effect of environmental factors on the direction and rate of the process.

The Sulfur Cycle in Lakes

The processes that constitute the sulfur cycle are more evident in lake waters with a greater sulfate content. By the application of radioactive isotopes, notably S^{35}, it became possible to determine the rate of the reduction and oxidation of sulfur compounds. Only speculations could be made in this field before the introduction of the isotope method. Figure 155 shows schematically the sulfur cycle in lakes.

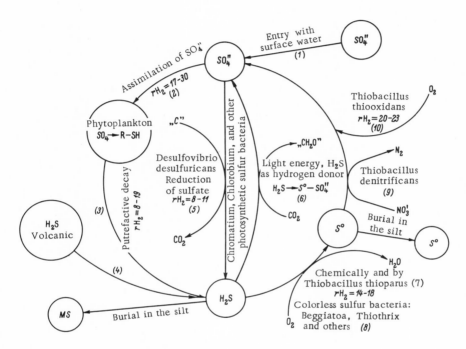

FIGURE 155. Scheme of the sulfur cycle in lakes.

Explanation in the text.

In most cases, sulfur arrives in lakes in the form of sulfate with surface or underground waters (1), though the water of some volcanic lakes receives hydrogen sulfide together with fumarole gases entering through the lake bottom (4).

The phytoplankton assimilates sulfate (2) and converts it to reduced sulfur as a protein ingredient, which escapes in the form of hydrogen sulfide during putrefaction (3). Alternatively, sulfate is reduced to sulfide by biologic agents (5). The reduction of sulfate takes place largely in the silt, which receives organic matter in the form of dead phytoplankton (Kuznetsov, 1952, 1965; Ivanov and Terebkova, 1959a, 1959b). Thus ends the reductive stage of the sulfur cycle.

The oxidation of hydrogen sulfide can proceed anaerobically and in aerobic conditions. The first step in the anaerobic oxidation of sulfide to molecular sulfur is due to the activity of purple sulfur bacteria, which require light (6).

This process is prominent in a number of Soviet lakes, including Belovod', Mogil'noe, and Chernoe-Kucheer.

In microaerophilic conditions, the oxidation of sulfide to sulfur is performed by thiobacilli (7), notably Thiobacillus thioparus, and by colorless sulfur bacteria (8). These organisms are most active at the border between the oxygen and hydrogen sulfide zones of water. The daily rate of the oxidation of hydrogen sulfide can reach 0.5 mg/L. Higher rates occur in lakes having a turbid water and an intensive reduction of sulfate in the silt. Examples are the lakes Solenoe and Sernoe, where hydrogen sulfide arrives from mineral sources (Ivanov, 1957; Ivanov and Terebkova, 1959a, 1959b).

Finally, the oxidation of molecular sulfur to sulfate can also proceed in anaerobic and aerobic conditions.

In the former case, there is a simultaneous reduction of nitrate (9). Thiobacillus denitrificans is widespread in nature. Its physiology is well known, but we possess no evidence of a simultaneous presence of appreciable amounts of hydrogen sulfate and nitrate in a natural water body. In other words, this group of organisms does not find suitable ecological conditions for a large-scale oxidation of sulfur.

Aerobic oxidation of molecular sulfur to sulfuric acid occurs at a fast rate in volcanic lakes, whose water mass obtains hydrogen sulfide from underwater fumaroles. Thus, M. V. Ivanov and G. I. Karavaiko (1964) found large quantities of Thiobacillus thiooxidans in Lake Kipyashchee and especially in Lake Goryachee on Kunashir Island. This microorganism (10) oxidizes colloidal sulfur, and the sulfuric acid formed in the process lowers the pH of the lake water to 3.5.

The Iron and Manganese Cycles in Lakes

Manganese and iron have similar properties. Both belong to the fourth period of Mendeleev's system, having the atomic numbers 25 and 26 respectively. Consequently, the compounds of these elements often occur together in nature, and the cycle of iron in lakes has much in common with that of manganese. The transformations of iron in lakes are better known, partly because the analysis of ferrous and ferric compounds is much simpler than in the case of manganese. For this reason we shall deal mainly with the iron cycle, giving supplementary data on its manganese counterpart.

Manganese and iron usually arrive in lakes from the catchment basin in an oxidized state as dissolved salts or suspensions; from the water mass, they settle in the silt. The role of microorganisms in the cycle of these elements begins with the reduction of the respective compounds to diffusible forms, mostly hydrocarbonates of iron and manganese. These compounds diffuse from the silt back to the water mass, where they undergo a secondary oxidation by specific groups of bacteria. Depending on the oxygen regime of the lake, the oxidation of ferrous and manganous compounds can take place in the surface layer of silt (oligotrophic lakes) or in the water mass (meso-trophic and eutrophic lakes).

Because of their chemical similarity, iron and manganese often occur together, the Mn/Fe ratio in eruptive rocks being usually between $\frac{1}{10}$ and $\frac{1}{100}$ (Krauskopf, 1963).

Neutral and acid solutions can contain high concentrations of ferrous (Fe^{2+}) and manganous (Mn^{2+}) ions. In alkaline conditions these ions can precipitate as hydroxides, carbonates, silicates, or sulfides. The bivalent ions of these metals can be oxidized by moderately strong oxidizing agents. Oxidation with atmospheric oxygen proceeds slowly and is more complete in an alkaline solution; at any given pH, the oxidation of iron is more rapid and complete than that of manganese. Krauskopf (1963) gives diagrams of the oxidation-reduction stability fields of different iron and manganese compounds in relation to pH and the oxidation-reduction potential of the medium. The oxidation yields free energy that can be utilized, theoretically at least, by some chemosynthetic bacteria.

The iron cycle in lakes is closely associated with the transformations of phosphorus and sulfur. Ohle (1956) explains as follows the mechanism of this process. Iron precipitates from the water mass in the form of ferric phosphate. When a reduction of sulfate begins in the silt, the hydrogen sulfide resulting from this reaction reduces the iron to a ferrous form. The latter is buried as sulfide or undergoes transformation into soluble ferrous phosphate or bicarbonate, which reenters the water mass. Thus, adequate knowledge of the iron cycle requires data on the stratification of this element during the summer and the seasonal course of its concentration.

Hydrochemical and Hydrographical Characterization of Lakes on the Basis of Their Iron and Manganese Content

Many authors have studied the summer distribution of iron in lakes all over the globe (V. D. Konshin, 1959).   Some of the most systematic observations were made by Yoshimura (1931, 1936c), who examined more than 150 Japanese lakes, and by Stangenberg (1936), who made similar analyses in 162 lakes in the Suwalki District of Poland.   Moreover, Ohle (1934) studied the relations of iron in 21 lakes in the northern part of West Germany.

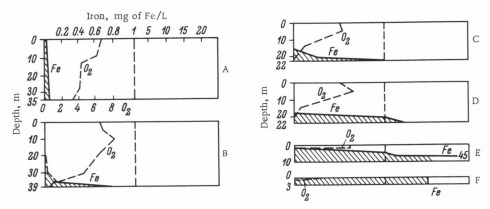

FIGURE 156. Summer stratification of iron in different types of Japanese lakes (after Yoshimura, 1937):

A) Akana-ko, an oligotrophic lake; B) Penke-ko, an oligotrophic lake; C) Koshiguchinoike, a mesotrophic lake; D) Ooike, a dystrophic lake; E) Shindenmaenuma, a eutrophic lake; F) Akanuma, an acidotrophic lake on the Bandai volcano.

It became evident from these analyses that the concentration of iron in lakes does not exceed 0.2—0.3 mg/L, except in those of the dystrophic type, while the water of oligotrophic lakes is often iron-free.   Greater concentrations of iron occur in the bottom water, especially in the absence of dissolved oxygen.

Figure 156 shows the vertical distribution of iron in different types of Japanese lakes during the summer stagnation (Yoshimura, 1936). Yoshimura exhaustively examined the seasonal dynamics of iron in the small eutrophic pond Takasuka in 1931; similar studies were made in Lake Beloe in Kosino (V. S. Ivlev, 1937) and in Lake Glubokoe (A. P. Shcherbakov, 1967a).   Striving to determine the dynamics of iron in Lake Beloe, V. S. Ivlev traced not only the transformations of this element in the water mass but also the exchange of diffusible forms of iron between the water and silt of the lake. Figure 157 shows the seasonal course of the vertical distribution of the total iron content of the water mass.

During the fall overturn in 1931, the water mass of the lake had a uniform iron content that did not exceed 0.1 mg/L.

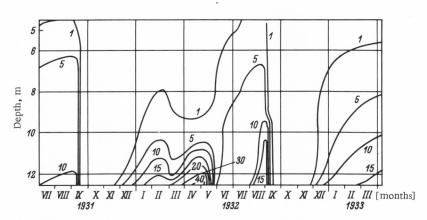

FIGURE 157. Seasonal changes in the vertical distribution of the total iron content of the water mass of Lake Beloe in Kosino (after Ivlev, 1937).

The figures on the curves indicate the concentration of iron in mg/L.

The winter stagnation ushered in a migration of iron from the bottom to the lowermost water layer. Such migration usually begins after the establishment of an oxygen minimum and a low pH in the bottom water layer. Later, the iron gradually spreads to higher water layers at a velocity that depends on the presence of suitable conditions for the existence of soluble iron. The iron content of the bottom water reached the considerable figure of 40 mg/L, during the winter of 1932. In the spring, after the thaw of the ice cover, the overturn enriched the water with oxygen and the ferrous bicarbonate was oxidized and precipitated as ferric hydroxide, thus increasing the iron content of the surface silt.

In eutrophic lakes, the summer stagnation causes a gradual impoverishment of the oxygen content of the hypolimnion, a certain lowering of the pH of the lower layers, and an increase in the concentration of dissolved iron (Figure 158).

Although the concentration of dissolved oxygen in summer is slightly lower than in winter, the distribution of this element in the hypolimnion is more uniform. Accordingly, the iron content of the lake as a whole is much greater in summer, reaching 1,000 kg in Lake Beloe (Figure 159).

During the fall, the thermocline sinks, while the iron-containing layers become richer in oxygen. Under such circumstances the iron undergoes oxidation and precipitates as hydroxides, which sink. Part of these iron compounds can be reduced to a ferrous form while still in the water mass (V. S. Ivlev, 1937). Finally, iron precipitates again from the water mass and reaches the surface silt during the fall overturn (Figures 157, 159).

The iron becomes reduced after reaching the bottom, and ferrous compounds diffuse from the sediment into the water mass. This continuous exchange of iron between bottom and water mass involves approximately

25 cm of upper silt. This follows from the distribution of iron in the silt (Figure 160).

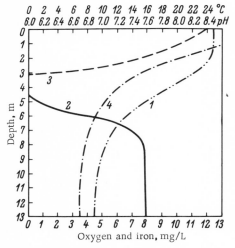

FIGURE 158. Vertical distribution of temperature (1), total iron (2), oxygen (3), and pH (4) at the end of the summer stagnation in Lake Beloe in Kosino (after Ivlev, 1937).

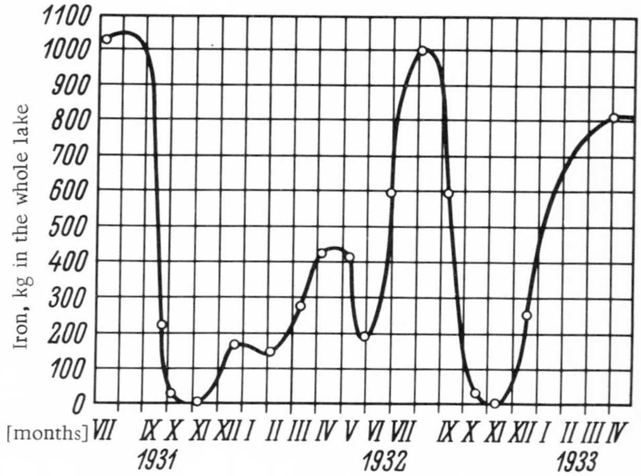

FIGURE 159. Seasonal changes of the total iron content of Lake Beloe in Kosino, kg of iron in the whole lake (after Ivlev, 1937).

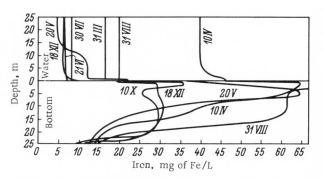

FIGURE 160. Distribution of iron in the bottom water layer and bottom solution of Lake Beloe in Kosino (after Ivlev, 1937).

As shown in Figure 160, the concentration of iron in the bottom solution decreases with depth, and at a depth of 25 cm it remains stable throughout the year. The iron in the bottom solution is in dynamic equilibrium with the iron absorbed by the bottom. This might explain the lack of seasonal regularity in the distribution of iron in the bottom solution. At any rate, the surface film of silt in eutrophic lakes prevents the penetration of oxygen and thus protects the silt mass from oxidation even during overturns, when the whole water mass becomes saturated with oxygen.

Ivlev's detailed studies of the concentration of total iron at different depths in the silt and in the overlying water proved beyond doubt that iron migrates from the bottom to the water mass during the stagnation periods and moves back to the bottom in the form of precipitate during the overturns (Table 103).

The relationship between the cycles of iron and phosphorus was thoroughly investigated by O. E. Fatchikhina (1948) in the small eutrophic Lake Chernoe (in Kosino), which has an area of about 2 hectares and an average depth of 4 m. Here the silt is rich in organic matter and undergoes a partial breakdown with the formation of lake gas.

The concentrations of total iron and ferrous and ferric compounds were determined from March 4, 1937 to September 22, 1938.

TABLE 103. Seasonal changes in the iron content (mg of Fe) of columns of water and bottom covering an area of 1 dm^2 in Lake Beloe (after Ivlev, 1937)

Date of analysis	Total iron content of column		Difference between two successive analyses	
	in the bottom	in the water	in the bottom	in the water
April 8, 1932	3,038	750	+436	−390
May 17, 1932	3,461	360	−174	+190
August 2, 1932	3,290	550	+496	−550
October 10, 1932	3,786	0	−674	+610
March 3, 1933	3,112	610		

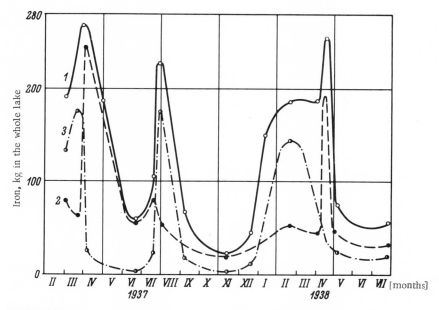

FIGURE 161. Seasonal changes in the total iron content of Lake Chernoe in Kosino, kg of iron in the whole lake (after Fatchikhina, 1948):

1) total iron; 2) trivalent iron; 3) bivalent iron.

369

O. E. Fatchikhina found that the concentration of iron in this lake reached at times 4—5 mg/L even in the surface water. At the end of the stagnation period it was 1 mg/L in the surface layers and 40 mg/L in the bottom water. The seasonal changes in the iron content of the water mass closely followed the picture observed by V. S. Ivlev (1937) in Lake Beloe.

The iron content of the bottom water reached a peak in the absence of oxygen during periods of peak concentration of inorganic phosphorus (Figure 190). Figure 161 shows the iron content of the lake as a whole. There is a peak of iron content at the end of the stagnation period, while the minima correspond with the overturns. The seasonal changes of the total phosphorus content of the water closely follow the iron curve.

The dynamics of the distribution of iron in mesotrophic lakes is essentially similar to the pattern presented by eutrophic lakes. A.P. Shcherbakov (1967a) determined the total iron content at different depths in Lake Glubokoe during a three-year period from 1950 until 1953. Figure 162 shows the results obtained in 1950—1951.

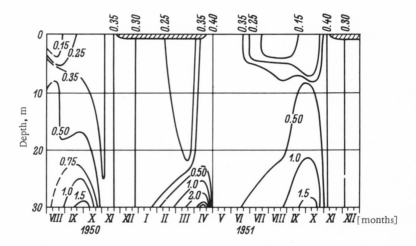

FIGURE 162. Seasonal dynamics of the total iron content of Lake Glubokoe.

The figures on the isolines show the amount of total iron, mg of Fe/L, while the shaded areas indicate the position of ice.

In summer, with the establishment of the thermal stratification and the disappearance of oxygen from the bottom water, the concentration of iron there begins to rise, reaching 1.5—3.5 mg/L as a result of the migration of this element from the bottom to the water mass. Such a phenomenon occurs also in winter, when the concentration of iron in the bottom water attains 4—14 mg/L (Fe). During the summer, iron spreads from the bottom layer as high as the thermocline, while in winter it does not rise above a depth of 20—22 m (Figure 162).

The concentration of iron rises in the bottom water during periods of stagnation; at the same time it decreases in the surface layers from 0.4 to 0.2 mg/L in winter and sometimes to zero during the summer.

The total iron content of the whole water mass of Lake Glubokoe shows two annual peaks, which coincide with the ends of the two stagnation periods. Being rather sudden (Figure 179), this rise in the total iron content of the water mass cannot be attributed entirely to diffusion from the lake profundal. It appears that bound iron in the silt passes into a free state during these periods, though evidence in support of this assumption is not yet available.

In ultraoligotrophic lakes (Figure 156, A), iron shows a perfectly uniform distribution throughout the water mass (Yoshimura, 1936). On the other hand, the water mass of most oligotrophic lakes contains only a few hundredths of a milligram of iron and manganese per liter; some lakes of this type may even lack such elements. Lake Baikal, for example, contains no iron. It appears that upon entering the water mass from the catchment basin these elements are converted into insoluble trivalent compounds that immediately precipitate in the slightly alkaline water in the form of hydroxides or phosphates. In such lakes, a microstratification of iron may develop in the bottom water only, corresponding to the fall of the oxygen content.

As Perfil'ev (1927) notes in his study of silt monoliths from Lake Segozero, ferric hydroxide is generated at all depths within the silt. He observed iron-rich streaks 0.7 mm thick interlaid with silt and white layers of quartz sand. This author assumes that the deposition of iron recurs every year, while the layers of quartz sand correspond to stormy spells, during which the surf action strongly erodes the sandy littoral of the lake.

Perfil'ev associates the microzonation of iron with secondary processes in the silt, where the iron can be converted to ferrous form, which circulates together with the silt solution. The iron precipitates again upon entering the oxidized zone and forms ochre-colored layers rich in ferric hydroxide.

There is no stratification in acidotrophic lakes, even in the presence of anaerobic conditions at the bottom (Figure 156, E). Lake Akanuma on the Bandai volcano can be taken as an example. The water of this lake is muddy, reddish green, with an iron content of up to 12.8 mg/L at the surface (Yoshimura, 1936).

Of particular interest in this respect is the meromictic Lake Shinaribetsu-ko, which has a depth of 92.5 m. This lake receives an undercurrent of salt groundwaters, because of which its deepest layers have a high density and do not participate in the circulation of water. Oxygen spreads to a depth of 90 m only; it is lacking in the bottom layer, where the concentrations of iron and manganese reach respectively 87 and 25.7 mg/L. These are the highest figures ever recorded in a freshwater lake.

Kjensmo (1967) described a number of iron-containing meromictic freshwater lakes in Norway. Thus, the bottom layer of Lake Storeaaklungen has an iron content of more than 300 mg/L (Figure 163).

The meromictic Lake Okha-Lampi on the Karelian isthmus has an area of 15.4 hectares and a maximal depth of 16 m (Kuz'menko, 1964; Dubinina and Deryugina, 1969). Here the lower waters have a high specific weight, and the circulation of water does not extend below a depth of 13 m. Oxygen is lacking in the hypolimnion; hydrogen sulfide has not been detected, and the bottom water has an iron content of 94 mg/L (Figure 164). Reduction of sulfate takes place in the silt, where all the hydrogen sulfide resulting from this process is bound as iron sulfides, and in the upper hypolimnion below the zone of iron bacteria. In the latter layer, the presence of hydrogen

sulfide could only be determined organoleptically (G. A. Dubinina and
Z. P. Deryugina, 1969).

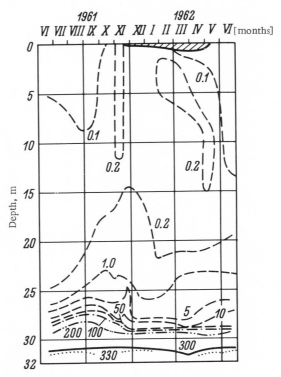

FIGURE 163. Seasonal changes in the total iron content
of the meromictic Lake Storeaaklungen in Norway.

The figures on the isolines show the iron content in mg/L;
the shaded areas indicate the period of ice cover.

The seasonal dynamics of iron and manganese in artificial reservoirs
was studied by A. V. Frantsev (1959) and M. N. Vilenkina and M.M.Sakharova
(1963). In the Ucha and Mozhaisk artificial reservoirs, the observed pattern is roughly the same as in the mesotrophic Lake Glubokoe. The concentrations of iron and manganese in the bottom layers of these reservoirs
rise to a peak during the stagnation periods (0.35—1.65 mg of Fe/L and
0.7—0.2 mg of Mn/L) and decline to a minimum during the spring and fall
overturns. A. V. Frantsev (1959) determined the manganese budget of the
Ucha Artificial Reservoir over a period of twelve years. This task was
facilitated by the regular monthly determinations of the water balance of
the artificial reservoir. During these twelve years, the artificial reservoir
received an annual average of about 38.7 tons and lost about 30 tons of manganese. The actual figures, however, varied considerably from one year to
another. Of particular interest are the data on the concentration of dissolved manganese in the water mass at the peak of the summer stratification.

With the maturation of the reservoir, its oxygen regime improved, and the quantity of dissolved manganese dropped from 235 tons in 1937 (the second year after the start of the flooding) to 7.5 tons in 1955. According to Frantsev, bacteria play a major role in the precipitation of manganese from the water mass.

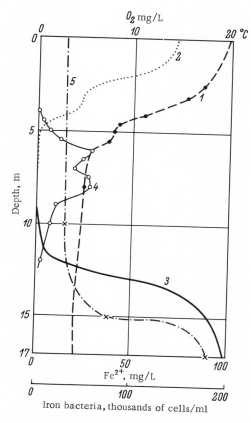

FIGURE 164. Vertical distribution of temperature (1), oxygen (2), ferrous salts (3), iron bacteria (4), and electric conductivity (5) in the meromictic Lake Okha-Lampi, Leningrad Region.

Morphology and Special Physiology of the Microorganisms that Participate in the Iron and Manganese Cycles

The reduction and oxidation of iron and manganese compounds proceed mainly in biological systems. The transformations of these compounds involve microorganisms belonging to different taxonomic groups. Some of these microorganisms selectively oxidize iron compounds, others do so with manganese compounds, while a third group can precipitate the hydroxides of iron and manganese. Before speaking of the geochemical function of these microorganisms, we shall outline their morphology and physiology.

Microorganisms that Reduce Compounds of Oxidized Iron and Manganese

The reduction of iron and manganese is closely associated with the activity of the bottom microflora as a whole, since the latter lowers the oxidation-reduction potential of its environment, especially in the silt. The state of iron depends closely on the oxidation-reduction regime of the environment. One would expect on these grounds that a lowering of the oxidation-reduction potential would readily produce ferrous compounds by purely chemical reactions.

Halvorson and Starkey (1927) showed, however, that there is no reduction of $Fe(OH)_3$ in sterile soil, a mere lowering of the oxidation-reduction potential being insufficient to reduce this compound even at pH 3.0.

Roberts (1947) isolated 265 strains capable of reducing ferric compounds in the presence of glucose; of these bacteria, only B a c. p o l y m y x a showed this ability as a specific trait. Of the bacteria isolated by Bromfield, B a c. p o l y m y x a and B a c. c i r c u l a n s were most active in reducing iron compounds.

Using Bromfield's medium with sucrose, Troshanov (1964) studied the reduction of natural iron-manganese compounds. He determined the pH, the E_h, and the concentration of oxygen in the cultures. No reduction of iron or manganese was observed in the sterile control, where the pH was 6.3 and the E_h varied from +370 to +405 mV during the fifteen days of the test. On the other hand, various strains of B a c. c i r c u l a n s reduced these compounds.

At approximately the same values of pH and E_h, strain No. 4 reduced manganese only. Strains Nos. 5 and 6 reduced both manganese and iron at the same pH, lowering the value of E_h to +150 and +200 mV. On the fifteenth day, the concentration of Mn^{++} reached 468 and 526 mg/L, and that of Fe^{++} 240 and 244 mg/L, respectively. The cultures of B a c. p o l y m y x a lowered the oxidation-reduction potential to $E_h = -300$ mV but accumulated comparatively small quantities of Mn^{++} and Fe^{++} — respectively, 226 and 7.5 mg/L. Clearly, there is no direct relationship between the oxidation-reduction potential and the rate of the reduction of manganese and iron. Bromfield (1954) believes that iron-reducing bacteria must possess a dehydrogenase system and form specific organic acids by means of which the comparatively insoluble ferric compounds enter the solution as ions or metalloorganic compounds. According to N. G. Kholodnii (1949), the reduction of iron and manganese oxides proceeds readily in the presence of some amount of hydrogen sulfide, which is frequently found in silt. In his view, the process can be expressed as follows

$$Fe_2O_3 + 3H_2S = 2FeS + 3H_2O + S;$$

$$FeS + 2H_2CO_3 = Fe(HCO_3)_2 + H_2S.$$

These reactions undoubtedly involve sulfate-reducing and spore-forming bacteria, such as B a c. c i r c u l a n s and B a c. p o l y m y x a.

Microorganisms that Precipitate Iron and Manganese Compounds from the Solution

Iron and manganese compounds precipitate mainly as hydroxides. At neutral pH, the formation of these hydroxides results not only from the direct physiologic activity of bacteria but also from their indirect influence by changing the chemistry of the environment. According to Baier (1937), organisms capable of using the energy released in the oxidation of manganous compounds can also oxidize ferrous compounds, but not all the iron bacteria can oxidize manganese compounds. This statement must be revised in view of recent evidence.

The organisms that precipitate iron and manganese from their solutions can be divided into four main groups.

To the first group belong the iron bacteria or manganese bacteria in the strict sense, that is, the microorganisms capable of utilizing the energy of the oxidation of ferrous or manganous compounds according to the equations:

$$4Fe(HCO_3)_2 + 6H_2O + O_2 \rightarrow 4Fe(OH)_3 + 4H_2CO_3 + 4CO_2 + 58,000 \text{ cal.}$$

$$4MnCO_3 + O_2 \rightarrow 2Mn_2O_3 + 2CO_2 + 76,000 \text{ cal.}$$

However, direct evidence of chemosynthesis in these bacteria is not available. This group includes Leptothrix ochracea, Gallionella, Metallogenium, Siderococcus, Caulococcus, and Ochrobium tectum.

The second group consists of heterotrophic microorganisms possessing a slime capsule that can absorb bivalent and trivalent iron or manganese compounds from the solution. The reduced forms of these elements are oxidized in the sheath or in the slime capsule, which they impregnate as hydroxides. These microorganisms do not utilize the energy liberated in the oxidation.

To this group belong several species of filamentous bacteria of the genus Cladothrix, notably C. dichotoma and C. issatchenkoi, which deposit iron, and C. discophora, which accumulates manganese compounds. Lyngbya martensiana, another member of the group, accumulates abundant quantities of iron that may even impede its normal development. Being motile, L. martensiana then glides out of its ferruginous sheath, until its slime develops a new iron coat.

The third group comprises microorganisms that can utilize the organic moiety of iron humates. One of its typical representatives is Siderocapsa treubii, which is widespread in humic waters (Hardman and Henrici, 1939). Here belong also Pedomicrobium ferrugineum and P. manganiferum (Aristovskaya, 1965). Feeding on the organic part of the humic complex, these bacteria precipitate the liberated iron on their own surfaces. In terms of bacterial biomass, the amount of iron precipitated by these bacteria is much smaller than in the autotrophic bacterium Siderococcus.

The fourth group includes some higher plants and filamentous algae, such as Conferva. During periods of intensive photosynthesis, these organisms utilize the carbon of the bicarbonates of iron, calcium, or manganese. This causes an alkalinization of the environment and a precipitation of iron and manganese as hydroxides. In some waters the process is so intensive that the whole aquatic vegetation becomes clad in a brown or ochre-colored film. Such mass precipitation of manganic compounds was observed on Elodea leaves in the Ucha Artificial Reservoir (A. V. Frantsev and S. K. Lebedeva, 1941).

Main species of iron bacteria capable of autotrophic life. S.N. Vinogradsky (1888) demonstrated that Leptothrix ochracea derives energy from the oxidation of ferrous to ferric compounds:

$$4FeCO_3 + 6H_2O + O_2 \rightarrow 4Fe(OH)_3 + 4CO_2; \quad \Delta F = -58,000 \text{ cal.}$$

He used the same method as in the case of filamentous sulfur bacteria. Several filaments of iron bacteria situated inside their ferruginous sheaths were placed in a drop of water from an iron-bearing source. The filaments with a fresh rusty tone readily lost color when washed in water saturated with CO_2. In iron-bearing water, the sheaths develop a color only in the presence of L. ochraceae cells; empty sheaths remain colorless. The organisms do not develop in the absence of ferrous compounds. On the other hand, frequent changes of water containing $Fe(HCO_3)_2$ cause a reproduction of the bacteria, whose sheaths become brown with oxidized iron. Bacterial growth stops when the ferrous compound is completely oxidized with atmospheric oxygen but resumes after the introduction of ferrous bicarbonate.

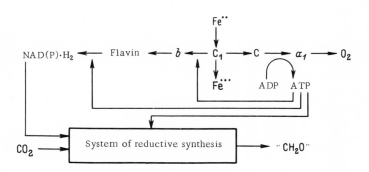

FIGURE 165. Scheme of the autotrophic assimilation of carbon dioxide in iron bacteria (after Tikhonova et al., 1967).

Vinogradsky's view of the chemoautotrophy of iron bacteria was criticize by Molisch, who used peptone media for the isolation of filamentous bacteria capable of encrusting their sheaths with iron salts. This microorganism was undoubtedly the heterotrophic L. crassa or, as Razumov (1957, 1961c) thinks, Cladothrix; at any rate, Molisch and Vinogradsky did not work with the same species. The views of Molisch exerted a major influence in this field of bacteriology, although he did not refute or even repeat Vinograd sky's experiment with a glass slide containing a Leptothrix ochracea culture, which represents the main proof of the autotrophic nature of iron bacteria.

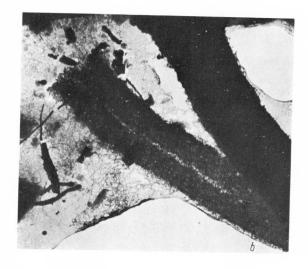

FIGURE 166. Leptothrix ochracea:

a) cells leaving their sheath (photograph by Kholodnyi);
b) structure of the sheath under the electron microscope (photograph by G.A.Dubinina).

Among the iron bacteria capable of autotrophic life are several Gallio-nella species: G. ferruginea, G. minor, G. major, and the new species G. filamenta (Balashova, 1967). Direct determinations of the ability of Gallionella to fix carbon dioxide at the expense of energy derived from the oxidation of ferrous to ferric iron were made only by Lieske (1912), who demonstrated a direct increment of bacterial carbon and found that the process has an efficiency of 8%. His work was later criticized because of insufficient proofs of the purity of the culture and also because the medium used in his experiments allowed the growth of nitrifying bacteria.

The enzymatic mechanism involved in the oxidation of iron is still unknown. At any rate, there are two conditions for the existence of autotrophic organisms (Wolfe, 1964): they must produce ATP for biosynthetic reactions and be able to lower the intracellular oxidation-reduction potential to $E_h = -0.326$ V, the level required for the conversion of DPN to the reduced form; as an alternative, an additional source of energy must be available for the reduction of DPN to DPN-H_2, which serves for the reduction of CO_2 to cell carbon. What remains to be found is the manner in which this process occurs in autotrophic bacteria where the ferrous ion is oxidized at a positive potential. One possible pathway is a reversible oxidative phosphorylation for the production of reduced dipyridine nucleotide, that is,

DPN-H_2 (N. N. Lyalikova, 1968). The synthesis of ATP is also a mystery because we do not know which stage of the enzymatic oxidation yields an amount of energy sufficient for the formation of an anhydride phosphate bond. As shown by G. V. Tikhonova (1967) and other authors working on the electron transfer in the oxidative activity of T. ferrooxidans, substrates poorer in energy cause a smaller change of the potential on the way of the electron from substrate to oxygen. In iron bacteria, the oxidation of Fe^{++} to Fe^{+++} yields only about 11,000 calories of free energy, which is barely enough for the formation of one mole of ATP. Since the chemosynthetic assimilation of CO_2 requires the presence of NAD·H_2, it follows that the ATP-producing system of iron bacteria needs much greater amounts of energy for the back transfer of electrons from the substrate (Fe^{++}) to NAD.

As shown by G. V. Tikhonova, iron bacteria indeed possess a large array of oxidative electron carriers: Thiobacillus ferrooxidans has cytochrome c, cytochrome oxidase, cytochromes c_1 and b_1, nicotinamide nucleotide and, probably, flavin and ubiquinone Q_6. In addition, iron bacteria contain a pigment whose reduced form has an absorption peak at 585 nm. Figure 165 shows the probable sequence of the electron carrier in the respiratory chain.

Experiments involving the inhibition of different stages of the oxidative system showed that the direct transfer of electrons in iron bacteria is via cytochromes c_1, c, and cytochrome oxidase, and the back transfer by means of cytochrome b and flavin.

Filamentous iron bacteria. The filamentous iron bacterium Leptothrix ochracea, is capable of some measure of autotrophic life. In nature, it occurs wherever there is an undercurrent of groundwaters containing ferrous compounds. This microorganism is responsible for the formation of a loose ferruginous sediment in pure water bodies (N.G. Kholodnyi, 1953). Under the microscope, the ochraceous sediment appears as a mass of cylindrical sheaths 2—3 μ wide and up to 1 cm long, with an inner cavity about 1 μ in diameter.

The filaments of L. ochracea swim freely in the water and never attach to a substrate. The bacteria are best observed in fresh material. For this purpose, N. G. Kholodnyi recommends that iron-bearing water containing sheaths of L. ochracea be placed in a wide open vessel. Within a few hours, a loose ferruginous sediment of young filaments of L. ochracea develops on the bottom of the resting vessel. Microscopic examination of a smear of the sediment stained with fuchsin reveals chains of stained bacteria within their sheaths, which take up little or no stain (Figure 166, a).

The filaments leave the sheaths naked; later they secrete a thin sheath that gives a distinct reaction for ferric ferrocyanide. Iron is deposited within the sheath.

Electron micrographs show that the whole sheath represents a fabric of fine fibrils (Figure 166, b). In contrast to Cladothrix, the gonidia of L. ochracea are immotile (Razumov, 1961a, 1961c).

Several species of Gallionella are widespread in nature, often as large masses of coiled, interwoven ferruginous filaments, sometimes with bean-shaped terminal cells on the stalks. This is the only classic iron bacterium of proven autotrophic habits.

Gallionella was first grown in an artificial medium by Lieske (1912). Much later, continuous cultures of it were prepared by the Perfil'ev method. Following the instructions of Van Niel, Wolfe and co-workers afterward tried to cultivate this genus in a medium containing FeS as source of energy. They obtained optimal growths in tubes whose lower part contained 0.75% agar-agar with freshly precipitated FeS, this mixture being overlaid with a mineral medium through which CO_2 was bubbled. Gallionella developed here at some depth, that is, in a zone with optimal concentrations of FeS and O_2. At room temperature, visible growth was obtained within a few days, the tube walls becoming lined with fine whitish clouds of Gallionella filaments.

Pure cultures of Gallionella in artificial media were obtained only recently. The earliest studies of the morphology and developmental cycle of this genus were made by B. V. Perfil'ev (1926), later in cooperation with D. R. Gabe (Perfil'ev and Gabe, 1961, 1964). As long ago as 1922, Perfil'ev found that the Gallionella filaments contain sparsely set cell units shaped as coccobacteria and established the existence of a motile unicellular stage. Contrary to the view of N. G. Kholodnyi, he was convinced by 1927 that the main element of Gallionella is its filaments and rodlike cells, whose transverse division yields filaments and zoogloeae. The terminal cells, regarded by N. G. Kholodnyi as the only live element of Gallionella, apparently develop only during the transition to the motile stage.

Gallionella can be observed in square capillary canals during the formation of a secondary microzonal profile in silt samples from some iron-ore lakes (B. V. Perfil'ev and D. R. Gabe, 1964). By the use of light and electron microscopy, a number of authors have established the following developmental stages of Gallionella (B. V. Perfil'ev and D.R. Gabe, 1964; van Iterson, 1958; G. A. Zavarzin, 1965; Wolfe, 1964).

1. Filamentous stage (Figure 167, a). Careful removal of the iron from the Gallionella stems leaves fine interwoven filaments that are clearly visible in the electron microscope. According to van Iterson, these filaments have a protein structure.

2. Buds. Buds or cells (Figure 167, b) can develop terminally or at any other site on the filaments. The fibers connected with these cells retain their spiral configuration. This speaks against the view of Kholodnyi, who maintains that the fibers are excreted by the cell and coil up owing to the activity of the latter.

3. Cell stage. Some Gallionella filaments bear vibrioid terminal cells that have a corrugated surface in certain species. The cells of the motile stage bear a polar flagellum. On the concave side lies a nipple, which is connected with the fibers of the stalk of the immotile stage (Figure 167, c).

However, Hanert (1968) did not find bean-shaped cells in a pure culture of Gallionella growing in a mineral medium. He observed instead that the stalks bear separate buds comparable to those reported by G.A. Zavarzin and van Iterson in cultures (Figure 167, b), and by Dubinina and Deryugina (1969) in natural material from Lake Okha-Lampi.

4. Membraneous sacs. Van Iterson (1958) and G. A. Zavarzin (1965) found that Gallionella cultures form large membraneous sacs several microns in diameter. The sacs are joined with one another by means of filaments. Their physiologic function remains obscure (Figure 167, d).

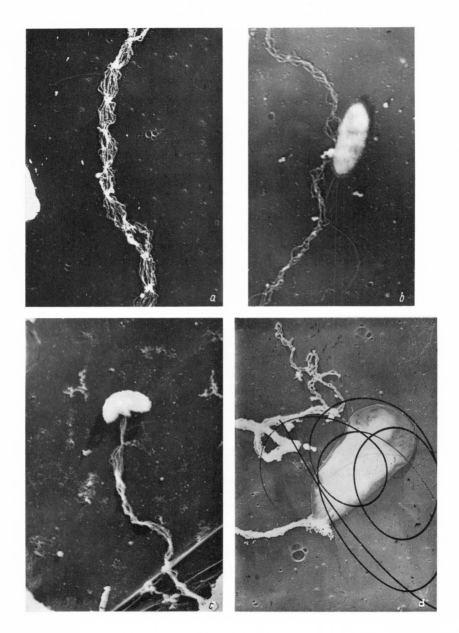

FIGURE 167. Different stages of the developmental cycle of Gallionella (micrographs by Zavarzin and Balashova):

a) filamentous form; b) formation of normal cells on a well-differentiated filament; c) growth of a filament from a nipple on the inner side of a Gallionella cell; d) membraneous sacs.

The observations of G. A. Zavarzin (1965), confirmed by V. V. Balashova (1968) and other workers, show that the filaments of Gallionella consist of protein fibers, which are semitransparent to electrons, and bear deposits of iron hydroxide, which is opaque to electrons. The development of cells and membraneous sacs on the Gallionella stems and the growth of deposits of iron hydroxides on the delicate protein fibers prove that the stalk fibers constitute the living organism, as Perfil'ev noted in 1926. Since iron is not deposited around the Gallionella cells of the motile stage, Perfil'ev regards the latter as heterotrophic.

Gallionella forms buds and membraneous sacs in addition to live elements shaped as delicate fibers about 0.01 micron thick. Moreover, it grows poorly in synthetic media. All these properties suggest that Gallionella should perhaps be removed from Bacteriales and placed in another order, namely Mycoplasmatales. In an attempt to solve this problem, V. V. Balashova (1968) observed that Gallionella cultures in Wolfe's medium are invariably accompanied by bacterial satellites. Removal of these satellites stopped the growth of Gallionella. Inoculation of an ultrafiltrate from an enrichment culture into medium with horse serum resulted in growth of Mycoplasma. A pure culture of the latter could be obtained by inoculation on a solid medium. Finally, transfer of material from this culture to Wolfe's medium with a small amount of horse serum led to a typical growth of Gallionella.

It appears that the bacterial contaminants of Gallionella cultures serve as hosts in which one of the developmental stages of this genus parasitizes.

Whether Gallionella is capable of chemosynthesis cannot be easily answered, since the necessary experiments must be made with labeled carbon dioxide ($C^{14}O_2$), whose radioactivity can hardly be determined in the negligible biomass of this bacterium; moreover, the iron hydroxide that precipitates from the solution shows a considerable self-absorption.

In a study of the capacity of Gallionella for autotrophic life, Hanert (1968) obtained a culture that grew satisfactorily in a strictly mineral medium containing iron sulfide. The absence of contaminant microorganisms was demonstrated by control inoculations of peptone-containing media. Experiments with $Na_2C^{14}O_3$ proved the existence of CO_2 fixation and consequently the ability of Gallionella for autotrophic life.

Toxothrix ferruginea was described by Molisch (1910). This species deposits iron hydroxide in the form of bundles containing numerous thin fibers. Some filaments bear buds.

N. G. Kholodnyi assumed that the ferruginous fibers lie around a separate bacterial filament and that the cells glide away from the bundle in adverse conditions. On these grounds he placed this organism in the genus Leptothrix and named it L. trichogenes. The careful studies of V. V. Balashova (1968) showed, however, that the fine ferruginous fibers are independent organisms that can be cultured outside any filamentous bacteria (Figure 168). The Toxothrix filaments form buds and closely resemble Gallionella filamenta. This organism appears to be similarly capable of autotrophic life.

Dubinina and Deryugina (1969) found large quantities of T. ferruginea at the edge of the oxygen zone, 6.5 m deep in Lake Okha-Lampi (Figure 164). As shown in the electron micrograph (Figure 168), the whole bundle consists of fine ferruginous threads.

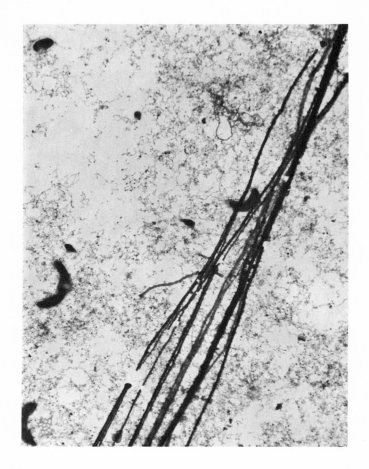

FIGURE 168. Toxothrix ferruginea. The thin fibers are covered with
iron. Material from Lake Okha-Lampi (electron micrograph by T.A.Dubinina).

Unicellular colonial iron bacteria. It appears that a number of
colonial forms can utilize the energy liberated in the oxidation of ferrous
compounds, though direct evidence in support of this assumption is still lacking. To this category belong S i d e r o c o c c u s   l i m o n i t i c u s,   O c h r o-
b i u m   t e c t u m,   B l a s t o c a u l i s   k l j a s m i e n s i s, and some B l a s t o-
b a c t e r species.

S i d e r o c o c c u s   l i m o n i t i c u s was described by Dorff (1935). It
grows poorly in synthetic media and is therefore little known. According
to electron micrographs (G. A. Zavarzin, 1965), the colonies of this species
represent aggregates of small cocci that measure 0.2–0.5 microns and
bear fine filiform processes. S i d e r o c o c c u s   l i m o n i t i c u s probably
reproduces by budding and comprises a motile stage. Its colonies, composed of 6–15 coccoid cells, are immersed in abundant deposits of iron oxide

Ochrobium tectum Perf. (Figure 169) produces iron in the zoogloea stage. Its motile stage sometimes develops in large numbers in lakes during the summer, creating a yellow color in the water. The cells are oval or cylindrical, with rounded ends, up to 5μ long and 1.5—3μ wide. They are enclosed in a gelatinous capsule where the oxidation of ferrous compounds takes place. There is a flagellum on one side of the cell.

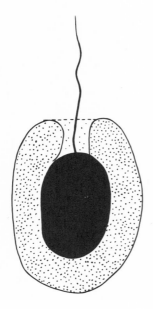

FIGURE 169. Scheme of the cell morphology of Ochrobium tectum (after Perfil'ev).

Blastocaulis planctonica Razumov (Figure 170) has spherical cells 0.3—0.5μ in diameter, resting at the ends of thin stalks that constitute a spherical colony with up to fifty cells. The stalks are composed of iron oxides and do not stain with erythrosine. The presence of an inner protoplasmic filament has not been demonstrated. This species was found in lakes and artificial reservoirs; during some periods of the year it develops in masses, reaching 6% of the total bacterial count.

G. A. Sokolova (1959) found in the plankton of Lake Glubokoe a colonial organism that appears to be capable of autotrophic life. In the center of the colony lies an irregular mass of iron hydroxide measuring from 1 to 11μ. On one side of this deposit is situated an aggregate of spherical, slightly elongate cells 1—1.5μ long. Some of these cells lie directly on the ferruginous deposit; others are situated at some distance from it, and the nature of their relationship to the iron hydroxide could not be determined under the light microscope. The cells reproduce by lengthwise division and budding (Figure 171). All these signs are reminiscent of the genus Pasteuria. This organism was also found in the Gorki Artificial Reservoir (by E. P. Rozanova).

Biogenic oxidation of manganous compounds. B. V. Perfil'ev and D. R. Gabe (1961, 1964) studied in square capillaries the development and microscopic structure of several organisms that participate in the formation of iron-manganese concretions and appear to be capable of autotrophic

life. To this group belong Metallogenium personatum, Kusnezovia polymorpha, Caulococcus manganifer, Siderococcus
limoniticus, and other species.

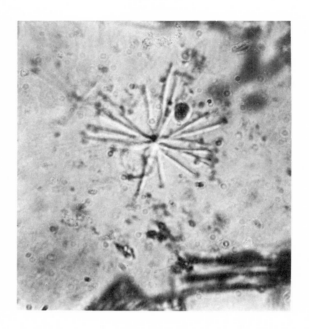

FIGURE 170. Blastocaulis planctonica (from a micrograph
by A.S. Razumov).

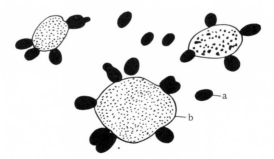

FIGURE 171. Scheme of the structure of the coenobia
of Pasteuria (after G.A. Sokolova-Dubinina, 1959):

a) cells; b) ferric hydroxide.

Metallogenium personatum is taxonomically related to
Gallionella. It represents a polymorphic organism that deposits

manganese and some amounts of iron on its exterior. After a study of Metallogenium growths in capillary preparations with a subsequent removal of the manganese oxides by dissolution in oxalic acid, Perfil'ev concluded that the various microcolonies of this species consist of small coccoid cells resting on thin filaments.

B. V. Perfil'ev and D. R. Gabe placed Metallogenium in the genus Hyphomicrobium on the basis of its morphology and developmental cycle, notably the presence of separate cells on thin filaments.

Metallogenium personatum has not yet been cultured in an artificial medium. However, G. A. Zavarzin (1961b, 1964a) obtained a similar organism in agar media with manganese acetate or in liquid ones containing starch and manganese carbonate. He named this bacterium M. symbioticum, because it grows only in symbiosis with molds or other organisms.

Electron micrographs show that the vegetative body of Metallogenium symbioticum consists of thin filaments that measure about 0.01μ across and form buds resting on short stalks (Figure 172). In a growing culture, these filaments depart from a single center, while the microcolony assumes the shape of a web. The stalked buds split open and give rise to a freely swimming stage. This happens synchronously, creating turbidity in the culture. The freely swimming stage represents a coccoid cell 0.5μ in diameter (Perfil'ev and Gabe, 1961). After settling or while still suspended in the medium, these cells begin to develop fine filaments measuring only $10-20 m\mu$ in diameter. Obviously, such thin filaments cannot possess a cell wall. They produce new cocci that begin to bud in various directions, forming lobate colonies clad in manganese oxides.

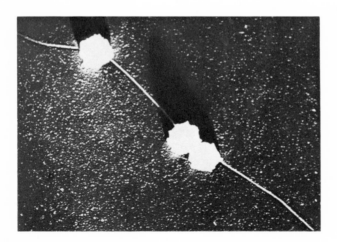

FIGURE 172. Metallogenium symbioticum. Filament with grown buds (electron micrograph by G. A. Zavarzin).

B. V. Perfil'ev distinguishes between three stages in the formation of the microcolony in parallel with the growth of the motile flagellated zoogonidium: trichosphere, dense zoogloea, and loose zoogloea.

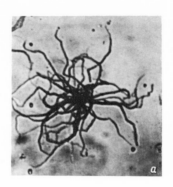

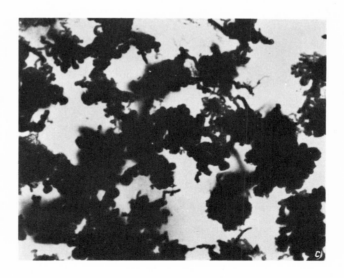

FIGURE 173. Stages in the development of a colony of Metallogenium personatum (micrographs by B.V. Perfil'ev):

a) trichospherical stage; b) radially lobate stage; 3) rounded-tuberose stage.

The outgrowths of the trichospherical colony (Figure 173, a) thicken with manganese oxide deposits and form a radially lobate microcolony (Figure 173, b). Later, the fusion of lobes creates rounded tuberose colonies (Figure 173, c). In the absence of manganese, the only stage is the symbiotic one, analogous to the buds.

The presence of growth in forms that lack a cell wall and the requirement for an imperfect fungus in the medium raise the question as to whether Metallogenium belongs to the order Mycoplasmatales. G. A. Dubinina (1969) approached this problem in the following manner.

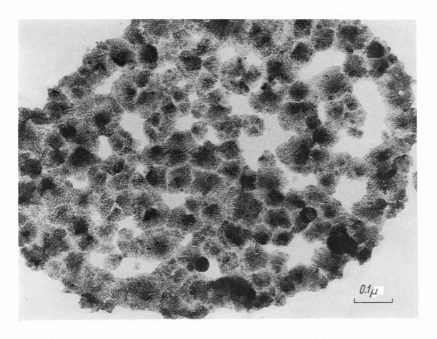

FIGURE 174. Metallogenium. Colonylike growth in a medium for mycoplasmas. Each cell breaks down to a mass of minute bodies that pass through an asbestos filter.

A nutrient medium for mycoplasmas containing 0.5% horse serum was inoculated with material from a culture of Metallogenium symbioticum growing together with a mold. Typical mycoplasmatic growth was obtained. It is known that mycoplasmas produce coccoid growth forms 5—10 mμ in diameter, which pass through asbestos filters. Accordingly, Dubinina filtered part of the liquid culture through an asbestos filter and inoculated the filtrate in a solid medium with horse serum. The result was typical mycoplasmatic colonies (Figure 174). Material from this culture was transferred in a liquid medium with manganese carbonate and horse serum. Here developed a trichospherical culture of Metallogenium with deposits of manganic compounds around fine hyphalike cell outgrowths.

Figure 175 shows the deposition of manganese oxides on the thin mycoplasmatic filaments, which corresponds to the typical growth of the trichospherical stage of Metallogenium. Typical mycoplasmatic growth was
obtained again after a back transfer to a medium with horse serum.

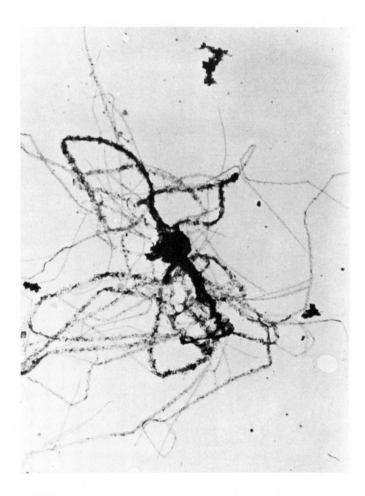

FIGURE 175. Metallogenium. Three-hour culture in a medium with
manganese carbonate — trichospherical stage. The inoculum was a filtrate
of a mycoplasmatic growth stage that passed through an asbestos filter (electron
micrograph by G.A. Dubinina, ×12,000).

G. A. Dubinina showed further why Metallogenium requires the
presence of fungal or bacterial contaminants. All the species of the order
Mycoplasmatales pass through a stage of intracellular parasitism.
According to G. A. Dubinina, the fungus serves as host of one of the developmental stages of Metallogenium.

Thus, in the view of G. A. Dubinina, Metallogenium should be assigned to the order Mycoplasmatales.

We conclude, therefore, that Gallionella, the closely related genus Toxothrix (synonym: Leptothrix trichogenes), and Metallogenium belong to the order Mycoplasmatales.

Kusnezovia polymorpha forms immotile coenobia shaped as microscopic goblets with toothed edges and attached to the substrate by means of a stalk. The variety of colonial forms depends on the aggregation of small coccoid cells and large budding ones, held by thin filaments. The growing coenobium of this species deposits manganese and iron oxides around itself, as B. V. Perfil'ev and D. R. Gabe (1961) demonstrated in peloscopic capillaries.

Caulococcus manganifer is likewise a polymorphic organism that oxidizes mainly manganese compounds. Its colony consists of a mass of minute coccoid cells held together by fine filaments; it is covered with abundant deposits of manganese oxides. The microcolonies reproduce by means of solitary motile coccoid cells. The iron-manganese deposits of this species have a typical reticulocostate structure. The taxonomic position of these organisms is still obscure.

Heterotrophic and Mixotrophic Organisms that Deposit Iron and Manganese Hydroxides

Filamentous iron bacteria. Some twenty years after S. N. Vinogradsky (1888) demonstrated the ability of Leptothrix ochracea to utilize the energy of the oxidation of ferrous compounds, this topic was reexamined by Molisch (1910); later studies were published by V. O. Kalinenko (1940, 1945, 1946), Hohnl (1955), Mulder and van Veen (1963), and others.

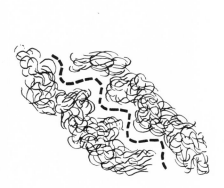

FIGURE 176. Spirothrix pseudovacuolata (scheme of the growth after a photograph by G. A. Sokolova).

FIGURE 177. Cladothrix dichotoma, syn. Leptothrix crassa (after Kholodnyi, 1926).

In contrast to S. N. Vinogradsky, these authors used organic media for the isolation of filamentous iron bacteria, whose sheaths are encrusted with iron hydroxides. Not surprisingly, they obtained heterotrophic organisms from the very beginning. The confusion about the ability of the filamentous iron bacteria to live as autotrophic organisms was further aggravated by the unsatisfactory state of the taxonomy of the group.

A. S. Razumov (1957, 1961a, 1961b, 1961c) introduced some order in this field. After a thorough study of the morphology and ecology of Sphaerotilus, Cladothrix, and Leptothrix, he concluded that some of their species are transitional forms whose generic position is a matter of controversy among the authors. For example, Molisch worked with Cladothrix but was convinced that the species in question was Leptothrix ochracea, that is, the bacterium of Vinogradsky, while Kalinenko (1945, 1946) described forms of Cladothrix as new Leptothrix species, namely L. issatchenkoii and L. mosquensis.

TABLE 104. Cultural characteristics of the main species of filamentous iron bacteria (after Razumov, 1957, 1961a, 1961b, 1961c)

Commonest species of genus	Nitrogen sources	Characteristics of species
Genus Sphaerotilus		
Sphaerotilus natans, Cladothrix dichotoma. Polysaprobic.	Only organic nitrogen compounds; NH_4^+ and NO_3^- not assimilated. Reduce little or no nitrate.	Capable of attachment; sparse branching; gonidia motile. Do not deposit iron or slime.
Genus Cladothrix		
Leptothrix crassa, L. discophora, Spirothrix pseudovacuolata. Found in mesosaprobic waters.	Organic and inorganic nitrogen compounds. Reduce nitrate.	Capable of attachment and branching; gonidia motile. Deposit iron in the sheaths of the filaments when grown in media containing organic or inorganic iron. In such cases, the empty sheaths are indistinguishable from those of Leptothrix ochracea. Grows satisfactorily in different organic media.
Genus Leptothrix		
Leptothrix ochraceae. Oligosaprobic.	Mineral and organic compounds	Autotrophic in water containing a very low concentration of organic matter. Filaments not attached; gonidia immotile; sheaths impregnated with iron or manganese hydroxides. Myxotrophic.

Note: The generic names are after Razumov, and those in the subheadings are from the accepted nomenclature.

A. S. Razumov proposes the following criteria for the distinction between species of Sphaerotilus, Cladothrix, and Leptothrix: (1) the relationship to nitrogen sources, (2) the saprobic category of the water body in which the bacterium is found, (3) the nature of the deposition of iron in the sheaths of the filaments, and (4) the motility of the gonidia. A brief characterization of the bacteria on the basis of these criteria appears in Table 104.

According to A. S. Razumov, the main species that can live as heterotrophs and deposit iron in their sheaths are S p i r o t h r i x p s e u d o - v a c u o l a t a, L e p t o t h r i x c r a s s a, and L. s i d e r o p u s.

S p i r o t h r i x p s e u d o v a c u o l a t a (Figure 176) forms spiral filaments up to 250μ long, with very thick sheaths where the amount of iron deposits varies from negligible to abundant. In lakes, this species can develop in the oxygen-free zone (Sokolova, 1959).

L e p t o t h r i x c r a s s a (Figure 177) should be placed in the genus C l a d o t h r i x (syn. C l a d o t h r i x d i c h o t o m a). Here the ferruginous sheaths are much shorter than in L e p t o t h r i x o c h r a c e a, but they vary considerably in thickness and adhere to the substrate. Basally up to 15μ long, they taper toward the other end and consist of a granular substance. Branched forms are common. Reproduction is by motile cells — zoospores.

L e p t o t h r i x d i s c o p h o r a Dorff (1935). According to Razumov (1961a), this bacterium belongs to the genus C l a d o t h r i x. Filamentous unbranched bacterium whose lower end is attached to the substrate by means of a wide disk encrusted with iron or manganese hydroxides. Iron or manganese not deposited in the sheath proper. The filaments are capable of a vibratory movement. Reproduction by motile gonidia.

C r e n o t h r i x p o l i s p o r a Cohn is a firmly attached filamentous bacterium that reproduces by means of motile gonidia. The sheath is thin, initially colorless, later brownish with iron deposits. These bacteria can multiply in masses in water pipes, which they may fill completely together with other iron bacteria and in the presence of iron bicarbonate.

L i e s k e e l l a b i f i d a Perf. forms double spiral jointed filaments composed of rods and performing a continuous gliding movement. The filaments are covered with iron hydroxide. The taxonomic position of this species remains obscure (Perfil'ev and Gabe, 1961).

Unicellular iron bacteria. S i d e r o c a p s a m a j o r Mol. is a mass of cocci that measure $0.7-1.8\mu$ in diameter. The zoogloea, which consists of cocci, is usually surrounded by a rusty film of iron hydroxide. The form and size of the ferruginous deposits do not depend on the dimensions of the zoogloea. Kholodnyi questions the position of the genus S i d e r o c a p s a among the iron bacteria.

S i d e r o c a p s a c o r o n a t a was described by Redinger (1931) as a planktonic form that occurs in many lakes. Redinger established definitely that the genus S i d e r o c a p s a belongs to the iron bacteria.

S i d e r o m o n a s c o n f e r v a r u m Chol. represents an accumulation of coccobacilli situated on filamentous algae and shaped as a gelatinous mass encrusted with iron hydroxide.

Heterotrophic and mixotrophic bacteria that oxidize manganese compounds. In his study of the oxidation of manganous compounds, Beijerinck (1922) isolated an organism that he named B a c. m a n g a n i c u s. Bromfield and Skerman (1950) and Bromfield (1956) repeated this work and confirmed the ability of bacteria to oxidize manganous compounds in symbiotic cultures containing corynebacteria and chromobacteria. Finally, G. A. Zavarzin (1962) isolated two species related to P s e u d o m o n a s e i s e n b e r g i i and

P. rathonis. When grown together, these bacteria oxidized manganous compounds in a medium of leached-out agar or in a siliceous gel with added yeast hydrolysate at a concentration not exceeding 1:10,000. Colonies growing in such conditions became surrounded with a brown ring of oxidized manganese compounds. The presence of yeast hydrolysate at a concentration of less than 1:40,000 was necessary; the addition of various organic compounds inhibited the oxidation process.

Although these organisms were not studied further, their ability to grow on meat peptone agar and the inhibitory effect of organic compounds on the oxidation of manganous carbonate speak of a mixotrophic nature.

Microorganisms that Utilize the Organic Component of Iron Humates

By the use of epiphyte glass slides, Hardman and Henrici (1939) obtained an organism that showed all the signs of Siderocapsa. The ferruginous capsule surrounding the colony of this microorganism was often the only sediment of iron on the glass. These authors note that the bacterium in question shows several transitional forms between Siderocapsa treubii and S. major. Consequently, they unite these two species into one, S. treubii.

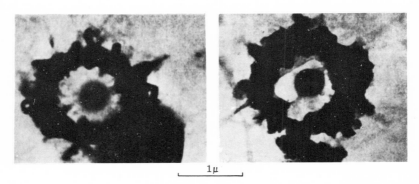

FIGURE 178. Siderocapsa annulata. A slime capsule is visible between the cell and the iron deposit (electron micrograph by Kalbe et al., 1965).

Siderocapsa annulata is related morphologically and physiologically to S. treubii (Figure 178). This planktonic bacterium was described by Kalbe, Keil, and Theile (1965). The coenobium consists of a single cell, 0.2 by 0.5μ, surrounded by an orange-yellow ferruginous ring that accumulates as a result of the utilization of humic acids from the iron humates. One of the daughter cells leaves the ferruginous capsule, whose diameter ranges from 1.2 to 1.9μ. This species attains a density of 30,000 cells per ml in Kummerow Lake (German Democratic Republic). According to Kalbe and co-workers (Kalbe, Keil, and Theile, 1965), S. annulata resembles S. treubii in being able to grow in hard waters where the iron can be retained in the form of humates.

T. V. Aristovskaya (1961) described the new species Pedomicrobium ferrugineum and P. manganiferum, which can utilize the organic component of fulvic acids and at the same time precipitate iron and manganese from their complexes with humates. These species are widespread in soil; it can be assumed that they are also common in lakes with humic waters, like Siderocapsa treubii.

Pedomicrobium Arist. forms round or oval cells 0.2 to 2.0μ long, connected by thin branched filaments. It stains irregularly. Reproduction is mainly by budding. One cell produces from one to four filaments, each with a terminal bud that develops into a daughter cell. The latter give rise to new filaments with daughter cells. As T. V. Aristovskaya notes, reproduction can also take place by division of cells.

On these grounds, G. A. Zavarzin (1961) places the genus Pedomicrobium Arist. in the family Hyphomicrobiaceae, namely in the group of budding bacteria.

Hirsch (1968) points out that budding bacteria which deposit iron are widespread in fresh and marine waters. The bacterium isolated by this author has the growth characteristics of Pedomicrobium. This microorganism can grow in iron-free media containing methylamine as source of organic matter. In the presence of an iron wire, the filaments and hyphae develop sheaths of iron hydroxide. This bacterium also grows satisfactorily in Wolfe's mineral medium (1958) with iron sulfide at a lower concentration of oxygen. According to Hirsch (1968), the ability of Pedomicrobium sp. for autotrophic life is still an open question because of insufficient evidence. At any rate, this organism is a mixotroph. It remains to be established whether it can utilize humic acids as the only source of organic matter.

Tyler and Marshall (1967) isolated several cultures of budding bacteria of the family Hyphomicrobiales from manganese deposits in water pipes and from different freshwater bodies in Tasmania. They note the considerable pleomorphism of this microbial group. For example, the variation of Hyphomicrobium and Pedomicrobium in pure culture and in nature goes beyond the characteristics of the different species. Tyler and Marshall believe, therefore, that Pedomicrobium cannot be regarded as an independent species.

Distribution of Iron Bacteria in Lakes

Various methods have been employed for the detection of iron bacteria in lakes: counting of the bacteria in the net plankton, analysis of the sediment on membrane filters, and examination of overgrowth glasses.

Ochrobium tectum often grows to large numbers in eutrophic lakes just before the spring overturn. Examples are Lake Chernoe in Kosino and the Ivan'kovo Artificial Reservoir (Kuznetsov, 1952), some Swedish lakes (Dorff, 1935), and a number of lakes near Lunz, Austria (Ruttner, 1962).

Masses of Leptothrix ochracea and L. crassa developed on glass slides submerged at the lower boundary of the oxygen-saturated waters

of the Toksovo eutrophic lakes during the summer stagnation
(A. G. Salimovskaya-Rodina, 1936).

Collini (1939) reports the presence of iron bacteria in the water of twelve oligotrophic, siderotrophic, and dystrophic lakes in southwestern Sweden. These lakes contain iron sediments. Leptothrix discophora, L. ochracea, and Ochrobium tectum occurred in surface samples of net plankton from nearly all the lakes, while the ferruginous sediments contained Gallionella ferruginea, Leptothrix ochracea, and L. trichogenes.

Other widespread unicellular iron bacteria are the Siderocapsa species, isolated from water by Molisch in 1909. N. G. Kholodnyi questioned the place of these microorganisms among the mixotrophic iron bacteria; he assumed that they develop in places where iron is deposited by factors unrelated to their own activity. Naumann (1928) isolated another species, Siderocapsa monoica, and Redinger (1931) described S. coronata as a planktonic organism occurring in various lakes. These findings confirmed the position of Siderocapsa among the iron bacteria.

Hardman and Henrici (1939) examined about two thousand overgrowth glasses from twelve lakes and two rivers. They found that Siderocapsa treubii occurs in rivers and running lakes with hard, alkaline water but is absent from stagnant lakes with soft, acid, or neutral water. In lakes with a thermocline, S. treubii was found in the epilimnion at an iron content of 0.03 mg/L but was absent from the hypolimnion, which lacked oxygen but had an iron content of 0.35 mg/L. Hardman and Henrici (1939) regard the pH of the environment as the main ecologic factor for S. treubii. In an alkaline medium, iron can remain in solution only in the form of complex compounds with fulvic acids. Therefore, the presence of iron deposits around the S. treubii colonies can be explained in only one way, namely, that this bacterium utilizes the fulvic acid of the metallo-organic complex, leaving iron hydroxide as a by-product around the colony.

Thus, heterotrophic and mixotrophic iron bacteria are widespread in lakes. The biologic precipitation of iron hydroxide appears to be a continuous process that assumes greater proportions during overturns or at the edge of the oxygen zone in deep eutrophic lakes. However, the oxidation of ferrous compounds can also proceed along purely chemical routes. This follows from the rapid and complete migration of iron from the water mass to the silt during the spring and fall overturns. The seasonal changes in the density and specific composition of iron bacteria were studied by A. S. Razumov (1962) and G. A. Sokolova (1959, 1961).

The distribution of Blastocaulis planctonica in the Klyazma Artificial Reservoir was examined quantitatively during different seasons of the year (A. S. Razumov, 1962). The density of this bacterium attained a peak of almost 80,000 cells per ml in July and August, which corresponded to about 4.6% of the total bacterial population as determined by direct count.

The seasonal changes of the distribution of different species of iron bacteria were thoroughly analyzed in the mesotrophic Lake Glubokoe (Moscow Region), where A. P. Shcherbakov (1967a) made chemical analyses and took microbiologic samples, which were examined by G. A. Sokolova.

Using the volume scale prepared by S. D. Muraveisky (1934) for Lake Glubokoe, G.A. Sokolova (1959, 1961) compared the seasonal changes of the total iron content and the population of iron bacteria in the whole water mass of the lake.

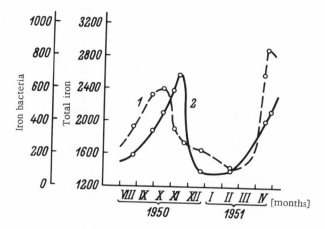

FIGURE 179. Seasonal changes of the total iron content and the number of iron bacteria in Lake Glubokoe, Moscow Region (after G.A. Sokolova):

1) total iron, kg in the whole lake; 2) total number of iron bacteria in the whole lake, 10^{15} organisms.

TABLE 105. Density (thousands of cells per ml) and percentage of iron bacteria in Lake Glubokoe (after Sokolova, 1961)

Depth, m	Aug.24, 1950		Sept.27, 1950		Nov.3, 1950		Dec.23, 1950		Feb.15, 1951		April 16, 1951	
	total density	percentage of iron bacteria	total density	percentage of iron bacteria	total density	percentage of iron bacteria	total density	percentage of iron bacteria	total density	percentage of iron bacteria	total density	percentage of iron bacteria
0	1,460	0.5	1,040	0.98	900	4.5	1,650	1.1	340	1.3	1,400	3.7
5	1,440	1.2	1,040	3.4	1,660	5.2	1,460	0.23	970	1.8	—	—
10	980	1.1	680	0.3	1,450	8.7	1,060	3	940	1.5	1,620	7
15	750	5	640	12	1,170	13.0	1,300	1.1	890	1.4	—	—
20	2,000	1.2	890	16	960	9	1,110	2.3	770	2	920	3.6
25	1,340	8	380	56	1,450	5	1,310	2.1	760	7	—	—
30	3,630	6.5	950	43	1,950	9	1,890	5.5	3,060	1.9	1,500	20
Average		3.4		18.8		7.8		2.2		2.4		4.9

After the spring overturn of 1950 (Figure 179), the lake water did not contain more than 1,600 kg of iron. This quantity increased to 2,450 kg during the summer stagnation and fell to 1,700 kg in the second half of October at the time of the fall overturn, which was characterized by a mass growth of iron bacteria. The iron content remained low throughout the winter and rose sharply in March owing to the disappearance of oxygen from the bottom water. Just before the spring overturn, the lake contained 2,800 kg of iron. The lowering of the iron content of the water mass during the spring overturn of 1951 was again accompanied by a sharp rise in the density of iron bacteria, which precipitated the soluble forms of iron.

Working with membrane filters, G. A. Sokolova determined not only the total number of bacteria but also the density and specific composition of iron bacteria.

As shown in Table 105, iron bacteria account for about 10% of the total bacterial count in Lake Glubokoe. This proportion, however, reached 55% at a depth of 25—30 m during the fall overturn in 1950.

G. A. Sokolova (1959) identified eleven species of iron bacteria, whose seasonal distribution is shown in Figure 180.

Spirothrix pseudovacuolata was constantly present in the plankton. At the lake bottom it grew in the form of threads up to 250μ long, with thick ferruginous sheaths. Largely confined to the oxygen-free zone, this species attained a peak density during overturns, when it was found throughout the water mass of the lake.

Gallionella ferruginea, another common form, did not occur in the oxygen-free zone, in contrast to Spirothrix pseudovacuolata.

Metallogenium personatum was absent from the epilimnion in February 1950; at that time, its density in the lower 15-m layer was 340,000 coenobia per ml.

Siderocapsa coronata developed in large numbers during periods of overturn, when the water became richer in oxygen. S. treubii, which mineralizes humates, appeared during rain periods, when large quantities of iron humates reached the lake from the neighboring swamps.

The work of G. A. Sokolova demonstrated the important function of iron bacteria in the iron cycle of mesotrophic lakes. Such processes as the mineralization of iron humates, the oxidation of ferrous compounds, and the precipitation of the oxidized products are due largely to the activity of certain species of iron bacteria. The circulation of iron is repeated twice a year, and only a small fraction of this element is buried in the form of sulfid

The work of G. A. Sokolova demonstrated that dense populations of iron bacteria precipitate iron from the solution and identified the bacterial species involved in this process.

Metallogenium shows a peculiar distribution pattern in the meromictic Lake Gek-Gel' (Yu. I. Sorokin, 1968).

This lake is about 70 m deep. The circulation of its water does not extend below a depth of 20 m. During the summer of 1964, the thermocline lay at a depth of 10—12 m in a zone of a metalimnial maximum of oxygen. The water contained oxygen to a depth of 24 m to the upper boundary of the denser deep water, which contained 1.1 mg of hydrogen sulfide per liter

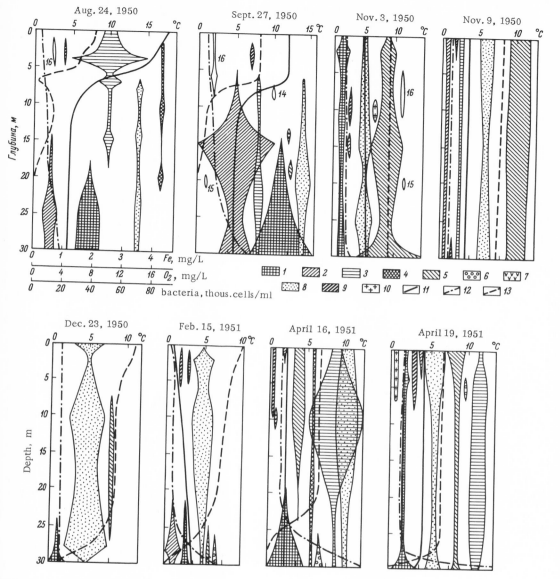

FIGURE 180. Distribution of iron bacteria in Lake Glubokoe (after G.A. Sokolova):

1) Spirothrix pseudovacuolata; 2) Metallogenium personatum; 3) Ochrobium tectum;
4) Siderocapsa treubii; 5) S. coronata; 6) Leptothrix ochracea; 7) L. crassa; 8) Gallionella ferruginea; 9) Blastocaulis planctonica; 10) a new organism of the genus Pasteuria;
11) temperature, °C; 12) total iron, mg/L; 13) oxygen, mg/L.

(Figure 181). Metallogenium reached a density of 15,000 coenobia
per ml in the contact zone between the oxygen and hydrogen sulfide layers;
this lowered the oxidation-reduction potential to $rH_2 = 16$, or $E_h = +70$ mV.

As Sorokin points out, Lake Gek-Gel' receives the waters of a brook, which contain up to 5 mg of manganese per liter. The abundance of Metallogenium is undoubtedly due to this supply of manganese salts.

Role of Microorganisms in the Formation of Iron and Manganese Lake Ores

In the USSR, iron ore lakes lie in the vicinity of outcrops of Precambrian rocks of the Baltic Crystalline Shield (L. L. Rossolimo, 1964; Fedorova, 1964a, 1964b). All these lakes belong to the oligotrophic type; at any rate, considerable quantities of dissolved oxygen are present throughout the year in the bottom water of these lakes near the iron ore deposits, and the oxidation-reduction potential of the surface silt approximates $rH_2 = 30$. This stabilizes the iron in the silt and prevents the migration of reduced iron into the water mass.

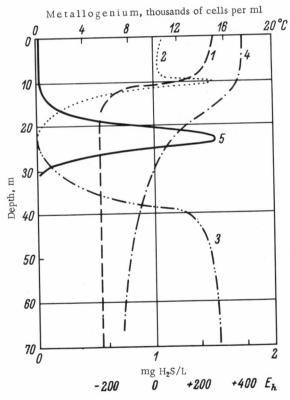

FIGURE 181. Distribution of Metallogenium personatum in Lake Gek-Gel' (after Sorokin):

1) temperature, °C; 2) oxygen; 3) hydrogen sulfide; 4) E_h; 5) Metallogenium.

The manner in which iron enters the silt may vary from one lake to another. In lakes with colored water, part of the iron supply arrives in the form of humates, whose mineralization enriches the bottom with iron precipitate. Another route supplies ferrous compounds with groundwaters and leads to a deposition of iron (N. I. Semenovich, 1958). Finally, iron and manganese compounds also enter into lakes in the form of fine suspensions together with flood waters from the neighboring slopes and settle in the deepest and quietest parts of the bottom (L. L. Rossolimo, 1964). There can be no other explanation of the formation of ore fields in the deep waters of lakes in the Kola Peninsula.

N. I. Semenovich (1958) examined the factors that determine the accumulation of iron-manganese ore in Lake Punnus-Yarvi, situated in the central part of the Karelian isthmus. The annual course of the vertical distribution of iron compounds in the water of this lake and the associated processes of coagulation and precipitation were later studied by E. A. Stravinskaya (1966), who found a uniform distribution of iron throughout the water mass during the ice-free period, with higher concentrations in the bottom water during the brief periods of summer stratification (Figure 182). The latter fact reflects a diffusion of iron from the sediment to the bottom water. The circulation of water brings the iron to higher layers, where part of it undergoes oxidation, precipitates, and falls to the bottom, while another part travels with bottom currents to the ore zone and joins the lake ore. In winter, iron-bearing water traverses the lake beneath the ice cover without mixing with its water mass (owing to the difference of temperature) and flows on to Lake Kirka-Yarvi.

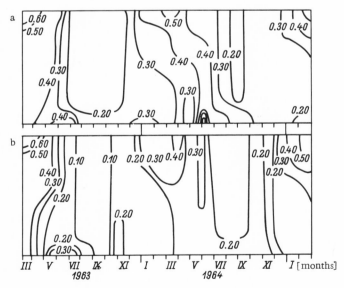

FIGURE 182. Seasonal changes in the concentration of iron in the water of Lake Punnus-Yarvi (after Stravinskaya):

a) total iron; b) soluble forms of iron. The figures on the isolines show the concentration of iron, mg/L.

Iron and manganese lake ores are manifestations of ore formation. Since the formation of lake ore is a recent process, iron ore lakes provide excellent possibilities for the study of the genesis of iron and manganese concretions. The latter contain up to 80% iron and manganese oxides. Their size ranges from fractions of a millimeter (powder ore) to spheres a few centimeters in diameter, or flat bodies (plate ore) (Figure 183).

FIGURE 183. Manganese concretions from Lake Punnus-Yarvi (reduced by six times).

B. V. Perfil'ev and D. R. Gabe (1964) note that the literature dealing with the role of microorganisms in the formation of these concretions gives no clear idea of the course of the biogenic processes. The works published on this topic contain many contradictions and do not discuss the geochemical conditions of ore formation. To this category belong the publications of V. S. Butkevich (1928), V. O. Kalinenko (1946, 1949, 1952), N. G. Kholodnyi (1953), Gryaznova (1964), Bonatti and Nayudi (1965), Manheim (1965), Nauman (1922), and Molisch (1910).

According to B. V. Perfil'ev and D. R. Gabe, the inaccuracies and contradictions in the current concepts of the role of iron bacteria in the formation of iron-manganese deposits stem mainly from the fact that standard microbiological procedures are unsuitable for a study of the distribution and specific composition of the organisms that take part in the ore formation. Indeed, these microorganisms do not grow in standard media and can be detected with great difficulty under the microscope because of the masses of iron and manganese hydroxides they produce.

This problem can be solved by the use of square capillary microscopy (B. V. Perfil'ev and D. R. Gabe, 1952, 1959, 1961, 1964). By inserting capillary tubes with plane-parallel walls into silt samples from different lakes, these authors were able to observe the live microbial flora of natural iron-manganese deposits at the very beginning of the reproduction of the microbial population during the formation of a secondary diagenetic profile in the

400

silt. Their numerous studies of the microbial population of silt showed that many microbes grow within a narrow zone of silt because of their requirement for a specific oxidation-reduction potential. Dense populations of such bacteria often deposit yellow or black streaks of iron hydroxides or manganese oxides respectively.

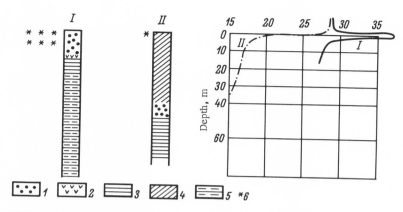

FIGURE 184. Microzonal distribution of microorganisms that reduce and oxidize iron and manganese compounds in the silts of Lake Punnus-Yarvi, in relation to the oxidation-reduction potential of the silt rH_2 (after G.A. Dubinina):

I) ore field; II) maximal depth of lake; 1) ore; 2) sand; 3) clay; 4) silt; 5) banded clay; 6) presence of Metallogenium and manganese-oxidizing bacteria.

When the physical-chemical conditions in the microzones become unfavorable, these organisms produce motile forms that migrate along the glass capillary to a site with optimal conditions for growth. B. V. Perfil'ev demonstrated in this manner that the following bacteria take part in the formation of lake ore: Metallogenium personatum Perf., Kusnezovia polymorpha Perf., and Caulococcus manganifer Perf.— and Siderococcus limoniticus Dorff. in the case of iron ore.

Microorganisms participate in two stages of the formation of lake ore: (1) reduction of oxidized iron and manganese compounds, involving a conversion to a diffusible stage; (2) secondary oxidation, which yields a precipitate in the form of lake ore. The first stage of this process will be discussed below.

Distribution of Microorganisms that Reduce Iron and Manganese Compounds in Silt

The reduction of iron and manganese compounds is due mainly to the activity of Bac. circulans, Bac. polymyxa, and sulfate-reducing bacteria. G. A. Sokolova-Dubinina and Z. P. Deryugina (1967) examined the distribution of these species in Lake Punnus-Yarvi and other lakes in the Karelian isthmus. Monoliths of silt samples with inclusions of oxidized and reduced iron and manganese compounds were taken from the 0—1, 1—3, 3—5, and 10—15 cm microzones; also tested were washings from ore concretions.

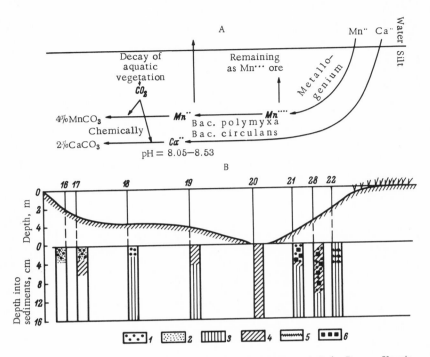

FIGURE 185. (A) Scheme of the formation of rhodochrosite in Lake Punnus-Yarvi; (B) lithological characteristics of silt from Punnus-Ioki Bay:

1) ore; 2) sand; 3) black silt; 4) gray silt; 5) peaty silt; 6) $MnCO_3$.

Analysis of the different strata showed that the bacteria that reduce iron and manganese compounds occur mainly in the 0—10-cm layer of silt. Such bacteria were also found inside the ore concretions and in sandstone, where the oxidation-reduction potential was $rH_2 = 37$ owing to the presence of higher oxides of manganese. The number of manganese-reducing bacteria ranged from 100 to 1,000 per gram of silt or ml of washings. Figure 184 shows the distribution of these bacteria in lake silt within and outside the ore bed.

Sulfate-reducing bacteria play an important role in the reduction of iron and manganese compounds. Their density attains 100 cells per gram of silt. Like Bac. polymyxa and Bac. circulans, these bacteria appear to be inhabitants of organic aggregates in microzones of silt and ore concretions. Silts from the ore bed and from the middle part of the lake invariably contain streaks and microzones of hydrotroilite (Figure 184) which has a very low oxidation-reduction potential. The reduction of manganese oxides requires the participation of specific bacteria (D. R. Gabe et al., 1964; E. P. Troshanov, 1964). This was confirmed later by direct analysis (G. A. Dubinina and Z. P. Deryugina, 1967). In the profundal part of the lake, reduced manganese compounds diffuse from the silt to the water. The concentration of bivalent manganese attains 1.4 mg/L in the bottom layer of the lake profundal. From here, water currents carry these compounds to the shallow zone, where they undergo oxidation to lake iron ore.

According to G. A. Dubinina and Z. P. Deryugina (1969), ore and silt from various parts of the lake contain small quantities of calcium and manganese carbonates. The concentration of manganese carbonate can be as high as 2—4% in the coarser fractions of lake ore. Rhodochrosite (manganese carbonate) is confined to a small area of the lake bottom. This can be explained as follows. At the site of the rhodochrosite beds accumulate remnants of higher vegetation, which create favorable conditions for the growth of manganese-reducing bacteria, namely B a c . c i r c u l a n s and B a c . p o l y - m y x a, while the carbon dioxide liberated during the decay of the organic matter causes the precipitation of the bivalent manganese as rhodochrosite. In favor of this hypothesis is the low solubility of manganese carbonate — 3—11 mg/L.

To sum up, the high oxidation-reduction potential of the silt rules out any chemical reduction of the oxidized manganese compounds. This fact, combined with the physiology of manganese-reducing bacteria, leads to the conclusion that the rhodochrosite deposits are of biological origin. Figure 185 shows the scheme of the formation of rhodochrosite in Lake Punnus-Yarvi.

Role of Microorganisms in the Formation of Iron-Manganese Concretions

In order to understand the origin of lake iron ore concretions, it is necessary (1) to examine the conditions of abiogenic precipitation of iron and manganese compounds from the solution; (2) to determine whether the necessary conditions for the biogenic process are available; and (3) to confirm the formation of concretions in the laboratory.

Numerous measurements of the oxidation-reduction potential of silt from the depths of a lake have shown that iron-manganese ores have a high oxidation-reduction potential, $rH_2 = 28 - 37$; near the silt border the concretions become fine and silted-up, and the silt has an $rH_2 = 16 - 24$. The deep water silt lacks ore concretions; here the oxidation-reduction potential is $rH_2 = 14 - 21$. In hydrotroilite microzones it is as low as 6—8.

E. I. Sokolova (1961) regards the formation of manganese ore in Lake Punnus-Yarvi as a strictly physical-chemical process. In her view, the high oxidation-reduction potential and the neutral reaction of the ore zone cause the sedimentation of manganese in the form of psilomelane. According to L. P. Listova (1961) and Krauskopf (1963), bivalent manganese is highly stable under such circumstances, namely at $rH_2 = 25$ and pH 6—7, and cannot be expected to undergo chemical oxidation at the concentration at which it occurs in the silt solution of Lake Punnus-Yarvi (10 mg/L). It follows that a chemogenic formation of manganese concretions in the lake cannot occur.

The flora involved in the oxidation of manganese was studied in samples of bottom monoliths from different parts of Lake Punnus-Yarvi and other lakes in the Karelian isthmus. The examinations were made by inoculating silt and washings from manganese concretions into bacteriologic media and by microscopic analysis.

In a study of the distribution of manganese-oxidizing organisms, G. A. Deryugina (1967) found that Metallogenium occurs constantly in all samples from the ore bed and from the profundal silts of Lake Punnus-Yarvi. In the central part of the lake, however, Metallogenium is confined to the surface layer of silt, which it probably reaches by sedimenting from the water mass. This bacterium can be easily recognized under the microscope, since its growth on separate sand grains from the zone of partly cemented sand forms brown lobate spots, such as in the square capillaries (Perfil'ev and Gabe, 1961).

The ore-forming microorganisms develop in microaerophilic conditions (Perfil'ev and Gabe, 1961). Direct examinations of the silt profile show not only the bacteria but also the presence of reduced iron and manganese compounds and the existence of suitable conditions for the development of these bacteria.

Finally, a few words on the biogenic formation of the concretions in laboratory conditions. G. A. Dubinina and Z. D. Deryugina (1969) examined in the laboratory the formation of microconcretions in silt samples from Lake Punnus-Yarvi. Silt monoliths kept for several months at a temperature of 8°C developed compact spherical dark-brown concretions up to 1 mm in diameter. Inoculation of this material into bacteriologic media yielded cultures of Metallogenium. No growth of this bacterium could be obtained by control inoculations of concretion-free parts of the same sample. This proves the biogenic nature of the concretions. Microscopical examination of thin sections of these concretions revealed the presence of radially lobate colonies of Metallogenium.

Some authors assume that the formation of manganese ore results from a catalytic oxidation of manganese carbonate. To test this hypothesis, G. A. Dubinina (1969) transferred material from an enrichment culture of Metallogenium into an inorganic medium containing manganese carbonate and 0.1% starch. The experiment was performed in a shaker. The control consisted of the same medium with pieces of sterile manganese ore as catalyst. As it turned out, oxidation of manganese and formation of concretions took place in the presence of the bacteria but were absent in the control, despite the presence of the catalyst.

All these facts speak clearly in favor of the biogenic formation of lake ore. The following scheme shows the formation of manganese ore in Lake Punnus-Yarvi.

Scheme of the Biogenic Formation of Manganese Lake Ore

G. A. Dubinina and Z. P. Deryugina propose the following scheme for the formation of manganese ore (Figure 186). Reduced manganese compounds arrive in the lake via the tributaries in a dissolved form at a concentration of 0.1—1 mg/L, while the oxides come mainly as suspensions and colloids with the surface waters. Owing to dilution in the lake water, the concentration of manganese drops to 0.01 mg/L. The reduced manganese compounds are oxidized by Metallogenium in the water mass, and the oxides formed by this process settle on the bottom together with the suspensions and colloids. In the silt, Bac. circulans and Bac. polymyxa reduce these compounds, and reduced manganese compounds begin to diffuse into the water, reaching a concentration of 1.4 mg/L in the bottom water. The lake is drained via a shallow bay. Here the oxidation-reduction potential of the silt is high enough to allow a biogenic oxidation of the manganese compounds carried by the draining current. This process leads to iron-manganese lake ore. Even in these conditions, however, Bac. circulans and Desulfovibrio desulfuricans perform a microzonal reduction of manganese compounds to rhodochrosite within the concretions. The above scheme of the formation of manganese lake ore is based on a comparative study of the manganese cycle in lakes of different trophic categories but of similar climate, all being situated in the Karelian isthmus. The biogenic formation of manganese ore took place in the presence of a steady inflow of this element from the catchment basin and in constant oxidative conditions in the surface layer of silt. This stability of the oxidative regime was due to the adequate aeration of the littoral zone and the absence of an intensive bacterial reduction of manganese.

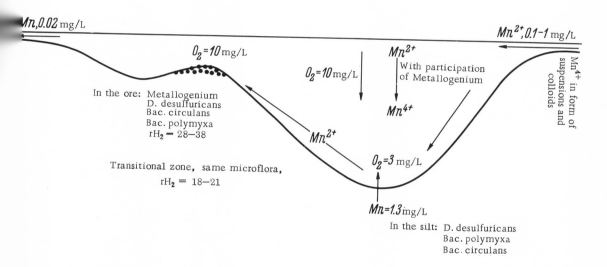

FIGURE 186. Scheme of the formation of lake ore (after G.A. Dubinina and Z.P. Deryugina).

Scheme of the Cycles of Iron and Manganese in Lakes

The cycles of iron and manganese in eutrophic lakes are characterized by the fact that the salts of these metals move comparatively fast from the silt to the water mass during periods of stagnation. In oligotrophic lakes, on the other hand, the surface silt accumulates iron and manganese, which do not take part in further transformations.

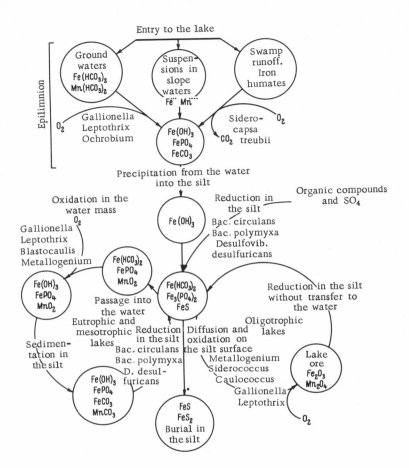

FIGURE 187. Scheme of the iron cycle in lakes.

Explanation in the text.

Thus, all types of lakes behave in a uniform manner with respect to the early stages of the iron cycle, namely inflow into the lake, sedimentation, and reduction in the silt. They differ, however, in the fate of the reduced compounds and of those formed by a secondary oxidation. Figure 187 shows schematically the transformations of iron in lakes.

Iron arrives in the lake as soluble ferrous compounds or humates, though surface waters from the slopes of the lake also bring suspensions of oxidized iron. Siderocapsa treubii destroys the iron humates, while the reduced forms of iron and manganese are oxidized by Blastocaulis planctonica, Metallogenium personatum, Gallionella ferruginea, Ochrobium tectum, and other bacteria before they reach the silt.

In the silt, Desulfovibrio desulfuricans, Bac. circulans, Bac. polymyxa, and some other microorganisms cause the reduction of iron and manganese compounds. Part of the iron and manganese is buried in the silt, while another part is converted to ferrous and manganous phosphates and hydrocarbonates, which ionize and diffuse toward the silt surface.

In eutrophic lakes, these compounds in equilibrium with their ion dissociation diffuse from the silt to the bottom water and accumulate in the oxygen-free zone by the end of the stagnation period. With the start of water circulation, they spread throughout the water mass of the lake and undergo a rapid oxidation by the above-mentioned iron bacteria and oxygen depending on pH. The resulting phosphates, hydroxides, or carbonates settle again on the bottom. Thus ends the cycle of iron and manganese in eutrophic or mesotrophic lakes.

In oligotrophic lakes, iron and manganese undergo similar transformations up to the stage of precipitation and reduction inside the silt. Then the hydrocarbonates of these metals diffuse toward the silt surface; upon reaching the oxygen-rich water of the lake, they are oxidized by the respective bacteria and oxygen and form microzones of high concentrations of oxidized iron and manganese compounds. The latter become subjected to repeated reduction by such bacteria as Bac. circulans, Bac. polymyxa, and Desulfovibrio desulfuricans, while fresh terrigenic sediments settle over the microzones. Thus reduced, the iron and manganese become ionized and diffuse to the silt surface, to be oxidized there by Metallogenium personatum, Caulococcus manganifera, and Siderococcus limoniticus.

The formation of a ferruginous microzone or iron-manganese lake ore on the silt surface depends on the supply of iron and manganese to the lake, the organic content of the silt, and the oxidation-reduction potential of the sediment.

The Phosphorus Cycle in Lakes

Phosphorus participates in a variety of mineral and organic compounds found in the water, silt, plankton, and microorganisms of the lake. It ranks second (after nitrogen) in the list of nutrient requirements of plants and microorganisms. The physiologic role of phosphorus lies mainly in the formation of energy-rich compounds that store and supply energy in the metabolism of the cell.

Microorganisms can bring about a number of transformations of phosphorus compounds. More important among these processes are the following: (1) increase of the solubility of inorganic phosphorus compounds; (2) mineralization of organic compounds and formation of orthophosphate; (3) transformation of the assimilable inorganic phosphate anion into organic phosphorus as a protoplasmic ingredient, that is, immobilization of phosphorus; (4) reduction of orthophosphate to hydrogen phosphide.

Hydrochemical and Hydrographical Characteristics of the Distribution of Phosphorus in Lakes

Composition of Organic Phosphorus Compounds

In lakes, organic phosphorus originates mainly from dead vegetation and plankton, which contain from 0.05 to 0.5% of this element. Plants possess a variety of phosphorus compounds, such as phytin, phospholipids, nucleic acids, nucleoproteins, phosphorylated sugars, coenzymes, etc. Cell vacuoles may contain phosphorus in the form of orthophosphate.

While the assimilation of nitrogen and sulfur involves reduction to amino- or sulfhydryl groups, the valence of inorganic phosphorus remains unchanged as this element in the form of phosphate enters the protoplasm and becomes an ingredient of phytin, phospholypids, or nucleic acids.

Phytin is the calcium magnesium salt of phytic acid, which represents inositolhexaphosphoric acid:

Phytic acid

In phospholipids, phosphorus is combined with fats. This type of compound includes the phosphatides, where phosphate participates in an ester linkage with the nitrogenous base. Lecithin, for example, consists of glycerol, fatty acids, phosphate, and choline:

```
H2—C—O—R
    |
H—C—O—R
    |        O
    |        ‖
H2—C—O—P—O—CH2—CH2—N—(CH3)3
         |                    +
         O
         |        R — fatty acid
              Lecithin-type compounds
```

Nucleoproteins are compounds of proteins with nucleic acids. The latter contain a number of purine and pyrimidine bases, pentose, and phosphate. The following formulas show the units that constitute the RNA and DNA molecules:

```
 N=C—NH2                      Pentose sugar
 |    |                   ┌────────O────────┐
H—C   C—N                 |                 |
 ‖    ‖    >CH—CH—CHOH—CH—CH—CH2OH
 N—C—N                    |
 |                        O
Purine                    |
base                   HO—P—OH
                          ‖
                          O

              RNA
```

```
 O=C—N—H
   |   |          Pentose sugar
H3C—C  C=O    ┌────────O────────┐        OH
   ‖    |     |                 |         |
H—C—N───CH—CH2—CHOH—CH—CH2—O—P=O
Pyrimidine                              |
base                                    OH
              DNA
```

A large proportion of the phosphorus of bacterial cells (from $\frac{1}{3}$ to $\frac{1}{2}$) is bound in ribonucleic acid (RNA). Further quantities (from 15 to 25% of the total phosphorus content) appear in the form of acid-soluble compounds, namely, ortho- and metaphosphates, phosphorylated sugars, some coenzymes, and adenosine phosphates. Phospholipids and DNA rarely account for more than 10% each. There is no reliable evidence of the presence of phytin in microbial cells.

Composition of Inorganic Phosphorus Compounds

The total phosphorus content of lake silts can reach 1.75% P_2O_5 of the dry ash weight. Here belong the above-mentioned organic phosphorus compounds, but iron and calcium phosphates can also be present in considerable quantities. The solubility of $Ca_3(PO_4)_2$ depends on the pH, while that of iron phosphates varies also with the form of the oxide. Ferrous phosphate dissolves readily; in the absence of oxygen from the hypolimnion, it diffuses rapidly from the surface silt to the water.

TABLE 106. Percentage of different phosphorus compounds in the surface water layer of different types of lakes (after Rigler, 1964)

Lake	Hardness of water, mg of CaCO$_3$/L	Color, degrees on platinum-cobalt scale	pH	Total phosphorus, µg/L	Distribution of total phosphorus (percent)		
					inorganic	organic dissolved	seston
Grenadier	232	12	8.7	133	4.8	12.5	82.7
Heard · · · ·	136	23	8.4	44	4.8	27.8	64.7
Teapot · · ·	92	42	7.7	33	5.0	29.6	65.2
Mary · · · · ·	176	11	8.5	27	6.8	25.0	68.2
Eos · · · · · ·	27	162	6.5	18	4.8	28.1	67.1
Costello · ·	25	30	6.7	12	7.2	28.8	64.0
Opeongo · ·	23	20	7.2	7	5.5	31.7	62.8
Lake of Two Rivers · · ·	17	24	6.8	7	5.3	28.9	61.8
Find · · · · · ·	28	6	6.9	5	7.8	30.0	62.2

Rigler (1964) has published comparative data on the concentrations of inorganic and organic phosphorus compounds in nine lakes of different types. This group included hard-water lakes in the Toronto area and soft-water lakes in the Algonquin Provincial Park. The pH of water was 7.7—8.7 in the hard-water lakes and 6.7—7.3 in the acid ones. The water of Lake Eos was the most strongly colored (162° on the platinum-cobalt scale), while that of Lake Find was least colored (6° on the color scale). The concentration of total phosphorus ranged from 133 µg/L in Lake Grenadier to 5 µg/L in Lake Find. No direct relationship could be found between the color, the hardness, and the concentration of different forms of phosphorus. Table 106 shows the average distribution of the different phosphorus fractions during the summer.

Vertical Distribution of Inorganic Phosphorus during the Summer Stagnation in Lakes of Different Types

Ohle (1962) examined the distribution of phosphorus in a number of Holstein lakes of different trophic categories. His data appear in Figure 188 Figure 117 shows the distribution of phosphorus-bound nitrogen.

Small quantities of ammonium salts and phosphates accumulate in the hypolimnion of the Schöhsee by the end of the summer stagnation, the proportion of these two components being close to that found in the precipitating plankton. A sharp deficit of oxygen developed in the metalimnion of this lake, but the bottom layers still contained traces of oxygen. In addition, there was a slight increase of the phosphate content of the bottom water. In the much deeper Schleinsee, the concentration of oxygen dropped below 1 mg/L in the bottom layer only and formed a minimum in the metalimnion. Nitrate was totally exhausted in the epilimnion, but considerable amounts of it remained in the middle hypolimnion. The neglig ible accumulation of phosphate in the depth indicates that phosphate was bound with iron, whose diffusion from the silt to the water was prevented by the presence of oxygen at the zone of contact between water and silt.

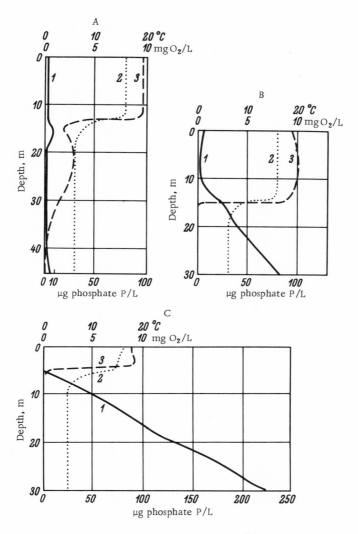

FIGURE 188. Vertical distribution of temperature (2), oxygen (3), and mineral phosphorus (1) in Holstein lakes:

A) Schleinsee, a mesotrophic lake; B) Schöhsee, a mesotrophic lake; C) Plussee, a eutrophic lake.

The relations of oxygen and phosphate are quite different in the eutrophic lake Plussee. Here the metalimnion and hypolimnion lacked oxygen owing to the abundance of phytoplankton and the decomposition of the latter in the deep waters. Considerable amounts of phosphates were present in the anaerobic zone of this lake. The intensive ammonification that took place in the hypolimnion from the bottom to a depth of 15 m and higher led to the accumulation of ammonium salts. In the epilimnion, on the other hand, free nitrate and phosphate ions were absent owing to the rich growth of phytoplankton. The concentration of ammonium nitrogen in the bottom layers was 1.86 mg/L; that of phosphate phosphorus was 0.285 mg/L, obviously as a result of the mineralization of organic phosphorus and the diffusion of this element from the silt to the water mass (Figure 117).

Annual Dynamics of the Total and Inorganic Phosphorus in Eutrophic Lakes

The dynamics of phosphorus in lakes was studied by Einsele (1936, 1938), Ohle (1958, 1962), Hutchinson and Bovin (1950), and Hayes and Coffin (1951). The phosphorus cycle is closely associated with those of iron and sulfide. The relationship between phosphorus and iron in eutrophic lakes was first established by Einsele and was later studied in detail by O. E. Fatchikhina (1948) in the eutrophic Lake Chernoe (in Kosino). Einsele found that the iron of eutrophic lakes undergoes oxidation during overturns, causing a nearly complete precipitation of phosphorus in the form of ferric phosphate. If the Fe:P ratio exceeds 10:4, phosphorus precipitates as $FePO_4$; an excess of iron causes the precipitation of ferric hydroxide in addition to ferric phosphate.

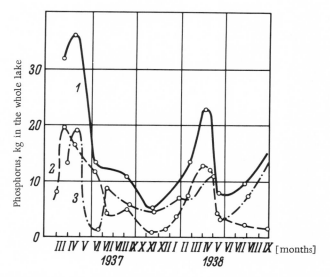

FIGURE 189. Seasonal changes in the quantities of total, organic, and inorganic phosphorus (kg in the whole lake) in Lake Chernoe, Kosino (after Fatchikhina):

1) total phosphorus; 2) inorganic phosphorus; 3) organic phosphorus.

412

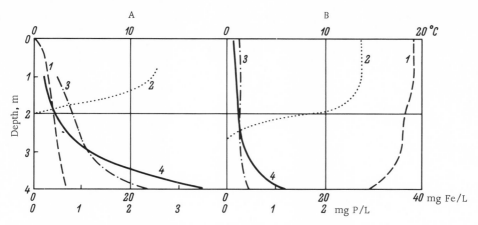

FIGURE 190. Vertical distribution of mineral phosphorus and iron in Lake Chernoe in Kosino (after Fatchikhina):

1) temperature, °C; 2) oxygen; 3) phosphorus; 4) iron; A) March 25, 1937; B) July 22, 1938.

O. E. Fatchikhina found that the Fe:P ratio in the water of Lake Chernoe varies considerably, not only in the vertical sense but also from one season to another. However, it never drops below 10:4, and in some cases it may be as high as 50:1, which causes a complete precipitation of phosphorus together with ferric hydroxide.

During stagnation periods, the disappearance of oxygen from the hypolimnion leads to a conversion of iron to ferrous form, which migrates from the silt to the water mass, releasing mineral phosphorus at the same time. Speaking of the annual changes in the concentration of the different forms of phosphorus in the lake, Fatchikhina notes that dissolved mineral and organic phosphorus accumulate in the bottom water during the winter stagnation; the phosphorus content of the whole water mass rises to a peak by the beginning of the overturn, largely as a result of the diffusion from the silt and the decomposition of dead plankton. A similar phenomenon occurs during the summer stagnation.

The concentration of soluble inorganic phosphorus in lake water decreases sharply during overturns. Figure 189 shows the concentration of total organic and inorganic phosphorus in the lake during different seasons. A similar pattern of inorganic phosphorus was found in the mesotrophic Lake Glubokoe, though in a less pronounced form (Shcherbakov, 1967a).

The changes in the vertical distribution of phosphorus are closely related to those of iron (Figure 190).

Ohle (1964) examined the relations of phosphorus in Grosser Plöner See during the summer stagnation of 1962 (Figure 191). In July, the hypolimnion still contained about 3 mg of oxygen per liter and was poor in phosphorus, whose concentration reached 90 μg/L in the bottom water only. Oxygen vanished from the hypolimnion in August, leaving favorable conditions for the presence of ferrous phosphate in solution; the concentration of phosphate rose accordingly throughout the hypolimnion, reaching 220 mg of P per liter one month later.

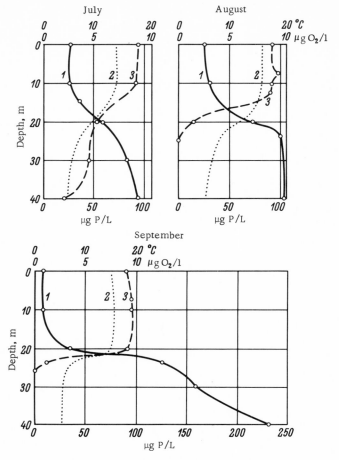

FIGURE 191. Phosphorus dynamics in Grosser Plöner See:
1) phosphorus; 2) temperature, °C; 3) oxygen.

Role of Microorganisms in the Phosphorus Cycle of Lakes

Mineralization of Organic Phosphorus Compounds

The rate of the mineralization of organic phosphates increases as the pH of the medium approaches the optimal range for microbial growth. Among the organic phosphorus compounds, nucleic acids are readily dephosphorylated; phytin breaks down very slowly, and lecithins occupy an intermediate position in this respect. The phosphorus of bacterial cells is rapidly mineralized, and their acid-soluble organic phosphates — phospholipids and DNA — undergo a fast dephosphorylation. On the other hand, RNA phosphorus is mineralized more slowly. Carbon is mineralized in parallel with phosphorus at the rate of 100—300 carbon molecules per molecule of phosphorus.

It is generally assumed that microorganisms that break down organic phosphorus compounds must possess the enzyme phosphatase. Clear zones appear around the colonies of such bacteria in media containing glucose, nucleic acid, and calcium carbonate. To this category belong many saprophytes, notably Rhizobium, Pseudomonas, and Bacterium (Minenko, 1965). Certain spore-forming bacteria, such as Bac. glutinosus, Bac. megatherium, Bac. simplex, and Bac. angulans, produce considerable amounts of phosphatase. This was confirmed by Surman (1961) and other workers who found that the ability to mineralize organic phosphate is widespread among microorganisms and does not characterize any specific group.

Panosyan and co-workers (1960) tried to determine the density of bacteria capable of utilizing lecithin or nucleic acid as a phosphorus source in the water of Lake Sevan (Table 107).

TABLE 107. Density of bacteria capable of mineralizing organic phosphorus compounds in the water and bottom of Lake Sevan (number of cells per ml of water or gram of bottom) (after Panosyan et al., 1960)

Origin of sample	Depth, m	May	August	September	October	December
Malyi Sevan, water	5	0	0	10	0	8
	10	0	3	133	2	6
	20	0	16	80	6	0
	40	0	8	55	0	0
	65	0	16	47	0	0
Bol'shoi Sevan, water ...	5	0	0	11	0	0
	10	10	88	8	0	0
	20	0	11	34	0	0
	35	1	11	34	2	0
Sand		4,670	770	375	0	0
Calcareous sand		2,280	900	0	80	15,100
Brown silt		1,250	3,450	124	0	14,000
Black silt		1,560	1,350	246	4,240	0

As shown in the table, the water mass of the lake contains small numbers of these bacteria. Their density is usually highest in the thermocline zone, where an accumulation of dead phytoplankton can be expected. The corresponding counts in the surface silt are much higher, especially during periods of planktic death.

The authors isolated about one hundred strains, all of them common saprophytes of the species Bac. megatherium and the genera Pseudomonas and Chromobacterium. This shows once again that the entire saprophyte microflora is responsible for the mineralization of organic forms of phosphorus and the liberation of free phosphate.

The mineralization of organic phosphorus in silt was examined by Shapiro (1967) in a series of experiments with active silt from purification plants, which can be regarded as analogous to the surface silt of lake sediments. The flakes of active silt contained Zooglea ramigera,

Escherichia intermedium, Bac. cereus, Flavobacterium sp. sp., and various species of Pseudomonas.

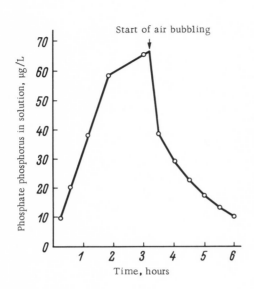

FIGURE 192. Absorption of phosphate by active silt in aerobic conditions and release of phosphate in anaerobic conditions (the experiment was made with 6 grams of sediment per liter at a temperature of 35°) (after Shapiro).

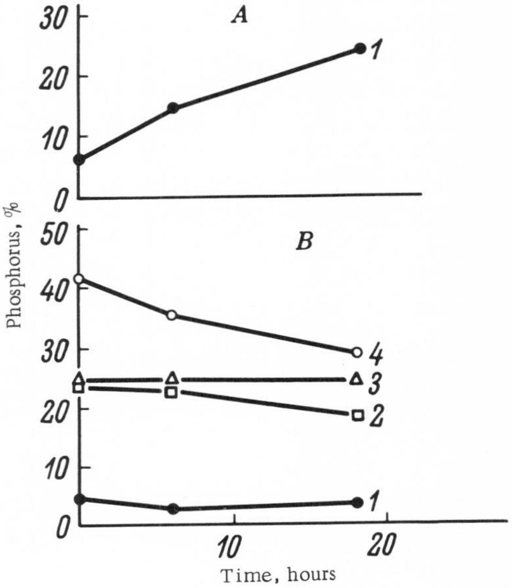

FIGURE 193. Release of mineral phosphorus into the solution in anaerobic conditions (after Shapiro):

A) percentage of the total phosphorus released from the active silt in form of orthophosphate;
B) distribution of the residual phosphorus in the solid phase as percentage of the total phosphorus; 1) lipids; 2) DNA, RNA; 3) proteins; 4) acid-soluble phosphorus.

In anaerobic conditions there was a rapid increase in the concentration of dissolved mineral phosphorus. Within 182 minutes, the 6 grams of active silt gave up 65 mg of phosphate phosphorus. With the beginning of aeration, the phosphorus content of the solution began to decrease at a similar rate and reached 55 mg/L after 172 minutes (Figure 192). All the changes in the dry weight of the sediment concerned phosphorus only; the percentages of carbon, nitrogen, and hydrogen in the organic matter remained unchanged. It appears that all the released phosphorus was in the form of phosphate and originated from readily hydrolyzable compounds. This process results from the activity of a nonspecific saprophyte microflora, since neither mineralization of organic phosphorus nor absorption of mineral phosphorus occurred in sterile conditions.

The organic fractions that yielded phosphate were determined as follows Samples were taken at regular intervals of time. The active silt suspension was centrifuged and inorganic phosphorus was determined in the filtered supernatant, while analyses for the four forms of organic phosphorus were made in the washed centrifugate of the precipitate, which contained the microbial population of the active silt.

As shown in Figure 193, inorganic phosphorus first appears from the organic fraction that enters the solution during treatment with weak acid. Indeed, the concentration of this organic fraction first began to decrease in the washed sediment of the centrifugate. The breakdown of nucleic acids began some six hours later, while the phosphorus of proteins and phospholipids underwent little or no mineralization throughout the twenty hours of the test.

Thus, the metabolism of phosphorus in microorganisms is a reversible process that depends largely on aeration conditions. The anaerobic liberation of phosphorus proceeds also in the presence of 0.001 M $HgCl_2$ and KCN, which indicates an autolytic mineralization of the readily hydrolyzable organic compounds of phosphorus. Clearly, such reactions can take place during the anaerobic breakdown of plankton in the silt.

Dissolution of Iron Phosphates Precipitated in the Silt

Microorganisms exert an indirect influence on the dissolution of $FePO_4$. To become soluble, ferric phosphate must be reduced to the ferrous form. Such reactions are more intensive in eutrophic lakes with an appreciable sulfate content. The silt of such lakes is rich in organic matter and shows a reduction of sulfate. The hydrogen sulfide or calcium hydrosulfide formed in these reactions reduce the ferric phosphate to soluble ferrous phosphate or insoluble ferrous sulfide. In this case, $FePO_4$ and calcium hydrosulfide yield the soluble calcium hydrosulfide, which likewise migrates from the silt to the water mass:

$$2CaSO_4 + 2"C" + H_2O \rightarrow Ca(HS)_2 + CaCO_3 + CO_2 \ (Desulfovibrio);$$

$$2FePO_4 + 2Ca(HS)_2 \rightarrow 2FeS + 2CaHPO_4 \ (chemically);$$

$$2FePO_4 + H_2S \rightarrow 2FeHPO_4 + S^0 \ (chemically).$$

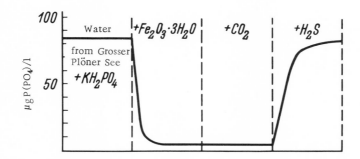

FIGURE 194. Scheme of the set-up for determining the effect of microorganisms on the release and dissolution of mineral phosphate from the silt (after Ohle).

In anaerobic laboratory conditions, silt from the Plussee yields up to 350 μg of phosphate phosphorus per liter (Ohle, 1954).

Figure 194 shows schematically the role of sulfide in the liberation of soluble phosphate from the silt. This scheme was confirmed in laboratory conditions.

KH_2PO_4 was added to water from the Grosser Plöner See to a concentration of about 85 μg of phosphate phosphorus per liter. The addition of $Fe_2O_3 \cdot 3H_2O$ caused a precipitation of phosphorus, whose concentration accordingly dropped to 8 μg of phosphate phosphorus per liter. Bubbling of carbon dioxide did not increase the concentration of phosphate in the solution, but the addition of hydrogen sulfide immobilized iron and raised the concentration of phosphate to the original value. The process followed the above formula. Since the formation of hydrogen sulfide by sulfate-reducing bacteria is a common phenomen in lake silts, there can be no doubt that sulfate-reducing bacteria represent a major factor in the release of bound phosphorus and the migration of this element from the silt to the water mass.

Dissolution of Calcium Phosphates

The role of microorganisms in the dissolution of inorganic phosphorus compounds is largely indirect. Various species of Pseudomonas, Mycobacterium, Micrococcus, Flavobacterium, Penicillium, and Aspergillus can produce acids on organic substrates and convert $Ca_3(PO_4)_2$ to soluble secondary phosphate.

No conceivable conversion of tribasic calcium phosphate to soluble form via nitric or sulfuric acid as a result of the activity of nitrifying bacteria or thiobacilli has ever been observed.

To sum up, the phosphorus that enters a lake, where the depth becomes anaerobic, participates continuously in the chemical transformations without being buried to any appreciable extent in the silt. Since this element often represents a limiting factor in the growth of aquatic vegetation, an increase of its concentration causes an irreversible eutrophication of the lake and a deterioration of the quality of water (Rossolimo, 1967).

Binding of Inorganic Phosphorus

The organic binding of inorganic phosphorus in lakes is due mainly to the growth of phytoplankton. Bacteria likewise assimilate inorganic phosphorus, though on a much smaller scale since their biomass is many times smaller than that of the phytoplankton per unit volume of water.

The phosphorus content of bacteria ranges from 1.5 to 2.5% in terms of dry weight; the corresponding percentages in fungi are 0.5—1.0%. Cellulose bacteria assimilate from 0.16 to 0.36 parts of phosphorus per 100 parts of oxidized cellulose.

Biological Oxidation and Reduction of Phosphorus

Phosphorus, like nitrogen and sulfur, has several valences, which range from P^{-3} in hydrogen phosphide (PH_3) to P^{+5} in orthophosphoric acid. In contrast to these two elements, however, the ability of microorganisms to oxidize or reduce phosphorus has been largely neglected.

Adams and Conrad (1953) observed a biological conversion of phosphorus to phosphoric acid in soil, the amount of phosphoric acid formed being equivalent to the loss of phosphorous acid:

$$HPO_3^= \rightarrow HPO_4^=.$$

The process was stopped by the addition of toluene, which proves its biological nature. Many heterotrophic bacteria, fungi, and actinomycetes can utilize salts of phosphorous acid as sources of phosphorus by incorporating these compounds in the protoplasm in the form of phosphates. It is still unknown whether microorganisms can utilize the energy derived from the oxidation of reduced phosphorus compounds; in fact, such experiments have not yet been positive. There are indications, on the other hand, that microorganisms living in anaerobic conditions can reduce phosphate to hydrogen phosphide in the presence of organic compounds.

The loss of phosphoric acid during the maturation of manure can amount to 40% of the original quantity (Egorov, 1925). In his studies of the biogenic reduction of phosphoric acid, K. I. Rudakov (1926, 1928) isolated from soil a non-spore-forming rod that reduced salts of phosphoric acid to phosphorous acid and further to hydrogen phosphide in an anaerobic medium with mannitol. The anaerobic decomposition of mannitol yielded butyric acid and 180 ml of gas, which had the following composition: CO_2 59.58 ml, H_2 114.66 ml, CH_4 2.16 ml, N_2 5.40 ml. Qualitative analysis revealed the presence of PH_3 in the gas; of the original quantity of 1.333 grams of P_2O_5, 0.248 gram was reduced to H_3PO_3 and H_3PO_2.

There was no further reduction of phosphoric acid in the culture, although the experiment lasted twenty days. The presence of sulfate in the medium inhibited the reduction of phosphate. Nitrates were reduced first. From the biochemical viewpoint the process is analogous to denitrification.

The data of K. I. Rudakov have not been verified, although they were published more than forty years ago.

If such reduction of phosphate can occur at all in lakes, it will be only in the anaerobic environment of the silt.

Mechanism of the Phosphorus Cycle in Lakes

The use of labeled phosphorus compounds makes it possible to determine the rate of the distribution of phosphorus in lakes, the rate of its assimilation by different aquatic organisms, and the exchange of phosphates between the silt and water mass of the lake.

Hayes and Coffin (1951) examined the relations of phosphorus in two small lakes. During the summer, the water of one of these lakes performed a complete overturn, while the other lake showed a distinct stratification of the water mass. Both lakes had an area of about 2—3 hectares. Radioactive phosphorus at a concentration of 100 mCi was placed directly in the surface water (McKarter et al., 1952).

The first of these lakes is bogged up. At the time of the introduction of radioactive phosphorus, the thermocline lay at a depth of 0—2 m. Among other signs, the absence of water circulation was evident from the position of an oxygen maximum at a depth of 1 m.

Analyses of silt, made at certain intervals, showed that the radioactive phosphorus did not reach the silt in the presence of a normal stratification.

Within thirty days, practically all the radioactive phosphorus was absorbed by the aquatic vegetation and the plankton, and the concentration of phosphorus in the water returned to its original level.

The concentration of labeled phosphorus peaked after one week in the zooplankton and after two weeks in fish, indicating that the latter obtain phosphorus by trophic ways.

A quantity of 100 mCi P^{32} was placed at a depth of 1 m above the silt on the hypolimnion of the second lake, where the thermal stratification was similarly well defined. Samples were taken for a period of three months. Phosphorus penetrated very slowly through the cold water to the bottom. It migrated horizontally in the hypolimnion, traversing a distance of 48 m for two months until it reached the shore; at the same time the vertical advance did not exceed 4.8 m. The plankton of the epilimnion showed a low radioactivity throughout the experiment, although its radioactivity could have increased 40,000 times. On the other hand, the silt became highly radioactive, which indicates that it had received most of the labeled phosphorus.

The last experiment was made in a lake of a totally different nature, with an area of about 8 hectares and a depth of approximately 7.5 m. This lake was poor in plankton and had no coastal vegetation. The mixed water extended to the bottom; oxygen and temperature were uniform throughout the depth range of the lake. A quantity of 1,000 mCi P^{32} was placed on the water surface. The distribution of phosphorus became uniform three days later, after which its activity began to decrease rapidly throughout the water mass, though at a decreasing rate (Figure 195).

This phenomenon can be attributed to a rapid establishment of an equilibrium between the consumption of phosphorus by the silt and vegetation, on the one hand, and the liberation of this element into the water, on the other. In fact, if the phosphorus content of the silt and vegetation is 1,000 times greater than that of water, the introduced phosphorus must be distributed according to the same proportion, that is, 1,000 parts in the silt for every part in the water. If the water alone is considered, this would appear as a major loss of phosphorus. The slope of the curve (Figure 195) shows, however, that about 7% of the phosphate is liberated daily from the silt, which means a complete exchange of this element every two weeks.

The authors believe that much of the phosphorus escapes from the water mass into the silt in the form of ferric phosphate. Figure 196 shows schematically the exchange of phosphorus between the water and silt of the lake.

In the absence of oxygen, the hypolimnion can receive phosphate in the form of $Fe_3(PO_4)_2$ from the silt. Upon reaching the oxidized zone, the ferrous phosphate is oxidized to insoluble ferric phosphate and returns to the si

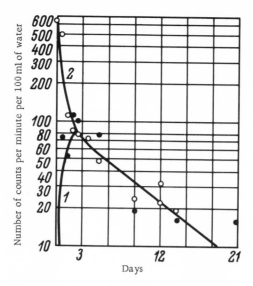

FIGURE 195. Distribution of phosphorus in the water mass of
Bluff Lake on the basis of experiments involving the introduction
of radioactive phosphorus:

1) bottom water; 2) surface water; the black circles indicate
analyses of radioactive bottom water, the white ones of radioactive
surface water.

Hutchinson and Bowen (1950) examined the exchange of phosphorus
between the water, the silt, and the population of the eutrophic Linsley Pond.
Radioactive phosphorus in the form of $K_2HP^{32}O_4$ was placed in the surface
water, and its distribution in the lake was observed for four weeks. The
lake had a distinct thermal stratification and an oxygen-free hypolimnion
during the experiment.

In the littoral zone of the epilimnion, the phosphorus was rapidly consumed by the aquatic vegetation and began to precipitate from the epilimnion to the hypolimnion. Upon reaching the bottom, however, it was converted to a soluble form and returned to the water.

A similar exchange of phosphorus was observed in the littoral vegetation
of the lake. Throughout the experiment, the littoral contained immobile
forms of phosphorus that showed low activity and mobile ones of high activity.
The circulation of phosphorus in the lake could be calculated on the basis
of observations made between August 1 and 15, when an equilibrium was
established. The authors gave the following figures (in kg per week):

Observed increase of the phosphorus content of the epilimnion	0.26
Migration from the epilimnion to the hypolimnion	1.55
Total inflow from the littoral to the epilimnion	1.81
Observed increase of the phosphorus content of the hypolimnion	3.75
Migration from the epilimnion	1.55
Migration from the silt to the hypolimnion	2.20

421

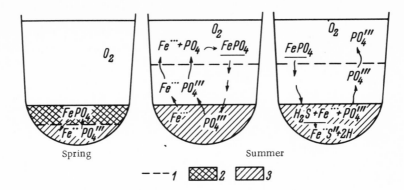

FIGURE 196. Scheme of the exchange of mineral phosphorus between the water
and silt of a lake with a complete overturn of water (after Hayes and Coffin):

1) limit of oxygen zone; 2) oxidized layer of silt; 3) reduced layer of silt.

Since the average phosphorus content of the epilimnion was 5.82 kg, the
observed rate of migration to the hypolimnion — 2.2 kg per week — corresponded to one-third of the whole amount. In other words, a complete exchange of phosphorus between the water, on the one hand, and the silt and
aquatic population, on the other, requires three weeks.

By summing up the absorption and liberation of phosphorus by the solid
phase, it can be seen that these processes are proportional to the amount
of phosphorus present in the water and in the solid phase. These relations
are presented in Table 108 (Hutchinson, 1957).

TABLE 108. Turnover time and mobile phosphorus in three lakes studied experimentally with radiophosphorus
(Hutchinson, 1957)

Lake	Area, km^2	Maximal depth, m	Turnover time, water, days	Turnover time, sediment, days	Total mobile P : phosphorus in lake
Bluff	0.4	7	5.4	39	6.4
Punch Bowl ...	0.3	6.2	7.6	37	4.8
Crecy	2.04	3.8	17	176	8.7

In this table, the turnover time is the time taken to absorb from the
water or liberate from the solid phase under steady-state conditions a mass
of phosphorus equal to the stationary mass present, respectively, in the
water or the solid phase. The quantity in the last column represents the
ratio of the total phosphorus taking part in exchange, either in sediments
or in the water, to that in the water alone. Despite the major differences in
the morphometry of the lakes and the time required for a complete cycle
through the water and silt, this ratio remains rather uniform.

According to Hutchinson (1957), the phosphorus cycle in lakes includes
the following processes: (1) liberation of phosphorus into the epilimnion
from the littoral, largely from the decay of littoral vegetation; (2) uptake of

phosphorus from the water by the littoral vegetation; (3) uptake of the liberated phosphorus by phytoplankton; (4) loss of phosphorus as a soluble compound, less assimilable than ionic phosphate from the phytoplankton, probably followed by slow regeneration of ionic phosphate; (5) sedimentation of phytoplankton and other phosphorus-containing seston into the hypolimnion; (6) liberation of phosphorus from sedimenting seston in the hypolimnion or when it arrives at the mud-water interface; (7) diffusion of phosphorus from the sediments into the water at those depths at which the superficial layer of mud lacks an oxidized microzone.

Thus, the role of microorganisms in the phosphorus cycle of lakes consists in the assimilation of phosphate, the mineralization of organic phosphorus compounds by a nonspecific microflora, and the dissolution of phosphorus from ferric phosphate by means of biogenic hydrogen sulfide.

Deposition of Calcium Carbonate in Lakes

Conditions of the Deposition of Calcium Carbonate in Lake Silts

Discussing the formation of carbonaceous rocks, N. M. Strakhov (1960) expressed the view that the only facial areas in humid zones where such rocks exist at all are terminal runoff basins, and in the vast majority of cases — seas.

Freshwater lakes with soft water contain little or no calcium carbonate. Thus, calcium carbonate is practically absent from the silt of such lakes as Baikal, Onega, and Ladoga. Matters are different in hard-water lakes situated at the boundary between the humid and arid zones. Calcium carbonate accumulates here in considerable amounts, especially in the littoral zone, which is occupied by littoral vegetation. Such distribution was observed by Passarge (cited from Strakhov, 1960) in the Lychen lake group in West Germany, namely: coastal sand 4.73—10.25% $CaCO_3$; deeper into the silty sand 34.73%; at a depth of 2—3 m inside the silt beneath growths of C h a r a an average of 72.4%; at a depth of 3—7 m beneath other plants an average of 49.4%; inside the silt at a depth of 16 to 49 m an average of 37.1%. A similar distribution of calcium carbonate was observed in the silt of lakes Michigan and Ontario, while the Bodensee shows less difference between the calcium carbonate contents of the coastal silt and the profundal.

A number of authors (V. V. Alabyshev, 1932; N. M. Strakhov, 1951) believe that, in lakes of the humid zone, an accumulation of calcium carbonate in the silt is possible in regions with abundant carbonaceous rocks. In this connection, R. V. Nikolaeva (1964) examined the conditions of the accumulation of calcium carbonate in several lakes in the Middle Volga area in the Mari Autonomous SSR. She reached the same conclusion, namely, that this process cannot be used in the classification of lakes situated in the humid zone. On the basis of data from the literature, Nikolaeva prepared a table showing the amount of calcium carbonate in the silt of lakes situated in different regions of the European part of the USSR (Table 109).

Most lakes in the temperate latitudes belong to the hydrocarbonate type. Accordingly, the calcium cycle in such lakes is associated with the conversion of calcium hydrocarbonate to carbonate and vice versa. Calcium carbonate is much less soluble than the hydrocarbonate or sulfate. For this reason, the precipitation and dissolution of $CaCO_3$ can be expressed by the following equation:

$$CaCO_3 + H_2O + CO_2 \rightleftarrows Ca^{\cdot\cdot} + 2HCO'_3.$$

TABLE 109. Calcium content (% of dry silt, 0-20-cm layer) of recent sediments of lakes (after Nikolaeva, 1964)

Republic or region	Number of examined lakes	CaO	Republic or region	Number of examined lakes	CaO
Murmansk Region	22	0.4—2.0	Novgorod Region	1	0.6—1.5
	7	2.4—4.8	Kalinin Region	17	0.7—2.9
Karelian Autonomous SSR	10	0.1—2.5		7	3.2—7.4
Arkhangel'sk Region	5	0.7—2.3	Moscow Region	8	0.5—2.1
Leningrad Region	2	0.6—1.3		2	4.0—6.0
Latvian SSR	7	0.8—2.5	Yaroslavl Region	1	3.0
Lithuanian SSR	5	2.0—10.0	Kostroma Region	4	2.8—4.6
Pskov Region	2	1.4—1.6		2	5.0—7.4

The precipitation of calcium carbonate from the solution depends entirely on physical-chemical factors, namely, the equilibrium between Ca^{++}, HCO_3, and carbon dioxide. These relations can be expressed by the Kolthoff formula

$$K = \frac{|Ca^{\cdot\cdot}| \times |HCO_3^-|^2 \alpha^3}{|CO_2|} = 1.13 \cdot 10^{-4},$$

where $Ca^{\cdot\cdot}$ is the concentration of calcium ions in gram equivalents; $|HCO_3'|$ the concentration of HCO_3' ions in gram equivalents; $|CO_2|$ the concentration of carbon dioxide in gram moles per liter; α the activity of the ions, which is close to unity; and K the equilibrium constant.

Calcium carbonate will dissolve if the experimentally found constant K is less than the equilibrium constant K. If K_e is greater than K, the solution is supersaturated with calcium carbonate and the latter will precipitate. In the latter case the consumption of HCO_3 ions or the supply of carbon dioxide will favor the precipitation of calcium carbonate from the solution until the establishment of the equilibrium $K = 1.13 \times 10^{-4}$.

Table 110 shows the values of K_e in different lakes and the presence or absence of calcium carbonate in their silts.

It is evident from the table that $CaCO_3$ precipitates only when K_e is much greater than the Kolthoff constant.

These relationships are illustrated in Lake Balkhash, which lies in the eastern part of Central Kazakhstan — an area of sharply continental, dry climate. Being drainless, this lake has a steadily rising salinity as a result of evaporation. It is very elongate, having a length of about 600 km and a maximal width of approximately 60 km. Most of its water supply (up to 80%) comes from the Ili River, which discharges in the west end of the lake. Because of evaporation, salinity increases from 1,261 mg/L at the west end of the lake to 5,243 mg/L at the east end. The proportion between the concentrations of CO_2, $Ca^{\cdot\cdot}$ and HCO_3' also changes in the same direction (Table 110) (V. D. Konshin, 1945). Thus, the concentration of calcium carbonate in the water rises at first from 34.2 to 64.2 mg/L in the central part of the lake and decreases again to one-half in the eastern part, while the concentration of calcium ions drops from 57.4 to 14 mg/L. These changes reflect the formation of calcareous and calcareous-dolomitic sediments, especially in the eastern part of the Lake Balkhash.

TABLE 110. Relationship between $Ca^{..}$ and HCO_3' ions and free carbon dioxide (K_e) after the Kolthoff formula in water of different lakes and presence of $CaCO_3$ in silt

Lake	pH	CO_2, mg-moles	Concentration		K_e	Presence of $CaCO_3$ in silt
			HCO_3', milligram-equivalents	$Ca^{..}$, milligram-equivalents		
Glubokoe	7.6	0.044	0.54	0.43	$0.02 \cdot 10^{-4}$	−
Onega	7.15	0.081	0.394	0.27	$0.5 \cdot 10^{-6}$	−
Baikal	7.2	0.068	1.14	0.59	$1.13 \cdot 10^{-5}$	−
Valdaiskoe	−	0.045	1.62	1.51	$0.88 \cdot 10^{-4}$	−
Shem-er (Mari Autonomous SSR)	7.1	0.96	2.09	1.71	$0.78 \cdot 10^{-4}$	−
Iz-er (Mari Autonomous SSR) ···	7.7	0.3	3.15	1.45	$0.4 \cdot 10^{-4}$	−
Kuzh-er (Mari Autonomous SSR):						
surface water	7.2	0.075	2.6	1.75	$0.18 \cdot 10^{-4}$	−
bottom water	7.0	0.55	2.87	2.05	$0.30 \cdot 10^{-4}$	−
Morskoi Glaz (Mari Autonomous SSR)	−	0	3.42	1.57	∞	+
Belovod':						
littoral	8.2	0.02	4.1	8.0	$67 \cdot 10^{-4}$	+
pelagial	7.2	0.5	3.9	10.2	$25 \cdot 10^{-4}$	+
Balkhash						
west end	8.3	0.1	4.8	2.73	$44 \cdot 10^{-4}$	+
east end	9.15	0	10.87	0.70	∞	+
Sevan	8.7	0	7.69	1.69	∞	+
Issyk-Kul	9.0	0	3.99	5.65	∞	+

Note: The plus sign indicates the presence of $CaCO_3$ in the silt, the minus sign its absence.

Role of Microorganisms in the Precipitation of Calcium Carbonate

Calcium carbonate can appear in the water mass and settle on the lake bottom not only by strictly chemical processes but also as a result of the physiologic activity of many organisms such as mollusks, foraminifers, and probably, bacteria. Contradictory views have been expressed about the role of bacteria in this phenomenon.

Drew (1911), Molisch (1925), and Nadson (1928) speak of "calcium bacteria" as specific microorganisms that produce calcite. This definition is misleading. After a more thorough study of the role of bacteria in the formation of calcite, Lipman (1931) and Bavendam (1932) found that the formation of this mineral cannot be associated with any specific group of bacteria, since various bacteria can bring about the same result.

The definition of calcium bacteria must be based on their physiology. However, calcium carbonate appears in certain environmental conditions and is not utilized by bacteria. Consequently, there is no justification in uniting different bacterial species into one group on the basis of such a sign as the precipitation of calcium carbonate around the colony on meat peptone agar containing soluble calcium salts.

There is no evidence that microorganisms represent a major factor in the formation of calcite (Baier, 1937). A possible exception are the calcium carbonate sediments at the sources of the Loa in the Loa River valley, so observed by Wetzel. Here the granite blocks of the river bed are covered with calcium carbonate incrustations consisting of a thick felt of blue-green algae and filamentous bacteria, probably C r e n o t h r i x, whose sheaths were incrusted with calcite and terrigenous particles of river mud.

The only indication of a possible link between bacterial physiology and the precipitation of calcium carbonate can be found in the work of Brussoff (1933, 1935), who isolated an organism from the Aachen hot springs. Brussoff observed deposits of calcium carbonate in the cell wall of this bacterium, which he named B a c t. a q u i g r a n a e; for the deposits he proposed the name "bacteriospherites" or "biospherites."

The stony sediments of the Aachen hot springs were produced by cocci and chain-forming bacteria whose slime capsules were filled with calcite crystals. Brussoff also found S i d e r o b a c t e r c a l c e u m Nauman — a motile rod that deposits ferric hydroxide and, when the latter is absent, calcium carbonate. An intracellular formation of calcium carbonate crystals was observed in several species of sulfur bacteria (Bersa, 1926) and in A c h r o m a t i u m (West and Griffiths, 1913).

A precipitation of calcite in laboratory conditions was first observed by Murray and Irvine (1890) during the putrefaction of meat in sea water. Later, Nadson (1903) isolated pure cultures of B a c t. v u l g a r i s, B a c. s u b - t i l i s, B a c. m y c o i d e s, and other bacteria that caused the precipitation of calcium carbonate in liquid media containing peptone and calcium chlorite or deposited calcium carbonate around the colony on solid media. Molisch (1925) examined this process in greater detail and isolated two species, P s e u d o m o n a s c a l c i p r e a c c i p i t a n s and P. c a l c i p h i l a. B a c t. s e w a n e n s e was isolated in a similar manner from the silt of Lake Sevan (Kalantarian and Petrosian, 1932; L. A. Erzinkyan, 1949). A number of other authors obtained analogous cultures (B. L. Isachenko, 1948; V. O. Kalinenko, 1949a, 1952; L. A. Rozenberg, 1950).

Since the work of Molisch (1925), many microbiologists have sought to associate specific bacteria with the precipitation of calcium carbonate in salt and fresh waters and have drawn conclusions about the formation of calcite in nature on the basis of the above experiments. These works were critically reviewed by Baier (1937) and N. M. Strakhov (1948, 1951). The main objection is that the concentration of nutrient salts in laboratory cultures is tens or hundreds of times greater than that found in nature. Because of this, the experimental results do not necessarily apply to natural conditions.

Calcite can be formed by three processes. First, the mineralization of peptone by bacteria yields ammonia, which alkalinizes the medium and converts $Ca(HCO_3)_2$ to $CaCO_3$. Second, microbial attack on calcium salts of organic acids produces carbon dioxide and calcium carbonate. Third, the reduction of sulfate yields calcium sulfide, which reacts with carbonic acid to form calcium carbonate (Nadson, 1903, 1928):

1) $Ca(HCO_3)_2 + 2NH_3 \rightarrow CaCO_3 + (NH_4)_2CO_3;$

2) $Ca(CH_3COO)_2 + 4O_2 \rightarrow CaCO_3 + CO_2 + 3H_2O;$

3) $CaSO_4 + 4H_2 \rightarrow CaS + 4H_2O;$

$CaS + H_2CO_3 \rightarrow CaCO_3 + H_2S.$

In all these processes, the primary reaction is performed by bacteria that decompose organic compounds or reduce sulfate, while $CaCO_3$ precipitates secondarily in a strictly chemical reaction determined by the proportion of the $Ca^{\cdot\cdot}$ and HCO_3' ions and the concentration of carbonic acid.

Although laboratory experiments do not necessarily explain the natural processes, they shed light on the early stage of the formation of calcite ($CaCO_3$).

Formation of Calcite by Microorganisms in Laboratory Conditions

The union of Ca and CO_3 ions into calcite does not yield free energy. Consequently, the very process of calcite formation cannot serve as source of energy to any specific group of organisms. It appears, therefore, that microorganisms can pay only a secondary role in the sedimentation of calcium carbonate. By utilizing the carbon dioxide of hydrocarbonate for the construction of organic matter, bacteria (and especially the photosynthetic ones) shift the equilibrium in favor of calcium carbonate. Obviously, the conditions of the precipitation of calcium carbonate in natural waters differ sharply from those existing in laboratory cultures of bacteria, where the concentrations of organic matter, calcium ions, and other nutrients are hundreds of times greater than in nature. Laboratory tests can provide a partial explanation of the early stages of calcite formation, notably the appearance of microcrystals that later develop into large crystals in lake water supersaturated with calcium carbonate.

Several workers have observed the formation of calcite crystals in bacterial cultures (B. L. Isachenko, 1948; V. O. Kalinenko, 1949a; L.A.Rozenberg 1950; Greenfield, 1963). They conclude that many bacteria that yield ammonia in peptone media can precipitate calcium carbonate in the presence of large concentrations of calcium salts. The process can be described briefly as follows. The mineralization of peptone by bacteria yields ammonia, which alkalinizes the medium and converts $Ca(HCO_3)_2$ to $CaCO_3$:

$Ca(HCO_3)_2 + 2NH_3 \rightarrow CaCO_3 + (NH_4)CO_3 .$

A film of bacteria develops at first on the surface of the medium. The bacterial slime, being an adsorbent, serves as site for the initial deposition of calcium carbonate, at first in the form of small, dropletlike bodies of "colloidal calcite," which grow steadily. Thus, the earliest deposits of calcite in the culture are amorphous. Crystals of calcite appear within a few days together with concentrically layered ooliths of calcium carbonate and radial spheroliths. These formations are especially conspicuous in agar cultures of Bact. precipitatum (V. O. Kalinenko, 1949a). According to B. L. Isachenko, the amorphous bodies give rise to the calcite crystals and concretions described above. Microscopic examination of the concretions reveals their constituent bodies, which contain inclusions of bacteria.

After extensive analyses of the media of Bact. precipitatum cultures, L. A. Rozenberg (1951) concluded that the alkalinization of a sterile medium causes a precipitation of calcium carbonate at a higher pH than in the bacterial culture. Indeed, microzones of calcium carbonate developed around the bacterial colonies, although the concentration of free carbonic acid in the culture was much greater than in the sterile control, and the pH of the medium was 7.25. Rozenberg attributes the formation of calcite in the culture to a change in the chemical equilibrium around the colony in favor of a microzonal crystallization of calcium carbonate. According to Greenfield (1963), such microcrystals of calcium carbonate can serve as crystallization centers of calcite from supersaturated solutions.

Role of Microorganisms in the Formation of Calcium Carbonate Sediments in Nature

The alpine Lake Sevan can be taken as a typical example of a precipitation of calcium carbonate in the littoral and in the deep-water silt. This lake lies in Georgia at an altitude of almost 2,000 m in an arid region. Its area and maximal depth were respectively 1,413 km^2 and 60 m. Evaporation is very great; it accounts for about 90% of the water supplied by precipitation and river runoff. Each year, 28,660 tons of calcium carbonate settle on the bottom of the lake (S. Ya. Lyatti, 1929, 1932a, 1932b).

The water of the lake feeds an electric power station, as a result of which its level has dropped in recent years by 16 m, baring the littoral, the shallow creeks, and the coastal silts. The latter are invariably white and contain a high percentage of calcium carbonate. The deep-water silts of the lake also contain up to 30% $CaCO_3$ (S. Ya. Lyatti, 1932b) (Figure 197).

Calcite crystals in the sediments of the lake attain a size of 7 cm at a depth of 60 m, where the scarcity of light prevents any photosynthesis (Figure 198). Consequently, Lake Sevan serves as an excellent object for the study of calcite formation in natural conditions.

The view that the calcite crystals of Lake Sevan are of biological origin was first expressed by P. B. Kalantaryan (1932). Later, it was confirmed by B. L. Isachenko and L. A. Erzinkyan (1949). Adopting the approach of Molisch, the latter authors inoculated silt in the medium of Molisch with peptone and a high concentration of $CaCl_2$; they obtained bacteria that precipitated $CaCO_3$. B. L. Isachenko successfully used remnants of higher

FIGURE 197. Calcium carbonate deposits on littoral rocks in Lake Sevan. The photograph was taken after the water level of the lake dropped by 9 m.

FIGURE 198. Calcium carbonate macrocrystals from a depth of 50 m in Lake Sevan.

aquatic vegetation as an organic ingredient. He assumed on these grounds that remnants of higher aquatic vegetation move down the slope from the littoral to the profundal, where they create favorable conditions for the growth and activity of $CaCO_3$-precipitating bacteria.

However, analysis of the sublittoral and profundal silts of the lake did not reveal any plant remnants whose breakdown could produce the quantity of ammonia necessary for the growth of calcite crystals (see.p. 214). Thus, the precipitation of $CaCO_3$ cannot be attributed to any specific "calcium bacteria."

S. I. Kuznetsov (1966) made further studies of the formation of calcite in Lake Sevan. The water of this lake is alkaline, having a pH of 8.7—9.0; here the equilibrium constant K_e equals infinity because the denominator in the Kolthoff formula (which includes the concentration of carbon dioxide) is equal to zero. In such conditions, the photosynthetic activity of the phytoplankton removes carbon dioxide from calcium hydrocarbonate and converts the latter into carbonate:

$$Ca(HCO_3)_2 - CO_2 = CaCO_3 + H_2O.$$

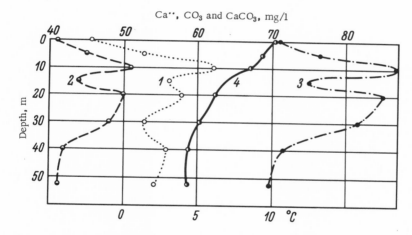

FIGURE 199. Vertical distribution of temperature (4), $Ca^{··}$ (1), CO_3^- (2), and $CaCO_3$ (3) in the water of Lake Malyi Sevan.

Microscopic analysis of the net phytoplankton revealed small crystals of calcium carbonate; in the presence of dilute hydrochloric acid, these dissolved with the release of gas bubbles.

Analysis of the vertical distribution of total calcium, bicarbonate, and carbonate in the lake water (Figure 199) shows that the concentrations of total calcium and carbonate increase with depth from a minimum at the surface to a peak just above the thermocline, that is, where the density of water rises sharply and the sedimentation rate of the minute crystals of calcium carbonate slows down.

The deep-water silts of Lake Sevan consist entirely of diatom shells and crystals of calcium carbonate. The water of this lake represents a supersaturated solution of calcium carbonate. This fact and the presence of crystallization centers in the photosynthetic zone explain the growth of the crystals on their way to the bottom.

It follows from the Kolthoff equation that the release of carbon dioxide from the silt must favor the growth of the calcium carbonate crystals in the specific conditions of the lake. Measurements of the oxidation-reduction potential show a sharp drop of rH_2 even at the very surface of the silt (Kuznetsov, 1966). This reflects an intensive decomposition of organic matter settled from the water mass. Moreover, the lowest pH values were found at the silt surface — 8.3 compared with 8.75 deeper inside the silt and 8.96—9.0 in the water. The comparatively low pH value of 8.3 at the silt surface indicates a release of carbonic acid, which can exist in a free state at such pH and thus create a supersaturated solution of $CaCO_3$ in the surface layer of silt.

Experiments involving the incubation of silt in laboratory conditions have shown that silts containing large crystals of calcite produce the largest quantities of carbon dioxide (S. I. Kuznetsov, 1966). In other words, the large crystals have developed in conditions that favored a maximal supersaturation of the calcium carbonate solutions.

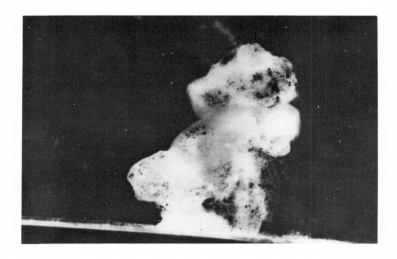

FIGURE 200. Formation of calcite crystals in square capillaries inserted in the surface layer of silt from Lake Sevan (×200).

To determine the possibility of the formation of calcite crystals in the surface silt of Lake Sevan without any external influences, S.I. Kuznetsov used the procedure of capillary microscopy as proposed by Perfil'ev and Gabe (1961). Surface silt from Lake Sevan was placed in a jar, which was filled with Sevan water. After mixing and settling the silt, capillaries with plane parallel walls and a lumen of 50×400 microns were inserted vertically in it and were left for 6—8 months in such a manner that part of the capillary projected from the silt into the water.

Control experiments showed that only small particles of detritus and remnants of the valves of diatom algae can penetrate into the capillaries as these are being inserted into the silt, while calcite crystals do not enter.

Macroscopic examination of the lumen of the capillaries eight months after the beginning of the experiment revealed a considerable amount of calcite crystals (Figure 200) that were attached to the inner side of the walls and remained there even after water was passed through the capillary. This proves once again that the formation of calcite crystals in the silt of Lake Sevan is due to crystallization from a supersaturated solution of calcium carbonate, while bacterial processes play only an indirect role by changing the equilibrium of the $Ca^{..}$ and HCO_3' ions and the concentration of free carbonic acid.

To sum up, the formation of calcium carbonate sediments in lakes with hard water and an alkaline reaction can be outlined as follows. Calcite crystals appear in the surface water owing to the photosynthetic activity of the phytoplankton, which utilizes the carbon dioxide of hydrocarbonate. These crystals grow as they sink in the water mass if the proportion between the calcium and hydrocarbonate ions is such that $K_e > K$. In the bottom sediments, the further growth of the crystals is probably due to the liberation of carbon dioxide from decaying organic matter until the concentrations of $Ca^{..}$, HCO_3' and CO_2 satisfy the equation $K_e = K = 1.13 \times 10^{-4}$.

In the meromictic Lake Belovod' (Vladimir Region), the generation of calcium carbonate in the silt is associated with a reduction of sulfate. Belovod' is a sink lake that receives considerable amounts of underground waters with a high calcium sulfate content.

The lake littoral is overgrown with C h a r a algae, which utilize the carbon dioxide of $Ca(HCO_3)_2$ and deposit $CaCO_3$. Consequently, the silt is white and contains a large proportion of calcite. Microscopical analysis of the silt from the lake littoral shows that the loose surface layer contains large amounts of algae and masses of amorphous calcite, while the deeper layers contain calcite crystals (Kuznetsov, 1958b).

The deep-water silts of the lake are black, in contrast to the littoral ones, because they contain a considerable proportion of iron sulfides. The surface layer of the deep-water silt is rich in remnants of chitinous shells of zooplankton and diatom valves. At a depth of 5—7 cm below the surface, the silt contains a much larger amount of calcium carbonate crystals. In other words, calcium carbonate crystals are formed at a depth of more than 3—5 cm from the silt surface. D e s u l f o v i b r i o d e s u l f u r i c a n s is present in these silts, where sulfate undergoes reduction at a daily rate of 0.17 mg of H_2S per liter of silt. The profundal silt has a pH of 8.4 (M. V. Ivanov, 1956), which means that free carbonic acid is absent and calcite crystals can develop according to the Kolthoff formula.

Figure 201 presents photographs of calcite crystals from the silt of Lake Belovod', where this mineral is formed by the reduction of sulfate.

Such precipitation of $CaCO_3$ as a result of the reduction of sulfate is even more pronounced in Lake Solenoe, situated near the city of Sol'vychegodsk in Arkhangelsk Region. Here the formation of calcite was examined

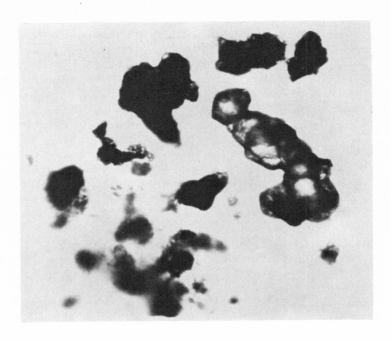

FIGURE 201. Calcite crystals formed by the reduction of sulfate at a depth of 7—10 cm from the silt surface in Lake Belovod' (×200).

in detail by M. V. Ivanov and V. M. Gorlenko (1969). The silt of this lake produces hydrogen sulfide at a rate of 2—3 mg per liter, though in some places this figure can be as high as 19 mg per liter per day (Ivanov and Terebkova, 1959a).

TABLE 111. Formation of calcium carbonates in the silts of Lake Solenoe as a result of the reduction of sulfates

Depth from silt surface, cm	pH	Rate of reduction of sulfate, mg of H_2S per kg of moist silt per day	Concentration per liter of silt solution			Kolthoff constant, K_e	Concentration of calcium carbonate, grams per kg of moist silt
			$Ca^{..}$, mg-equiv.	HCO_3', mg-equiv.	CO_2, mg-moles*		
0—1	8.32	11.36	36.13	26.2	1.2	$206.5 \cdot 10^{-4}$	22.84
1—2	8.56	—	36.09	29.5	0.94	$334 \cdot 10^{-4}$	35.43
2—4	8.25	—	36.33	37.0	1.82	$274 \cdot 10^{-4}$	41.32
4—6	8.30	8.52	32.64	40.5	1.84	$293 \cdot 10^{-4}$	43.57
10—12	8.20	3.76	31.14	45.7	2.38	$276 \cdot 10^{-4}$	51.34
15—17	8.19	—	27.35	54.2	2.74	$295 \cdot 10^{-4}$	55.35

* The free carbon dioxide is calculated from the values of the pH, HCO_3, and CO_3.

Table 111 is based on data placed at our disposal by M. V. Ivanov and V. M. Gorlenko. It shows that the silts of this lake contain large amounts of calcium carbonate, while the proportion of the calcium and carbonic acid ions (K_e) permits the precipitation of calcite.

Scheme of the Calcium Cycle of Lakes

Figure 202 shows schematically the calcium cycle of lakes. Calcium ions enter the lake as bicarbonate or sulfate. When the proportion between the $Ca^{..}$ and HCO_3' ions and carbon dioxide equals the Kolthoff equilibrium constant

$$K = \frac{\left|Ca^{..}\right| \times \left|HCO_3^-\right|^2 \times \alpha^3}{\left|CO_2\right|} = 1.13 \cdot 10^{-4},$$

the system is in equilibrium and calcium carbonate does not precipitate. In this equation, carbon dioxide is of particular importance as an independent variable. In water bodies with a rich population, the equilibrium between $CaCO_3$ and $Ca(HCO_3)_2$ depends on respiration and on the assimilation of carbon dioxide. An increase in the concentration of carbon dioxide converts $CaCO_3$ from a solid to a dissolved state until the proportion between the concentrations of $Ca^{..}$, HCO_3', and CO_2 becomes again equal to 1.13×10^{-4}.

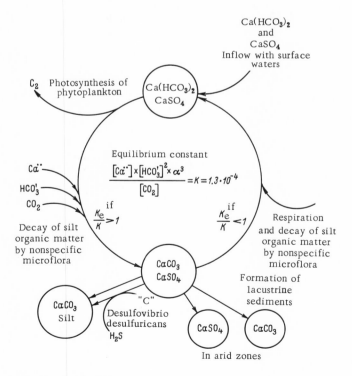

FIGURE 202. Scheme of calcium cycle in lakes.

A deficit of carbon dioxide causes an opposite shift, namely, the decomposition of $Ca(HCO_3)_2$ to $CaCO_3$. However, an unstable state can persist for an indefinite period because $CaCO_3$ tends to form supersaturated solutions. The restoration of the equilibrium requires a catalyst, such as the microscopic calcite crystals that exist in suspension and in the slime on the surface of photosynthetic phytoplankton cells. Under such circumstances the calcite crystals grow steadily as they sink to the bottom of the water body. According to the Kolthoff equilibrium, the formation of calcium occurs at the expense of the reduction of $CaSO_4$ in Desulfovibrio desulfuricans. In arid zones, in lakes joining to the sea, the NaCl concentration, as well as the concentration of other salts dissolved in sea water, starts to increase at high summer temperatures. At 5% NaCl, the chemogenic deposition of calcium carbonate starts and then crystals of calcium sulfate, gypsum, are precipitated.

CONCLUSION

V. I. Vernadsky, the founder of geochemistry in the USSR, wrote the following about the role of microorganisms in geochemical processes: "Our concepts of the 'Universe,' 'nature,' or 'integrity,' of which so much was spoken during the eighteenth and the first half of the nineteenth centuries, are undergoing rapid changes before our very eyes..." "Not only the theories and scientific hypotheses -- fleeting creations of the mind -- but also the valuable new empiric facts and generalizations force us to alter and reconstruct our picture of nature, which had remained intact and almost unchanged during several generations of scientists and thinkers. And if the roots of modern knowledge can be traced back to the atoms and to the elements of ancient science and philosophy, they are so thoroughly changed today that only their names link them with the past. Facts have dictated the establishment of new scientific disciplines, which do not have the static concepts of the old ones" (Vernadsky, 1934, p. 758). Geochemistry is one of these new sciences.

In Vernadsky's words, geochemistry "deals with the chemical elements, that is, the atoms of the earth's crust and, as far as possible, of the whole planet. It studies their history, distribution, and movement in space and time, their genetic relationships on our planet" (p. 9).

Vernadsky regarded living organisms as important factors in geochemistry: "From the geochemical viewpoint, living organisms are not an accidental factor in the chemical organization of the earth's crust but represent an integral and essential part of it. They are closely associated with the inert material of the earth's crust, with minerals and rocks" (Ibid, p.38).

Vernadsky notes that, in studying the live organisms, biologists have largely ignored the close relationship that exists between the organism and its environment. "Concentrating on the structure and function of the organism, they have neglected the organization of the environment, that is, the biosphere. This environment cannot be regarded as inert, 'cosmic,' or independent of the organism. Viewed in such light, the organism ceases to be a natural body and becomes an ideal product of the mind (Ibid, p.38).

"An organism, its form and biology cannot be understood without reference to the environment" (p. 39). According to Vernadsky, "the geochemical manifestations of organisms can only be studied in terms of the overall effect of their physiological activity, which thus becomes a planetary phenomenon" (p. 41).

The geochemical activity of microorganisms is especially evident in the hydrosphere, which includes lakes. One of our tasks was to demonstrate the close relationship between the lake environment and the activity of different groups of microorganisms.

The geochemical activity of microorganisms depends largely on the chemical composition of lake water, which reflects the mineral and organic content of surface and underground waters entering the lake.

An increase in the concentration of biogenic elements — mineral salts of nitrogen and phosphorus — leads to a greater production of organic matter as a result of photosynthesis by the phytoplankton, which in turn accelerates the bacterial mineralization of organic compounds. In sufficiently deep lakes, these processes occur even if aerobic conditions return to the organic cycle. This "lesser cycle" lasts about one week.

The geochemical activity of anaerobic bacteria is concentrated in the silt. Here, too, the specific composition of the microflora and the course of the breakdown of organic matter depend on the concentration of the latter in the silt. These processes yield hydrogen, methane, and free nitrogen. Thus, bacterial activity causes major changes in the environment.

However, the microflora does not affect merely the chemistry of the environment. Dissolved organic matter is assimilated into new bacterial biomass, which in turn serves as food for the zooplankton.

The magnitude of the geochemical activity of bacteria can be illustrated in the case of the Rybinsk Artificial Reservoir. During the summer, the photosynthetic activity of the phytoplankton produces here about 100—110 thousand tons of organic matter, while the bacterial population develops a biomass of 160 thousand tons. The phytoplankton fixes about 4,000 tons of atmospheric nitrogen within the same period.

The geochemical activity of the aquatic microflora of lakes is even more obvious in the processes of the sulfur cycle. Practically all the hydrogen sulfide of lakes is of biological origin, regardless of whether it comes from putrefaction or from the reduction of sulfate. Laboratory tests have shown that the reduction of sulfate to hydrogen sulfide in natural conditions requires the presence of sulfate-reducing bacteria. The rate of sulfate reduction was determined by the use of radioactive isotopes. This process takes place mainly in the silt, yielding up to 20 mg of hydrogen sulfide per day per kg of silt.

However, the reduction of sulfate is not the only geochemical manifestation of bacteria. Depending on the environment, part of the hydrogen sulfide can be oxidized chemically, either by thiobacilli or by pigmented sulfur bacteria. The oxidation proceeds to sulfate or stops at molecular sulfur; examples of the latter are the syngenetic deposits of sulfur, formed in recent and past geological time.

The role of microorganisms in the formation of iron and manganese deposits is still a matter of controversy among geologists. At any rate, this geochemical process occurs today with the direct participation of microorganisms, as shown by studies of the microflora of iron-manganese lake ores.

Inland water bodies permit a more thorough ecological study of ore-forming microorganisms. The analysis of ore formation in such environments has shed light on all the processes involving the precipitation of manganese from dilute solutions, the reduction of this element by microorganisms in the silt, and its secondary oxidation from more concentrated solutions on the silt surface.

Comparison of the experimental results with analyses of the microflora and chemistry of water and silt in natural conditions has confirmed the words of Vernadsky on the geochemical role of microorganisms.

Vernadsky maintained that microorganisms are not accidental factors in the geochemistry of the earth's crust but represent an essential and integral part of it. This view was fully confirmed by recent knowledge on the chemical transformations in inland waters.

BIBLIOGRAPHY

Publications in Russian

Afanas'ev, G. D.   Donnye otlozheniya ozera Sevan (Bottom Sediments of Lake Sevan). — Sovet po Izucheniyu Proizvoditel'nykh Sil.   Seriya Zakavkazskaya, No. 6.   Bassein Ozera Sevan, 3(2):59—153. Leningrad, Izd. AN SSSR i Upravlenie vodokhranilishch SSR Armenii. 1933.

Akimov, V. A.   Obshchaya chislennost' mikroorganizmov v vode rybovodnykh prudov pri intensivnom udobrenii i kormlenii ryby (Total Numbers of Microorganisms in Fishponds with Intensive Fertilization and Fish Feeding). — Trudy Vsesoyuznogo Nauchno-Issledovatel'skogo Instituta Prudovogo Rybnogo Khozyaistva, Vol. 14:185—189. 1966.

Akimov, V. A.   Izuchenie protsessov raspada organicheskogo veshchestva v rybovodnykh prudakh pri vnesenii mineral'nykh udobrenii i kormlenii ryby (Decomposition Processes of Organic Matter in Fishponds with Mineral Fertilization and Fish Feeding).   Author's Summary of Candidate Thesis. Institut Mikrobiologii AN SSSR. Moskva. 1967a.

Akimov, V. A.   Razlozhenie organicheskogo veshchestva ilovykh otlozhenii rybovodnykh prudov (Decomposition of the Organic Matter in Muddy Sediments of Fishponds). — Trudy Vsesoyuznogo Nauchno-Issledovatel'skogo Instituta Prudovogo Rybnogo Khozyaistva, Vol. 15:221—227. 1967b.

Alabyshev, V. V.   Zonal'nost' ozernykh otlozhenii (Zonation of Lake Sediments). — Izvestiya Sapropelevogo komiteta, No. 6:1—44. 1932.

Aleev, B. S.   Vydelenie vodoroslyami organicheskikh veshchestv v okruzhayushchuyu sredu (Excretion of Organic Matter by Algae into the Environment). — Trudy Instituta Vodosnabzheniya. 1933.

Aleev, B. S.   K voprosu o mekhanizme vydeleniya vodoroslyami organicheskikh veshchestv (On the Mechanism of Excretion of Organic Matter by Algae). — Biokhimiya, 1(1):94—100. 1936.

Aleev, B. S. and K. A. Mudretsova. Rol' fitoplanktona v dinamike azota v vode "tsvetushchego" vodoema (The Role of Phytoplankton in Nitrogen Dynamics in a "Blooming" Water Body). — Mikrobiologiya, Vol. 6:329—338. 1937.

Alekin, O. A.   Obshchaya gidrokhimiya (General Hydrochemistry), p. 42. Leningrad, Gidrometizdat, 1948.

Aleshina, V. I.   Razrushenie khinina bakteriyami, vosstanavlivayushchimi sul'faty, i izmeneniya okislitel'no-vosstanovitel'nykh uslovii v protsesse vosstanovleniya sul'fatov (Decomposition of Quinine by Sulfate-Reducing Bacteria and Fluctuations of Oxidation-Reduction Conditions in the Sulfate-Reduction Process). — Mikrobiologiya, 7(7):850—859. 1938.

440

Alipova, M. G.   O roli azotobaktera v pishchevykh vzaimootnosheniyakh zoonaseleniya rybkhoza "Yamat" (The Role of Azotobacter in Food Relationships of Zoopopulation at the "Yamat" Fish Farm). — Trudy Instituta Mikrobiologii AN SSSR, No. 4:207—212. 1955.

Aliverdieva, L. A.   Sravnitel'noe izuchenie mikroflory osnovnykh tipov ozer Dagestana (Comparative Study of the Microflora of the Main Types of Lakes of Dagestan). — Mikrobiologiya, 33(3):494—500. 1964.

Aliverdieva, L. A.   Mikrobiologicheskaya kharakteristika osnovnykh tipov ozer Dagestana (Microbiological Description of the Main Types of Lakes of Dagestan).   Author's Summary of Candidate Thesis.   AN AzSSR, otdel biologicheskikh nauk. Makhachkala. 1965.

Aristovskaya, T. V.   Akkumulyatsiya zheleza pri razlozhenii organo-mineral'nykh kompleksov gumusovykh veshchestv mikroorganizmami (Iron Accumulation with Decomposition of Organic and Mineral Complexes of Humus by Microorganisms). — Doklady AN SSSR, 136(4):954—957. 1961.

Balashova, V. V.   Nakopitel'naya kul'tura Gallionella filamenta n. sp. (Cumulative Culture of Gallionella filamenta n. sp). — Mikrobiologiya, 36(4):646—650. 1967.

Balashova, V. V.   K taksonomii roda Gallionella (Taxonomy of the Genus Gallionella). — Mikrobiologiya, 37(4):715—724. 1968.

Belyaev, S. S.   Rasprostranenie gruppy Caulobacter v vodokhrani-lishchakh Volgo-Dona (Distribution of the Group Caulobacter in Volga-Don Reservoirs). — Mikrobiologiya, 36(1):157—162. 1967.

Belyaeva, M. I.   Khimizm usvoeniya uglekislogo gaza i rol' fosfatov pri avtotrofnoi assimilyatsii ugleroda vodorodnymi bakteriyami (Chemistry of Carbon Dioxide Assimilation and the Role of Phosphates in Autotrophic Assimilation of Carbon by Hydrogen Bacteria). — Uchenye Zapiski Kazanskogo Universiteta, Biologiya, 114(1):3—12. 1954.

Belyatskaya-Potaenko, Yu. S.   Kolichestvennye dannye po bakterial'-nomu pitaniyu zooplanktona (Quantitative Data on the Bacterial Diet of Zooplankton). — In Sbornik: Biologicheskie osnovy rybnogo khozyaistva na vnutrennikh vodoemakh Pribaltiki. Trudy X nauchnoi konferentsii po izucheniyu vnutrennikh vod Pribaltiki, pp. 227—282. Minsk. 1964.

Berval'd, E. A.   Opyt izucheniya prevrashchenii organicheskogo veshchest-va v presnovodnom vodoeme (ozero Piyavochnoe Vyshnevolotskogo raiona) (An Experimental Study of the Transformation of Organic Matter in a Freshwater Body (Lake Piyavochnoe of the Vyshnii-Volochek Area)). — In Sbornik: Nauchnye studencheskie raboty MGU, No. 6. 1939.

Bogoslovskii, B. B.   Ozerovedenie (Limnology). Izd. MGU. 1960.

Bokova, E. N.   Ob obrazovanii gazoobraznykh produktov pri biokhimiche-skom razlozhenii organicheskogo veshchestva ila, pochvy i porody (Formation of Gaseous Products in the Biochemical Decomposition of Organic Matter in Mud, Soil and Rocks). — Trudy Nauchno-Issledovatel'skogo Instituta Geofizicheskikh i Geokhimicheskikh Metodov Razvedki, No. 2:59—67. 1954.

Braksht, N., L. Dubova, and K. Logina.   Sapropelevye otlozheniya vodoemov Latviiskoi SSR (Sapropelic Sediments of Water Bodies of the Latvian SSR). Riga, Izd. "Znanie." 1967.

Butkevich, V. S.   Obrazovanie morskikh zhelezo-margantsevykh otlozhenii i uchastvuyushchie v nem mikroorganizmy (Formation of Iron and Manganese Sediments in the Sea and Participating Microorganisms).— Trudy Morskogo Nauchnogo Instituta, 3(3):1—81. 1928.

Butkevich, V. S.   O bakterial'nom naselenii Kaspiiskogo i Azovskogo morei (The Bacterial Population of the Caspian Sea and Sea of Azov).— Mikrobiologiya, 7(9/10):1021—1055. 1938a.

Butkevich, V. S.   O bakterial'nom naselenii morskikh vod v vysokoshirot-nykh arkticheskikh oblastyakh (The Bacterial Population of Seawaters of High-Latitude Arctic Regions). — Doklady AN SSSR, 19(8):651. 1938b.

Butkevich, V. S. and I. V. Bogdanova. Nekotorye osobennosti naseleniya arkticheskikh morei (Some Features of the Population of Arctic Seas). — Mikrobiologiya, 8(9/10):1073—1095. 1939.

Bylinkina, V. N.   K poznaniyu pochvennoi mikroflory kak konstitutsionnoi chasti bioorganomineral'nogo kompleksa pochv (Contribution to the Study of Soil Microflora as a Constituent of the Bioorganic-Mineral Complex of Soils). — Mikrobiologiya, 9(2):129—142. 1940.

Daukshta, A. S.   Dannye mikrobiologicheskogo obsledovaniya nekotorykh ozer Latviiskoi SSR. Biologiya vnutrennikh vod (Data of the Micro-biological Investigation of Some Lakes of the Latvian SSR.   Biology of Inland Waters). — Informatsionnyi Byulleten', No. 1:20—22. 1968.

Daukshta, A. S.   Mikrobiologicheskaya kharakteristika osnovnykh tipov ozer Latviiskoi SSR (Microbiological Description of the Main Types of Lakes of the Latvian SSR). Author's Summary of Thesis. 1969.

Deksbakh, N. K.   O khimicheskom sostave ilov nekotorykh ozer Moskovskoi oblasti (Chemical Composition of Mud of Some Lakes of the Moscow Region). — Trudy Sapropelevogo Instituta, Vol. 1:213—221. 1934.

Deksbakh, N. K.   O khimicheskom sostave zheleznoi rudy ozera Idolom-skogo bliz goroda Kostromy (Chemical Composition of Iron Ore of Lake Idolomskoe near Kostroma). — Uchenye Zapiski Moskovskogo Universiteta, Biologiya, No. 8:172—173. 1936.

Dianova, E. V. and A. A. Voroshilova. Azotobakter-podobnye bakterii v pochve (Azotobacter-like Bacteria in the Soil). — Nauchno-Agronomicheskii Zhurnal, 7(4):259—270. 1930.

Dolgov, G. I.   Sobinskie ozera (Sobinka Lakes). — Trudy Vsesoyuznogo Gidrobiologicheskogo Obshchestva, Vol. 6:193—204. 1955.

Doman, N. G. and A. K. Romanova. K voprosu o puti ugleroda pri khemosinteze (The Pathway of Carbon in Chemosynthesis). — Doklady AN SSSR, 128(5):1076—1079. 1959.

Doman, N. G., A. K. Romanova and Z. A. Terent'eva. Put' ugleroda pri khemosinteze. O prirode rannego produkta khemosinteza vodorod-nykh bakterii (Carbon Pathway in Chemosynthesis.   The Nature of the Early Product of Chemosynthesis of Hydrogen Bacteria). — Doklady AN SSSR, 138(6):1456—1459. 1961.

Doman, N. G., Z. A. Vasil'eva, A. K. Romanova, and G. A. Zavarzin. O putyakh assimilyatsii ugleroda monokarbonovykh soedinenii pochkuyushchimisya bakteriyami Hyphomicrobium vulgare Stutz et Hartleb (Carbon Assimilation of Monocarboxylic Compounds by Budding Bacteria Hyphomicrobium vulgare Stutz et Hartleb). — Mikrobiologiya, 34(1):3—11. 1965.

Dostalek, M.   Propanokislyayushchie bakterii (Propane-Oxidizing Bacteria). — Biologiya, 3(3): 173—182. 1954.

Drabkova, V. G.   Dinamika chislennosti bakterii, vremya generatsii i produktsiya bakterii v vode ozera Krasnogo (Punnus-Yarvi) (Population Dynamics, Generation Time and Bacterial Production in Waters of Lake Krasnoe (Punnus-Yarvi)). — Mikrobiologiya, 34(6):1063—1069. 1965.

Dragunov, S. S., N. N. Zhelokhovtseva, and E. I. Strelkova.   Sravnitel'noe issledovanie pochvennykh i torfyanykh guminovykh kislot (Comparative Study of Soil, Peat and Humic Acids). — Pochvovedenie, No. 7:409-420. 1948.

Dubinina, G. A.   O prinadlezhnosti roda Metallogenium k poryadku Mycoplasmatales (The Genus Metallogenium Belonging to the Mycoplasmatales) — Doklady AN SSSR, 184(6):1433—1436. 1969.

Dubinina, G. A. and Z. P. Deryugina.   Mikrobiologicheskie protsessy prevrashcheniya form zheleza v meromikticheskom ozere (Microbiological Processes of Transformation of Iron Forms in a Meromictic Lake). — Zhurnal Obshchei Biologii, 30(5):602—610. 1969.

Dukel'skii, V. M.   Fiziko-khimicheskie nablyudeniya na Teletskom ozere letom 1928 g. (Physicochemical Observations in Lake Teletskoe in the Summer of 1928). — Izvestiya Gosudarstvennogo Gidrologicheskogo Instituta, No. 28:42. 1930.

Dymchishina-Kriventsova, T. D.   Bakterioplankton malykh vodokhranilishch Moldavii (Bacterioplankton of Small Reservoirs of Moldavia). — In Sbornik: Biologicheskie resursy vodoemov Moldavii, No. 2:68—81. Kishinev, Izd. Cartea Moldoveneasca. 1964.

Dzens-Litovskii, A. I.   Mineral'nye ozera Iletskogo solyanogo kupola i ikh termicheskii rezhim (Mineral Lakes of the Sol'-Iletsk Salt Dome and their Thermal Regime). — Trudy Laboratorii Ozerovedeniya AN SSSR, Vol. 2:108—138. 1953.

Dzyuban, I. N.   Nekotorye dannye o mikrobakteriyakh volzhskikh vodokhranilishch (Some Data on the Bacteria of the Volga Reservoirs). — Byulleten' Instituta Biologii Vodokhranilishch, No. 5:7—8. 1959.

Egorov, M. A.   Fosfornaya kislota navoza pri razlichnykh usloviyakh ego khraneniya (Phosphoric Acid of Manure under Various Conditions of Storage). Gosudarstvennoe Izdatel'stvo Ukrainy. 1925.

Egorova, A. A.   Mikrobiologicheskie issledovaniya ozera Belovod' (Microbiological Investigations of Lake Belovod'). — Mikrobiologiya, 20(2): 103—112. 1951.

Egorova, A. A., Z. P. Deryugina, and S. I. Kuznetsov.   Kharakteristika saprofitnoi mikroflory vody ozer razlichnoi stepeni trofii (Characteristics of the Saprophytic Microflora of Waters of Lakes of Various Trophic Degrees). — Trudy Instituta Mikologii AN SSSR, No. 2:139—149. 1952.

Ekzertsev, V. A.   Opredelenie moshchnosti mikrobiologicheski aktivnogo sloya ilovykh otlozhenii nekotorykh ozer (Determining the Thickness of the Microbiologically Active Layer of Silt Sediments of Some Lakes). — Mikrobiologiya, 17(6):476—483. 1948.

Eleonskii, A. N.   Osnovy rybovodstva (Fundamentals of Fish Culture). Moskva. 1932.

Epikhina, V. V. and G. A. Zavarzin. Okislitel'no-vosstanovitel'nyi potentsial pri razvitii Metallogenium (Redox Potential for the Development of Metallogenium). — Mikrobiologiya, 32(2):227—230. 1963.

Ermachenko, V. A. Morfologicheskie formy Nitrosomonas europae i ikh fiziologicheskie osobennosti (Morphological Forms of Nitrosomonas europae and their Physiological Properties). — Izvestiya AN SSSR, Seriya Biologicheskaya, No. 4:539—548. 1966.

Erzinkyan, L. A. K voprosu biogennogo obrazovaniya travertinov i kristallov ozera Sevan (On the Biogenic Formation of Travertines and Crystals in Lake Sevan). — Mikrobiologicheskii sbornik, AN ArmSSR, No. 4:127—147. 1949.

Fatchikhina, O. E. Metod opredeleniya okislyaemosti vody khromovoi smes'yu (Potassium Dichromate Determination of the Oxidizability of Water). — Gidrokhimicheskie Materialy, Vol. 15:205—212. 1948a.

Fatchikhina, O. E. Dinamika soderzhaniya fosfora i zheleza v Chernom ozere (Dynamics of Phosphorus and Iron Content in Lake Chernoe). — Gidrokhimicheskie Materialy, Vol. 15:180—204. 1948b.

Fedorova, E. O. Ozernoe zhelezonakoplenie v predelakh Baltiiskogo kristallicheskogo shchita (Lacustrine Iron Accumulation within the Limits of the Baltic Crystalline Shield). — In Sbornik: Nakoplenie veshchestva v ozerakh, pp. 164—193. Moskva, Izd."Nauka." 1964a.

Fedorova, E. O. Kharakteristika zhelezorudnykh ozer Kol'skogo poluostrova (Characteristics of Iron-Ore Lakes of the Kola Peninsula). — In Sbornik: Nakoplenie veshchestva v ozerakh, pp. 59—77. Moskva, Izd. "Nauka." 1964b.

Fedosov, M. V. Metodika izucheniya obogashcheniya biogennymi elementami naddonnoi vody (Methods of Studying Enrichment of Near-Bottom Waters by Biogenic Elements). — Doklady po biologii sistematiki i pitaniyu ryb, VNIRO, Vol. 1:152—154. 1950.

Filimonova, N. A. Bakterioplankton i bakterial'nyi perefiton v razlichnykh biotopakh Syamozera (Bacterioplankton and the Bacterial Periphyton in Various Biotopes of Lake Syamozero). — Mikrobiologiya, 34(1):133—139. 1965.

Fortunatov, M. A. Tsvetnost' i prozrachnost' vody Rybinskogo vodokhranilishcha kak pokazateli ego rezhima (Color and Transparency of the Water of the Rybinsk Reservoir as Parameters of its Regime). — Trudy Instituta Biologii Vodokhranilishch, 2(5):246—357. 1959.

Fotiev, A. V. K izucheniyu gumusa gruntovykh vod (Study of Humus of Ground Waters). — Pochvovedenie, No. 11:115—117. 1966.

Frantsev, A. F. and S. K. Lebedeva. Khimizm vody Uchinskogo vodokhranilishcha (Chemistry of the Water of the Ucha Reservoir). — Trudy Zoologicheskogo Instituta AN SSSR 7(1):31—52. 1941.

Frantsev, A. V. Opyt otsenki gidrobiologicheskoi proizvoditel'nosti moskvoretskoi vody (An Experiment to Estimate the Hydrobiological Efficiency of the Water of the Moskva River). — Mikrobiologiya, 1(2):112—130. 1932.

Frantsev, A. V. Marganets v Uchinskom vodokhranilishche (Manganese in the Ucha Reservoir) — Trudy Vsesoyuznogo Gidrobiologicheskogo Obshchestva, Vol. 9:13—28. 1959.

Gabe, D.R. and V.A. Rabinovich. Fiziko-khimicheskie usloviya razvitiya Metallogenium Perf. v ilu (Physicochemical Conditions of the Development of Metallogenium Perf. in Mud).— In Sbornik: Rol' mikroorganizmov i obrazovanii zhelezo-margantsevykh ozernykh rud, pp. 54—70. Moskva—Leningrad, Izd. "Nauka." 1964.

Gabe, D.R., E.P. Troshanov, and E.E. Sherman. Obrazovanie margantsevo-zhelezistykh prosloek v ile kak biogennyi protsess (Formation of Manganese-Iron Strata in Mud as a Biogenous Process). — In Sbornik: Rol' mikroorganizmov v obrazovanii zhelezo-margantsevykh ozernykh rud, pp. 95—117. Moskva—Leningrad, Izd. "Nauka." 1964.

Gaevskaya, N.S. Trofologicheskoe napravlenie v gidrobiologii, ego ob"ekt, nekotorye osnovnye problemy i zadachi (The Trophologic Trend in Hydrobiology, its Object and Some Major Problems and Tasks). — Sbornik, posvyashchennyi pamyati S.A. Zernova, pp. 27—47. Moskva—Leningrad, Izd. AN SSSR. 1948.

Gaevskii, P.M. Zheleznye ozernye rudy Olonetskogo kraya i ikh ispol'-zovanie (Lake Iron Ores of the Olonets Territory and their Exploitation). — In Sbornik: Proizvoditel'nye sily raiona Murmanskoi zheleznoi dorogi. Petrozavodsk. 1923.

Gambaryan, M.E. Obshchaya kharakteristika protsessov prevrashcheniya azota, chislennost' i biomassa bakterii v ozere Sevan (General Characteristics of Transformation Processes of Nitrogen; Numbers and Biomass of Bacteria in Lake Sevan). — Trudy Sevanskoi Gidrobiologicheskoi Stantsii AN Armyanskoi SSR. Vol. 15:5—45. 1957.

Gambaryan, M.E. O produktsii fitoplanktona i khemoavtotrofnykh bakterii v ozere Sevan (Phytoplanktonic Production and Chemoautotrophic Bacteria in Lake Sevan). — In Sbornik: Pervichnaya produktsiya morei i vnutrennikh vod, pp. 218—222, Minsk, Izd. Ministerstva vysshego obrazovaniya Belorusskoi SSR. 1961.

Gambaryan, M.E. Mikrobiologicheskie protsessy krugovorota sery v ozere Sevan (Microbiological Processes of the Sulfur Cycle in Lake Sevan). — Trudy Sevanskoi Gidrobiologicheskoi Stantsii, Vol. 16:5—14. 1962.

Gambaryan, M.E. Rol' biologicheskikh protsessov v sovremennom kislorodnom rezhime ozera Sevan (The Role of Biological Processes in the Contemporary Oxygen Regime in Lake Sevan). — Izvestiya AN Armyanskoi SSR, Biologicheskie Nauki, 16(9):7—16. 1963.

Gambaryan, M.E. Opredelenie intensivnosti fotosinteza i destruktsii organicheskogo veshchestva i biotipicheskii balans vodnoi tolshchi ozera Sevan (Determination of the Intensity of Photosynthesis and Decomposition of Organic Matter and the Biotypic Balance of the Water Column of Lake Sevan). — In Sbornik: Radioaktivnye izotopy v gidrobiologii i metody sanitarnoi gidrobiologii, pp. 3—10. 1964.

Gerasimov, E.G. Karstovye yavleniya Vladimirskoi gubernii (Karst Phenomena in Vladimir Province) — Trudy Vladimirskogo Obshchestva Lyubitelei Estestvoznaniya, Vol. 4:79. 1916.

Godnev, T.I. and G.G. Vinberg. O pigmentakh zelenoi bakterii (The Pigments of Green Sulfur Bacteria) — Doklady AN SSSR, 76(6):909—912. 1951.

Gorbunov, K. V.   Rasprostranenie A z.   chroococcum v vodoemakh
     i pochvakh del'ty Volgi i ego znachenie kak faktora produktivnosti
     (Distribution of A z. chroococcum in Water Bodies and Soils
     of the Volga Delta and its Significance as a Factor of Productivity). —
     Mikrobiologiya, 20(3):231—244. 1951.

Gorbunov, K. V.   Raspad ostatkov vysshikh vodnykh rastenii i ego ekologi-
     cheskaya rol' v vodoemakh nizhnei zony del'ty Volgi (Decomposition
     of the Remains of Higher Aquatic Plants and its Ecological Role in
     Water Bodies of the Lower Zone of the Volga Delta). — Trudy
     Vsesoyuznogo Gidrobiologicheskogo Obshchestva, Vol. 5:158—202.
     1953.

Gorlenko, V. M.   Novyi vid zelenykh serobakterii (A New Species of Green
     Sulfur Bacteria). — Doklady AN SSSR, 179(5):1229—1231. 1968a.

Gorlenko, V. M.   Vliyanie okislitel'no-vosstanovitel'nykh uslovii sredy i
     kisloroda na razvitie okrashennykh serobakterii v prirode (The Effect
     of Oxidation-Reduction Conditions of the Environment and of Oxygen
     on the Development of Sulfur Bacteria in Nature). — Mikrobiologiya,
     27(1):26—30. 1968b.

Gorlenko, V. M.   Rol' fiziko-khimicheskikh faktorov v raspredelenii
     fotosinteziruyushchikh bakterii (The Role of Physicochemical Factors
     in the Distribution of Photosynthetic Bacteria).   Author's Summary
     of Candidate Thesis.   Institut Mikrobiologii AN SSSR.   Moskva.
     1969a.

Gorlenko, V. M.   Sporoobrazovanie u pochkuyushcheisya fotogeterotrofnoi
     bakterii (Spore Formation in Budding Photoheterotrophic Bacteria). —
     Mikrobiologiya, 38(1):126—133. 1969b.

Gorlenko, V. M. and M. V. Ivanov.   Mikrobiologicheskoe obrazovanie
     karbonata kal'tsiya v ilakh ozera Solenogo (Microbiological Formation
     of Calcium Carbonate in Mud of Lake Solenoe).   (In Press.)

Gorlenko, V. M. and V. A. Kuznetsova.   Bakterial'noe vosstanovlenie
     sul'fatov pri sovmestnom kul'tivirovanii Desulfovibrio
     desulfuricans i uglevodorod okislyayushchikh bakterii na
     mineral'noi srede s neft'yu (Bacterial Reduction of Sulfates with
     Associated Cultivation of Desulfovibrio desulfuricans and
     Hydrocarbon Oxidizing Bacteria on Mineral Medium with Petroleum). —
     Prikladnaya Biokhimiya i Mikrobiologiya, 2(3):264—270. 1966.

Goryunova, S. V.   Kharakteristika rastvorennykh organicheskikh
     veshchestv v vode Glubokogo ozera (Characteristics of Dissolved
     Organic Matter in the Water of Lake Glubokoe). — Trudy Instituta
     Mikrobiologii AN SSSR, No. 2:166—179. 1952.

Greze, V. N.   Taimyrskoe ozero (Lake Taimyr). — Izvestiya Vsesoyuznogo
     Geograficheskogo Obshchestva, 79(3):289—302. 1947.

Grichuk, V. P.   Karstovye ozera (sovremennye i iskopaemye) doliny reki
     Teshi (Karst Lakes (Recent and Fossil) of the Valley of the Tesha
     River) — Zemlevedenie, 39(1):44—57. 1937.

Gryaznov, V. I.   Genezis margantsevykh rud (Genesis of Manganese
     Ores). — In Sbornik: Nikopol'skii margantsevorudnyi bassein,
     pp. 271—284. 1964.

Gurfein, L. N.   Metody kolichestvennogo ucheta bakterii v vode (Methods
     of Counting Bacteria in Water). — Arkhiv Biologicheskikh Nauk,
     Vol. 30, Nos. 5—6. 1930.

Guseva, K. A.   Tsvetenie Uchinskogo vodokhranilishcha (Bloom of the
    Ucha Reservoir). — Trudy Zoologicheskogo Instituta AN SSSR, 7(1):
    89—121. 1941.
Imshenetskii, A. A.   Mikrobiologiya tsellyulozy (Microbiology of
    Cellulose). Moskva, Izd. AN SSSR. 1953.
Imshenetskii, A. A. and L. I. Solntseva.   Ob aerobnykh tsellyuloznykh
    bakteriyakh (Aerobic Cellulose Bacteria). — Izvestiya AN SSSR,
    Seriya Biologicheskaya, No. 6:1115—1172. 1936.
Imshenetskii, A. A. and L. I. Solntseva.   O miksobakteriyakh,
    razlagayushchikh kletchatku (On Myxobacteria Decomposing Cel-
    lulose). — Mikrobiologiya, 6(1):3—15. 1937.
Isachenko, B. L.   Issledovaniya nad bakteriyami Severnogo Ledovitogo
    okeana (Study of Bacteria of the Arctic Ocean). — Trudy Murmanskoi
    Nauchno-Promyshlennoi Ekspeditsii, 1906. Petrograd. 1914.
Isachenko, B. L.   O gipoteze Brandta i o denitrifitsiruyushchikh
    bakteriyakh Chernogo i Mramornogo morei (Brandt's Hypothesis
    and Denitrifying Bacteria of the Black Sea and Sea of Marmara). —
    Zhurnal Mikrobiologii, Vol. 3:53—60. 1916.
Isachenko, B. L.   Mikrobiologicheskie issledovaniya nad gryazevymi
    ozerami (Microbiological Investigations of Mud Lakes). — Trudy
    Geologicheskogo Komiteta, Novaya Seriya, No. 148; Izbrannye Trudy,
    Vol. 2:26—142. 1927 (1951).
Isachenko, B. L.   O biogennom obrazovanii karbonata kal'tsiya (Biogenous
    Formation of Calcium Carbonate). — Mikrobiologiya, Vol. 17, No. 2.
    1948. Izbrannye Trudy, Vol. 2:226—233. Moskva—Leningrad, Izd.
    AN SSSR 1951.
Isachenko, B. L. and A. G. Salimovskaya.   K morfologii i fiziologii
    tionovykh bakterii (Morphology and Physiology of Sulfur Bacteria). —
    Izvestiya Gosudarstvennogo Gidrologicheskogo Instituta, Nos. 21, 61;
    Izbrannye Trudy, Vol. 2:176—189. Moskva—Leningrad. 1928.
Ivanov, M. V.   Opredelenie vremeni generatsii vodnykh bakterii v ryb-
    khoze del'ty reki Volgi (Determining the Generation Time of Bacteria
    in the Water of Fisheries of the Volga River Delta). — Trudy Instituta
    Mikrobiologii AN SSSR, No. 3:213—220. 1954.
Ivanov, M. V.   Metod opredeleniya produktsii bakterial'noi biomassy v
    vodoeme (Determination of the Production of Bacterial Biomass in
    a Water Body). — Mikrobiologiya, 24(1):79—89. 1955.
Ivanov, M. V.   Primenenie izotopov dlya izucheniya protsessa reduktsii
    sul'fatov v ozere Belovod' (Using Isotopes for Studying the Process
    of Sulfate Reduction in Lake Belovod'). — Mikrobiologiya, 25(3):
    305—309. 1956.
Ivanov, M. V.   Rol' mikroorganizmov v obrazovanii otlozhenii sery v
    serovodorodnykh istochnikakh Sergievskikh mineral'nykh vod (The
    Role of Microorganisms in the Formation of Sulfur Deposits in
    Hydrosulfide Sources of Sergievsk Mineral Waters). — Mikro-
    biologiya, 24(3):338—345. 1957.
Ivanov, M. V.   Izuchenie intensivnosti protsessa krugovorota sery v ozerakh
    s pomoshch'yu radioaktivnoi sery (The Study of the Intensity of Sulfur
    Cycle Processes in Lakes Using Radioactive Sulfur). — Trudy VI
    soveshchaniya po problemam biologii vnutrennikh vod, pp. 152—158.
    Moskva—Leningrad. 1959.

Ivanov, M. V. Rol' mikrobiologicheskikh protsessov v genezise mesto-
rozhdenii sery (The Role of Microbiological Processes in the Genesis
of Sulfur Deposits). — Moskva—Leningrad, Izd. "Nauka." 1964.

Ivanov, M. V. and G. I. Karavaiko. Rol' avtotrofnykh bakterii v okislenii
vulkanicheskoi sery (The Role of Autotrophic Bacteria in Oxidation of
Volcanic Sulfur). — In Sbornik: Avtotrofnye mikroorganizmy
(Yubileinyi sbornik 80 let akademika V. N. Shaposhnikova); Trudy
Obshchestva Ispytatelei Prirody, Vol. 24:221—228. 1964.

Ivanov, V. I. and N. N. Lyalikova. O sistematike zhelezookislyayushchikh
tionovykh bakterii (Classification of Iron-Oxidizing Sulfur Bacteria). —
Mikrobiologiya, 31(3):468—469. 1962.

Ivanov, M. V. and L. S. Terebkova. Izuchenie mikrobiologicheskikh
protsessov obrazovaniya serovodoroda v Solyanom ozere (Study of
Microbiological Processes of Hydrogen Sulfide Formation in Lake
Solyanoe). Communication I. — Mikrobiologiya, 28(2):251—256.
1959a.

Ivanov, M. V. and L. S. Terebkova. Izuchenie mikrobiologicheskikh
protsessov obrazovaniya serovodoroda v Solyanom ozere (Study of
Microbiological Processes of Formation of Hydrogen Sulfide in
Lake Solyanoe). Communication II. — Mikrobiologiya, 28(3):413—418.
1959b.

Ivlev, V. S. Materialy po izucheniyu balansa veshchestva v ozerakh.
Balans zheleza (Contributions to the Study of Element Balance in
Lakes. Iron Balance). — Trudy Limnologicheskoi Stantsii v Kosine,
No. 21:21—60. 1937.

Ivlev, V. S. Biologicheskaya produktivnost' vodoemov (Biological
Productivity of Water Bodies). — Uspekhi Sovremennoi Biologii,
Vol. 19:99—120. 1945.

Kalinenko, V. O. Vydelenie chistoi kul'tury Leptothrix ochracea
(Isolation of a Pure Culture of Leptothrix ochracea). —
Mikrobiologiya, 9(6):615—619. 1940.

Kalinenko, V. O. Novaya zhelezobakteriya reki Enisei (New Iron
Bacterium from the Yenisei River). — Mikrobiologiya, 14(4):292—296.
1945.

Kalinenko, V. O. Rol' bakterii v formirovanii zhelezo-margantsevykh
konkretsii (The Role of Bacteria in Formation of Iron-Manganese
Nodules). — Mikrobiologiya, 15(5):364—369. 1946.

Kalinenko, V. O. Geterotrofnye bakterii v roli nitrofikatorov (Heterotrophic Bacteria as Nitrogen Fixers). — Pochvovedenie, No. 6:
357—363. 1948.

Kalinenko, V. O. Bakterial'noe osazhdenie kal'tsiya v more (Bacterial
Sedimentation of Calcium in the Sea). — Trudy Instituta Okeanologii
AN SSSR, Vol. 3:200—215. 1949a.

Kalinenko, V. O. Proiskhozhdenie zhelezo-margantsevykh konkretsii
(Origin of Iron-Manganese Nodules). — Mikrobiologiya, 28(6):528—532.
1949b.

Kalinenko, V. O. Geokhimicheskaya deyatel'nost' bakterial'noi kolonii
(Geochemical Activity of a Bacterial Colony). — Izvestiya AN SSSR,
Seriya Geologicheskaya, No. 1:145—150. 1952.

Karzinkin, G. S. K izucheniyu bakterial'nogo perefitona (The Study of Bacterial Periphyton). — Trudy Limnologicheskoi Stantsii v Kosine, No. 17:21—48. 1934.

Karzinkin, G. S. Osnova biologicheskoi produktivnosti vodoemov (Fundamentals of the Biological Productivity of Water Bodies). Pishchepromizdat. Moskva. 1952.

Karzinkin, G. S. and S. I. Kuznetsov. Novye metody v limnologii (New Methods in Limnology). — Trudy Limnologicheskoi Stantsii v Kosine, Nos. 13—14:47—68. 1931.

Karzinkin, G. S. and Z. I. Kuznetsova. Izuchenie bakterial'nogo perefitona v vodakh raznoi stepeni zagryazneniya (Study of the Bacterial Periphyton in Waters with Various Degrees of Contamination). — Trudy Limnologicheskoi Stantsii v Kosine, No. 18:91—107. 1934.

Karzinkin, G. S., S. I. Kuznetsov, and Z. I. Kuznetsova. K vyyasneniyu prichin dinamiki kisloroda v vode Glubokogo ozera (Elucidation of Oxygen Dynamics in the Water of Lake Glubokoe). — Trudy Gidrobiologicheskoi Stantsii na Glubokom Ozere, 6(5):9—27. 1930.

Kastal'skaya-Karzinkina, M. A. Opyt primeneniya metoda ucheta zhivykh i otmershikh komponentov v izuchenii planktona Glubokogo ozera (Experimental Estimation of Living and Dead Components in a Study of the Plankton of Lake Glubokoe). — Trudy Limnologicheskoi Stantsii v Kosine, No. 21:143—170. 1937.

Kazakov, E. I. and B. A. Tovbin. Khimicheskii sostav pelogena i sapropelya ozer Belogo i Kolomno (Chemical Composition of the Pelogen and Sapropel of Lakes Beloe and Kolomno). — Trudy Laboratorii Genezisa Sapropeliya, No. 1; Materialy po izucheniyu genezisa ilovykh otlozhenii, pp. 165—172. 1939.

Khartulari, E. M. Bakteriologicheskie i khimicheskie issledovaniya ryada podmoskovnykh ozer v svyazi s voprosom razlozheniya ila s obrazovaniem gazov (Bacteriological and Chemical Investigations of a Number of Moscow Area Lakes in Connection with the Problem of Mud Decomposition and Gas Formation). — Trudy Limnologicheskoi Stantsii v Kosine, No. 22:115—127. 1939.

Khartulari, E. M. and S. I. Kuznetsov. Rezul'taty proschetov obshchego chisla bakterii v vode ryada ozer Vyshne-Volotskogo raiona (Results of Counting Bacteria in the Water of a Number of Lakes of the Vyshnii-Volotchek Area). — Trudy Limnologicheskoi Stantsii v Kosine, No. 21:117—124. 1936.

Kholodnyi, N. G. K morfologii zhelezobakterii Gallionella i Spirophyllum (Morphology of the Iron Bacteria Gallionella and Spirophyllum). — Russkii Arkhiv Protistologii, 3(3/4):4—95. 1925.

Kholodnyi, N. G. Bakterii, okislyayushchie i nakoplyayushchie zhelezo (Bacteria Oxidizing and Accumulating Iron). — In Sbornik: Sredi prirody i v laboratorii, No. 15:59—67. Izd. Moskovskogo obshchestva ispytatelei prirody. 1949.

Kholodnyi, N. G. Zhelezobakterii (Iron Bacteria). Moskva, Izd. AN SSSR. 1953.

Klachko, M. A.   Solyanye vodoemy raiona Bol'shoi El'by i nekotorye
    voprosy migratsii solei (Saline Water Bodies of the Elbe River Area
    and Some Problems of Salt Migration). — Priroda, No. 5:73—83. 1934.

Kondrat'eva, E. N.   Fotosinteziruyushchaya aktivnost' purpurnykh
    bakterii (Rhodopseudomonas sp.) i okislitel'no-vosstanovitel'nyi
    potentsial sredy.   Problemy fotosinteza (Photosynthetic Activity of
    Purple Bacteria (Rhodopseudomonas sp.) and Oxidation-
    Reduction Potential of the Medium.   Problems of Photosynthesis),
    p. 373. Moskva—Leningrad, Izd. AN SSSR. 1959.

Kondrat'eva, E. N.   Fotosinteziruyushchie bakterii (Photosynthesizing
    Bacteria). Moskva, Izd. AN SSSR. 1963.

Kondrat'eva, E. N. and E. V. Ramenskii.   Razvitie anaerobnykh
    fotosinteziruyushchikh bakterii v zavisimosti ot okislitel'no-vosstano-
    vitel'nykh uslovii sredy (Development of Anaerobic Photosynthesizing
    Bacteria in Relation to Oxidation-Reduction Conditions of the
    Medium). — Nauchnye Doklady Vysshei Shkoly, Biologicheskie Nauki,
    No. 4:155—159. 1961.

Kononova, M. M.   Problema pochvennogo gumusa i sovremennye zadachi
    ego izucheniya (The Problem of Soil Humus and Current Tasks of
    its Study). Moskva—Leningrad, Izd. AN SSSR. 1951.

Kononova, M. M., I. V. Aleksandrova, N. P. Bel'chikova, and
    N. A. Titova.   Gumus tselinnykh i osvoennykh pochv (Humus of
    Virgin and Developed Soils). — Doklady VIII Mezhdunarodnogo
    kongressa pochvovedov. Moskva, Izd. "Nauka." 1964.

Konshin, V. D.   Formy azota v ozernykh ilovykh otlozheniyakh (Forms of
    Nitrogen in Lacustrine Mud Sediments). — Trudy Limnologicheskoi
    Stantsii v Kosine, No. 22:105—114. 1939.

Konshin, V. D.   Metamorfizatsiya vody ozera Balkhash (Metamorphi-
    zation of Water of Lake Balkhash). — Doklady AN SSSR, 48(5):
    355—357. 1945.

Konshin, V. D.   Balans azota v Chernom ozere v Kosine (Nitrogen Balance
    in Lake Chernoe in Kosino). — Doklady AN SSSR, 66(5):941—943. 1949.

Konshin, V. D.   Gidrokhimiya zheleza v poverkhnostnykh vodakh sushi
    (Hydrochemistry of Iron in Inland Surface Waters). — Trudy Mos-
    kovskogo Tekhnicheskogo Instituta Rybnoi Promyshlennosti, No. 10:
    21—42. 1959.

Kopp, F. I. and E. L. Limberg.   Mikrobiologicheskie issledovaniya ozer
    severnogo Kazakhstana (Microbiological Investigations of Lakes of
    Northern Kazakhstan). — Mikrobiologiya, 14(4):281—286. 1945.

Korol'kov, K. N.   Raspad osadka v anaerobnykh usloviyakh (Decompo-
    sition of Sediments in Anaerobic Conditions). — Trudy Soveshchaniya
    po ochistke stochnykh vod pri Upravlenii kanalizatsii MKKh, No. 8. 1926.

Korsakova, M. P.   Vliyanie aeratsii na protsess vosstanovleniya nitratov
    (The Effect of Aeration on Nitrate Reduction). — Mikrobiologiya,
    10(2):163—178. 1941a.

Korsakova, M. P.   Vosstanovlenie nitratov do ammiaka nekotorymi
    fakul'tativnymi i obligatnymi anaerobami (Reduction of Nitrates to
    Ammonia by Some Facultative and Obligatory Anaerobes). —
    Mikrobiologiya, 10(3): 299—313. 1941b.

Korsakova, M.P.   Denitrifitsiruyushchie mikroorganizmy (obzor). (Denitrifying Bacteria (Survey)). — Mikrobiologiya, 22(2):215—227. 1953.

Kostychev, S.   Fiziologiya rastenii. Chast' 1. Khimicheskaya fiziologiya (Plant Physiology. Part 1. Chemical Physiology). Leningrad, Gosizdat. 1924.

Kostychev, S.P. and O.G. Shul'gina.   Vesovoe soderzhanie mikroorganizmov v pochvakh (Weight Content of Microorganisms in Soils). — Trudy Otdela Sel'skokhozyaistvennoi Mikrobiologii Gosudarstvennogo Instituta Opytnoi Agronomii, Vol. 2:109—112. 1927.

Krasheninnikova, S.A.   Mikrobiologicheskie protsessy raspada vodnoi rastitel'nosti v litorali Rybinskogo vodokhranilishcha (Microbiological Decomposition of Aquatic Vegetation in the Littoral of the Rybinsk Reservoir). — Byulleten' Instituta Biologii Vodokhranilishch, No. 2:3—6. 1958.

Krasheninnikova, S.A.   O raspredelenii metanokislyayushchikh bakterii v Rybinskom vodokhranilishche (Distribution of Methane Bacteria in the Rybinsk Reservoir). — Byulleten' Instituta Biologii Vodokhranilishch, No. 3:9—12. 1959.

Krasheninnikova, S.A.   Mikrobiologicheskaya kharakteristika Gor'kovskogo vodokhranilishcha vo vtoroi god ego sushchestvovaniya (Microbiological Characteristics of the Gorki Reservoir in its Second Year). — Trudy Instituta Biologii Vodokhranilishch, 3(6):9—20. 1960.

Krasil'nikov, N.A.   Novyi vid geterotrofnykh fiksatorov Azotomonas fluorescens (New Species of Heterotrophic Azotomonas fluorescens). — In Sbornik: Referaty rabot OBN, AN SSSR za 1945g. Moskva, Izd. AN SSSR. 1945.

Krasil'nikov, N.A. and N.I. Nikitina.   Vliyanie razlagayushchikhsya kornei na sostav mikroflory v pochve (The Effect of Decomposing Roots on the Composition of Microflora in the Soil). — Pochvovedenie, No. 2:131—135. 1945.

Krasina, N.N.   Fiziologiya bakterii, razlagayushchikh murav'inuyu kislotu s obrazovaniem gaza (Physiology of Bacteria Decomposing Formic Acid with Gas Formation). — Mikrobiologiya, Vol. 5:669—678. 1936.

Krauskopf, K.B.   Separation of Manganese and Iron by Precipitation. — In Sbornik: Geokhim. litogeneza, pp. 259—293. (Russian translation) Moskva. 1963 (1957).

Kravtsov, P.V. and Yu. I. Sorokin.   Obrazovanie serovodoroda za schet vosstanovleniya sulfatov v Kuibyshevskom vodokhranilishche (Formation of Hydrogen Sulfide by Sulfate Reduction in Kuibyshev Reservoir). — Trudy Instituta Biologii Vodokhranilishch, 2(5):191—196. 1959.

Kudrina, E.S.   Vliyanie guminovoi kisloty na nekotorye gruppy pochvennykh mikroorganizmov i ee znachenie dlya etikh organizmov kak istochnika pitatel'nykh veshchestv (The Effect of Humic Acid on Certain Groups of Soil Bacteria and its Significance for these Organisms as a Source of Nutrients). — Trudy Pochvennogo Instituta im. Dokuchaeva, Vol. 38:184—253. 1951.

Kudryashov, V. V.   Osnovnye momenty istorii Kosinskikh ozer (Main Factors in the History of Kosino Lakes). — Trudy Kosinskoi Biologicheskoi Stantsii, 1(1):5—15. 1924.

Kudryavtsev, V. M.   Mikrobiologicheskaya i gidrologicheskaya kharakteristika Volgogradskogo vodokhranilishcha (Microbiological and Hydrological Characteristics of the Volgograd Reservoir). Institut Biologii Vnutrennikh Vod i Kazanskii Universitet. (Thesis). 1966.

Kukharenko, T. A.   Issledovanie ligninov khemosorbtsionnym sposobom (Investigation of Lignin by the Chemisorption Method). — Zhurnal Prikladnoi Khimii, 21(3):291—294. 1948.

Kuznetsov, N. I.   Ob ozerakh Pokrovskogo uezda Vladimirskoi gubernii (On the Lakes of Pokrov County of Vladimir Province). — Izvestiya Russkogo Geograficheskogo Obshchestva, Vol. 43:111—138. 1907.

Kuznetsov, S. I.   Rezul'taty bakteriologicheskikh issledovanii vody Glubokogo ozera (Results of Bacteriological Examination of the Water of Lake Glubokoe). — Trudy Gidrobiologicheskoi Stantsii na Glubokom ozere, 6(2/3):46—53. 1925.

Kuznetsov, S. I.   Sravnitel'noe izuchenie azotnogo, fosfornogo i kislorodnogo rezhima Glubokogo i Belogo ozer (Comparative Study of Nitrogen, Phosphorus and Oxygen Regimes in Lakes Glubokoe and Beloe). — Trudy Limnologicheskoi Stantsii v Kosine, No. 17:49—69. 1934a.

Kuznetsov, S. I.   Mikrobiologicheskie issledovaniya pri izuchenii kislorodnogo rezhima ozer (Microbiological Investigations for Studying the Oxygen Regime of Lakes). — Mikrobiologiya, 3(4):486—505. 1934b.

Kuznetsov, S. I.   Okislitel'no-vosstanovitel'nyi potentsial v ozerakh i metod ego kolorimetricheskogo opredeleniya (Oxidation-Reduction Potential in Lakes and Colorimetric Determination). — Trudy Limnologicheskoi Stantsii v Kosine, No. 20:55—65. 1935.

Kuznetsov, S. I.   Vliyanie zapasa legko gidrolizuemogo azota v ilu na obshchii kharakter vosstanovitel'nykh protsessov v razlichnykh ozerakh (The Effect of a Reserve of Slightly Hydrolysed Nitrogen in Mud on the General Character of Reduction Processes in Different Lakes). — Mikrobiologiya, Vol. 6:186—201. 1937.

Kuznetsov, S. I.   Opredelenie intensivnosti pogloshcheniya kisloroda iz vodnoi massy ozera za schet bakteriologicheskikh protsessov (Determining the Intensity of Oxygen Uptake from the Water Mass of a Lake Due to Bacteriological Processes). — Trudy Limnologicheskoi Stantsii v Kosine, No. 22:53—74. 1939.

Kuznetsov, S. I.   Krugovorot sery v ozerakh (The Sulfur Cycle in Lakes). — Mikrobiologiya, 11(5/6):218—241. 1942.

Kuznetsov, S. I.   Biologicheskii metod otsenki bogatstva vodoema biogennymi elementami (A Biological Method for Assessing the Biogenic Resources in a Water Body). — Mikrobiologiya, 14(4):248—253. 1945.

Kuznetsov, S. I.   Raspredelenie v ozerakh bakterii, okislyayushchikh gazoobraznye i zhidkie uglevodorody (Distribution in Lakes of Bacteria Oxidizing Gaseous and Liquid Hydrocarbons). — Mikrobiologiya, 16(5):429—436. 1947.

Kuznetsov, S. I.   Osnovnye itogi i ocherednye zadachi mikrobiologicheskikh issledovanii raspada organicheskogo veshchestva v ozernykh ilovykh otlozheniyakh (Main Results and Further Tasks of Microbiological Examination of Organic Matter Decomposition in Lacustrine Mud Deposits). — Trudy Russkogo Gidrobiologicheskogo Obshchestva, No. 1:73—90. 1949a.

Kuznetsov, S. I.   Primenenie mikrobiologicheskikh metodov k izucheniyu organicheskogo veshchestva v vodoemakh (Application of Microbiological Methods for Studying Organic Matter in Water Bodies). — Mikrobiologiya, 18(3):203—214. 1949b.

Kuznetsov, S. I.   Mikrobiologicheskie issledovaniya ozer Kokchetavskoi, Tyumenskoi i Kurganskoi oblastei. I. Mikrobiologicheskaya kharakteristika protsessov mineralizatsii organicheskogo veshchestva v ozerakh razlichnoi stepeni solenosti (Microbiological Investigations of Lakes of the Kokchetav, Tyumen and Kurgan Regions. I. Microbiological Characteristics of Mineralization Processes of Organic Matter in Lakes with Various Degrees of Salinity). — Trudy Laboratorii Sapropelevykh Otlozhenii, No. 4:5—14. 1950a.

Kuznetsov, S. I.   Mikrobiologicheskie issledovaniya ozer Kokchetavskoi, Tyumenskoi i Kurganskoi oblastei. II. Mikrobiologicheskaya kharakteristika raspada organicheskogo veshchestva v ilovykh otlozheniyakh (Microbiological Investigations of Lakes of the Kochetav, Tyumen and Kurgan Regions. II. Microbiological Characteristics of Decomposition of Organic Matter in Mud Sediments). — Trudy Laboratorii Sapropelevykh Otlozhenii, No. 4:15—28. 1950b.

Kuznetsov, S. I.   Sravnitel'naya kharakteristika biomassy bakterii i fitoplanktona v poverkhnostnom sloe vody Srednego Baikala (A Comparison of the Biomasses of Bacteria and Phytoplankton in the Surface Water Layer of Central Baikal). — Trudy Baikal'skoi Limnologicheskoi Stantsii. AN SSSR, Vol. 13:217—224. 1951.

Kuznetsov, S. I.   Rol' mikroorganizmov v krugovorote veshchestv v ozerakh (The Role of Microorganisms in the Cycle of Elements in Lakes). Moskva, Izd. AN SSSR. 1952.

Kuznetsov, S. I.   Osnovnye podkhody k izucheniyu sootnoshenii mezhdu pervichnoi produktsiei organicheskogo veshchestva v vodoeme i biomassoi bakterii (Basic Approaches toward Studying the Relation between Primary Production in a Water Body and the Bacterial Biomass). — Trudy Problemnykh i Tematicheskikh Soveshchanii. ZIN AN SSSR, No. 2; Problemy Gidrobiologii Vnutrennikh Vod, pp. 202—212. 1954.

Kuznetsov, S. I.   Ispol'zovanie radioaktivnoi uglekisloty C^{14} dlya opredeleniya sravnitel'noi velichiny fotosinteza i khemosinteza v ryade ozer razlichnykh tipov (Utilization of Radioactive Carbon Dioxide C^{14} for Determining the Comparative Intensity of Photosynthesis and Chemosynthesis in a Number of Lakes of Different Types). — In Sbornik: Izotopy v mikrobiologii, pp. 126—135. Moskva, Izd. AN SSSR. 1955.

Kuznetsov, S. I.   Mikrobiologicheskaya kharakteristika vod i gruntov Baikala (Microbiological Characteristics of the Water and Types of

Bottom in Lake Baikal). — Trudy Baikal'skoi Limnologicheskoi Stantsii AN SSSR, Vol. 15:388—396. 1956.

Kuznetsov, S. I. Osnovnye puti obrazovaniya osadkov karbonatov kal'tsiya v presnykh vodoemakh i rol' mikroorganizmov v etom protsesse (The Main Pathways of Formation of Calcium Carbonate Sediments in Fresh Waters and the Role of Microorganisms in this Process). — Trudy Instituta Mikrobiologii AN SSSR, No. 5:170—185. 1958b.

Kuznetsov, S. I. Mikrobiologicheskaya kharakteristika volzhskikh vodo- khranilishch (Microbiological Characteristics of the Volga Reservoirs). — Trudy Instituta Biologii Vodokhranilishch, 1(4):69—81. 1959a.

Kuznetsov, S. I. Osnovnye faktory formirovaniya bakterial'nogo naseleniya volzhskikh vodokhranilishch (Main Factors in the Formation of the Bacterial Population of the Volga Reservoirs). — Trudy Soveshchanii Ikhtiologicheskogo Komiteta AN SSSR, No. 10; Trudy Vsesoyuznogo Soveshchaniya po Biologicheskim Osnovam Rybnogo Khozyaistva i Osvoeniya Vodokhranilishch: 114—118. 1961.

Kuznetsov, S. I. Chislennost' bakterii v Rybinskom vodokhranilishche v 1959 i 1960 gg. (Numbers of Bacteria in the Rybinsk Reservoir in 1959 and 1960). — Byulleten' Instituta Biologii Vnutrennikh Vod AN SSSR, No. 13:3—6. 1962.

Kuznetsov, S. I. Osnovnye puti primeneniya radioaktivnykh i stabil'nykh izotopov pri izuchenii krugovorota veshchestv v vodoemakh (Main Methods of Radioactive and Stable Isotope Studies of the Cycle of Elements in Water Bodies). — Trudy Instituta Biologii Vnutrennikh Vod, 9(12):210—232. 1965.

Kuznetsov, S. I. Rol' mikroorganizmov v krugovorote veshchestv v ozerakh (The Role of Microorganisms in the Cycle of Elements in Lakes). — In Sbornik: Krugovorot veshchestva i energiya v ozernykh vodoemakh, pp. 148—171, Moskva, Izd. "Nauka." 1967.

Kuznetsov, S. I. and S. N. Duplakov. Fiziko-khimicheskie issledovaniya na Glubokom ozere i vertikal'noe raspredelenie planktona v nem (Physicochemical Investigations and Vertical Distribution of Plankton in Lake Glubokoe). — Russkii Gidrobiologicheskii Zhurnal, 2(8/10): 149—163. 1923.

Kuznetsov, S. I. and I. N. Dzyuban. Ispol'zovanie guminovykh veshchestv pri razvitii mikobakterii (Utilization of Humic Matter for Development of Mycobacteria). — Byulleten' Instituta Biologii Vodokhranilishch, No. 7:3—5. 1960a.

Kuznetsov, S. I. and I. N. Dzyuban. Ispol'zovanie pektinovykh veshchestv v kachestve istochnika ugleroda pri razvitii mikobakterii (Utilization of Pectins as a Carbon Source in Development of Mycobacteria). — Byulleten' Instituta Biologii Vodokhranilishch, Nos. 8—9:3—4. 1960b.

Kuznetsov, S. I. and M. E. Gambaryan. Opredelenie produktsii organicheskogo veshchestva v protsesse fotosinteza v ozere Sevan (Determination of Primary Production in Lake Sevan). — Izvestiya AN Armyanskoi SSR, Biologicheskie Nauki, 13(4):63—69. 1960.

Kuznetsov, S. I., M. V. Ivanov, and N. N. Lyalikova. Vvedenie v geologicheskuyu mikrobiologiyu (Introduction to Geological Micro- biology). Moskva, Izd. AN SSSR. 1962.

Kuznetsov, S. I. and E. M. Khartulari. Mikrobiologicheskaya kharak- teristika protsessov anaerobnogo raspada organicheskogo veshchestva dlya Belogo ozera v Kosine (Microbiological Aspects of Anaerobic Decomposition of Organic Matter in Lake Beloe in Kosino). — Mikrobiologiya, 10(7/8):834—849. 1941.

Kuznetsov, S. I. and N. S. Karpova. Dinamika chislennosti bakterii v Rybinskom vodokhranilishche v 1961 i 1962 gg. (Bacterial Population Dynamics in the Rybinsk Reservoir in 1961 and 1962). — In Sbornik: Produtsirovanie i krugovorot organicheskogo veshchestva vo vnutrennikh vodoemakh; Trudy Instituta Biologii Vnutrennikh Vod, Nos. 13 (16): 117–122. 1966.

Kuznetsov, S. I. and G. S. Karzinkin. Metod kolichestvennogo ucheta bakterii v vode (Counting Bacteria in Water). — Russkii Gidrobiologicheskii Zhurnal, Vol. 9:85—89. 1930.

Kuznetsov, S. I., G. S. Karzinkin, A. A. Egorova, M. A. Kastal'skaya, A. A. Karasikova, M. V. Ivanov, G. A. Zavarzin, and Z. P. Deryugina. Zhestkaya rastitel'nost' kak zelenoe udobrenie dlya povysheniya ryboproduktivnosti nerestovo-vyrostnykh khozyaistv (Coarse Vegetation as Green Fertilizer for Increasing Fish Productivity in Spawning and Nursery Farms). — Voprosy Ikhtiologii, No. 5:119—137. 1955.

Kuznetsov, S. I. and Z. I. Kuznetsova. Bakteriologicheskie i khimicheskie issledovaniya ozernykh ilov v svyazi s donnym gazootdeleniem (Bacteriological and Chemical Investigations of Lake Mud with Respect to Gas Liberation from the Bottom). — Trudy Limnologicheskoi Stantsii v Kosine, No. 19:127—144. 1935.

Kuznetsov, S. I. and V. I. Romanenko. Mikrobiologicheskoe izuchenie vnutrennikh vodoemov (Microbiological Study of Inland Water Bodies). — Laboratornoe rukovodstvo. Moskva—Leningrad, Izd. AN SSSR. 1963a.

Kuznetsov, S. I. and V. I. Romanenko. Okislitel'no-vosstanovitel'nyi potentsial v poverkhnostnykh sloyakh ilovykh otlozhenii ozer razlichnogo tipa (Oxidation-Reduction Potential in Surface Layers and Mud Sediments of Different Types of Lakes). — Doklady AN SSSR, 151(3): 679—682. 1963b.

Kuznetsov, S. I. and V. I. Romanenko. Mikrobiologicheskaya kharakteristika Tsimlyanskogo vodokhranilishcha (Microbiological Characteristics of the Tsimlyansk Reservoir). — In Sbornik: Mikroflora, fitoplankton i vysshie rasteniya vnutrennikh vodoemov; Trudy Instituta Biologii Vnutrennikh Vod, Nos. 15(18):3—16. 1967.

Kuznetsov, S. I. and V. I. Romanenko. Mikroflora Sivasha i isparitel'nykh basseinov solyanykh promyslov (Microflora of Sivash and of Salt Evaporation Ponds). — Mikrobiologiya, 37(6):1104—1108. 1968.

Kuznetsov, S. I., V. I. Romanenko, and I. V. Glazunov. Produktsiya organicheskogo veshchestva za schet fotosinteza fitoplanktona v ozere Baikal (Primary Production of Phytoplankton in Lake Baikal). — Doklady AN SSSR, 156(6):1444—1447. 1964.

Kuznetsov, S. I., V. I. Romanenko, and N. S. Karpova. Chislennost' bakterii i produktsiya organicheskogo veshchestva v vodnoi masse Rybinskogo vodokhranilishcha v 1963 i 1964 gg. (Bacterial Population and Production of Organic Matter in the Rybinsk Reservoir in 1963 and 1964). — In Sbornik: Produtsirovanie i krugovorot organicheskogo veshchestva vo vnutrennikh vodoemakh; Trudy Instituta Biologii Vnutrennikh Vod, Nos. 13(16):123—132. 1966.

Kuznetsov, S. I., V. I. Romanenko, and N. S. Karpova. Chislennost' bakterii i produktsiya organicheskogo veshchestva v Rybinskom vodokhranilishche v 1965 g. (Bacterial Population and Production of Organic Matter in the Rybinsk Reservoir in 1965). — In Sbornik: Mikroflora, fitoplankton i vysshie vodnye rasteniya vnutrennikh vodoemov; Trudy Instituta Biologii Vnutrennikh Vod, Nos. 15(17):17—25. 1967.

Kuznetsov, S. I., T. A. Speranskaya, and V. D. Konshin. Sostav organicheskogo veshchestva ilovykh otlozhenii razlichnykh ozer (Organic Composition of Mud Sediments of Various Lakes). — Trudy Limnologicheskoi Stantsii v Kosine, No. 22:75—104. 1939.

Kuznetsova, Z. I. Metod vydeleniya planktonnykh i perefitonnykh bakterii i prilozhenie ego k izucheniyu dinamiki bakteriologicheskikh protsessov v vodoeme (A Method for Identifying Planktonic and Periphytonic Bacteria and its Application to the Study of the Dynamics of Bacteriological Processes in a Water Body). — Trudy Limnologicheskoi Stantsii v Kosine, No. 21:89—104. 1937.

Kuz'menko, K. N. Raspredelenie i kolichestvennoe razvitie bentofauny v raznotipnykh malykh ozerakh Karel'skogo peresheika (Distribution and Quantitative Development of Zoobenthos in Different Types of Small Lakes in the Karelian Isthmus). — In Sbornik: Ozera Karel'-skogo peresheika, pp. 89—100. Moskva—Leningrad, Izd. "Nauka." 1964.

Lastochkin, D. A. Stoyachie vodoemy (ozera i prudy) (Standing Water Bodies (Lakes and Ponds)). Ivanovo, Izd. "Osnova." 1925.

Lastochkin, D. A., N. V. Korde, N. I. Tseshinskaya, and V. V. Gorsh-kova. Valdaiskoe ozero (Lake Valdai). — Trudy Ivanovo-Voznesen-skogo Gubernskogo Obshchestva Kraevedov, No. 2. 1924.

Lazareva, M. F. Pryamoi schet bakterii pri reshenii zadach tekhnicheskoi mikrobiologii (Direct Bacterial Counts for Determining Questions of Technical Microbiology). — Informatsionnye Materialy, No. 1. Laboratoriya biologicheskoi ochistki stochnykh vod. Moskva, Izd. VODGEO. 1953.

Lebedev, A. F. Issledovanie khemosinteza u Bacillus hydrogenes (Investigation of Chemosynthesis in Bacillus hydrogenes). Odessa. 1910.

Lees, H. Biochemistry of Autotrophic Bacteria. (Russian translation.) 1950.

Lepneva, S. G. Termika, prozrachnost', tsvet i khimizm vody Teletskogo ozera (Heat, Transparency, Color and Chemistry of Lake Teletskoe). — Issledovaniya Ozer SSSR, No. 9:3—105. 1937.

Lepneva, S. G. Zhizn' v ozerakh (Life in Lakes). — Zhizn' Presnykh Vod, Vol. 3. Chapter 25: 257—552. 1950.

Levina, R. I. Antagonizm mezhdu protokokkovymi vodoroslyami i koliti-foznoi gruppoi mikroorganizmov (Antagonism between Protococcal Algae and Coli Microorganisms). — Mikrobiologiya, 33(5):887—893. 1964a.

Levina, R. I. Vzaimootnosheniya razlichnykh vidov protokokkovykh vodoroslei i ikh bakteritsidnoe deistvie pri sovmestnom vyrashchivanii (Relationship of Various Protococcal Algae Species and their Bactericida

Effect in Mixed Cultures). — Mikrobiologiya, Vol. 33:140—147. 1964b.

Listova, L. P. Fiziko-khimicheskie issledovaniya uslovii obrazovaniya okisnykh i karbonatnykh rud margantsa (Physicochemical Investigations of Conditions of Formation of Oxide and Carbonate Ores of Manganese). Moskva, Izd. AN SSSR. 1961.

Lopatik, M. D. Izuchenie sposobnosti mikobakterii okislyat' uglevodorody (A Study of the Capacity of Mycobacteria to Oxidize Hydrocarbons). — Mikrobiologiya, 33(2):236—238. 1964.

Lozinov, A. B. and V. A. Ermachenko. Pigmentirovannaya forma Nitrosomonas europae (A Pigmented Form of Nitrosomonas europae). — Mikrobiologiya, 29(4):523—528. 1960.

L'vov, N. P. Svobodnodvizhushchie azotfiksiruyushchie mikroorganizmy dernovopodzolistoi pochvy (Autotrophic Nitrogen-Fixing Microorganisms of Sod-Podzolic Soil). Author's Summary of Candidate Thesis. Moskovskaya Sel'skokhozyaistvennaya Akademiya im. K. A. Timiryazeva. 1964.

Lyalikova, N. N. Izuchenie protsessa usvoeniya svobodnoi uglekisloty purpurnymi serobakteriyami v ozere Belovod' (Study of CO_2 Assimilation by Purple Sulfur Bacteria in Lake Belovod'). – Mikrobiologiya, 26(1):92—98. 1957.

Lyalikova, N. N. Izuchenie protsessa khemosinteza u Thiobac. ferrooxidans (Study of Chemosynthesis in Thiobacillus ferrooxidans). — Mikrobiologiya, 27(5):556—559. 1958.

Lyalikova, N. N. Osobennosti fiziologii mikroorganizmov, okislyayushchikh sul'fidy metallov (Physiological Characteristics of Microorganisms Oxidizing Sulfides of Metals). — Materialy soveshchanii po bakterial'nomu vyshchelachivaniyu tsvetnykh metallov. Moskva, Izd. Instituta tsvetnykh metallov. 1968.

Lyatti, S. Ya. Gidrokhimicheskie issledovaniya ozera Sevan (Hydrochemical Investigations of Lake Sevan). — Byulleten' Byuro Gidrometeorologicheskikh Issledovanii na Ozere Sevan, Nos. 7—8. Leningrad. 1929.

Lyatti, S. Ya. Grunty ozera Sevan (Types of Bottom in Lake Sevan). — Materialy po Issledovaniyu Ozera Sevan i ego Basseina, Part 4, No. 4. Tiflis, Izd. Sevanskogo gidrometbyuro. 1932a.

Lyatti, S. Ya. Gidrokhimicheskii ocherk ozera Sevan (Hydrochemical Survey of Lake Sevan). — Materialy po Issledovaniyu Ozera Sevan i ego Basseina, Part 4, No. 2. Leningrad. 1932b.

Lyubimov, V. I. Nitritnye bakterii v gruntakh ozer i vodokhranilishch (Nitrobacteria in Bottoms of Lakes and Reservoirs). — Mikrobiologiya, 6(3):351—360. 1937.

Maksimova, I. V. and M. N. Pimenova. Priroda organicheskikh soedinenii, vydelyaemykh v sredu rastushchimi kul'turami zelenykh vodoroslei (The Nature of Organic Compounds Released into the Environment by Growing Cultures of Green Algae). — Mikrobiologiya, 35(4):623—632. 1966.

Maksimovich, G. A. Khimicheskaya geografiya vod sushi (Chemical Geography of Inland Waters). Moskva, Geografgiz. 1955.

Manuilova, E. F. K voprosu o svyazi razvitiya Cladocera s pishchevym faktorom (On the Relation between the Development of Cladocera and the Nutrient Factor). — Doklady AN SSSR, 90(6):1155—1158. 1953.

Margolina, G. L. Mikrobiologicheskaya kharakteristika Cherepovetskogo vodokhranilishcha v pervyi god ego stanovleniya (Microbiological Characteristics of the Cherepovetsk Reservoir during its First Year). — Mikrobiologiya, 34(6):720—726. 1965.

Messineva, M. A. and A. I. Gorbunova. Izmenenie soderzhaniya azotistykh soedinenii v sapropele pod vliyaniem mikroorganizmov (Variation in Nitrogen Compound Content of Sapropel Due to Microorganisms). — Mikrobiologiya, 9(7/8):685—694. 1940.

Messineva, M. A. and A. I. Gorbunova. Protsess razlozheniya makrofitov presnykh ozer i uchastie ikh ostatkov v formirovanii ozernykh ilovykh otlozhenii (Decomposition of Macrophytes of Freshwater Lakes and the Role of the Residues in Formation of Lake Mud Sediments). — Izvestiya AN SSSR, Otdel Biologicheskikh Nauk, No. 5:565—580. 1946.

Mikheeva, I. V. Dinamika chislennosti bakterii v vodnoi tolshche Kuibyshevskogo vodokhranilishcha v 1960—1961 gg. (Population Dynamics of Bacteria in the Water Column of the Kuibyshev Reservoir in 1960—1961). — Trudy Instituta Biologii Vnutrennikh Vod, Nos. 13(16):204—207, 1966.

Minenko, A. K. Nekotorye voprosy ekologii i fiziologii fosformineralizuyushchikh mikroorganizmov (Some Problems of Ecology and Physiology of Phosphorus-Mineralizing Microorganisms). Author's Summary of Candidate Thesis. MGU. 1965.

Mishustin, E. N. O roli sporonosnykh bakterii v pochvennykh protsessakh (The Role of Sporogenic Bacteria in Soil Processes). — Mikrobiologiya, 17(3):201—207. 1948.

Mishustin, E. N. and D. I. Nikitin. Atakuemost' guminovykh kislot pochvennoi mikrofloroi (Humic Acid Decomposition by Soil Microflora). — Mikrobiologiya, 30(5):841—848. 1961.

Mishustin, E. N. and M. I. Pertsovskaya. Mikroorganizmy i samoochishchenie pochvy (Microorganisms and Self-Purification of the Soil). Moskva, Izd. AN SSSR. 1954.

Mishustin, E. N. and V. K. Shil'nikova. Biologicheskaya fiksatsiya atmosfernogo azota (Biological Fixation of Free Nitrogen). Moskva, Izd. "Nauka." 1968.

Mishustin, E. N., I. S. Vostrov, D. I. Nikitin, and N. S. Erofeev. Rol' aerobioza v obrazovanii gumusovykh soedinenii (The Role of Aerobiosis in Formation of Humic Compounds). — Mikrobiologiya, 34(3):497—501. 1965.

Mishustina, I. E. Oligonitrofil'nye mikroorganizmy pochvy (Oligonitrophilic Microorganisms of the Soil). — Trudy Instituta Mikrobiologii, AN SSSR, No. 4:110—129. 1955.

Molchanov, A. A. Ozera Srednei Azii (Lakes of Soviet Central Asia). — Trudy Sredne-Aziatskogo Gosudarstvennogo Universiteta, Ser. 12a, Geografiya, No. 3:12. Tashkent. 1929.

Monakov, A. V. and Yu. I. Sorokin. K voprosu ob usvoenii tsiklopami protokokkovykh vodoroslei (The Problem of Assimilation of Protococcal Algae by Cyclops). — Byulleten' Instituta Biologii Vodokhranilishch, No. 3:24—27. 1959.

Monteverde, N. A. and B. V. Perfil'ev. O pigmente iz gruppy khlorofilla u "zelenoi bakterii" Pelodiction (A Chlorophyll Pigment in the "Green Bacterium" Pelodiction). — Zhurnal Mikrobiologii 1(3—5):199—208. 1914.

Mudretsova, K. A. and B. S. Aleev. Tsvetenie vody i metody ego predskazaniya (Water Blooms and their Forecasting). — Vodosnabzhenie i Sanitariya, 14(3):17—20. 1939.

Muraveiskii, S. D. Morfologiya Glubokogo ozera (Morphology of Lake Glubokoe). — Trudy Limnologicheskoi Stantsii v Kosine, Nos. 13—14: 29—42. 1934.

Muraveiskii, S. D. Puti postroeniya teorii biologicheskoi produktivnosti vodoemov (Ways of Theoretical Determination of Biological Productivity of Water Bodies). — Zoologicheskii Zhurnal, 15(4):563—584. 1936.

Nadson, G. A. Mikroorganizmy, kak geologicheskie deyateli (Microorganisms as Geological Agents). — Trudy Komissii issledovanii mineral'nykh ozer goroda Slavyanska. Sankt-Peterburg. 1903.

Nadson, G. A. Mikrobiologicheskie ocherki. I. Chlorobium limicola Nads., zelenyi mikroorganizm s nefunktsioniruyushchim khlorofillom (Microbiological Essays. I. Chlorobium limicola Nads., a Green Microorganism with Nonfunctional Chlorophyll). — Izvestiya Imperatorskogo S.-Peterburgskogo Botanicheskogo Sada, 12(2/3): 55—89. 1912.

Nechaeva, N. B. Mikobakteriya, okislyayushchaya ammiak v nitrity (Mycobacteria Oxidizing Ammonia to Nitrites). — Mikrobiologiya, 16(5): 418—428. 1947.

Nechaeva, N. B. Dva vida mikobakterii, okislyayushchikh metan (Two Species of Mycobacteria Oxidizing Methane). — Mikrobiologiya, 18(4):310—317. 1949.

Nechaeva, N. B. and A. G. Salimovskaya-Rodina. Mikrobiologicheskii analiz donnykh otlozhenii Baikala (Microbiological Analysis of Bottom Deposits of Baikal). — Trudy Baikal'skoi Limnologicheskoi Stantsii, Vol. 6:5—14. 1935.

Nekhotenova, T. I. Elektrometricheskie opredeleniya okislitel'novosstanovitel'nogo potentsiala v vodoemakh (Electrometric Determination of the Oxidation-Reduction Potential in Water Bodies). — Mikrobiologiya, 7(2):186—197. 1938.

Nikitin, D. I. Razlozhenie pochvennykh guminovykh kislot mikroorganizmami (Decomposition of Soil Humic Acids by Microorganisms). — Izvestiya AN SSSR, Seriya Biologicheskaya, No. 4:618—625. 1960.

Nikitin, D. I. and S. I. Kuznetsov. Primenenie elektronnoi mikroskopii dlya izucheniya vodnoi mikroflory (Application of Electronic Microscopy for Studying Aquatic Microflora). — Mikrobiologiya, 36(5):938—941. 1957.

Nikitin, D. I., L. V. Vasil'eva, and R. A. Lokhmacheva. Novye i redkie formy pochvennykh mikroorganizmov (New and Rare Forms of Soil Microorganisms). Moskva, Izd. "Nauka." 1966.

Nikitinskii, Ya. Ya. Stigeoclonium tenue. — Trudy Instituta Vodosnabzheniya. Moskva. 1930.

Nikitinskii, Ya. Ya.   Nekotorye itogi v oblasti sanitarno-tekhnicheskoi gidrobiologii (Some Results in the Field of Sanitary-Technical Hydrobiology). — Mikrobiologiya, 7(1):3—35. 1938.

Nikolaeva, R. V.   Nakoplenie kal'tsiya v sovremennykh ozernykh otlozheniyakh (Calcium Deposits in Contemporary Lake Sediments). — In Sbornik: Nakoplenie veshchestva v ozerakh, pp. 78—101. 1964.

Nikol'skii, G. V.   O dinamike chislennosti stada ryb i o tak nazyvaemoi probleme produktivnosti vodoemov (Population Dynamics of the Fish Stock and the Problem of Water Body Productivity). — Zoologicheskii Zhurnal, 29(6):489—500. 1950.

Novobrantsev, P. V.   Razvitie bakterii v ozerakh v zavisimosti ot nalichiya legkousvoyaemogo organicheskogo veshchestva (Development of Bacteria in Lakes in Relation to the Availability of Easily Assimilated Organic Matter). — Mikrobiologiya, 6(1):28—36. 1937.

Novozhilova, M. I.   Dinamika chislennosti i biomassy bakterii v vodnoi tolshche Rybinskogo vodokhranilishcha (Population Dynamics and Bacterial Biomass of Bacteria in the Water Column of the Rybinsk Reservoir). — Mikrobiologiya, 24(6):710—717. 1955.

Novozhilova, M. I.   Vremya generatsii bakterii i produktsiya bakterial'- noi biomassy v vode Rybinskogo vodokhranilishcha (Generation Time and Production of Bacterial Biomass in Waters of the Rybinsk Reservoir). — Mikrobiologiya, 26(2):202—209. 1957.

Novozhilova, M. I.   Opredelenie veroyatnoi oshibki pri uchete bakterii v vodoemakh metodom pryamogo scheta (Determining the Probable Error in Bacterial Counts in Water Bodies Using the Direct Count Method). — Trudy IV soveshchaniya po probleme biologii vnutrennikh vod, pp. 569—573. 1959.

Olifan, V. I.   Biologiya planktona i fiziko-khimicheskii rezhim Gigirevskogo pruda (Biology of Plankton and the Physicochemical Regime of the Gigirevskii Pond). — Trudy Zvenigor. gidrofizicheskoi stantsii. Institut eksperimental'noi biologii: Primenenie metodov fiziko-khimicheskikh k izucheniyu biologii presnykh vodoemov, pp. 288—351. 1928.

Omelyanskii, V. L.   O vodorodnom brozhenii tsellyulozy (Hydrogen Fermentation of Cellulose). — Arkhiv Biologicheskikh Nauk, 7(5):1; Izbrannye Trudy, Vol. 1:34—54. Moskva, 1899 (1953).

Omelyanskii, V. L.   O metanovom brozhenii kletchatki (Methane Fermentation of Cellulose). — Arkhiv Biologicheskikh Nauk, Vol. 9, No. 3; Izbrannye Trudy, Vol. 1:55—74. 1902 (1956).

Omelyanskii, V. L.   O vydelenii metana v prirode pri biologicheskikh protsessakh (Liberation of Methane by Biological Processes in Nature). — Arkhiv Biologicheskikh Nauk, Vol. 12; Izbrannye Trudy, Vol. 1:427—440. 1906 (1953).

Omelyanskii, V. L.   Bakteriologicheskie issledovaniya ila ozer Beloe i Kolomno (Bacteriological Investigations of the Mud of Lakes Beloe and Kolomno). — Zhurnal Mikrobiologii, Vol. 4, No. 3; Izbrannye Trudy, Vol. 1:461—467. 1917 (1953).

Omelyanskii, V. L.   Svyazyvanie atmosfernogo azota pochvennymi mikrobami (Fixation of Free Nitrogen by Soil Bacteria). — Petrograd, Izd. Komissii po izucheniyu proizvoditel'nykh sil Rossii AN; Izbrannye Trudy, Vol. 1:175—366. 1923 (1953).

Omelyanskii, V. L. Zametki o sapropele (Notes on Sapropel). — Izvestiya Sapropelevogo Komiteta, No. 2:11—15; Izbrannye Trudy, Vol. 2:394—397. 1925 (1953).

Osnitskaya, L. K. Rasprostranenie gnilostnykh, tionovykh, metanokislya-yushchikh i vodorodokislyayushchikh bakterii v gruntakh Severnogo Kaspiya (Distribution of Putrescent, Thionic, Methane, and Hydrogen Bacteria in Bottoms of the Northern Caspian). — Mikrobiologiya, 22(4):399—407. 1953.

Panosyan, A. Kh., M. E. Gambaryan, and G. S. Babayan. O fosforo-prevrashchayushchikh mikroorganizmakh ozera Sevan (On Phosphorus-Mineralizing Microorganisms of Lake Sevan). — Izvestiya AN Armyanskoi SSSR, Biologicheskie Nauki, 13(10):3—12. 1960.

Pel'sh, A. D. O neodnorodnosti zhidkoi fazy ila (Heterogeneity of the Liquid Phase of Mud). — Uchenye Zapiski LGU, No. 30; Trudy Boro-dinskoi Presnovodnoi Biologicheskoi Stantsii v Karelii, No. 8:5—46. 1939.

Perfil'ev, B. V. O khlorofillonosnoi "zelenoi bakterii" Pelodictyon clathratiforme Lauterb. (Chlorophyll-Containing "Green Bacterium" Pelodictyon clathratiforme Lauterb.). — Zhurnal Mikrobiologii, 1(3/5):179—198. 1914a.

Perfil'ev, B. V. K ucheniyu o simbioze Chlorochromatium aggre-gatum Lauterborn (Chloronium mirabile Buder) Cylin-drogloea bacterifera gen. nov. sp. nov. (Study of the Symbio-sis of Chlorochromatium aggregatum Lauterborn (Chloronium mirabile Buder) and Cylindrogloea bac-terifera gen. nov. sp. nov.). — Zhurnal Mikrobiologii, 1(3/5): 209—224. 1914b.

Perfil'ev, B. V. Novye dannye o roli mikrobov v rudoobrazovanii (New Data on the Role of Bacteria in Ore Formation). — Izvestiya Geologi-cheskoi Kommissii, 45(7):795—820. 1926.

Perfil'ev, B. V. K metodike izucheniya ilovykh otlozhenii (A Method for Studying Mud Sediments). — Trudy Borodinskoi Presnovodnoi Biolo-gicheskoi Stantsii v Karelii, No. 5:135—166. 1927.

Perfil'ev, B. V. Biologiya lechebnykh gryazei (Biology of Therapeutic Muds). — Osnovy Kurortologii, Vol. 1:210—233. Gosmedizdat. 1932.

Perfil'ev, B. V. Izuchenie zaileniya vodoemov i absolyutnaya geokhro-nologiya (A Study of Silting of Water Bodies and Absolute Geochro-nology). — Izvestiya Vsesoyuznogo Geograficheskogo Obshchestva, 84(4):333—349. 1952.

Perfil'ev, B. V. Novyi biologicheskii tip bakterii s khishchnym sposobom pitaniya (A New Biological Type of Bacteria with a Predatory Form of Nutrition). — Doklady AN SSSR, 98(5):845—848. 1954.

Perfil'ev, B. V. Kapillyarnyi metod mikrobnogo peizazha v geomikro-biologii (The Capillary Method of Microbial Landscape in Geomicro-biology). — In Sbornik: Rol' mikroorganizmov v obrazovanii zhelezo-margantsevykh ozernykh rud, pp. 6—15. Moskva—Leningrad, "Nauka." 1964.

Perfil'ev, B. V. and D. R. Gabe. Kapillyarnye metody izucheniya mikroorganizmov (Capillary Methods for Studying Microorganisms). Moskva—Leningrad, Izd. AN SSSR. 1961.

Perfil'ev, B. V. and D. R. Gabe. Izuchenie metodom mikrobnogo peizazha bakterii, nakoplyayushchikh marganets i zhelezo v donnykh otlozheniyakh (A Study Using the Method of Microbial Landscape of Bacteria Depositing Manganese and Iron in Bottom Sediments). — In Sbornik: Rol' mikroorganizmov v obrazovanii zhelezo-margantse-vykh ozernykh rud, pp. 16—53. Moskva—Leningrad, "Nauka." 1964.

Pervol'f, Yu. V. Bioanizotropnye ozera Yaponii (Bioanisotropic Lakes of Japan). — Priroda, No. 7:87. 1939.

Pervol'f, Yu. V. Kislye ozera Yaponii (Acidic Lakes of Japan). — Priroda, Nos. 1—2:69—71. 1944.

Pontovich, V. E. Razlozhenie guminovykh veshchestv mikroorganizmami (Decomposition of Humic Substances by Microorganisms). — Mikro-biologiya, Vol. 7:696—707. 1938.

Posokhov, E. V. Solyanye ozera Kazakhstana (Saline Lakes of Kazakhstan). Moskva, Izd. AN SSSR. 1955.

Potaenko, Yu. S. Sezonnaya dinamika obshchei chislennosti i biomassy bakterii v vode Narochanskikh ozer (Seasonal Dynamics of the Numbers and Biomass of Bacteria in Water of Naroch' Lakes). — Mikrobiologiya, 37(4):540—547. 1968.

Preobrazhenskii, I. A. Usoiskii zaval (Usoi Avalanche). — Materialy po Obshchei i Prikladnoi Geologii, No. 14:1—20. 1920.

Razumov, A. S. Pryamoi metod ucheta bakterii v vode. Sravnenie ego s metodom Kokha (Direct Counting of Bacteria in Water. Comparison with Koch's Method). — Mikrobiologiya, 1(2):131—146. 1932.

Razumov, A. S. Metody mikrobiologicheskikh issledovanii vody (Methods of Microbiological Investigations of Water). — VODGEO, Izd. Ministerstva stroitel'stva predpriyatii tyazheloi industrii. 1947.

Razumov, A. S. Vzaimootnosheniya mezhdu saprofitnymi bakteriyami i planktonom v vodoemakh (Relationships between Saprophytic Bacteria and the Plankton in Water Bodies). — In Sbornik: Voprosy sanitarnoi bakteriologii, pp. 30—43. Izd. AMN SSSR. 1948a.

Razumov, A. S. Bakterial'nyi plankton Klyaz'minskogo vodokhranilishcha (Bacterial Plankton of the Klyaz'ma Reservoir). — In Sbornik: Zagryaznenie i samoochishchenie vodoemov, No. 1. Institut Obshchei i Kommunal'noi Gigieny AMN SSSR, pp. 100—109. 1948b.

Razumov, A. S. Gallionella klasmiensis (sp. n.) kak komponent bakterial'nogo planktona (Gallionella klasmiensis (sp. n.) as a Component of the Bacterial Plankton). — Mikrobiologiya, 18(5): 442—446. 1949.

Razumov, A. S. K voprosu o khemosinteze u zhelezobakterii (The Problem of Chemosynthesis in Iron Bacteria). — Mikrobiologiya, 26(3):394—396. 1957.

Razumov, A. S. Mikrobial'nye pokazateli saprobnosti vodoemov, zagryaz-nennykh promyshlennymi stokami. I. Nitchatye bakterii iz roda Cladothrix (Microbial Indicators of Saprobicity of Water Bodies Polluted by Industrial Wastes. I. Filamentous Bacteria of the Genus Cladothrix). — Mikrobiologiya, 30(3):515—524. 1961a.

Razumov, A. S. Mikrobial'nye pokazateli saprobnosti vodoemov zagryaz-nennykh promyshlennymi stokami. II. Fiziologiya i ekologiya nitcha-tykh bakterii iz roda Cladothrix (Microbial Indicators of Saprobicity of Water Bodies Polluted by Industrial Wastes. II. Physiology and Ecology of Filamentous Bacteria of the Genus C l a d o t h r i x). — Mikrobiologiya, 30(5):938—945. 1961b.

R a z u m o v, A. S. Mikrobial'nye pokazateli saprobnosti vodoemov, zagryaznennykh promyshlennymi stokami. III. O sistematike nitchatykh bakterii (Microbial Indicators of Saprobicity of Water Bodies Polluted by Industrial Wastes. III. Taxonomy of Filamentous Bacteria). — Mikrobiologiya, 30(6):1088—1096. 1961c.

R a z u m o v, A. S. Mikrobial'nyi plankton vody (Microbial Plankton of Water). — Trudy Vsesoyuznogo Gidrobiologicheskogo Obshchestva, Vol. 12:60—190. 1962.

R o d i n a, A. G. Opyty po pitaniyu D a p h n i a m a g n a (Experiments on the Feeding of D a p h n i a m a g n a). — Zoologicheskii Zhurnal, 25(3): 237—244. 1946.

R o d i n a, A. G. Vodorosli kak pishcha Cladocera (Algae as Food for Cladocera). — Doklady AN SSSR, 59(2):345—347. 1948.

R o d i n a, A. G. Bakterii kak pishcha vodnykh zhivotnykh (Bacteria as Food of Aquatic Animals). — Priroda, No. 10:23—26. 1949.

R o d i n a, A. G. O roli otdel'nykh grupp bakterii v produktivnosti vodoemov (The Role of Certain Groups of Bacteria in the Productivity of Water Bodies). — Trudy Problemnykh i Tematicheskikh Soveshchanii ZIN SSSR, No. 1. Problemy Gidrobiologii Vnutrennikh Vod, pp. 23—33. 1951.

R o d i n a, A. G. Vodnye spirilly, fiksiruyushchie molekulyarnyi azot (Aquatic Nitrogen-Fixing Spirillas). — Mikrobiologiya, 25(2):145—149. 1956.

R o d i n a, A. G. Vozmozhnost' ispol'zovaniya metoda mechenykh atomov dlya resheniya voprosa o vybornosti pishchi u vodnykh zhivotnykh (Use of Radioactive Isotopes in Determining Food Selectivity in Aquatic Animals). — Zoologicheskii Zhurnal, 6(3):337—343. 1957.

R o d i n a, A. G. O rasprostranenii serobakterii v presnykh vodakh i meste ikh v sisteme pokazatel'nykh organizmov Kol'kvitsa i Marssona (Distribution of Sulfur Bacteria in Fresh Waters and their Position in the System of Indicator Organisms of Kolkwitz and Marsson). — Mikrobiologiya, 30(6):1080—1083. 1961.

R o d i n a, A. G. Serobakterii detrita ozer Priladozh'ya (Sulfur Bacteria of Detritus of Lakes in the Ladoga Area). — Mikrobiologiya, 32(4): 675—682. 1963a.

R o d i n a, A. G. Soderzhanie bakterii v detrite ozer Priladozh'ya (Bacteria Content in Detritus of Lakes of the Ladoga Area). — Mikrobiologiya, Vol. 32:1031—1037. 1936b.

R o d i n a, A. G. and N. K. K u z ' m i t s k a y a. Chislennost' i raspredelenie bakterioplanktona v Ladozhskom ozere (Population and Distribution of Bacterioplankton in Lake Ladoga). — Mikrobiologiya, 32(2):288—295. 1963.

R o d i n a, A. G. and N. K. K u z ' m i t s k a y a. Vidovoi sostav geterotrofnykh mikroorganizmov vodnoi tolshchi Ladozhskogo ozera (Species Composition of Heterotrophic Microorganisms of the Water of Lake Ladoga). — Mikrobiologiya, 33(6):1010—1017. 1964.

R o m a n e n k o, V. I. Uchet metanokislyayushchikh bakterii v vode metodom radioavtografii kolonii s membrannykh fil'trov (Counts of Methane

Bacteria in the Water by Radioautography of Colonies on Membrane Filters). — Byulleten' Instituta Biologii Vodokhranilishch, No. 5:40—42. 1959.

Romanenko, V. I.   Kolichestvo letuchikh zhirnykh kislot v ilakh Rybinskogo vodokhranilishcha, opredelennoe metodom khromatografii (Chromatographic Determination of Volatile Fatty Acids in Mud of the Rybinsk Reservoir). — Byulleten' Instituta Biologii Vodokhranilishch, No. 13: 39—43. 1962.

Romanenko, V. I.   Geterotrofnaya assimilyatsiya CO_2 bakterial'noi floroi vody (Heterotrophic Assimilation of CO_2 by Bacterial Flora of Water).— Mikrobiologiya, 33(4):679—683. 1964a

Romanenko, V. I.   Potentsial'naya sposobnost' mikroflory ilovykh otlozhenii k geterotrofnoi assimilyatsii uglekisloty i k khemosintezu (Capacity of Microflora of Mud Sediments for Heterotrophic CO_2 Assimilation and Chemosynthesis). — Mikrobiologiya, 33(1):134—139. 1964b.

Romanenko, V. I.   Mikrobiologicheskie protsessy v vodokhranilishchakh razlichnykh tipov (Microbiological Processes in Reservoirs of Different Types). Author's Summary of Candidate Thesis. Institut Mikrobiologii AN SSSR. Moskva. 1964c.

Romanenko, V. I.   Mikrobiologicheskoe obsledovanie Onezhskogo ozera, Vygozerskogo vodokhranilishcha i ozer Belomoro-Baltiiskogo kanala (Microbiological Survey of Lake Onega, Vygozero Reservoir and Lakes of the White Sea-Baltic Canal). — Mikrobiologiya, 34(2):350—356. 1965.

Romanenko, V. I.   Kharakteristika mikrobiologicheskikh protsessov obrazovaniya i razrusheniya organicheskogo veshchestva v Rybinskom vodokhranilishche (Characteristics of Microbiological Processes of Formation and Decomposition of Organic Matter in the Rybinsk Reservoir). — In Sbornik: Produtsirovanie i krugovorot organicheskogo veshchestva vo vnutrennikh vodoemakh; Trudy Instituta Biologii Vnutrennikh Vod, Nos. 13(16):133—153. 1966.

Romanenko, V. I., S. I. Kuznetsov, and A. S. Daukshta.   Mikrobiologicheskie protsessy v ozerakh Latvii (Microbiological Processes in Lakes of Latvia). — In Sbornik: Biologiya i produktivnost' presnovodnykh organizmov. Trudy Instituta Biologii Vnutrennikh Vod, Nos. 20(23). 1969.

Romanova, A. P.   Intensivnost' razvitiya bakterial'noi flory na litorali ozera Baikal (po plastinkam obrastaniya) (Intensity of Development of Bacterial Flora on the Littoral of Lake Baikal (from Layers of Fouling)). — Mikrobiologiya, 27(5):634—640. 1958a.

Romanova, A. P.   Sezonnaya dinamika bakterioplanktona, ego gorizontal'-noe i vertikal'noe raspredelenie v yuzhnoi chasti Baikala (Seasonal Dynamics of Bacterioplankton, its Horizontal and Vertical Distribution in the Southern Part of Baikal). — Izvestiya SO AN SSSR, No. 7: 114—124. 1958b.

Romanova, A. P.   K mikrobiologii ozera Baikal; sezonnaya dinamika chislennosti bakterii i protsessov krugovorota azota v vodnoi tolshche i gruntakh Yuzhnogo Baikala (The Microbiology of Lake Baikal; Seasonal Dynamics, Bacterial Numbers and Nitrogen Cycle Processes

in the Waters and Bottoms of Southern Baikal).—Author's Summary
of Candiate Thesis. Irkutskii Gosudarstvennyi Universitet, 1961.

Rossolimo, L. L. Morfometriya Kosinskikh ozer (Morphometry of
Kosino Lakes). — Trudy Kosinskoi Biologicheskoi Stantsii, No. 2:3—24.
1925.

Rossolimo, L. L. Materialy po gidrologii i planktonu nekotorykh vodoemov
Meshcherskoi nizmennosti (Ryazanskoi gubernii) (Data on the
Hydrology and Plankton of Some Water Bodies of Meshchera Lowland
(Ryazan Province)). — Trudy Kosinskoi Biologicheskoi Stantsii,
Nos. 7—8:51—56. 1928.

Rossolimo, L. L. Termika donnykh otlozhenii Belogo ozera v Kosine
(Heat Regime of Bottom Sediments of Lake Beloe in Kosino). —
Trudy Limnologicheskoi Stantsii v Kosine, No. 15:44—66. 1932a.

Rossolimo, L. L. Yavleniya gazootdeleniya na Belom ozere v Kosine
(The Phenomena of Gas Liberation in Lake Beloe in Kosino). —
Trudy Limnologicheskoi Stantsii v Kosine, No. 15:67—84. 1932b.

Rossolimo, L. L. Zadachi i ustanovki limnologii kak nauki (Tasks and
Purposes of Limnology as a Science). — Trudy Limnologicheskoi
Stantsii v Kosine, No. 17:5—19. 1934.

Rossolimo, L. L. Ocherki po geografii vnutrennikh vod SSSR (Geographical Surveys of Inland Waters of the USSR). Moskva, Uchpedgiz.
1953.

Rossolimo, L. L. Nekotorye cherty iz proshlogo Glubokogo ozera (Some
Historical Features of Lake Glubokoe). — In Sbornik: Voprosy
golotsena, pp. 285—307. Vilnius. 1961.

Rossolimo, L. L. Osnovy tipizatsii ozer i limnologicheskogo raioniro-
vaniya (Fundamentals of Lake Classification and Limnological
Zoning). — In Sbornik: Nakoplenie veshchestva v ozerakh, pp. 5—46.
Moskva, Izd. "Nauka." 1964.

Rossolimo, L. L. Teoreticheskie osnovy osvoeniya ozernykh resursov
(Theoretical Principles of Tapping Lake Resources). — In Sbornik:
Krugovorot veshchestva i energii v ozernykh vodoemakh, pp. 5—13.
Moskva, Izd. "Nauka." 1967a.

Rossolimo, L. L. Neobratimye tipologicheskie izmeneniya ozer kul'-
turnykh landshaftov (Irreversible Typological Variations of Lakes of
Cultivated Regions). — In Sbornik: Tipologiya ozer, pp. 5—27.
Moskva, Izd."Nauka. " 1967b.

Rossolimo, L. L. and Z. I. Kuznetsova. Donnoe gazootdelenie, kak
faktor kislorodnogo rezhima ozer (Bottom Gas Liberation as a Factor
in the Oxygen Regime of Lakes). — Trudy Limnologicheskoi Stantsii
v Kosine, No. 17:87—112. 1934.

Rozanova, E. P. Kharakteristika bakterial'nogo naseleniya Gor'kovskogo
vodokhranilishcha v pervyi god ego sushchestvovaniya (Characteristics
of the Bacterial Population of the Gorki Reservoir during its First
Year). — Byulleten' Instituta Biologii Vodokhranilishch, No. 3:5—8.
1959.

Rozanova, E. P. Ispol'zovanie uglevodorodov mikroorganizmami
(Utilization of Hydrocarbons by Microorganisms). — Uspekhi
Mikrobiologii, No. 4:61—96. 1967.

R o z e n b e r g, L. A.   Fiziko-khimicheskie usloviya bakterial'nogo osazhdeniya kal'tsiya (Physicochemical Conditions of Bacterial Precipitation of Calcium). — Mikrobiologiya, 19(5):410—417. 1950.

R u b a n, E. L.   Fiziologiya i biokhimiya nitrifitsiruyushchikh mikroorganizmov (Physiology and Biochemistry of Nitrifying Microorganisms). Moskva, Izd. AN SSSR. 1961.

R u b e n c h i k, L. I.   Sulfatredutsiruyushchie bakterii (obzor) (Sulfate -
Reducing Bacteria (Review)). — Mikrobiologiya, 15(5):443—456. 1946.

R u b e n c h i k, L. I.   Mikroorganizmy i mikrobial'nye protsessy v solyanykh
vodoemakh USSR (Microorganisms and Microbial Processes in Saline
Water Bodies of the Ukrainian SSR). Kiev, Izd. AN USSR. 1948.

R u b e n c h i k, L. I. and D. G. G o i k h e r m a n.   K mikrobiologii gryazevykh
ozer. II.   Issledovanie Kuyal'nitskogo limana (Microbiology of Mud
Lakes. II.   Investigation of Kuyal'nik Liman). — Mikrobiologiya,
4(3):403—420. 1935.

R u b e n c h i k, L. I. and D. G. G o i k h e r m a n.   K mikrobiologii bioanizo-
tropnykh solenykh vodoemov.   Issledovanie Slavyanskikh ozer
(Microbiology of Bioanisotropic Saline Water Bodies.   Investigation
of Slavyansk Lakes). — Mikrobiologiya, 8(5):533—549. 1939.

R u b e n c h i k, L. I. and D. G. G o i k h e r m a n.   K mikrobiologii gryazevykh
ozer. III.   Vertikal'noe rasprostranenie bakterii v donnykh otlozheniyakh Repnogo ozera (Microbiology of Mud Lakes. III.
Vertical Distribution of Bacteria in Bottom Sediments of Lake
Repnoe). — Mikrobiologiya, 9(1):39—44. 1940.

R u b e n c h i k, L. I. and D. G. G o i k h e r m a n.   K mikrobiologii gryazevykh
ozer. IV.   Issledovanie Molochnogo limana (Microbiology of Mud
Lakes. IV.   Investigations of Molochnyi Liman). — Mikrobiologiya,
10(3):323—332. 1941.

R u d a k o v, K. I.   Vosstanovlenie mineral'nykh fosfatov biologicheskim
putem (Biological Reduction of Inorganic Phosphates). — Vestnik
Bakterial'no-Agronomicheskoi Stantsii, No. 24:171—188. 1926.

R u d a k o v, K. I.   Vosstanovlenie mineral'nykh fosfatov biologicheskim
putem. 2-e soobshchenie (Biological Reduction of Inorganic Phosphates.   Second Communication). — Vestnik Bakterial'no-Agronomicheskoi Stantsii, No. 25:203—232. 1928.

R u s a k o v a, G. S. and V. S. B u t k e v i c h.   Denitrifikatsiya bez ispol'-
zovaniya nitratrov v kachestve istochnika azota (Denitrification without
Using Nitrates as a Source of Nitrogen). — Mikrobiologiya, 10(2):
137—162. 1941.

R u s s k i i, M.   Limnologicheskie issledovaniya v Srednem Povolzh'e (ozera
severo-zapadnoi chasti Kazanskoi gubernii) (Limnological Investigation
in the Middle Volga (Lakes of the Northwestern Part of Kazan
Province)). — Izvestiya Tomskogo Universiteta, Vol. 65:1. 1916.

S a l i m o v s k a y a - R o d i n a, A. G.   Mikrobiologicheskie issledovaniya Onezhskogo ozera v 1930 i 1931 gg. (Microbiological Investigations of Lake
Onega). — In Sbornik: Issledovaniya ozer SSSR, No. 1:53—75. 1932.

S a l i m o v s k a y a - R o d i n a, A. G.   Opyt primeneniya metoda plastinok
obrastaniya k izucheniyu bakterial'noi flory vody (Experimental
Use of Layers of Fouling for Studying Aquatic Bacterial Flora). —
Mikrobiologiya, 5(4):487—493. 1936.

Salimovskaya-Rodina, A. G. O vertikal'nom raspredelenii bakterii v vode ozer (The Vertical Distribution of Bacteria in Lake Waters). — Mikrobiologiya, 7(6):789—803. 1938.

Salimovskaya-Rodina, A. G. Mestonakhozhdenie azotobaktera v presnykh vodakh (Azotobacter Deposits in Fresh Waters). — Doklady AN SSSR, 25(5):448—450. 1939.

Salmanov, M. A. Kharakteristika obshchego chisla bakterii v Kuibyshev-skom vodokhranilishche v pervye gody ego zapolneniya (Character-istics of Bacterial Numbers in the Kuibyshev Reservoir during its First Years of Filling). — Byulleten' Instituta Biologii Vodokhranilishch, No. 1:15—18. 1958.

Salmanov, M. A. Sravnitel'noe izuchenie mikrobiologicheskikh protsessov pri formirovanii Kuibyshevskogo i Mingichaurskogo vodokhranilishch (Comparative Study of Microbiological Processes in the Formation of the Kuibyshev and Mingichaursk Reservoirs). Author's Summary of Candidate Thesis. Baku. 1959.

Samoilov, Ya. V. and A. G. Titov. Zhelezo-margantsevye zhelvaki so dna Chernogo, Baltiiskogo i Barentseva morei (Iron-Manganese Nodules from the Bottom of the Black, Baltic and Barents Seas). — Trudy Geologicheskogo i Mineralogicheskogo Muzeya im. Petra Velikogo. Rossiiskaya Akademiya Nauk, Vol. 3:25—112. 1922.

Savel'eva, N. D. and T. N. Zhilina. K sistematike vodorodnykh bakterii (The Taxonomy of Hydrogen Bacteria). — Mikrobiologiya, 37(1):84—91. 1968.

Selivanov, L. S. Materialy po biogidrokhimii reki Klyaz'my III. Bio-gidrokhimiya kal'tsiya i gazov (Contribution to the Study of the Biohydro-chemistry of the Klyazma River. III. Biohydrochemistry of Calcium and Gases). — Zapiski Bol'shevskoi Biologicheskoi Stantsii, Nos. 7—8:3—41. 1935.

Selivanov, L. S. Materialy po gidrokhimii i gidrografii reki Klyaz'my (Data on the Hydrochemistry and Hydrography of the Klyazma River). — Zapiski Bol'shevskoi Biologicheskoi Stantsii, No. 10:3—48. 1937.

Semenovich, N. I. Limnologicheskie usloviya nakopleniya zhelezistykh osadkov v ozerakh (Limnological Conditions for Accumulation of Iron Deposits in Lakes). — Trudy Laboratorii Ozerovedeniya, Vol. 6, Trudy Limnologicheskoi Stantsii AN SSSR na ozere Punnus-Yarvi, No. 1:1—186. Leningrad. 1958.

Semenovich, N. I. K voprosu izucheniya khimicheskogo obmena mezhdu donnymi otlozheniyami i vodnoi massoi ozer (Study of the Chemical Exchange between Bottom Sediments and Waters of Lakes). — Trudy 5-i nauchnoi konferentsii po izucheniyu vnutrennikh vodoemov Pribaltiki, pp. 55—63. 1959.

Semenovich, N. I. Issledovaniya okislitel'no-vosstanovitel'nogo potentsiala i aktivnoi reaktsii donnykh otlozhenii Ladozhskogo ozera (Investigations of Oxidation-Reduction Potential and Active Reaction of Bottom Sediments of Lake Ladoga). — In Sbornik: Elementy rezhima Ladozh-skogo ozera (Trudy Laboratorii Ozerovedeniya), pp. 45—56. 1964.

Semenovich, N. I. Donnye otlozheniya Ladozhskogo ozera (The Bottom Sediments of Lake Ladoga). Moskva—Leningrad, Izd. "Nauka." 1966.

Shabarova, N. T.   Azotistye veshchestva sapropelya (Nitrogenous Matter of Sapropel). — Trudy Laboratorii Sapropelovykh Otlozhenii, No. 4: 40—54. 1950.

Shaposhnikov, V. N. and R. M. Balitskaya. Ispol'zovanie serovodoroda i organicheskikh soedinenii zelenymi serobakteriyami Chloro- pseudomonas ethylicum v zavisimosti ot intensivnosti sveta (Utilization of Hydrogen Sulfide and Organic Compounds by Green Sulfur Bacteria Chloropseudomonas ethylicum with Respect to Light Intensity). — Mikrobiologiya, 33(3):385—389. 1964.

Shaposhnikov, V. N., E. N. Kondrat'eva, and V. D. Fedorov. K izu- cheniyu zelenykh serobakterii roda Chlorobium (Study of Green Sulfur Bacteria of the Genus Chlorobium). — Mikrobiologiya, 27(5):529—535. 1958.

Shcherbakov, A. P.   O kontsentratsii vodorodnykh ionov v Glubokom ozere (The Concentration of Hydrogen Ions in Lake Glubokoe). — Trudy Gidrobiologicheskoi Stantsii na Glubokom Ozere, 6(4):41—50. 1928.

Shcherbakov, A. P.   O pogloshchenii kisloroda nekotorymi planktonnymi rakoobraznymi (Oxygen Uptake by Some Planktonic Crustaceans). — Trudy Limnologicheskoi Stantsii v Kosine, No. 19:67—89. 1935.

Shcherbakov, A. P.   Ozero Glubokoe. Gidrobiologicheskii ocherk (Lake Glubokoe. Hydrobiological Survey). Moskva, Izd. "Nauka. " 1967a.

Shcherbakov, A. P.   Rol' zooplanktona v destruktsii organicheskogo veshchestva v ozere (The Role of Zooplankton in the Decomposition of Lacustrine Organic Matter). — Zhurnal Obshchei Biologii, 28(2): 131—139. 1967b.

Shternberg, L. E.   O biogennykh strukturakh v margantsevykh rudakh (The Biogenic Structures in Manganese Ores). — Mikrobiologiya, 36(4):110—111. 1967.

Shternberg, L. E., E. S. Bazilevskaya, and T. A. Chigireva. Karbonaty margantsa i zheleza v donnykh otlozheniyakh ozera Punnus- Yarvi (Manganese and Iron Carbonates in Bottom Sediments of Lake Punnus-Yarvi). — Doklady AN SSSR, 170(3):691—694. 1966.

Shturm, L. D.   K voprosu aerobnogo razlozheniya kletchatki bakteriyami (The Problem of Aerobic Decomposition of Cellulose by Bacteria). — Izvestiya Sapropelogo Komiteta, No. 4:29—40. 1928a.

Shturm, L. D.   Razlozhenie kletchatki bakteriyami sapropelei ozer Belogo, Kolomny i Samro i ila ozera Kirenskogo (Decomposition of Cellulose by Bacteria of Sapropels of Lakes Beloe, Kolomna and Samro and of Mud of Lake Kirensk). — Izvestiya Sapropelogo Komiteta, No. 4: 41—60. 1928b.

Shturm, L. D.   Predvaritel'nyi otchet o zimnei ekspeditsii v Galichskii, Chukhlomskii i Semenovskii raiony v 1931 g.   (Preliminary Report of the Winter Expedition to the Galich, Chukhloma and Semenov Regions in 1931). — Izvestiya Sapropelogo Komiteta, Vol. 6:71—74. 1931.

Shturm, L. D.   Issledovaniya Alakul'skogo ozera i vopros o proiskhozhdenii balkhashita (Investigations of Lake Alakul and the Problem of the Origin of Balkhashite). — Trudy Sapropelogo Instituta, Vol. 1:167—200. 1934.

Shturm, L. D. Issledovanie mikroflory ozer po metodu plastinok obrastaniya (Investigation of Lake Microflora Using the Method of Fouling
Layers). — AN SSSR. Trudy Laboratorii Genezisa Sapropela, No. 1:
149—163. 1939a.

Shturm, L. D. Ozera Zaluch'ya i ikh ilovye otlozheniya (kharakteristika
po rezul'tatam rabot kompleksnoi rekognostsirovannoi ekspeditsii
IGI AN SSSR) (Zaluch'e Lakes and their Mud Sediments. Results of
the Comprehensive Reconnaissance Expedition of the IGI AN SSSR). —
Trudy Laboratorii Genezisa Sapropela, Vol. 1:137—200. 1939b.

Shturm, L. D. and N. P. Fedorovskaya. Izuchenie prevrashcheniya
zhirovykh veshchestv v svyazi s genezisom ilovykh otlozhenii (Study
of Transformation of Fatty Substances in Connection with the Genesis
of Mud Sediments). — Trudy Laboratorii Genezisa Sapropela, No. 2:
93—114. 1941.

Shturm, L. D. and Z. A. Kanunnikova. Raspredelenie mikroorganizmov
v presnodovnykh ilovykh otlozheniyakh (Distribution of Microorganisms
in Freshwater Mud Sediments). — Mikrobiologiya, 14(4):260—264. 1945.

Shturm, L. D., M. A. Messineva, and N. P. Fedorovskaya. Mikrobiologicheskoe issledovanie ilovykh otlozhenii ozera Borkovskogo
(Microbiological Investigations of Mud Sediments of Lake Borkov-
skoe). — Trudy Laboratorii Genezisa Sapropela, No. 2:115—129. 1941.

Shturm, L. D. and S. I. Orlova. O prevrashchenii zhira, parafina i
pal'mitinovoi kisloty pod vliyaniem mikroorganizmov iz Alakul'skogo
ozera (Transformation of Fat, Paraffin and Palmitic Acid by Microorganisms from Lake Alakul). — Mikrobiologiya, Vol. 6:754—772. 1937.

Shturm, L. D. and S. I. Orlova. Serobakterii i ekologicheskie usloviya
vodoema, soputstvuyushchie ikh obil'nomu razvitiyu (Sulfur Bacteria
and Ecological Conditions in the Water Body Accompanying Mass
Development). — Trudy Instituta Mikrobiologii AN SSSR, No. 3:176—184.
1954.

Shturm, L. D. and T. A. Simakova. Materialy po bakterial'nomu issledovaniyu sapropelevykh otlozhenii (Data for a Bacterial Investigation
of Sapropel Sediments). — Izvestiya Sapropelogo Komiteta, No. 5:81—
116. 1929.

Skadovskii, S. N., A. P. Shcherbakov, and G. G. Vinberg. Predvaritel'-
noe soobshchenie o rezult'tatakh gidrobiologicheskogo i fiziko-
khimicheskogo issledovaniya Petrovskikh ozer Tverskoi gubernii
(Preliminary Communication on the Results of Hydrobiological and
Physicochemical Investigations of the Petrovskie Lakes of Tver
Province). — Trudy Zvenigorodskoi Gidrofizicheskoi Stantsii, pp. 215—
239. 1928.

Slobodchikov, B. Ya. Gidrologicheskii ocherk ozer sistemy reki Kemi:
Verkhnego, Srednego i Nizhnego Kuito (Hydrological Survey of Lakes
of the System of the Kem' River: Upper, Central and Lower Kuito). —
Trudy Karel'skoi Nauchno-Issledovatel'skoi Rybokhozyaistvennoi
Stantsii (KNIPS), Vol. 1:43—102. 1935.

Slobodchikov, B. Ya. Gidrokhimicheskii rezhim ozera Sevan po dannym
1947—1948 gg. (Hydrochemical Regime of Lake Sevan from Data of
1947—1948). — Trudy Sevanskoi Gidrobiologicheskoi Stantsii, Vol. 12:
5—28. 1951.

Slobodchikov, B. Ya. and G. Shaposhnikova. Nauchno-promyslovoe issledovanie ozer basseina reki Kemi: Nizhnego i Srednego Kuito (Scientific-Commercial Investigation of Lakes of the Kem' River Basin: Lower and Central Kuito). — Rybnoe Khozyaistvo Karelii, No. 2:18—47. 1933.

Sokolov, D. V. O mikroorganizmakh v podpochvennykh sloyakh i o biokhimicheskikh faktorakh vyvetrivaniya (Microorganisms in Subsoil Layers and the Biochemical Factors of Weathering). — Izvestiya AN SSSR, Ser. 7, Otdel Matematiki i Estestvennykh Nauk, No. 5:693. 1932.

Sokolova, E. I. Fiziko-khimicheskie issledovaniya osadochnykh zhelez-nykh i margantsevykh rud i vmeshchayushchikh ikh porod (Physico-chemical Investigations of Sedimentary Iron and Manganese Ores and of the Enclosing Rocks). Moskva, Izd. AN SSSR. 1962.

Sokolova, G. A. Izuchenie mikrobiologicheskikh protsessov v Gor'kovskom vodokhranilishche v pervyi god ego sushchestvovaniya (Study of Microbiological Processes in the Gorki Reservoir in its First Year). Institut Biologii Vodokhranilishch AN SSSR i Kafedra Mikrobiologii MGU. (Thesis.) 1957.

Sokolova, G. A. Zhelezobakteria ozera Glubokogo (Iron Bacteria of Lake Glubokoe). — Mikrobiologiya, 28(2):245—250. 1959.

Sokolova, G. A. Rol' zhelezobakterii v dinamike zheleza v Glubokom ozere (The Role of Iron Bacteria in the Dynamics of Iron in Lake Glubokoe). — Trudy Vsesoyuznogo Gidrobiologicheskogo Obshchestva, Vol. 11:5—11. 1961.

Sokolova-Dubinina, G. A. and Z. P. Deryugina. Rol' mikro-organizmov v obrazovanii rodokhrozita v ozere Punnus-Yarvi (The Role of Microorganisms in the Formation of Rhodochrosite in Lake Punnus-Yarvi). — Mikrobiologiya, 36(3):535—542; 36(6):1066—1076. 1967.

Sokolova-Dubinina, G. A. and Z. P. Deryugina. Vliyanie uslovii ozernoi sredy na mikrobiologicheskoe obrazovanie margantsevoi rudy (Effect of Lacustrine Environmental Conditions on Micro-biological Formation of Manganese Ore). — Mikrobiologiya, 37(1): 148—154. 1968.

Sokolova, G. A. and G. I. Karavaiko. Biogennoe okislenie sery rozdel'-skoi rudy v laboratornykh usloviyakh (Biological Oxidation of Sulfur of Rozdol Ore in Laboratory Conditions). — Mikrobiologiya, 31(6): 984—989. 1962.

Sokolova, G. A. and G. I. Karavaiko. Fiziologiya i geokhimicheskaya deyatel'nost' tionovykh bakterii (Physiology and Geochemical Activity of Sulfur Bacteria). Moskva, Izd. "Nauka." 1964.

Sokolova, G. A. and Yu. I. Sorokin. Bakterial'noe vosstanovlenie sul'fatov v ilakh Rybinskogo vodokhranilishcha (Bacterial Reduction of Sulfates in Mud of the Rybinsk Reservoir). — Mikrobiologiya, 26(2):194—201. 1957.

Sokolova, G. A. and Yu. I. Sorokin. Opredelenie intensivnosti bakterial'-nogo vosstanovleniya sul'fatov v gruntakh Gor'kovskogo vodokhranili-shcha s primeneniem S^{35} (S^{35}-Determination of Bacterial Reduction of Sulfates in Bottoms of the Gorki Reservoir). — Doklady AN SSSR, 118(2): 404—406. 1958.

Solov'ev, M. M.   Problema sapropela v SSSR (The Problem of Sapropel in the USSR).   Moskva, Izd. AN SSSR. 1932.

Solov'eva, N. F.   K voprosu o dinamike solevogo balansa Aral'skogo morya. Materialy po ikhtiofaune i rezhimu vod basseina Aral'skogo morya (Dynamics of the Salt Balance of the Aral Sea.   Materials on the Ichthyofauna and Water Regime of the Aral Sea Basin). — Materialy k Poznaniyu Fauny i Flory SSSR, Novaya Seriya, Otdel Zoologicheskii, Nos. 19(34):62—69. 1950.

Sorokin, Yu. I.   Khimizm protsessa vodorodnoi reduktsii sul'fatov (Chemistry of Hydrogenous Reduction of Sulfates). — Trudy Instituta Mikrobiologii, No. 3:21—34. 1954.

Sorokin, Yu. I.   Produktivnost' khemosinteza v ilovykh otlozheniyakh (Productivity of Chemosynthesis in Mud Sediments). — Doklady AN SSSR, 103(5):875—877. 1955a.

Sorokin, Yu. I.   O bakterial'nom khemosinteze v ilovykh otlozheniyakh (Bacterial Chemosynthesis in Mud Sediments). — Mikrobiologiya, 24(4):393—399. 1955b.

Sorokin, Yu. I.   K teorii khemoavtotrofii (The Theory of Chemoautotrophy). — Mikrobiologiya, 25(3):363—375. 1956.

Sorokin, Yu. I.   Rol' khemosinteza v produktsii organicheskogo veshchestva v vodoemakh. I. Podlednyi khemosintez v vodnoi tolshche Rybinskogo vodokhranilishcha (The Role of Chemosynthesis in the Production of Organic Matter in Water Bodies. I. Chemosynthesis under Ice in Waters of the Rybinsk Reservoir). — Mikrobiologiya, 26(6):736—744. 1957.

Sorokin, Yu. I.   Pervichnaya produktsiya organicheskogo veshchestva v vodnoi tolshche Rybinskogo vodokhranilishcha (Primary Production in Waters of the Rybinsk Reservoir). — Trudy Biologicheskoi Stantsii "Borok," Vol. 3:66—88. 1958a.

Sorokin, Yu. I.   Rol' khemosinteza v produktsii organicheskogo veshchestva v vodokhranilishchakh. III. Produktivnost' khemosinteza v vodnoi tolshche v letnii period (The Role of Chemosynthesis in the Production of Organic Matter in Reservoirs. III. Chemosynthetic Productivity in the Water Column in Summer). — Mikrobiologiya, 27(3): 357—365. 1958b.

Sorokin, Yu. I.   Rol' khemosinteza v produktsii organicheskogo veshchestva v vodokhranilishchakh. IV. Pitanie vodnykh bespozvonochnykh avtotrofnymi bakteriyami, okislyayushchimi metan i vodorod (The Role of Chemosynthesis in the Production of Organic Matter in Reservoirs. IV.   Feeding of Aquatic Invertebrates on Autotrophic Bacteria Oxidizing Methane and Hydrogen). — Mikrobiologiya, 28(6):916—920. 1959a.

Sorokin, Yu. I.   O vliyanii stratifikatsii vodnykh mass na pervichnuyu produktsiyu fotosinteza v more (Effect of Stratification of Water Masses on Primary Production in the Sea). — Zhurnal Obshchei Biologii, 20(6):455—463. 1959b.

Sorokin, Yu. I.   Metan i vodorod v vode volzhskikh vodokhranilishch (Methane and Hydrogen in the Water of Volga Reservoirs). — Trudy Instituta Biologii Vodokhranilishch, 3(6):50—58. 1960.

Sorokin, Yu. I.   Geterotrofnaya assimilyatsiya uglekislot mikroorganizmami (Heretotrophic Assimilation of CO_2 by Microorganisms). — Zhurnal Obshchei Biologii, 22(4):265—272. 1961a.

Sorokin, Yu. I. Rol' khemosinteza v produktsii organicheskogo veshchestva v vodokhranilishchakh. Izuchenie produktsii khemosinteza v Kuibyshevskom vodokhranilishche v 1958—1959 gg. (The Role of Chemosynthesis in the Production of Organic Matter in Reservoirs. Study of Chemosynthetic Production in the Kuibyshev Reservoir in 1958—1959). — Mikrobiologiya, 30(5):928—937. 1961b.

Sorokin, Yu. i. Rol' khemosinteza v trofike vodoemov (The Role of Chemosynthesis in the Trophics of Water Bodies). — In Sbornik: Pervichnaya produktsiya morei i vnutrennikh vod, pp. 363—368. Minsk, Izd. Ministerstva vysshego obrazovaniya BSSR. 1961c.

Sorokin, Yu. I. Pervichnaya produktsiya i ee utilizatsiya v morskikh i presnykh vodoemakh (Primary Production and its Utilization in Marine and Fresh Water Bodies). Author's Summary of Candidate Thesis. Institut Biologii Vnutrennikh Vod AN SSSR. 1963.

Sorokin, Yu. I. Rol' temnovoi bakterial'noi assimilyatsii uglekisloty v trofike vodoemov (The Role of Bacterial Assimilation of CO_2 in the Dark in the Trophics of Water Bodies). — Mikrobiologiya, 33(5): 880—886. 1964a.

Sorokin, Yu. I. K voprosu o metodike mikrobiologicheskikh rabot v more v svete sovremennykh zadach morskoi mikrobiologii (On a Methodology for Microbiological Studies in the Sea in the Light of Current Tasks of Marine Microbiology). — Okeanologiya, 4(2):349—353. 1964b.

Sorokin, Yu. I. Issledovanie konstruktivnogo obmena sul'fatredutsiruyushchikh bakterii s pomoshch'yu C^{14} (Study of Constructive Exchange of Sulfate-Reducing Bacteria Using C^{14}). — Mikrobiologiya, 35(6): 967—977. 1966a.

Sorokin, Yu. I. Vzaimosvyaz' mikrobiologicheskikh protsessov krugovorota sery i ugleroda v meromikticheskom ozere Belovod' (Interrelationship of Microbiological Processes of the Sulfur Cycle and Carbon in the Meromictic Lake Belovod'). —In Sbornik: Plankton i bentos vnutrennikh vodoemov; Trudy Instituta Biologii Vnutrennikh Vod AN SSSR, Nos. 12(15):332—355. 1966b.

Sorokin, Yu. I. O primenenii radioaktivnogo ugleroda dlya izucheniya pitaniya i pishchevykh svyazei vodnykh zhivotnykh (Use of Radioactive Carbon for Studying the Feeding and Food Relations of Aquatic Animals). — In Sbornik: Plankton i bentos vnutrennikh vodoemov; Trudy Instituta Biologii Vnutrennikh Vod AN SSSR, Nos. 12(15):75—119. 1966c.

Sorokin, Yu. I. Pervichnaya produktsiya i mikrobiologicheskie protsessy v ozere Gek-Gel' (Primary Production and Microbiological Processes in Lake Gek-Gel'). — Mikrobiologiya, 37(2):345—354. 1968.

Sorokin, Yu. I. and L. B. Klyashtorin. Pervichnaya produktsiya v Atlanticheskom okeane (Primary Production in the Atlantic Ocean). — Trudy Vsesoyuznogo Gidrobiologicheskogo Obshchestva, Vol. 11: 265—284. 1961.

Sorokin, Yu. I. and A. N. Meshkov. O primenenii radioaktivnogo ugleroda dlya izucheniya pitaniya vodnykh bespozvonochnykh (Use of Radioactive Carbon for Studying the Feeding of Aquatic Invertebrates). — Trudy Instituta Biologii Vodokhranilishch, No. 5:7—14. 1959.

Sorokin, Yu. I., A. V. Monakov, E. D. Mordukhai-Boltovskaya, E. A. Tsikhon-Lukanina, and R. A. Rodova. Opyt primeneniya radiouglerodnogo metoda dlya izucheniya troficheskoi roli sinezelenykh vodoroslei (Experimental Use of the Radiocarbon Method for Studying the Trophic Role of Blue-Green Algae). — In Sbornik: Ekologiya i fiziologiya sinezelenykh vodoroslei, pp. 235—240. Moskva—Leningrad, Izd. "Nauka." 1965.

Sorokin, Yu. I., E. P. Rozanova, and G. A. Sokolova. Izuchenie pervichnoi produktsii v Gor'kovskom vodokhranilishche s primeneniem C^{14} (Study of Primary Production in Gorki Reservoir Using C^{14}). — Trudy Vsesoyuznogo Gidrobiologicheskogo Obshchestva, Vol. 9:351—359. 1959.

Sorokina, V. A. Obrazovanie bakterial'noi plenki na poverkhnosti ozernykh ilov i vliyanie ee na obmen veshchestvom mezhdu ilom i vodoi (Formation of a Bacterial Film on the Surface of Lake Mud and its Effect on the Metabolism between Mud and Water). — Mikrobiologiya, 7(5):579—591. 1938.

Speranskaya, T. A. Dannye po izucheniyu organicheskogo veshchestva ozernykh ilovykh otlozhenii (A Contribution to the Study of Organic Matter of Lake Mud Sediments). — Trudy Limnologicheskoi Stantsii v Kosine, No. 20:67—80. 1935.

Stal'makova, G. A. O pogloshchenii kisloroda donnymi otlozheniyami nekotorykh ozer Zaluch'ya (Oxygen Uptake by Bottom Sediments of Zaluch'e Lakes). — Trudy Laboratorii Genezisa Sapropela. No. 2: 35—43. 1941.

Strakhov, N. M. Zhelezorudnye fatsii i ikh analogi v istorii zemli (Iron Facies and their Analogues in the History of the Earth). — Trudy Geologicheskikh Nauk AN SSSR, No. 73, Geologicheskaya Seriya, No. 22. 1947.

Strakhov, N. M. Ob istinnoi roli bakterii v obrazovanii karbonatnykh porod (The Role of Bacteria in the Formation of Carbonate Rocks). — Izvestiya AN SSSR, Seriya Geologicheskaya, No. 3:9. 1948.

Strakhov, N. M. Izvestkovo-dolomitovye fatsii sovremennykh i drevnikh vodoemov (Calcareous-Dolomitic Facies of Recent and Ancient Water Bodies). — Trudy Instituta Geologicheskikh Nauk, No. 124, Geologicheskaya Seriya, No. 45. 1951.

Strakhov, N. M. Osnovy teorii litogeneza, t. II. Zakonomernosti sostava i razmeshcheniya gumidnykh otlozhenii (Fundamentals of the Theory of Lithogenesis, Vol. 2. Patterns of the Composition and the Distribution of Humic Deposits). Moskva, Izd. AN SSSR. 1960.

Strashchuk, M. F., V. A. Suprychev, and M. S. Khitraya. Mineralogiya, geokhimiya i usloviya formirovaniya donnykh otlozhenii Sivasha (Mineralogy, Geochemistry and Conditions of Formation of Bottom Sediments of Sivash). Kiev, Izd. "Naukova dumka." 1964.

Stravinskaya, E. A. O raspredelenii zheleza v vode ozera Krasnogo (The Distribution of Iron in the Water of Lake Krasnoe). — Doklady AN SSSR, 168(4):908—910. 1966.

Suchenya, L. M. Kolichestvennye issledovaniya troficheskikh vzaimootnoshenii presnovodnogo zoo- i fitoplanktona (Quantitative Investigations of Trophic Interrelationships of Freshwater Zooplankton and Phytoplankton). Author's Summary of Candidate Thesis. Belorusskii Gosudarstvennyi Universitet. Minsk. 1958.

Surman, K. I. Razlozhenie trudnodostupnykh rastenii soedinenii fosfora silikatnymi bakteriyami (Decomposition of Little Accessible Phosphorus-Compound Plants by Silicate Bacteria). — In Sbornik: Mikroorganizmy i effektivnoe plodorodie pochvy; Trudy INMI, No. 11: 269—274. 1961.

Sysueva, A. F. Mikrobiologicheskie issledovaniya Kremenchugskogo vodokhranilishcha v period ego stanovleniya (Microbiological Investigations of the Kremenchug Reservoir during its Formation). Author's Summary of Candidate Thesis. INMI AN USSR. Kiev. 1963.

Tauson, V. O. Osnovnye polozheniya rastitel'noi bioenergetiki (The Basic Theories of Plant Bioenergetics). Moskva—Leningrad, Izd. AN SSSR. 1950.

Tauson, V. O. and V. Aleshina. O vosstanovlenii sulfatov bakteriyami v prisutstvii uglevodorodov (Reduction of Sulfates by Bacteria in the Presence of Hydrocarbons). — Mikrobiologiya, 1(3):229—261. 1932.

Tikhonova, G. V., L. L. Lisenkova, N. G. Doman, and V. P. Skulachev. Puti perenosa elektronov u zhelezookislyayushchikh bakterii Thiobac. ferooxidans (Electron Transfer in the Iron Bacteria Thiobac. ferooxidans). — Biokhimiya, 32(4):725—732. 1967.

Titov, E. M. O khimicheskom sostave zoly ural'skikh sapropelei i k voprosu ob obrazovanii izvestkovistykh sapropelei (The Chemical Composition of Ash of the Urals Sapropels and the Problem of Formation of Calcareous Sapropels). — Trudy Laboratorii Sapropelovykh Otlozhenii, No. 3:29—52. 1949.

Tomilov, A. A. Materialy po gidrobiologii nekotorykh glubokovodnykh ozer Olekmi-Vitimskoi gornoi strany (Contribution to the Study of Hydrobiology of Some Deep-Water Lakes of Olekmo-Vitim Highland). — Trudy Irkutskogo Gosudarstvennogo Universiteta, Vol. 11:3—88. 1954.

Trifonova, N. A. Opredelenie velichiny vydeleniya obshchego i mineral'nogo azota gruntami Rybinskogo vodokhranilishcha (Determination of Total and Inorganic Nitrogen in Bottoms of the Rybinsk Reservoir). — Byulleten' Instituta Biologii Vodokhranilishch, No. 11:49—52. 1961.

Trifonova, N. A. Obmen rastvorimymi formami azota mezhdu gruntom i pridonnym sloem vody (Exchange of Soluble Nitrogen Compounds between the Bottom and Near-Bottom Waters). — In Sbornik: Materialy po biologii i gidrologii volzhskikh vodokhranilishch, pp. 110—116. 1963.

Troshanov, E. P. Bakterii, vosstanavlivayushchie marganets i zhelezo v donnykh osadkakh (Manganese- and Iron-Reducing Bacteria in Bottom Sediments). — In Sbornik: Rol' mikroorganizmov v obrazovanii zhelezo-margantsevykh ozernykh rud, pp. 118—122. Moskva—Leningrad, Izd. "Nauka." 1964.

Tyurin, I. V. and M. M. Kononova. O novom metode opredeleniya potrebnosti pochv v azote (New Method of Determining Nitrogen Requirement in Soils). — Trudy Pochvennogo Instituta im. Dokuchaeva, 18(4):49. 1934.

Uspenskii, E. E. K voprosu o zadachakh i putyakh mikrobiologii v svyazi s razvitiem gorodskogo vodosnabzheniya i v osobennosti pri stroitel'stve vodokhranilishch (Tasks and Methods of Microbiology in Relation to the Development of Urban Water Supply and in Particular in the Construction of Reservoirs). — Mikrobiologiya, 1(2):89—111. 1932.

Uspenskii, E. E. K energetike zhiznennykh protsessov (The Energetics of Life Processes). Sbornik: "Pamyati K. A. Timiryazeva, " pp. 127—170. — In Sbornik: Fiziko-khimicheskie usloviya sredy kak osnova mikrobiologicheskikh protsessov, pp. 198—226. Moskva—Leningrad, Izd. AN SSSR. 1936 (1963).

Vereshchagin, G. Yu. Nekotorye dannye o rezhime glubinnykh vod Baikala v raione Maritua (Some Data on the Regime of Deep Waters of Baikal in the Mariti Village Area). — Trudy Komissii po Izucheniyu Ozera Baikala, Vol. 2:77—138. 1927a.

Vereshchagin, G. Yu. Gidrokhimicheskie nablyudeniya v Yuzhnom Baikale letom 1926 g. (Hydrochemical Observations in Southern Baikal in the Summer of 1926). — DAN SSSR, Seriya A-20, pp. 327—332. 1927b.

Vereshchagin, G. Yu. Baikal. Nauchno-populyarnyi ocherk (Lake Baikal. Scientific-Popular Survey). Irkutsk. 1948.

Vernadskii, V. I. Ocherki geokhimii (Review of Geochemistry). Leningrad, Nauchno-tekhnicheskoe izdatel'stvo. 1934.

Vilenkina, M. N. and M. M. Sakharova. Khimizm vody, bakterial'noe naselenie i fitoplankton Mozhaiskogo vodokhranilishcha i izmenenie ikh v reke Moskve (Chemistry of Water, Bacterial Population and Phytoplankton of Mozhaisk Reservoir and their Variation in the Moskva River). — In Sbornik: Uchinskoe i Mozhaiskoe vodokhranilishcha, pp. 389—406. 1963.

Vinberg, G. G. Opyt izucheniya fotosinteza i dykhaniya v vodnoi masse ozera. K voprosu o balanse organicheskogo veshchestva. Soobshchenie I. (Experimental Study of Photosynthesis and Respiration in Lacustrine Water. The Problem of the Balance of Organic Matter. Communication I). — Trudy Limnologicheskoi Stantsii v Kosine, No. 18:5—24. 1934.

Vinberg, G. G. K voprosu o balanse organicheskogo veshchestva v vodoemakh. Soobshcheniya I—V (On the Balance of Organic Matter in Water Bodies. Communications I—V). — Trudy Limnologicheskoi Stantsii v Kosine, No. 18. 1934; No. 20,.1935; No. 21, 1937; No. 22, 1939. 1934—1939.

Vinberg, G. G. Nekotorye obshchie voprosy produktivnosti ozer (Some General Problems of the Productivity of Lakes). — Zoologicheskii Zhurnal, Vol. 15:587—603. 1936a.

Vinberg, G. G. Nekotorye nablyudeniya na gumusovykh ozerakh. K voprosu o balanse organicheskogo veshchestva. Soobshchenie IV. (Some Observations on Humic Lakes. The Problem of the Balance of Organic Matter. Communication IV). — Trudy Limnologicheskoi Stantsii v Kosine, No. 21:75. 1936b.

Vinberg, G. G. Nablyudeniya nad intensivnost'yu dykhaniya i fotosinteza planktona rybovodnykh prudov. K voprosu o balanse organicheskogo veshchestva. Soobshchenie III (Observations on the Intensity of Respiration and Photosynthesis of Plankton of Fishponds. The Problem of the Balance of Organic Matter. Communication III). — Trudy Limnologicheskoi Stantsii v Kosine, No. 2:61—74. 1937a.

Vinberg, G. G. Nekotorye nablyudeniya na gumusovykh ozerakh (Petrovskie ozera). K voprosu o balanse organicheskogo veshchestva.

Soobshchenie IV (Some Observations on Humic Lakes (Petrov Lakes). The Problem of the Balance of Organic Matter. Communication IV). — Trudy Limnologicheskoi Stantsii v Kosine, No. 2:75—88. 1937b.

Vinberg, G. G. Intensivnost' dykhaniya bakterii (Intensity of Bacterial Respiration). — Uspekhi Sovremennoi Biologii, Vol. 21:401—413. 1946.

Vinberg, G. G. Boticheskii balans Chernogo ozera (Biotic Balance of Lake Chernoe). — Byulleten' Moskovskogo Obshchestva Ispytatelei Prirody, otdel biologicheskii, Vol. 53:10—19. 1948.

Vinberg, G. G. Intensivnost' obmena i razmery rakoobraznykh (Rate of Metabolism and the Size of Crustaceans). — Zhurnal Obshchei Biologii, 11(5):367—380. 1950.

Vinberg, G. G. Obshchie zadachi i nekotorye metody gidrobiologicheskikh issledovanii na rybokhozyaistvennykh prudakh (General Tasks and Some Methods of Hydrobiological Investigations on Fishponds). — Trudy Biologicheskoi Stantsii na Ozere Naroch', No. 1:3—22. Minsk. 1958.

Vinberg, G. G. Pervichnaya produktsiya vodoemov (Primary Production of Water Bodies). Minsk, Izd. AN BSSR. 1960.

Vinberg, G. G. and A. I. Ivanova. Opyt izucheniya fotosinteza i dykhaniya vodnoi massy ozera. Soobshchenie II (Experimental Study of Photosynthesis and Respiration in Lacustrine Waters. Communication II). — Trudy Limnologicheskoi Stantsii v Kosine, No. 20:5—34. 1935.

Vinberg, G. G., V. S. Ivlev, T. Platova, and L. L. Rossolimo. Metodika opredeleniya organicheskogo veshchestva i opyt kaloricheskoi otsenki kormovykh zapasov vodoema (Determination of Organic Matter and Experimental Caloric Appraisal of Food Resources of a Water Body). — Trudy Limnologicheskoi Stantsii v Kosine, No. 18:25—39. 1934.

Vinberg, G. G., G. A. Pechen' and E. A. Shushkina. Produktsiya planktona rakoobraznykh v trekh ozerakh raznogo tipa (Production of Plankton and Crustaceans in Three Different Types of Lakes). — Zoologicheskii Zhurnal, 48(5):676—687. 1965.

Vinberg, G. G. and T. P. Platova. Biomassa planktona i rastvorennoe organicheskoe veshchestvo v vode ozer (Planktonic Biomass and Soluble Organic Matter in Lake Waters). — Byulleten' Obshchestva Ispytatelei Prirody, otdel biologicheskii, 56(2):24—37. 1951.

Vinberg, G. G. and T. N. Sivko. Nekotorye nablyudeniya nad "zelenoi bakteriei" (Some Observations on a "Green Bacterium"). — Mikrobiologiya, 21(2):139—145. 1952.

Vinberg, G. G. and L. I. Yarovitsina. Razmnozhenie bakterii i poglo-shchenie kisloroda v vode (Reproduction of Bacteria and Oxygen Uptake in the Water). — Mikrobiologiya, 15(6):499—508. 1946.

Vinberg, G. G. and I. S. Zakharenkov. K kolichestvennoi kharakteristike roli planktona v krugovorote veshchestv v ozerakh (Quantitative Appraisal of Plankton in the Cycle of Elements in Lakes). — DAN SSSR, 73(5):1037—1039. 1950.

Vinogradskii, S. N. Serobakterii. I. (Sulfur Bacteria. I.). — Mikrobiologiya Pochvy, pp. 32—47. Moskva. Izd. AN SSSR. 1887 (1952).

Vinogradskii, S. N. O zhelezobakteriyakh (The Iron Bacteria). — Mikrobiologiya Pochvy, pp. 57—60. Moskva, Izd. AN SSSR. 1888 (1952).

Vinogradskii, S. N.   Izuchenie nitrifitsiruyushchikh organizmov (Study of Nitrifying Organisms). — Mikrobiologiya Pochvy, pp. 151—193. Moskva, Izd. AN SSSR. 1890 (1952).

Vinogradskii, S. N.   Ob usvoenii mikrobami gazoobraznogo azota atmosfery (The Uptake of Atmospheric Nitrogen by Bacteria). — Mikrobiologiya Pochvy, pp. 336—340. Moskva, Izd. AN SSSR. 1893, 1894 (1952).

Vinogradskii, S. N.   O razrushenii tsellyulozy v pochve (The Decomposition of Cellulose in the Soil). — Mikrobiologiya Pochvy, pp. 485—522. Moskva, Izd. AN SSSR. 1929 (1952).

Vinogradskii, S. N.   O sinteze ammiaka azotobakterom (The Synthesis of Ammonia by Azotobacter). — Mikrobiologiya Pochvy, pp. 641—643. Moskva. Izd. AN SSSR. 1930 (1952).

Vinogradskii, S. N.   Ocherki po pochvennoi mikrobiologii. 9-e soobshchenie.   K morfologii i ekologii azotobaktera (Surveys on Soil Microbiology.   Ninth Communication.   The Morphology and Ecology of Azotobacter). — Mikrobiologiya Pochvy. pp. 691—724. Moskva, Izd. AN SSSR. 1938 (1952).

Vinogradskii, S. N. and V. L. Omelyanskii.   Vliyanie organicheskikh veshchestv na deyatel'nost' nitrifitsiruyushchikh mikroorganizmov (Effect of Organic Matter on the Activity of Nitrifying Microorganisms). — Mikrobiologiya Pochvy, pp. 201—228. Moskva, Izd. AN SSSR. 1899 (1952).

Visloukh, S. M.   Biologicheskii analiz vody (Biological Analysis of Water). — In: Uchenie o mikroorganizmakh. Edited by Ch. P. Zlatogorov, pp. 225—306. Petrograd, Izd. "Prakticheskaya meditsina." 1916.

Vlasov, N. A., L. I. Pavlova, and L. A. Chernysheva.   Osobennosti formirovaniya i rezhima mineral'nykh ozer Vostochnoi Sibiri (Features of the Formation and the Regime of Mineral Lakes of Eastern Siberia). — Izvestiya Fiziko-Khimicheskogo Nauchno-Issledovatel'skogo Instituta pri Irkutskom Universitete, 6(1):176—191. 1964.

Voronin, V. V.   O bakterial'nykh issledovaniyakh planktona (Bacterial Investigations of Plankton). — Trudy Otdela Ikhtiologicheskogo Obshchestva Akklimatizatsii Zhivotnykh i Rastenii, Vol. 2:231. 1897.

Voronkov, N. V.   Vertikal'noe raspredelenie kisloroda v Glubokom ozere i nekotorye drugie svedeniya po khimizmu poslednego (Vertical Distribution of Oxygen in Lake Glubokoe and Other Information on its Chemistry). — Trudy Gidrobiologicheskoi Stantsii na Glubokom Ozere, 5(1):36—39. 1913.

Zakharov, N. G. and E. F. Konstantinova.   Ochistitel'nye prudy na Lyublinskikh polyakh fil'tratsii v 1919—1920 gg.   (Purification Ponds on the Lublin Filtration Fields in 1919—1920). — Trudy Soveshchaniya po Ochistke Stochnykh Vod, No. 11:11—14. 1929.

Zakharova, T. M.   O denitrifikatsii v zavisimosti ot reaktsii sredy v svyazi s izvestkovaniem pochvy (Denitrification in Relation to the Reaction of the Medium with Respect to Soil Calcification). — Trudy NIU, No. 29. 1925.

Zaslavskii, A. S.   O solelyubivykh tionovokislykh bakteriyakh solyanykh vodoemov (Halophilic Sulfur Bacteria in Saline Water Bodies). — Mikrobiologiya, 21(1):31—35. 1952.

Z a v a r z i n, G. A.   O vozbuditele vtoroi fazy nitrifikatsii. III. Morfologiya vozbuditelya vtoroi fazy nitrifikatsii (The Stimulant of the Second Phase of Nitrification. III. Morphology of the Stimulant of the Second Phase of Nitrification). — Mikrobiologiya, 27(6):679—686. 1958a.

Z a v a r z i n, G. A.   Vozbuditel' vtoroi fazy nitrifikatsii (The Stimulant of the Second Phase of Nitrification). Author's Summary of Candidate Thesis. INMI AN SSSR. Moskva. 1958b.

Z a v a r z i n, G. A.   Tsikl razvitiya i yadernyi apparat H y p h o m i c r o b i u m v u l g a r e Start et Hartleb (Developmental Cycle and the Nucleic Apparatus of H y p h o m i c r o b i u m v u l g a r e Start et Hartleb). — Mikrobiologiya, 29(1):38—42. 1960.

Z a v a r z i n, G. A.   Pochkuyushchiesya bakterii (Budding Bacteria). — Mikrobiologiya, 30(5):952—975. 1961a.

Z a v a r z i n, G. A.   Simbioticheskaya kul'tura novogo okislyayushchego marganets mikroorganizma (Symbiotic Culture of a New Manganese-Oxidizing Microorganism). —Mikrobiologiya, 30(3):393—395. 1961b.

Z a v a r z i n, G. A.   Simbioticheskoe okislenie margantsa dvumya vidami P s e u d o m o n a s (Symbiotic Oxidation of Manganese by Two Species of P s e u d o m o n a s). — Mikrobiologiya, 31(4):586—588. 1962.

Z a v a r z i n, G. A.   Stroenie M e t a l l o g e n i u m (The Structure of M e t a l l o- g e n i u m). — Mikrobiologiya, 32(6):1020—1023. 1963.

Z a v a r z i n, G. A.   K mekhanizmu osazhdeniya margantsa na rakovinakh mollyuskov (The Mechanism of Manganese Precipitation on Mollusk Shells). — Doklady AN SSSR, 154(4):944—945. 1964a.

Z a v a r z i n, G. A.   Khemosintez i anorgoksidatsiya (Chemosynthesis and Inorganic Oxidation). — In Sbornik: Uspekhi mikrobiologii, No. 1: 30—60. Moskva. 1964c.

Z a v a r z i n, G. A.   Khemoavtotrofnye mikroorganizmy (Chemoautotrophic Microorganisms). Author's Summary of Doctoral Thesis. Moskva. 1965.

Z a v a r z i n a, N. B.   Razrabotka metodiki polucheniya kul'tur S c e n e d e s- m u s q u a d r i c a u d a i D a p h n i a l o n g i s p i n a, pomechennykh radioaktivnym fosforom (The Method of Obtaining Cultures of S c e n e d e s m u s q u a d r i c a u d a and D a p h n i a l o n g i s p i n a Labeled with Radioactive Phosphorus). — Mikrobiologiya, 24(1): 31—35. 1955a.

Z a v a r z i n a, N. B.   Izuchenie prichin, zaderzhivayushchikh razvitie mikroorganizmov v tolshche ilovykh otlozhenii v ozere Biserovo (Factors Inhibiting Development of Microorganisms inside Mud Sediments in Lake Biserovo). — Mikrobiologiya, 24(5):573—579. 1955b.

Z a v a r z i n a, N. B.   Izuchenie prichin, vliyayushchikh stimuliruyushchim obrazom ili zaderzhivayushchim obrazom na razvitie fitoplanktona (Stimulating and Inhibiting Factors of the Development of Phyto-plankton). — Trudy Vsesoyuznogo Gidrobiologicheskogo Obshchestva, Vol. 6:104—109. 1955c.

Z a v a r z i n a, N. B.   O veshchestvakh, tormozyashchikh razvitie S c e n e- d e s m u s q u a d r i c a u d a (Inhibitors of S c e n e d e s m u s q u a d r i- c a u d a). — Trudy Vsesoyuznogo Gidrobiologicheskogo Obshchestva, Vol. 9:195—205. 1959.

Z e l e n k o v a - P e r f i l' e v a, M. V.   K gidrokhimii Konchezerskoi gruppy ozer (The Hydrochemistry of the Konchozero Group of Lakes). —

Trudy Borodinshoi Biologicheskoi St., Vol. 5:177—183. 1927.

Zelenov, K. K.   Ul'trakislye vody tropicheskoi zony na primere vulkana Kava Idzhen (Vostochnaya Yava) (Ultra-Acid Waters of the Tropics, as Exemplified by the Volcano Kava Idjen (Eastern Java)). — Problemy Vulkanizma, pp. 285—287. Petropavlovsk-Kamchatskii, Dal'-nevostochnoe Izd. 1964.

Zelenov, K. K., R. I. Tkachenko, and M. A. Kanakina.   Pereraspredelenie rudoobrazuyushchikh elementov v protsesse gidrotermal'noi deyatel'nosti vulkana Ebeko (o. Paramushir) (Redistribution of Ore-Forming Elements by the Hydrothermal Activity of the Volcano Abeko (Paramushir Island)). — Trudy GIN, No. 141. 1965.

Zelinskii, N. D. and E. M. Brusilovskii.   O serovodorodnom brozhenii v Chernom more i Odesskikh limanakh (Hydrogen Sulfide Fermentation in the Black Sea and Odessa Limans). — Yuzhnorusskaya Meditsinskaya Gazeta, Nos. 18—19. 1898.

Zenkevich, L. A.   Retsenziya na knigu Karzinkina "Osnovy biologicheskoi produktivnosti vodoemov" (A Review of Karzinkin's Book "Fundamentals of Biological Productivity of Water Bodies"). — Uspekhi Sovremennoi Biologii, 36(2):117—126. 1953.

Zhadin, V. I.   Sovremennoe sostoyanie i zadachi gidrobiologii v svete ucheniya Vil'yamsa-Michurina-Lysenko (Current State and Tasks of Hydrobiology in the Light of the Doctrines of Williams, Michurin and Lysenko). — Zoologicheskii Zhurnal, 28(3):197—212. 1949.

Publications in Other Languages

Aberg, B. and W. Rodhe.   Über die Milieufaktoren in einigen Süd-schwedischen Seen. — Symb. bot. upsal., 5(3):5—256. 1942.

Adams, M. E. and J. R. Postgate.   On Sporulation of Sulphate-Reducing Bacteria. — J. gen. Microbiol., Vol. 24:291—294. 1961.

Ahrens, R. and G. Rheinheimer.   Über einige sternbildende Bakterien aus der Ostsee. — Kieler Meeresforsch., 23(2):127—136. 1967.

Alexander, M.   Introduction to Soil Microbiology. N. Y. and London. John Wiley and Sons INC. 1961.

Alexander, M.   Biochemical Ecology of Soil Microorganisms. — An. Rev. Microbiol., Vol. 18:217—252. 1964.

Allgeier, R. J., B. C. Hafford, and C. Juday.   Oxidation-Reduction Potentials and pH of Lake Waters and of Lake Sediments. — Trans. Wis. Acad. Sci. Arts. Lett., Vol. 33:115—133. 1941.

Alsterberg, G.   Die Sauerstoffschichtung der Seen. — Lund, Bot. Notiser. 1927.

Alsterberg, G.   Neue Beiträge zur Sauerstoffschichtung der Seen. Lund. 1928.

Anagnostidis, K. and J. Overbeck.   Methanoxydirer und hypolimnische Schwefelbakterien. Studien zur ökologischen Biocönotik der Gewässermikroorganismen. — Ber. dt. bot. Ges., 79(3):163—174. 1966.

479

Arnon, D.I. Ferredoxin and Photosynthesis. An Iron-Containing Protein as a Key Factor in Energy Transfer during Photosynthesis.— Science, 149(3691):1460—1470. 1965.

Arnon, D.I., M. Losada, M. Nozaki, and K. Tagawa. Photofixation of Nitrogen and Photoproduction of Hydrogen by Thiosulphate during Bacterial Photosynthesis.— Biochem. J., 77(3):23. 1960.

Arnon, D.I., M. Losada, M. Nozaki, and K. Tagawa. Photoproduction of Hydrogen, Photofixation of Nitrogen and Unified Concept of Photosynthesis.— Nature, 190(4776):601—606. 1961.

Aubert, I., G. Milhaud, and I. Millet. Métabolisme du carbone dans la chimioautotrophie. Mode d'incorporation de l'anhydride carbonique.— C. r. Acad. Sci. Paris, 242(16):2058. 1956.

Aubert, I.P., G. Milhaud, and I. Millet. Le métabolisme du carbone dans la chimioautotrophie. Fixation de l'anhydride carbonique sur l'acide phosphoénolpyruvique.— C. r. Acad. Sci. Paris, 244(3):398—401. 1957.

Auerbach, M., W. Maerker, and J. Schamalz. Hydrographisch-biologische Bodensee-Untersuchungen.— Arch. Hydrobiol., Suppl., Vol. 3:587—738. 1924.

Baalsrud, K. and K.S. Baalsrud. The Role of Phosphate in CO_2 Assimilation of Thiobacilli.— Symp. on Phosph. Metabolism Baltimore, Vol. 2:544—576. 1952.

Baalsrud, K. and K.S. Baalsrud. Studies on Thiobacillus Denitrificans. — Arch. Mikrobiol., 20(1):26—34. 1954.

Baars, I.K. Over sulfaatreductie door bacterien. Delft. 1930.

Baas-Becking, L.G.M. On the Cause of High Acidity in Natural Waters, Especially in Birnes.— Proc. K. ned. Akad. Wet., 41(10):1074—1085. 1938.

Baas-Becking, L. and G. Parks. Energy Relation in the Metabolism of Autotrophic Bacteria.— Physiol. Rev., Vol. 7:85—106. 1927.

Baas-Becking, L.G.M. and I.R. Kaplan. The Microbiological Origin of the Sulphur Nodules of Lake Eyre.— Trans. R. Soc. S. Aust., Vol. 79:52—65. 1956.

Baas-Becking, L.G.M., I.R. Kaplan, and D. Moore. Limits of the Natural Environment in Terms of pH and Oxidation-Reduction Potentials.— J. Geol., 68(3):243—284. 1960.

Bach, H. and F. Sierp. Untersuchungen zur Frage der Sumpfgasbildung aus Abwasserklärschlamm.— Zentrbl. Bakt. ParasitKde, Sect. 2, 60(14/17):318. 1923—1924.

Bachmann, H. Hydrobiologische Untersuchungen am Rotsee.— Z. Hydrol. Hydrogr. Hydrobiol., Vol. 5:39. 1931.

Bahr, H. and W. Schwartz. Untersuchungen zur Ökologie farbloser fädiger Schwefelmikroben.— Biol. Zbl., 75(7/8):451—464. 1956.

Baier, C.R. Wesen und Bedeutung hydrobakteriologischer Forschung.— Die Biologie, 4(3):73—75. 1935.

Baier, C.R. Über die Bedeutung von Spurenelementen und Kolloiden bei der Deckbildung von Azotobacter und über seinen Nachweis in Wasser.— Zentrbl. Bakt. ParasitKde, Sect. 2, Vol. 95:97—102. 1936.

Baier, C.R. Die Bedeutung der Bakterien für den Kalktransport in den Gewässern.— Geologie Meere Binnengewäss., 1(1):75—105. 1937.

Baier, C.R. Die Bedeutung der Bakterien für die Bildung oxydischer

Eisen- und Manganerze. — Geologie Meere Binnengewäss., 1(2/3): 325—348. 1937.

B a r k e r , H. A. Bacterial Fermentations. New York, John Wiley INC. London, Chapman and Hall Ltd. 1956.

B a s s h a m , J. A. and M. C a l v i n .   The Path of Carbon in Photosynthesis.— Handbuch der Pflanzenphysiologie (Die CO_2- Assimilation). Part 1, Vol. 5:884—922, Berlin, Springer Verlag. 1960.

B a v e n d a m m , W. Die farblosen und roten Schwefelbakterien des Süss - und Salzwassers. Jena. 1924.

B a v e n d a m m , W. Die Frage der bakteriologischen Kalkfällung in der tropischen See.— Ber. dt. bot. Ges., Vol. 49:282. 1931.

B a v e n d a m m , W. Die mikrobiologische Kalkfällung in der tropischen See.— Arch. Mikrobiol., Vol. 3:205—276. 1932.

B e c k , J. V. A Ferrous Ion- Oxidizing Bacterium. I. Isolation and some General Physiological Characteristics. — J. Bact. , Vol. 79: 502—509. 1960.

B e i j e r i n c k , M. W. Ueber S p i r i l l u m   d e s u l f u r i a n s als Ursache von Sulfatreduction.— Zentrbl. Bakt. ParasitKde. , Sect. 2, Vol. 1:1—9, 49—59, 104—114. 1895.

B e i j e r i n c k , M. W. Über oligonitrophile Mikroben.— Zentrbl. Bakt. ParasitKde. , 1, Sect. 2, Vol. 7:561—582. 1901.

B e i j e r i n c k , M. W. Über die Bakterien, welche sich im Dunkeln mit Kohlensäure als Kohlenstoffquelle ernähren können.— Zentbl. Bakt. ParasitKde., Sect. 2, Vol. 11:593—599. 1904.

B e i j e r i n c k , M. W. and A. V a n D e l d e n . Über die Assimilation des freien Stickstoffs durch Bakterien.— Zentbl. Bakt. ParasitKde., Sect. 2, Vol. 9:3—43. 1902.

B e r e , R. Numbers of Bacteria in Inland Lakes of Wisconsin as Shown by the Direct Microscopic Method.— Int. Revue ges. Hydrobiol. Hydrogr., Vol. 29:248—263. 1933.

B e r s a , E. Über das Vorkommen von kohlensaurem Kalk in einer Gruppe von Schwefelbakterien.— Ber. dt. bot. Ges., Vol. 44. 1926.

B i r g e , E. A. and C. J u d a y . Solar Radiation and Inland Lakes.— Trans. Wis. Acad. Sci. Arts. Lett., Vol. 27:523—562. 1932.

B i r g e , E. A. and C. J u d a y . Particulate and Dissolved Organic Matter in Inland Lakes.— Ecol. Monogr., 4(4):440—474. 1934.

B i r g e , E., Ch. J u d a y , and M a r c h . The Temperature of the Bottom Deposits of Lake Mendota.— Trans. Wis. Acad. Sci. Arts. Lett., Vol. 23:187—231. 1928.

B i s s e t , K. A. and J. B. G r a c e . The Nature and Relationships of Autotrophic Bacteria.— Autotrophic Microorganisms 4th Sympos. of Soc., Gen. Microbiol., pp. 28—53. London. 1954.

B l a c k , A. P. and R. F. C h r i s t m a n . Chemical Characteristics of Fulvic Acids.— J. Am. Wat. Wks, Ass., Vol. 55:897—912. 1963.

B o n a t t i , E. and Y. R. N a y u d u . The Origin of Manganese Nodules on the Ocean Floor.— Am. J. Sci., 263(1):17—39. 1965.

B r o m f i e l d , S. M. Reduction of Ferric Compounds by Soil Bacteria.— J. gen. Microbiol., Vol. 11, No. 1. 1954.

B r u s s o f f , A. Über ein Kieselbakterium. — Arch. Mikrobiol. , 4(1):1—22. 1933.

B r u s s o f f , A. Ein kalkfällendes Stäbchen und ein Eisen- und kieselspeichernder Coccus als Gesteinsbildner.— Arch. Mikrobiol., 6(5):471—474. 1935.

Bryant, M. P., E. A. Wolin, M. J. Wolin, and R. S. Wolfe. Methano-
bacillus omelianskii a Symbiotic Association of Two Species
of Bacteria.— Arch. Mikrobiol., 59(1/3):20—31. 1967.

Buchanan, R. E. and E. I. Fulmer. Physiology and Biochemistry of
Bacteria, Vol. 2:709; Vol. 3:154. Wilans and Wilkins Co. Baltimore.
1930.

Buchanan, V. V., M. C. W. Evans, and D. J. Arnon. Ferrodoxin-Dependent Carbon Assimilation in Rhodospirillum rubrum. —Arch.
Mikrobiol., 59(1/3):32—40. 1967.

Burton, S. D. and R. Y. Morita. Effect of Catalase and Cultural Conditions of Growth of Beggiatoa.— J. Bact., 88(6):1755—1761. 1964.

Buswell, A. M. Anaerobic Fermentation.— Illinois St. Wat. Surv. Bull.,
No. 32. 1939.

Buswell, A. M. and L. Neaves. Laboratory Studies of Sludge Digestion.—
Illinois St. Wat. Surv. Bull., No. 30. 1930.

Butlin, K. R., M. E. Adams, and M. Thomas. The Isolation and Cultivation of Sulphate-Reducing Bacteria.— J. gen. Microbiol., Vol. 3:46—
—59. 1949.

Butlin, K. R. and J. R. Postgate. Microbiological Formation of Sulphide
and Sulphur.— Symposium Microbiol. Metabolism. Proc. Inst.
superiore di sanita, pp. 126—143. Roma. 1953.

Butlin, K. R. and J. R. Postgate. The Microbiological Formation of
Sulphur in Cyrenaican Lakes.— Symposium of Productivity of Hot and
Cold Deserts: 112—121. Institute of Biology. London. 1954.

Butterfield, C. T. Experimental Studies of Natural Purification in
Polluted Waters. III. A Note on the Relation between Food Concen-
tration in Liquid Media and Bacterial Growth.— Rep. U. S. publ. Hlth.
Serv., Vol. 44:2865—2872. 1929.

Campbell, L. L., H. A. Frank, and E. R. Hall. Studies on Thermophilic
Sulfate Reducing Bacteria. I. Identification of Sporovibrio
desulfurians as Clostridium nigrificans.— J. Bact.,
Vol. 73:516—521. 1957.

Campbell, L. L., M. Kasprzycki, and J. R. Postgate. Desulfovibrio africanus sp., a New Dissimilatory Sulfate-Reducing
Bacterium.— J. Bact., 92(4):1122—1127. 1966.

Carpenter, P. L. Microbiology. Saunders Co. Philadelphia. 1963.

Cataldi, M. S. Aislamiento de Beggiatoa alba en cultivo puro.—
Revta Inst. bact., B. Aires, 9(4):393—423. 1940.

Chibnall, A. C. The Constitution of the Primary Alcohols, Fatty Acids
and Paraffins Present in Plant and Insect Waxes.— Biochem. J.,
Vol. 28:2189—2208. 1934.

Christman, R. F. The Chemistry of Color in Water.— The Trend in
Engineering at Un. Wisconsin, 16(4):10—14, 1964.

Clark, W. M. The Determination of Hydrogen Ions. p. 262. Wil. Wilk.
Co. Baltimore. 1925.

Clausen, P. Studien über anaerobe Zellulosebazillen unter besonderer
Berücksichtigung der Züchtungstechnik.— Zentbl. Bakt. ParasitKde.,
Sect. 2, Vol. 84:20. 1931.

Clayton, R. K. Symposium on Autotrophy. Vol. III. Recent Development in
Photosynthesis.— Bact. Rev., Part 1, Vol. 26(2):151—164. 1962.

Cobret, A.S. The Formation of Hyponitrous Acid as an Intermediate Compound in the Biological or Photochemical Oxidation of Ammonia to Nitrous Acid. I. Chemical Reactions.— Biochem. J., Vol. 28: 1575. 1934.

Coffin, C.C., F.R. Hayes, L.N. Jodrey, and S.G. Whiteway. Exchange of Materials in Lakes as Studied by the Addition of Radioactive Phosphorus.— Can. J. Res., D, Vol. 27: 207—222. 1949.

Collet, L.W. Les lacs, leur mode de formation, leurs eaux, leur destin.— Elements de Hydrogéologie. Paris. 1925.

Collini, B. Hydrogeographische Beobachtungen an einigen Seen im Südwesten Schwedens.— Sver. geol. Unders. Afh., Ser. C., 33, No. 5. 1939.

Colmer, A.R. and M.H. Hinkle. The Role of Microorganisms in Acid Mine Drainage.— Science, 106(2751): 253—256. 1947.

Colmer, A.R., K. Temple, and M.E. Hinkle. An Iron-Oxidizing Bacterium from the Drainage of Some Bituminous Coal Mines.— J. Bact., Vol. 59: 317—328. 1949.

Cooper, R.C. Evidence for the Presence of Certain Tricarboxylic Acid Cycle Enzymes in Thiobacillus thioparus.— J. Bact., 88(3): 624—629. 1964.

Czeczuga, B. Primary Production of the Green Hydrosulphuric Bacteria, Chlorobium limicola Nad. (Chlorobacteriaceae). —Photosynthetica, 2(1): 11—15. 1968.

Davis, J.B. Microbial Decomposition of Hydrocarbons.— Ind. Engng. Chem., Part 1., 48(9): 1444—1448. 1956.

Davis, J.B., H.H. Chase, and R.L. Raymond. Mycobacterium paraffinicum n. sp., a Bacterium Isolated from Soil.— Appl. Microbiol., 4(6)310—315. 1956.

Davis, J.B., V.F. Coty, and J.P. Stanley. Atmospheric Nitrogen Fixation by Methane-Oxidizing Bacteria.— J. Bact., 88(2): 468—472. 1964.

De P.K. The Role of Blue-Green Algae in Nitrogen Fixation in Rice Fields.— Proc. R. Soc., Ser. B, Vol. 127: 121—139. 1939.

Deevey, E.S., M. Stuiver, and N. Nakai. Isotopes of Carbon and Sulphur as Tracers of Lake Metabolism.— Verh. Int. Ver. Limnol., 15(1): 291—292. 1964.

Delden, A. van. Beitrag zur Kenntnis der Sulfatreduction durch Bakterien.— Zentbl. Bakt. ParasitKde., Vol. 11: 81—94, 113—118. 1904.

Dorff, P. Biologie des Eisen- und Mangankreislaufs. Berlin. 1935.

Drew, G.H. The Action of Some Dentrifying Bacteria in Tropical and Temperate Seas.— J. mar. Biol. Ass. U.K., New. Ser., Vol. 9, No. 2. 1911.

Drews, K. Über die Assimilation des Luftstickstoffs durch Blaualgen.— Zentbl. Bakt. ParasitKde., Sect. 2, 76(1/7): 88—101. 1928.

Dubos, R. The Decomposition of Cellulose by Aerobic Bacteria.— J. Bact., Vol. 15: 223. 1928.

Dugan, P.R. and D.G. Lungdren. Energy Supply for the Chemoautotroph Ferrobacillus ferrooxidans.— J. Bact., Vol. 89: 825——834. 1965.

Dugdale, R., V. Dugdale, J. Nees, and J. Goering. Nitrogen Fixation in Lakes.— Science, Vol. 130: 859—860. 1959.

Dugdale, R.C., D.W.Menzel, and J.H.Ryther. Nitrogen Fixation in the Sargasso Sea.— Deep Sea Res., Vol. 7:298—300. 1961.

Dugdale, Y.A. and R.C.Dugdale. Nitrogen Metabolism in Lakes. The Role of Nitrogen Fixation in Sanctuary Lake.— Pennsylvania Limnol. a. Oceanograph., 7(2)170—177. 1962.

Duggeli, M. Bakteriologische Untersuchungen am Ritomsee.—Zeitschrift für Hydrobiol., Vol. 2:65—205. 1924.

Dussart, B.H. Les grands lacs d'Europe occidentale.— Annls. Biol., 2(11/12):499—572. 1963.

Dworkin, M. Biology of the Myxobacteria.— A. Rey. Microbiol., Vol. 20: 75—106. 1966.

Dworkin, M. and I.W.Foster. Studies on Pseudomonas methanica (Söhngen) nov. comb.— J.Bact., 72(5):649—659. 1956.

Eberly, W.R. Further Studies on the Metalimnetic Stuoxygen Maximum with Special Reference to its Occurrence throughout the World.— Invest. Indiana Lakes and Streams, Vol. 6:103—139. Aug. 1964.

Edmonson, W.T. Pacific Coast and Great Basin.— Limnology in North America, pp. 371—392. 1963.

Einsele, W. Über die Beziehungen des Eisenkreislaufs zum Phosphatkreislauf in eutrophen Seen.— Arch. Hydrobiol., Vol. 29:664—686. 1936.

Einsele, W. Über chemische und kolloidschemische Vorgänge in Eisen-Phosphat Systemen under limnochemischen und limnogeologischen Gesichtspunkten.— Arch. Hydrobiol., Vol. 33:361—387. 1938.

Eisden, S.R. The Utilization of Organic Compounds by Photosynthetic Bacteria. Autotrophic Microorganisms.— 4th Symp. Soc. gen. Microbiol., p.202. London, Cambridge Univ. Press. 1954.

Eiseter, H.J. Das limnologische Seetypensystem, Rückblick und Ausblick.— Verh. int. Verein, theor. angew. Limnol., Vol. 13:101—120. 1958.

Emmerich, R. Über die Bedeutung des Wassers vom bakteriologischen Standpunkte.— Z. Unters. Nahr.- u. Genussmittel, Vol. 14. 1904.

Evans, M.C.W., B.B.Buchanan, and D.I.Arnon. A New Ferrodoxin-Dependent Carbon Reduction Cycle in a Photosynthetic Bacterium.— Proc. natn. Acad. Sci. U.S.A., 55(4):928—934. 1966.

Faust, L. and Wolfe. Enrichment and Cultivation of Beggiatoa alba. — J.Bact., Vol. 81:99—106. 1961.

Findenegg, I. Produktionsbiologische Planktonuntersuchungen an Ostalpenseen.— Int. Revue ges. Hydrobiol. Hydrogr., 49(3):381—416. 1964.

Fischer, F., R.Lieske, and K.Winzer. Biologische Gasreaktionen. I. Die Umsetzungen des Kohlenoxyds.— Biochem. Z., Vol. 236:247—267. 1931.

Fischer, F., R.Lieske, and K.Winzer. Biologische Gasreaktionen. II. Mitteilung über die Bildung von Essigsäure bei der biologischen Umsetzung von Kohlenoxyd und Kohlensäure mit Wasserstoff zu Methan.— Biochem. Z., 245(1/3):1—12. 1932.

Fischer, G., B.Bizzimi, M.Raynand, and A.R.Prevot. Études sur les bactéries lignolitiques. II. Caractéristiques des bactéries lignolitiques isolées du sol.— Annls. Inst. Pasteur. Paris, 88(618): 1—454. 1955.

Fischer, R. Die Bakterien des Meeres nach den Untersuchungen der Planktonexpedition unter gleichzeitiger Berücksichtigung einiger älterer und neuerer Untersuchungen.— Zentbl. Bakt. ParasitKde, Vol. 15:657—666. 1894.

Fogg, G. E. and M. Wolfe. The Nitrogen Metabolism of the Blue-Green Algae (Myxophyceae). Autotrophic Microorganisms.— 4th Symp. Soc. gen. Microbiol., pp. 99—125, London. Cambridge Univ. Press. 1954.

Fogg, G. E. and D. E. Westlake. The Importance of Extracellular Products of Algae in Fresh Waters.— Verh. int. Verein, theor. angew. Limnol., Vol. 12:219—231. 1955.

Fogg, G. E. and W. D. Watt. The Kinetics of Release of Extracellular Products of Photosynthesis by Phytoplankton.— Memorie Ist. ital. Idrobiol., Suppl. Vol. 18:165—174. 1965.

Fogg, G. E., C. Nalewajko, and W. D. Watt. Extracellular Products of Phytoplankton Photosynthesis.— Proc. R. Soc., Ser. B, 162(989): 517—534. 1965.

Forti, G. Light Energy Utilization in Photosynthesis.— Memorie Ist. ital. Idrobiol., Suppl., Vol. 18:17—35. 1965.

Fortunatov, M. A. Les travaux limnologiques de la station du lac Sevan sur les lacs des montagnes du Transcaucase.— Arch. Hydrobiol., Vol. 24:449—484. 1932.

Foster, J. W. Alcohol Oxidation by Photosynthetic Purple Bacteria.— J. Bact., 42(1):8. 1942.

Foster, J. W. Oxidation of Alcohols by Non-Sulphur Photosynthetic Bacteria.— J. Bact., Vol. 47:355. 1944.

Foster, J. W. Hydrocarbons as Substrates for Microorganisms.— Journ. Antonie van Leeuwenhock, Vol. 28:241—274. 1962.

Foster, J. W. and R. H. Davis. A Methane-Dependent Coccus, with Notes on Classification and Nomenclature of Obligate, Methane-Utilizing Bacteria.— J. Bact., 91(5):1924—1931. 1966.

Fred, B. E., F. C. Wilson, and A. Davenport. The Distribution and Significance of Bacteria in Lake Mendota.— Ecology, Vol. 5:322. 1924.

Frey, P. G. (Ed.). Limnology in North America. Madison, Univ. of Wisconsin Press. 1963.

Fuchs, A. and G. J. Bonde. The Availability of Sulphur for Clostridium perfringens and an Examination of Hydrogen Sulphide Production.— J. gen. Microbiol., 16(2):330—340. 1957.

Fuhs, G. W. Der mikrobielle Abbau von Kohlenwasserstoffen. Sammelbericht.— Arch. Mikrobiol., Vol. 39:374—422. 1961.

Gemerden, H. van. On the Bacterial Sulphur Cycle of Inland Waters.— Hydrobiological Institute Nicuwersluis. The Netherlands. Thesis Ph. D. Dissertation, Univ. of Leiden. 1967.

Génovèse, S. Données sur les conditions physico-chimiques de l'étang de Faro.— Rapp. P. -v. Réun, Commn. int. Explor. scient. Mer. Mediterr., 17(3):775—778. 1963a.

Génovèse, S. The Distribution of the H_2S in Lake of Faro (Messina) with Particular Regard to the Presence of "Red Water".— Symposium on Marine Microbiology, pp. 194—204, compiled and edited by C. H. Oppenheimer. Springfield, Ill. C. C. Thomas. 1963b.

Goldman, C. R. Primary Productivity in Cirque Lakes of the Klamath Mountains (Abst.).— Bull. ecol. Soc. Am., Vol. 42:141. 1960.

Goldman, Ch. R. Primary Productivity and Micronutrient Limiting Factors in Some North American and New Zealand Lakes.— Verh. Int. Verein. Limn., 15(1):365—373. 1964.

Goldman, C. R. and R. G. Wetzel. A Study of the Primary Productivity of Clear Lake, Lake Country, California. — Ecology, 44(2):283—294. 1963.

Greenfield, L. I. Metabolism and Concentration of Calcium and Magnesium and Precipitation of Calcium Carbonate by a Marine Bacterium.— Ann. N. Y. Acad. Sci., 109(1):23—45. 1963.

Griesel, R. Physikalische und chemische Eigenschaften des Himmelsdorfer Sees bei Lübeck.— Mitt. geogr. Ges. naturh. Mus. Lübeck, Series 2, No. 28-39. 1921.

Grohman, G. Zur Kenntnis Wasserstoff-oxydierenden Bakterien.— Zentbl. Bakt. ParasitKde., Sect. 2, Vol. 61:256—271. 1924.

Grossman, J. P. and J. R. Postgate. Cultivation of Sulphate-Reducing Bacteria.— Nature, Vol. 171:600—605. 1953.

Halbfass, W. Grundzüge einer vergleichenden Seenkunde. Berlin. 1923.

Halvorson, H. O. and R. L. Starkey. Studies on the Transformation of Iron in Nature, Part II. Concerning the Importance of Microorganisms in the Solution and Precipitation of Iron. — Soil Sc., Vol. 24:381—402. 1927.

Hanert, H. Untersuchungen zur Isolierung. Stoffwechselphysiologie und Morphologie von Gallionella ferruginea Ehrenberg.— Arch. Mikrobiol., 60(4):348—376. 1968.

Happold, F. C. and A. Key. The Bacterial Purification of Gas-Works Liquors. II. The Biological Oxidation of Ammonium Thiocyanate.— Biochem. J., Vol. 31(8):1323. 1937.

Happold, F. C., K. I. Johnstone, and H. J. Rogers. An Examination of Bacterium thiocyanoxidans. — Nature, 169(4295):332. 1952.

Harder, E. C. Iron Depositing Bacteria and their Geologic Relations.— Prof. Pap. U. S. geol. Surv., 113. 1919.

Hardman, Y. and A. T. Henrici. Studies on Freshwater Bacteria. The Distribution of Siderocapsa treubii in Some Lakes and Streams.— J. Bact., Vol. 37:97—105. 1939.

Hasler, A. D. Fish Biology and Limnology of Crater Lake. Oregon.— J. Wildl. Mgmt., Vol. 2:94—103. 1938.

Hayes, F. R. and C. C. Coffin. Radioactive Phosphorus and Exchange of Lake Nutrients.— Endeavour, 10(38):78—81. 1951.

Hayes, F. R., J. A. McCarter, M. L. Cameron, and D. A. Livingstone. On the Kinetics of Phosphorus Exchange in Lakes.— J. Ecol., Vol. 40:202—216. 1952.

Heer, E. and R. Bachofen. Pyruvatstoffwechsel von Clostridium butyricum. — Arch. Mikrobiol., 54(1):1. 1966.

Henrici, A. T. and D. A. Johnson. Studies of Freshwater Bacteria. II. Stalked Bacteria, A New Order of Scizomucetes.— J. Bact., 30(1): 61—88. 1935.

Henrici, A. and E. McCoy. The Distribution of Heterotrophic Bacteria in the Bottom Deposits of Some Lakes.— Trans. Wis. Acad. Sci. Arts Lett., Vol. 31:324—361. 1938.

Heukelekian, H. and A. Heller. Relation between Food Concentration and Surface for Bacterial Growth.— J. Bact., Vol. 40:547—558. 1940.

Hinze, G. Thiophysa volutans, ein neues Schwefelbakterium.— Ber. dt. bot. Ges., Vol. 21:309—316. 1903a.

Hinze, G. Über Schwefeltropfen im Innern von Oscillarien.— Ber. dt. bot. Ges., Vol. 21:394—398. 1903b.

Hinze, G. Beiträge zur Kenntnis der farblosen Schwefelbakterien. —Ber. dt. bot. Ges., Vol. 31:189—202. 1913.

Hirsch, P. Biology of Budding Bacteria. IV. Epicellular Deposition of Iron by Aquatic Budding Bacteria.— Arch. Mikrobiol., Vol. 60:201— —216; Vol. 62:289—306. 1968.

Hobbie, J. E. Carbon 14 Measurements of Primary Production in Two Arctic Alaska Lakes.— Verh. int. Verein. theor. angew. Limnol., 15(1):360—364. 1964.

Hobbie, J. E. and R. T. Wright. Competition between Planctonic Bacteria and Algae for Organic Solutes.— Memorie Ist. ital. Idrobiol., Suppl., Vol. 18:175—185. 1965.

Hoch, G. E., O. H. Owens, and B. Kok. Photosynthesis and Respiration.— Archs. Biochem. Biophys., Vol. 101:171. 1963.

Hock, C. H. Decomposition of Chitin by Marine Bacteria.— Biol. Bull., Vol. 79:199—206. 1940.

Honhl, G. Ein Beitrag zur Physiologie der Eisenbakterien.— Vom. Wass., Vol. 22:176—193. 1955.

Horie, S. Morphometric Features and the Classification of All the Lakes in Japan.— Mem. Coll. Sci. Kyoto Univ., Ser. B., 29(3):191—262. 1962.

Hough, J. L. Geologic Framework. Great Lakes Basin Sympos. of Amer. Ass. Agv. Sci., pp. 3—27. 1959.— Am. Ass. Av. Sci. Wash. 1962.

Hutchinson, G. E. The Biogeochemistry of Phosphorus.— In: The Biology of Phosphorus, pp. 1—35. Ed. L. E. Wolterink, Michigan State College Press. 1952.

Hutchinson, G. E. A Treatise on Limnology, Vol. 1. J. Wiley. N. Y. 1957.

Hutchinson, G. E. and V. T. Bowen. Limnological Studies in Connecticut IX. A Quantitative Radiochemical Study of the Phosphorus Cycle in Linsley Pond.— Ecology, Vol. 31: 194—203. 1950.

Hutchinson, G. E., E. S. Deevey, and A. Wollack. The Oxidation-Reduction Potential of Lake Waters and its Ecological Significance.— Proc. natn. Acad. Sci. U. S. A., Vol. 25:87—90. 1939.

Hutchinson, H. and J. Clayton. On the Decomposition of Cellulose by an Aerobic Organism (Spirochaeta cytophaga n. sp.).— J. agric. Sci., Camb., Vol. 9:141. 1919.

Hutton, W. E. and C. E. ZoBell. The Occurrence and Characteristics of Methane-Oxidizing Bacteria in Sediments.— J. Bact., Vol. 58: 463—473. 1949.

Hutton, W. E. and C. E. ZoBell. Production of Nitrite from Ammonia by Methane-Oxidizing Bacteria.— J. Bact., Vol. 65:216—219. 1953.

Iterson, W. van. Gallionella ferruginea (Ehrenberg) in a Different Light. Thesis. Amsterdam. 1958.

Ivanov, M. V. and G. I. Karavaiko. The Role of Microorganisms in the Sulphur Cycle in Crater Lakes of the Golovnin Caldera.— Z. allg. Mikrobiol., 6(1):10—22. 1966.

Jannasch, H. W. Studies on Planktonic Bacteria by Means of a Direct Membrane Filter Method.— J. gen. Microbiol., 28(3):609—620. 1958a.

Jannasch, H.W. Schwellenkonzentration verschiedener Stickstoffquellen
    für die Vermehrung einiger Bakterien aus nährstoffarmen
    Gewässern.— Arch. Mikrobiol., Vol. 32:114—124. 1958b.

Jannasch, H.W. Die kontinuierliche Kultur in der experimentellen
    Ökologie mariner Mikroorganismen.— Kieler Meeresforsch., 18(3):
    67—73. 1962.

Jannasch, H.W. Bakterielles Wachstum bei geringen Substratkonzentra-
    tionen.— Arch. Mikrobiol., Vol. 45:323—342. 1963.

Järnefelt, H. Einige Randbemerkungen zur Seetypennomenklatur. —
    Schweiz. Z. Hydrol., 15(1):198—212. 1953.

Jenkin, P.M. Report of the Percey Sladen Expedition to Some Rift Valley
    Lakes in Kenya in 1929. VII. Summary of the Ecological Results, with
    Special Reference to the Alkaline Lakes.— Ann. Mag. nat. Hist. Ser.
    10, Vol. 18:133—181. 1932.

Jimbo, T. Die Verbreitung der Purpur- und Grünbakterien in Yumoto
    (Nikko) in Beziehung zur Schwefelwasserstoffkonzentration.— Sci.
    Rep. Tohoku Imp. Univ., Ser. Biology, 13(3):229—233. 1938a.

Jimbo, T. Beobachtungen einiger thiotropher Seen Japans mit besonderer
    Berücksichtigung der Schwefelbakterien. I.— Sci. Rep. Tohoku Imp.
    Univ., Ser. Biology, 13(3):259—269. 1938b.

Jimbo, T. Beobachtungen einiger thiotropher Seen Japans mit besonderer
    Berücksichtigung der Schwefelbakterien. II.— Sci. Rep. Tohoku Imp.
    Univ., Ser. Biology, 15(1):7—11. 1940.

Johnson, F.H. and R.F. Baker. The Electron and Light Microscopy of
    Beggiatoa. — J. cell. comp. Physiol., Vol. 30:131—146. 1947.

Juday, C. and E.A. Birge. Dissolved Oxygen and Oxygen Consumed in
    the Lake Waters of Northeastern Wisconsin.— Trans. Wis. Acad. Sci.
    Arts. Lett., Vol. 27:415—486. 1932.

Juday, C., E.A. Birge, and V. Meloche. The Carbon Dioxide and
    Hydrogen Ion Content of the Lake Waters of Northeastern Wisconsin.
    — Trans. Wis. Acad. Sci. Arts. Lett., Vol. 29:1—82. 1935.

Juday, C., E.A. Birge, and V.W. Meloche. Mineral Content of Lake
    Waters of Northeastern Wisconsin.— Trans. Wis. Acad. Sci. Arts.
    Lett., Vol. 31:223—276. 1938.

Kalantarian, P.B. and A.P. Petrossian. Über ein neues kalk-
    fällendes Bakterium aus dem Sewan See (Goktschasee) Bac. Sew-
    anese. — Zentbl. Bakt. ParasitKde., Sect. 2, Vol. 85:431. 1932.

Kalbe, L., R. Keil, and M. Theile. Licht- und elektronenmikroskopische
    Studien an Arten von Leptothrix, Siderocapsa und Plankto-
    myces.— Arch. Protistenk., Vol. 108:29—40. 1965.

Kandler, O. Reported at the 10th Bot. Congress. Edinburgh. 1964.

Kaserer, H. Die Oxidation des Wasserstoffes durch Mikroorganismen.—
    Zentbl. Bakt. ParasitKde., Sect. 2., Vol. 16:681—696, 769—775. 1906.

Kaserer, H. Über die biologische Reizwirkung natürlicher Humus-
    stoffe. — Zentbl. Bakt. ParasitKde., Sect. 2, Vol. 31:577—578.
    1911.

Keil, F. Beiträge zur Physiologie der farblosen Schwefelbakterien.—
    Zeitsch. Biol. d. Pflanzen (Cohn's), Vol. 2:335—372. 1912.

Keys, A., E. H. Christensen, and A. Krogh. The Organic Metabolism of Seawater with Special Reference to the Ultimate Food Cycle in the Sea.— J. mar. biol. Ass. U. K., Vol. 20:181—196. 1935.

Kjensmo, J. The Development and Some Main Features of "Iron-Meromectic" Soft Water Lakes.— Arch. Hydrobiol., Supp., 32(2):137—312. 1967.

Kleerekoper, H. The Mineralization of Plankton.— J. Fish. Res. Bd. Can., 10(5):238—291. 1953.

Kleiber, A. Qualitative und quantitative bakteriologische Untersuchungen des Zürichseewassers. Zürich. 1894.

Kluyver, A. J. Some Aspects of Nitrate Reduction.— Symposium Microbial Metabolism, p. 71, Rome. 1953.

Kluyver, A. J. and A. Manten. Some Observations on the Metabolism of Bacteria Oxidizing Molecular Hydrogen.— Antonie van Leeuwenhoek Journ. Microbiol., Vol. 8:71—85. 1942.

Knaysi, C. A Cytological and Microchemical Study of Thiobacillus thiooxidans.— J. Bact., Vol. 46:451—461. 1943.

Kolkwitz, R. and M. Marsson. Grundsätze für die biologische Beurteilung des Wassers nach seiner Flora und Fauna.— Mitt. aus d. Königl. Prüfungsanstalt für Wasserversorgung und Abwasserbeseitigung, No. 1. 1902.

Kossowitsch, P. Untersuchungen über die Frage wie die Algen freien Stickstoff fixieren.— Bot. Zeitschr., Sect. 1, Vol. 52:95. 1894.

Koyama, T. Gaseous Metabolism in Lake Sediments and Paddy Soils.— Adv. org. Geochem., pp. 363—375. Oxford-London-New York-Paris, Pergamon Press. 1964.

Kran, G., F. W. Schlote, and H. G. Schlegel. Cytologische Untersuchungen an Chromatium okenii Perty.— Naturwissenschaften, 50(24):728—730. 1963.

Krogh, A. and E. Lange. Quantitative Untersuchungen über Plankton, Kolloide und gelöste organische und anorganische Substanzen in dem Furesee.— Int. Revue ges. Hydrobiol. Hydrolog., 26(1/2):20—53. 1931.

Kucera, S. and R. S. Wolfe. A Selective Enrichment Method for Gallionella ferruginea.— J. Bact., Vol. 74:344—349. 1957.

Kudrjaschow, W. W. Zur Geschichte der Seen in postglazialer Zeit.— Verh. int. Verein. theor. angew. Limnol., 3(2):246. 1927.

Kusnetzow, S. I. Die Rolle der Mikroorganismen bei der Bildung von Calcitkristallen im Schlamm des Sewan-Sees.— Z. allg. Mikrobiol., 6(4):289—295. 1966.

Kusnetzow, S. I. and G. S. Karzinkin. Direct Method for the Quantitative Study of Bacteria in Water and Some Considerations on the Causes which Produce a Zone of Oxygen-Minimum in Lake Glubokoe.— Zentbl. Bakt. ParasitKde., Sect. 2, Vol. 83:169—174. 1931.

Kusnetzow, S. I. Die Rolle der Mikroorganismen im Stoffkreislauf der Seen.— VEB. Deutscher Verlag der Wissenschaften. Berlin. 1959.

Kusnetzow, S. I. Die Rolle der Mikroorganismen bei der Bildung von Calcitkristallen im Schlamm des Sewan-Sees.— Z. allg. Mikrobiol., 6(4):289—295. 1966.

Kuznetzov, S.I.   A Study of the Size of Bacterial Populations and of Organic Matter Formation Due to Photo- and Chemosynthesis in Water Bodies of Different Types.— Verh. int. Verein, theor. angew. Limnol., Vol. 13:156—169. 1958a.

Larsen, H.   On the Culture and General Physiology of the Green Sulphur Bacteria.— J. Bact. 64(2):187. 1952.

Larsen, H.   On the Microbiology and Biochemistry of the Photosynthetic Green Sulphur Bacteria.— K. norske Vidensk. Selsk. Skr., p. 1. Trondheim, Brun. 1953.

Larsen, H.   The Photolitho-Autotrophic Bacteria and their Energy Relations.   Autotrophic Microorganisms.— 4th Symp. Soc. gen. Microbiol., pp. 186—201. London, Cambridge Univ. Press. 1954.

Larsen, H.   Chemosynthesis (General).— Handbuch der Pflanzenphysiologie, Vol. 5. Die CO_2-Assimilation, Part 2, pp. 613—648. Berlin-Göttingen-Heidelb., Springer Verlag. 1960.

Larsen, H.   Halophilism. The Bacteria, a Treatise on Structure and Function, Vol. 4. The Physiology of Growth, pp. 297—342. 1962.

Larsen, H., S. Omang, and H. Steensland.   On the Gas Vacuoles of the Halobacteria.— Arch. Mikrobiol., 59(1/3):197—203. 1967.

Leadbetter, E. R. and I. W. Foster.   Bacterial Oxidation of Gaseous-Alkanes.— Arch. Mikrobiol., 35(1):92—104. 1960.

Leadbetter, E. R. and J. W. Foster.   Studies on Some Methane-Utilizing Bacteria.— Arch. Mikrobiol., 30(1):91—118. 1958.

Leathen, W., S. Braley, and L. McIntyre.   The Role of Bacteria in the Formation of Acid from Certain Sulphuric Constituents Associated with Bituminous Coal.— Appl. Microbiol., 1(2):61—64, 65—68. 1953.

Leathen, W. W., N. A. Kinsel, and E. A. Braley.   Ferrobacillus ferroxidans.   A Chemosynthetic Autotrophic Bacterium.— J. Bact., 72(5):700—704. 1956.

Lees, H.   The Biochemistry of the Nitrifying Bacteria.   Autotrophic Microorganisms.— 4th Symp. Soc. gen. Microbiol., pp. 84—98. London, Cambridge. 1954.

Lieske, R.   Beiträge zur Kenntnis der Physiologie von Spirophyllum ferrugineum, einem typischen Eisenbakterium.— Jb. wiss. Bot., Vol. 49:91—127. 1912a.

Lieske, R.   Untersuchungen über die Physiologie denitrifizierender Schwefelbakterien.— Ber. Deutsch. bot. Ges., Vol. 30:12—22. 1912b.

Lieske, R.   Zur Ernährungsphysiologie der Eisenbakterien.— Zentbl. Bakt. ParasitKde., Sect. 2, Vol. 49:413—425. 1919.

Likens, G. E. and A. D. Hasler.   Movements of Radiosodium Na[24] within an Ice-Covered Lake.— Limnol. Oceanogr., 7(1):48—56. 1962.

Littlewood, D. and J. R. Postgate.   On the Osmotic Behaviour of Desulfovibrio desulfuricans.— J. gen. Microbiol., Vol. 17:596—603. 1957.

Lloyd, B.   Bacteria of the Clyde Sea Area: A Quantitative Investigation.— J. mar. biol. Ass. U. K., Vol. 16:879—907. 1930.

London, J.   Thiobacillus intermedius nov. sp.   A Novel Type of Facultative Autotrophy.— Arch. Mikrobiol., Vol. 46:329—337. 1963.

Longinelli, A. and H. Craig.   Oxygen-18 Variations in Sulfate Ions in Seawater and Saline Lakes.— Science, 156(3771):56—59. 1967.

Lönnerblad, G.   Über die Sauerstoffabsorption des Bodensubstrates in
        einigen Seetypen.— Bot. Notiser, pp. 53—60. 1930.
Lönnerblad, G.   O$_2$-Absorption des Bodensubstrates der Seen im Anebo-
        dagebiet.— Int. Revue ges. Hydrobiol. Hydrogr. Hydrol., Vol. 25:155.
        1931a.
Lönnerblad, G.   Über den Sauerstoffhaushalt der dystrophen Seen.—
        Lunds Universitets Årsskrift, N. F., 27(14):1—53. 1931b.
Losada, M., A. V. Trebst, S. Ogata, and D. I. Arnon.   Equivalence of
        Light and Adenosine Triphosphate in Bacterial Photosynthesis.—
        Nature, 186(4727):753. 1960.
Lukins, H. B.   On the Utilization of Hydrocarbons Methylketons and
        Hydrogen by Mycobacteria.— Ph. Diss. Univ. Texas. Quoted after
        J. W. Foster. 1962.
Lundgren, D. G., K. J. Andersen, C. C. Remsen, and Mahoney.
        Culture, Structure and Physiology of the Chemoautotroph Ferro-
        bacillus ferrooxidans.— Devs. ind. Microbiol., Vol. 6:250—
        —259. 1964.
Lundqvist, G.   Bodenablagerungen und Entwicklungstypen der Seen.—
        Die Binnengewässer, Vol. 2. Stuttgart. 1927.
MacGinitie, G. E.   The Role of Bacteria as Food for Bottom Animals.—
        Science, Vol. 76:490. 1932.
Mahoney, R. P. and R. E. Mercedes.   Fine Structure of Thiobac
        thiooxidans.— J. Bact., 92(2):487—495. 1966.
Malacinski, G. and W. A. Konetzka.   Bacterial Oxidation of Orto-
        phosphite.— J. Bact., 91(2):578—582. 1966.
Manheim, F. T.   Manganese-Iron Accumulations in the Shallow Marine
        Environment.— Symposium on Marine Geochemistry, Narragansett
        Marine Laborat. Graduate School of Oceanography University of
        Rhode Island. Occasional Publications, No. 3:217. 1965.
Marca, A.   Contribution à l'étude de la flore bactérienne du lac de
        Genève.— Thèse Inst. Bot. Univer. Geneva. 1927.
Marco, J. de, J. Kurbel, J. M. Symons, and G. Robeck.   Influence of
        Environmental Factors on the Nitrogen Cycle in Water.— J. Am. Wat.
        Wks. Ass., 59(5):580—592. 1967.
Marre, E., G. Forti, R. Bianchetti, and B. Parisi.   Utilization of
        Photosynthetic Chemical Energy for Metabolic Processes Different
        from CO$_2$ Fixation.— In: "La Photosynt." p. 556. Centre National de
        la Recherche Scientifique. Paris. 1963.
McCarter, J. A., F. R. Hayes, L. N. Jardrey, and M. L. Cameron.
        Movements of Materials in the Hypolimnion of the Lake as Studied
        by the Addition of Radioactive Phosphorus. —Can. J. Zool., 30(2):
        128—133. 1952.
McKenna, E. J. and R. E. Kallio.   The Biology of Hydrocarbons.— A.
        Rev. Microbiol., Vol. 19:183—208. 1965.
Meiklejohn, J.   Aerobic Denitrification.— Ann. appl. Biol., Vol. 27:
        568—573. 1940.
Meyerhof, O.   Untersuchungen über den Atmungsvorgang nitrifizierender
        Bakterien. — Pflugers Arch. ges. Physiol., Vol. 164:353—427.
        1916.
Meyerhof, O.   Untersuchungen über den Atmungsvorgang nitrifizierender
        Bakterien.— IV. Die Atmung des Nitritbildners und ihre Beeinflussung

durch chemische Substanzen.— Pflugers Arch. ges. Physiol., Vol. 166:240—280. 1917.

Minder, L. Zur Hydrophysik des Zürich- und Walensees nebst Beitrag zur Hydrochemie und Hydrobakteriologie des Zürichsees.— Arch. Hydrobiol., Vol. 12, No. 1. 1918.

Minder, L. Studien über den Sauerstoffgehalt des Zürichsees.— Arch. Hydrobiol., Suppl., Vol. 3:107—155. 1923.

Miyadi, D. Oxygen Absorption of the Lake Deposit.— Proc. imp. Acad. Japan, Vol. 10:236—239. 1934.

Mohr, V. and H. Larsen. On the Structural Transformations and Lysis of Halobacterium solinarium in Hypotonic and Isotonic Solutions.— J. gen. Microbiol., Vol. 31:267—280. 1963.

Molisch, H. Die Eisenbakterien. Jena. 1910.

Molisch, H. Über Kalkbakterien und andere kalkfällende Pilze.— Zentbl. Bakt. ParasitKde., Sect. 2, Vol. 65:130—139. 1925.

Morita, R. Y. and P. S. Stave. Electron Micrograph of an Ultrathin Section of Beggiatoa.— J. Bact., Vol. 85:940—942. 1963.

Mortimer, C. H. The Exchange of Dissolved Substances between Mud and Water in Lakes.— J. Ecol., Vol. 29:280—329. 1941; Vol. 30:147—201. 1942.

Mulder, E. G. and W. L. van Veen. Investigation on the Sphaerotilus-Leptothrix Group.— Antonie van Leeuwenhoek, Vol. 29:121—153. 1963.

Müller, F. M. On the Metabolism of the Purple Sulphur Bacteria in Organic Media.— Arch. Mikrobiol., Vol. 4:131—166. 1933.

Munro, A. L. and T. D. Brock. Distinction between Bacterial and Algal Utilization of Soluble Substances in the Sea.— J. gen. Microbiol., Part 1, Vol. 51:35—42. 1968.

Münz, E. Zur Physiologie der Methanbakterien.— Mag. Dissertation. Halle. 1915.

Murray, J. and R. Irvine. On Coral Reefs and Other Carbonate of Lime Formation in Modern Seas.— Nature, Vol. 42. London Proc. R. Soc. Edinb., Vol. 17. 1890.

Nadson, G. A. Beitrag zur Kenntnis der bakteriogenen Kalkablagerungen.— —Arch. Hydrobiol., Vol. 19. 1928.

Nakamura, H. Über das Auftreten des Schwefelkügelchen im Zellinnern von einigen niederen Algen.— Bot. Mag., Tokyo, Vol. 51:529. 1937.

Naumann, E. Über die See- und Sumpferze Süd- und Mittelschwedens.— Sver. geol. Ünders. Afh., Vol. 13. 1922.

Naumann, E. Ziel und Hauptprobleme der regionalen Limnologie.— Bot. Notiser., pp. 81—103. 1927.

Naumann, E. Siderogene Organismen und die Bildung von See-Erz.— Ber. dt. bot. Ges., Vol. 48. 1928.

Naumann, E. Limnologische Terminologie. 1931.

Naumann, E. Grundzüge der regionalen Limnologie.— Die Binnegewässer, Vol. 11. 1932.

Nees, J. C., R. C. Dugdale, V. A. Dugdale, and J. Goering. Nitrogen Metabolism in Lakes. I. Measurement of Nitrogen Fixation with N^{15}.— Limnol. Oceanogr., 7(2): 163—169. 1962.

Nelson, D. Isolation and Characterization of Nitrosomonas and Nitrobacter.— Zentbl. Bakt. ParasitKde., Sect. 2, Vol. 83:208. 1931.

Niel, C. B. van. On the Morphology and Physiology of the Purple and Green Sulphur Bacteria.— Arch. Mikrobiol., 3(1):1—118. 1931.

Niel, C. B. van. On the Metabolism of the Thiorhodaceae.— Arch. Mikrobiol., Vol. 7:323—358. 1936.

Niklewski, B. Ein Beitrag zur Kenntnis wasserstoffoxydierender Mikroorganismen.— Zentbl. Bact. ParasitKde., Sect. 2., Vol. 20:469—473. 1908.

Niklewski, B. Über die Wasserstoffoxydation durch Mikroorganismen.— Jb. wiss. Bot., Vol. 48:113—142. 1910.

Oginsky, E. L. and W. W. Umbreit. An Introduction to Bacterial Physiology. Freeman Co. San Francisco. 1959.

Ohle, W. Chemisch-stratigraphische Untersuchungen der Sedimentmetamorphose eines Waldsees.— Naturwissenschaften, Vol. 21:397——400. 1933.

Ohle, W. Chemische und physikalische Untersuchungen norddeutscher Seen.— Arch. Hydrobiol., Vol. 26:386—464 and 584—658. 1934.

Ohle, W. Sulfat als "Katalisator" des limnischen Stoffkreislaufes.— Vom. Wass., Vol. 21:13—32. 1954.

Ohle, W. Beiträge zur Produktionsbiologie der Gewässer.— Arch. Hydrobiol., Suppl., 22(3/4):456—479. 1955.

Ohle, W. Die Stoffwechseldynamik der Seen in Abhängigkeit von der Gasausscheidung ihres Schlammes.— Vom Wass., Vol. 25:127—194. 1958.

Ohle, W. Blick in die Tiefe des grossen Plöner Sees mit Fernseh- und Photo-Kameras.— Natur Volk, 89(6):177—188. 1959.

Ohle, W. Fernsehen, Photographie und Schallortung der Sedimentoberfläche in Seen.— Arch. Hydrobiol., 57(1/2):135—160. 1960.

Ohle, W. Der Stoffhaushalt der Seen als Grundlage einer allgemeinen Stoffwechseldynamik der Gewässer.— Kieler Meeresforsch., 18(3):107—120. 1962 (Special issue).

Okafor, N. Ecology of Microorganisms on Chitin Buried in Soil.— J. gen. Microbiol., 44(3):311—327. 1966.

Ooyama, J. and J. W. Foster. Bacterial Oxidation of Cycloparaffinic Hydrocarbons.— Antonie van Leeuwenhoek, 31(3):45—65. 1965.

Overbeck, J. Über Anreicherung und Isolierung methanoxydierender Bakterien aus dem Süsswasser.— Zentbl. Bakt. ParasitKde., Suppl. 1, Anreicherungskultur und Mutantenauslese, pp. 139—147. 1966.

Overbeck, J. and W. Ohle. Contributions to the Biology of Methane Oxidizing Bacteria.— Verh. Int. Verein, Limnol., Vol. 16:535—543. 1964.

Pacheco, G. and G. A. Costa. Hydrogen Sulfide Production, a General Property of Heterotrophic Bacteria.— Mems. Inst. Oswaldo Cruz, Vol. 35:381—397. 1940.

Parejko, R. A. and P. W. Wilson. Taxonomy of Azotomonas Species.——J. Bact., 95(1):143—146. 1968.

Parker, C. D. Species of Sulphur Bacteria Associated with the Corrosion of Concrete.— Nature, Vol. 159:439—440. 1947.

Parker, C. D. and T. Prisk.   The Oxidation of Inorganic Sulphur Compounds by Various Bacteria.— J. gen. Microbiol., 8(13):344—364. 1953.

Pearsall, W. H. and C. H. Mortimer.   Oxidation-Reduction Potentials in Waterlogged Soils, Natural Waters and Muds.— J. Ecol., Vol. 27: 483—501. 1929.

Peck, H. D.   The ATP-Dependent Reduction of Sulphate with Hydrogen in Extracts of Desulfovibrio desulfurians.— Proc. natn. Acad. Sci. U. S. A., Vol. 45:701—708. 1959.

Peck, H. D.   The Role of Adenosine 5-Phosphosulphate in the Reduction of Sulphate to Sulphide by Desulfovibrio desulfuricans.— J. biol. Chem., 237(1):198—203. 1962a.

Peck, H. D.   Comparative Metabolism in Organic Sulphur Compounds in Microorganisms.— Bact. Rev., Vol. 26:67—94. 1962b.

Perfiliev, B. W.   Zur Mikrobiologie der Bodenablagerungen. — Verh. int. Verein. theor. angew. Limnol., Vol. 4:107—143. 1929.

Perfiliev, B. W.   Das Gesetz der Periodizität der Schlammbildung und die Tiefwasserbohrung.— Verh. int. Verein. theor. angew. Limnol., Vol. 5:298—306. 1931.

Peterson, W., E. Fred, and B. Domogalla.   The Occurrence of Amino Acids and Other Organic Nitrogen Compounds in Lake Water.— J. biol. Chem., Vol. 23:287—295. 1925.

Pfennig, N.   Photosynthetic Bacteria.— A. Rev. Microbiol., Vol. 21: 285—324. 1967.

Pfennig, N. and G. Cohen-Bazire.   Some Properties of the Green Bacterium Pelodictyon clathratiforme.— Arch. Mikrobiol., 59(1/3):226—236. 1967.

Pfenniger, A.   Beiträge zur Biologie des Zürichsees.— Z. Gewässerk., Vol. 4. 1902.

Phillips, J. E.   The Ecological Role of Phosphorus in Waters with Special Reference to Microorganisms.   Principles and Application in Aquatic Microbiology.— Research Confer. Rutgers Univers. New Brunswick, pp. 61—81. 1964.

Poindexter, J. S.   Biological Properties and Classification of the Caulobacterial Group.— Bact. Rev., 28(3):231—295. 1964.

Porter, J. R.   Bacterial Chemistry and Physiology. N. Y., John Wiley Co. 1946.

Postgate, J. R.   Sulphate Reduction by Bacteria.— A. Rev. Microbiol., Vol. 13:505—520. 1959.

Postgate, J. R. and L. L. Campbell.   Classification of Desulfovibrio Species, the Nonsporulating Sulphate-Reducing Bacteria.— Bact. Rev., 30(4):732—738. 1966.

Pratt, R., T. Daniels, J. Eiler, J. Gunnison, W. Kummler, J. Oneto, H. Spoehr, G. Hardin, H. Milner, J. Smith, and H. Strain.   Chlorellin, an Antibacterial Substance from Chlorella.— Science, Vol. 99:351—352. 1944.

Prazmowskii, A.   Azobacter-Studien. II. Physiologie und Biologie.— Bull. Intern de l'Ac. de Cracovie. Math. Nat. Cl. Sci., B., No. 7: 855—950. 1912.

Prescott, S. C. and C. E. A. Winslow.   Elements of Water Bacteriology. N. Y. Wiley. 1931.

Pringsheim, E. G. Taxonomy of Green Bacteria.— Nature, 172(4369): 167—168. 1952.

Pringsheim, E. G. Die Stellung der grünen Bakterien im System der Organismen.— Arch. Mikrobiol., 19(3):353—364. 1953.

Pringsheim, E. G. Die Mixotrophie von Beggiatoa.— Arch. Mikrobiol., 59(1/3):247—254. 1967.

Quayle, J. R. Metabolism of C_1 Compounds in Autotrophic and Heterotrophic Microorganisms.— A. Rev. Microbiol., Vol. 15:119—152. 1961.

Rabinowitch, E. Photosynthesis and Related Processes, Vol. 1. 1945.

Rahn, O. Physiology of Bacteria. Philadelphia, P. Blackston. 1932.

Rakestrow, N. W. and A. Hallender. Photochemical Oxidation of Ammonia in Sea Water.— Science, Vol. 84, Nos. 442—443. 1936.

Raymond, J. C. and V. R. Sistom. The Isolation and Preliminary Characterization of Halophilic Photosynthetic Bacterium.— Arch. Mikrobiol., 59(1/3):255—268. 1967.

Redinger, F. Siderocapsa coronata Redinger, eine neue Eisenbakterie aus dem Lunzer Obersee.— Arch. Hydrobiol., Vol. 22:410——414. 1931.

Renn, C. E. Bacteria and the Phosphorous Cycle in the Sea.— Biol. Bull., Vol. 72:190—195. 1937.

Reuser, H. W. Marine Bacteria and their Role in the Cycle of Life in the Sea. III. The Distribution of Bacteria in the Ocean Waters and Muds about Cape Cod.— Biol. Bull., Vol. 45:480—487. 1933.

Rigler, F. H. A Tracer Study of the Phosphorous Cycle in Lake Water.— Ecology, Vol. 37:550—562. 1956.

Rigler, F. H. The Phosphorus Fractions and the Turnover Time of Inorganic Phosphorus in Different Types of Lakes.— Limnol. Oceanogr. 9(4):511—518. 1964.

Roberts, J. L. Reduction of Ferric Hydroxide by Strains of Bacillus polymyxa.— Soil Sci., Vol. 63. 1947.

Rodhe, W. Primarproduktion und Seetypen.— Verh. int. Verein. theor. angew. Limnol., Vol. 13:121—141. 1958.

Rodhe, W., J. E. Hobbie, and R. Wright. Phototrophy and Heterotrophy in High Mountain Lakes.— Verh. Intern. Verein. Limn., Vol. 16: 302—313. 1966.

Rodina, A. G. On the Forms of Existence of Bacteria in Water Bodies.— Arch. Hydrobiol., 63(2):238—242. 1967.

Roelefsen, P. A. On Photosynthesis of the Thiorodaceae.— Mag. Diss. Univ. Utrecth. 1935.

Rossolimo, L. Die Boden-Gasausscheidung und das Sauerstoffregime der Seen.— Verh. int. Verein. theor. angew. Limnol., Vol. 7:539—561. 1935.

Ruhland, W. Beiträge zur Physiologie der Knallgasbakterien. — Jb. Wiss. Bot., Vol. 63:321—389. 1924.

Ruhle, E. Sedimentaktivität.— Limnologica (Berlin), Vol. 4(2):323—332. 1966.

Ruttner, F. Grundriss der Limnologie (Hydrobiologie des Süsswassers). 3rd edition. Berlin. 1962.

Sacks, L. E. and H. A. Barker. The Influence of Oxygen on Nitrate and Nitrite Reduction.— J. Bact. Vol. 58:11. 1949.

495

Santarius, K. A., U. Heber, W. Ulbrich, and W. Urbach. Intracellular Translocation of ATP, ADP and Inorganic Phosphate in Leaf Cells of Elodea densa.— Biochem., Biophys. Res., Comm., 15(2):139. 1964.

Santer, M. and W. Vishniac. CO_2-Incorporation by Extracts of Th. thioparus.— Biochem. biophys. Acta, 18(1):157—158. 1955.

Saunders, G., F. Trama, and R. Bachmann. Evaluation of a Modified C^{14} Technique for Shipboard Estimation of Photosynthesis in Large Lakes.— Great Lakes Research Division Publication, No. 8. 1962.

Schewiakoff, W. Über einen bakterienähnlichen Organismus des Süsswassers.— Verh. naturh.-med. Ver. Heidelb., Vol. 5:44—79. 1897.

Schlegel. H. G. Untersuchungen über den Phosphatstoffwechsel der wasserstoffoxydierenden Bakterien.— Arch. Mikrobiol., 21(2): 127—155. 1954a.

Schlegel, H. G. Zur Frage der gleichzeitigen Oxydation von molekularem Wasserstoff und organischen Substraten durch Knallgasbakterien.— Wiss. Z. Martin-Luther-Univ. Halle Wittenberg., 4(1):95—98. 1954b.

Schlegel, H. G. Die Eisenbakterien.—Handb. Pflphysiol., Part 2, Vol. 5: 649—663. 1960a.

Schlegel, H. G. Die wasserstoffoxydierenden Bakterien.— Handb. Pflphysiol. Part 2, Vol. 5:687—714. 1960b.

Schlegel, H. G. Die Rolle des Kohlendioxyds im Stoffwechsel der Mikroorganismen.— Zentbl. Bakt. ParasitKde., Sect. 1, Orig., Vol. 191: 177—190. 1963.

Schlegel, H. G. Allgemeine Microbiologie.— Verlag Thieme, Stuttgart. 1969.

Schlegel, H. G. and N. Pfennig. Die Anreicherungskultur einer Schwefelpurpurbakterien.— Arch. Mikrobiol., Vol. 38:1—39. 1961.

Schwartz, W. and A. Müller. Methoden der Geomikrobiologie Freiberger Forschungshefte C 48.— Angewandte Naturwissenschaften. 1958.

Scotten, H. L. and J. L. Stokes. Isolation and Properties of Beggiatoa.— Arch. Mikrobiol., 42(4):353—368. 1962.

Senez, J. Some Considerations on the Energetics of Bacterial Growth.— Bact. Rev. Vol. 26:95—107. 1962.

Shapiro, J. Chemical and Biological Studies on the Yellow Organic Acids of Lake Water. —Limnol. Oceanogr., Vol. 2:161—179. 1957.

Shapiro, J. Effect of Yellow Organic Acids on Iron and Other Metals in Water. —J. Am. Wat. Wks. Ass., 56(8):1062—1082. 1964.

Shapiro, J. Induced Rapid Release and Uptake of Phosphate by Microorganisms. —Science, 155(3767):1269—1271. 1967.

Silverman, M. P. and Lundgren. Studies on the Chemoautotrophic Iron Bacterium Ferrobacillus ferrooxidans. I. An Improved Medium and a Harvesting Procedure for Securing High Cell Yields.— J. Bact., Vol. 77:642—647. 1959.

Sisler, F. D. and C. E. ZoBell. Hydrogen-Utilizing Sulphate-Reducing Bacteria in Marine Sediments.— J. Bact., Vol. 60:747—756. 1950.

Sisler, F. D. and C. E. ZoBell. Hydrogen Utilization by Some Marine Sulphate-Reducing Bacteria.— J. Bact. Vol. 62:117—127. 1951.

Skarzynski, B., W. Ostrowski, and A. Krawczyk. Investigations on the Metabolism of Sulphur in Thiobacillus thioparus with Radioactive Sulphur S^{35}.— Bull. Acad. pol. Sci. Cl. II. Ser. Sci. biol., 5(5/6):159—164. 1957.

Snow, L. M. and E. B. Fred. Some Characteristics of Bacteria of Lake Mendota.— Trans. Wis. Acad. Sci. Arts. Lett., Vol. 22:143—154. 1926.

Söhngen, N. L. Über Bakterien, welche Methan als Kohlenstoffnährung und Energiequelle gebrauchen.— Zentbl. Bakt. ParasitKde., Sect. 2, Vol. 15:513—517. 1906.

Sperber, J. I. Release of Phosphate from Soil Minerals by Hydrogen Sulphide.— Nature, Vol. 181:394. 1958.

Stadtman, T. and H. Barker. Studies on the Methane Fermentation. VI. Tracer Experiments on Mechanism of Methane Fermentation.— Archs. Biochem., 21(2):256—264. 1949.

Stadtman, E. R. and H. Barker. Fatty Acid Synthesis by Enzyme Preparation of Clostridium kluyver. III. The Activation of Molecular Hydrogen and the Conversion of Acetylphosphate and Acetate to Butyrate.— J. biol. Chem., Vol. 180:1117—1124. 1949.

Stadtman, T. C. and H. A. Barker. Studies on the Methane Fermentation. VIII. Tracer Experiments on Fatty Acid Oxidation by Methane Bacteria.— J. Bact., 61(1):67—80. 1951.

Staley, J. T. Prosthecomicrobium and Ancalomicrobium, New Prosthecate Freshwater Bacteria.— J. Bact., 95(5):1921—1942. 1968.

Stanier, R. Y. Photosynthetic Mechanisms in Bacteria and Plant Development of a Unitary Concept.— Bact. Rev., 25(1):1—17. 1961.

Stapley, E. O. and R. Starkey. Transformations of Cysteic Acid and Taurine by Soil Microorganisms.— Bact. Proc., p. 125. 1959.

Stark, W. H. and E. McCoy. Distribution of Bacteria in Certain Lakes of Northern Wisconsin.— Zentbl. Bakt. ParasitKde., Sect. 2, Vol. 98:201. 1938.

Starkey, R. Isolation of Some Bacteria which Oxidize Thiosulphate.— Soil Sci., 39(3):197—220. 1935.

Starkey, R. L. Microbial Transformation of Some Organic Sulphur Compounds.— Principles and Applications in Aquatic Microbiology, pp. 405—429. edited by Heukelkian. J. Wiley, N. Y. and London. 1964.

Starkey, R. L. and H. O. Halvorson. Studies on the Transformation of Iron in Nature. II. Concerning the Importance of Microorganisms in the Solution and Precipitation of Iron.— Soil Sci., Vol. 24: 381——402. 1927.

Starr, M. P. and N. Baigent. Parasitic Interaction of Bdellovibrio bacteriovorus with Other Bacteria.— J. Bact., 91(5):2006—2017. 1966.

Steemann-Nielsen, E. Measurement of the Production of Organic Matter in the Sea by Means of Carbon-14.— Nature, Vol. 167: 684—685. 1951.

Steemann-Nielsen, E. The Use of Radioactive Carbon (C^{14}) for Measurement of Organic Production in the Sea.— Journ. du Conseil de l'exploration de la mer, 18(2):117—140. 1952.

Steiner, M. Zur Kenntnis des Phosphatkreislaufes in Seen.— Naturwissenschaften, Vol. 44. 1938.

Stocks, P. K. and C. S. McCleskey. Morphology and Physiology of Methanomonas methanooxidans.— J. Bact., 88(4):1071——1077.1964.

Ström, K. M. Production Biology of Temperate Lakes.— Int. Revue ges. Hydrobiol. Hydrogr., Vol. 19:329—348. 1928.

Ström, K. M. Limnological Observations of Norwegian Lakes.— Arch. Hydrobiol., Vol. 21:97—124. 1930.

Ström, K. M. Tyrifjord, a Limnological Study.— Skr. norske Vidensk-Akad. Mat. - naturv. Kl., No. 3. 1932.

Ström, K. M. Nordfiord Lakes. A Limnological Survey.— Skr. norske Vidensk-Akad. Mat. - naturv. Kl., 1932(8):1—56. 1933.

Ström, K. M. Flakevatn. A Semi-Arctic Lake of Central Norway.— Skr. norske Vidensk-Akad. Mat. - naturv. K., 1933(10):1—7. 1934.

Ström, K. M. Land-Locked Waters (Hydrography) and Bottom Deposits in Badly Ventilated Norwegian Fjords with Remarks upon Sedimentation under Anaerobic Conditions.— Skr. norske Vidensk-Akad. Mat. - naturv. Kl., Vol. 1, No. 7. 1936.

Ström, K. Trapped Seawaters.— New Scient., 13(274):384—386. 1962.

Stuiver, M. The Sulphur Cycle in Lake Waters during Thermal Stratification.— Geochim. cosmochim. Acta, Vol. 31:2151—2167. 1967.

Stumpf, P. K., J. M. Bove, and Goffeau. Fat Metabolism in Higher Plants. XX. Relation of Fatty Acid Synthesis and Photophosphorylation in Lettuce Chloroplasts.— Biochim. biophys. Acta, Vol. 70:260. 1963.

Suzuki, I. and C. H. Werkman. Phosphoenolpyruvate Carboxylase in Extracts of Th. denitrificans, a Chemoautotrophic Bacterium.— Archs. Biochem. Biophys., Vol. 72:514. 1957.

Suzuki, I. and C. H. Werkman. Chemoautotrophic Fixation of Carbon Dioxide by Th. thiooxidans.— Iowa St. Coll. J. Sci., 32(4):475. 1958a.

Suzuki, I. and C. H. Werkman. Chemoautotrophic Carbon Dioxide Fixation by Extracts of Th. thiooxidans. II. Formation of Phosphoglyceric Acid. — Archs. Biochem. Biophys., Vol. 77:112. 1958b.

Suzuki, S. The Microbial Population in Lake Katanuma, a Very Strong Acid Water Lake in Japan.— Jap. J. Limnol., 22(4):201—207. 1961.

Tanaka, A. and R. Hosino. Limnological Survey of the Lakes in the Southwestern Part (South of 44°N. lat.) of Kunasiri-sima.— Jap. J. Limnol., 3(4):95—108. 1934.

Taylor, C. B. Bacteriology of Fresh Water. I. Distribution of Bacteria in English Lakes.— J. Hyg., Camb., Vol. 40:616—640. 1940.

Taylor, C. B. Bacteriology of Fresh Water. II. The Distribution and Types of Coliform Bacteria in Lakes and Streams.— J. Hyg., Camb., Vol. 41:17—38. 1941.

Taylor, C. B. and A. G. Lockhead. Qualitative Studies of Soil Microorganisms. II. A Survey of the Bacterial Flora of Soils Differing in Fertility.— Can. J. Res., Sec. C., Vol. 16:162—173. 1938.

Temple, K. L. and E. W. Delchamps. Autotrophic Bacteria and the Formation of Acid in Bituminous Coal Mines.— Appl. Microbiol., 1(5):255—261. 1953.

Thienemann, A. Die Binnengewässer Mitteleuropas. Eine limnologische Einführung.— Die Binnengewässer, Vol. 1. 1925.

Thienemann, A. Der Sauerstoff in eutrophen und oligotrophen Seen.— Die Binnengewässer, Vol. 4. 1928.

Thimann, K. V. The Life of Bacteria, their Growth, Metabolism and Relationships. Macmillan Co. N. Y. 1963.

Trautwein, K. Beitrag zur Physiologie and Morphologie der Thionsäure-bakterien (Omelianski).— Zentbl. Bakt. ParasitKde., Sect. 2, 53(22/24):513—548. 1921.

Trautwein, K. Physiologie und Morphologie der fakultativ autotrophen Thionsäure-Bakterien unter heterotrophen Ernährungsbedingungen.— Zentbl. Bakt. ParasitKde., Sect. 2, Vol. 61:1—5. 1924.

Trudinger, P. A. Phosphoglycerate Formation from Pentose Phosphate by Extracts of Th. denitrificans.— Biochim. biophys. Acta, Vol. 18:581—582 (Sheffield). 1955.

Trudinger, P. A. Fixation of Carbon Dioxide by Extracts of Strict Autotroph Thiobacillus denitrificans.— Biochem. J., 64(2):274—286. 1956.

Tyler, P. A. and K. C. Marshall. Form and Function in Manganese-Oxidizing Bacteria.— Arch. Mikrobiol., Vol. 56:344—353. 1967.

Uéno, M. Acid Water Lakes in North Shinano.— Arch. Hydrobiol., Vol. 27:571—584. 1934.

Umbreit, W. and E. McCoy. The Occurrence of Actinomycetales of the Genus Micromonospora in Inland Lakes.— A Symposium on Hydrobiology, pp. 106—114. Wiscons. Univ. Press. 1941.

Umbreit, W. W. and T. F. Anderson. A Study of Th. thiooxidans with the Electron Microscope.— J. Bact., Vol. 44:317. 1942.

Umbreit, W., H. Vogler, and K. G. Vogler. The Significance of Fat in Sulphur Oxidation by Thiobacillus thiooxidans.— J. Bact., Vol. 43:141—148. 1942.

Uphof, J. C. Th. Zur Oekologie der Schwefelbakterien in den Schwefel-quellen Mittelfloridas.— Arch. Hydrobiol., Vol. 18:71. 1927.

Vallentyne, J. R. Geochemistry of the Carbohydrates. Calgary, Alberta. 1959.

Vatter, A. E. and R. S. Wolfe. Observations on the Growth and Mor-phology of Gallionella ferruginea.— Bact. Proc., p. 35a. 1955.

Vatter, A. E. and R. S. Wolfe. Electron Microscopy of Gallionella ferruginea.— J. Bact., Vol. 72:248—252. 1956.

Vishniac, W., B. Horecker, and S. Ochoa. Enzymic Aspects of Photosynthesis.— Adv. Enzymol., 19(1):1—77. 1957.

Vishniac, W., B. Horecker, and S. Ochoa. Enzymic Aspects of Photosynthesis.— Adv. Enzymol.

Vishniac, W. and M. Santer. The Thiobacilli.— Bact. Rev., 21(3):195—213. 1957.

Vogler, K. G. The Presence of an Endogenous Respiration in Autotrophic Bacteria.— J. gen. Physiol., Vol. 25:617. 1941.

Vogler, K. G., G. A. LePage, and W. W. Umbreit. The Respiration of Thiobacillus thiooxidans on Sulphur.— J. gen. Physiol., Vol. 26:89—102. 1942.

Vogler, K. and W. Umbreit. The Necessity for Direct Contact in Sulphur Oxidation by Thiobacillus thiooxidans.— Soil Sci., Vol. 51:331—339. 1941.

Wagner, E. and W. Schwartz. Geomikrobiologische Untersuchungen. IV. Untersuchungen über die mikrobielle Verwitterung von Kalkstein im Karst.— Z. allg. Mikrobiol., 5(1): 52—76. 1965.

Waksman, S. A. The Role of Bacteria and Other Microorganisms in the Decomposition of Cellulose in Nature.— J. Bact., Vol. 30: 441. 1935.

Waksman, S. A. Aquatic Bacteria in Relation to the Cycle of Organic Matter in Lakes.— Univ. Wisconsin Sympos. Hydrobiol., pp. 86—105. Madison. Univ. Wisc. Press. 1941.

Waksman, S. and M. Allen. Decomposition of Polyuronides by Fungi and Bacteria. II. Decomposition of Alginic Acid by Bacteria and Formation of the Enzyme Alginase.— J. Am. chem. Soc., Vol. 56: 2701. 1934.

Waksman, S. A., C. L. Carey, and M. C. Allen. Bacteria Decomposing Alginic Acid.— J. Bact., Vol. 28: 213—220. 1934.

Waksman, S. and C. Carey. Decomposition of Organic Matter in Sea Water by Bacteria. I. Bacterial Multiplication in Stored Sea Water.— J. Bact., Vol. 29: 531—543. 1935.

Waksman, S. A. and M. Hotchkiss. On the Oxidation of Organic Matter in Marine Sediments by Bacteria.— J. mar. Res., Vol. 1: 101—118. 1938.

Waksman, S. A. and J. S. Joffe. Microorganisms Concerned in the Oxidation of Sulphur in the Soil. II. Thiobacillus thiooxidans, a New Sulphur Oxidizing Organism Isolated from the Soil.— J. Bact., Vol. 7: 239—256. 1922.

Waksman, S. and Ch. E. Renn. Decomposition of Organic Matter in Sea Water by Bacteria. III. Factors Influencing the Rate of Decomposition.— Biol. Bull., Vol. 70: 472—483. 1936.

Waksman, S. A. and R. L. Starkey. On the Growth and Respiration of the Sulphur-Oxidizing Bacteria.— J. gen. Physiol., Vol. 5: 285—310. 1923.

Waksman, S. A., J. L. Stokes, and R. Butler. Relations of Bacteria to Diatoms in Sea Water.— J. mar. biol. Ass. U. K., Vol. 22: 359—373. 1937.

Waksman, S. A. and Tenney. The Composition of Natural Organic Materials and their Decomposition in the Soil.— Soil Sci., Vol. 24. 1927.

Watt, W. D. and F. R. Hayes. Tracer Study of the Phosphorous Cycle in Sea Water.— Limnol. Oceanogr., Vol. 8: 276—285. 1963.

Weber, C. I. A Study of Photosynthesis in Clear Lake Iowa.— Proc. Iowa Acad. Sci., Vol. 70: 79—97. 1963.

Weindling, R. Microbial Associations and Antagonism.— Ind. Engng. Chem., Part 1, 48(9): 1407. 1956.

Welch, P. S. Limnology. McGraw Hill Book Co. N. Y. 1952.

Welch, P. S. Limnological Methods. Philad. - Toronto, Blakiston. 1948.

Werkman, C. H. and H. G. Wood. Heterotrophic Assimilation of Carbon Dioxide.— Adv. Enzymol., Vol. 2: 135—182. 1942.

West, G. S. and B. M. Griffiths. The Lime-Sulphur Bacteria of the Genus Hillhousia.— Ann. Bot., Vol. 27: 83—91. 1913.

Weston, W. H. The Role of the Aquatic Fungi in Hydrobiology.— A Symposium on Hydrobiology, pp. 129—151. 1941.

Wetzel, R. G. Variations in Productivity of Goose and Hypereutrophic Sylvan Lakes, Indiana.— Invest. Indiana Lakes Streams, Vol. 7: 147—184. 1966.

Whipple, G. C. The Microscopy of Drinking Water. J. Wiley and Sons, N. Y. 1927.

Wiame, I. M. Le cycle du soufre dans la nature.— Handb. Pfl Physiol., Vol. 9:103—120. 1958.

Wieland, Th., G. Griss, and B. Haccius. Untersuchungen zur mikro-biellen Benzoloxydation. I. Nachweis und Chemismus des Benzol-abbaus.— Arch. Mikrobiol., Vol. 28:383—393. 1958.

Wieringa, K. T. The Formation of Acetic Acid from Carbon Dioxide and Hydrogen by Anaerobic Spore Forming Bacteria.— Antonie van Leeuwenhoek; J. Microbiol., Vol. 6:251—262. 1940.

Wight, K. M. and R. Starkey. Utilization of Hydrogen by Sulphate-Reducing Bacteria and its Significance in Anaerobic Corrosion.— J. Bact., 50(2):238. 1954.

Wilken, T. Untersuchungen über Methangärung und die dabei wirksamen Bakterien.— Arch. Mikrobiol., 11(3):312—317. 1940.

Williams, F. T. and E. McCoy. The Microflora of the Mud Deposits of Lake Mendota.— J. sedim. Petrol., 5(1):31—36. 1935.

Williams, W. D. A Contribution to Lake Typology in Victoria, Australia.— Verh. Int. Ver. Limnol., 15(1):158—168. 1964.

Williams, W. and B. Siebert. The Chemical Composition of Some Surface Waters in Central Australia.— Aust. J. mar. Freshwat. Res., 14(2):166—175. 1963.

Wilson, L. G. Metabolism of Sulphate: Sulphate Reduction.— A. Rev. Pl. Physiol., Vol. 13:201. 1962.

Wimmer, R. Beiträge zur Kenntnis der Nitrifikationsbakterien.— Z. Hyg. Infekt. Krankh., Vol. 48:135. 1904.

Winogradsky, S. Sur l'étude microscopique du sol.— C. r. Acad. Sci., Paris, Vol. 179. 1924.

Wolfe, M. The Effect of Molybdenum upon the Nitrogen Metabolism of Anabaena cylindrica. Ph. D. Thesis, University of London. 1953.

Wolfe, R. S. Cultivation Morphology and Classification of the Iron Bacteria. — J. Am. Wat. Wks. Ass., Vol. 50:1241—1249. 1958.

Wolfe, R. S. Iron and Manganese Bacteria. Principles and Applications in Aquatic Microbiology.— Proc. of Conference Rutgers Univ. N. Brunswick, pp. 82—97. 1964.

Wright, R. T. and J. E. Hobie. The Uptake of Organic Solutes in Lake Water.— Limnol. Oceanogr., Vol. 10:22—28. 1965.

Wyss, O. Microbial Adaptation.— Ind. Engng. Chem., Part 1, 48(9): 1404—1406. 1956.

Yoshimura, S. Horizontal Distribution of Dissolved Oxygen and Hydrogen Ion Concentration in Several Japanese Lakes.— Geophys. Mag., 3(1):27—35. 1930.

Yoshimura, S. Contribution to the Knowledge of Hydrogen Ion Concen-tration in the Lake Waters in Japan.— Proc. imp. Acad. Japan, 7(5):195—197. 1931a.

Yoshimura, S. Seasonal Variation of Iron and Manganese in the Water of Takasuka-Numa, Saitama.— Jap. J. Geol. Geogr., 7(4):269—279. 1931b.

Yoshimura, S. Limnological Reconnaissance Lake Busyu, Hukui, Japan.— Sci. Rep. Tokyo Bunrika Daig, Sec. C, Vol. 1:1—27. 1932a.

Yoshimura, S. Contributions to the Knowledge of Nitrogenous Compounds and Phosphate in the Lake Waters of Japan.— Proc. imp. Acad. Japan, 8(3):94—97. 1932b.

Yoshimura, S. Seasonal Variation in Content of Nitrogenous Compounds and Phosphate in the Water of Takasuka Pond, Saitama, Japan.— Arch. Hydrobiol., Vol. 24:155—176. 1932c.

Yoshimura, S. Vertical Distribution of the Amount of Sulphate Dissolved in Water of Lakes Suigetu and Hiruga with Reference to the Origin of Hydrogen Sulphide in their Bottom Water.— Geophys. Mag., 6(4):315—321. 1932d.

Yoshimura, S. Kata-Numa, a Very Strong Acid Water Lake on Volcano Kata-numa Miyadi Prefecture, Japan.— Arch. Hydrobiol., Vol. 26: 197—202. 1934.

Yoshimura, S. Contribution to Knowledge of Iron in Lake Waters of Japan, Second Report.— Jap. J. Geol. Geogr., Vol. 13:39—56. 1936a.

Yoshimura, S. Limnology of Lake Wakuike, Nagano Prefecture, Japan.— Proc. imp. Acad. Japan, Vol. 12:245—247. 1936b.

Yoshimura, S. Soundings of Deep Japanese Lakes.— Jap. J. Limnol., 8(3/4):173—194. 1938a.

Yoshimura, S. and D. Miyadi. Limnological Observations of Two Crater Lakes of Miyake Island, Western North Pacific.— Jap. J. Geol. Geogr., 13(3/4):339—352. 1936.

Yoshimura, S. Dissolved Oxygen in the Lake Waters of Japan.— Sci. Rep. Tokyo Bunrika, Daig., Sec. C, 2(8):63—277. 1938b.

Youatt, I. B. Studies on the Metabolism of Thiobacillus thiocyanoxidans.— J. gen. Microbiol., 11(2):139—149. 1954.

Zawarzin, G. A. Metallogenium symbioticum.— Z. allg. Mikrobiol., 4(5):390—395. 1946b.

Zih, Al. and F. Ruttner. Beiträge zur Bakteriologie der Lunzer Seen.— Rev. d. g. Hydrobiol., Vol. 26:431—443. 1932.

ZoBell, C. E. Microbiological Activities at Low Temperatures with Particular Reference to Marine Bacteria.— Q. Rev. Biol., 9(4):460. 1934.

ZoBell, C. E. Oxidation-Reduction Potential and the Activity of Marine Nitrifiers.— J. Bact., Vol. 29:78. 1935.

ZoBell, C. E. Occurrence and Activity of Bacteria in Marine Sediments, Recent Marine Sediments, Circulation.— Bull. Am. Ass. Petrol. Geol., pp. 416—427. September 1939.

ZoBell, C. E. Some Factors which Influence Oxygen Consumption by Bacteria in Lake Water.— Biol. Bull., 78(3):388—402. 1940a.

ZoBell, C. E. The Effect of Oxygen Tension on the Rate of Oxidation of Organic Matter in the Sea Water by Bacteria.— J. mar. Res., Vol. 3:211—223. 1940b.

ZoBell, C. E. Bacteria of the Marine World.— Scient. Mon., Vol. 55: 320—330. 1942.

ZoBell, C. E. The Effect of Solid Surfaces upon Bacterial Activity.— J. Bact., Vol. 46:39—56. 1943.

ZoBell, C.E.   Marine Microbiology. A Monograph on Hydrobacteriology. Wiltham Mass. U.S.A., Chronica Botan. Comp. 1946.

ZoBell, C.E.   Ecology of Sulphate Reducing Bacteria.— Producers Mon. Penn. Oil Prod. Ass., 22(7):21—29. 1958.

ZoBell, C.E. and D.Q.Anderson.   Observations on the Multiplication of Bacteria in Different Volumes of Stored Sea Water and the Influence of Oxygen Tension and Solid Surfaces.— Biol. Bull., Vol. 71: 324—342. 1936.

ZoBell, C.E. and C.B.Feltham.   Preliminary Studies on the Distribution and Characteristics of Marine Bacteria.— Bull. Scripps. Instn. Oceanogr., techn. Ser., Vol. 3:279—296. 1934.

ZoBell, C.E. and C.B.Feltham.   Bacteria as Food for Certain Marine Invertebrates.— J. mar. Res., 1(4):312—327. 1938.

ZoBell, C.E. and C.W.Grant.   Bacterial Activity in Dilute Nutrient Solutions.— Science, Vol. 96:189. 1942.

ZoBell, C.E. and C.W.Grant.   Bacterial Utilization of Low Concentrations of Organic Matter.— J. Bact., 45(4):555—564. 1943.

ZoBell, C.E., C.W.Grant, and H.F.Haas.   Marine Microorganisms which Oxidize Petroleum Hydrocarbons.— Bull. Am. Ass. Petrol. Geol., Vol. 27:1175—1193. 1943.

ZoBell, C.E. and S.C.Rittenbergs.   Sulphate-Reducing Bacteria in Marine Sediments.— J. mar. Res., (Saars Foundation), Vol. 7: 602—617. 1948.

ZoBell, C.E. and J.Stadler.   The Effect of Oxygen Tension on the Oxygen Uptake of Lake Bacteria.— J. Bact., 39(3):307—322. 1940.

Zuelzer, M.   Zur Kenntnis der biologischen Wasserbeurteilung. Ein Sammelbericht.— Int. Revue ges. Hydrobiol. Hydrogr., Vol. 1: 439—446. 1908.